OCÉANO ATLÁNTICO

LAS BAHAMAS

La Habana

CUBA
Morón

Guantánamo

Santiago de Cuba

REPÚBLICA DOMINICANA

Santiago de los Caballeros

HAITÍ

Santo Domingo

San Juan
Río Piedras
Mayagüez • Ponce
PUERTO RICO

Guadalupe

JAMAICA

Martinica

MAR CARIBE

Aruba
Curazao
La Guaira
Caracas

Trinidad

ONDURAS
gucigalpa

NICARAGUA

Managua

Lago de Nicaragua

COSTA RICA
San José
Sarchí

Canal de Panamá
Islas de San Blás

Colón
Panamá
PANAMÁ

VENEZUELA

COLOMBIA

¡Claro que sí!

¡Claro que sí!

Introductory Course in Spanish

Instructor's Annotated Edition

Lucía Caycedo Garner
University of Wisconsin–Madison

Debbie Rusch

Marcela Domínguez
University of California, Los Angeles

HOUGHTON MIFFLIN COMPANY   BOSTON
Dallas   Geneva, Illinois   Palo Alto   Princeton, New Jersey

Components of *¡Claro que sí!*

For the Student
Student Text (hardbound)
Workbook/Lab Manual, with Workbook
   Answer Key

Audiocassettes (Parts 1 and 2)
Video Workbook

For the Instructor
Instructor's Annotated Edition
Instructor's Audiocassettes
   Listening Comprehension (Chapter
   conversations)
   Testing (Oral portions of tests and quizzes)
Tapescript/Answer Key to Lab Manual
Test and Quiz Bank, including Answer Key

Overhead Transparencies
Instructor's Edition Video Workbook

Audiocassettes (Parts 1 and 2)
Four RTVE Videos
Computer Study Modules (IBM)

Cover photograph by Pam Haller
Credits for photos, illustrations, and realia can be found following the index of
this book.

Printed in the U.S.A.

Student Text ISBN: 0-395-51540-8

Instructor's Annotated Edition ISBN: 0-395-51541-6

Library of Congress Catalog Card Number: 89-81004

CDEFGHIJ-D-9987654321

Contents of the Instructor's Annotated Edition

Instructor's Guide

Aims, Components, and Organization

¡Claro que sí! is an eclectic, functional 4-skills approach for beginning students of Spanish. It is an integrated skills approach, developing both receptive and productive skills simultaneously. The primary objective of the program is to offer students an opportunity to acquire communication skills while developing an awareness and appreciation of Hispanic culture.

The following are the leading principles that inspired the creation of *¡Claro que sí!:*

1. *We learn by doing.* Only by practicing all skills can students acquire a high degree of proficiency.
2. *Language development is based on skill integration.* Each skill reinforces the other; therefore, students learn to comprehend and speak the language while practicing specific strategies for reading and writing from the beginning of the course.
3. *Language is culture and culture is reflected in language.* By being exposed to real-life situations and by comparing the new culture with their own, students acquire an awareness and respect for other peoples.
4. *Self-expression in the language contributes to attaining proficiency.* Opportunities for extended discourse and for expressing their own ideas, needs, and wants help students develop proficiency.
5. *Recycling of material is essential to move from learning to acquisition.* Continuous reentry of previously learned material leads students to acquisition of language functions.
6. *Learning is enhanced when it is enjoyable.* If the material presented places the students in a relaxed, pleasant atmosphere, and if students enjoy class activities, their rate of success is increased.

Program Components

Student Text

The student text consists of:

- a preliminary and eighteen chapters
- four full-color photo essays
- a reference section with verb conjugation charts, information on accentuation and syllabication, answers to the grammar questions

- maps of the Hispanic world
- a Spanish-English end vocabulary
- an index

See page IAE x for a detailed description of the student text.

Instructor's Annotated Edition

The Instructor's Annotated Edition includes the entire student text, this Instructor's Guide, and annotations overprinted in a second color on the student text pages. The annotations contain suggestions for practicing pronunciation, mechanical drills for practicing grammar topics, additional grammatical and cultural information, and suggestions for extra oral and written practice.

Instructor's Cassettes: Listening Comprehension and Testing

Cassettes containing the conversations from the textbook and the listening portions of the quizzes and tests are available for the instructor. The recordings of the chapter conversations are intended for classroom use in order to develop listening skills and to allow students to hear a variety of different native speaker voices.

Workbook/Lab Manual

The Workbook/Lab Manual provides additional practice in reading, writing, and listening. The Workbook reinforces chapter vocabulary, grammar, and functions, and provides additional writing practice. Each chapter progresses from mechanical exercises (intended for use upon completion of each grammar explanation section) to communicative activities. The Lab Manual is keyed to the recordings and contains the instructions for all taped activities, as well as written material and illustrations coordinated with the recordings. The Lab Manual exercises are to be done after completing the second grammar explanation section. An Answer Key to the workbook exercises is located at the back of the Workbook/Lab Manual.

Cassettes, Parts 1 and 2

The recording program provides explanations of Spanish sounds, pronunciation practice, numerous listening comprehension activities, and the chapter conversations. The listening comprehension activities simulate real-life listening experiences that include conversations in varied situations, monologues, announcements, ads, and answering machine messages. The recordings provide students the opportunity to hear native speakers from a number of different countries.

The cassettes are packaged in two parts (Part 1: Preliminary Chapter–Chapter 9; Part 2: Chapters 10–18) and are available for student purchase. Approximate timings for each chapter are provided in the Tapescript/Answer Key.

Tapescript/Answer Key

The Tapescript contains the complete script for all recorded activities and an answer key for the Lab Manual activities.

Overhead Transparencies

A set of twenty-four overhead transparencies contains maps of the Hispanic world and varied scenes taken from the text illustrations to serve as the basis for vocabulary and conversation practice. A correlation sheet provides a listing of the transparencies with references to the chapters in which they might be used. The transparencies can be used to present or review vocabulary, as a conversation stimulus, or as the basis for testing. Map transparencies can be used to illustrate and discuss the location of the action in the chapter conversations, to locate places mentioned in the **Nuevos horizontes** readings, or to review countries, capitals, and cardinal points.

Test and Quiz Bank

The Test and Quiz Bank offers two ready-to-copy versions (A and B) of each quiz and test, which cover listening, reading, vocabulary, and grammar. The tests follow Chapters 3, 6, 9, 12, 15, and 18 and each covers three chapters. Quizzes are provided for the intervening chapters. Both quizzes and tests include a suggested point breakdown. An Answer Key is provided at the back of the Test and Quiz Bank. Suggestions for testing oral skills and open-ended writing are given at the beginning of the Test and Quiz Bank. The instructor's cassettes contain the listening portions of the quizzes and tests.

Videos from RTVE

Four videos of varying duration consist of excerpted programs broadcast by Radio Televisión Española. They include programs such as ads, documentaries, interviews, a soap opera, and a game show, and present material about several Hispanic countries.

Video Workbook, with Instructor's Edition

The Video Workbook contains varied activities for pre-, ongoing, and post-viewing of the video programs. The programs are divided into manageable segments, and activities are geared for the beginning student.

Scripts for each segment are provided. The Instructor's Edition includes chapter correlations with *¡Claro que sí!* and additional suggestions for using the videos.

Computer Study Modules

The computer program accompanying *¡Claro que sí!* consists of two parts: Flash and Foundation. Flash provides a variety of flash-card type exercises, entirely in Spanish, to practice vocabulary and grammar. Foundation contains fill-in and multiple-choice exercises practicing vocabulary, grammar, and reading comprehension. The computer program is available for IBM and IBM-compatible PCs.

Student Text: Description and Chapter Organization

The Preliminary Chapter gives students input in listening and includes an introduction to some basic language functions, cognates, the geography of the Hispanic world, and punctuation and accentuation, as well as useful classroom expressions.

Chapters 1 to 17 are divided as follows:

Chapter Opener. Each chapter opens with a statement of the chapter objectives and illustrations accompanied by brief activities that set the stage for the theme of the lesson. The objectives are expressed in functional terms, as expected outcomes.

Core Material. The core material section generally consists of a conversation involving one or more of the main characters in the text. A loose story line is carried throughout the text and takes the characters to different parts of the Hispanic world. All chapter conversations are recorded on a separate cassette available to the instructor to facilitate development of listening skills. The conversations contain approximately 80 per cent familiar material, and introduce new functions and vocabulary to be practiced in the chapter. Most conversations are accompanied by an illustration that leads students to anticipate the action and that serves as an aid for a pre-listening activity. A screened box preceding the conversation contains two or three high-frequency expressions from the conversation, which will become an integral part of the students' everyday active vocabulary. An ongoing listening activity focuses the attention of the students and prepares them to listen for basic information contained in the conversation. Post-listening activities check for comprehension and allow for personalization and active student participation while practicing new functions and expressions.

Lo esencial. This section contains a thematic presentation of high-frequency vocabulary through illustrations and use of realia. The presentation is followed by activities that include practice of the vocabulary in natural, everyday situations.

Hacia la comunicación. Grammar, viewed as a key to communication, is represented by the illustration of a key accompanying each grammar section. Grammatical concepts often are introduced or followed by questions designed to aid the students' comprehension of the concept being studied. Grammar explanations are concise and emphasize the syntactical points needed for communication. Mechanical practice is included in the instructor's annotations and in the Workbook. Activities following the grammar explanations are mainly communicative, encouraging self-expression; they also continuously reenter previous grammar and functions.

Nuevos horizontes. This section introduces reading strategies to be practiced while reading passages such as newspaper clippings, letters, interviews, etc., that deal with various aspects of Hispanic culture, both past and present. It also serves as the basis for introducing writing strategies beginning in Chapter 3. Activities stress application of the strategies presented.

¿Lo sabían? Brief cultural readings generally appear two to four times in each chapter to explain cultural references contained in the conversations, vocabulary presentations, and activities. Beginning in Chapter 4, the **¿Lo sabían?** sections are in Spanish to maximize student contact with the language.

Student Annotations. Student annotations that maintain a dialogue between the authors and the students appear throughout the chapters in color-screened boxes in the margin. They serve to point out some of the main functions in the chapter conversations, to provide helpful learning hints, and to call students' attention to, clarify, and expand on material in the text.

The rest of the chapter consists of a second **Lo esencial** section, a core text (usually in the form of a conversation), and a second **Hacia la comunicación** section, each followed by activities. The final activity in each chapter integrates skills and usually culminates in writing.

A summary listing of the active vocabulary closes each chapter.

Chapter 18 allows students to assimilate previously presented material and has a slightly different format from earlier chapters: two sections of core material, a vocabulary presentation, a one-act play, and a variety of activities that review functions presented in the text.

Four full-color photo essays complement the cultural information in the text and contain pair and group activities designed to broaden students' cultural appreciation of the Hispanic world.

Teaching Successfully with *¡Claro que sí!*

Suggested Strategies and Techniques

In this section, you will find specific ideas and suggestions for working with the different parts of the chapters.

Chapter Opener

Each chapter begins with a two-page opener which serves to set the scene for the chapter. Focus on the illustrations, using yes/no, either/or, information, or opinion questions to help the students see where the chapter will take place or understand the setting and theme. Point out the chapter objectives, which highlight the main linguistic and functional material students will learn and practice.

Core Material

The core material is intended to help develop listening skills. In order to facilitate the acquisition of these skills, follow these steps:

1. Use the drawing/photo and the introduction to the conversation as a pre-listening activity to set the scene.
2. Focus on the expressions presented in the screened box and practice them in meaningful context. Specific suggestions are given in the annotations.
3. The activity preceding the conversation is an ongoing listening activity. Have students read the instructions and the activity in its entirety before listening to the conversation. Then play the tape once and check the activity. Students should not look at the conversation in their texts until after the listening phase.
4. Play the tape again and do the first activity following the conversation. If students are unable to answer all questions, either play the tape again or have the students scan the conversation for the answers.
5. Personalized activities follow. Expand on these activities, keeping in mind the interests and backgrounds of your individual students.

The conversations are intended to give listening input and are not intended to be memorized. Reading sections aloud can be done for pronunciation and intonation practice or to point out or contrast functions or structures. For core material readings (a letter, a memo, a selection about El Dorado), recycle strategies used in the **Nuevos horizontes** sections of the book.

Pronunciation and Intonation

Pronunciation and intonation practice is provided in the tape program. Specific suggestions for practicing discrete points are given in the annotations accompanying the chapter conversations, and are intended for use after completion of the conversation. Here are some general tips:

1. Isolate the sound and demonstrate its articulation.
2. Have the students listen and repeat.
3. Practice the sound in the context of a phrase or sentence.
4. Practice auditory discrimination of sounds by comparing and contrasting sounds, by giving short instructor-student dictations and short student-student dictations, etc.
5. Use tongue twisters, proverbs, and short poems to practice pronunciation and intonation.
6. Emphasize correction of this particular sound during the chapter.
7. Do not neglect sounds from previous chapters since the process of building good pronunciation is ongoing.

Lo esencial

Vocabulary is presented in thematic groups related to the plot in the chapter. It is seeded in the core material and formally presented in the **Lo esencial** sections. The presentation of vocabulary in the text is usually done with drawings or realia. To respond to different learning styles and to bring variety into the class, present vocabulary using audio-visual materials (photo files, transparencies, slides, music, etc.), or using the resources you have in the class (e.g., when teaching the word **alto,** use the tallest students to illustrate the meaning). Begin, using either/or or yes/no questions before asking students to use the words themselves. Help the students to retain meaning by giving word associations and word families, by pointing out prefixes and suffixes, etc. The activities in the book offer situations in which the students can practice vocabulary words in meaningful context. The vocabulary items can be presented in class or assigned as homework and later practiced in class.

The following two specific techniques can be used to present vocabulary:

Gouin Series

In a Gouin Series, students relate words to actions, thus internalizing and retaining the words or concepts more easily. A Gouin Series is a set of not more than seven short sentences (each seven or eight syllables in length) that describes a specific series of actions; for example, when presenting vocabulary for the kitchen you can have a series such as the following: **Entro en la cocina. Tomo una taza. Lavo la taza. Seco bien la taza. Sirvo café. Tomo el café.**

1. Mime the actions and say the sentences while the students listen.
2. Say the lines and have the students begin imitating the actions.
3. Have the students incorporate the words, until they can perform the series as a group or alone without your help.

4. To practice different persons of a verb, ask one student to model while the others say what he/she is doing: **Él entra en la cocina ...** , etc.

Total Physical Response

Use commands as a basis for teaching vocabulary. Here is an example using articles of clothing:

1. Display photos of people on the chalkboard.
2. Give commands; for example, **Dale a Ricardo la foto de la mujer que lleva una falda. Pon la foto del hombre que lleva una corbata en el escritorio de Ana.** (etc.)
3. Personalize; for example, **Si Uds. llevan una camisa de algodón, caminen a la pizarra. Habla con una persona que lleva un suéter.**

Hacia la comunicación

The functions introduced in the chapter conversations are explained in this section. Grammatical structures are presented briefly and clearly; the explanations should be assigned as homework. Questions preceding or following many explanations help students anticipate or reflect on what they are studying. Answers to these questions are in Appendix B at the back of the book.

Mechanical practice is an essential step in the ladder to communication. The annotations provide suggestions for mechanical exercises for in-class drilling after students have studied the grammar explanation. This skill-getting phase is the time for correcting errors and helping the students form good linguistic habits. Additional mechanical practice is supplied in the Workbook and is separated in two parts that correspond to the two grammar sections in each chapter.

To be successful when drilling in class:

1. Give clear instructions and model carefully.
2. Maintain a rapid pace, but be sure every student participates.
3. Practice words or structures in context, not in isolation.
4. Keep sentences short and **easy** to remember.
5. Practice one point at a time.
6. Alternate group and individual response.

Some types of mechanical practice are:

1. *Substitution:* One word in the sentence is replaced by another: **Claudia está en España. (Claudia y Teresa)** → **Claudia y Teresa están en España.** (etc.)

   Or, for multiple substitution: **Claudia está en España. (Claudia y Teresa)** → **Claudia y Teresa están en España. (Nicara-**

gua) → **Claudia y Teresa están en Nicaragua. (Mi amigo)** →
Mi amigo está en Nicaragua. (etc.)

2. *Transformation:* A sentence is changed from affirmative to negative, from singular to plural, from a statement to a question, etc.: **La casa es blanca y grande. (las casas)** → **Las casas son blancas y grandes.**

3. *Integration:* Two sentences are combined into one: **Pablo es un chico. Vive en México.** → **Pablo es un chico que vive en México.**

4. *Chain Drill:* Each student repeats and expands on what has been said by the previous student: S1: **Marcos es alto.** S2: **Marcos es alto y moreno.** S3: **Marcos es alto, moreno e inteligente.** (etc.)

5. *Expansion:* A word is added at the corresponding place in the sentence: **Llegué tarde. (muy)** → **Llegué *muy* tarde.**

6. *Stand-up Drills:* The entire class stands up and students sit down as each one performs a specific task correctly, such as answering a question, giving a verb form, etc. This is a quick way of checking to see whether the students have assimilated the material presented, to make sure that no one is neglected, and to break the monotony.

   For a difficult structure, drilling may be necessary for short periods over several days. Drilling of previously presented structures may be needed occasionally as reentry.

"Mechanicative" and Communicative Activities

The activities that follow the grammar explanations usually fall into two main categories:

1. "Mechanicative" activities in which you can predict what student A will say and what student B will respond, even though the students may not be aware of this. These activities ask the students to use the language to carry out a specific task. Therefore, error prediction is simple. For an example of a "mechanicative" activity, see Chapter 5, **Actividad 10: La agenda de Álvaro.**

2. Communicative activities in which you know what functions students will try to express and the vocabulary and grammar needed to do so, but you are unaware of the exact message the students will want to convey. You may want to have students brainstorm before asking them to begin some communicative activities; for example, before asking students to give advice to a new college freshman entering their school, have them brainstorm advice commonly given to college students. While doing communicative activities, error correction should be done only if it is absolutely necessary, if it is an error that is likely to be repeated frequently, or if meaning is impaired. For an example of a communicative activity see Chapter 16, **Actividad 12: El dilema.**

Many of the activities in the text are done as class mingles, in small groups or in pairs to maximize student participation. The following offers specific tips to help these activities run effectively:

Small Group and Pair Work

Small group and pair work encourage student participation in class while reducing anxiety and giving the students the opportunity to socialize on a personal level. Suggestions for successful small group or pair activities are:

1. Make sure students understand what to do. Model properly.
2. Form the groups quickly and vary groups from day to day or activity to activity.
3. To reduce anxiety, use imagination (e.g., have students sit back-to-back for a phone conversation, or use a pen as a microphone for an interview).
4. Specify a time limit for the activity. Give less time than you believe is necessary to force the students to work intensively.
5. Insist on the use of Spanish only.
6. Monitor, making sure students are on task and to note or correct errors. You should not be a member of a group.
7. Extend the time if the activity is working well. Interrupt the activity when a few groups have finished.
8. Have students report their findings to the class, have a pair role play the situation when finished, do spot checks, etc., to hold students responsible for work done in pairs and small groups.

Mingling in the Classroom

Activities that require students to "mingle" or stand up and move around the classroom to accomplish a specific linguistic task (such as finding out everyone's phone number to practice numbers) are very successful if:

- students understand what to do.
- each student speaks to one student for one conversational exchange and then moves on to speak with others.
- time is carefully controlled. (The activity should be ended when a few students have finished. The objective is not for all to finish, but for all to participate.)
- students know there will be a check and that they will be responsible for carrying out a task.

Recycling and Reentry

"Mechanicative" and communicative activities allow for natural recycling of material to occur, providing constant review of previously presented material. The Table of Contents includes a list of the main topics recycled in the chapter activities.

Nuevos horizontes

Besides giving an overview of Hispanic culture, the **Nuevos horizontes** section includes a step-by-step development of reading and writing skills, integrated into the learning process.

Reading Strategies

Discuss the chapter reading strategy and compare it with how students read in their own language. Have the students do the pre-reading activities. Also, as a pre-reading activity, bring, or have the students bring, related cultural materials and information to class for discussion. For example, in the chapter dealing with ecology, discuss the contamination problem in the world, nuclear plants, oil spills, etc. After reading the selection, check for comprehension, see how the students applied the reading strategy, and discuss the cultural aspect presented in the reading. The readings are not intended to be read aloud in class except for segments you may want to use to practice pronunciation and intonation.

Writing Strategies

Prepare the students for writing by helping them understand the writing strategy presented in the chapter. Help them understand that the process of writing is as important as the product itself and that writing should be used as a learning tool. Encourage the students to recognize and develop their own process to approach writing and help them develop the habit of draft writing, allowing time between drafts. When reviewing students' writing, correct grammar and spelling mistakes, and separate content from form, reacting to the writing itself.

Peer Editing

You shouldn't need to correct all of the writing activities suggested in *¡Claro que sí!* Students learn if they have the opportunity to analyze and react to others' writing. By doing peer editing, the students are forced to look critically at someone else's work and suggest revisions and corrections. Students can peer edit in class or as homework, but they must be aware that successful peer editing is more than mere correction of simple errors. When peer editing, instruct students to focus on content, organization, tone and style, and language (grammar, spelling, etc.). Peer-edited material may be spot-checked later.

¿Lo sabían?

Have students analyze their own culture to better understand others. Encourage students to apply previously studied reading strategies when reading the **¿Lo sabían?** sections. Check comprehension by asking either/or, yes/no, information, or opinion questions.

Sample Lesson Plan

¡Claro que sí! was written keeping in mind different programs and teaching situations. The text can be covered in semester or quarter programs that meet three, four, or five times a week. Classes meeting four times a week over two semesters or three quarters, can spend five to six days per chapter, with less time for the preliminary chapter. Classes meeting three times a week can spend four to five days per chapter and do most of the writing activities and peer editing as homework.

Suggestions for warm-up activities are given in the annotations. You can use those provided or create activities that stress areas where your students need extra practice. Possibilities include rapid-fire question/answer; student-led activities; pronunciation practice; reviews based on magazine clippings, photos, overhead transparencies, etc.; student-generated activities based on homework assignments; and puzzles, riddles, and vocabulary games based on previously studied material.

Capítulo 1

Day 1

1. Warm-up: Review material from the Preliminary Chapter. (6 minutes)

- Have students mingle, greeting one another, finding out names, and taking leave. Allow students 2 minutes to do this. When finished, quiz students on the names of their classmates, using yes/no and either/or questions followed by **¿Cómo se llama él/ella?** This will serve as an introduction to the third person singular.

- Review classroom commands from the Preliminary Chapter, using TPR.

- Instruct all students to stand up. In order to sit down they must correctly answer questions dealing with capitals: **¿Cuál es la capital de Perú? San José es la capital de Puerto Rico, ¿no?** (etc.)

2. Do the chapter opener, pages 14–15. (5 minutes)

- Read the chapter objectives to focus the students' attention on the functions that will be learned.

- Focus students' attention on the photograph and ask the accompanying questions.

- Work with the registration card by asking the questions in the caption. Discuss, briefly, items suggested in the annotations.

3. Presentation of core material, pages 16–17. (12 minutes)

Pre-listening activity

- Set the scene by having students look at the photo and read the introduction to the conversation.
- Pre-teach the expressions in the screened box. Follow suggestions in the annotations.

Ongoing listening activity

- Have students read **Actividad 1.** Model and have students repeat lines of the activity for pronunciation practice.
- Have students cover the conversation printed in the text (to avoid reading it while listening) and play the tape once.
- Check **Actividad 1.**

Post-listening activities

- Play the tape again. When finished, have students do **Actividad 2.** If they cannot answer the questions, allow them to refer back to the written text.
- Have students read and discuss the **¿Lo sabían?** section. (Beginning in Chapter 4, these cultural readings will be in Spanish to provide additional input for students.)

4. Present and practice the sounds for the chapter. (5 minutes)

- Follow suggestions in the annotations.
- Continue stressing these sounds throughout the chapter when dictated by the needs of your individual students.

5. Do the follow-up activities for the core material: **Actividades 3–7,** pages 18–19. (10 minutes)

- Remember: Introduce these activities by modeling with one student, set up pairs quickly (with an uneven number, have one group of three students), set time limits, have students change roles so that all ask and answer questions, circulate and offer assistance.
- Check by having one or two groups perform for the class.
- Give three minutes for writing **Actividad 7.** Circulate and correct errors. Have some students read; ask others about what they have heard.

6. Practice vocabulary in the **Lo esencial** section, pages 19–20. (10 minutes)

- Teach the numbers by modeling and having the students repeat. Stress pure vowel sounds. Be attentive to the incorrect use of the schwa.
- Follow suggestions in the annotations for practicing numbers.
- In future chapters you may want to assign the vocabulary as homework the night before.
- Do **Actividades 8–10.**

Assignment: 1) Study **Hacia la comunicación.** 2) Do the corresponding **Práctica mecánica, Parte I,** in the Workbook. 3) Have students prepare logical series of numbers (as in **Actividad 8**) to use as a warm-up the next day.

Day 2

1. Warm-up: Review material studied the day before. (10 minutes)

- Rapid-fire, ask yes/no, either/or questions based on people in the class and the character Teresa, who was introduced in the core material. Extend this to include questions on other characters by having the students look at page 13 while you ask questions.
- Have some students do their homework math sequences for their peers while the others guess the correct responses.
- Write − **menos;** + **y;** x **por;** and ÷ **dividido por** on the board and do math problems with the students orally.

2. Drill the grammar points, pages 20–22. (20 minutes)

- Follow the suggestions in the annotations.
- While drilling, focus on accuracy.
- Stress clear pronunciation.

3. Do **Actividades 11–14,** pages 22–24, and **¿Lo sabían?,** page 22. (15 minutes)

- Follow suggestions in the annotations.
- Use the realia to its fullest. After following the suggestions in the annotations, ask questions such as **¿El padre de Helena es el Sr. Castro o el Sr. Castañeda?**
- During pair work, circulate and correct errors; change pairs frequently.

Assignment: 1) Review accentuation, Appendix C. 2) Do the **Práctica comunicativa, Actividades 1–3,** in the Workbook, corresponding to the grammar and vocabulary studied. 3) Prepare math problems to quiz a partner during the next class session.

Day 3

1. Warm-up: Review items from the last class and the Preliminary Chapter. (12 minutes)

- Use TPR to review classroom expressions. These can proceed from simple **(Levántense)** to complex **(Abre el libro del estudiante de Denver en la página 5).**
- Do three chain drills, using **llamarse, ser de,** and **tener años.**
- In groups of three, have students quiz each other with their math problems from the homework.

2. Peer edit **Actividad 2** from the homework. (4 minutes)

- Spot check while students peer edit.
- Have one or two students read their responses.

3. **Nuevos horizontes** section, pages 24–25. (15 minutes)

- After reading about the strategy, ask students what types of texts they scan.

Pre-reading activity
- Have the students read the **ficha.** In order to focus their attention on the type of information they will be seeking from the application form, have students say what they would put in the lines for themselves.

Ongoing reading activity
- Give students 4 or 5 minutes to complete this task.
- Have them compare answers with a partner.
- Check as a group.

Post-reading activity
- Discuss the cultural points mentioned in the annotations.
- Have students identify cognates.
- Ask students why **número, teléfono,** and **admisión** have accents and why **pasaporte** and **ciudad** don't.

NOTE: Beginning in Chapter 3, a writing strategy will be explained and practiced. To make the best use of class time, you may want to assign the vocabulary in the **Lo esencial** section for homework and practice it the following day with the core material.

4. Introduce vocabulary from the **Lo esencial** section, pages 26–27. (10 minutes)

- Use visuals to present the vocabulary. Begin by giving short narratives while holding up two pictures: **Es Carlos. Carlos es economista. Está en una oficina. Ella se llama Carmen. Carmen es abogada. Es amiga de Perry Mason.** Then ask: **¿Cómo se llama él/ella? ¿Él es abogado? ¿Es economista? ¿Quién es abogada?** Have students respond with simple one-word responses (**Carlos, Carmen, él, ella, sí, no**) before asking them to say the professions.
- Drill masculine/feminine forms.

5. Do **Actividades 16–17,** page 27. (6 minutes)

- Give additional professions as dictated by the needs of the students.

Assignment: 1) Review the vocabulary for **ocupaciones** and the expressions preceding the conversation on page 28. 2) Write the names of famous people to associate them with occupations; for example, **Iacocca = hombre de negocios.** Write 5 questions to ask a partner in class: **¿Qué hace (Lee Iacocca)?** 3) Write the names of three famous people and where they are from.

Day 4

1. Warm-up (15 minutes)

- Do a pronunciation review focusing on the vowel sounds. Have students contrast sounds to avoid the schwa by doing multiple repetitions of words like **Coca-Cola,** accentuating the mouth positions.
- In groups of three, have students refer to their homework and quiz each other about the origin of famous people.
- In pairs, have students ask each other their homework questions on occupations.
- Use visuals to review occupations.
- Do associations based on homework as a student-led drill. Have individuals give names and class respond with each person's occupation.

2. Do the core material, pages 28–29. (25 minutes)

Pre-listening activities

- Set the scene by reading the introduction to the conversation and discussing the drawing. Ask questions such as **¿Hay una cafetería en tu colegio mayor? ¿Hay café? ¿Hay Coca-Cola? ¿Hay alcohol? ¿Hay sándwiches?**
- Discuss the cultural differences mentioned in the annotations.

- Practice the expressions in the screened box; follow the suggestions in the annotations.

Ongoing listening activity

- Give instructions for **Actividad 18.** Have students cover the conversation in the book so they cannot refer to it. Have them focus on the drawing.
- Play the dialogue and check **Actividad 18.**

Post-listening activities

- Play the dialogue again and do **Actividad 19.**
- Preview the next **Hacia la comunicación** section by drawing the students' attention to the plural verb forms and **ellos/ellas.** Write the forms on the board: **son, se llaman, tienen.** Ask questions about the students: **¿Cómo se llama él? ¿Cómo se llaman ellos?** (etc.)
- Have students work in pairs to redo the conversation from the point of view of Vicente and Juan Carlos. Have some groups perform for the class.
- Do **Actividad 20.** Have some groups perform for the class.

3. Review accents. (5 minutes)

- To review accent rules, dictate the lines in the dialogue that contain the following words: **América, también, Córdoba, Gómez, inglés.**

Assignment: 1) Study **Hacia la comunicación.** 2) Write five questions using different question words and ways of asking questions. 3) Do the corresponding **Práctica mecánica, Parte II,** in the Workbook. 4) Students can begin to listen to the tapes for Chapter 1.

Day 5

1. Warm-up (10 minutes)

- Have students get in groups of three and say as much as they can about individual members of the class: name, origin, age, parents' occupations. Check by asking specific questions about individuals: **¿Cómo se llama él? ¿De dónde es ella? ¿Cuántos años tiene Paul?** Convert this into a student-led check by having students ask questions.
- Review different types of questions: information, yes/no, either/or, and tag.
- In pairs, have students ask and answer the questions they wrote as homework.

2. Drill grammar from **Hacia la comunicación,** pages 30–31. (20 minutes)

- Follow the suggestions in the annotations to drill the grammar points.
- While drilling, stress accuracy.
- Inform students whether or not you will teach and test the **vosotros** form.

3. Do **Actividades 21–27,** pages 32–34. (20 minutes)

- Follow suggestions in the annotations.
- Change pairs at least once during these activities.
- Before peer editing **Actividad 27,** explain the advantages of cooperative learning: learning from one's mistakes, helping someone, etc. You may wish to collect these paragraphs.

Assignment: 1) Do **Práctica comunicativa, Actividades 4–9,** in the Workbook. 2) Have students write where famous people are from (extension of **Actividad 21** to be used as a warm-up) 3) Finish lab work for this chapter. 4) Tell students when they will have their chapter quiz (See the Test and Quiz Bank).

The following shows a typical chapter breakdown over 5 class periods:
Day 1: Chapter opener, core material, presentation of the sound for the chapter, and the first **Lo esencial**

Day 2: **Hacia la comunicación**
Day 3: **Nuevos horizontes** and a short preview of the second vocabulary
Day 4: Second **Lo esencial,** core material, and sound (if given)
Day 5: Second **Hacia la comunicación** and review

References

Asher, James J. *Learning Another Language Through Actions.* Los Gatos, CA: Sky Oaks Productions, 1982.

Gaudiani, Claire. *Teaching Writing in the Foreign Language Curriculum.* Washington, D.C.: Center for Applied Linguistics, 1981.

Grellet, Françoise. *Developing Reading Skills.* New York: Cambridge University Press, 1981.

Krashen, Stephen D. and Tracy D. Terrell. *The Natural Approach.* Hayward, CA: The Alemany Press, 1983.

Omaggio, Alice C. *Teaching Language in Context.* Boston: Heinle and Heinle, Inc., 1986.

Rivers, Wilga, Milton Azevedo, and William Heflin, Jr. *Teaching Spanish: A Practical Guide.* Skokie, Ill.: National Textbook Company, 1988.

Seelye, H. Ned. *Teaching Culture.* Skokie, Ill.: National Textbook Company, 1981.

¡Claro que sí!

¡Claro que sí!

Introductory Course in Spanish

Lucía Caycedo Garner
University of Wisconsin–Madison

Debbie Rusch

Marcela Domínguez
University of California, Los Angeles

HOUGHTON MIFFLIN COMPANY BOSTON
Dallas   Geneva, Illinois   Palo Alto   Princeton, New Jersey

Cover photograph by Pam Haller

The authors and editors would like to thank the following authors and publishers for granting permission to use copyrighted material:

"Getting to Know One Another" from *Pair Work for Effective Communication* by Peter Watcyn-Jones (Penguin Books, 1981), Copyright © Peter Watcyn-Jones, 1981 pp. 9–10. Reproduced by permission of Penguin Books Ltd.

Selected definitions. Copyright © 1987 by Houghton Mifflin Company. Reprinted by permission from the *American Heritage Larousse Spanish Dictionary,* paperback edition.

"If you want a big new market . . . ," by Julia Lieblich, *Fortune,* November 21, 1988, pp. 181–188. Copyright © 1988 Time Inc. All rights reserved.

"Cuadros y ángulos" by Alfonsina Storni. Reprinted by permission of the government of Argentina.

Brochure text from the exposition "Fernando Botero, Pinturas, Dibujos, Esculturas." Reprinted by permission of the Ministry of Culture, Spain.

"A la luz de la luna." Reprinted by permission of the Department of Liberal Studies, Division of University Outreach, University of Wisconsin-Madison.

Credits for photos, illustrations, and realia can be found following the index of this book.

Printed in the U.S.A.

Student Text ISBN: 0-395-51540-8

Instructor's Annotated Edition ISBN: 0-395-51541-6

Library of Congress Catalog Card Number: 89-81004

CDEFGHIJ-D-9987654321

Contents

Capítulo 7   170

Capítulo 8   198

Capítulo 9   226

To the Student

Learning a foreign language means learning skills, not just facts and information. *¡Claro que sí!* is based on the principle that **we learn by doing** and, therefore, offers a variety of activities designed to practice and develop your skills in listening, speaking, reading, and writing in Spanish. *¡Claro que sí!* also provides an overview of the Spanish-speaking world — its peoples and places — so that you can better understand others and their ways of doing things. Knowledge of another culture, including the aspects that may be similar to or different from your own, is an integral part of learning a language.

In order to make the most of *¡Claro que sí!*, read the following description of the chapter parts and the study tips provided.

Chapter Opener

The first two pages of each chapter contain a list of objectives and illustrations that help set the scene for the rest of the chapter. The objectives, stated as language functions or uses, identify the linguistic and communicative focus for the chapter.

Story Line

In *¡Claro que sí!* you will get to know a series of characters and will follow them through everyday events in their lives. This is usually done through listening to a conversation. The chapter conversations present vocabulary and language functions that you will practice in the chapter and they provide a base for learning more about the Spanish-speaking world. They consist of approximately 80 percent known material and 20 percent new material, and are accompanied by listening and speaking activities.

In order to develop good listening skills, follow these tips:

1. Do not read the conversation before listening to it.
2. Visualize the setting of the conversation (a café, a theater, a hotel, etc.) and think of things that might be said in the situation presented.
3. Keep in mind what you know about the recurring characters who are speaking.
4. You will usually hear the conversation twice. The first time you will be asked to listen for certain basic information and, the second time, for a more detailed understanding. Try to focus on the task at hand.

5. It is not important to understand all the words spoken. You may listen to the conversation again in the language lab. All conversations from the textbook are recorded at the end of the corresponding chapter tape.

Lo esencial

Knowing vocabulary is fundamental to learning a language. In *¡Claro que sí!*, vocabulary is presented in thematic groups, such as sports or entertainment, to aid you in the learning process. Vocabulary presentations are followed by activities that include practice of the new words in situations common to daily life.

There are many ways to learn vocabulary; you may use the following strategies or others that work for you:

1. Say words aloud while studying.
2. Study vocabulary while walking to class, riding the bus, etc. Practice by saying to yourself in Spanish what you are doing or what you see.
3. Associate words with things that are meaningful to you, for example, *expensive* = your friend's new red sports car. Form sentences with the words you are learning: John's car is *expensive*.
4. Make lists of the words that you have a difficult time remembering and look at the list frequently.

Hacia la comunicación

Grammar explanations in *¡Claro que sí!* are written in English so that you can study them at home. Concise explanations are illustrated by examples, and many are preceded or followed by questions to help you process the information you are studying. Answers to the questions are given at the back of the book. The activities that follow the explanations ask you to use what you are learning while interacting with classmates.

Here are some tips for studying grammar:

1. Remember that knowledge of grammar is the key to communication. Knowing grammar rules is not an end, but rather a means to enable you to express yourself in another language.
2. Focus on the title of each topic presented to see what language use is being emphasized—expressing likes, describing people and places, etc.
3. Read the examples carefully.
4. Create sentences of your own, using the grammar point presented to carry out the language function emphasized.

Developing speaking skills is reinforced throughout the chapters in this text. In order to learn how to speak Spanish, you need to have ample opportunity to express yourself orally. You will be asked to do many activities in pairs and small groups to maximize your speaking time. Here are a few tips to help you develop good speaking skills:

1. Speak loudly and clearly; avoid mumbling.
2. Work cooperatively while in pairs or small groups. Correct or help your classmates when necessary.
3. Be aware of exactly what you are to do and the focus of each activity—what grammar and vocabulary you will need to carry out the task.
4. Volunteer frequently to maximize your own personal speaking time.
5. Use Spanish before and after class with your peers and instructor.

Nuevos horizontes

This section has three goals: to teach you how to read in Spanish, how to write, and to expand your understanding of the Hispanic world. Specific techniques are discussed and practiced to develop your reading and writing skills in Spanish.

Here are some tips to help you become a more proficient reader and writer in Spanish:

1. Focus on the technique being taught.
2. Use techniques taught in early chapters while reading selections from later chapters.
3. Write frequently in Spanish (notes to yourself about what you have to do, a diary, etc.).
4. When reading and writing, look up only those words that are essential to understanding the message. List these words on a separate sheet of paper for reference.

After the **Nuevos horizontes** section, the sections from the first part of the chapter repeat, with a change in sequence: **Lo esencial,** a story line section, **Hacia la comunicación.** For easy reference, each chapter ends with a summary of the new vocabulary presented.

Ancillaries

Workbook/Lab Manual

The Workbook/Lab Manual is designed to give you needed practice in listening, reading, and writing in order to help develop these skills. Each chapter in the Workbook is divided as follows:

- *Mechanical Practice, Parts I and II.* Parts I and II are to be done upon completion of the first and second grammar explanation sections, respectively. The exercises give you practice manipulating each grammar topic in isolation.

- *Communicative Practise.* This section allows you to express yourself in a less controlled way and to practice the language functions covered in the chapter. The activities in this section include the main grammar points and vocabulary presented in the chapter. They should be done after completing the second grammar explanation section and before any quizzes or exams. An Answer Key to the Workbook exercises is given at the back of the Workbook/Lab Manual so that you can check your answers.

The Lab Manual is keyed to nine cassettes of recorded activities, which are available for purchase in two parts. Each chapter in the Lab Manual contains the following material:

- *Pronunciation.* An explanation of the sound or sounds to be focused on is followed by practice exercises.

- *Listening Comprehension Activities.* Each chapter contains numerous activities that include conversations in different settings and circumstances, and varied types of ads, announcements, and messages.

- *The Chapter Conversations.* Each chapter tape ends with the chapter conversations from the text, so that you can listen to them outside of class. The recorded activities should be done after the second grammar explanation section and before any quizzes or exams. The Lab Manual contains the instructions for all activities as well as the written portions that you need to work with while listening to the tapes.

Computer Study Modules

The computer software that accompanies *¡Claro que sí!* provides practice of the vocabulary and grammar of each chapter. It also incorporates reading comprehension practice. The program gives immediate feedback of responses so that you can check your progress in Spanish and learn where you may need further practice. The Computer Study Modules are available for IBM and IBM-compatible computers.

Video Workbook

The Video Workbook accompanies a series of authentic videos from Radio Televisión Española, the national Spanish television station. The videos contain programs about a number of countries in the Hispanic world to expose you to the culture and language in a variety of natural settings. The Video Workbook provides activities to be done before, while, and after viewing the videos to help you expand your knowledge of Hispanic culture. The topics range from historic themes to art to everyday aspects of culture. Although the language has not been simplified for a beginning student of Spanish, you will be amazed at how much you can understand when you combine your knowledge of language with the visual images provided by video.

Acknowledgments

The authors and publisher thank the following people for their contributions reviewing portions of the manuscript during the development of *¡Claro que sí!*

Alurista, *California Polytechnic State University, San Luis Obispo*
Roman Alvarez, *Moorhead State University*
Debra Andrist, *Baylor University*
Elisabeth Boyce, *University of Houston*
M. Cecilia Colombi, *University of Massachusetts, Amherst*
Jeanette Harker, *Florida Atlantic University*
Francisco Hinojos, *Skyline College*
John Kelly, *North Carolina State University, Raleigh*
John Lipski, *University of Florida, Gainesville*
James Maloney, *Pan American University*
Keith Mason, *The University of Michigan, Ann Arbor*
Jaime Montesinos, *Manhattan Community College/CUNY*
Douglas Morgenstern, *Massachusetts Institute of Technology*
David F. Pardess, *Los Angeles Mission College*
Richard A. Raschio, *College of Saint Thomas*
Ana Roca, *Florida International University, Tamiami Campus*
Berardo Valdes, *Iowa State University*

We dedicate this book to George and André, Andy, and Norma and Pete Selly, who gave us both inspiration and food for thought.

We are especially grateful to the following people and organizations for their valuable assistance during the development of this project: Guiomar Borrás-Azpurua for selecting and obtaining permission for realia and for contributions to some of the *Nuevos horizontes* sections; Adán Griego for preparing the index; Victoria Junco de Meyer, Olga Tedias Montero, Almerindo Ojeda, and the native Spanish-speaking graduate students and teaching assistants of the Spanish Department at the University of Wisconsin-Madison for helping assure the linguistic and cultural accuracy of the book; the participants of the Spanish for Spanish Teachers course at the University of Wisconsin-Milwaukee, especially Kathy Solórzano and Jane Spector, and the Center for Latin America at the University of Wisconsin-Milwaukee; all our students for their role in testing activities; Beverly Fuller; the Monona Grove School District.

¡Hola!
Guadalajara, México

Capítulo preliminar

Chapter objectives

After studying this chapter, you will know how to:

- tell your name and where you are from
- ask others their name and where they are from
- tell the names of many countries and their capitals

- recognize a number of classroom expressions, commands and some Spanish words that are similar to English
- greet someone and say good-by

What is happening in this scene? What could these people be saying?

Las presentaciones

A: ¿Cómo te llamas?
B: Me llamo Marisa. ¿Y tú?
A: Martín.

A: ¿Cómo se llama usted (Ud.)?
B: Me llamo Tomás Gómez. ¿Y Ud.?
A: Silvio Rivera.

> ### ¿Lo sabían?
>
> Spanish has two forms of address to reflect different levels of formality. **Usted (Ud.)** is generally used when talking to people whom you would address by their last name (Mrs. Smith, Mr. Jones) or with the words "sir" and "madam." (What would you like, sir?) **Tú** is used when speaking to a young person and to people whom you would call by their first name.

Actividad 1: ¿Cómo te llamas?

Try to meet as many people in your class as you can in three minutes by asking their names. Remember as many names as you can. Follow the model.

> **A:** ¿Cómo te llamas?
> **B:** Me llamo . . .

Actividad 2: ¿Cómo se llama Ud.?

Choose the name of a president, actor/actress, or famous athlete. Introduce yourself to three other famous personalities in your class. Follow the model.

> **A:** ¿Cómo se llama Ud.?
> **B:** Me llamo . . .

Have students compare the two situations and the use of **tú** and **Ud.**

El origen

A: ¿De dónde eres?
B: Soy de Laredo, Texas.
A: Yo soy de Madrid.

A: ¿De dónde es Ud.?
B: Soy de Los Ángeles.
A: Yo soy de Puerto Rico.

Informal = **¿De dónde eres?**

Actividad 3: ¿De dónde eres?

Ask four or five classmates where they are from. Follow the model.

 A: ¿De dónde eres?
 B: Soy de (Cincinnati, Ohio). ¿Y tú?

Formal = **¿De dónde es usted?**

Act. 4: After doing Act. 4, tell students to meet other members of the class and to find out their names and where they are from. To practice both **tú** and **Ud.**, have students address classmates who are blond or wearing red, for example, with **Ud.**

Actividad 4: ¿De dónde es Ud.?

You are a businessman/businesswoman at a cocktail party and you are talking to two other guests. Find out their names and where they are from. Follow the model.

 A: ¿Cómo se llama Ud.?
 B: . . . ¿y Ud.?
 A: ¿De dónde es?
 B: . . .

Los saludos y las despedidas

A: ¡Hola Pedro! ¿Cómo estás?
B: Bien, gracias. ¿Y tú?
A: Bien.

A: Hasta luego, Sra. Ramírez. ¡Buen viaje!
B: Adiós, señorita. Muchas gracias.

Los saludos *(Greetings)*

Hola. Hi.
Buenos días. Good morning.
Buenas tardes. Good afternoon / evening.

Buenas noches. Good evening.

¿Cómo estás?
¿Cómo está (Ud.)? } How are you?
¿Qué tal?
  (informal)

¡Muy bien! Very well!
Bien. O.K.
Más o menos. So, so.
Regular. Not bad.
Mal. Lousy. / Awful.

Discuss the **abrazo,** kiss, and handshake when saying good-by. Explain the use of **adiós** vs. **hasta luego.**

Las despedidas *(Saying Good-by)*

Hasta luego.   See you later.
Hasta mañana.   See you
  tomorrow.
Buenas noches.   Good night.

Adiós.   Good-by.
Chau. / Chao.   By. / So long.

¿Lo sabían?

Adiós is also used as a greeting when two people pass each other on the street and just want to say "Hi," but have no intention of stopping to chat.

Is the greeting formal or informal?

Actividad 5: ¡Hola! ¿Cómo estás?

In pairs, take one of the roles in each of the situations in the drawing (roles A, C, E, and G or roles B, D, F, and H). Greet each other, ask how you are, and then say good-by.

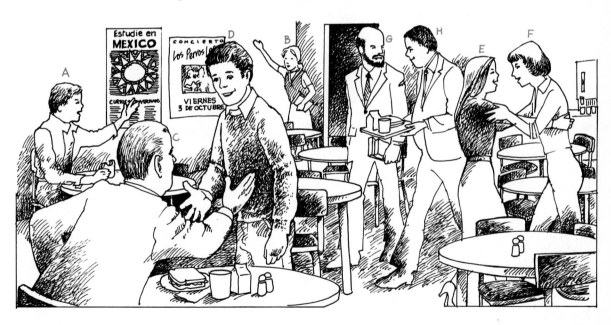

Act. 6: Set a time limit. Monitor the activity and see that all students have had a chance to meet. Check by seeing how many names and home towns they can remember.

Actividad 6: En una fiesta

You are at a get-together at your dorm. You know only some of the guests. Walk around and greet the people you know and introduce yourself to people you don't know. Ask their names and where they are from, and then take leave; say that you will see them later.

Países y sus capitales

Salidas – Departures			
Iberia	508	MADRID	8:35 A.M.
Viasa	359	CARACAS	8:55 A.M.
AA	622	SAN JUAN	9:25 A.M.

Llegadas – Arrivals			
LanChile	203	SANTIAGO	9:00 AM
Aeroperú	199	LIMA	9:50 AM
Avianca	875	BOGOTÁ	10:20 AM

Model the pronunciation of the countries and their capitals as you look at the maps. Have students pronounce them after you. Note: **Sucre = la capital oficial de Bolivia; La Paz = la sede del gobierno.**

Note: **Suramérica, Sudamérica,** and **América del Sur** are all correct. Point out that **Sudamérica** and **Suramérica** are written as one word. **Suramérica** will be used in this text due to high-frequency usage.

Option 1: Drill students on capitals by giving true/false statements: **San Juan es la capital de Costa Rica.** Have students correct the false statements.
Option 2: Ask, **¿Cuál es la capital de ...? Santiago es la capital de Chile, ¿no?**
Option 3: In pairs, students quiz each other with true/false statements based on the departure and arrival boards: S1: **Caracas es la capital de Colombia.** S2: **No, ...**

Act. 7: Have students switch roles in pair activities.

Países hispanos y sus capitales

Use the maps on the inside cover of your text to learn the names of Hispanic countries and their capitals. Follow the directions of your instructor.

Otros países y sus capitales

Alemania Occidental	Bonn
Alemania Oriental	Berlín
Brasil	Brasilia
Canadá	Ottawa
Estados Unidos	Washington
Francia	París
Inglaterra	Londres
Italia	Roma
Portugal	Lisboa

Actividad 7: Capitales hispanas

In pairs, take three minutes to memorize the capitals of the countries on either the front or back inside cover of the book. Your partner will memorize the opposite cover. Then turn to the cover that your partner has studied and take turns asking the capitals of these countries. Follow the model.

A: *(Looking at the back inside cover)* ¿Cuál es la capital de Chile?
B: Santiago.

B: *(Looking at the front inside cover)* ¿Cuál es la capital de Costa Rica?
A: . . .

Actividad 8: Capitales del mundo

Ramiro likes to travel around the world and has visited these capitals: Bogotá, Ottawa, Montevideo, La Paz, Londres, San José, and Tegucigalpa. In pairs, take turns asking the correct question for each capital he has visited. Follow the model.

A: Bogotá
B: ¿Cuál es la capital de Colombia?

Expresiones para la clase

Learn the following commands **(mandatos)** so that you can react to them when they are used by your instructor.

Mandatos

Abre/Abran el libro en la página . . . Open your book to page . . .

Cierra/Cierren el libro. Close your book.

Mira/Miren el ejercicio/la actividad . . . Look at the exercise/the activity . . .

Escucha./Escuchen. Listen.

Escribe./Escriban. Write.

Lee/Lean las instrucciones. Read the instructions.

Saca/Saquen papel/bolígrafo/ lápiz. Take out a paper/pen/ pencil.

Repite./Repitan. Repeat.

Siéntate./Siéntense. Sit down.

Levántate./Levántense. Stand up.

[Vicente], pregúntale a [Ana] . . . [Vicente], ask [Ana] . . .

[Ana], contéstale a [Vicente] . . . [Ana], answer [Vicente] . . .

[María], repite la respuesta, por favor. [María], repeat the answer, please.

[María], dile a [Jorge] . . . [María], tell [Jorge] . . .

The following expressions will be useful in the classroom:

¿Cómo se dice _____ en español? How do you say _____ in Spanish?

¿Cómo se escribe _____? How do you spell _____?

¿Qué quiere decir _____? What does _____ mean?

¿En qué página, por favor? What page, please?

No entiendo. / No comprendo. I don't understand.

No sé [la respuesta]. I don't know [the answer].

Más despacio, por favor. More slowly, please.

(Muchas) gracias. Thank you (very much).

De nada. You're welcome.

Act. 9: 1. **Pablo, pregúntale a Ana de dónde es. Ana, contéstale.** 2. **John, levántate. Susan, levántate. John y Susan, levántense.** (etc.)

Actividad 9: Los mandatos

Listen to the commands your instructor gives you and act accordingly.

Actividad 10: ¿Qué dirías tú?

What would you say in the following situations?

1. The instructor is speaking very fast.
2. The instructor asks you a question but you don't know the answer.
3. You do not understand what the word **azafata** means.
4. You do not understand what the instructor is telling you.
5. You did not hear the page number.
6. You want to know how to say *table* in Spanish.

Los cognados

You already know more Spanish than you may think. Many Spanish words are similar in spelling and meaning to English words, for example: **capital** – *capital*, **instrucciones** – *instructions*. These words are called cognates **(cognados).** Your ability to recognize them will help you understand Spanish.

Actividad 11: Anuncios

Look at the following newspaper clippings and tell what each is about or advertises. Look for cognates to help you.

Actividad 12: ¿Qué entiendes?

The following ad was taken from the yellow pages in San Gabriel, California. Look at it quickly, then try to answer the questions.

1. What is this ad advertising?
2. Why is there a picture of a family?
3. Who is Gregory Robins?
4. How many telephone numbers can you call?
5. How many offices are there? Where are they located?
6. Name two services offered.

Other false cognates: **fútbol** = soccer; **lectura** = reading; **actual** = current, present.

¡OJO! *(Watch out!)* There are some words that have similar forms in Spanish and English but have very different meanings **(cognados falsos).** Context will usually help you determine whether the word is a cognate or a false cognate. Look at the following examples.

María está muy contenta porque el médico dice que está **embarazada.**	*María is very happy because the doctor says she is **pregnant**.*
Necesito ir a la **librería** para comprar los libros del semestre.	*I need to go to the **bookstore** to buy books for the semester.*

ca, co, cu: c is pronounced like *c* in *cat*.
ce, ci: c is pronounced like *c* in *center*.
ga, go, gu: g is pronounced like *g* in *go* or softer, as in *egg*.
ge, gi: g is pronounced like *h* in *hot*.
H is silent.

Listen to the tape for each chapter to practice pronunciation.

Go through the ABCs pronouncing letters. Drill the letters, stressing pure vowel sounds.

Contrast the [g] and [c] sounds.

Point out the pronunciation of the **z** and **c** in Spain.

Point out to students the **che, ll, ñ,** and **rr** and their alphabetization.

Pronunciation will be explained and practiced in the lab program and specific sounds will be highlighted for practice in each chapter.

Pronunciando y deletreando palabras: El alfabeto

Letter	Name	Example
A	a	**A**rgentina
B	be, be larga, be grande, be de burro	**B**arcelona
C	ce	**C**entroamérica, **C**anadá
Ch	che	**Ch**ile
D	de	Santo **D**omingo
E	e	**E**cuador
F	efe	**F**ilipinas
G	ge	Carta**g**ena, **G**uatemala
H	hache	**H**onduras
I	i	Las **I**slas Canarias
J	jota	San **J**osé
K	ca	**K**ansas
L	ele	**L**ima
LL	elle	Marse**ll**a
M	eme	**M**ontevideo
N	ene	**N**icaragua
Ñ	eñe	Espa**ñ**a
O	o	**O**viedo
P	pe	**P**anamá
Q	cu	**Q**uito
R	ere	**P**erú
RR	erre, doble ere	Sie**rr**a Nevada
S	ese	**S**antiago
T	te	**T**oledo
U	u	**U**ruguay
V	uve, ve chica, ve corta, ve de vaca	**V**enezuela
W	doble uve, doble ve, doble u	**W**ashington
X	equis	E**x**tremadura
Y	i griega, ye	**Y**ucatán
Z	zeta	**Z**aragoza

Notes:

1. The Spanish alphabet has thirty letters. Each letter (except for the **rr,** which never occurs at the beginning of a word) has its own separate entry in dictionaries.
2. The **k** and **w** are usually used with words of foreign origin.
3. All letters are feminine, for example: **las letras son la** *a***, la** *b***, la** *c***,** etc.

Briefly explain gender. It will be dealt with formally in Ch. 1.

Actividad 13: Usen el diccionario

In pairs, see who can locate the following words more quickly in the dictionary at the back of the book: **carro, loco, cara, compañero, charla, lluvia, calle.**

Actividad 14: ¿Cómo se escribe . . . ?

Find out the names of two classmates and ask them to spell their last names. Follow the model.

|●| **A:** ¿Cómo te llamas?
    B: Teresa Domínguez Schroeder.
    A: ¿Cómo se escribe "Schroeder"?
    B: Ese-che-ere-o-e-de-e-ere.

For more information on syllabication and accentuation, see Appendix C.

Discuss syllabication when presenting accentuation.

Acentuando palabras *(Stressing Words)*

In order to pronounce words correctly, you will need to know the stress patterns of Spanish.

a. If a word ends in **n, s,** or a *vowel* **(vocal),** stress falls on the *next-to-last syllable* **(penúltima sílaba).**
    re**pi**tan   **lla**mas   **ho**la

b. If a word ends in any *consonant* **(consonante)** other than **n** or **s,** stress falls on the *last syllable* **(última sílaba).**
    espa**ñol**   us**ted**   regu**lar**

c. Any exception to rules *a* and *b* has a written accent mark **(acento ortográfico)** on the stressed vowel.
    televi**sió**n   te**lé**fono   **lá**piz

Note: There are two other sets of words that require accents:

1. Question words: **cómo, de dónde, cuál,** etc., always have accents.
2. Certain words change meaning when written with an accent although pronunciation remains the same: **tú** = you, **tu** = yours, **él** = he, **el** = the.

Actividad 15: Acentos

Indicate the syllable where the stress falls in each word of the following sentences. Listen while your instructor pronounces each sentence.

1. ¿Có-mo es-tá, Se-ñor Pé-rez?
2. La ca-pi-tal de Pe-rú es Li-ma.
3. ¿Có-mo se es-cri-be "Ne-bras-ka"?
4. Re-pi-tan la fra-se.
5. No com-pren-do.
6. Más des-pa-cio, por fa-vor.

Act. 16: Do a listening exercise, dictating U.S. place names: **Nevada, San Francisco, Los Ángeles, San Agustín, Orlando, Boca Ratón, El Paso, Los Álamos, San José, Sacramento, Toledo,** etc. Check for correct placement of written accents when finished. Continue to practice accents in beginning chapters.

Actividad 16: Más acentos

Read the following words, stressing the syllables in bold type. Place a written accent mark over the appropriate vowel when necessary.

1. **ra**pido	5. profe**sor**	9. **Me**xico	13. pi**za**rra
2. Sala**man**ca	6. tele**gra**ma	10. doc**to**ra	14. **can**cer
3. **la**piz	7. ca**fe**	11. **pa**gina	15. Bogo**ta**
4. profe**sion**	8. na**cio**nes	12. universi**dad**	

Vocabulario funcional

Las presentaciones (Introductions)

¿Cómo te llamas?   What's your name? (informal)
¿Cómo se llama (usted)?   What's your name? (formal)
Me llamo . . .   My name is . . .
¿Y tú/usted?   And you?

El origen

¿De dónde eres?   Where are you from? (informal)
¿De dónde es usted?   Where are you from? (formal)
Soy de . . .   I am from . . .

Países hispanos y sus capitales

¿Cuál es la capital de . . . ?   What is the capital of . . . ?

México   México D.F. (Distrito Federal) } América del Norte

Costa Rica   San José
El Salvador   San Salvador
Guatemala   Guatemala
Honduras   Tegucigalpa   } América Central
Nicaragua   Managua
Panamá   Panamá

Argentina   Buenos Aires
Bolivia   La Paz/Sucre
Colombia   Bogotá
Chile   Santiago
Ecuador   Quito   } América del Sur
Paraguay   Asunción
Perú   Lima
Uruguay   Montevideo
Venezuela   Caracas

Cuba   La Habana
Puerto Rico   San Juan   } El Caribe
República Dominicana   Santo Domingo

España   Madrid } Europa

Los saludos y las despedidas   Expresiones para la clase

See pages 4–5   See page 7

See pages 4–5
See page 7

Point out to students that **don** and **doña** are titles of respect that have no English equivalent. They are used with first names in direct discourse: **Don Jorge, Doña Inés.**

Los protagonistas

These are the main characters you will be reading about throughout *¡Claro que sí!*

1. Teresa Domínguez Schroeder, 22, Puerto Rico
2. Vicente Mendoza Durán, 26, Costa Rica
3. Claudia Dávila Arenas, 21, Colombia
4. Juan Carlos Moreno Arias, 24, Perú
5. Marisel Álvarez Vegas, 19, Venezuela
6. Álvaro Gómez Ortega, 23, España
7. Diana Miller, 25, Los Estados Unidos
8. Isabel Ochoa Hermann, 24, Chile
9. Don Alejandro Domínguez Estrada, 55, Puerto Rico

Madrid, España.

¿Sí o no?
¿Es un hotel?; ¿Es un hospital?; ¿Es una universidad?; ¿Qué es?

Explain that this is a **colegio mayor** by giving names of dorms at your university. Contrast this with names of hotels and hospitals.

A dorm is referred to as a **colegio mayor** in Spain and as a **residencia** in most of Hispanic America. The word **dormitorio** is used by some Spanish speakers in the Caribbean.

¿De dónde es el pasaporte de Teresa?

Capítulo 1

Note:
1. People from Puerto Rico have U.S. passports and are U.S. citizens, even though they consider themselves Puerto Ricans. They travel freely to the U.S. and can legally obtain jobs there.
2. The use of 2 last names: first = father's, second = mother's.
3. Many Mexican-Americans commonly use the mother's last name as a middle name.

Chapter Objectives

After studying this chapter, you will know how to:

- introduce yourself
- give your age
- tell where you are from

- tell what you do
- identify others and tell their age, origin, and occupation

Look at the registration card (**ficha de inscripción**) and answer the following questions:
¿Cómo se llama la persona?
¿Es Teresa la señorita (**Srta.**) Domínguez o la Srta. Schroeder?
¿De dónde es ella?
¿Es Ponce una ciudad o un país?

Colegio Mayor Hispanoamericano

Nombre T E R E S A

Apellidos D O M Í N G U E Z   S C H R O E D E R

Edad 2 2   País de origen P U E R T O   R I C O

Número de pasaporte 0 2 3 1 5 3 6 4 4

Dirección C A L L E   D E L   P A R Q U E   2 N 3 6

Ciudad P O N C E

País P U E R T O   R I C O   Código postal 0 0 7 3 1

Prefijo 8 0 9   Teléfono 8 3 3 7 3 1 4

En el Colegio Mayor Hispanoamericano

Refer to the Tapescript or Lab Manual for a description of the sound(s) practiced in each chapter. Dedicate extra time to troublesome sounds.

When practicing dialogue lines or sounds within sentences, draw students' attention to and practice proper intonation and linking.

Act. 1: Do not allow students to look at the dialogue while you play the tape.

Student registering at the **Universidad Autónoma de Madrid,** Spain.

Pronunciation: **a, e, i, o, u**
1. Model the sounds and have students repeat after you.
2. Alert students that there is no schwa (*uh* sound) for unstressed vowels in Spanish. Pronounce **banana** in Spanish and in English and have students identify, then repeat the Spanish.
3. Have students practice the sounds in syllables: **ma, ta, sa; me, te, se,** etc.

> Read the phrases before listening so that you know what to listen for.

4. Practice word pairs such as **buenas-buenos, malas-malos.**
5. Ask students to find words in the dialogue that contain specific vowels, and have them say these words aloud. Write the words on the board and have the class repeat them.

¿Cómo?	What? / What did you say?
No hay de qué.	Don't mention it. / You're welcome.

Teresa has just arrived in Madrid. She has come to Spain to study tourism and to help her uncle at his travel agency. In the following dialogue, Teresa is registering at the dorm **(colegio mayor)** where she will be living.

Actividad 1: ¿Qué escuchas?

Listen to the conversation between Teresa and the receptionist, Andrés Pérez, and check only the phrases that you hear.

✔	Buenos días.	_____	Buenas tardes.
_____	¿Cómo te llamas?	✔	¿Cómo se llama Ud.?
✔	Sí, soy de Puerto Rico.	_____	Sí, es de Puerto Rico.
_____	¿Cuál es su dirección?	✔	¿Cuál es su número de pasaporte?

Is this a formal or informal conversation?

Recepcionista	Un momento . . . ¿Sí? Buenos días.
Teresa	Buenos días.
Recepcionista	¿Cómo se llama Ud.?
Teresa	Soy Teresa Domínguez Schroeder.
Recepcionista	Domínguez . . . Domínguez . . . ¿Cómo? ¿Cómo es el segundo apellido?
Teresa	Schroeder.
Recepcionista	¿Cómo se escribe?
Teresa	Ese-che-ere-o-e-de-e-ere.
Recepcionista	Emmm . . . Domínguez Sánchez, Domínguez Salinas, ¡ah, Domínguez Schroeder! Usted es de Puerto Rico, ¿no?
Teresa	Sí, soy de Puerto Rico.
Recepcionista	¿Cuál es su número de pasaporte?
Teresa	Cero-dos-tres-uno-cinco-tres-seis-cuatro-cuatro (023153644).
Recepcionista	Bien, su habitación es la ocho (8), señorita.
Teresa	¿Cómo?
Recepcionista	La ocho.
Teresa	¡Ah! Muchas gracias, señor. Hasta luego.
Recepcionista	Adiós. No hay de qué.

Discussing origin

Asking for a repetition

Ask questions related to the preliminary chapter, pretend not to hear the response, and ask, **¿Cómo?** Then, ask the students something quickly or in a soft voice so they will ask you, **¿Cómo?**

Have students find all the questions the receptionist asks Teresa. Then direct students to use only these questions and create a role play.

Act 2: Encourage students to correct false statements.

Actividad 2: ¿Cierto o falso?

After listening to the conversation write **C** if the statement is true **(cierto)** or **F** if the statement is false **(falso).**

1. _____ Teresa es de Costa Rica.
2. _____ Ella se llama Teresa Schroeder Domínguez.
3. _____ El número de su habitación es ocho.
4. _____ Teresa está en un hotel.

The ¿**Lo sabían?** sections serve as the basis for comparison between cultures. Encourage students to analyze their own culture to better understand others.

¿Lo sabían?
In Hispanic countries, when students attend a university or college outside their hometown, it is customary for them to stay with relatives who live in that city. When this is not possible, they may live in a dorm **(colegio mayor, residencia)** that is usually independent from the university. Since in some countries dorms are almost nonexistent, it is possible to rent a room in a **pensión,** which is similar to a boarding house. A small number of students rent apartments. What do students do in the United States?

Act. 3: Point out that usually, when meeting someone, a person only gives the first last name. Model this activity with a student before beginning. Encourage students to stand up, mingle, and shake hands.

Act. 4: Model with a student. Encourage students to shake hands when they meet, adopt a country, and act like business people. Have them reverse roles when finished.

Point out if needed: **Me llamo John Smith** is correct: **Soy el Sr. Smith** is correct; **Me llamo el Sr. Smith** is incorrect.

Remember: If there is an odd number of students, it is preferable to have 1 group of 3 so that you can monitor.

Act. 5: This may be a competition. Ask students to keep score. When they finish, have them quiz you.

> If you don't know, say, **No sé.**

Act. 6: Allow time for students to meet a number of classmates, especially in a large class. Have them use questions from Act. 5 to expand conversation. Option 1: Have students use **Ud.** for classmates with long hair or for those wearing red, and **tú** with others in the class. Option 2: Set a time limit for students to mingle and pose questions. After they have finished, quiz students in rapid-fire fashion to see how many names they have learned.

Actividad 3: ¿Cómo te llamas?

Meet three classmates. Introduce yourselves and ask each other where you are from. Follow the model.

A: ¿Cómo te llamas?
B: . . . ¿Y tú?
A: . . .
B: Mucho gusto.
A: Igualmente.
B: ¿De dónde eres?
A: Soy de . . . ¿Y tú?
B: Yo también soy de . . . / Soy de . . .

Actividad 4: ¿Cómo se llama Ud.?

In pairs, pretend that you are Hispanic business people visiting the United States. Introduce yourselves, and ask each other where you are from, following the model. This is a formal dialogue.

A: ¿Cómo se llama Ud.?
B: Me llamo . . . ¿Y Ud.?
A: . . .
B: Encantado/a.
A: Igualmente.
B: ¿De dónde es Ud.?
A: De . . . ¿Y Ud.?
B: Soy de . . .

Actividad 5: ¿Cómo se llama?

In pairs, ask each other questions to see how many of the other students' names you can remember. Also, tell where they are from. Follow the model. Note that there are two dialogue possibilities.

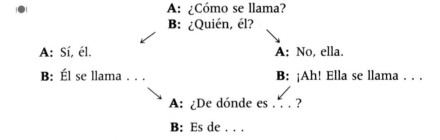

A: ¿Cómo se llama?
B: ¿Quién, él?

A: Sí, él.
B: Él se llama . . .

A: No, ella.
B: ¡Ah! Ella se llama . . .

A: ¿De dónde es . . . ?
B: Es de . . .

Actividad 6: Conversación

Combine what you have learned so far and greet a classmate that you have not yet met. Find out his/her name and where he/she is from.

Actividad 7: Tú y él/ella

In pairs, write a few sentences introducing yourself and introducing your partner. State your names and where each of you is from.

Lo esencial

Los números del uno al cien

(0	cero)				
1	uno	11	once	21	veintiuno
2	dos	12	doce	22	veintidós . . .
3	tres	13	trece	30	treinta, treinta y uno . . .
4	cuatro	14	catorce	40	cuarenta, cuarenta y uno . . .
5	cinco	15	quince	50	cincuenta, cincuenta y uno . . .
6	seis	16	dieciséis	60	sesenta, sesenta y uno . . .
7	siete	17	diecisiete	70	setenta, setenta y uno . . .
8	ocho	18	dieciocho	80	ochenta, ochenta y uno . . .
9	nueve	19	diecinueve	90	noventa, noventa y uno . . .
10	diez	20	veinte	100	cien, ciento uno, ciento dos . . .

Actividad 8: Numerológica

Use logic to find the next number in the series.

1. tres, seis, nueve, . . .
2. seis, doce, dieciocho, . . .
3. dos, cuatro, ocho, dieciséis, . . .
4. setenta, sesenta y tres, cincuenta y seis, cuarenta y nueve, . . .
5. cien, noventa, ochenta y uno, setenta y tres, . . .

Act. 9: Another common way to say this phone number would be **dos, tres, tres,** *(pause)* **seis, cinco, cero, cuatro.**

Act. 10: Call out numbers at random. Make sure to write down numbers already called so that you can check when a student gets a bingo. There may be four separate bingos: horizontal, vertical, diagonal, and the entire card. Note that **horizontal, vertical** and **diagonal** are cognates.

Actividad 9: ¿Cuál es tu número de teléfono?

Mingle with your classmates and ask and answer the following question.

A: ¿Cuál es tu número de teléfono?
B: Mi número de teléfono es 2-33-65-04 (dos, treinta y tres, sesenta y cinco, cero cuatro).

Actividad 10: ¡Bingo!

Complete the bingo card below using randomly selected numbers in the following manner. Column B: between 1 and 19, column I: between 20 and 39, column N: between 40 and 59, column G: between 60 and 79, and column O: between 80 and 99. Then cross out the numbers as you hear them.

B	I	N	G	O

Hacia la comunicación

Gramática

Answers to questions are in Appendix B.

Explain the importance of the title of this section: grammar is the key to communication. It is a means, not an end.

I. Introductions: Subject Pronouns and *llamarse*

After having used Spanish to communicate with your classmates, answer the following questions to see what you have learned.

- What is the difference between **él se llama** and **ella se llama?**
- How would you tell someone your name?
- What are two ways to ask someone his/her name?
- How would you ask the Dean of Students of your institution his/her name?

I. Drill subject pronouns:
1. Point to one or several students while establishing eye contact with the other students. For example, look at the class, point to yourself, and say, **yo;** look directly at one student, point to another, female student, and say, **ella,** etc. Have students supply the appropriate pronoun.
2. Ask students if they would use **tú** or **Ud.** to address the following people: **George Bush, un amigo, una profesora, tu madre.**

Explain that *it* uses the third person singular form of the verb.

I. Drill **llamarse:**
1. Do a chain drill. S1: **Me llamo Frank.** S2: **Me llamo Jody y él se llama Frank.** S3: **Me llamo Bill, ella se llama Jody y él se llama Frank.** (etc.)
2. Bring in pictures of famous people and have students say, **Él se llama George Bush.**
3. Have students ask each other what their mother's or father's name is. Remind students that **llamarse** is used only with a name and not with a title: **Me llamo Juan Gómez.** vs. **Soy el Sr. Gómez.**

II. Drill **ser de:**
1. Ask where famous people are from.
2. Use classroom objects and ask where things are from: **¿De dónde es tu lápiz/ bolígrafo/mochila/etc.?**
3. Do a chain drill combining names and origin. S1: **Me llamo Pete y soy de Chicago.** S2: **Él se llama Pete y es de Chicago. Me llamo Ann y soy de Detroit.**

To summarize what you have learned, the singular subject pronouns are the following:

yo	I
tú	you (familiar, singular)
usted (Ud.)	you (formal, singular)
él	he
ella	she

The singular forms of the verb **llamarse** (*to call oneself*) are the following:

Llamarse	
yo	**Me llamo** Miguel.
tú	¿Cómo **te llamas?**
Ud.	¿Cómo **se llama** Ud.?
él	¿Cómo **se llama** él?
ella	Ella **se llama** Carmen.

Note: Subject pronouns in Spanish are optional and are generally used only for clarification, emphasis, and contrast. In most cases the conjugated verb forms indicate who the subject is. **Usted,** unlike other subject pronouns, is frequently used to indicate politeness.

II. Giving One's Origin: *Ser + de*

Answer the following questions based on what you have practiced.

- How would you ask your new roommate where he/she is from?
- How would you ask a professor where he/she is from?
- How would you say where your mother is from? **Mi madre . . .**
- How would you say where your boyfriend/girlfriend is from? **Mi novio/novia . . .**

The singular forms of the verb **ser + de** (*to be from*) are the following:

Ser de	
yo	**Soy de** Ecuador.
tú	¿**Eres de** Nicaragua?
Ud.	¿**De** dónde **es** Ud.?
él	Él **es de** San Francisco.
ella	Ella **es de** Colorado.

III. Drill **tener + años:**
1. Have students give ages of people in the news.
2. Have students ask each other how old their partners' mothers or fathers are.

III. Indicating One's Age: *Tener*

One of the uses of the verb **tener** is to indicate one's age. The following are the singular forms of the verb **tener** in the present indicative:

Tener	
yo	**Tengo** treinta años.
tú	¿Cuántos años **tienes?**
Ud.	¿Cuántos años **tiene** Ud.?
él	Él **tiene** diecinueve años.
ella	Ella **tiene** veintiún años.*

Do mechanical drills, Workbook, Part I.

*Note: The number **veintiuno** loses its final **-o** when followed by a masculine noun. When the **-o** is dropped, an accent is placed over the **u.**

Actividad 11: ¿Cuántos años tienes?

Use the verb **tener** to ask several of your classmates their age. Then look at p. 33 and, in pairs, guess the age of the people in the photographs.

◖●| **A:** ¿Cuántos años tienes?   **A:** ¿Cuántos años tiene él?
 B: Tengo . . .   **B:** Tiene . . . años.
                                     A: Sí. / No, él tiene . . . años.

¿Lo sabían?

In Hispanic countries it is not proper to ask someone, especially middle-aged and older women, their age. Moreover, age is not commonly given in Hispanic newspaper articles when describing brides and grooms, political candidates, criminals, or even in obituaries. Do any of these "rules" apply in the United States?

Realia: Ask students what the clipping announces. Discuss the absence of ages. Have students identify cognates.

UNION DE CASTRO CASTAÑEDA Y RODRIGUEZ RODRIGUEZ

Helena De Castro Castañeda y Francisco Rodríguez Rodríguez, se casaron por la religión católica, en la Capilla de Nuestra Señora del Carmen, en Campo Alegre. La encantadora novia fue conducida al altar por su padre, luciendo un bellísimo vestido confeccionado en santug de seda. Cursaron las invitaciones para la boda los padres de ambos contrayentes.
La novia es hija de Eduardo de Castro Benedetti y de Finita Castañeda de Castro, y el novio de Francisco Rodríguez Sobral y de Berta Rodríguez de Rodríguez.
La recepción fue celebrada en la Quinta Campo Claro.

Actividad 12: ¿Qué recuerdas?

In pairs, take turns saying as much as you can about several members of the class.

● Ella 'se llama Elvira, es de Chicago y tiene veintidós años.

Actividad 13: Dos diálogos

Act. 13: Encourage students to listen, memorize their line, establish eye contact, then say their line. Have them repeat the dialogue, using different degrees of loudness: shouting, whispering, etc. Set a scene where this dialogue could take place (a singles' bar, first day of class, etc.) and have students act it out.

In pairs, student "A" covers Column B and student "B" covers Column A. Carry on a dialogue with your partner by listening and choosing an appropriate response from each box in your column. There are two dialogue possibilities.

A   B

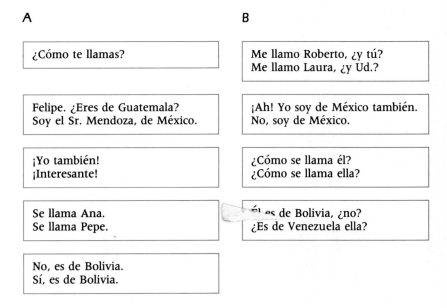

A	B
¿Cómo te llamas?	Me llamo Roberto, ¿y tú? Me llamo Laura, ¿y Ud.?
Felipe. ¿Eres de Guatemala? Soy el Sr. Mendoza, de México.	¡Ah! Yo soy de México también. No, soy de México.
¡Yo también! ¡Interesante!	¿Cómo se llama él? ¿Cómo se llama ella?
Se llama Ana. Se llama Pepe.	Él es de Bolivia, ¿no? ¿Es de Venezuela ella?
No, es de Bolivia. Sí, es de Bolivia.	

Actividad 14: En el colegio mayor

Act. 14: Make sure students cover their partner's information. To simulate a real registration, have partners stand with a desk between them. After students complete the activity, choose a pair to role play in front of the class.

Select role (papel) A or B and follow the instructions for that role. Do not look at the information given for the role your partner plays. When you finish, role play the second situation.

Papel A

You are Juan Carlos Moreno Arias and you are registering at a dorm. Give the necessary information to the receptionist when he/she asks you. This is the information you will need:

Juan Carlos Moreno Arias   Perú   24 años
Número de pasaporte: 5-66-45-89

Papel B

You are the receptionist and have to ask the new student the questions to fill out this registration card. Remember to show the new student respect by using the **usted** form.

Colegio Mayor Hispanoamericano

Nombre

Apellidos

Edad   País de origen

Número de pasaporte

Papel A

You are the receptionist and have to ask the new student questions to fill out this registration card. Remember to show the new student respect by using the **usted** form.

Papel B

You are Isabel Ochoa Hermann and you are registering at a dorm. Give the necessary information to the receptionist when he/she asks you. This is the information you will need:

Isabel Ochoa Hermann   Chile   24 años
Número de pasaporte: 8749652-40

Nuevos horizontes

Ask students what types of readings they scan and why they scan them. This will help them understand when to use *scanning* (reading for specifics: a phone book, application forms, etc.), as opposed to *skimming* (reading to get the gist: newspaper articles, instructions, junk mail, etc.).

Estrategia de lectura: *Scanning*

In this book, you will learn specific techniques that will help you to become a proficient reader in Spanish. In this chapter, the focus is on a technique called *scanning*. When scanning, you are looking for specific bits of information as if you were on a search-and-find mission. Your eyes function as radar, ignoring superfluous information and zeroing in on the specific details that you set out to find.

Actividad 15: Completa la ficha

Look at the following registration card to see what information is requested. Then scan Claudia's application form to the **Colegio Mayor Hispanoamericano** to find the information you need, and fill out Claudia's registration card. Check your answers with a partner.

Colegio Mayor Hispanoamericano

Nombre

Apellidos

Edad ☐☐   País de origen

Número de pasaporte

Dirección

Ciudad

País

Prefijo ☐☐   Teléfono

Discuss the way the numerals 1 and 7 are written.

Mention the elaborate way many Hispanics sign their names.

Colegio Mayor Hispanoamericano
No 78594
Solicitud de admisión para estudiantes extranjeros

Sr./Sra/Srta. _Claudia Dávila Arenas_ hijo/a
de _Jesús María Dávila Cifuentes_ y
de _Elena Arenas Peña_, nacido/a en la ciudad
de _Cali_, _Colombia_ el _15_ de _febrero_
de _1970_, de nacionalidad _colombiana_,
estado civil _soltera_[1], número de pasaporte
_AL 674283_ de _Colombia_,
con domicilio en
Calle 8 No. 15-25 Apto. 303,
de la ciudad de _Cali_, en el país de _Colombia_,
teléfono: prefijo _23_, número _67-15-52_,
solicita admision en el Colegio Mayor Hispanoamericano con fecha de entrada del _2_ de _julio_ de _1992_ y permanencia hasta
el _30_ de _junio_ de _1993_.

Firmado el día _29_ de _enero_ de _1992_

1. Single

Lo esencial

Las ocupaciones

Provide Spanish for other occupations students want to know.

1. el actor/la actriz
2. el/la atleta
3. el/la dentista
4. el/la director/a
5. el/la economista
6. el/la estudiante
7. el/la ingeniero/a
8. el médico / el/la doctor/a
9. el/la recepcionista

Otras ocupaciones

el/la abogado/a   lawyer
el/la agente de viajes   travel agent
el ama de casa (f.)*   housewife
el/la camarero/a   waiter/waitress
el/la dependiente/a   store clerk

*Note: Since **ama** begins with a stressed **a,** the article **el** is used even though the word is feminine.

el/la dueño/a de un negocio owner of a business
el hombre/la mujer de negocios businessman/businesswoman
el/la programador/a de computadoras computer programmer
el/la secretario/a secretary

Act. 16: Supply **está jubilado/a** if necessary.

Actividad 16: ¿Qué hace tu familia?

In pairs, role play the parts of Claudia and Vicente. Student "A" covers Column B and student "B" covers Column A. You are meeting each other for the first time. Introduce yourselves and ask questions about each other's families, asking their names, where they are from, what they do, etc. Ask questions such as the following:

Teach **¿Que hace ... ?** as a set phrase. **Hacer** is presented formally in Ch. 4. Have students use the singular only in both Act. 16 and 17.

A: ¿Qué hace tu padre?
B: Mi padre es economista.

A   B

Los Dávila de Colombia   Los Mendoza de Costa Rica

Claudia—21 años estudiante

Vicente—26 años estudiante

madre—46 años ama de casa | padre—48 años médico

madre—49 años abogada | padre—57 años economista

Actividad 17: ¿Qué hacen tus padres?

Interview several classmates and ask them what their parents do.

En la cafetería del colegio mayor

Practice **¿Qué hay?** and **¡Oye!** in meaningful context: When a student is talking or not looking up, get his/her attention by saying, **¡Oye!** Go around the room using different greetings: **hola, buenos días, ¿Qué hay?**

In some countries—Chile, for example—**¡Escucha!** is used instead of **¡Oye!**

Since this dialogue takes place in Spain, explain that the Spanish dorms have a dining room (**comedor**) where meals are served and a bar/snack bar (**cafetería**) where one can get a sandwich, coffee, soda, beer, wine, etc.

¿Qué hay?	What's up?
¡Oye!	Hey!
entonces	then

After settling in at the dorm, Teresa goes to the snack bar where she joins her new friend, Marisel Álvarez Vegas, who is from Venezuela. Marisel has lived at the dorm for a while and is telling Teresa who everyone is.

Actividad 18: ¿Quién con quién?

Look at the scene in the snack bar. Listen to the conversation and find out who is talking with whom. The names of the people are Juan Carlos, Diana, Marisel, Teresa, Álvaro, and Vicente.

Teresa	Hola, Marisel.
Marisel	¿Qué hay?
Teresa	Oye, ¿quién es ella?
Marisel	¿La chica? Es Diana.
Teresa	¿Es de España?
Marisel	No, es de los Estados Unidos.
Camarero	¿Qué toman Uds.?
Teresa	Una Coca-Cola.
Marisel	Yo también.
Teresa	¿Y ellos? ¿Quiénes son?
Marisel	Se llaman Juan Carlos y Vicente. Juan Carlos es de Perú y Vicente es de Costa Rica.
Teresa	¡Uy! ¡Entonces todos somos de América!
Marisel	No, el chico que está con Diana es de España, de Córdoba.
Teresa	¿Cómo se llama?
Marisel	Álvaro Gómez.
Teresa	Todos son estudiantes, ¿no?
Marisel	Sí y no, son estudiantes, pero Diana también es profesora de inglés.
Camarero	Las dos Coca-Colas, 180 pesetas,[1] por favor.
Marisel	Gracias.
Camarero	No hay de qué.

1. Spanish monetary unit

Negating

Giving information

Expressing amazement

Asking for a confirmation

Note: The word **cafetería** varies in meaning from country to country: a restaurant, a self-service restaurant, or just a place to have coffee.

In Spain, most dorms are not coed. In the summer, however, they may be rented to both males and females in order to remain open.

Be sure students understand that the word **América** includes the northern and southern hemispheres.

Act. 19: After completing the activity, have students work in pairs, pretending they are Vicente and Juan Carlos. They inquire about people in the snack bar. V: **¿Quiénes son ellas?** JC: **Son ...** V: **¿De dónde son ...?**

Actividad 19: Completa la información

Listen to the conversation again and complete the following chart.

Nombre	País
Diana	Estados Unidos
Juan Carlos	Perú
Álvaro	España
Vicente	Costa Rica

Actividad 20: Presentaciones

From the people you have met in your class, choose two from the same city or state. Introduce them to your classmates and say where they are from.

Hacia la comunicación

I. Talking About Yourself and Others

A. Subject Pronouns in the Singular and Plural

Vosotros/as is used only in Spain.

Point out that in Hispanic America **Uds.** is the plural formal and informal form of address.

yo	I	**nosotros** / **nosotras**	we
tú	you (informal)	**vosotros** / **vosotras**	you (plural informal)
Ud. (usted)	you (formal)	**Uds. (ustedes)**	you (formal/informal)
él	he	**ellos**	they
ella	she	**ellas**	

B. Singular and Plural Forms of the Verbs *llamarse, ser,* and *tener*

Llamarse

Note accents on question words.

yo	**Me llamo** Teresa.	nosotros / nosotras	**Nos llamamos** los Celtics.
tú	¿Cómo **te llamas?**	vosotros / vosotras	¿Cómo **os llamáis?**
Ud.	¿Cómo **se llama** Ud.?	Uds.	¿Cómo **se llaman** Uds.?
él	**Se llama** Vicente.	ellos	**Se llaman** Vicente y Diana.
ella	**Se llama** Diana.	ellas	**Se llaman** Teresa y Marisel.

I.B. Drill **ser** by doing a substitution drill:
**Juan es de Panamá.
Yo ...
Ellos ...
... Bolivia.** (etc.)

Ser

yo	**Soy** dentista.	nosotros / nosotras	**Somos** de Chile.
tú	¿De dónde **eres?**	vosotros / vosotras	¿De dónde **sois?**
Ud.	¿Quién **es** Ud.?	Uds.	¿Quiénes **son** Uds.?
él	Él **es** Vicente.	ellos	**Son** de Perú.
ella	Ella **es** Diana.	ellas	

In this chapter you have seen three uses of the verb **ser.**

1. **Ser + de** + city/country   to indicate origin

2. **Ser +** name   to identify a person **(=llamarse)**

3. **Ser +** occupation   to identify what someone does for a living

Tener			
yo	**Tengo** 20 años.	nosotros nosotras	**Tenemos** 20 años.
tú	¿Cuántos años **tienes?**	vosotros vosotras	¿Cuántos años **tenéis?**
Ud.	Ud. **tiene** 25 años, ¿no?	Uds.	Uds. **tienen** 25 años, ¿no?
él ella	**¿Tiene** 19 años?	ellos ellas	**¿Tienen** 19 años?

II. Drill question formation:
1. Do rapid-fire questions and answers: **Te llamas Juan, ¿no? Él es de Miami, ¿no?**
2. Give students time to write as many questions as they can, including tag questions, and to practice them in pairs.
3. Give statements and have students form all possible questions.

Note: Students can be made aware of simple intonation questions which do not invert word order: **¿Carlos es de Guatemala?** This will not be practiced actively at this point, since it may lead students to make the error, **¿De dónde Carlos es?**

II. Asking and Giving Information: Question Formation

1. Information questions begin with question words such as **cuántos, de dónde, cuál, cómo, qué,** and **quién/es.** Note the word order in the question and in the response.

¿Question word + verb + subject? ⟶ Subject + verb.
¿De dónde es Álvaro? (Él) es de España.
¿Cómo se llama (ella)? (Ella) se llama Teresa.

2. Questions that elicit a yes/no response are formed as follows:

¿Es Isabel? Sí, es Isabel.
¿Es Isabel de Chile?
 ¿Es de Chile Isabel? } Sí, Isabel es de Chile.

Another possibility is to add the tag **¿no?** or **¿verdad?** at the end of a statement.

Isabel es de Chile, ¿no? Sí, Isabel es de Chile.

III. Negating

1. Simple negation.

Ellos **no** son de México.
No se llama Marisel.

2. Answering a question with negation.

¿Son ellas de Perú? { **No,** ellas **no** son de Perú.
 No, ellas son de Panamá.

After reading the grammar explanations, answer these questions:

- How many questions can you formulate that would elicit the following responses? There are several possibilities for each.
  a. **Soy de Quito.** b. **No, soy de Quito.** c. **No, no soy de Quito.**
- How many different ways can you think of to respond to the following question: **¿Son de Guatemala ellos?**

Do mechanical drills, Workbook, Part II.

Actividad 21: ¿De dónde son?

In pairs, say where the following people are from.

1. Julio Iglesias y Seve Ballesteros
2. Margaret Thatcher
3. Steffi Graf y Boris Becker
4. Fernando Valenzuela
5. Gabriela Sabatini y Guillermo Vilas
6. Gabriel García Márquez y Juan Valdés

Actividad 22: ¿Toledo o Toledo?

Vicente and Juan Carlos are talking about their friends. Choose the correct responses and practice the dialogue with a partner.

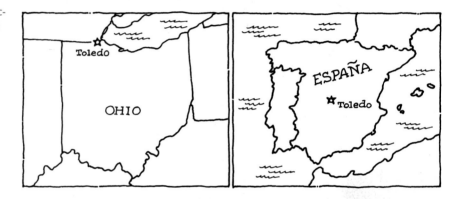

Vicente

| ¿Quiénes son ellas? |

Juan Carlos

| A. Son Diana y Álvaro.
B. Son Diana y Teresa.
C. Es Diana. |

| Teresa es de Suramérica, ¿no? |

| A. No, no es de Puerto Rico.
B. No, es de Puerto Rico.
C. No. Él es de Puerto Rico. |

| Y Diana, ¿también es de Puerto Rico? |

| A. No, es de Toledo.
B. No, no es de España.
C. No es de Puerto Rico. |

| ¡Ah! Es de España. |

| A. No, no es de los Estados Unidos.
B. No es de Ohio.
C. No, es de Toledo, Ohio. |

Act. 23: Repeat, using the **vo-sotros** form.

Actividad 23: Vecinos en el colegio mayor

Assume a Hispanic name. In pairs, talk with other pairs and pretend you are with your roommate, meeting your new neighbors at the dorm. Get to know them by asking questions to elicit the following information.

1. nombre   2. origen   3. edad

A: ¡Hola! Somos sus vecinos. Yo me llamo . . .
B: Y yo me llamo . . . ¿Y Uds., cómo se llaman?
C: . . .

> Remember: ¿ ... ? and accents on question words.

Actividad 24: Preguntas y respuestas

Using the question words you have learned **(qué, cuántos, cómo, quién/es, cuál, de dónde),** write as many questions as you can about the characters that you have met in this chapter (Teresa, Claudia, Juan Carlos, Vicente, Diana, Isabel, Álvaro, and Marisel). You have three minutes. Then, maintain a dialogue with your partner, using the questions you have written.

Act. 25: Encourage students to guess freely. Point out that all photos are of Hispanics. Elicit student reactions, and comment on any misconceptions. Top (left to right): Nicaragua, Puerto Rico, Peru. Bottom: Venezuela, Peru, Spain, Puerto Rico.

Actividad 25: ¿De dónde son estas personas?

Look at the following pictures and try to guess where the people are from.

Actividad 26: ¡Hola! Soy nuevo

In pairs, imagine one of you is a new student who has just transferred into the class. Ask your partner questions to learn about other students. Use questions such as **¿Cómo se llaman ellos? ¿De dónde es él? ¿Quiénes son ellas?**, etc.

Actividad 27: ¡Qué grupo!

You have five minutes to write a brief paragraph identifying a group of people in your class.

Vocabulario funcional

El origen

¿De dónde es él?   Where is he from?   **ser + de**   to be from

Las personas *(People)*

el/la chico/a boy/girl
la madre, la mamá mother, mom
el/la novio/a boyfriend/girlfriend
el padre, el papá father, dad
señor/Sr. Mr.

el señor the man
señora/Sra. Mrs./Ms.
la señora the woman
señorita/Srta. Miss/Ms.
la señorita the young woman

Pronombres personales *(Subject Pronouns)*

See page 30

La posesión

mi my
tu your (informal)
su his/her/your (formal)

Las presentaciones

¿Cómo se llama él/ella? What's his/her name?
¿Quién es él/ella? Who's he/she?
Encantado/a. / Mucho gusto. Nice to meet you.
Igualmente. Nice to meet you, too. / Same here.

el nombre (de pila) first name
el primer apellido first last name (father's name)
el segundo apellido second last name (mother's maiden name)

Agradecimientos *(Thanking)*

No hay de qué. Don't mention it. / You're welcome.

Los números del uno al cien

See page 19

Expresiones relacionadas con los números

el año year
¿Cuál es tu/su número de . . . ?
  What is your . . . number?
¿Cuántos años tiene él/ella?
  How old is he/she?

el pasaporte passport
el teléfono telephone
tener . . . años to be . . . years
  old

Las ocupaciones

See pages 26–27

Palabras y expresiones útiles

la cafetería cafeteria/bar/short-
  order restaurant
el colegio mayor/la residencia
  dormitory
¿Cómo? What? / What did you say?
la dirección address
entonces then
no; ¿no? no; right? isn't it?
¡Oye! Hey!

por favor please
—¿Qué hace él/ella? —Es . . .
  What does he/she do? He/she
  is a . . .
¿Qué hay? What's up?
sí yes
también too, also
todos all
¿verdad? right?
y and

A store in San José, Costa Rica. What do they sell in this store? How do you think Spanish speakers would say Disneyland?

Café de Colombia

¿De dónde es el café?
¿Te gusta el café?

Discuss importance of coffee in the economies of Colombia, El Salvador and Costa Rica.

Ask, **¿Cómo se llama el señor de la foto?**

Do you have the following items: **computadora, calculadora, radio, televisor?**
¿Tienes calculadora? Sí, tengo calculadora. / No, no tengo calculadora.

Ask questions to practice cognates presented here and to recycle professions: **¿Quién tiene computadora, un abogado o un camarero?**

Capítulo 2

¿Es una IBM?
¿Qué computadora te gusta más: la IBM, la Macintosh o la Atari?

Si puede tener un león, ¿por qué conformarse con un simple ratón?

¡Me gusta mucho!

Pronunciation: **d**
1. Contrast the stop [d] sound (**día, condición**) with the fricative [ð] (**todo**): **dónde** vs. **de dónde.**
2. Practice minimal pairs: **cada-cara, todo-toro,** etc.
3. Have students supply occupations that contain the letter **d** and identify, then pronounce, stops (**director**) and fricatives (**agente de viajes, abogado**).
4. Practice the sounds in sentences: **¿De dónde es el estudiante? ¿Dónde está el estudiante? Don Alejandro está en Madrid.**
5. Have students dictate to a classmate 5 words from the dialogue with stop [d] and 5 with fricative [ð].

Practice **claro, por supuesto,** and **¿De veras?** in meaningful context. Use rejoinders: **George Bush es el presidente de los Estados Unidos, ¿no? Tengo $100,00.** (etc.)

Claro.	
¡Claro que sí! }	Of course.
Por supuesto.	
¿De veras?	Really?

Marisel is studying in her room. Teresa is taking a study break and comes to Marisel's room looking for a cup of coffee and some conversation.

Bring in salsa music if possible.

Actividad 1: ¿Qué escuchas?

Listen to the conversation and place a check mark next to the topics that you hear.

✓	computadoras	_____	calculadoras
✓	música salsa	_____	música rock
_____	té	✓	café

Marisel	Sí, pasa.
Teresa	Hola. ¿Cómo estás?
Marisel	Bien. ¿Y tú?
Teresa	Más o menos, tengo que estudiar mucho. ¡Oye! ¿Tienes café?
Marisel	¡Claro que sí!
Teresa	¡Ah! Tienes computadora.
Marisel	Sí, es una Macintosh.
Teresa	A mí me gusta más la IBM porque es más rápida.
Marisel	¿De veras?
Teresa	Sí, mi papá tiene una IBM.
Marisel	Pues a mí me gusta más la Macintosh porque tiene ratón. ¡Oye! ¿Te gusta el café solo o con leche?
Teresa	Solo. . . . Mmm. Me gusta mucho. ¡Ah! ¡Qué música tan buena tienes!
Marisel	Tengo muchos discos de salsa. ¿Te gusta la salsa?
Teresa	Por supuesto. ¿Tienes discos de Rubén Blades?
Marisel	Claro, y de Willie Colón, Oscar de León, Wilfrido Vargas . . .

Getting someone's attention

Expressing preferences

Asking preferences

Papá/mamá and **papi/mami** are commonly used in Latin America. In Spain, **papi/mami** are terms of affection used only by children.

Although **ratón** and **mouse** are used, **mouse** is more prevalent. It is pronounced just as in English.

Rubén Blades (Panama) singer, songwriter, actor; **Willie Colón** (Puerto Rico) trombonist; **Oscar de León** (Venezuela) vocalist and bass player; **Wilfrido Vargas** (Dominican Republic) singer, trumpet player, and **merengue** band leader.

Actividad 2: Preguntas

After listening to the conversation answer the following questions.

1. ¿Qué computadora le gusta a Teresa? ¿Y a Marisel?
2. ¿Tiene computadora Teresa? ¿Y Marisel?
3. ¿Qué significa **ratón** en inglés?
4. ¿Cómo le gusta el café a Teresa, solo o con leche?
5. ¿Quién tiene discos de salsa, Teresa o Marisel?

Act. 3: Have students quiz each other about musical categories: Bach→ **música clásica,** Chuck Mangione→ **jazz,** AC/DC→ **rock ácido,** etc.

Actividad 3: ¿Y tú?

In pairs, ask your partner the following questions.

1. ¿Qué computadora te gusta?
2. ¿Tienes computadora? ¿Qué computadora tienes?
3. ¿Tienes discos de salsa?
4. ¿Qué tipos de discos tienes? ¿Rock? ¿Jazz? ¿Música clásica? ¿Música country? ¿Rock ácido?

Actividad 4: ¡Claro!

In pairs, find out if your partner has the following things. Follow the model.

A: ¿Tienes televisor?
B: ¡Claro! / ¡Por supuesto! / ¡Claro que sí! / No, no tengo.

1. calculadora	4. radio
2. estéreo	5. guitarra
3. vídeo	6. teléfono

Lo esencial

La habitación de Vicente

To learn vocabulary, think of the word **champú** when you are washing your hair, **jabón** when you wash your hands, etc. Say the words aloud.
Idle time = study time.

La cinta/el cassette/el casete, la computadora/el computador, el vídeo/video are all accepted in Spanish.

Articles for items 1–13: Have students quiz each other on gender after studying the grammar section.

Remind students of study hints: Short frequent study periods help long-term memory. Use personal flash cards, preferably with drawings, to avoid translation. Say the words aloud as you use the items: **champú, jabón,** etc.

1. toalla	6. silla	11. plantas
2. cepillo de pelo	7. cámara	12. estéreo
3. cama	8. máquina de escribir	13. guitarra
4. escritorio	9. periódico	
5. lámpara	10. radiorreloj	

Otras cosas

Note: **Agua** takes the article **el** since the first **a** is stressed.

el agua de colonia cologne
la calculadora calculator
el cepillo de dientes
  toothbrush
la cinta/el cassette tape,
  cassette
la computadora computer
la crema de afeitar shaving
  cream
el champú shampoo
el diccionario dictionary
el disco/disco compacto
  record/compact disc
la grabadora tape recorder
el jabón soap

el kleenex Kleenex
la máquina de afeitar electric
  razor
la mesa table
la novela novel
la pasta de dientes
  toothpaste
el peine comb
el perfume perfume
el radio radio
la revista magazine
el sofá sofa, couch
el teléfono telephone
el televisor television set
el vídeo VCR; video-cassette

"VIDEO CASSETTES"
Panasonic
● PV-2800
2 cabezales
Precio Sug. $325 **255**⁸⁹
● PV-3802K
Tres cabezales
Precio Sug. $425 **289**⁸⁹

SOFAS CAMA SIMMONS
● Bridgeport 3/3
Precio Sug. $809 **599**⁸⁹
● Dale 4/6
Precio Sug. $899 **619**⁸⁹
● Angela 5/0
Precio Sug. $839 **629**⁸⁹

What are some Hispanic products sold in the U.S.?

Act. 5: Students may think of other products and lead a warm-up in class the next day to reenter the vocabulary.

Actividad 5: Asociaciones

Associate the following brand names with objects.

◖●◗ Prell   Prell es un champú.

1. Panasonic
2. Colgate
3. Nikon
4. Memorex
5. Norelco

6. Olivetti
7. Zenith
8. Chanel Número 5
9. RCA
10. Palmolive

Actividad 6: ¿Tiene computadora Vicente?

In pairs, look at the picture of Vicente's room and ask what things he has, using the following model.

◖●◗ **A:** ¿Tiene vídeo Vicente?
   B: Sí, tiene vídeo. / No, no tiene vídeo.

Act. 7: After having finished Act. 6, give students 3 minutes to individually write a brief list of what Vicente has that the student doesn't have, what they both have, and what the student has that Vicente doesn't.

Actividad 7: ¿Qué tienes en tu habitación?

In pairs, ask your partner what he/she has in his/her room. Make a list of what you have and what your partner has and be prepared to report back to the class. Follow the model.

    A: ¿Tienes estéreo?
   B: Sí, tengo estéreo. / No, no tengo estéreo.

Have students try to think of other English words that come from Spanish: rodeo, lariat, guitar, etc.

¿Lo sabían?

There are many words commonly used by Spanish speakers that come directly from English. You have already seen one example: *kleenex.* Other words that fall into this category are **la xerox** *(photocopy),* **el jumbo** *(a jumbo jet or the largest size of a product),* **el hall, el lobby, el pub,** and **el ticket.** Different Hispanic countries borrow different words from English. Although they may have varying pronunciations, these words are easy to understand for a native speaker of English. These words are normally masculine in gender. On the other hand, English borrows words from Spanish, such as **barrio, aficionado, patio,** and **taco.** Are you aware of other Spanish words that are used in English?

Hacia la comunicación

Gramática

I. Using Correct Gender and Number

All nouns in Spanish are either masculine or feminine (gender) and singular or plural (number). Nouns referring to males are masculine and those referring to females are feminine. The definite article **(el, la, los, las)** agrees in gender and in number with the noun it modifies.

In many languages, nouns have gender. Even in English we refer to a friend's new car, saying, "She runs really well."

A. Gender

1. Nouns ending in the letters **-l, -o, -n,** or **-r** are usually masculine.

   el pape**l**   el jabó**n**
   el cepill**o**   el televiso**r**

Common exceptions include **la mano** *(hand),* **la foto (fotografía), la moto (motocicleta).**

2. Nouns that end in **-e** are usually masculine, but there are high-frequency words that are exceptions: **la tarde, la noche, la clase, la gente, la parte.**

3. Nouns ending in **-a, -ad, -ción** and **-sión** are usually feminine.

la novel**a**   la composi**ción**   la universid**ad**   la televi**sión**

Common exceptions include **el día** and nouns of Greek origin ending in **-ma, -pa,** and **-ta,** such as **el problema, el programa, el mapa,** and **el planeta.**

4. Most nouns ending in **-e** or **-ista** that refer to people can be masculine or feminine in gender. Context or modifiers such as articles generally help you determine whether the word refers to a male or female.

el estudiant**e**   la estudiant**e**   el art**ista**   la art**ista**
el pian**ista**   la pian**ista**

Note: The definite article is used with titles, such as **Sr., Sra., Srta., Dr., profesora,** etc., except when speaking directly to the person.

La Sra. Ramírez es de Santo Domingo.
BUT: ¿De dónde es Ud., Sr. Leyva?

B. Number: Plural Formation

Singular Definite Article	Plural Definite Article
el	los
la	las

Singular Indefinite Article	Plural Indefinite Article
un	unos
una	unas

1. Nouns ending in a vowel generally add **-s.**

la revista **las** revista**s**   el presidente **los** presidente**s**
el disco **los** disco**s**

2. Nouns ending in a consonant add **-es.**

el profesor **los** profesor**es**   el examen **los** exámen**es**
la mujer **las** mujer**es**   la nación **las** nacion**es**
la ciudad **las** ciudad**es**

3. Nouns ending in **-z** change **z** to **c** and add **-es.**

el lápi**z**   **los** lápi**ces**

II. Indicating Possession

Before studying the grammar explanation, answer the following questions:

- How would you say that you have a radio?
- How would you say that you and your roommate have a television set?
- How would you ask your instructor whether he/she has a stereo?
- How would you say that your friends don't have a clock radio?

Note the absence of an article.

II. Note: The indefinite article is used only when number is important or if the word is modified, for example, **¿Tienes un kleenex?** or **¿Tienes un bolígrafo rojo?**

Drill possession:
1. Ask students questions such as, **¿Tienes lápiz?** Then take the object and say, **Gracias.**
2. Using the students' objects taken in (1), ask students, **¿De quién es el lápiz?** Then return objects to the owners.

Point out the difference between English and Spanish word order when expressing possession.

1. **Tener** is not only used to indicate age, but also to show possession as in **tengo televisor, ¿tienes discos?**

> Tener *(to have)*
>
> **Tengo** radio.
> Juan Carlos **tiene** dos guitarras.
> **¿Tienes** discos de jazz?
> Nosotros **tenemos** televisor y vídeo.
> **Tienen** calculadora.

2. The preposition **de** indicates possession in Spanish:

El estéreo **de** Alfredo

Alfredo*'s* stereo

¿De quién es el estéreo?
Las cintas **de** la chica son de Japón.
¿De quiénes son las revistas?
Es el televisor **de la** señora Viñals.
BUT: Es el televisor **del** señor Viñals. **(de + el = del)**

Look at the examples to help you answer. See answers in Appendix B.

After studying the grammar explanation, answer the following questions:

- What is the Spanish equivalent of the English *'s*?
- How would you say that the record belongs to Carlos? To Mr. González? To Miss López? To the students?
- How would you ask someone whose towel it is?
- How would you ask someone whose plants they are?

III. Drill **gustar:**
1. Have students state preferences for cities, states, and brands. You may wish to use the list of brands in Act. 5.
2. Ask either/or questions: **¿Te gusta San Diego o San Francisco? ¿Te gustan las computadoras o las máquinas de escribir?** (etc.)

III. Likes and Dislikes: *Gustar*

1. In order to express your likes and dislikes you use the construction **me gusta +** *article* **+** *noun.* The noun that follows the verb **gustar** determines whether the form of the verb is singular or plural.

Me gusta (el libro.)　　(The book) *is pleasing to me.*
　　　　　　　　　　　　　(I like the book.)

Me gustan (los libros.)　(The books) *are pleasing to me.*
　　　　　　　　　　　　　(I like the books.)

After having studied the preceding explanation, answer the following question:

● How would you say that you like the following things: **la revista, los periódicos de Nueva York, el vídeo, el estéreo de Carmen?**

2. To talk about the likes and dislikes of others, you need to change only the beginning of the sentence. In the examples that follow, the words in parentheses are optional; they are used for emphasis or clarification. When using **le/s gusta,** clarification is especially important because **le** or **les** can refer to several people.

(A mí) no **me** gusta el libro.	**(A nosotros)** no **nos** gusta el libro.
¿**(A ti) te** gustan las revistas?	¿**(A vosotros) os** gustan las revistas?
(A él) le gustan los discos de Ana.	**(A ellos) les** gustan los discos de Ana.
¿**(A ella) le** gusta el café?	¿**(A ellas) les** gusta el café?
(A Ud.) no **le** gusta el vídeo.	**(A Uds.)** no **les** gusta el vídeo.

Note: **A** Miguel **le** gusta el vino.
　　　　A la Sra. Ferrer **le** gusta el vino.
BUT: **Al** Sr. Ferrer **le** gusta el vino. **(a + el = al)**

Do mechanical drills, Workbook, Part I.

After studying the grammar explanation, answer these questions:

● How would you say that Raúl doesn't like the novel? What would you have to change to say that he doesn't like the novels?
● Give all possible translations for **Le gusta el té.**
● How would you clarify that Tomás, not Elena, likes music?
● How would you say that Mr. Porta likes Coca-Cola and that Mrs. Bert does not?

Actividad 8: La habitación de Vicente

In pairs, quiz each other by looking at the list of things that Vicente has in his room (p. 40).

- **A:** ¿Tiene vídeo?
  B: Sí, tiene. / No, no tiene.

Actividad 9: ¿Qué tienen?

In pairs, write a list of the ten most common items students have in their rooms.

- Nosotros tenemos . . .

Check your list for validity by polling other members of your class. Ask questions such as **¿Tienes radio?** Then, report your findings to your partner.

Actividad 10: Las habitaciones de los estudiantes

In pairs, student "A" covers the drawing of Vicente and Juan Carlos's room; student "B" covers the drawing of Marisel and Diana's room. Then, find out what they have in their rooms by asking your partner questions. Follow the model.

- **A:** ¿Tienen computadora Vicente y Juan Carlos?
  B: No, no tienen computadora.

Marisel y Diana

Vicente y Juan Carlos

Act. 11: Have students invent other questions based on their favorite musicians, athletes, painters, writers, actors, cities, etc.

Discuss the importance of Hispanics in sports and the entertainment industry. Have students brainstorm names of other famous Hispanics.

Basquetbol/baloncesto/ basket(bol) are all used.

La radio = radio broadcast, radio station. In some countries, **el radio** is used. **El/La radio** = radio (apparatus).

Actividad 11: Tus gustos

In pairs, find out your partner's preferences and jot down his/her answers. Follow the model.

● **A:** ¿Te gusta más Gabriela Sabatini o Steffi Graf?
   B: Me gusta más . . .

1. Rubén Blades o Julio Iglesias
2. Nueva York o Los Ángeles
3. Charlie Sheen o Emilio Estévez
4. Andrés Galarraga o José Canseco
5. el béisbol o el basquetbol
6. Oprah Winfrey o Geraldo Rivera
7. MTV o CNN
8. la televisión o la radio
9. el jazz o el rock

Actividad 12: Más gustos

Continue to find out more about your partner's preferences. Follow the model.

● **A:** ¿Te gustan más los Yanquis o los Dodgers?
   B: . . .

1. las revistas o los libros
2. las computadoras o las máquinas de escribir
3. las cintas o los discos
4. las novelas de Danielle Steele o las novelas de Agatha Christie
5. los vídeos de horror o los vídeos de romance
6. los periódicos o las revistas
7. los conciertos de rock o los conciertos de música clásica
8. las fotografías o los vídeos

Actividad 13: Compatibles

Keeping in mind the responses given by your partner in Activities 11 and 12, interview a third person to see if he/she is or isn't compatible with your partner. Be prepared to report back findings to the class. Remember the use of definite articles with common nouns. Use sentences such as the following.

● Ellos son compatibles porque les gusta la televisión.
   Ellos no son compatibles porque a él le gustan las novelas y a ella le gustan las revistas.

Actividad 14: Los artículos de baño

Some of the women at the dorm have left things lying about in the bathroom. In pairs, student "A" covers the information in Column B and student "B" covers the information in Column A. Ask your partner questions to find out who owns some of the items in the bathroom.

A: ¿De quién es la pasta de dientes?
B: Es de . . .

B: ¿De quiénes son . . . ?
A: Son de . . .

A

jabones – Claudia y Teresa
champú – Marisel
peines – Teresa y Diana
cepillos de dientes – Diana, Marisel, Teresa y
   Claudia

B

kleenex – Claudia
pasta de dientes – Marisel
toallas – Diana y Teresa
perfume – Marisel

Act. 15: Before doing this activity, take students' belongings and give them to other students. Have students say, **Tengo el cuaderno de Peter,** etc.

Actividad 15: Las preferencias

Juan Carlos and Vicente are roommates. Read about their preferences and decide what items belong to whom.

LOS CONTRASTES Y LA DIVERSIDAD

Contraste geográfico

(1) El valle del Cauca, Colombia
(2) Los Andes, Chile   (3) La
Patagonia, Argentina

Actividad

Uds. tienen que ir a vivir a uno de
estos lugares. En grupos de cuatro,
escojan el lugar que más les gusta
y digan por qué.

1

2

3

4

5

6

7

8

Diversidad étnica

(4) Perú   (5) España   (6) Ecuador   (7) Uruguay
(8) España   (9) Guatemala

Actividad
En grupos de tres, escojan dos de estas fotos e imagínense un día completo en la vida de estas personas.

9

Diversidad en el trabajo y el transporte

(10) Barcos de pesca, Valparaíso, Chile
(11) Investigación del aceite de oliva, Madrid,
España   (12) Cargando una llama, Latacunga,
Ecuador   (13) Autopista en Madrid, España
(14) El lago Titicaca, entre Perú y Bolivia

Actividad
En grupos de cuatro, escojan tres adjetivos para
describir cada foto.

12

13

14

15

Contraste urbanístico

(15) El barrio de La Boca, Buenos Aires, Argentina   (16) *Bolívar desnudo*,
Pereira, Colombia

Actividad
En grupos de tres, comenten sobre el ritmo de vida en estos dos barrios. Usen
la imaginación.

16

Have you read any books by Hemingway or Michener about Hispanic countries?

By Ernest Hemingway: *Death in the Afternoon* (on bullfighting), *For Whom the Bell Tolls* (Spanish Civil War), *The Old Man and the Sea* (set in Cuba). By James A. Michener: *Iberia* (Spain).

Act. 16: Have students read their paragraphs and see how their self-descriptions compare with what others wrote about them.

A Juan Carlos le gusta mucho la música y a Vicente le gustan los libros. Entonces, ¿de quién son estas cosas? Por ejemplo:

|●| El libro de Hemingway: El libro de Hemingway es de Vicente porque a él le gustan los libros.

1. guitarra
2. diccionario
3. revistas
4. grabadora
5. novelas de James Michener
6. discos y cintas
7. estéreo
8. periódicos

Actividad 16: Descripción

Complete the following paragraph, describing yourself.

Me llamo _____ y soy de _____ .
Tengo _____ años y me gusta _____ ;
por eso tengo _____ en mi habitación. También me gustan _____ , pero no tengo _____ .

Redo this paragraph, describing another person in your class. Make all the necessary changes.

Nuevos horizontes

Stress that this reading will be easy to understand because it is about a theme familiar to students.

This book will emphasize similarities between cultures and will look at the similarities as a springboard to discuss the differences.

Discuss the role of Hispanics, not only in the United States, but also in the world. Mention César Chávez, Javier Pérez de Cuéllar, Fidel Castro, Daniel Ortega, Gabriel García Márquez, etc.

Estrategia de lectura: *Activating Background Knowledge*

We read for many different reasons, but they all fall into two broad categories: pleasure reading and information seeking. We employ different reading strategies depending on our purpose and the type of text. When we read, we interact with the text depending on the background knowledge we have on the topic. It is for this reason that two readers might interpret the same text differently. For example, a lawyer and a lay person may not have the same perceptions when reading a legal document.

Before doing the reading in this chapter, you will do two prereading activities that will help you activate your background knowledge by focusing on two topics related to the text: television and music. These two activities will prepare you to obtain a global understanding of the reading selection. It is not important to understand every word; just try to capture the general meaning.

What Spanish songs have
been popular in the U.S.?

Act. 17: Play Hispanic music as
students enter the classroom.

Actividad 17: La música

Read the following questions, then scan the hit parade list from Puerto
Rico to answer them.

¿Cuántos discos son de los Estados Unidos o de Inglaterra?
¿Cuántos son de países hispanos?

Hit Parade   (del 25 de diciembre de 1988
al 2 de enero de 1989)

Cantante	Selección
1. Los Hispanos	Las campanas de la catedral
2. Whitney Houston	One Moment in Time
3. José Nogueras	Hay fiesta
4. Grupo Jataca	Jibarita mía
5. Phil Collins	Groovy Kind of Love
6. George Michael	Faith
7. Nano Cabrera	Brincando badenes
8. Danny Rivera	Salve
9. Beach Boys	Kokomo
10. Roberto Carlos	Si el amor se va

Name 5 or 6 Hispanic actors
and compare your list with
a partner's.

Actividad 18: La televisión

Scan this portion of a Spanish TV guide to answer the question that
follows.

¿Cuáles son los programas de los Estados Unidos?

14 de noviembre de 1988

LUNES

Hora	tve1	tve2
7'00	7,00 A MEDIA TARDE «Safari por el idioma» Después de leer «Las minas del Rey Salomón», los jugadores se convierten en exploradores del lenguaje. 7,25 DE PELICULA «Festival de Valladolid» Presentación: Marina Saura.	
8'00	8,30 TELEDIARIO-2	
9'00	9,00 EL TIEMPO 9,15 EL PRECIO JUSTO Presentación: Joaquín Prat. Concurso en el que se realizan una serie de juegos relacionados con el precio de regalos heterogéneos y que, tras sucesivas eliminaciones, queda un solo vencedor.	«El fugitivo». TV-1, 3,15 horas. 9,00 EL MIRADOR Informativo cultural. 9,20 CINE CLUB. CICLO: E. QUEREJETA
10'00	11,05 JUZGADO DE GUARDIA «Cuadrángulo amoroso» La llegada de Suzanne, una nueva ayudanta del discrito, provoca el primer enfrentamiento serio entre los tres hombres del juzgado.	10.00 REMINGTON STEELE «Mi querido Steele» Ross Crocket, un hombre de negocios que ve cercana su muerte, contrata a Steele con el fin de encontrar a Tracy.

Los hispanos y sus gustos

El español es la lengua[1] oficial de veinte países del mundo.[2] En total, hay más de 320 millones de personas que hablan español, incluyendo[3] unos 19 millones en los Estados Unidos; por eso, la población hispana es un mercado consumidor[4] muy significativo.

En los países hispanos, casi todas[5] las familias tienen radio y televisor y hoy muchas tienen vídeo. A muchos hispanos les gustan su música folklórica, la música clásica, el rock y el jazz. La música folklórica combina influencias indígenas, africanas y europeas y, por eso, es muy rítmica. La música hispana más popular en los Estados Unidos es la salsa y muchos norteamericanos tienen discos de cantantes como Rubén Blades, Willie Colón y Oscar de León.

La televisión también es importante en los países hispanos y hay muchos teleadictos. Los hispanos tienen sus propios[6] programas de noticias,[7] de música, comedias y telenovelas, pero también hay muchos programas de los Estados Unidos. Las comedias "M*A*S*H" y "La hora de Cosby" y telenovelas como "Dallas", "Falcon Crest" y "Dinastía", son muy populares, pero tienen una diferencia: ¡Joan Collins no habla inglés, habla español! En algunas ciudades de los Estados Unidos como Nueva York, Miami, Los Ángeles y Chicago, hay canales de televisión en español (27 en total). Las dos cadenas[8] hispanas de televisión en los Estados Unidos son Telemundo y Univisión; también hay más de doscientas emisoras de radio para los hispanos en este país.

---

1. language 2. world 3. including 4. **mercado** . . . consumer market 5. **casi** . . . almost all 6. own 7. news 8. networks

Actividad 19: Los gustos hispanos

Answer the following questions based on what you have just read. You may need to refer back to the text to scan for specific information.

1. ¿En cuántos países es el español la lengua oficial?
2. ¿Tenemos programas de televisión en español en los Estados Unidos?
3. ¿Tienen programas de los Estados Unidos en los países hispanos?
4. ¿Dónde hay canales de televisión en español en los Estados Unidos y cuántos hay?
5. ¿Tienen Uds. un canal de televisión o una estación de radio en español en su ciudad o estado?
6. ¿Qué significa **teleadicto** en inglés?
7. ¿Te gusta la música hispana?
8. ¿Tienes un disco de música hispana?

Lo esencial

I. Acciones

1. bailar	5. hablar
2. beber	6. cantar
3. comer	7. salir
4. escuchar	

Have students mime actions as you go over the list of verbs.

Otras acciones

caminar   to walk
comprar   to buy
correr   to run
escribir   to write
esquiar   to ski
estudiar   to study
leer   to read

llevar   to carry, take along; to wear
mirar   to look (at)
nadar   to swim
trabajar   to work
visitar   to visit

Act. 20: Encourage originality.

Actividad 20: Asociaciones

Associate the actions in the preceding lists with words that you know.

◉ leer—libro   nadar—Hawai   estudiar—estudiante

Actividad 21: ¿Te gusta bailar?

In pairs, use the actions in the preceding lists to find out what activities your partner likes to do. Follow the model.

◉ **A:** ¿Te gusta bailar?
B: Sí, me gusta bailar. / No, no me gusta bailar.

> **Note: Days of the week are not capitalized in Spanish.**

II. Point out that Spanish calendars often start with the first day of the workweek, **lunes,** and end with the Christian day of rest, **domingo.**

Drill days of the week:
1. Ask questions such as, **Si hoy es lunes, ¿qué día es mañana?**
2. Ask what days of the week popular TV shows are on: **¿Qué día es el programa de Cosby?**

II. Los días de la semana *(The Days of the Week)*

lunes	viernes
martes	sábado
miércoles	domingo
jueves	

Expresiones de tiempo *(Time Expressions)*

el fin de semana weekend
el lunes on Monday
los lunes (los sábados) on Mondays (Saturdays)
esta tarde/noche this afternoon/evening

hoy today
la semana que viene next week
mañana tomorrow
la mañana morning

Actividad 22: El calendario

Look at a calendar for this year and say on what days of the week the following events fall.

◉ El día de San Patricio es el 17 de marzo. El 17 es viernes.

1. tu cumpleaños *(your birthday)*
2. el 4 de julio
3. Navidad *(Christmas)*
4. el día de San Valentín
5. Halloween
6. Año Nuevo *(New Year's Day)*

Think of other superstitions that are common in the U.S.

Again, cultural similarities are stressed before differences in order to make students more apt to accept rather than criticize.

¿Lo sabían?

In the United States, Friday the 13th evokes feelings of anxiety in some people. In Hispanic countries, bad luck is associated with Tuesday the 13th. That is why the movie *Friday the 13th* was translated into Spanish as *Martes 13.*

There is a saying in Spanish that refers to Tuesday as being the day of bad luck: **"Martes, ni te cases, ni te embarques, ni de tu casa te apartes."** *(On Tuesdays, don't get married, don't take a trip, and don't leave your family.)*

Planes para una fiesta de bienvenida

Pronunciation: [p], [t], [k]
1. Have students hold a piece of paper in front of their mouths and produce the aspirated and unaspirated sounds. Tell them that there is no puff of air in Spanish.
2. Have students raise one finger when they hear the English (aspirated) sounds and two fingers when they hear the Spanish (unaspirated) sounds in words such as: too-**tú**, papa-**papá**, Kay-**qué**.
3. Pronounce Spanish words with and without aspiration and have students repeat correct pronunciation only: **tomate, casa, claro, Pepe,** etc.

Practice **no importa, vale,** and **O.K.** in meaningful contexts such as: **Tengo tu lápiz. (No importa.)**

Vale is used in Spain; **O.K.,** throughout Latin America; and **está bien,** everywhere.

No importa.	It doesn't matter.
Vale./O.K.	O.K.

Marisel has decided to have a welcoming party for her new friend, Teresa. She and Álvaro are now discussing some of the arrangements.

Discuss the importance of music and dance at Hispanic parties.

Discuss the role of alcoholic beverages in Hispanic cultures: the lack of a drinking age in many Hispanic countries; the lack of pressure to drink quickly and a lot; the fact that U.S. franchises abroad (McDonald's, etc.) may sell beer or wine; and the importance of wine as a part of daily life and as an export for Chile and Spain.

Stating an obligation

Expressing agreement

Offering an option

Expressing agreement

Expressing future actions

Point out differences in lexical items between Spanish-speaking countries: **vale/O.K.** and **patatas/papas.** Draw analogies between British and American English: lorry/truck, lift/elevator, queuing for the loo/waiting in line for the bathroom, etc.

Act. 24: **Sangría** = wine, club soda or 7-UP, fruit, sugar, cinnamon; other liquors are optional.

Actividad 23: Cosas para la fiesta

Listen to the dialogue and match the following items with the people who are going to take them to the party. Some are taking more than one item. When you finish, report to the class using this pattern:

Álvaro va a llevar . . .

Álvaro	la tortilla de patatas
Vicente	los ingredientes para la sangría
Marisel	la guitarra
Juan Carlos	la grabadora
Claudia	la Coca-Cola
	las papas fritas
	las cintas

Marisel	Bueno, Álvaro, la fiesta es mañana.
Álvaro	¿Mañana es sábado?
Marisel	Sí, claro. Tenemos que preparar todo.
Álvaro	Yo voy a llevar la música.
Marisel	¿Tienes estéreo o grabadora?
Álvaro	Tengo grabadora y muchas cintas de rock y salsa.
Marisel	¡Fantástico! Yo tengo guitarra. ¿Y de beber?
Álvaro	¿Qué te gusta más, la cerveza o el vino?
Marisel	¿Qué tal una sangría?
Álvaro	Sí, sí . . . sangría. ¿Quién va a comprar los ingredientes para mañana?
Marisel	Juan Carlos, quizás.
Álvaro	¿Moreno?
Marisel	Sí, Juan Carlos Moreno.
Álvaro	Vale. Y también tenemos que tener Coca-Cola.
Marisel	Ah sí, por supuesto. Claudia va a llevar la Coca-Cola y las papas fritas.
Álvaro	Vale. Y Vicente va a llevar la tortilla de patatas.
Marisel	¡Es tortilla de PAPAS!
Álvaro	¡Bueno! Papas o patatas, no importa.

Actividad 24: Preguntas

In groups of four, answer the following questions based on information from the dialogue and common knowledge.

1. ¿Cómo se dice *potato* en España? ¿Y en Hispanoamérica?
2. ¿Tiene alcohol la sangría?
3. ¿Cuál es el ingrediente principal de la sangría?
4. ¿Cuándo es la fiesta de Marisel y Álvaro? ¿Cuándo son, en general, las fiestas de Uds.?

Actividad 25: La ópera

This is a dialogue between Teresa and Vicente about opera. Arrange the lines in a logical order. The first two have already been done for you. When you finish, read the dialogue with a partner.

7	Me gustan los dos, pero tengo tres discos de Domingo.
3	Voy a comprar un disco de ópera.
1	¿Qué hay?
13	El sábado.
5	De Plácido Domingo. ¿Te gusta?
6	Sí, pero a mí me gusta más José Carreras. ¿Y a ti?
2	¡Ah! Vicente. ¿Qué vas a hacer hoy?
9	Oye, ¿vas a mirar el recital de Monserrat Caballé en la televisión?
11	No importa, pues yo sí.
4	¿De quién?
12	¿Cuándo es?
8	Yo también tengo cintas de Domingo.
10	No tengo televisor.

¿Lo sabían?

Plácido Domingo, Montserrat Caballé, and José Carreras are three world-renowned Spanish opera stars. Plácido Domingo, a tenor, also sings popular music. He moved to Mexico in 1950. Montserrat Caballé is well known for the purity of her soprano voice. She became popular in the United States after singing in Carnegie Hall in 1965. José Carreras was a rising opera star when he was struck with leukemia. Luckily his illness is in remission after treatment in the United States, and he is appearing in theaters throughout the world.

José Carreras performs at the Royal Opera House in London. Have you ever gone to the opera?

Hacia la comunicación

Gramática

I. Drill **gustar**:
1. Have students answer either/or questions: **¿Te gusta esquiar o nadar? ¿Te gusta estudiar o leer?**
2. Ask what famous people like to do: Mark Spitz, James Michener, Mary Decker-Slaney.

You can also use **tener que** to give an excuse.

II. Drill **tener que**:
1. Do a chain drill.
2. Have students answer yes/no questions: **¿Tienes que estudiar/salir esta noche?**
3. Have students ask and answer: **¿Qué tienes que hacer el lunes/el viernes?** (etc.)

III. Drill **ir a** + infinitive:
1. Have students answer the question, **¿Cuándo vas a estudiar/comer/trabajar/nadar?**
2. In pairs, have students ask and answer, **¿Qué vas a hacer el sábado/el domingo? ¿Qué va a hacer ... el viernes?**

Contrast **tener que** with **ir a**. Give students a situation: They are lazy and always goof off. Ask them what they have to do tomorrow and what they are going to do: **Tenemos que ..., pero vamos a ...**

Do mechanical drills, Workbook, Part II.

I. Expressing Likes and Dislikes: *Gustar*

The verb **gustar** may be followed by infinitives or by nouns with articles.

¿Qué te gust**a hacer**?	*What do you like to do?*
A Juan le gust**a esquiar.**	*Juan likes to ski.*
A Jesús y a Ramón no les gust**a bailar.**	*Jesús and Ramón don't like to dance.*
Al Sr. Moreno le gust**an las cintas** de jazz.	*Mr. Moreno likes jazz tapes.*

II. Expressing Obligation: *Tener que*

To express obligation, use a form of the verb **tener + que** and the necessary infinitive.

Tengo que estudi**ar** mañana.	*I have to study tomorrow.*
Tenemos que compr**ar** vino.	*We have to buy wine.*
¿Qué **tienes que** hac**er**?	*What do you have to do?*
¿Cuándo **tiene que** trabaj**ar** él?	*When does he have to work?*

III. Making Plans: *Ir a*

Before studying the grammar explanation, answer the following question based on the dialogue.

- When Álvaro says, **"¿Quién va a comprar los ingredientes para mañana?"**, is he referring to a past, present, or future action?

To express future plans, use a form of the verb **ir + a** and the necessary infinitive.

Ir *(to go)*		
voy	vamos	
vas	vais	+ a + *infinitive*
va	van	

Voy a esqui**ar** mañana.	*I'm going to ski tomorrow.*
Juan **va a** estudi**ar** hoy.	*Juan is going to study today.*
Ellos **van a** nad**ar** el sábado.	*They are going to swim on Saturday.*
¿Qué **van a** hac**er** Uds.?	*What are you going to do?*

Actividad 26: Las preferencias

In groups of five, find out which of the following things the members of your group prefer. Have one person take notes and report the results back to the class. Use the following model.

 |●| **A:** ¿Te gusta esquiar?
     B: Sí/No . . .

     (To report results) A ellos les gusta escuchar música clásica y a nosotros nos gusta escuchar rock.

1. bailar
2. beber Coca-Cola
3. beber Pepsi
4. cantar
5. correr
6. escuchar música clásica
7. escuchar rock
8. esquiar
9. estudiar
10. leer novelas
11. nadar
12. trabajar

Act. 27: This activity can be done in pairs, small groups, or as a class. Encourage imagination and different types of questions, including tags.

Actividad 27: La agenda de Claudia

Look at Claudia's calendar for the week and form as many kinds of questions as you can about her activities. Then ask your classmates questions.

 |●| ¿Cuándo van a . . . Claudia y Juan Carlos?
     Va a . . . el lunes, ¿no?
     ¿Tiene que . . . el viernes o el sábado?
     ¿Qué tiene que hacer el . . .?

abril	actividades
lunes 6	nadar, escribir una composición, comer con Álvaro
martes 7	comprar discos, leer la lección 4 para historia
miércoles 8	visitar el Museo de Arte Contemporáneo
jueves 9	escribir a Rosita, estudiar para el examen de literatura
viernes 10	correr, comprar papas fritas y la Coca-Cola, salir con Juan Carlos
sábado 11	ir a la fiesta, llevar las papas fritas y la Coca-Cola
domingo 12	ir a Toledo con Diana, visitar la catedral

Actividad 28: ¿Qué tienes que hacer hoy y mañana?

Tell what you and others *have to* do today and what you and others are *going to* do tomorrow, using one cue from each of these columns.

◖◗ Hoy tengo que trabajar, pero mañana voy a esquiar.

	Hoy	Mañana
yo	estudiar	cantar
nosotros	trabajar	bailar
Carlos y Vicente	leer el libro de	comer en un restaurante
tú	economía	escuchar discos
ella y yo	hacer la tarea	nadar
Uds.	hablar con el	correr
Teresa	profesor	mirar un vídeo
		salir con Marisel
		esquiar

Actividad 29: Tu futuro

Make a list of five things that you *have to* do next week and five things that you are *going to* do with your friends for fun. Then, in pairs, compare your lists to see whether you are going to do similar things.

Actividad 30: ¡Hola! Soy Álvaro

Read this paragraph and be prepared to answer questions.

Hola. Soy Álvaro Gómez de Córdoba, una ciudad del sur de España que tiene muchos turistas. Me gusta mucho Córdoba, pero ahora tengo que estudiar en Madrid. Voy a ser abogado.

Mosque **(Mezquita)**, Córdoba, Spain. A fine example of Arab architecture.

Act. 30: Assign a time limit of 15 seconds to read the paragraph. Have students close their books. Ask, **¿Cómo se llama? ¿De qué ciudad es? Córdoba tiene muchos artistas, ¿no? A Álvaro, ¿le gusta o no le gusta Córdoba? ¿Qué tiene que hacer? ¿Va a ser médico o abogado?**

Discuss Córdoba: **los moros, la mezquita, Julio Romero de Torres**, etc. Bring in more photos if possible.

Act. 31: After the activity is finished, discuss Barcelona: the 1992 Olympics, Cristóbal Colón, Salvador Dalí, Antonio Gaudí, etc. If possible bring in more photos of Barcelona.

Actividad 31: ¡Qué hay! Me llamo Diana

Read this paragraph. Then your instructor will read it to you again with some changes. Be ready to correct him/her when the information is not accurate.

¡Qué hay! Me llamo Diana Miller. Mi padre es de los Estados Unidos pero mi madre es de Barcelona, España. Voy a estudiar para el *masters* de literatura en España. En los Estados Unidos soy profesora de español, pero en España tengo que enseñar inglés porque no tengo mucho dinero.

View of **La Sagrada Familia,** Barcelona, Spain. This masterpiece was designed by Antonio Gaudí (1852–1926), an innovative Spanish architect, who died before the church could be completed.

Act. 31: Give students 20 seconds to read the paragraph, then have them close their books. Act **despistado/a** and confuse the contents of the paragraph by saying, **Él se llamo Duane Miller, ¿no?** *(Students correct.)* **Ah, gracias, entonces ella se llama Diana Milton.** *(Students correct.)* **¿Cómo?** *(Students repeat.)* **Vale, gracias. Ella se llama Diana Miller y su padre es de España...,** etc. Try to incorporate words like **gracias, vale, perdón,** and **cómo.**

Students could do extra credit projects on Córdoba, Barcelona, Spanish opera singers, salsa, etc.

Vocabulario funcional

La posesión

¿De quién/es? Whose?   **tener** to have

Los gustos *(Likes)*

gustar to like, be pleasing   **¿Qué?** What?
más more

Las obligaciones *(Obligations)*

tener que + infinitive   to have to . . .

Los planes *(Plans)*

¿Cuándo? When?
ir a + infinitive   to be going to . . .

Los días de la semana *(The Days of the Week)*

See page 53

Expresiones de tiempo *(Time Expressions)*

See page 53

Los artículos de la habitación y del baño

See pages 40–41

Comidas y bebidas *(Food and Drink)*

el café coffee   **la sangría** sangria (a wine punch)
la cerveza beer   **el té** tea
las papas/patatas fritas potato   **la tortilla** omelette (in Spain)
 chips   **el vino** wine

Las acciones

See page 52

Palabras y expresiones útiles

Claro. / ¡Claro que sí! Of course.   **o** or
¿De veras? Really?   **por eso** therefore
el, la, los, las the   **Por supuesto.** Of course.
la habitación room   **la tarea** homework
hacer to do   **un, una; unos, unas** a/an, some
mucho a lot   **Vale. / O.K.** O.K.
No importa. It doesn't matter.

¿Es una ciudad colonial o
moderna?

The Andes provide the setting
for Quito, the capital of
Ecuador.

Capítulo 3

Chapter Objectives

After studying this chapter, you will know how to:

- describe people and things
- identify a person's nationality
- discuss your classes and other activities that you do every day
- state location and where you are going
- indicate possession

¿Va Teresa a la clase de geografía los lunes? ¿Estudia Teresa inglés o francés? ¿Qué días va Teresa a la clase de historia? ¿Que asignaturas tienes tú en común con Teresa?

	LUNES	MARTES	MIÉRCOLES	JUEVES	VIERNES
9:00-9:50	Geografía	Arquitectura	Geografía	Arquitectura	Geografía
10:00-10:50	Lengua (FRANCÉS)	Lengua (FRANCÉS)		Lengua (FRANCÉS)	
11:00-11:50	Historia		Historia		Historia
12:00-12:50					
1:00-1:50		Arte (Museo del Prado)		Arte (Museo del Prado)	
2:00-2:50					

Una llamada de larga distancia

Llamada de larga distancia =
conferencia (Spain).

| No tengo idea. | I don't have any idea. |
| demasiado | too much |

Practice these words in meaningful context. Ask questions to elicit desired responses. T: **¿Cuál es la capital de Zambia?** S1: **No tengo idea.** T: **¿Estudias poco o demasiado?** S2: **Estudio demasiado.**

Claudia is talking long distance to her parents who have gone from Bogotá to Quito for a convention. They are talking about Claudia's classes and her new roommate, Teresa.

Actividad 1: La familia de Teresa

Listen to the conversation and complete the following chart about Teresa's family.

	Origen	Ocupación
Teresa	Puerto Rico	estudiante/agente de viajes
Padre	Puerto Rico	actor
Madre	Estados Unidos	

Discussing the future

Conferencia can also mean *session* at a conference.

Claudia	Y la convención, ¿qué tal?
Padre	¡Fantástica! Una doctora mexicana va a hablar de medicina nuclear esta tarde.
Claudia	¡Qué interesante!
Padre	Sí, muy interesante, pero ahora tengo que ir a una conferencia. Adiós, hija. Aquí está tu mamá.

Describing

Stating profession and origin

Explain that diminutives are used as terms of endearment and to denote size. They are more common in the Americas than in Spain. General formation: -ito/a/os/as for words ending in -a, -o, -l; -cito/a/os/as for words ending in -e and consonants other than -l. Mention possible regional variations: -ico, -illo, etc.

Asking about plans

Pronunciation: flap [r], trilled [R]
1. Contrast the flap [r] with the trilled [R] (no English equivalent). Have students pronounce *Betty* several times quickly for the flap [r] sound.
2. Do minimal pairs: **pero-perro, moro-morro, caro-carro,** etc.
3. Ask students to name common objects that contain these sounds: flap [r] = **la lámpara, el perfume;** trilled [R] = **el radio, la guitarra,** etc.
4. Have students find words that contain flap [r] and trilled [R] in the dialogue. In pairs, they can dictate to each other the words, or the sentence in which the sound occurs.

Act. 3: Have students sit back-to-back to simulate a phone call.

Claudia	Adiós, papi . . . ¿Mami?
Madre	Sí, mi hijita. ¿Cómo estás?
Claudia	Muy bien, ¿y tú?
Madre	Muy bien aquí en Quito. Y tus clases, ¿qué tal?
Claudia	Muy bien. Tengo una clase de economía fabulosa y otra de historia con un profesor excelente.
Madre	¿Y las otras clases?
Claudia	Regulares.
Madre	¿Y quién es tu compañera en la residencia?
Claudia	Se llama Teresa Domínguez.
Madre	Domínguez ¿qué?
Claudia	Domínguez Schroeder; su papá es un actor famoso de Puerto Rico y su mamá es de los Estados Unidos.
Madre	Ah . . . ¿pero ella es puertorriqueña?
Claudia	Sí, es de Ponce.
Madre	¿Y qué estudia en España?
Claudia	Estudia turismo y trabaja en una agencia de viajes. Pero, ¿y Uds., qué van a hacer en Quito?
Madre	Vamos a visitar la parte colonial esta noche y el sábado vamos al pueblo de Santo Domingo de los Colorados.
Claudia	Uds. viajan y yo estudio . . . Bueno mami, tengo que ir a la biblioteca.
Madre	¡Estudias demasiado, Claudia!
Claudia	Es que tengo un examen de economía mañana. ¿Cuándo regresan Uds. a Bogotá?
Madre	No tengo idea, pero posiblemente la semana próxima.
Claudia	Bueno mami, entonces hablamos la semana próxima.
Madre	Bueno, un beso. Adiós.

Actividad 2: La familia de Claudia

After listening to the conversation, answer the following questions.

1. ¿Qué piensas tú que hace el padre de Claudia?
2. ¿Qué estudia Claudia?
3. ¿Qué van a visitar los padres de Claudia?
4. ¿Adónde tiene que ir hoy Claudia?
5. ¿Qué tiene Claudia mañana?

Actividad 3: Los papeles

In pairs, role play a conversation between Teresa and her mother about Claudia. Include information about Claudia's occupation, origin, and family.

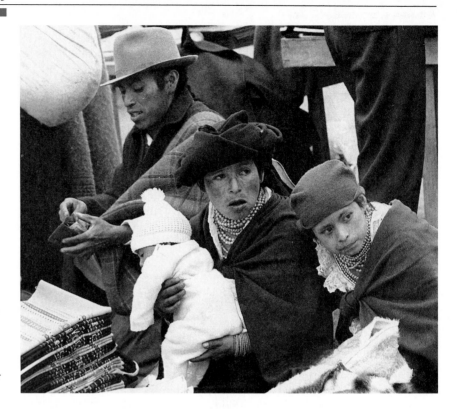

A family of Otavalan Indians
sells their wares at an outdoor
market in Ecuador.

Bring in pictures of Ecuador.

¿Lo sabían?

The setting of Quito, the capital of Ecuador, is breathtaking. The city lies in
a beautiful valley at the base of a volcano. Even though it is close to the
equator, Quito enjoys a moderate climate all year round since it is almost
10,000 feet above sea level. The combination of colonial and modern architecture creates a fascinating contrast in the city.

   A large percentage of Ecuador's population is of Indian origin. East of
Quito is the Indian town of Santo Domingo de los Colorados. The men of
this town are well known by their hair, which they cover with red clay and
shape in the form of a leaf. The **Otavalos,** another Indian group, are very
industrious. In Quito, their work is valued because they are considered to be
some of the best construction workers in the area.

Actividad 4: ¿Estudias arte?

Mingle and ask people in the class what subjects **(asignaturas)** they are
studying **(biología, matemáticas, sociología, historia, economía,
literatura).** Follow the model.

   A: ¿Estudias arte?
   B: Sí, estudio arte. / No, no estudio arte. / No, estudio historia.

Lo esencial

Adjectives of nationality are not capitalized in Spanish.

Play word association games for practice: **Salvador Dalí = español;** **Lady Di = inglesa;** etc.

Make flash cards of things you associate with each country: **tangos argentinos, enchiladas mexicanas,** etc.

I. Check student belongings to see where they are from: **La calculadora de Mike es japonesa.**

I. Las nacionalidades *(Nationalities)*

Soy español.   Soy mexicana.   Somos bolivianos.   Somos argentinas.

Otras nacionalidades y adjetivos regionales

africano/a*	dominicano/a	indio/a	puertorriqueño/a
asiático/a	ecuatoriano/a	italiano/a	ruso/a
brasileño/a	europeo/a	panameño/a	salvadoreño/a
colombiano/a	guatemalteco/a	paraguayo/a	uruguayo/a
chileno/a	hondureño/a	peruano/a	venezolano/a

*Note: Adjectives of nationality ending in **-o** and **-a** form their plural by adding **-s.** For example: african**os**, african**as**.

alemán/alemana	inglés/inglesa	portugués/portuguesa
francés/francesa*	irlandés/irlandesa	

Review accent rules. See Appendix C.

*Note: Adjectives of nationality ending in a consonant add **-es** to form the masculine plural. The feminine singular form adds **-s** to form the plural. For example: frances**es**/frances**as.** Note that only the masculine singular form has a written accent: ingl**és** — ingl**esa**; ingl**eses** — ingl**esas**; alem**án** — alem**ana**; alem**anes** — alem**anas**.

Point out dieresis in **nicara-güense.**

árabe*   costarricense   nicaragüense
canadiense   estadounidense

*Note: Adjectives of nationality ending in **-e** can be masculine or feminine. The plural is formed by adding **-s.** For example: árab**es.**

¿Lo sabían?

How people from the United States are referred to varies in Hispanic countries. **Americanos** is a misnomer, since all people from the Americas are Americans. In some Hispanic countries (such as Colombia, Venezuela, Peru, and Chile) they are usually called **gringos,** which is not necessarily a derogatory term. But in Mexico, for example, **gringo** has a negative connotation. In countries such as Spain, Mexico, and Argentina, they are called **norteamericanos.** These terms are used since the word **estadounidenses** is somewhat cumbersome. **Estadounidense** is used primarily in formal writing, when filling out forms, or in formal speech, such as newscasts.

Act. 5: Ask students to explain who specific people are if any names are unfamiliar. Answers: **inglés, alemán, estadounidenses, francés, francesa, españoles, canadiense, rusos, mexicano.**

Have students suggest more names for a student-led warm-up.

Actividad 5: ¿De dónde son estas personas?

In pairs, take turns telling where these people are from.

1. Monty Python
2. Henry Kissinger
3. Janet Evans y Florence Griffith-Joyner
4. Jacques Cousteau
5. Paloma Picasso
6. Plácido Domingo y Monserrat Caballé
7. Michael J. Fox
8. Mikhail y Raisa Gorbachev
9. Fernando Valenzuela

Page through the book if necessary.

Actividad 6: ¡Qué memoria!

In groups of three, have a competition by trying to remember the characters you have met so far in the book. State where they are from and their nationality. Follow the model.

◖●◗ Teresa es de Puerto Rico, entonces es puertorriqueña.

Remember: **Origen** refers to one's heritage, not to where one was born.

Actividad 7: El origen de tu familia

In groups of five, find out the ancestry of your group members. Follow the model.

Act. 7: The question, **¿De dónde eres?,** asks only where you were born.

◖●◗ **A:** ¿Cuál es el origen de tu familia?
B: Mi familia es de origen italiano y alemán.

II. Lugares *(Places)*

1. el cine
2. la iglesia
3. la playa
4. el supermercado
5. la escuela
6. la librería

> Identify places while walking or riding through town: **el parque, el cine,** etc. Idle time = study time.

Otros lugares

la agencia de viajes travel agency

la biblioteca library

la oficina office

el parque park

la piscina pool

el teatro theater

la tienda store

II. Do word associations with places in your city: Li'l Peach = **una tienda.**

Actividad 8: Acción y lugar

Act. 8: Point out the difference between **a la** and **al** in model sentences.

Choose an action from Column A and a logical place to do this action from Column B. Form sentences, following the models.

▢ Me gusta nadar; por eso voy a la piscina.
Tienen que comer; por eso van al restaurante.

A	B
Me gusta nadar	la piscina
Tienen un examen	el parque
Tiene que estudiar	la biblioteca
Necesito dinero *(money)*	el restaurante
Tenemos que comprar papas	la universidad
Tienen que comer	la farmacia
Me gusta caminar	el banco
Tienes que comprar aspirinas	el supermercado
Me gusta el arte	el museo
	la playa
	la cafetería

Act. 9: In parts of Latin America (Chile, Dominican Republic, Panama and some others), **voy a la casa** = I'm going home. In many other countries, **voy a casa** = I'm going home.

Actividad 9: Después de clase

Mingle with your classmates and find out where **(adónde)** others are going after class and with whom **(con quién)** they are going. Follow the model.

  A: ¿Adónde vas?
B: Voy a casa.
A: ¿Con quién vas?
B: Voy solo/a. / Voy con . . .

Hacia la comunicación

Gramática π☐

I. Expressing Destination: *Ir + a + place*

To say where you are going, you need to use a form of **ir + a** and the destination. Remember to use **al** when the destination noun is masculine.

Note that prepositions precede the question word.

Vamos al Museo de Antro-pología.	*We are going to the Museum of Anthropology.*
Cuando necesito aspirinas, **voy a la** farmacia.	*When I need aspirin, I go to the drugstore.*
¿A**dónde vas?**	*Where are you going (to)?*
¿Con quién **vas a la** fiesta?	*With whom are you going to the party?*

Practice **ir a** and **estar en** by reporting your actions to yourself as you do them.

II. Use the sentences presented to do a substitution drill.

I./II. Practice **ir a/estar en** + place: Bring in pictures and ask questions with **¿Adónde va?** and **¿Dónde está?**

Memorize verb infinitives. Make lists of **-ar, -er,** and **-ir** verbs.

Practice automatic pairs: **¿Trabajas? / Sí, trabajo. ¿Trabaja ella? / Sí, ella trabaja. ¿Trabajan Uds.? / Sí, trabajamos.**

II. Indicating Location: *Estar + en + place*

Estar			
yo	**estoy**	nosotros/as	**estamos**
tú	**estás**	vosotros/as	**estáis**
Ud. él/ella	**está**	Uds. ellos/ellas	**están**

Las secretarias **están en** la oficina.*   *The secretaries are in the office.*
Mamá, **estoy en** el hospital.   *Mom, I'm in/at the hospital.*

*Note: The preposition used in Spanish to express being *in* or *at* a place is **en: Estamos *en* el cine.** *(We're at the movies.)*

III. Talking About the Present: Present Indicative of Regular Verbs and the Verbs *Hacer* and *Salir*

1. In Spanish, there are three classes of verbs depending upon the ending of the infinitives: **-ar (trabajar), -er (beber),** and **-ir (escribir).** The stems **(trabaj-, beb-, escrib-)** of regular verbs do not change. The endings vary according to the subject of the sentence, which can be expressed or not: **(yo) trabajo, (tú) trabajas,** etc. In order to talk about daily or future activities or about an action in progress, you use the following endings:

Trabaj**ar** *(to work)*			
yo	trabaj**o**	nosotros/as	trabaj**amos**
tú	trabaj**as**	vosotros/as	trabaj**áis**
Ud. él/ella	trabaj**a**	Uds. ellos/as	trabaj**an**

Mañana **yo** trabaj**o**.   *I work tomorrow.*
Mi madre habl**a** español.   *My mother speaks Spanish.*

Beb**er** *(to drink)*			
yo	beb**o**	nosotros/as	beb**emos**
tú	beb**es**	vosotros/as	beb**éis**
Ud. él/ella	beb**e**	Uds. ellos/as	beb**en**

¿Beb**es** vino o cerveza?   *Do you drink wine or beer?*
Nosotros com**emos** en la cafetería.   *We eat in the cafeteria.*

III. Drill regular verbs:
1. Do a Gouin series: **Leo la lección, aprendo las palabras, escribo la tarea, miro la televisión, hablo por teléfono, salgo con un amigo.**
2. Have some students mime actions; others say what they are doing.
3. Do chain drills based on different verbs.
4. Use rapid-fire questions and answers: T: **¿Hablas español?** S1: **Sí, hablo español.** T: **¿Hablan ellos español?** S2: **Sí, hablan español.** (etc.)
5. Have students write 10 questions and 10 answers. Then have them work in pairs, asking and answering questions.
6. Begin a story and have students complete it. For example, T: **Blanca es muy activa. Todos los días ...** *(Students continue.)* T: **Blanca sale con Raúl. Él ...** *(Students continue.)*

Do mechanical drills, Workbook, Part I.

Act. 10: Extend activity by having students invent more people or places.

Escribir *(to write)*			
yo	escrib**o**	nosotros/as	escrib**imos**
tú	escrib**es**	vosotros/as	escrib**ís**
Ud. él/ella }	escrib**e**	Uds. ellos/as }	escrib**en**

Nosotros viv**imos** en Lima.   *We live in Lima.*
Isabel Allende escrib**e** novelas.   *Isabel Allende writes novels.*
¿Recib**es** tus cartas aquí?   *Do you receive your letters here?*

In order to choose the correct ending for a verb, you need to know two things: (1) the infinitive of the verb **(-ar, -er, -ir),** and (2) the subject of the sentence. For example:

(1) beb**er**   (2) nosotros = Nosotros beb**emos** Coca-Cola.

2. The following verbs, and most of those you learned in Chapter 2, are regular verbs and therefore follow the pattern of **trabaj*ar*, beb*er*,** and **escrib*ir*.**

aprender to learn	**regresar** to return
comprar to buy	**tocar** to play (an
desear to want; to desire	instrument); to touch
molestar to bother	**usar** to use
necesitar to need	**vender** to sell
recibir to receive	**vivir** to live

3. The verbs **hacer** *(to do; to make),* and **salir** *(to leave; to go out)* have an irregular **yo** form: **yo ha*go*, yo sal*go*.** However, both verbs follow the pattern of regular verbs in all other present indicative forms.

Ha**go** la tarea.   *I do my homework.*
¿Qué hac**en** Uds.?   *What are you doing?*
Sal**go** con Ramona.   *I go out with Ramona.*
Ella sal**e** de la clase.   *She is leaving the class.*

Actividad 10: ¿Dónde están?

In pairs, ask and state where the following people or things are located.

1. el presidente de los Estados Unidos
2. la Torre Eiffel y el Arco de Triunfo
3. Bogotá
4. la Estatua de la Libertad y Woody Allen
5. el Vaticano
6. Machu Picchu y Lima

Remember the endings for **-ar, -er,** and **-ir** verbs and the subject-verb agreement.

Actividad 11: El verano

In pairs, discuss what you and your partner do during the summer (**el verano**). Use the following verbs: **nadar, esquiar, bailar, estudiar, comer en un restaurante, mirar la televisión, escuchar música, salir con amigos.** Follow the model.

A: ¿Nadas?
B: Sí, nado todos los días.
A: ¿Dónde nadas?
B: En la piscina de la universidad.

Actividad 12: ¡Una carta de Miguel!

This is a letter from a Honduran student who is studying in the United States. He is describing his daily activities to his parents. Complete the letter with the appropriate conjugated forms of the following verbs: **bailar, correr, escribir, estudiar, hablar, ir, salir, ser, tener.**

Why is **exámenes** written with an accent and **examen** without? See Appendix C for explanation.

Queridos papás:

¿Cómo están? Yo, bien. Me gusta la universidad y ___tengo___ muchos amigos. Voy a las clases, ___escribo___ composiciones y ___estudio___ mucho porque ___tengo___ demasiados exámenes; el jueves tengo un examen importante de biología. Los viernes y los sábados yo ___estudio___ en la biblioteca y por la noche ___salgo___ con un grupo de amigos. Ellos ___son___ mexicanos, venezolanos y de los Estados Unidos. Los mexicanos siempre ___hablan___ de política con los venezolanos.

Yo también ___voy___ a una discoteca los martes porque tienen música latina; entonces yo ___bailo___ con Santa, una chica puertorriqueña. Ella ___baila___ bien porque es bailarina profesional.

Bueno, tengo que terminar porque voy a correr. ¡___Corro___ ocho kilómetros al día!

Abrazos y besos,

Miguel

Act. 12: Elicit from students equivalency: 8 km = 5 m.

P.D. Gracias por los $$$dólares$$$.

Act. 13: Have groups quiz other groups. One group gives names; the other forms sentences.

Actividad 13: Gente famosa

In groups of three, name famous people who do the following things: **cantar, bailar, escribir novelas, correr, tocar la guitarra, nadar, esquiar.**

◉ Gabriel García Márquez escribe novelas.

Actividad 14: Nosotros y nuestros padres

In groups of three, discuss what students and parents do in a typical week. Think of at least five examples. Follow the model.

◉ Nosotros bailamos los fines de semana y nuestros padres van al cine.

Act. 15: Have students stand to simulate the interview. After completion, ask students to report their findings to the class.

Actividad 15: El cuestionario

In pairs, imagine that you are working for an advertising agency. You have to conduct a "person-on-the-street" interview on people's likes and dislikes based on the following questionnaire. Use complete questions to elicit responses and remember to use the **Ud.** form: **¿Es Ud. estudiante? ¿Qué periódico lee Ud.?** When finished, exchange roles. Be prepared to report back to the class. The "person on the street" should not look at the book.

Cuestionario
Nacionalidad: _____
Edad: _____
Sexo: Masculino _____ Femenino _____
Estudiante: _____ Si contesta que sí:
               ¿Dónde? _____
Trabajador/a: _____ Si contesta que sí:
               Ocupación _____
Vive con: Familia _____ Amigo/a _____ Solo/a _____
Gustos: Leer _____ Si contesta que sí:
                  ¿Qué lee? _____
               Mirar la televisión _____ Si contesta que sí:
                  ¿Qué tipos de programas? _____
               Escuchar música _____ Si contesta que sí:
                  ¿Qué tipo de música? _____
               Usar: Perfume _____ Agua de colonia _____
               Nada _____
               Escribir con: Computadora _____
                  Bolígrafo _____ Máquina de escribir _____
                  Lápiz _____

Nuevos horizontes

Estrategias de lectura: *Skimming* and *Word Order*

One of the reading strategies to be focused on in this chapter is *skimming*. When you skim you read quickly to get the main ideas of a text. You do not stop to wonder about the meaning of unknown words.

In Spanish word order, the subject normally precedes the verb, but it can sometimes follow the verb or not be expressed at all. In cases where there is one form for more than one subject **(Ud./él/ella bebe)**, context should help you deduce the subject. So, when you read a selection in Spanish, look before and after the verb to find the subject, and look at the ending of the verb.

Actividad 16: Ideas principales

Each paragraph in the following letter expresses one of these main ideas. Skim through the letter and put the correct paragraph number next to its corresponding idea.

   2   las actividades de Mario   1   las preguntas a Teresa

   4   la familia de Mario   3   la composición étnica

A street in Old San Juan, Puerto Rico. What Spanish influences do you see in this photo?

Carta de Puerto Rico

Teresa recibe cartas *(letters)* de sus amigos puertorriqueños. La siguiente carta es de su amigo Mario. Él vive con su padre y su madre en San Juan, Puerto Rico.

San Juan, 20 de octubre

Querida Teresa:

Por fin tengo tiempo para escribir. ¿Cómo estás? Espero que bien. Tengo muchas preguntas porque deseo saber cómo es tu vida en España y cuáles son tus planes y actividades. ¿Te gusta Madrid? ¿Tienes muchos amigos? ¿De dónde son y qué estudian? ¿Qué haces los sábados y los domingos? Escribe pronto y contesta todas las preguntas; todos deseamos recibir noticias de nuestra querida Teresa.   5

Yo estoy muy bien. Voy a la universidad todas las noches y trabajo por las mañanas en un banco. Soy cajero y me gusta mucho el trabajo. Por las tardes voy a la biblioteca y estudio con Luis Sosa. ¿Te acuerdas de él? Necesito estudiar dos años más y termino mi carrera; voy a ser hombre de negocios. ¿Te gusta la idea? A mí me gusta mucho.   10

Por cierto, uno de mis cursos es geografía social de Hispanoamérica y es muy interesante, pero tengo que memorizar muchos datos. Por ejemplo, en Argentina son de origen europeo la mayoría de las personas y solamente un 2% tiene mezcla[1] de blancos, indios y negros; pero en México sólo un 5% es de origen europeo; el 25% de los mexicanos son descendientes de indios y el 60% son mestizos.[2] Necesito tener buena memoria porque hay mucha variedad en todos los países, ¿verdad?   15

Por aquí, todos bien. Mis padres y yo vivimos ahora en la Calle Sol en el Viejo San Juan. Nos gusta mucho el apartamento. Los amigos están bien. Marta estudia y trabaja todo el día. Tomás, el atleta profesional, practica béisbol ocho horas diarias y Carolina va a comprar una computadora Macintosh. Ahora escribe en mi computadora y quiere aprender todo en tres días, ¡como siempre! Bueno, no tengo más noticias.   20

Teresa, espero recibir carta muy pronto. Contesta todas las preguntas, ¿O.K.? Adiós.   25

Cariños,

Mario

P.D. La dirección nueva es: Calle Sol, Residencias "Margaritas", Apto. 34, San Juan, Puerto Rico 00936

---

1. mixture   2. of mixed parentage (white and Indian)

Actividad 17: ¿Quién es el sujeto?

To whom do the following verbs refer? Go back to the letter and note the verb endings and the context given before choosing an answer.

1. "¿De dónde son y qué **estudian**?" (línea 4)
   a. Teresa y Mario
   b. los amigos de Teresa
   c. los amigos de Teresa y Mario
2. "**Necesito** estudiar dos años más y termino mi carrera." (línea 10)
   a. Mario   b. Teresa   c. Marta
3. "Por ejemplo, en Argentina **son** de origen europeo . . ." (línea 13)
   a. los amigos de Mario
   b. la mayoría de las personas
   c. los hispanoamericanos
4. "Ahora **escribe** en mi computadora . . ." (línea 23)
   a. Marta   b. Tomás   c. Carolina
5. "Teresa, **espero** recibir carta muy pronto." (línea 25)
   a. Mario   b. Teresa   c. Carolina

Actividad 18: Preguntas

Act. 18: Discuss ethnic make-up of different countries. Puerto Rico: the lack of Indian heritage due to fatal diseases brought by Europeans. Basques in Spain: their unknown origin; the fact that Basque is unrelated to other world languages; the disproportionally high number of people with Rh negative blood. Peru: 100 different Indian groups, each having its own customs and language; a relatively large Chinese population. (etc.)

Answer the following questions based on the letter you have just read.

1. ¿Dónde trabaja Mario y qué hace?
2. ¿Qué practica Tomás todos los días?
3. ¿Qué va a comprar Carolina?
4. ¿Cuál es el origen de los argentinos?
5. En México, ¿qué porcentaje de personas son mestizas?

What do you know about the ethnic make-up of other Hispanic countries?

Estrategia de escritura: *Brainstorming*

One of the many techniques that can help you write successfully is brainstorming. Brainstorming is mainly a group activity in which you write down whatever comes to your mind related to the topic at hand. These thoughts do not need to be organized. This activity helps you to learn from others and to develop your own ideas as a starting point for your written work.

Act. 19: Encourage students to accept all ideas given in their group and to not be judgmental. This is only to generate ideas; many will be disregarded.

Actividad 19: Una carta a Mario

Use the following steps in order to write a letter to Mario.

Note the format and punctuation in the letter from Mario when writing your own letter.

1. In groups of five, imagine that you are Teresa and brainstorm a list of ideas you could write in your letter to Mario.
2. On your own, choose the best ideas and organize them.
3. Write a letter to Mario.

Lo esencial

I. Las descripciones: *Ser* + adjective

I./II. Practice **ser/estar** + adjective:
1. Use students as models in presentations. Contrast **corto** and **bajo**.
2. Create a picture file to use with adjectives: (a) Describe a picture and have students tell you which picture it is; (b) Have them describe pictures; (c) Do a student-led group writing, describing a picture. This picture file can be reused when teaching clothes or other adjectives.

1. **Ella** es al**ta**.
2. **Ella** es baja.
3. **Ellos** son gord**os**.
4. **Ellos** son delgad**os**. **(Ellos** son flac**os**.)
5. **Él** es joven.
6. **Él** es viej**o**.
7. **Ellas** son moren**as**.
8. **Ellas** son rubi**as**.

Otros adjetivos

simpático/a nice
guapo/a good looking
bonito/a pretty
bueno/a good
inteligente intelligent
grande large, big
largo/a long

antipático/a unpleasant, disagreeable
feo/a ugly
malo/a bad
estúpido/a, tonto/a stupid
pequeño/a small
corto/a short (in length)

Actividad 20: ¿A quién describo?

In groups of four, take turns describing other people in your class, and have the rest of the group guess who they are.

Adjectives, including adjectives of nationality, agree in number and in gender with the noun modified.

Act. 21: Extend the activity with examples given by students.

Act. 22: You might have students try to predict a partner's answers.

Actividad 21: ¿Cómo son?

Describe the following people using one or two adjectives.

1. el/la profesor/a
2. Joan Collins
3. Tom Cruise y Mel Gibson
4. Frankenstein
5. el capitán Kirk
6. Sigourney Weaver y Meryl Streep
7. tu madre o tu padre

Actividad 22: ¿Cómo eres?

The following descriptive adjectives are cognates. Circle the four that best describe you and underline the four that least describe you. When finished, compare your answers with those of a friend.

activo/a	idealista	optimista	reservado/a
artístico/a	indiferente	paciente	responsable
atlético/a	informal	pesimista	serio/a
conservador/a	intelectual	político/a	sociable
cómico/a	liberal	realista	tímido/a
formal	nervioso/a	religioso/a	tradicional

II. Las descripciones: *Estar* + adjective

1. Él está **contento.**
2. Ella está **triste.**
3. Ellos están **enamorados.**
4. Ella está **enferma.**
5. Ella está **aburrida.**
6. Él está **enojado.**

Otros adjetivos

borracho/a   drunk
cansado/a   tired
preocupado/a   worried

Actividad 23: ¿Cómo estoy?

In pairs, act out the different adjectives and have your partner guess how you feel, then switch roles.

Actividad 24: ¿Cómo estamos?

Discuss in what situations you and other people have the following feelings.

1. Estoy aburrido/a cuando . . .
2. Estoy triste cuando . . .
3. Estoy cansado/a cuando . . .
4. Una persona está borracha cuando . . .
5. Mis amigos están enojados cuando . . .
6. Estoy contento/a cuando . . .

Act. 25: Encourage students to be creative.

Actividad 25: ¿Cómo están ellos?

Look at the drawing and answer the following questions.

1. ¿Cómo es él?
2. ¿Cómo es ella?
3. ¿Cómo está él?
4. ¿Cómo está ella?

Hay familias . . . y . . . FAMILIAS

Practice **¿por qué?/porque** by having students ask and answer questions: **¿Por qué estudias español? ¿Por qué miras la televisión? ¿Por qué vas al restaurante/bar ...** *(Fill in name)?*

me gustaría	I would like
¿Por qué? Porque . . .	Why? Because . . .
No te preocupes.	Don't worry.

Teresa and Vicente have started going out together. Don Alejandro, Teresa's uncle, wants to meet Vicente to "check him out." Teresa is trying to convince Vicente to meet her uncle.

Act. 26: Before students listen to the tape or complete this activity, have them suggest adjectives they think will apply to Teresa's uncle.

Actividad 26: ¿Cómo es el tío de Teresa?

Study the following list, then listen to the dialogue and check the adjectives that apply to Teresa's uncle.

El tío de Teresa es:

✔	alto	_____	bajo
✔	moreno	_____	rubio
_____	delgado	✔	gordo
✔	simpático	_____	antipático
_____	pesimista	✔	optimista
_____	cómico	✔	serio
✔	liberal	_____	conservador

Inviting

Vicente	¿Te gustaría ir al cine el jueves?
Teresa	Me gustaría, pero antes tenemos que tomar un café con mi tío.
Vicente	Pero, ¿por qué?
Teresa	Porque es mi tío y por eso, es mi papá en España.

Giving a reason

Giving physical description

Describing personality traits

Expressing feelings

Vicente	Estoy nervioso. ¿Cómo es?
Teresa	No te preocupes. Es alto, moreno, un poco gordo . . .
Vicente	¡No, no! Pero, ¿cómo es? ¿Simpático? ¿Antipático?
Teresa	Es muy simpático, es un hombre optimista y siempre está contento.
Vicente	Pero . . . es tu familia . . . y las familias . . .
Teresa	Y las familias, ¿qué?
Vicente	No sé, pero, estoy nervioso. ¿Es tradicional tu tío?
Teresa	No, hombre. Es un poco serio, pero muy liberal.
Vicente	Bueno, voy, pero después vamos al cine, ¿O.K.?
Teresa	Sí, por supuesto, pero con mi tío, ¿no?
Vicente	¿Cómo? ¿Estás loca?

Actividad 27: Preguntas

Answer the following questions based on the dialogue.

1. ¿Adónde van a ir Teresa y Vicente el jueves?
2. ¿Con quién van a ir?
3. ¿Cómo está Vicente?
4. Vicente le dice a Teresa, "¿Estás loca?"; ¿Por qué?

¿Lo sabían?

Since Teresa's parents are in Puerto Rico and her uncle is in Madrid, it is normal for him to consider her welfare an important responsibility. Teresa's duty is to respect him as if he were her father.

The word *family* has different connotations in different cultures. For Hispanics, the word **familia** suggests not only the immediate family, but also grandparents, uncles and aunts, as well as close and distant cousins. What does the word *family* mean to you?

Actividad 28: Comparación

Look back at the description of Teresa's uncle and compare him to your father or to one of your uncles. Follow the model.

⏺ Mi padre es bajo, pero el tío de Teresa es alto.

Actividad 29: Una invitación y una excusa

In pairs, invite your partner to go somewhere or to do something. Your partner should give an excuse. Then switch roles. Follow the model.

⏺ **A:** ¿Te gustaría ir al cine/a bailar/. . . ?
B: Me gustaría, pero estoy . . ./tengo que . . ./necesito . . .

A large family gathers for a picnic in Chapultepec Park, Mexico City. Describe some of the people physically.

Hacia la comunicación

Gramática

I. Describing Yourself and Others: Descriptive Adjectives

Before studying the grammar explanation, answer these questions:

- What would you have to change in the sentence **Eduardo está cansado** if the subject were Carmen instead of Eduardo?
- Since both **ser** and **estar** mean *to be* in English, what is the difference between **¿Cómo es ella?** and **¿Cómo está ella?**
- Even though you may not know these adjectives in Spanish, would you use **ser** or **estar** to say that a person is generous? Courageous? Interesting? Upset? Honest? Elated? Explain your choices.

I. A. Drill adjective agreement: Do a transformation drill: Opposites attract. State, **Juan es alto, pero Juana ...**, etc.

A. Agreement of Adjectives

1. Adjectives that end in **-o** agree in gender (masculine/feminine) and in number (singular/plural) with the nouns they modify.

Francisco es baj**o** pero **Francisca** es alt**a**.
Ellos son delgad**os** y **ellas** son delgad**as**.

Remember: Professions that end in **-ista** also have two forms only: **artista/s.**

2. Adjectives that end in **-e** and in consonants agree in number (singular/plural) with the nouns they modify.

Ella está trist**e** y **ellos** también están trist**es.**
Camilo no es libera**l. Ana y Elisa** tampoco son libera**les.**

Note: j**o**ven — j**ó**venes

3. Adjectives that end in **-ista** agree in number with the nouns they modify.

Rafael es real**ista** y **Emilia** es ideal**ista.**
Ellos son optim**istas.**

B. *Ser* and *estar* + adjective

I. B. To illustrate the use of **ser** and **estar** + *adjective,* have a student get in front of the class; have the class describe him: **Es alto. Es guapo. Es inteligente.** Make him frown: **Está triste.** Make him look bored: **Está aburrido,** etc. Show that even though he is sad, bored, etc., he never stopped being tall, good-looking, and intelligent.

Drill **ser** and **estar:**
1. Use pictures and ask, **¿Cómo es? ¿Cómo está?**
2. In pairs, have students mime and describe emotions. S1: *(Pouts.)* S2: **Estás triste.**
3. Contrast meaning by having students finish these sentences: **El vino es bueno porque ...** **El vino está bueno porque ...** **La estudiante es lista porque ... Ella está lista porque ...**

1. **Ser** + *adjective* is used to describe *the being:* what someone or something *looks like* or *is like* to someone who is not familiar with them. You use **ser** when describing someone's personality (**Él es inteligente/optimista,** etc. . . .); or when describing a person physically (**Ella es alta, delgada,** etc.)

2. **Estar** + *adjective* is used to describe the *state of being:* it indicates how people or things are or describes a particular condition: **Él está enfermo.**

3. Certain adjectives convey different meanings depending on whether they are used with **ser** or **estar.**

El político **es aburrido.**	*The politician is boring.*
Ellos **están aburridos.**	*They are bored.*
Ella **es lista.**	*She is clever.*
Él **está listo.**	*He is ready.*
El vino **es bueno.**	*Wine is good (for you).*
El vino **está bueno.**	*The wine tastes good.*
El café **es malo.**	*Coffee is bad (for you).*
El café **está malo.**	*The coffee tastes lousy.*
Verónica **es bonita**.	*Veronica is pretty.*
¡Hoy Verónica **está bonita**!	*Veronica is (looks) especially pretty today!*

II. Expressing Possession: Possessive Adjectives

II. The long forms **de él/ella/ ellos/ellas** are used instead of **su** in some countries, such as Argentina and Colombia.

You already know two ways of expressing possession: **de** + *noun* (**el vídeo es de Juan Carlos/es el vídeo de Juan Carlos**) and **tener** + *noun* (**tengo calculadora**). Possession can also be expressed using possessive adjectives *(her, their, our,* etc.). In Spanish, **mi, tu,** and **su** agree in number with the thing or things possessed; **nuestro** and **vuestro** agree in gender and number with the thing or things possessed.

Possessive Adjectives

mi/s	my	**nuestro/a/os/as**	our
tu/s	your (informal)	**vuestro/a/os/as**	your (informal)
su/s	{your (formal) / his, her	**su/s**	{your (in/formal) / their

—¿Son los discos de Mario?　　—No, no son **sus discos,** son **mis discos.**

—¿De quiénes son las guitarras?　—Son **nuestras guitarras.**

—¿Es el televisor de Ana y Luis?　—Sí, es **su televisor.**

III. Position of Adjectives

1. Possessive adjectives and adjectives of quantity (including indefinite articles) precede the noun they modify.

Mi madre es arquitecta.*　　*My mother is an architect.*
Tengo **tres televisores**.　　*I have three TV sets.*
Bebo **mucha Coca-Cola.**　　*I drink a lot of Coca-Cola.*
¿Tienes **pocos o muchos amigos?**　*Do you have few or many friends?*

*Note: The indefinite articles *(un, una, unos, unas—a/an, some)* are used with occupations only when they are modified by an adjective.

Mi padre es **ingeniero.** Mi padre es **un** ingeniero **fantástico.**

2. Descriptive adjectives normally follow the nouns they modify.

Tenemos un **examen importante** en la clase de literatura.

We have an *important exam* in literature class.

Actividad 30: ¿Adónde vas cuando . . . ?

In pairs, ask your partner where he/she goes when in the following moods or situations. Follow the model.

A: ¿Adónde vas cuando estás enojado/a?
B: Cuando estoy enojado/a voy a mi habitación.

1. estar aburrido/a
2. necesitar comprar café
3. tener que trabajar
4. estar enfermo/a
5. necesitar estudiar
6. necesitar correr
7. estar contento/a
8. necesitar comprar periódicos
9. estar preocupado/a
10. estar con tu novio/a

Act. 31: Have students peer edit. Ask volunteers to read their paragraphs aloud.

Actividad 31: Tu amigo y su amiga

Read the following paragraph, then invent a story about a friend of yours and his girlfriend by completing the paragraph with the types of words indicated in parentheses. Remember that adjectives agree with the nouns they modify.

Mi amigo _____ es _____ y es
        (nombre)   (nacionalidad)
_____ . Él tiene _____ años y es
   (ocupación)   (número)
_____ , _____ y _____ .
  (adjetivo)   (adjetivo)   (adjetivo)
_____ amigo tiene una amiga que se llama
(adjetivo posesivo)
_____ y ella es _____ y
   (nombre)   (adjetivo)
_____ . Ellos son muy _____ , pero están
  (adjetivo)   (adjetivo)
_____ porque _____ .
  (adjetivo)   (?)

Actividad 32: Un compañero de clase

As a class, write a description of one of your classmates. Say what the person's name is, where he/she is from, what he/she looks like, what activities he/she likes to do, etc.

Act. 33: Students can earn 1 point for each clue given and 5 points for getting the correct response.

Actividad 33: ¿Quién es?

In groups of five, each one prepares descriptions of a famous man and a famous woman. When you finish the descriptions, read them aloud and have the rest of the group identify who is being described.

⦿ Es político.
    Es un político famoso.
    Es un político famoso de Massachusetts.
    Está en Washington.
    Su familia es de origen irlandés.

Act. 34: This can be expanded by having students write descriptions to go along with the drawings. Display drawings on the wall, and have students match the description to the drawing.

Actividad 34: El criminal

In groups of three, pretend that you have just witnessed a crime and are giving a description of the criminal to a police artist. Two people can describe the suspect while the third one draws.

Actividad 35: Los gustos

In pairs, discuss what TV programs, music, movies, etc., young kids like and compare their preferences with those of adults. Use as many descriptive adjectives as you can. Follow the model.

▐●▌ Sus programas favoritos son . . . , pero nuestros programas favoritos son . . . .

Actividad 36: La persona ideal

In groups of five, describe the ideal companion. When finished, share your description with the other groups.

▐●▌ Nuestro/a compañero/a ideal es . . .

Actividad 37: Dos diálogos

In pairs, student "A" covers Column B and student "B" covers Column A. Carry on a dialogue with your partner by listening and choosing an appropriate response from each box in your column. There are two dialogue possibilities.

A

Estás muy contento/a hoy. ¿Estás triste?

¿Por qué? ¿No trabajas hoy? ¿Por qué? ¿Tienes un problema?

¿Está enfermo? ¿Cómo es?

¿De dónde es? ¿Dónde está?

B

No, estoy preocupado/a. Sí, hoy no tengo problemas en la oficina.

Voy a trabajar con la Sra. Martínez. Sí, es mi padre.

Es simpática, joven y muy inteligente. Sí, está en el hospital y está solo.

Está en Miami y yo voy mañana. Es de Guadalajara.

Actividad 38: Autobiografía

Write an autobiographical sketch. Use these questions as a guide.

Párrafo *(paragraph)* 1

1. ¿Cómo te llamas, de qué nacionalidad eres y cuántos años tienes?
2. ¿Dónde estás y por qué estás allí *(there)*?

Listen, pick the appropriate sentence, look your partner in the eye, and say the line.

Act. 37: Students should maintain eye contact.

After practicing, have different students repeat the dialogue for specific situations. Remind them to vary their tones of voice accordingly: whispering in church, yelling across a busy street, talking loudly on the telephone because of a bad connection, etc.

Pay attention to accents and punctuation.

Act. 38: Peer edit, or collect and correct.

Párrafo 2

1. ¿Tienes muchos o pocos amigos? ¿Cómo son?
2. Si son estudiantes, ¿qué estudian? ¿Estudian mucho o poco?
3. Si trabajan, ¿qué hacen? ¿Dónde trabajan? ¿Trabajan mucho o poco?

Párrafo 3

1. ¿Qué te gusta hacer y con quién?
2. ¿Qué hacen Uds. los viernes y los sábados? ¿Adónde van?
3. ¿Estás contento/a cuando estás con tus amigos?

Vocabulario funcional

Las nacionalidades

See page 67

Lugares

¿**Adónde vas?**   Where are you going?
¿**Dónde estás?**   Where are you?
¿**Con quién vas?**   With whom are you going?
estar en   to be in/at
  la agencia de viajes   travel agency
  el banco   bank
  la biblioteca   library
  la casa   house/home
  el cine   movie theater
  la escuela   school
  la farmacia   drugstore

el hospital   hospital
la iglesia   church
la librería   bookstore
la oficina   office
el parque   park
la piscina   pool
la playa   beach
el restaurante   restaurant
el supermercado   supermarket
el teatro   theater
la tienda   store
la universidad   university

La descripción

Adjetivos con **ser: ¿Cómo es?**
aburrido/a   boring
alto/a   tall
antipático/a   unpleasant, disagreeable
bajo/a   short (in height)
bonito/a   pretty
bueno/a   good
corto/a   short (in length)
delgado/a   thin
estúpido/a   stupid
feo/a   ugly
flaco/a   skinny
gordo/a   fat

grande   large, big
guapo/a   good-looking
inteligente   intelligent
joven   young
largo/a   long
listo/a   clever
malo/a   bad
moreno/a   brunet/te; dark skinned
pequeño/a   small
rubio/a   blond/e
simpático/a   nice
tonto/a   stupid
viejo/a   old

Adjetivos con **estar:** **¿Cómo está?**

aburrido/a bored	**enojado/a** angry, mad
borracho/a drunk	**listo/a** ready
cansado/a tired	**preocupado/a** worried
contento/a happy	**solo/a** alone
enamorado/a in love	**triste** sad
enfermo/a sick	

Las asignaturas *(Subjects)*

la biología biology	**la literatura** literature
la economía economics	**las matemáticas** mathematics
la historia history	**la sociología** sociology

Más verbos

-ar

comprar to buy	**regresar** to return
desear to want; to desire	**tocar** to play (an instrument);
molestar to bother	to touch
necesitar to need	**usar** to use

-er

aprender to learn	**vender** to sell

-ir

recibir to receive	**vivir** to live

Los adjetivos posesivos

See page 85

Palabras y expresiones útiles

la clase lesson, class	**pero** but
con with	**el origen** origin
¿Cuál es el origen de tu familia? Where is your family from?	**poco/pocos** a little/few
	¿Por qué? Why?
demasiado too much	**porque** because
después after	**si** if
la familia family	**siempre** always
me gustaría I would like	**el tío** uncle
muy very	
No te preocupes. Don't worry.	
No tengo idea. I don't have any idea.	

Una arqueóloga trabaja en una excavación de ruinas precolombinas en la Ciudad de México. ¿Sabes en qué países están las ruinas aztecas, mayas e incas? ¿Qué hace la persona de la foto?

Capítulo 4

Chapter Objectives

After studying this chapter, you will know how to:

- describe what someone is doing
- discuss daily routines
- identify parts of the body
- talk about who and what you and others know and don't know
- tell what the weather is like

¿Cómo se llaman las montañas de Perú?

Noticias de una amiga

¡Qué + adjective!	How + *adjective!*
¡Qué inteligente!	How intelligent!
hay	there is/there are
deber + infinitive	should/must + *infinitive*
debes conocer	should/must know

Practice **deber** + *infinitive* by asking, **¿Qué debes hacer si eres estudiante? ¿Qué deben hacer los atletas profesionales?** (etc.)

José Manuel, un arqueólogo venezolano que está en Perú, recibe una carta de España de su amiga Marisel. José Manuel comenta con Rafael, otro arqueólogo venezolano.

Actividad 1: Cierto o falso

Escucha la conversación y escribe **C** si la oración es cierta y **F** si la oración es falsa.

1. ____F____ Rafael no conoce a Marisel.
2. ____F____ Marisel es arqueóloga.
3. ____C____ Marisel tiene una foto de José Manuel.
4. ____F____ Rafael practica andinismo.

Un hombre hace andinismo en una montaña muy rocosa de los Andes argentinos. ¿Te gusta hacer andinismo?

Being curious

Showing excitement

Reporting

Describing what someone is doing

Contrast: **Es loco** = He is a crazy man; **Está loco** = He is (acting) crazy.

Machu Picchu and the Incas are discussed in the **Nuevos horizontes** section.

Pronunciation: ñ
1. Have students repeat words that contain ñ: **año, señor, señora, montaña, piña.**
2. Have students create sentences that contain words with ñ and either say them aloud, or dictate them to a classmate.

Rafael	Hola, José Manuel. ¿A quién conoces en Madrid?
José Manuel	¿Por qué?
Rafael	Porque hay una carta de Madrid para ti.
José Manuel	¡Ay qué bueno! Es de Marisel.
Rafael	¿De quién?
José Manuel	De Marisel. Tú debes conocer a Marisel; es venezolana.
Rafael	Ah, sí. Estudia geología, ¿no? ¿Qué dice[1]?
José Manuel	A ver . . . Pregunta mucho sobre el proyecto en Machu Picchu: qué hago en el trabajo, cómo son las ruinas incaicas, si hablo con los indios sobre su cultura. Tú sabes, preguntas.
Rafael	¿Y qué más?
José Manuel	. . . También dice que tengo que afeitarme porque estoy feo con la barba que tengo y que estoy loco y voy a tener un accidente.
Rafael	¿Cómo sabe que tienes barba y por qué vas a tener un accidente?
José Manuel	Porque tiene una foto donde estoy haciendo andinismo. En la foto estoy subiendo una montaña totalmente vertical.
Rafael	¡Qué inteligente es Marisel! Porque, en realidad, tú estás loco.

1. What does she say?

Actividad 2: El amigo de Marisel

En grupos de tres, hablen de José Manuel. ¿Cómo es? ¿Qué hace? ¿Dónde está? Después, seleccionen tres adjetivos para describir al amigo de Marisel.

Actividad 3: La habitación de tu compañero/a

En parejas *(pairs)*, averigüen *(find out)* cinco cosas que su compañero/a *(partner)* tiene en su habitación. Sigan *(Follow)* el modelo.

A: ¿Hay vídeo en tu habitación?
B: Sí, hay. / No, no hay.

Actividad 4: Los comentarios

Caminas por la calle y ves a diferentes personas. Haz un comentario *(Make a comment)* sobre ellas. Por ejemplo: Ves a Brooke Shields y tu comentario es "¡Qué bonita!"

Roseanne Barr, Einstein, Tom Cruise, Cybill Shepherd, Beaver Cleaver, el tío de la familia Adams, Danny DeVito

Lo esencial

I. Acciones reflexivas

1. afeitarse
2. cepillarse los dientes
3. ducharse
4. peinarse
5. ponerse la ropa
6. quitarse la ropa

As you do these activities, narrate them in your mind: **Me ducho, me lavo,** etc. Remember: Idle time = study time.

I. Point out that some speakers say **lavarse los dientes** instead of **cepillarse los dientes.**

Do a Gouin series: **Me levanto, voy al baño, me ducho, me lavo el pelo, salgo de la ducha, me cepillo los dientes,** etc.

Contrast physically: **Me levanto. Levanto a mi niño.**

Otras acciones reflexivas

bañarse   to bathe
cepillarse el pelo   to brush one's hair
desayunarse   to have breakfast
lavarse   to wash up, wash (oneself)
levantarse   to get up
maquillarse   to put on make-up

Actividad 5: ¿En qué orden?

Di *(Tell)* en qué orden *(order)* haces estas acciones.

peinarse, bañarse, afeitarse, levantarse, desayunarse, cepillarse los dientes, ponerse la ropa

II. Las partes del cuerpo *(Parts of the Body)*

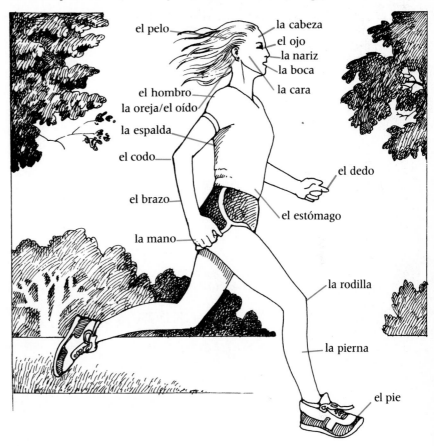

el pelo
la cabeza
el ojo
la nariz
la boca
la cara
el hombro
la oreja/el oído
la espalda
el codo
el dedo
el brazo
el estómago
la mano
la rodilla
la pierna
el pie

Otras partes del cuerpo

la barba	beard	**el diente**	tooth
el bigote	mustache	**los labios**	lips
el dedo del pie	toe	**la lengua**	tongue

Actividad 6: Relaciones

Relaciona la acción reflexiva con la parte correspondiente del cuerpo.

afeitarse   los ojos
lavarse   las manos
peinarse   la barba
maquillarse   el pelo
cepillarse   los dientes
                las piernas
                la cara
                la boca

Act. 7: Extend activity by having students think of other associations.

Answers: **piernas, pelo, orejas, ojos, barba, nariz, brazos, dientes, labios, pies**

Actividad 7: Asociaciones

En grupos de tres, digan qué partes del cuerpo Uds. asocian con estas personas o productos.

No Nonsense, Lady Godiva, Dumbo, Visine, Fidel Castro, Kleenex, Venus de Milo, Pepsodent, Mick Jagger, Reebok

Act. 8: Introduce this activity by describing 1 or 2 students.

Actividad 8: Adivina quién es

En parejas, el estudiante "A" describe a una persona de la clase y el estudiante "B" tiene que adivinar *(guess)* quién es. Después cambien de papel *(switch roles)*.

A: Esta persona tiene piernas largas, ojos grandes, pelo corto y rubio y tiene barba.

B: Es . . .

After reading **¿Lo sabían?**, create sentences that illustrate when to use these sayings. Say, for example, **Tengo un amigo que habla y habla y habla y no escucha.** Then ask, **¿Qué dicho relacionas con esta situación?**

¿Lo sabían?

Cada lengua *(language)* tiene sus dichos *(sayings)* y proverbios, y el español tiene muchos. Algunos están relacionados con las partes del cuerpo.

¡Ojo!	*Watch out!*
Ojo por ojo, diente por diente.	*An eye for an eye and a tooth for a tooth.*
Tengo la palabra en la punta de la lengua.	*I have the word on the tip of my tongue.*
Habla por los codos.	*He/She runs off at the mouth.*

¿En qué situaciones puedes usar estos dichos? ¿Conoces otros dichos en inglés relacionados con las partes del cuerpo?

Hacia la comunicación

Gramática

While watching TV, think about the actions taking place: **Están cantando,** etc.

I.   Discussing Actions in Progress: *Estar + -ando/-iendo*

To discuss actions in progress, you can use the present indicative, as you saw in Chapter 3, or the present progressive. In Spanish, the present progressive is used for actions that are taking place at the moment of speaking. This construction is made with a form of the verb **estar** and the present participle *(-ing)* of another verb. The present participle is formed by adding **-ando** to the stems of **-ar** verbs and **-iendo** to the stems of **-er** and **-ir** verbs.

—¿Qué haces?	*What are you doing?*
—**Estoy** trabaj**ando.**	*I'm working.*

—¿**Están** com**iendo**?	*Are they eating?*
—No, **están** escrib**iendo** una carta.	*No, they are writing a letter.*

Note: **-er** and **-ir** verbs whose stems end in a *vowel* substitute a **y** for the **i**: leer ⟶ le**y**endo.

II. Describing Daily Routines: Reflexive Verbs

A reflexive verb is used when the subject performs and receives the action of the verb. Study the difference between these three drawings:

Ella lava el carro.　　　Él se lava.　　　Él se lava las manos.

A. Form

In order to form reflexive verbs, you need to know the reflexive pronouns.

Levantar**se** *(to get up)*	
me levanto	**nos** levantamos
te levantas	**os** levantáis
se levanta	**se** levantan

Me levant**o** temprano.	*I get up early.*
Él **se** cepill**a** los dientes después de comer.	*He brushes his teeth after he eats.*
Nos desayun**amos** en la cafetería.	*We have breakfast in the cafeteria.*

B. Position

1. The reflexive pronoun precedes a simple conjugated verb form.

　　Todos los días **me levanto** temprano.　　*I get up early every day.*

2. When there is a conjugated verb + infinitive or present participle, the reflexive pronoun either precedes the conjugated verb or follows attached to the infinitive or present participle.

Mañana **me voy a levantar** tarde.⎫ *Tomorrow, I'm going to get up*
Mañana **voy a levantarme** tarde. ⎭ *late.*
Ella **se está bañando.**⎫
Ella **está bañándose.*** ⎭ *She is bathing.*

Review accent rules. See Appendix C.

*Note: When the pronoun is attached to the present participle, an accent is needed on the stressed vowel of the verb.

III. Verbs With Irregular *Yo* Forms

The following verbs are regular in the present indicative, except in the **yo** form.

hacer	to do; to make	yo ha**go**
poner/se	to put/put on	yo pon**go**/yo me pon**go**
salir	to leave; to go out	yo sal**go**
traer	to bring	yo tra**igo**
saber	to know (facts/how to do something)	yo **sé**
ver	to see	yo v**eo**
conocer*	to know (a person/place/thing)	yo cono**zco**
traducir*	to translate	yo tradu**zco**

Me pongo la ropa.   *I put on my clothes.*
Ellos siempre **traen** la música.   *They always bring the music.*
Sé cantar y también toco el piano.   *I know how to sing and I also play the piano.*

—¿**Conoces** Acapulco?   *Do you know Acapulco?*
—No, pero **conozco** Puerto Vallarta.   *No, but I know Puerto Vallarta.*

*Note: Most verbs that end in **-cer** and **-cir** follow the same pattern as **conocer** and **traducir**: **ofrecer** *(to offer)*, **establecer** *(to establish)*, **introducir** *(to introduce)*, **producir** *(to produce)*, etc.

IV. The Personal *a*

When a person receives the action of the verb directly (direct object), you need to use the personal **a.**

Maricarmen mira **a Juan.**
Maricarmen mira **al Sr. López.**

III. Drill irregular **yo** forms:
1. Do a chain drill. T: **¿Qué traes a clase?** S1: **Traigo mis libros.** T: **¿Qué traes a clase?** S2: **Traigo mi lápiz y él trae sus libros.** (etc.)
2. Have students talk about daily activities by completing sentences with these verbs: **conocer, hacer, ponerse, salir, traer,** and **ver.** Encourage creativity. (a) **Todos los días me levanto y ...** (b) **Para mis clases ...** (c) **Soy muy popular, por eso ...** (d) **Todos los días ...** (e) **Todas las noches ...**

Contrast: **introducir** vs. **presentar.**

IV. Work on identifying a direct object and contrast with a prepositional phrase: **Veo el cine. Veo a Carmen. Voy al cine.**

Drill personal **a:**
Do a substitution drill. **Veo a Juan, la iglesia. / Veo la iglesia,** etc. /

Remember to use **el, la los,** or **las** with titles such as **Sra., Dr.,** etc. when speaking about the person.

Maricarmen mira **a la profesora.**
BUT:
Maricarmen mira **la televisión.***

*Note: **Televisión** is not a person, therefore it does not take the personal **a. Tener** does not normally take the personal **a**: **Tengo un amigo.**

Do mechanical drills, Workbook, Part I.

Actividad 9: La familia Rosado

Di qué hace por la mañana la familia Rosado en un día típico.

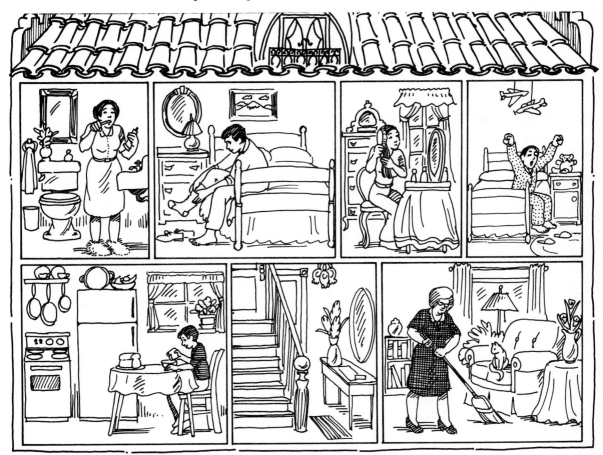

Actividad 10: ¿Qué vas a hacer?

Decide qué vas a hacer con estas cosas.

1. un peine
2. una bañera
3. un cepillo de dientes
4. una ducha
5. café y yogur
6. un jabón

Act. 11: Repeat activity a number of times. Have students sit back-to-back to simulate a phone conversation.

Answering the phone varies within countries and zones. Some examples: **¿Aló?** (Chile, El Salvador); **¿Diga?** (Spain); **¿Bueno?** (Mexico); **¿A ver?** (Colombia); **¿Hola?** (Argentina).

Act. 11: To practice the present progressive: Play the following game, which requires concentration. It is Marcel Marceau with a twist. All actions are valid; what follows is just an example. You may want to model this first with a student. S1: Mimes he/she is swimming. S2: **¿Qué estás haciendo?** S1: Responds while doing the actions for swimming. **Estoy peinándome.** S2: Mimes combing his/her hair. S1: **¿Qué estás haciendo?** S2: Responds while combing his/her hair. **Estoy corriendo.** (etc.)

Actividad 11: ¿Está Diana?

En parejas, "A" llama por teléfono para hablar con una persona, pero la persona está ocupada *(busy)*; "B" dice qué está haciendo. Después cambien de papel. Sigan el modelo.

    B: ¿Aló?
    A: Buenos días. ¿Está Diana?
    B: Sí, está, pero está duchándose.
    A: Ah, muchas gracias, adiós. / Ah, entonces llamo más tarde.

Actividad 12: Nuestra rutina

En parejas, ¿qué tienen que hacer Uds. por la mañana en un día típico?

    Nosotros tenemos que levantarnos . . . / Nosotros nos tenemos que levantar . . .

Actividad 13: ¿Qué hacen ellos?

Describe las actividades de estas personas formando oraciones con frases de las tres columnas. Por ejemplo: Ellos saben tu número de teléfono.

ellos	traducir	tu número de teléfono
Steven Spielberg	ofrecer	Alaska
yo	producir	libros del inglés al
mi tío bilingüe	(no) conocer (a)	español
muchas universidades	saber	películas *(movies)* de
	salir con	horror
	traer	trabajo *(jobs)* a los
	ver	estudiantes
		cursos de
		cinematografía
		programas de televisión
		una persona famosa
		música a la fiesta

Act. 14: Practice 2 or 3 questions before starting. Time the activity. When finished, ask questions so that students report about others in the class: **¿Quién va al cine todas las semanas?** Avoid questions that require answers in the **yo** form.

Actividad 14: La rutina

Pregúntales a tus compañeros si hacen las siguientes actividades. Tienes que encontrar *(find)* dos personas para cada acción.

1. ir al cine todas las semanas
2. preparar el desayuno todos los días
3. ver dos horas de televisión todas las noches
4. salir a bailar los sábados
5. levantarse temprano *(early)* los domingos
6. hacer gimnasia un mínimo de tres días por semana
7. correr todos los días

Act. 15: Before doing this activity, ask students what they remember about Juan Carlos and Claudia.

Why do **saxofón** and **también** have a written accent?

Act. 16: Ask students other places where they could be skiing. Encourage them to use proper nouns when they don't know the vocabulary: Vail, Jackson Hole, Steamboat for "ski slope"; Madison Square Garden for "concert hall"; Bob Dylan for "musician."

Actividad 15: El amor de Juan Carlos

Completa esta historia *(story)* sobre Claudia y Juan Carlos con **a, al, a la, a los** o **a las** sólo *(only)* si es necesario.

____A____ Juan Carlos le gusta mucho Claudia y desea salir con ella, pero no sabe si ella va ____a____ salir con él. Está nervioso y llama ____a____ Teresa porque ella conoce bien ____a____ Claudia. Teresa sabe cómo es Claudia y le explica que ____a____ Claudia le gusta ir ____al____ cine, que los sábados por la noche baila _____ rock con sus amigos en una discoteca y que toca el saxofón y por eso va ____a los____ bares donde tocan _____ jazz. También dice que ahora Claudia está visitando ____a los____ amigos de sus padres que viven en Ávila y que regresa mañana. Entonces Juan Carlos decide llamar ____a____ Claudia mañana por la tarde.

Actividad 16: Imagina

En parejas, cada persona selecciona tres dibujos. Después, usen la imaginación para explicarle a su compañero/a quiénes son las personas, qué están haciendo y dónde están.

▶ Son mis amigos Mike y Eric y están esquiando en Vail.

Nuevos horizontes

Estrategia de lectura: *Predicting*

Predicting is a reading skill that will help you start thinking about the theme of a selection even before you read it. You can predict or guess what a selection will be about by looking at its title, its subtitles and illustrations, as well as by using your general knowledge; that is, what you know about a topic before you read about it. The more you predict what the reading is about, the easier it will be for you to understand its main ideas.

In the following exercises, you will be asked some questions to make you aware of what you know and what you do not know about Machu Picchu and you will be asked to predict the topics of the selection.

Actividad 17: ¿Qué sabes de Perú?

Contesta estas preguntas sobre Perú. Mira el mapa de Suramérica al final del libro para contestar las preguntas uno a cuatro.

1. ¿Dónde está Perú?
2. ¿Cuál es la capital de Perú?
3. ¿Qué países limitan con *(border)* Perú?
4. ¿Dónde está Machu Picchu?
5. ¿Qué es Machu Picchu?
6. ¿Quiénes son los incas?

Actividad 18: Lee y adivina

Marisel recibe un libro con una nota de José Manuel.

1. Lee la nota de José Manuel e intenta *(try)* completar el título del libro.
2. Lee el título de esta sección de la guía. ¿Cuál es el tema?
3. Lee los cinco subtítulos y di cuál es la idea principal de cada párrafo.

Querida Marisel:
Aquí tienes una guía turística de Perú que incluye Machu Picchu, la ciudad misteriosa de los incas. ¿Te gustaría visitarme? Estoy enamorado de los Andes y a ti te gustarían mucho Lima, Cuzco y ¡por supuesto, Machu Picchu!

DE PERÚ

Machu Picchu: El lugar misterioso de los incas

Historia de Machu Picchu

En los Andes, a más de 2.500 metros está la ciudad sagrada[1] de los incas, Machu Picchu, que Hiram Bingham, arqueólogo norteamericano de la Universidad de Yale, descubrió en 1911. Según una versión sobre la historia de Machu Picchu, los incas construyeron la ciudad en una montaña para defender a las Mujeres Sagradas, esposas de su dios[2] el Sol. En este refugio de vírgenes, Bingham y otros arqueólogos descubrieron diez esqueletos de mujer por cada esqueleto de hombre.

Arquitectura

Machu Picchu es la construcción más perfecta de los incas. Las ruinas de la ciudad sagrada tienen bloques enormes de granito blanco colocados perfectamente y sin[3] cemento. Los arqueólogos no comprenden cómo construyeron los incas esta ciudad tan perfecta sin tener la rueda,[4] el hierro,[5] ni el cemento.

Cuzco, ciudad imperial

Para visitar Machu Picchu, es necesario pasar por Cuzco, capital del Imperio Incaico, ciudad construida por Manco Cápac, primer emperador de los incas. La mayoría de las personas que viven hoy en Cuzco son descendientes de los incas; mantienen sus costumbres y hablan quechua, la lengua de los incas.

---

1. sacred   2. god   3. without   4. wheel   5. iron

Machu Picchu, la ciudad sagrada de los incas del Perú.

Cómo ir a Machu Picchu

La aerolínea española, Iberia, tiene vuelos directos de Madrid a Lima y también es posible viajar a Lima desde Miami por AeroPerú. De Lima se va a Cuzco por avión, por tren o por autobús y de Cuzco sale un tren que viaja 117 kilómetros hasta el pie de la montaña donde está Machu Picchu. Aunque hay muchos hoteles en Cuzco y en Lima, hay pocos en Machu Picchu y, por eso, muchas personas regresan a Cuzco después de visitar la ciudad sagrada.

Hoteles

Algunos de los hoteles que hay en Machu Picchu son: el Hotel Turista que acepta Visa, American Express, cheques de viajero y tiene restaurante; el hotel Aguas Calientes y el Albergue Juvenil tienen electricidad y restaurante; y el hospedaje Los Camiones tiene agua y electricidad desde las 6:30 hasta las 10:00 de la noche.

Actividad 19: Cierto o falso

Después de leer el texto, di si estas oraciones son ciertas o falsas. Corrige *(correct)* las oraciones falsas.

1. Machu Picchu es la capital de los incas.
2. Machu Picchu está en Lima.
3. Un arqueólogo de los Estados Unidos descubrió Machu Picchu en 1911.
4. Las construcciones de esta ciudad tienen cemento.
5. La lengua de los incas es el quechua.
6. Las personas de Cuzco no hablan quechua.
7. Para visitar Machu Picchu, visitamos Cuzco primero.
8. Hay muchos hoteles en Machu Picchu.

Estrategia de escritura: *Outlining*

In Chapter 3, you encountered one of the first steps in the process of writing: *brainstorming*. The next step after brainstorming is usually *outlining*. Brainstorming helps you generate ideas about a topic. Outlining helps you plan your writing and therefore write a more organized paragraph or essay.

An outline is an organized list of what you plan to write that contains details from the general to the specific. For short compositions, you can use a topic outline: a list of topics you plan to cover without the details. For example, when the author of the Machu Picchu article was planning the first paragraph, he/she probably wrote the following outline:

I. Historia

    Dónde está Machu Picchu

    Arqueólogo norteamericano

    Función de Machu Picchu

Actividad 20: El plan del autor

En grupos de tres, escriban bosquejos *(outlines)* para los otros párrafos.

Actividad 21: El bosquejo

En grupos de cuatro, imagínense que Uds. son agentes de viajes. Una estudiante de Perú va a estar dos semanas en los Estados Unidos y va a visitar lugares turísticos. ¿Qué lugares de los Estados Unidos debe conocer o visitar esta estudiante? Hagan *(Make)* una lista de tres lugares que debe conocer la estudiante y organicen sus ideas en forma de bosquejo.

Lo esencial

Months: **septiembre** or **setiembre.**

Los meses, las estaciones y el tiempo *(Months, Seasons, and the Weather)*

Un año en la provincia de Mendoza, Argentina

el verano

En enero hace calor.   En febrero hace sol.   En marzo está nublado.

el otoño

En abril hace mal tiempo.   En mayo hace fresco.   En junio hace frío.

el invierno

En julio nieva.

En agosto hace viento.

En septiembre hace fresco.

la primavera

En octubre hace buen tiempo.

En noviembre hace sol.

En diciembre llueve.

> **Treinta días trae noviembre, con abril, junio y septiembre; de veintiocho sólo hay uno y los demás de treinta y uno.**

Expresiones relacionadas con el tiempo

centígrados	centigrade/Celsius
Está a _____ grados (bajo cero).	It's _____ degrees (below zero).
¿Qué tiempo hace?	What's the weather like?
la temperatura	temperature

Ayer

La temperatura mínima de ayer fue de 7,0 grados y se registró a las 07.15 horas, en tanto que la máxima alcanzó a los 25,0 grados y se anotó a las 16.00 horas.

Pronóstico

Despejado con temperaturas probables de 7 y 27 grados, anuncia para hoy en la Región Metropolitana la Dirección Meteorológica de la Fuerza Aérea.

Ask questions based on the realia: **¿Cuál es la temperatura máxima/mínima?**, etc.

¿Lo sabían?

En los países que están al sur de la línea del ecuador (*Equator*), las estaciones no son en los mismos meses que en los Estados Unidos. Por ejemplo, cuando es invierno en este país, es verano en Uruguay; por eso, en el hemisferio sur hace calor para la Navidad (*Christmas*). Hay clases desde el otoño, en marzo, hasta noviembre o diciembre en la primavera.

Expresiones de tiempo *(Time expressions)*

—**¿Cuál es la fecha?**	*What is the date?*
—**Hoy es el 20 de octubre.***	*Today is October 20th.*
—**¿Cuándo es la fiesta?**	*When is the party?*
—**Es el 21 de marzo.***	*It is on March 21st.*

*Nota: El **primero** de enero, pero **el dos/tres/cuatro** . . . de enero.

Act. 22: Point out that this realia comes from Chile and that terms used in weather reports may vary from country to country. Have students use the weather expressions from pp. 105–106 for this activity.

Actividad 22: Los meteorólogos

En parejas, imagínense que Uds. son meteorólogos que trabajan para Radio Popular. Hablen del tiempo que hace en el mundo, usando la siguiente información.

|●| Aquí en La Paz, Pepito Pérez. Hoy hace sol y la temperatura es de 16 grados centígrados. Ahora a nuestro amigo . . . en . . .

Match the terms in the weather report with the expressions you've just learned: **despejado = hace sol,** etc.

El Mundo

Las temperaturas están expresadas en grados Celsius
Los datos proporcionados son de hace 24 horas

Ciudad	Mín.	Máx.	Condiciones	Ciudad	Mín.	Máx.	Condiciones
Asunción	20	30	Despejado	México	10	23	Despejado
Atenas	6	16	Lluvioso	Miami	22	27	Despejado
Berlín	5	8	Nuboso	Montevideo	18	21	Despejado
Bonn	8	12	Nuboso	Moscú	2	6	Despejado
Bogotá	7	18	Nuboso	Nueva York	3	3	Despejado
Bruselas	7	14	Despejado	Panamá	30	32	Nuboso
Buenos Aires	18	22	Nuboso	París	9	14	Nuboso
Caracas	18	28	Despejado	Pekín	5	14	Despejado
Ginebra	-9	11	Nuboso	Quito	8	19	Nuboso
Guatemala	14	26	Despejado	Río de Janeiro	19	32	Despejado
La Habana	21	26	Nuboso	Roma	5	9	Despejado
La Paz	4	16	Despejado	San José	16	27	Despejado
Lima	19	25	Nuboso	San Juan	21	28	Nuboso
Lisboa	11	19	Nuboso	San Salvador	21	30	Despejado
Londres	6	13	Despejado	Santo Domingo	20	30	Despejado
Los Angeles	11	16	Nuboso	Tegucigalpa	21	33	Despejado
Madrid	5	20	Despejado	Tokio	6	17	Nuboso
Managua	21	32	Despejado	Viena	9	13	Soleado
				Washington	8	19	Despejado

Act. 23: Encourage students to introduce the next speaker: **Y ahora a ... en Honolulú.**

Actividad 23: El informe

En grupos de cuatro, escriban un informe *(report)* sobre el tiempo que va a hacer mañana en diferentes partes del país. Por ejemplo: Va a nevar/llover/hacer sol/estar nublado/etc. Al terminar, lean el informe a la clase, siguiendo el modelo de la Actividad 22.

| Estudiante A | Honolulú | Estudiante C | Anchorage |
| Estudiante B | Nueva York | Estudiante D | Seattle |

For practice, say dates that are important to your family: birthdates, anniversaries, etc.

Actividad 24: Las celebraciones

En parejas, pregúntenle a su compañero/a en qué mes o fecha específica son estas celebraciones.

|●| **A:** ¿Cuándo es el Día de San José?
B: Es el 19 de marzo.

1. el Día de San Valentín
2. el Día de la Independencia de los Estados Unidos
3. el Día de San Patricio
4. la Navidad
5. Año Nuevo
6. el Día de la Madre
7. el Día del Padre

El memo

favor de + infinitive	please . . .
favor de comprar	please buy
¿podrías + infinitive?	could you . . . ?
¿Podrías ir tú?	Could you go?

Teresa va a la agencia de viajes de su tío para trabajar y recibe un memo.

Act 25: Before reading the memo, ask students what a memo looks like, what type of format it has, and what kind of information it conveys.

Actividad 25: Lee y contesta

Mira la primera parte del siguiente memo y contesta estas preguntas.

1. ¿Quién escribe el memo?
2. ¿Quién recibe el memo?
3. ¿Cuál es el tema del memo?
4. ¿Cuál es la fecha del memo?

Entrada al metro Puerta del Sol en Madrid, España.

Which was written as a Roman numeral, the day or the month?

A: Teresa
DE: tu tío Alejandro
FECHA: 20/VI/90
EN RELACION A: información sobre un viaje a Argentina
HA LLAMADO: _____
LLAMAR A: _____

Tengo que ir a la librería La Casa del Libro pero no tengo tiempo. ¿Podrías ir tú? ¿Sabes dónde está? En la Gran Vía. Tomas el metro o el autobús número dos. Favor de llevar este paquete de información sobre vacaciones. El señor se llama Federico de Rodrigo y desea ir a esquiar con su familia a Mendoza, Argentina, el mes de agosto. Tú conoces al Sr. de Rodrigo, ¿no? Es bajo, un poco gordo y tiene la nariz larga. Trabaja en el segundo piso[1] en la sección de arte; en ese piso también se venden mapas. Favor de comprar una guía urbana de Madrid de este año. Gracias.

1. floor

Actividad 26: Preguntas

Después de leer el memo, contesta estas preguntas.

1. Teresa tiene que hacer dos cosas; ¿cuáles son?
2. ¿Dónde está la librería y cómo se llama?
3. Teresa tiene dos opciones para ir a la librería; ¿cuáles son?
4. ¿Qué se vende en el segundo piso de la librería?
5. ¿Adónde desea ir el Sr. de Rodrigo, con quiénes y por qué?

Actividad 27: Los favores

En parejas, pídanle (ask) favores a su compañero/a. Usen las expresiones **favor de + infinitivo** y **podrías + infinitivo**. Sigan el modelo.

⬤ **A:** Favor de comprar champú. / ¿Podrías comprar champú?
B: Con mucho gusto. / Por supuesto. / No puedo, tengo que estudiar.

Actividad 28: ¿Sabes esquiar?

En parejas, pregúntenle a su compañero/a si sabe hacer estas cosas. Averigüen tres cosas que su compañero/a sabe hacer y tres cosas que no sabe hacer. Sigan el modelo.

⬤ **A:** ¿Sabes bailar tango?
B: Sí, sé bailar tango. / No, no sé (pero me gustaría).

Actividad 29: ¿Conoces San Francisco?

Pregúntales a tus compañeros si conocen diferentes ciudades. Si contestan que sí, pregúntales cómo son. Sigan el modelo.

 —¿Conoces la ciudad de Chicago?
—Sí.
—¿Cómo es?
—Es muy bonita, pero hace mucho frío en invierno.

Hacia la comunicación

I.A./B. Drill demonstratives:
1. Use TPR: **Dame este libro.
Dale aquella pluma a Carlos.**
(etc.)
2. Practice by asking for objects and pointing; after modeling, have students lead the activity. T: **Deseo ese lápiz.** S1:
¿Cuál? ¿Éste? T: **No, ése.**

Demonstratives are frequently used with **aquí**
(here), **allí** (there), and
allá (there).

Este has a **t** and you can touch it, **ese** is over there, and **aquel** is so far away you have to **yell**.

I. Pointing Out: Demonstrative Adjectives and Pronouns

A. Demonstrative Adjectives

Estos discos son de jazz, **esos discos** son de música clásica y **aquellas cintas** son de rock.

In English there are two demonstrative adjectives: *this* and *that*. In Spanish there are three: **este** *(this)*, which indicates something near the speaker, **ese** *(that)*, which indicates something farther from the speaker, and **aquel** *(that)*, which usually indicates something far away from the speaker and the listener. It is common to use **ese** and **aquel** interchangeably. Many native speakers make no distinction between the two. Since **este, ese,** and **aquel** are adjectives, they must agree with the noun they modify in gender and in number.

est**e** libr**o**	est**os** libr**os**
est**a** grabador**a**	est**as** grabador**as**

es**e**, es**a**, es**os**, es**as**
aquel, aquel**la**, aquel**los**, aquel**las**

B. Demonstrative Pronouns

1. Demonstrative adjectives function as demonstrative pronouns when the nouns they modify are absent. When this occurs, an accent is placed over the stressed vowel of the demonstrative pronoun.

Este disco es bueno, pero **éste** es fantástico.	*This record is good, but this (other) one is fantastic.*

2. **Esto, eso,** and **aquello** are neuter demonstrative pronouns that refer to abstract concepts; they do not have accents.

¿Qué es **eso**?	*What's that?*

II. Generalizing: The Impersonal *se* and the Passive *se*

II.1. Drill **se**:
Give statements and have students react by saying **sí** or **no**:
Se habla español en Brasil.
(etc.)

1. The impersonal **se** + *a third person singular verb form* is used to express an indefinite subject, which would be expressed in English as *one, people, you,* or *they.*

Se dice que Cancún es muy bonito.	*They say Cancún is very pretty.*
En Chile **se esquía** en julio.	*In Chile, people ski in July.*

Note: You can express the same meaning by saying **Dicen que** . . . or **Esquían en** . . . .

II.2. With the passive **se,** the thing being acted upon is the subject.

2. The passive **se** + *third person verb form* is used when the person or persons doing the action are unknown or irrelevant. The action expressed by the verb is stressed. The verb agrees in number with the thing being acted upon.

Se abr**en las oficinas** de lunes a viernes.	*The offices are open from Monday through Friday.*
Se necesit**an vendedores.**	*Salespeople are needed.*
Se vend**e chocolate** en la tienda nueva.	*Chocolate is sold in the new store.*
Aquí **se** habl**a español.**	*Spanish is spoken here.*

III. Drill **saber** vs. **conocer**: Give items: have students decide whether to use **saber** or **conocer**: el número de páginas en el libro, la capital de Panamá, a Ramón, nadar bien, el disco nuevo de Bon Jovi, etc.

III. *Saber* versus *conocer*

Both **saber** and **conocer** mean *to know,* but they are used to express very different kinds of knowledge in Spanish.

A. Saber

1. **saber** + *infinitive* = to know how to do something

Claudia **sabe** tocar el saxofón.	*Claudia knows how to play the saxophone.*
Juan Carlos **sabe** esquiar.	*Juan Carlos knows how to ski.*

2. **saber** + *factual information* = to know something (by heart).

Teresa **sabe** el número de teléfono de Vicente.	*Teresa knows Vicente's telephone number.*
¿**Sabes** dónde está la Casa del Libro?	*Do you know where the "Casa del Libro" is?*
¿**Sabes** quién es ella?	*Do you know who she is?*

B. Conocer

1. **conocer a** + *person* = to know a person

Claudia **conoce al** tío de Teresa.	*Claudia knows Teresa's uncle.*
¿**Conoces a** Marisel?	*Do you know Marisel?*

2. **conocer** + *noun* = to be familiar with places and things

Teresa no **conoce** Buenos Aires.	*Teresa doesn't know Buenos Aires.*
¿**Conoces** el libro *Cien años de soledad* de Gabriel García Márquez?	*Do you know the book One Hundred Years of Solitude by Gabriel García Márquez?*

Gabriel García Márquez, Colombian, Nobel Prize for Literature in 1982.

Do mechanical drills, Workbook, Part II.

Actividad 30: Los arreglos

En parejas, estudiante "A" es el/la agente de un actor famoso. Estudiante "B" trabaja en un hotel. "A" necesita información sobre la ciudad, entonces le pregunta a "B". Sigan el modelo.

◖●◗ **A:** ¿Dónde se come bien?
   B: Se come bien en . . .

comprar aspirinas	tomar una cerveza
correr	comprar una novela
nadar	escuchar música buena

Actividad 31: Las tiendas

Completa estos letreros *(signs)* de diferentes tiendas con uno de estos verbos: **comer, comprar, hablar, necesitar, vender, vivir.**

1. En un apartamento:

> _____
> Tel. 446 55 68

4. En una cafetería:

> _____ camareros.

2. En una joyería *(jewelry store):*

> _____ oro
> *(gold)* y plata *(silver).*

5. En un restaurante:

> _____ bien
> aquí.

3. En una agencia de viajes:

> Aquí _____
> inglés.
> English spoken here.

6. En un edificio *(building)* de apartamentos:

> _____ como un
> rey *(king)* en los apartamentos
> Villarreal.

Actividad 32: Tu universidad

En parejas, díganle a un/a estudiante nuevo/a en su universidad los mejores lugares para comer, bailar, comprar libros, comer hamburguesas, etc.

|●| Se come bien en . . .

Act. 33: Instruct students to ask 1 question per classmate. Suggest they proceed directly from person to person in order to insure that the activity runs smoothly.

Actividad 33: Una persona que . . .

Busca *(Look for)* a las personas de tu clase que saben o conocen:

1. esquiar
2. San Francisco
3. la película *E.T.*
4. tocar el piano
5. el número de teléfono de la policía
6. cantar "La bamba"
7. Nueva York
8. una persona importante

Remember to use the personal **a** with **conocer.**

Act. 34: Use the drawing to talk about the 3 planes of **este, ese,** and **aquel.**

Actividad 34: ¿Éste, ése o aquél?

En parejas, el/la estudiante "A" cubre la información del/de la estudiante "B", y "B" cubre la información de "A". Uds. están en una fiesta y conocen a muchas personas, pero no a todas. Pregúntale a tu compañero/a si conoce a las personas que tú no conoces. Usa oraciones como: **¿Conoces a ese señor alto que está bailando?**

A

1. Ramón Paredes, hombre de negocios, el novio de Carmen
3. Carmen Barrios, estudiante universitaria, estudia biología
4. Miguel Jiménez, médico, 31 años, no tiene novia
6. Germán Mostaza, periodista, trabaja para *El Diario*, 27 años

B

2. Ramona Carvajal, dentista, argentina, amiga de Laura
5. Laura Salinas, economista, trabaja en el Banco Hispanoamericano
7. José Peña, geólogo, el novio de Begoña
8. Begoña Rodríguez, programadora de computadoras

Act. 35: Practice some questions before starting. The interviewee should not be looking at the questionnaire.

Actividad 35: La investigación

Trabajas para Barron's y vas a escribir un artículo para un libro que hace evaluaciones de universidades norteamericanas para hispanos. Habla con varios estudiantes para averiguar sus opiniones de la universidad. Pregunta, por ejemplo: **¿Se estudia mucho en esta universidad? / Se dice que se estudia mucho en esta universidad, ¿es verdad? / ¿Estudian mucho los estudiantes en esta universidad?**

La universidad

Se dice que . . .	Sí	No	No sé
se estudia mucho			
se aprende mucho			
se ofrecen muchas clases diferentes			
se hace mucha investigación			
hay muchas bibliotecas buenas			
los profesores conocen personalmente a los estudiantes			

La vida de los estudiantes

Se dice que . . .	Sí	No	No sé
hay piscinas y gimnasios para los estudiantes			
se vive bien en las residencias			
se come bien en las cafeterías			
se ofrecen conciertos buenos			
se bebe mucha cerveza en las fiestas			
se habla de política			
hay asociaciones estudiantiles			

Esta universidad es . . .
    excelente   buena   regular   mala

Estudio en esta universidad porque . . .

Pay attention to accents and punctuation.

Act. 36: Collect students' work or do peer editing. The students may also form a composite from the data.

Actividad 36: La evaluación

Usa la información de las entrevistas *(interviews)* y escribe el artículo. Sigue este bosquejo.

I. Introducción
    Nombre de la universidad y dónde está
    Si es buena o mala

II. La universidad y la vida académica
    Profesores y relaciones con los profesores
    Bibliotecas
    Clases e investigación

III. La vida de los estudiantes
    Residencias
    Diversiones

IV. Conclusión
    Evaluación global
    Citas *(quotes)* de los estudiantes

Vocabulario funcional

Verbos reflexivos

Ver página 94

Las partes del cuerpo

Ver página 95

Adjetivos y pronombres demostrativos

Ver páginas 110–111

Más verbos

conocer to know (a person/ place/thing)
poner to put
saber to know (facts/how to do something)

subir to go up
traducir to translate
traer to bring
ver to see

El tiempo

centígrados centigrade/Celsius
Está a _____ grados (bajo cero). It's _____ degrees (below zero).
está nublado it's cloudy
hace buen/mal tiempo it's nice/bad out
hace calor/frío it's hot/cold

hace fresco   it's chilly
hace sol   it's sunny
hace viento   it's windy
llover/llueve   to rain/it's raining
nevar/nieva   to snow/it's snowing
¿Qué tiempo hace?   What's the weather like?
la temperatura   temperature

Los meses y las estaciones

Ver páginas 105–106

Expresiones de tiempo

el año   year
el cumpleaños   birthday

la fecha   date
el mes   month

Palabras y expresiones útiles

allá   over there
allí   there
aquí   here
la carta   letter
deber + infinitive   should/must
  + *infinitive*
favor de + infinitive   please . . .

hay   there is/there are
no puedo   I can't
ocupado/a   busy
¿podrías + infinitive?   could
  you . . .
¡Qué + adjective!   how + *adjective!*

Cine en Madrid, España.

1. ¿Qué hay en esta foto-grafía?
2. ¿Cómo se llaman las películas *(movies)?*
3. ¿Cómo se llama el actor principal de la película *Ejecutor?*
4. ¿Sabes los títulos de las películas en inglés?

Capítulo 5

Chapter Objectives

After studying this chapter, you will know how to:

- express feelings
- tell the time
- discuss clothing
- indicate purpose, reason, and contrast

- specify the location of something
- discuss present and future events

1. ¿Hay películas de los Estados Unidos?
2. ¿Te gustaría ver una de estas películas? ¿Cuál?
3. Tienes que llevar a un grupo de niños de ocho años al cine. ¿Qué película van a ver Uds.?
4. A tu amigo le gustan las películas de suspenso. ¿A qué película va a ir?

CINE ARTE

ART MOVIES

PEPPERMINT, de Carlos Saura. 22 al 25 de Dic. 5 y 8 pm. Sala Margot Benacerraf.*

QUERELLE, de Reiner Fassbinder. Del 26 al 28 Dic. 5 y 8 pm. Sala Margot Benacerraf.*

REPULSION, DE ROMAN POLANSKI 29 y 30 Dic. 5 y 8 pm. Sala Margot Benacerraf.*

* Sala Margot Benacerraf. Ateneo de Caracas. Telf. 537.46.22.

CINE HOY

MOVIES

SOSPECHOSO, de Peter Yates, con Cher y Dennis Quaid.

WILLOW EN LA TIERRA DEL ENCANTO, de Ron Howard, con Val Kilmer, Joanne Halley, Wardick Davis y Billy Barty.

HIDDEN, de Jack Sholder.

PROXIMOS ESTRENOS

UPCOMING MOVIES

QUIEN ENGAÑO A RO-BERT RABBITT? de Robert Zemeckis, con Bob Hoskins, Christoper Lloyd, Stuby Kaye, Joanna Cassidy y Alan Tilvern. Es la historia de un hombre, una mujer y un conejo en un triángulo lleno de problemas. Un film donde personajes humanos y dibujos coexisten, frecuentan los mismos restaurantes, los mismos clubes de golf y comparten los mismos problemas.

Esta noche no estudiamos

En muchos cines hispanos la gente puede escoger asientos específicos cuando compran boletos, al igual que cuando van al teatro. (Cine en Madrid, España.)

Practice ¡No me digas/s! by telling students strange or incredible facts, and having them respond, ¡No me diga! Then have students tell facts. Respond by saying, ¡No me digas!

Me fascina/n.	I love it/them.
¡No me diga/s!	No kidding!

Juan Carlos y Claudia están en una cafetería haciendo planes para esta noche.

Actividad 1: Marca las películas

Escucha la conversación y marca sólo las películas que mencionan Juan Carlos y Claudia. ¡Ojo! Algunas no son películas.

__✔__ Vértigo   __✔__ Doña Bárbara
_____ Groucho   _____ María Félix
__✔__ Casablanca   _____ Psicosis

In pairs, have students read the dialogue, look up after each line, and say the line or phrase.

Inviting

Offering an option

Discussing future time

Telling time

Pronunciation: **ll, y**
1. Model and have students repeat after you words that contain [y]: **toalla, llueve, silla, yo, playa.** (You may want to point out different pronunciations of **ll** and **y**.)
2. Practice the following sentences: **La sombrilla amarilla a rayas está en la playa. Ella se llama Yolanda.**
3. In pairs, have students create sentences that contain words with [y]. Have them dictate the sentences to their classmates.

Act. 3: Add to this list if possible.

Juan Carlos	Bueno, entonces ¿qué te gustaría hacer?
Claudia	No sé.
Juan Carlos	¿Te gusta el jazz?
Claudia	¡Uy! Me fascina, pero esta noche no.
Juan Carlos	¿Y entonces? ¿Prefieres ir al cine?
Claudia	Sí, me gustaría ver una película vieja.
Juan Carlos	Bueno, puedo mirar en un periódico. Camarero. ¿Tiene Ud. un periódico de hoy? Y por favor, otra cerveza que tengo sed.
Camarero	Sí, cómo no, señor . . . Aquí está.
Juan Carlos	Gracias . . . Vamos a ver . . . En el Alphaville podemos ver *Vértigo* de Hitchcock.
Claudia	Es una película muy buena, pero ¿qué más hay?
Juan Carlos	*Doña Bárbara* está en el Cinestudio Groucho.
Claudia	¡Ay! No me gusta la actriz María Félix y es con ella, ¿no?
Juan Carlos	Sí . . . También está *Casablanca*.
Claudia	¡No me digas! ¡Qué bueno! Vamos a ésa.
Juan Carlos	¿Te gusta Humphrey Bogart?
Claudia	Sí, y me fascina Ingrid Bergman.
Juan Carlos	Bueno. La película empieza a las 9:35 en el Cine Luna.
Claudia	¡Uy! Y son las 8:30. Voy a llamar a Vicente y a Teresa para salir a comer después. Ellos también van al cine esta noche.
Juan Carlos	O.K. Podemos ir a un restaurante a comer comida china.
Claudia	¡Perfecto!

Actividad 2: Preguntas

Después de escuchar la conversación, contesta estas preguntas.

1. ¿Qué van a hacer esta noche Juan Carlos y Claudia?
2. ¿Dónde buscan *(look for)* información?
3. ¿Qué película van a ver?
4. ¿Conoces esta película? ¿Qué tipo de película es?
5. ¿Qué van a hacer Juan Carlos y Claudia después del cine?

Actividad 3: Películas norteamericanas

Adivina el nombre en inglés de estas películas norteamericanas.

1. La guerra de las galaxias
2. Lo que el viento se llevó
3. El graduado
4. El cartero llama dos veces
5. Los intocables
6. El hombre elefante
7. El joven Frankenstein
8. El último emperador

Act. 4: Set a time limit for each part of this activity.

Actividad 4: Una entrevista

Clasifica *(Rate)* los siguientes tipos de películas en una escala de uno a cinco.

1   no me gustan nada
2   no me gustan
3   me gustan
4   me gustan mucho
5   me fascinan

_____ románticas	_____ cómicas
_____ de horror	_____ dramáticas
_____ de ciencia ficción	_____ de Disney
_____ documentales	_____ de suspenso
_____ religiosas	_____ de violencia

Ahora, en parejas, entrevisten a su compañero/a para ver qué tipo de películas le gustan y cuáles son sus películas, actores, actrices y directores favoritos.

A: ¿Te gustan las películas de horror?
B: No, no me gustan nada.
A: . . .

Lo esencial

Every time you look at your watch think of the time in Spanish.

The hour may be written 3 different ways depending on the country:
10.00/10,00/10:00.

I. Write times on the board and ask, **¿Qué hora es?** or bring in a clock to give to students for a student-led drill.

I.   La hora, los minutos y los segundos

Es la una y cuarto.

Son las ocho
menos diez.

Es mediodía.

Es medianoche.

Son las cinco y media.

En el aeropuerto

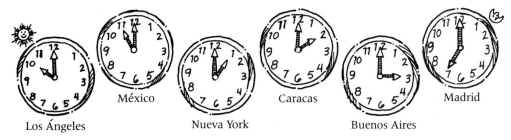

Los Ángeles   México   Nueva York   Caracas   Buenos Aires   Madrid

¿Qué hora **es** en Los Ángeles?   **Son las diez** de la mañana.
¿Qué hora **es** en Nueva York?   **Es la una** de la tarde.
¿Qué hora **es** en Madrid?   **Son las siete** de la tarde.

¡OJO! Son las once **de** la noche. (with a specific time)
      Nunca estudio **por** la noche. (with a general time period)

¿Lo sabían?

El uso de "buenas tardes" o "buenas noches" varía entre los países hispanos. En países como Ecuador, Colombia y Venezuela hay doce horas de día y doce horas de noche, porque estos países están cerca de la línea del ecuador. Por eso, la tarde empieza más o menos después de las 12:00 y termina más o menos a las 6:00 cuando ya no hay sol; después de esa hora, se dice "buenas noches". En cambio *(On the other hand)*, en España, por ejemplo, la tarde empieza como a las 3:00 después de comer y termina a las 10:00 cuando muchos españoles cenan. Por lo tanto, los españoles generalmente empiezan a decir "buenas noches" a partir de las 10:00.

Actividad 5: La hora en el mundo

En parejas, imagínense que Uds. están en el aeropuerto de México. Miren los relojes de la sección **En el aeropuerto** en esta página y pregúntenle a su compañero/a la hora en las diferentes ciudades. Después cambien de papel.

▶ 6:15 A.M.   ¿Madrid?

  A: Si en México son las 6:15 de la mañana, ¿qué hora es en Madrid?
  B: En Madrid son las 2:15 de la tarde.

Hora en México

1. 1:15 A.M.   ¿Nueva York?
2. 5:50 A.M.   ¿Caracas?
3. 4:25 P.M.   ¿Los Ángeles?
4. 3:30 P.M.   ¿Buenos Aires?

5. 7:16 A.M.   ¿Caracas?
6. 10:20 P.M. ¿Madrid?
7. 8:45 A.M.   ¿Nueva York?
8. 2:12 P.M.   ¿Madrid?

Note: **Son las 7:00** = It is 7:00; **El concierto es a las 7:00** = The concert is at 7:00. Practice this latter construction when reading movie schedules, TV guides, etc.

Act. 6: Practice **Es a las ...** vs. **Son las ...** prior to doing this activity. Reenter vocabulary for days of the week. T: **¿Cuándo es el programa de Cosby?** S1: **Es el jueves a las 7:00.**

Actividad 6: Programas de televisión

En grupos de tres, miren esta página de una guía de televisión y pregunten a qué hora son los diferentes programas.

⏺ **A:** ¿A qué hora es *La ley de Los Ángeles* con Jimmy Smits?
  B: Es a la/las . . .

TVE-1	TVE-2
NOCHE	**NOCHE**
8.30 Telediario-2.	9.00 Vía olímpica.
9.00 El tiempo.	*Gimnasia deportiva.*
9.15 La ley de Los Angeles.	9,05 Suplementos-4.
	Campo y mar.
	9.35 Todo motor.
Episodio 42. Leland se ve en el compromiso de defender a un amigo suyo que ha sido acusado de agredir a otro con una pierna ortopédica.	10.05 Jueves cine.
	La matanza de Texas (1974). Dirección: Tobe Hooper. Intérpretes: Marylin Burns, Allen Danzinger.
10.15 **Derecho a discrepar.** Coloquio moderado por Miguel Ángel Gozalo.	Un grupo de jóvenes que acude a visitar el cementerio de un pequeño pueblo tejano. se ve inmerso en una pesadilla de terror.
11.45 **A media voz.**	11.30 **Metrópolis.**
12.15 **Telediario-3.**	12.00 **Despedida y cierre.**
12.35 **Teledeporte.**	

Act. 7: 1. **60 minutos en una hora** 2. **52 semanas en un año** 3. **24 horas en un día** 4. **28 días en febrero** 5. **2 días en un fin de semana** 6. **12 meses en un año** 7. **7 días en una semana** 8. **4 semanas en un mes** 9. **30 días en noviembre, abril, junio y septiembre**

Actividad 7: Adivinanzas

En grupos de tres, completen estas adivinanzas *(guessing games)* sobre la hora y los meses.

⏺ 60 s. en un m. ⟶ 60 segundos en un minuto

1. 60 m. en una h.
2. 52 s. en un a.
3. 24 h. en un d.
4. 28 d. en f.
5. 2 d. en un f. de s.
6. 12 m. en un a.
7. 7 d. en una s.
8. 4 s. en un m.
9. 30 d. en n., a., j. y s.

II. Las sensaciones

1. Tienen frío.   2. Tiene calor.

4. Tienen hambre.   5. Tienen sed.

3. Tiene miedo.

6. Tiene sueño.   7. Tiene vergüenza.

II. Have students quiz each other using mime.

You may want to make students aware that although **el hambre** and **el agua** take the article **el,** they are feminine words: **El agua está fría.**

The article **el** in **el hambre, el agua,** etc. is a remnant of the feminine article **ela** which through the centuries has become **el** before feminine words starting with a stressed [a].

Actividad 8: ¿Cómo se sienten Uds.?

Di qué sensaciones tienen estas personas en estas situaciones.

 Si veo un ratón, tengo miedo.

1. Si estás en la playa, . . .
2. En el mes de enero, . . .
3. Después de correr cuatro kilómetros, . . .
4. Si tu amigo ve una película de horror, . . .
5. Si estudias toda la noche, . . .
6. Si voy al dentista, . . .
7. Si deseamos beber una Coca-Cola, . . .
8. Si no comes durante *(during)* ocho horas, . . .

Actividad 9: ¿Cuándo tienes miedo?

En parejas, pregúntenle a su compañero/a en qué situaciones tiene **frío, calor, miedo, sueño, sed, vergüenza** y **hambre.**

A: ¿Cuándo tienes vergüenza?
B: Cuando . . .

Hacia la comunicación

Gramática

Drill yourself on these forms.

Drill stem-changing verbs:
1. Use a Gouin series to present the concept of stem-changing verbs.
2. Use a transformation drill where Ramón always does the same thing we do: **Nosotros volvemos temprano a casa y Ramón ... Nosotros dormimos 8 horas cada noche y Ramón ...** Reverse the drill where we do everything Ramón does.
3. Do rapid-fire questions and answers.
4. Use pictures to elicit descriptions: **El niño está durmiendo. El camarero está sirviendo la comida. La señora vuelve de la tienda a casa.** (etc.)

Expressing Habitual and Future Actions and Actions in Progress: Stem-changing Verbs

1. Stem-changing verbs function the same as regular **-ar, -er,** and **-ir** verbs. In the present indicative, these verbs express habitual actions as well as actions in progress and future actions. They have the same endings as regular **-ar, -er,** and **-ir** verbs. They are different, though, in that there is a vowel change in the last syllable of the stem. You have already seen an irregular verb that has a stem change: **tener (tienes, tiene, tienen).** Stem-changing verbs are often referred to as *boot verbs* to help you remember in which persons the changes occur.

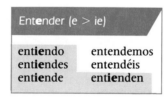

Entender (e > ie)

entiendo	entendemos
entiendes	entendéis
entiende	entienden

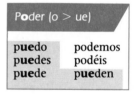

Poder (o > ue)

puedo	podemos
puedes	podéis
puede	pueden

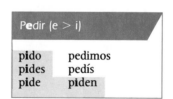

Pedir (e > i)

pido	pedimos
pides	pedís
pide	piden

Jugar (u > ue)

juego	jugamos
juegas	jugáis
juega	juegan

¿Entiendes la explicación?

Mañana no puedo ir.
Pedimos agua.
Los chicos juegan al fútbol.

Do you understand the explanation?
I can't go tomorrow.
We order (ask for) water.
The kids play soccer.

Stem-changing Verbs

e > ie

cerrar	to close	**entender**	to understand
comenzar	to begin	**pensar (en)**	to think (about)
despertar	to wake some- one up	**pensar** + infinitivo	to plan to
		perder	to lose
despertarse*	to wake up	**preferir**	to prefer
divertirse*	to have fun	**querer**	to want; to love
empezar	to begin	**sentarse***	to sit down
		venir**	to come

o > ue

acostar	to put some- one to bed	**dormirse***	to fall asleep
		encontrar	to find
acostarse*	to go to bed	**poder**	to be able, can
almorzar	to have lunch	**probar**	to taste
costar	to cost	**probarse***	to try on (clothes)
dormir	to sleep	**volver**	to return, come back

e > i

decir**	to say; to tell
pedir	to ask for
servir	to serve
vestirse*	to get dressed

u > ue

jugar	to play (a sport or game)

*Note: Verbs with an asterisk are reflexive verbs; for example, **sentarse: Yo me siento.**

Note: Verbs with two asterisks are conjugated the same as stem-changing verbs in the present indicative, except for a different **yo form: **digo, vengo.**

2. Stem-changing verbs that end in **-ir** have another change in the present participle.

o > ue > **u**   dormir ⟶ durmiendo
e > ie > **i**   divertirse ⟶ divirtiéndose
e > i > **i**   servir ⟶ sirviendo

El niño está durmiendo.   *The child is sleeping.*
Nos estamos divirtiendo mucho.   *We're enjoying ourselves a lot./ We're having fun.*

Ahora estoy sirviendo la comida. *I'm serving the meal now.*

Actividad 10: La agenda de Álvaro

En parejas, el/la estudiante "A" cubre la Columna B y el/la estudiante "B" cubre la Columna A. Para completar la agenda de Álvaro, pregúntenle a su compañero/a qué día va a hacer Álvaro las cosas de su lista y a qué hora empieza cada actividad.

> **A:** ¿Qué día es el examen de cálculo?
> **B:** Es el . . .
> **A:** ¿A qué hora empieza . . . ?
> **B:** . . .

> Remember: **¿A qué hora ... ?** refers to the time at which something takes place. **¿Qué hora es?** refers to present time.

A

1. el examen de cálculo
2. la película de Almodóvar en la televisión
3. el concierto de Les Luthiers

B

1. la fiesta de Vicente
2. la exhibición de Dalí
3. el torneo de tenis

Act. 10: Pedro Almodóvar directed the film **Mujeres al borde de un ataque de nervios.** Oscar nominee for best foreign film, 1989.

Les Luthiers, a comedic musical group from Argentina, is known throughout the Hispanic world for their humor, talent, and the strange instruments they play.

9 lunes
10 martes *5:30 exhibición de Dalí*
11 miércoles *12:45 torneo de tenis*
12 jueves
13 viernes
14 sábado *10:00 fiesta de Vicente*
15 domingo

9 lunes *3:15 examen de cálculo*
10 martes
11 miércoles
12 jueves *8:30 película de Almodóvar*
13 viernes *10:00 concierto de Les Luthiers*
14 sábado
15 domingo

Actividad 11: Los deportes

> **Fútbol americano** = football; **fútbol** = soccer.

Habla con varios estudiantes (un mínimo de cinco) y pregúntales si juegan al béisbol, al basquetbol, al fútbol americano, al fútbol, al tenis y al voleibol, y cuándo juegan estos deportes. Al terminar, tienes que decirle a la clase quiénes juegan al béisbol, al fútbol, etc.

Act. 11: **Jugar a** + *sport* and **jugar** + *sport* are both acceptable. The text will use the former.

The sports presented in this activity are not listed in the **Vocabulario funcional** because most of them are close cognates.

> **A:** ¿Juegas al béisbol?
> **B:** Sí, juego muy bien. / No, juego al golf. / No, prefiero jugar al tenis.
> **A:** ¿Cuándo juegas?
> **B:** En el verano. / Todos los días. / Los sábados. / Cuando hace buen tiempo, etc.

Actividad 12: La vida de Gloria

Completa esta historia sobre un día en la vida de Gloria con la forma correcta del verbo indicado y después pon *(put)* los párrafos en orden.

A la 1:30 _____ almuerzo _____ en una cafetería. Después voy a la
(almorzar)
universidad para estudiar. A las 6:00 yo _____ vuelvo _____
(volver)
a casa y mi niño y yo _____ nos divertimos _____ un poco. A las 7:00
(divertirse)
_____ sirvo _____ la comida y el niño _____ se acuesta _____ a las
(servir)   (acostarse)
8:30. Por fin yo _____ me siento _____ y estudio y a veces
(sentarse)
_____ me duermo _____ con el libro en la mano. Así es mi vida. ¿Te
(dormirse)
gusta? A mí, ¡me fascina . . . !

En las películas las personas siempre están contentas y tienen una
vida ideal. ¡Pero mi vida no es así! Yo _____ duermo _____ poco,
(dormir)
_____ me despierto _____ a las 5:30 de la mañana, _____ me ducho _____ y
(despertarse)   (ducharse)
_____ me visto _____. Siempre tengo mucha prisa. Después yo
(vestirse)
_____ despierto _____ a mi hijo de tres años y él _____ pide _____
(despertar)   (pedir)
el desayuno porque este niño siempre _____ tiene _____ hambre. A
(tener)
las 7:00 _____ viene _____ mi hermana para estar con el niño.
(venir)
Entonces yo _____ salgo _____ de la casa con mucho cuidado y
(salir)
_____ cierro _____ la puerta silenciosamente porque si el niño
(cerrar)
_____ sabe _____ que su madre sale, _____ empieza _____ a llorar
(saber)   (empezar)
porque _____ quiere _____ estar con su mamá.
(querer)
Al llegar a la oficina, los directores me _____ dicen _____ qué
(decir)
tengo que hacer. Siempre _____ piden _____ cosas imposibles y
(pedir)
_____ quieren _____ todo en cinco minutos. Nosotras, las secretarias,
(querer)

no _____podemos_____ beber café ni recibir llamadas personales.
                (poder)

___Pienso/Pensamos___ que los directores no son directores sino
          (pensar)

DICTADORES.

Act. 13: Before doing Act. 13,
brainstorm excuses and activities.

Actividad 13: Invitación y excusa

En parejas, inviten a su compañero/a a hacer una de las actividades que
a él/ella le gustan. El otro estudiante da una excusa *(gives an excuse)* diciendo por qué no puede.

▶   **A:** ¿Quieres ir a esquiar?

$$\left\{\begin{array}{l}\text{no tengo tiempo.}\\\text{no tengo dinero.}\\\text{necesito estudiar.}\\\text{vienen mis padres.}\\\text{(etc.)}\end{array}\right.$$

B: Me gustaría, pero no puedo porque

Act. 14: Have students sit back-
to-back to simulate a phone
conversation. When finished,
have them write Mr.
Fernández's schedule.

Actividad 14: El cantante salvadoreño

En parejas, escojan el papel A o B y lean las instrucciones para su papel.
Cubran las instrucciones para el papel de su compañero/a. Después,
mantengan *(have)* una conversación telefónica imaginaria, según las
indicaciones.

Papel A

Eres hispano/a y trabajas para el Madison Square Garden. Esta semana
tienes que recibir a un cantante de El Salvador, Nelson Fernández, que
es muy famoso pero también muy excéntrico. Tienes que organizar un
horario *(schedule)* de actividades para él. Necesitas saber qué le gusta
hacer y cuándo. Esta nota es de tu jefe *(boss)*.

Juan/Juana:
    Fernández is arriving on Sunday. His concert is on Tuesday, so you
need to entertain him on Monday. They say he's wacko. We need to
make him happy, so it's up to you. Phone him and find out the following information:

  1. When does he wake up?
  2. Breakfast: when and where?
  3. Preferences for a tour: (a) Greenwich Village, (b) Soho, (c) Empire
     State, (d) Wall Street
  4. Lunch: when and where?
  5. Shopping? Bloomingdale's, Saks, Macy's?
  6. Does he nap?

Specific plans: talk with David Letterman 5:30 and Geraldo Rivera 6:15. Party at Geraldo's 9:00

Papel B

Tú eres el señor Nelson Fernández, un cantante salvadoreño muy excéntrico. El domingo vas a Nueva York y vas a cantar en el Madison Square Garden el martes. No tienes que trabajar el lunes. Una persona del Madison Square Garden te llama por teléfono porque quiere saber qué te gustaría hacer ese día. A ti te gusta dormir muy tarde por las mañanas porque te acuestas a las 3:15 de la mañana todos los días. Siempre te desayunas en un parque. Quieres ver el metro de Nueva York y hablar con muchas personas. Sabes que tienes que hablar con unas personas de la televisión, pero quieres ir a un club a escuchar a Woody Allen tocar el clarinete.

Nuevos horizontes

Before reading this section, ask students what they do when they run across a word they don't know in English. List what they do and what techniques they use to find the meaning. For example, they may skip over the word, determine what part of speech it is, relate it to similar words, use their knowledge of suffixes, etc.

Brainstorm with students cognates they have seen in this text and others they may know.

Estrategia de lectura: *Dealing With Unfamiliar Words*

As was discussed in the Preliminary Chapter, there are many cognates in Spanish. These are words similar to English words that help you read and understand Spanish. However, there are other words that might be completely unfamiliar to you while important to the understanding of an idea. A natural tendency when encountering an unknown word is to look it up in the dictionary. What follows are alternate strategies you can use to deal with unfamiliar words. These strategies can be used while reading:

a. Identify the grammatical form of the word. For example, if it is a noun, it can refer to a person, place, or thing; if it is a verb, it can refer to an action or state.
b. Try to extract its meaning from context.
c. Check if the word or expression is explained by the writer.
d. Check if the word reappears in another context.

These strategies will help you make a reasonable guess regarding the word's meaning. If the meaning is still unclear, the next step would be to consult a dictionary. You will have a chance to practice these strategies after reading the selection.

Actividad 15: Lee y contesta

Lee el título del texto y contesta las siguientes preguntas.

1. ¿Sabes qué formas de gobierno hay en los países suramericanos?
2. ¿Son estables estos gobiernos?
3. ¿Conoces a alguien que no puede vivir en su país por motivos políticos? ¿Cuál era *(was)* la ocupación de esa persona en su país?

¿Democracia o dictadura?

Diálogo de sordos entre Gorbachov y Fidel Castro

Point out the use of the **presente histórico** to discuss past occurrences.

For further information see *La aventura de Miguel Littín, clandestino en Chile* by Gabriel García Márquez (1986).

La situación política en Suramérica varía de país a país, aunque en la década de los ochenta hay una tendencia general hacia la democracia. Por un lado, hay países como Colombia, donde existe la democracia desde principios de siglo, con sólo tres años y medio de dictadura. Por otro lado, se encuentran países como Argentina, Perú y Uruguay que alternan entre democracia y dictadura. La situación de Bolivia es más extrema, con más de cien golpes militares[1] en el siglo XX. Cuando hay golpes militares, muchas personas, especialmente artistas y profesionales, salen del país porque no pueden expresar sus ideas con libertad. Este éxodo se llama "fuga de cerebros".   10

Esta "fuga de cerebros" ocurre en Chile en 1973, después del golpe militar al gobierno democrático del presidente Allende. Es aquí cuando

5

---

1. **golpes . . .** coups d'état

En 1988 los chilenos manifiestan su preferencia política con un "sí" o un "no" a la continuación de la dictadura militar. (Santiago, Chile)

comienza la dictadura del general Pinochet. Entre las personas que salen del país está Miguel Littín, un director de cine. En 1985 él vuelve a Chile con una identidad falsa y con el pretexto de filmar un anuncio publici- 15 tario para Uruguay, pero su verdadero propósito es filmar un documental sobre los chilenos y la dictadura.

Littín usa tres grupos de filmación europeos, que como él, entran en Chile con diferentes pretextos artísticos. También trabajan jóvenes chilenos en el proyecto porque el director necesita ayuda extra. Littín 20 filma en Chile durante seis semanas y después de seis meses de revisiones en España, produce una película para el cine y otra para la televisión. Las dos películas tienen un gran éxito[2] en Europa.

En 1988, el director Littín entra en Chile, pero esta vez con su identidad real para votar en el referéndum sobre la continuación de la dic- 25 tadura militar. La mayoría de los ciudadanos votan "no" a la dictadura y por eso se esperan[3] elecciones para 1989. De esta manera, Chile se suma a la lista de los países suramericanos que tratan de lograr la restauración de la democracia.

---

2. success   3. are expected

Presionan a Pinochet
SANTIAGO DE CHILE

Recommend that students see the movies *Missing* and *La historia oficial* to gain an understanding of different political situations in Latin America.

Act. 16: Ask students to explain how they arrived at the meanings of these words.

Actividad 16: Palabras desconocidas

Busca las siguientes palabras en el texto que acabas de leer *(have just read)* y adivina sus significados usando las estrategias sugeridas bajo **Estrategia de lectura**. Después compara tus ideas con las de un/a compañero/a.

a. fuga de cerebros (línea 10)
b. verdadero propósito (línea 16)
c. ayuda (línea 20)
d. se suma (línea 27)

Actividad 17: ¿Cierto, falso o no se sabe?

Después de leer el texto, di si las siguientes oraciones son ciertas o falsas o si el texto no habla de ellas.

1. Uruguay es un país políticamente estable.
2. La dictadura de Pinochet comienza después de un golpe militar.
3. En 1985 Littín va a su país a hacer una película sobre los inmigrantes.
4. Las películas de Littín triunfan en Europa.
5. Los chilenos quieren tener democracia en su país.

Estrategia de escritura: *Writing a Synopsis*

There are times when we need to remember information that we find in written material. One way to help us remember is to write the information in the form of a list of facts or **cuadro sinóptico**, in which only the main facts are written in telegram-like form.

Actividad 18: La aventura de Littín

Completa el siguiente cuadro sinóptico sobre la aventura de Littín usando sólo información importante.

1973: Golpe, fin de Allende, dictadura de Pinochet, Littín sale

1985: _Littín vuelve a Chile con identidad falsa_

Verdadero propósito: _Filmar un documental_   Falso: _Filmar un anuncio_

Trabaja con: a. _Grupos de filmación europeos_

b. _Jóvenes chilenos_

Tiempo de trabajo: _6 semanas en Chile; 6 meses en España_

1988: Littín _entra en Chile con su identidad real_

Propósito: _Votar en el referéndum sobre la continuación de la dictadura_

Lo esencial

I. Los colores

Colors are adjectives and agree in gender and number with the noun they modify.

While walking down the street, identify, in Spanish, colors you see.

I. Help students to relate colors to items shown. Inform students that **castaño** (brown) is used to refer to hair color.

Option 1: Have students face each other, observe, then turn back-to-back and say what colors the other person is wearing from head to toe.

Option 2: Take students' notebooks, backpacks, etc. To get them back, students must describe the items using colors. Encourage the use of demonstrative adjectives.

1. rojo/a	4. verde	7. azul	10. negro/a
2. marrón	5. anaranjado/a	8. blanco/a	11. rosa, rosado/a
3. amarillo/a	6. morado/a	9. gris	

¿Lo sabían?

En español, como en inglés, los colores representan diferentes ideas. Por ejemplo, en inglés se dice *He/She's blue* cuando una persona está triste. Adivina qué significan estas expresiones en español: "ver todo color de rosa", "ver todo negro" y "un chiste *(joke)* verde". Mira las respuestas al pie de la página.

Logotipo de los JJ OO de Barcelona 92, obra de José María Trías.

JJ OO stands for **Juegos Olímpicos.**

Actividad 19: Asociaciones

En grupos de cinco, digan qué colores asocian Uds. con estas cosas.

1. el 14 de febrero
2. el elefante
3. la noche
4. la Coca-Cola
5. el chocolate
6. las plantas
7. el 25 de diciembre
8. el detective Clouseau y la pantera . . .
9. el arco de McDonald's
10. el café
11. el 4 de julio
12. la crema Nivea
13. el jabón Ivory
14. el 17 de marzo

Act. 20: Change teachers frequently.

Actividad 20: El profesor preguntón

En grupos de cinco, uno de Uds. es el profesor que pregunta los colores de cosas que hay en la clase.

Profesor: ¿De qué color es el bolígrafo de Peter?
Estudiante: Es rojo.

Respuestas: to see everything through rose-colored glasses; to be a pessimist; a dirty joke

II. La ropa y los materiales *(Clothes and Materials)*

A: Trajes informales de lana para todas las ocasiones: pantalones y saco. Colores: gris, azul o negro. B: Camisas de algodón de manga larga. Colores: blanco o azul. C: Corbatas de seda, de rayas verticales. Colores: azul o verde con blanco. D: Sombrero de cuero. E: Abrigo de lana. Color: beige. F: Gafas de sol Oscar de la Renta de metal. G: Zapatos 3 Coronas de Colombia.

A: Vestido de algodón, lavar a máquina. Colores: rosado, morado o amarillo. Talla: P, M, G, XG. B: Chaquetas de cuero. Colores: negro, marrón oscuro, marrón claro. C: Pañoletas de rayón. Colores: amarillo, rojo o azul. D: Botas de cuero Gacela de Chile con tacón bajo. Talla: 35−40

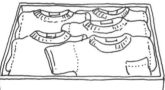
Camisetas de algodón

Medias de algodón y lana

Trajes de baño. Colores: rojo con lunares amarillos

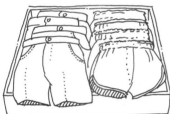
Para el día de los enamorados: calzoncillos blancos y rojos.

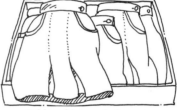
Faldas clásicas de lana en muchos colores.

Blusas de seda de Carolina Herrera.

Suéteres, lavar a mano, colores variados.

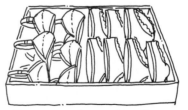
Sostenes y calzones de nailon.

Llama la atención con un bikini de colores brillantes.

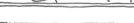

Un hombre de negocios con guayabera, Colombia.

Actividad 21: De compras

Tienes un amigo y una amiga que van a celebrar sus cumpleaños este mes. Decide qué vas a comprar del catálogo en la página 136: una cosa para él, una cosa para ella y otra cosa para ti. Después, en parejas, hablen de qué van a comprar, de qué colores y por qué van a comprar esas cosas. Usen oraciones como: **Voy a comprar una blusa de seda roja para mi amiga porque . . .**

Actividad 22: El pedido

En parejas, una persona va a llamar a la tienda del catálogo para pedir la ropa; la otra persona va a recibir la llamada. Lean la siguiente lista de expresiones que deben usar en la conversación.

A	B
¿Cuánto cuesta . . . ?	No tenemos la talla . . .
¿Tiene Ud. . . . en azul?	Cuesta . . .
¿Tiene Ud. . . . en talla . . . ?	¿De qué color quiere . . . ?
¿De qué material es . . . ?	¿Va a pagar con Visa, American Express o MasterCard?
Es muy caro/barato.	¿Cuál es el número de su tarjeta de Visa?
Me gustaría comprar . . .	¿Dónde vive Ud.?

¿Lo sabían?

Como en las zonas tropicales de Hispanoamérica hace calor, con frecuencia los hombres no llevan chaqueta; muchos prefieren llevar guayabera, que es un tipo de camisa muy fresca. Hay guayaberas para uso diario y también hay guayaberas muy elegantes que muchos hombres llevan en vez de traje con corbata.

Actividad 23: La noche de los Oscars

En parejas, Uds. están trabajando como reporteros en la ceremonia de los Óscars. Al llegar las estrellas, Uds. tienen que decir qué ropa llevan y con quién vienen.

A: Michael Jackson lleva unos pantalones de cuero y viene con Brooke Shields.
B: Ella lleva . . .

Las estrellas: Cher, Willie Nelson, Joan Collins, Bette Midler, Bill Cosby, Vanna White, Dan Ackroyd, Danny DeVito, Whoopi Goldberg, Steve Martin, etc.

De compras en San Juan

acabar de + infinitive	to have just + *past participle*
Acaban de llegar.	They have just arrived.
Cuesta un ojo de la cara.	It costs an arm and a leg.
Te queda bien.	It looks good on you. / It fits you well.

Un almacén *(department store)* en la Ciudad de México. ¿Es como un almacén en los Estados Unidos?

Teresa tiene vacaciones y vuelve a Puerto Rico para celebrar el aniversario de sus padres. Ahora Teresa y su hermano Luis están de compras en San Juan.

Act. 24: 1. a, b   2. b, c
3. b, d

Actividad 24: Escoge las opciones

Escucha la conversación y escoge todas las opciones correctas para cada oración.

1. Teresa quiere comprar . . . .
   - a. un vestido para su madre
   - b. un vestido elegante
   - c. un vestido de fiesta
   - d. un vestido caro
2. Luis quiere comprar una guayabera para . . . .
   - a. salir con Teresa
   - b. una fiesta de aniversario
   - c. ir a una cena
   - d. almorzar en un restaurante
3. Luis compra una guayabera . . . .
   - a. cara
   - b. barata
   - c. talla 38
   - d. de algodón

Indicating the recipient of an action

Teresa	Entonces, para mami vamos a comprar un vestido elegante para el aniversario y yo sé exactamente dónde.
Luis	Por favor, no en "Anaís" porque allí todo cuesta un ojo de la cara.
Teresa	¿Por qué no? Quiero comprar algo especial.

Indicating purpose

| Luis | Mira, allí en "González Padín" tienen una rebaja. Me gustaría comprar una guayabera nueva para la cena. ¿Tenemos tiempo? |

Plaza Las Américas = a mall in Hato Rey, on the outskirts of San Juan.

| Teresa | ¡Por supuesto! Y después, ¿qué tal si almorzamos en la terraza de Plaza Las Américas? En España, siempre pienso en la comida típica puertorriqueña. |

En la sección de caballeros de la tienda

| Luis | Por favor, busco una guayabera fina, para una ocasión especial. |
| Dependiente | Tenemos unas muy elegantes de seda de China que acaban de llegar y . . . también hay de algodón. |

Contradicting

Luis	Me gustaría ver una blanca de talla 40, pero no de algodón sino de seda.
Dependiente	Aquí tiene Ud. dos guayaberas muy finas.
Teresa	¿Por qué no te pruebas ésta? ¡Me gusta mucho! ¿Cuánto cuesta?

Asking prices

| Dependiente | Ciento noventa dólares. |
| Luis | ¡Cómo! ¿Ciento . . . ciento noventa? Creo que me pruebo una de algodón. |

Luis	¿Qué piensas?
Teresa	Te queda muy bien. Y ésta, ¿cuánto cuesta?
Dependiente	Cuesta ochenta dólares.
Luis	Bueno, me llevo ésta.
Teresa	Claro, es que a ti te gustan las tres "bes": **b**ueno, **b**onito y **b**arato. Y vamos, que tenemos que buscar el vestido todavía.

> The currency used in Puerto Rico is the U.S. dollar. In colloquial usage, **dólares** are called **pesos**.

Actividad 25: Preguntas personales

Contesta las siguientes preguntas.

1. ¿A qué tipo de tiendas te gusta ir de compras: a una tienda grande o a una boutique?
2. ¿Qué tipo de materiales prefieres usar?
3. ¿Qué prefieres: la ropa práctica o la ropa elegante?

> Act. 26: Bring in clothes or pictures of clothes to simulate a clothing store. As a check pick students at random to perform for the class once they have finished.

Actividad 26: Los padres de Teresa van de compras

En grupos de tres, dos personas son los padres de Teresa que van a una tienda a comprar ropa elegante para la fiesta de su aniversario. La otra persona es el/la dependiente/a. Mantengan la conversación en la tienda. Hablen de diferentes opciones, tallas, colores, materiales y precios. Los padres pueden usar expresiones como: **te queda bien, cuesta un ojo de la cara, voy a probarme.** El/La dependiente/a puede usar expresiones como: **¿en qué puedo servirle/s?** *(how may I help you?)*, **cuesta/n . . . , también hay en otros colores,** etc.

Hacia la comunicación

Gramática

> I. Drill **estar** vs. **ser:** Ask about famous people: **¿De dónde es Julio Iglesias? ¿Dónde está Julio Iglesias? Es de España, pero está en Miami.**

I. Indicating What Something Is Made of and Indicating Location: *Ser de* and *estar en*

1. You learned in Chapter 1 that **ser de** is used to indicate the origin of people and things. It is also used to indicate what things are made of.

   —¿Ese vestido **es de algodón**?   —No, **es de seda**.

2. **Estar en** is used to specify the location of people or things.

   Diana es de los Estados Unidos pero **está en** España.

I. Drill **estar en** and **ser en**: Brainstorm events taking place in your city or the world and names of people who are attending those events. List them on the board under **ser en** and **estar en**. Have students form sentences: **El concierto de Sting es mañana en el estadio y por eso, Sting está en Cleveland.** (etc.)

II. Drill **sino** vs. **pero**: Have students finish phrases in an original manner: **No estudio francés sino ... Mario habla ruso pero ...** (etc.) Encourage multiple responses.

III.A./B. Drill **para** vs. **por**: 1. An extraterrestrial comes to the classroom. Have students explain what pens, pencils, chalkboards, clocks, etc., are for. 2. Ask students to brainstorm answers to these questions: **¿Para qué estudia Felipe? ¿Por qué está triste Felipe?** 3. Brainstorm endings for these sentences: **Juego al fútbol para ... , Juego al fútbol por ...** 4. Brainstorm endings for these sentences: **Por ser inteligente ... , Por ser rico ...**

Because **por** and **para** are prepositions, verbs that follow them directly must be in the infinitive.

Note: **Ser en** is used to specify where an event *takes place* (a concert, a lecture, an exhibit, etc.).

La clase de arte es en el Museo de Arte Contemporáneo.
    La clase ⟶ *the class meeting takes place*
La clase está en el Museo de Arte Contemporáneo.
    La clase ⟶ *the students are in*

II. Contrasting: *Sino* and *pero*

When you want to contrast two objects, two persons, or two actions, you need to use **sino** or **pero**.

1. **Sino,** which means *but* in the sense of *but rather,* is used when contradicting a negative statement in the first part of the sentence. The first part of the sentence must be negative and the second cannot have a conjugated verb.

   Paco **no** compra faldas **sino pantalones**.
   Paco **no** quiere comprar **sino vender** faldas.
   Paco **no** está comprando **sino vendiendo** faldas.

2. **Pero**, which means *but* in the sense of *however,* is used for contrasting and can be used whether the preceding statement is affirmative or negative. **Pero** is frequently followed by a conjugated verb.

   Paco compra pantalones, **pero** no **compra** faldas.
   Paco no compra faldas, **pero** (sí) **compra** pantalones.
   Las faldas son baratas, **pero** bonitas.

III. Indicating Purpose, Reason, Destination, and Duration: *Para* and *por*

A. Para

1. To explain the purpose or recipient of an action

¿Para qué? = What for?	**¿Para qué** trabajas?
¿Para quién? = For whom?	**¿Para quién** trabajas?
para + infinitive = in order to	Trabajo **para tener** dinero.
para (ser) + occupation = to become + *occupation*	Paloma estudia **para (ser) bióloga.**

2. To indicate destination (physical or temporal)

   El libro es **para Ana**.
   La composición es **para mañana**.
   El autobús sale **para El Paso, Texas**.

B. Por

1. To indicate the reason or motivation for an action

III.B. Brainstorm everyday activities. In pairs, have students practice **por**/**durante** to express duration by asking each other how much time they will spend on these activities tomorrow. T: **¿Cuánto tiempo vas a estar hablando por teléfono?** S1: **Voy a estar hablando por teléfono por/durante 15 minutos.** (etc.)

¿**Por qué?** = Why?
porque = because
por = for the sake of

por = due to, because of

—¿**Por qué** trabajas?
—**Porque** necesito dinero.
Estudio **por** mis padres. *(They are the reason why I study.)*
Canto **por** cantar.
Por tener cinco años, el niño se acuesta temprano *(early).*

2. To express duration of an action*

Voy a estar en Caracas **por un año**.
Todas las tardes estudio **por dos horas**.

*Note: To express duration, you can also use **durante** or nothing at all before the time expression: **Voy a estar en Caracas** *durante* **un año.** / **Voy a estar en Caracas un año.**

Do mechanical drills, Workbook, Part II.

Actividad 27: El origen y el material

Act. 27: Encourage students to look at clothing tags. Give any names that may be needed: **Sri Lanka, Taiwán, Japón,** etc.

En grupos de cinco, averigüen de dónde y de qué material es la ropa de cada persona del grupo. Luego informen a la clase.

A: ¿De qué material es tu camisa?
B: Es de . . .

Actividad 28: Cultura general

Act. 28: Continue the activity with other place names: **la Casa Rosada, el Monte Everest, la Torre Inclinada de Pisa,** etc.

For a student-led warm-up activity, suggest students use the Spanish names of other commonly known places.

En grupos de tres, digan dónde están estas cosas.

1. la Estatua de la Libertad
2. el Museo del Prado
3. Machu Picchu
4. el Museo del Louvre y la Torre Eiffel
5. la Pequeña Habana
6. las Pirámides del Sol y de la Luna
7. el Vaticano
8. la Plaza Roja

Actividad 29: Una encuesta

Haz una encuesta *(poll)* preguntando a tus compañeros si hacen las siguientes cosas. Intenta encontrar a dos personas para cada ítem. Escoge **para** o **por** y haz *(ask)* preguntas como: **¿Trabajas para tu padre en el verano?** / **¿Para quién trabajas en el verano?**

1. compra una guayabera para/por su padre
2. estudia para/por ser hombre/mujer de negocios
3. siempre estudia para/por las noches

4. usa la biblioteca mucho para/por aprender
5. lee para/por leer
6. va a estar en la universidad para/por tres años más
7. trabaja mientras *(while)* estudia para/por tener dinero

Actividad 30: Los planes

En parejas, miren estos anuncios para unos eventos. Uds. tienen que hacer planes para esta noche. Decidan qué van a hacer, dónde y a qué hora.

A: ¿Te gustaría ir . . .? / ¿Qué tal si vamos . . .? / ¿Quieres ir al concierto de . . .?
B: Sí. ¿Dónde es?
A: Es en el estadio . . .

Segundo Festival de Grandes Solistas

Concierto en homenaje a Alirio Díaz
(premio Gabriela Mistral 1988)

Fecha: Domingo 27 de noviembre de 1988
Lugar: Sala Ríos Reyna / Teatro Teresa Carreño
Hora: 11:00 am.
Entrada general: Bs. 50
Estudiantes: Bs. 20

Sala de Conciertos Electricidad de Caracas
2ª Temporada 1988

Sinfonietta Caracas

Eduardo Marturet
Director

Margot Parés Reyna
Soprano

Próximo Miércoles 5 de Octubre
Hora: 8:30 p.m.

DOS ESTRENOS MUNDIALES
"Imágenes en movimiento"
Coreografía: Marisol Alemán
"Nosotros"
Coreografía: Pablo Denubila

CARMINA BURANA
Coreografía: John Butler
Música: Carl Orff
Versión para dos pianos y percusión

6, 7 y 8 octubre
Hora: 8:00 p.m.

Entradas a la venta:
Taquillas del Teatro

Teatro Teresa Carreño
Presentan
BALLET NUEVO MUNDO DE CARACAS
Dirección artística: Zhandra Rodríguez

Act. 31: Before doing this activity, remind students of the usage rule for **sino**: The first clause must be negative; the clause following **sino** cannot have a conjugated verb.

Actividad 31: Contrasta o contradice

Contrasta o contradice usando una frase de cada columna. Hay muchas posibilidades.

Yo no tengo mucho dinero		el domingo.
Nos gustaría ir al cine		ella sí.
Mi amigo no vuelve mañana	pero	él no.
No juegan hoy	sino	estoy contento/a.
Hoy no queremos estudiar		mañana sí.
Yo vivo en una ciudad fría		es tarde.
Ellos no están trabajando		ir al cine.
		me gusta mucho.
		divirtiéndose.

Actividad 32: Los regalos

En parejas, Uds. van a darles las cosas de esta lista a diferentes compañeros de la clase. Decidan para quiénes son estas cosas, para qué se usan y por qué son para estas personas. Por ejemplo: El peine es para Chuck, para peinarse porque tiene el pelo muy bonito.

1. estéreo
2. vídeo
3. cámara
4. máquina de afeitar
5. libro de filosofía
6. cinta del loco Al Yankovic
7. blusa de seda
8. camiseta de rock ácido
9. reloj
10. disco de Plácido Domingo

Act. 33: Point out that **modelo** can take the article **el** or **la**.

Assign as homework a description of the clothes students will wear to the next class session. Have students peer edit the descriptions. Create a fashion show: Each student hands his/her description to another student, who reads the paragraph(s) aloud while the outfit is modeled.

Actividad 33: El desfile de modas

En parejas, imagínense que están en un desfile de modas *(a fashion show)*. Observen a la otra persona y describan qué lleva. Escriban la descripción y después léanle esta descripción al resto de la clase.

Nombre del/de la modelo y su origen.

Qué lleva — mencionen colores, materiales, origen y para qué tipo de ocasión es el conjunto *(outfit)*.

Vocabulario funcional

Verbos con cambio de raíz

Ver página 127

La hora *(Telling Time)*

¿Qué hora es?   What time is it?
  Es la una menos cinco.   It's five to one.
  Es mediodía.   It's noon.
  Es medianoche.   It's midnight.
  Son las tres y diez.   It's ten after three.
¿A qué hora . . . ?   At what time . . . ?
A la una. / A las dos.   At one o'clock. / At two o'clock.
cuarto   quarter (of an hour)
la hora   hour
media   half (an hour)
el minuto   minute
el segundo   second

Las sensaciones

Ver página 125

La ropa

el abrigo coat
la blusa blouse
las botas boots
la camisa shirt
la camiseta T-shirt
los calzones/ women's/men's
 calzoncillos underwear
la corbata tie
la chaqueta jacket
la falda skirt
las gafas de sol sunglasses

las medias stockings
los pantalones pants
la pañoleta scarf
el saco sports coat
el sombrero hat
el sostén bra
el suéter sweater
el traje suit
el traje de baño bathing suit
el vestido dress
los zapatos shoes

Los colores

¿De qué color es? What color is it?
 amarillo/a yellow
 anaranjado/a orange
 azul blue
 blanco/a white
 gris gray
 marrón brown
 morado/a purple

negro/a black
rojo/a red
rosa, rosado/a pink
verde green
claro/a light
oscuro/a dark
vivo/a bright

Los materiales

¿De qué material/tela es? What material is it made out of?
 el algodón cotton
 el cuero leather
 la lana wool

el nailon/nilón nylon
la seda silk

Ir de compras

barato/a cheap, inexpensive
caro/a expensive
¿Cuánto cuesta/n . . . ?
 How much is/are . . . ?

la talla size
Te queda bien. It looks good on
 you. / It fits you well.

Palabras y expresiones útiles

acabar de + infinitive to have
 just + *past participle*
Cuesta un ojo de la cara. It costs
 an arm and a leg.
Me fascina/n. I love it/them.

¡No me digas! No kidding!
No me gusta nada I don't like it
 at all.
la película movie
el torneo tournament

Calle Florida, Buenos Aires, Argentina.

1. ¿Es una calle residencial o comercial?
2. ¿Conoces una calle como ésta en los Estados Unidos? ¿En qué son iguales o diferentes?

Remind students of the reversal of seasons by asking, **¿Qué mes puede ser?**

1. ¿Conoces un lugar como éste? ¿Cómo es?
2. ¿Qué están haciendo estas personas?
3. ¿Qué estación del año es?

Centro de esquí, Las Leñas, Argentina.

Capítulo 6

Chapter Objectives

After studying this chapter, you will know how to:

- talk about things you and others did in the past
- ask and give prices
- discuss the location of people and things
- describe family relationships

Una carta de Argentina

Pronunciation: [g]:
1. Model and have students repeat after you words that contain [g]: **gato, guitarra, guerra, algodón, gafas, abrigo.** Remind students that the **u** in **gue,** and **gui** is silent (except **güe, güi**).
2. Write **ga, gue, gui, go** and **gu** on the board and have students repeat after you.
3. Have students create sentences with the following words and then read them aloud: **gustar, preguntar, guitarra, amigo.**

La Casa Rosada, el edificio principal del gobierno de Argentina, y una manifestación de las Madres de la Plaza de Mayo, quienes protestan las injusticias de gobiernos anteriores.

Practice these expressions using visuals: —¡Qué **estudiante más alto! ¡Sí, es altísimo!**

¡Qué +noun + **más** + adjective!	What a + *adjective* + *noun!*
¡Qué hotel más lujoso!	What a luxurious hotel!
adjective + **ísimo**	
bello ⟶ bellísimo	very beautiful

Alejandro, el tío de Teresa, le lee a su esposa *(wife)* una carta de su amigo Federico de Rodrigo, que está viajando por Argentina.

Act. 1: 1. b   2. b   3. a   4. b

Actividad 1: Escoge opciones

Pronunciation: [k]
1. Model and have students repeat after you words that contain [k]: **caro, cuesta, cosa, qué, quiero.**
2. Write **ca, que, qui, co** and **cu** on the board and have students repeat after you.
3. Have students find words in the letter that contain [k] and dictate them to their classmates.

Escucha la siguiente carta y escoge la opción correcta.

1. La carta es de . . . .
   a. Buenos Aires   b. Las Leñas
2. Federico está viajando con . . . .
   a. unos amigos   b. su familia
3. El español de Argentina es . . . español de España.
   a. diferente del   b. igual al
4. La Recoleta es . . . .
   a. una zona de tiendas   b. una zona de cafeterías

Hotel Las Leñas

Reconquista 585
Mendoza, Argentina

Las Leñas, 20/7/90

Estimado Alejandro:

Aprovecho un rato libre para mandarles un saludo a ti y a tu familia desde Las Leñas, Mendoza, un centro de esquí muy bonito de la zona andina argentina. Los Andes son impresionantes y muy diferentes de los Pirineos españoles y el Aconcagua es realmente majestuoso. Las Leñas es un lugar excelente para esquiar. En este momento mi esposa y los niños están esquiando y por eso tengo unos minutos para escribir unas líneas.

Llegamos a Buenos Aires el 15 de este mes. Fuimos directamente al Hotel Presidente. ¡Qué hotel más lujoso! Comimos y salimos a ver la ciudad para no perder ni un minuto de nuestro viaje. Buenos Aires es una ciudad muy europea y bellísima. Nos divertimos escuchando hablar a los argentinos con ese acento tan bonito que tienen. Casi cantan al hablar y siempre dicen "che".

Al día siguiente Elena y los niños fueron a la Calle Florida y compraron muchas cosas. El cuero aquí es increíble y baratísimo. Una de las cosas que compró Elena fue un mate porque quiere aprender a beber "yerba". Cerca del hotel, a unos cinco minutos, Elena y yo bailamos tango toda la noche y nuestros hijos fueron a la Recoleta. Les llamó la atención ver esta zona de cafeterías y restaurantes enfrente de un cementerio donde están las tumbas de las personas más importantes del país. De veras que es curioso, ¿no?

Después de esquiar en Las Leñas, vamos a viajar a las Cataratas del Iguazú y después, como sabes, tenemos que regresar a Madrid la semana que viene. ¡Qué pena! Un millón de gracias a ti y a tu sobrina, Teresa, por organizarnos un viaje fantástico.

Como dicen aquí: un abrazo, "che", de tu amigo,

Federico

Actividad 2: ¿Comprendieron?

En grupos de tres, después de escuchar la carta, identifiquen o describan las siguientes cosas o lugares.

1. las montañas donde están Federico y su familia
2. el Hotel Presidente
3. un lugar de compras
4. el mate
5. la Recoleta
6. el itinerario de viaje de la familia

Dates can be written 20/VII/90, 20 de julio de 1990, or **20/7/90.**

A colon is preferable to a comma after the greeting, even in informal letters.

El Aconcagua = highest peak in the Western Hemisphere.

Talking about past events (Paragraphs 2 and 3)

Note that the city where the letter was written precedes the date.

Point out that the day precedes the month.

Discussing future plans

Note the closing. Discuss common, informal closings: **Un (fuerte) abrazo, un beso, saludos de tu amigo,** etc.

Act. 2: Ask students: **¿Te gustaría ir a una cafetería enfrente de un cementerio?**

Act. 3: The rules for adding
-ísimo will be covered in Ch. 12.

Have students continue to describe, using **¡Qué ciudad más
grande!** (etc.)

Hombre tomando mate en
Montevideo, Uruguay.

In Paraguay they often
drink **tereré,** or cold **mate.**

¿Lo sabían?

El mate es un té de yerba (hierba) que se toma especialmente en Argentina,
Paraguay, Uruguay y en algunas partes de Chile. Se bebe en un recipiente
también llamado mate, que puede ser una pequeña calabaza seca *(small
gourd)*, o en un recipiente de forma similar. Se usa también una bombilla *(a
special straw)*, y se pasa de persona a persona. Beber mate es una actividad
social y normalmente se toma con un grupo de amigos o con la familia.

Keep in mind subject-
adjective agreement. To
keep the **[k]** sound, final **c**
changes to **qu** before
adding **-ísimo/a:**
flaco/a → **flaquísimo/a.**

Actividad 3: ¡Qué exageración!

Describe de forma exagerada algunas cosas y personas que conoces,
usando estos adjetivos de una manera original: **altísimas, gordísimo,
guapísimos, feísimo, flaquísimo, simpatiquísima.**

◖●◗   grandísima: La ciudad de Nueva York es grandísima.

Lo esencial

The use of periods and
commas differs in English
and Spanish: 54.56 and
1,987,789 (Eng.) = **54,56**
and **1.987.789** (Sp.).

Note spelling of **quinien-
tos, setecientos,** and
novecientos.

I.   Los números del cien al millón

100	cien	700	setecientos
101, 102	ciento uno, ciento dos	800	ochocientos
200	doscientos	900	novecientos
300	trescientos	1.000	mil
400	cuatrocientos	2.000	dos mil
500	quinientos	1.000.000	un millón
600	seiscientos	2.000.000	dos millones

¿Lo sabían?

En muchos países hispanos la inflación es un problema muy grave. Como resultado, la moneda *(currency)* se devalúa rápidamente y por eso, se necesitan sumas extraordinarias, con muchos ceros, para pagar algo. En Argentina, en 1986, se cambió el nombre de la moneda, "peso argentino", por "austral" y se quitaron *(took off)* ceros, pues se pensó que una moneda nueva daría *(would give)* a los argentinos confianza en el valor de su dinero. Se usa la palabra "austral" porque Argentina es el país más austral *(southern)* del mundo.

Actividad 4: Los precios

En grupos de cinco, decidan cuánto cuestan generalmente estas cosas en dólares norteamericanos.

1. un estéreo bueno
2. estudiar un año en su universidad
3. un viaje de dos semanas a Hawaii
4. un televisor a color de trece pulgadas con control remoto
5. una cámara de vídeo
6. un BMW
7. una chaqueta de cuero
8. una blusa de seda

II. Preposiciones de lugar

a la derecha de   to the right of
a la izquierda de   to the left of
al lado de   beside
cerca de   near
lejos de   far from

encima de   on top of
debajo de   below
delante de   in front of
detrás de   behind
enfrente de   facing, across from

Actividad 5: La meca de la elegancia

En parejas, imagínense que están en "La meca de la elegancia". El/La estudiante "A" es un/a cliente y quiere comprar una cosa. El/La estudiante "B" es un/a dependiente/a.

A: Por favor, ¿(me dice) dónde está/n . . . ?
B: Está/n . . .
A: ¿Cuánto cuesta/n . . . ?
B: Cuesta/n . . .
A: . . .

Act. 6: Model first in a large group.

Actividad 6: La ciudad universitaria

En grupos de cinco, una persona describe dónde están los lugares importantes de su ciudad universitaria *(campus)* y los otros adivinan qué lugar es. La persona que adivina describe el siguiente lugar. Usen preposiciones de lugar, por ejemplo: Este lugar está cerca de la cafetería y a la derecha de Bascom Hall.

Hacia la comunicación

Gramática

All -ar and -er stem-changing verbs are regular in the preterit.

Note the use of accents.

Vosotros form = **tú** form + **is: bebiste +** **is = bebisteis.**

I. Point out the reasons for accents. Contrast: **Bailo mucho. / Bailó mucho.** Say a number of sentences; have students raise their right hands if they hear the preterit and their left to indicate the present indicative.

I. Talking About the Past: The Preterit

1. You have already seen in Chapter 5 how to discuss the immediate past using **acabar de +** *infinitive.* Now you will learn how to talk about completed past actions using the preterit. All regular verbs as well as stem-changing verbs ending in **-ar** and **-er** are formed as follows. (You will learn the preterit of stem-changing **-ir** verbs in Chapter 7.)

Cerr**ar**	
cerr**é**	cerr**amos**
cerr**aste**	cerr**asteis**
cerr**ó**	cerr**aron**

Com**er**	
com**í**	com**imos**
com**iste**	com**isteis**
com**ió**	com**ieron**

Escrib**ir**	
escrib**í**	escrib**imos**
escrib**iste**	escrib**isteis**
escrib**ió**	escrib**ieron**

Point out that **ver** is regular in the preterit and that it has no accents because **vi** and **vio** are monosyllables.

Point out that **-car, -gar, -zar** verbs are regular and have logical spelling changes to preserve the sounds.

Dar will be practiced more actively in the second part of this chapter with the introduction of indirect-object pronouns.

Note the lack of accents.

Note the **z** in **hizo.**

Drill preterit of regular verbs:
1. Do a transformation drill with present indicative and preterit: **Todos los días ellos comen en la cafetería, pero ayer ...**
2. Do a chain drill with what students did yesterday. S1: **Ayer comí en la cafetería.** S2: **Ayer Peter comió en la cafetería y yo corrí.** S3: **Ayer Peter comió en la cafetería, Ana corrió y yo ...**
3. Have students brainstorm endings for this sentence: **Antes de ir de vacaciones el verano pasado nosotros ...**
4. Mime a series of actions (silent Gouin series); when finished, ask students, **¿Qué hice?**

El viernes pasado **vi** una película.	*I saw a movie last Friday.*
Anoche no **estudiamos**.	*We didn't study last night.*
Ayer, Paco **almorzó** en un restaurante.	*Paco had lunch in a restaurant yesterday.*
¿**Trabajaste** mucho ayer?	*Did you work a lot yesterday?*
¿Cuándo **empezaron** las clases?	*When did classes begin?*

Note:

a. Regular **-ar** and **-ir** verbs have the same ending in the **nosotros** form in the present indicative and the preterit. Context helps determine the tense of the verb. For example: **No almorzamos ayer. Almorzamos todos los días.**

b. Verbs that end in **-car, -gar,** or **-zar** require a spelling change in the **yo** form: ju**gar** ⟶ ju**gué**, empe**zar** ⟶ empe**cé**, to**car** ⟶ to**qué**. For example: **Ayer *jugué* al fútbol y Juan también *jugó*.**

c. Regular reflexive verbs follow the same pattern as other regular verbs in the preterit. The reflexive pronoun precedes the conjugated form. For example: **Esta mañana me levanté temprano.**

2. Four common irregular verbs in the preterit are **ir** and **ser,** which have the same preterit forms, and **dar** *(to give)* and **hacer.**

Ir/Ser

fui	fuimos
fuiste	fuisteis
fue	fueron

Dar

di	dimos
diste	disteis
dio	dieron

Hacer

hice	hicimos
hiciste	hicisteis
hizo	hicieron

Ella no **fue** al concierto.	*She didn't go to the concert.*
¿Qué **hiciste** anoche?	*What did you do last night?*
Todos **hicieron** la tarea.	*All of them did their homework.*

3. The following time expressions frequently signal the use of the preterit to express a completed past action.

anoche last night
ayer yesterday
anteayer the day before yesterday
de repente suddenly
el sábado/mes/año pasado last Saturday/month/year
la semana pasada last week

II. Many compound prepositions indicate location of a person or thing. Remind students
that common prepositions of
location are listed in the preceding **Lo esencial.**

Point out that with the preposition **entre,** the subject-
pronoun forms are always
used: **Entre tú y yo no hay
mucha diferencia.**

Have a contest where students
guess who is being described:
**Esta persona está lejos de la
puerta, detrás de Amy y enfrente de mí.**

Tell students that verbs that
indicate the beginning of an
action or mental process, such
as **comenzar, aprender,** and
enseñar, are followed by the
preposition **a** + *infinitive.*

Practice verbs used with
prepositions in context:
1. Give names of famous
people and have students
say who married whom:
Madonna/Sean Penn, Liz
Taylor/Richard Burton, etc.
2. Ask students, **¿Cuáles son 5
cosas que aprendiste a hacer
en la escuela secundaria?**
(etc.)

You already used these
pronouns with **gustar.**
See p. 45.

II. Drill **conmigo:**
Have students invite each
other places and accept or reject invitations.

Here are some frequently used verbs that you will practice in the chapter activities.

abrir to open	**llegar** to arrive
aprender to learn	**llorar** to cry
asistir a to attend (class, church, etc.)	**pagar** to pay for
buscar to look for	**sacar** to get a grade; to take out
comenzar (e > ie) to begin	**terminar** to finish
decidir to decide	**tomar** to eat, have food or drink; to take (a bus, etc.)
dejar to leave behind; to let, allow	**viajar** to travel
gritar to shout, scream	

Terminé anoche a las 10:00.   *I finished last night at 10:00.*
Ayer dos alumnos no **asistieron**   *Two students didn't attend class*
 a clase.   *yesterday.*
El público **gritó** con entusiasmo.   *The audience shouted*
      enthusiastically.

II. Indicating Relationships: Prepositions and Prepositional Pronouns

1. Prepositions relate one word with another in a sentence. Common prepositions include **a, con, de, desde, en, hacia, para, por,** and **sin.**

   Él caminó **hacia** la playa.   *He walked towards the beach.*
   Prefiero ver el rodeo **desde** aquí.   *I prefer to see the rodeo from here.*
   Salimos **sin** tu permiso.   *We went out without your permission.*

2. When pronouns follow a preposition, the forms of the pronouns are the same as subject pronouns except for the forms corresponding to **yo** and **tú,** which are **mí** and **ti** respectively.

   —Tengo un regalo **para ti.**   —¿Vas a ir **sin Juan**?
   —¿**Para mí**? Gracias.   —No, no podemos ir **sin él.**

Note: With the preposition **con, mí** and **ti** become **conmigo** and **contigo.**

   —¿Quieres ir **conmigo**?   *Do you want to go with me?*
   —Sí, voy **contigo.**   *Yes, I'll go with you.*

3. When a preposition is immediately followed by a verb, the latter is always in the infinitive.

Después de comer, miraron la tele.　　　　　　*After eating, they watched TV.*

Antes de irse, vendieron la casa.　　　　　　*Before leaving, they sold the house.*

4. Note the prepositions used with the following verbs:

asistir a + lugar	to attend + *place*
casarse con + persona	to marry + *person*
entrar en + lugar	to enter + *place*
salir de + lugar	to leave + *place*

Note: The verbs **deber, desear, necesitar, poder,** and **querer** are directly followed by the infinitive.

Necesito estudiar porque tengo un examen.　　　　*I need to study because I have an exam.*

Debemos volver a casa.　　*We should return home.*

Actividad 7: Anoche

En tu clase probablemente hay personas que hicieron estas actividades ayer. Haz preguntas para encontrar a estas personas.

A: ¿Hiciste la tarea ayer?
B: Sí, hice la tarea. / No, no hice la tarea.

1. beber Pepsi
2. correr
3. bailar
4. recibir una carta
5. comer a las siete
6. ir al cine
7. tocar el piano
8. mirar TV

Actividad 8: La última vez

En parejas, pregúntenle a su compañero/a cuándo fue la última vez *(last time)* que hizo estas acciones.

1. ducharse
2. ir al médico
3. visitar a sus padres
4. sacar "A" en un examen
5. comer pizza
6. jugar al tenis

Actividad 9: Las últimas vacaciones

En parejas, pregúntenle a su compañero/a sobre las últimas vacaciones de sus padres, amigos, etc. Averigüen adónde fueron y qué hicieron.

II. Ask students: **¿Qué deseas hacer esta noche? ¿Qué necesitas hacer? ¿Qué debes hacer que no puedes hacer?**

Do mechanical drills, Workbook, Part I.

Act. 7: If needed, practice the questions first.

Instruct students to ask one question per person and then to proceed to the next person. This will help the activity run smoothly. If students receive a negative response from a classmate, encourage them to probe further by asking, **¿Qué hiciste entonces?**

If you can't remember, invent! Use the preterit to speak about the past and **ir a +** infinitive to speak about the future.

Actividad 10: ¿Qué hicieron estas personas?

Di qué hicieron tus padres, amigos o personas famosas el año pasado y qué van a hacer el año que viene. Usa la imaginación. Por ejemplo: Mi padre visitó Japón el año pasado y va a ir a Rusia el año que viene.

Actividad 11: Un episodio

Claudia está contando un episodio del viernes pasado. Completa el párrafo con la forma del verbo y tiempo *(tense)* correctos. Usa los siguientes verbos: **hablar, recibir, ir, llegar, encontrar, perder.**

El viernes pasado nosotros terminamos las clases y ___fuimos___ a la casa del tío de Teresa para celebrar la fiesta de cumpleaños de Carlitos. Juan Carlos ___fue___ conmigo, y Álvaro con Isabel. Ellos ___llegaron___ tarde porque, por fortuna, ___encontraron___ 150.000 pesetas en el Parque del Retiro. Álvaro e Isabel ___hablaron___ con un policía y él les explicó que si la persona que ___perdió___ el dinero no ___habla___ con la policía antes del lunes que viene, Álvaro e Isabel van a ___recibir___ el dinero.

Actividad 12: De compras

Imagínate que ayer fuiste de compras. En parejas, explícale a tu compañero/a adónde fuiste, quién fue contigo, qué hiciste, si compraste algo y para quién.

Act. 13: When students finish the activity, have them report back and tabulate responses on the board. Discuss the implications of their responses for the university. For example, if they all play sports, ask if there are enough sports facilities.

Actividad 13: La entrevista

La administración de tu institución quiere saber qué tipo de estudiantes asisten a esta universidad para hacer publicidad. En parejas, entrevisten a su compañero/a y luego informen al resto de la clase.

Pregúntenle . . .

1. en qué año empezó sus estudios universitarios.
2. si asistió a otras universidades. ¿Dónde? ¿Por cuánto tiempo?
3. por qué decidió venir aquí.
4. en qué año comenzó a estudiar en esta universidad.
5. si aprendió a usar computadoras en esta universidad, en otra universidad, en la escuela secundaria o en la escuela primaria *(elementary school)*.
6. qué hace después de sus clases todos los días.
7. si juega al tenis, al basquetbol, etc.
8. dónde y cuántas horas al día estudia.
9. en qué año va a terminar sus estudios.
10. qué piensa hacer después de terminar la universidad.

Nuevos horizontes

Evaluate your habits: Do you highlight or mark your textbooks? Do you buy used books with notes?

Estrategia de lectura: *Ongoing Prediction*

You have already seen that the reading technique of prediction can be used as a means of anticipating the content of a reading selection and have practiced this technique using titles and photographs. In addition, you can use prediction *while* reading, to guess what the author is going to say next. Then, based on what you read, you confirm or reject your predictions. Most of us are unaware of this interaction with the writer. There are, however, some readers that interact overtly with the writer by writing comments in the margins such as "so what?," "important," "don't get it," and "I agree."

You will have a chance to practice prediction as you read the selection.

Actividad 14: Mira y contesta

Lee el título del texto que sigue y contesta las siguientes preguntas.

1. ¿Qué entiendes por "belleza natural"?
2. ¿Recuerdas alguna belleza natural de Suramérica que se mencionó en este libro?
3. ¿Qué sabes del clima de Suramérica? ¿Qué regiones son frías o cálidas?
4. Mira las fotos que acompañan el texto. ¿Conoces lugares como éstos? ¿Están en tu país o en otro?

Actividad 15: Predicción

En el siguiente texto va a haber pausas. Cuando llegues a una pausa sigue estos pasos *(steps)*:

a. Usa lo que sabes del texto hasta ese momento para hacer una predicción sobre lo que va a decir después el autor.
b. Compara tu predicción con la de un/a compañero/a.
c. Continúa leyendo para confirmar o rechazar *(reject)* tu predicción.

You may want to put the text on an overhead transparency and reveal the contents up to the pauses. If not, have students cover the text with a piece of paper so they don't look ahead.

Suggest that students see the movie *The Mission*, part of which was filmed on location at Iguazú.

Suramérica y su belleza natural

Suramérica se caracteriza por la diversidad de su belleza natural. Esta belleza varía desde la selva amazónica en países como Ecuador y Perú hasta el árido desierto de Atacama en el norte de Chile. También se encuentran las playas blancas de Colombia, Venezuela y Uruguay que contrastan con los Andes y sus nieves eternas en **(PAUSA)** Argentina, Chile y Bolivia. Entre las bellezas naturales también están las Cataratas del

Iguazú y el Salto Ángel. **(PAUSA)** Éste último está en Venezuela y es la catarata más alta del mundo.

Las Cataratas del Iguazú se encuentran en el río del mismo nombre, en la frontera entre Argentina y Brasil. Tienen una caída de ochenta metros y son veinte metros más altas que las del Niágara. El salto más importante es la Garganta del Diablo.[1] Desde el lado brasileño hay una visión panorámica de las cataratas. **(PAUSA)** En el lado argentino se puede caminar muy cerca de cada salto o catarata.

Los indios de esta zona explican el origen de estas cataratas con una leyenda. **(PAUSA)** Ésta dice que el dios[2] de los indios eligió a Naipi, la hija del jefe de la tribu, como esposa, pero ella se enamoró del indio Tarob y un día Naipi y Tarob se fueron en una canoa por el río Iguazú ("agua grande" en la lengua indígena). Cuando el dios escuchó esto se enfureció y entonces decidió crear las cataratas para matar a los enamorados con su torrente de agua. Así terminó la vida de los dos jóvenes amantes.

Las cataratas no sólo son ricas en vegetación y animales sino que también son una fuente de electricidad para Argentina, Brasil y Paraguay. Hace aproximadamente veinte años **(PAUSA)** se terminó de construir en las cataratas una de las plantas hidroeléctricas más grandes del mundo. En 1984 la UNESCO declaró las Cataratas del Iguazú "patrimonio universal".

1. devil's throat   2. god

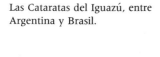

See the color photos in **Patrimonio cultural** for examples of other world-heritage sights.

Las Cataratas del Iguazú, entre Argentina y Brasil.

Desierto en Ecuador.

Act. 16: Some of the questions will be easily answered by students, some you will be able to answer, and others may need to be researched by students. The idea is, reading generates questions and arouses curiosity. This process provides stimuli for informative conversation and/or more reading.

Other linking words in the reading: **esta belleza, éste último, ésta** (referring to **una leyenda**), **cuando, así,** and **no sólo ... sino que.**

Act. 17: Peer edit. Have some students read their versions aloud.

Actividad 16: Tus preguntas

Después de leer el texto, prepara tres preguntas sobre cosas que no entendiste o cosas que el texto no explica en detalle y que te gustaría saber. Luego, en grupos de tres, háganles *(ask)* estas preguntas a sus compañeros.

Estrategia de escritura: *Linking Words*

When writing a sentence or paragraph, the writer uses connectors or *linking words* either to unite an idea or to provide smooth transitions from one idea to the next. Lack of linking words makes a paragraph choppy and difficult to follow.

In the text about South America, there are some linking words used, such as **entonces** and **también.** Can you find any others?

Actividad 17: La leyenda

En grupos de tres, inventen una nueva versión de la leyenda de las Cataratas del Iguazú con un final feliz. Tomen la leyenda original como modelo. Usen el siguiente formato:

- La leyenda dice que . . . , pero . . . . Un día, . . . y entonces, ... Cuando . . . y . . . para . . . .

159

Lo esencial

I. Medios de transporte

I. **Carro** is understood throughout most of Hispanic America, although in some countries, **auto** and/or **coche** are used; **coche** is used in Spain.

Autobús = **camión** (Mexico), **guagua** (Puerto Rico, Cuba), **ómnibus** (Peru), **camioneta** (Guatemala).

Iberia (Spain); **Lacsa** (Costa Rica); **VIASA** (Venezuela).

1. el carro/coche/auto
2. el taxi
3. el autobús
4. el avión
5. el barco

6. el camión
7. el metro
8. el tren
9. la bicicleta
10. la moto/motocicleta

¿Lo sabían?

Avianca, la aerolínea nacional de Colombia, fue la primera aerolínea de este hemisferio y comenzó en el año 1919. ¿Sabes de qué países hispanos son las aerolíneas Iberia, Lacsa y VIASA?

Actividad 18: Asociaciones

Di qué medios de transporte se asocian con estas palabras: Greyhound, Pee Wee Herman, Pan Am, Allied, el color amarillo, Porsche, Titanic, Amtrak, Kawasaki.

Actividad 19: Los transportes de tu ciudad

En parejas, hagan una lista de los medios de transporte de la ciudad donde Uds. estudian. Digan cuánto cuestan, qué zonas recorren y a qué hora empieza el servicio. Expliquen también qué medios de transporte hay, cuáles piensan que se necesitan y por qué.

II. Active vocabulary words are in boldface.

II. La familia de Marisel

Parientes = relatives; padres = parents.

Mª = abbreviation for María.

Esposo/marido = husband; esposa/mujer = wife.

La familia de Marisel es grande. Sus **abuelos** paternos son Francisco y Marina y sus **abuelos** maternos son Ramón y María Luisa. Su **padre** se llama Javier y su **madre,** Ana María. Marisel tiene un **hermano menor** que se llama Quico y ella, por supuesto, es la **hermana mayor.** Tiene cuatro **tíos:** Luis y Alicia son **hermanos** de su padre y Mª Rebeca y Marta, **hermanas** de su madre. Para Marta, Marisel es su **sobrina** favorita. Marisel también tiene dos **tíos políticos:** Rosa, la **esposa** de su tío Luis, y Tomás, el **esposo** de su **tía** Marta. Rosa y Luis tienen dos **hijos,** Inés y Diego, que son los **primos** de Marisel, pero su **primo** favorito es Tomasito.

Practice family vocabulary by forming sentences about your family and about fictional families on TV: **Beaver y Wally son hermanos.**

Actividad 20: La familia de Javier

En parejas, describan la familia en relación con Javier. Las siguientes palabras pueden ser útiles: suegro *(father-in-law)*, suegra *(mother-in-law)*, cuñado *(brother-in-law)*, cuñada *(sister-in-law)*. Por ejemplo: El padre de Javier se llama Francisco. Tiene dos hermanos, Alicia y Luis.

Ask students to determine the last names of the following people from the family-tree: **Javier, Ana María, Marisel,** and **Tomasito.**

¿Lo sabían?

Cuando se casa una mujer hispana, generalmente conserva sus apellidos y añade *(adds)* el primer apellido de su esposo. Por ejemplo, si Olga Tedias Araya se casa con Vicente Montero Salgado, ella se llama Olga Tedias (Araya) de Montero. Si tienen un hijo, sus apellidos van a ser Montero Tedias.

Act. 21: Have students ask one question per classmate and then move on.

Actividad 21: ¡Bingo!

O *(or)* becomes **u** before words beginning with **o** or **ho.**

Vas a jugar al Bingo. Tienes que hacer preguntas a diferentes personas de tu clase basándote en la información de las casillas *(boxes)*. Si ellas contestan que sí, escribe su nombre en la casilla correspondiente. La persona que completa primero una fila *(line)* en forma diagonal, vertical u horizontal es el/la ganador/a *(winner)*.

You can have 3 winners: 1 for a vertical, 1 for a horizontal, and 1 for a diagonal Bingo. You may also want to see if someone can fill the entire card.

B	I	N	G	O
1 hermano	cumpleaños en septiembre	madre alta	abuelo irlandés	tía enfermera
cumpleaños en febrero	padre gordo	no tiene hermanos	tía que se llama Ann	tiene primos
tiene 4 abuelos	un tío que se llama Bill	cumpleaños en julio	tiene esposo	hermano rubio
tiene hijo	abuela italiana	2 cuñados	tiene 1 sobrina	abuelo con poco pelo
2 hermanas	tiene sobrino	tiene hija	cumpleaños en el otoño	tiene esposa

Actividad 22: Oraciones incompletas

En tres minutos escribe oraciones incompletas sobre la familia. Por ejemplo: La madre de mi madre es mi _____ .

Luego, en grupos de tres, una persona lee sus oraciones incompletas y los compañeros tienen que completar esas oraciones.

El hotel secreto

Practice expressions: **¿Te gusta viajar por tren? ¿Qué tienes ganas de hacer?**

en/por + **barco/tren**/etc.	by boat/train/etc.
tener ganas de + infinitive	to feel like + -ing
Tengo ganas de viajar.	I feel like traveling.

Isabel fue a Chile por dos semanas para visitar a su familia y para asistir a la boda *(wedding)* de su mejor amiga con su primo favorito. Ahora está hablando con dos amigos, Andrés y Camila, sobre la boda, que fue ayer.

Una boda en Madrid, España.

Actividad 23: Marca los regalos

Escucha la conversación y marca sólo las cosas que recibieron los novios como regalos *(presents)* de boda. Indica también de quiénes las recibieron.

	¿Recibieron?	¿De quiénes?
una grabadora	_____	_____
un estéreo	✔	el abuelo de Isabel
un televisor	✔	un tío de Olga
unas toallas	_____	_____
muebles	✔	los papás de Olga
una casa	_____	_____
un viaje	✔	los papás de Nando

Andrés	Hola, Isabel. ¿Qué haces?
Isabel	Nada. Estoy cansadísima.
Andrés	¿Y por qué?
Isabel	Es que anoche fue el matrimonio de Olga y mi primo Nando y bailé muchísimo.
Camila	Los papás de Olga echaron la casa por la ventana.[1] ¡A mí me encantó ver a Nando entrando en la iglesia del brazo de tu tía. ¡Qué buen mozo estaba Nando! Y tu tía, ¡qué madrina[2] más elegante!
Andrés	¿Y sabes qué regalos les dieron?
Isabel	Un tío de ella les dio un televisor, mi abuelo les dio un estéreo y los papás de ella, los muebles de la casa.
Camila	Nando me dijo que los papás de él les pagaron el viaje de luna de miel.[3]
Andrés	¡No me digas! ¿Adónde?
Isabel	Hoy van a Santo Domingo y después van a viajar en barco por el Caribe.
Camila	¡Qué romántico! Yo tengo muchas ganas de ir a la República Dominicana; las islas del Caribe deben ser muy lindas.
Andrés	¿Y sabes en qué hotel se quedaron anoche?
Isabel	No sé. Creo que no le contaron nada a nadie. ¿Tú sabes algo, Camila?
Camila	¡Claro que no! Eso . . . no se dice nunca . . . .

1. to go all out   2. maid of honor   3. honeymoon

Boda = matrimonio (Chile).

The Dominican Republic is a desirable destination for tourists because of its beautiful beaches and low prices.

Note the use of **lindas** to mean *beautiful*. Ask students to give a synonym. **Lindo/a** is commonly used in Hispanic America.

Stating who gave what to whom

Discussing means of transportation

Expressing desires

Making negative statements

In Chile, it is common for newly-weds to spend the first night incognito in a hotel and begin their honeymoon the next day.

Actividad 24: Preguntas

Después de escuchar la conversación, contesta estas preguntas.

1. ¿Quiénes se casaron? ¿Quién es pariente de Isabel: el novio o la novia?
2. ¿Con quién entró el novio en la iglesia?
3. ¿Qué significa **echar la casa por la ventana**?
4. ¿Adónde fueron Nando y Olga para su luna de miel y cómo fueron?
5. ¿Qué tiene ganas de hacer Camila, la amiga de Isabel?

Los padrinos play an important role in Hispanic culture at baptisms, confirmations, and weddings. Most of the time they are members of the immediate or extended family.

¿Lo sabían?

Por lo general, en las bodas hispanas, los amigos de los novios no participan directamente en la ceremonia; en cambio, los padres de los novios son los "padrinos" y están en el altar acompañando a sus hijos. El novio entra en la iglesia del brazo de su madre y, como en los Estados Unidos, la novia entra del brazo de su padre. ¿Te gusta la idea de tener a los padres como padrinos en una boda?

E. Guillermo Muñoz Torres   Francisco Montero Salgado
Elsa Cabezón de Muñoz   Margarita Llanos de Montero

Participan a Ud. y *familia,* el matrimonio de sus hijos

Marcela   y   Francisco

y le invitan a la ceremonia religiosa que se efectuará en la Parroquia Santa Marta (Avda. Diego de Almagro 5225, Ñuñoa), el viernes 29 de enero, a las 20.00 horas.

Santiago, Enero de 1988

Actividad 25: La luna de miel

En parejas, pregúntenle a su compañero/a adónde fueron unos amigos para su luna de miel, qué hicieron y cómo viajaron. Si su compañero/a está casado/a, pregúntenle sobre su luna de miel.

Actividad 26: El viaje del año pasado

En grupos de cuatro, pregúntenles a sus compañeros adónde fueron de viaje el año pasado, por qué fueron y qué medios de transporte usaron. También pregúntenles qué tienen ganas de hacer el año que viene.

A: ¿Adónde fuiste el año pasado?   **B:** Fui en/por avión.
B: Fui a San Francisco.   **A:** . . .
A: ¿Cómo fuiste?

Hacia la comunicación

I. Using Indirect-Object Pronouns

Before studying the grammar explanation, answer these questions:

• When Isabel, Camila, and Andrés speak, to whom do the words in bold refer in the following sentences?

"¿Y sabes qué regalos **les** dieron?"

"Creo que no **le** contaron nada a nadie."

"Nando me dijo que los papás de él **les** pagaron el viaje . . ."

• Do the people indicated by the words in boldface perform the actions indicated by the verbs?

1. An indirect object indicates *to whom* or *for whom* an action is done. You have already learned the indirect-object pronouns with the verbs **gustar** and **fascinar.**

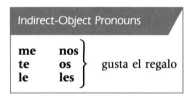

Indirect-Object Pronouns		
me	**nos**	
te	**os**	gusta el regalo
le	**les**	

—¿Quién **te** mandó dinero?   *Who sent you money?*
—Mi padre **me** mandó dinero.   *My father sent me money.*

2. Like the reflexive pronoun, the indirect-object pronoun precedes a conjugated verb or follows attached to a present participle or an infinitive.

Ayer **le** escribí una carta.   *I wrote him/her a letter yesterday.*
Ahora **le** estoy escribiendo   *I'm writing him/her a letter now.*
  (estoy escribi**é**ndo**le**) una carta.
Mañana **le** voy a escribir   *I'm going to write him/her a letter*
  (voy a escribir**le**) una carta.   *tomorrow.*

3. The meaning of an indirect-object pronoun can be emphasized or clarified by using the preposition **a** + *a noun* or *a prepositional pronoun.*

Le escribí una carta **a Juan**.   *I wrote a letter to Juan.*
Ella **les** explicó el problema   *She explained the problem to*
  a ellos.   *them.*

The following verbs are commonly used with indirect-object pronouns:

contar   to tell; to count
contestar   to answer
dar   to give
decir   to say; to tell
escribir   to write
explicar   to explain

hablar   to speak
mandar   to send; to command
ofrecer   to offer
preguntar   to ask (a question)
regalar   to give a present

Conjugate **ofrecer** like conocer: ofrezco, ofreces ...

Los padres de Nando **les ofrecieron** pagar el viaje.
La familia de Olga **les regaló** muchas cosas.

Nando's parents offered to pay for their trip.
Olga's family gave them many things.

II. Using Affirmative and Negative Words

II. Drill affirmative and negative words:
1. Tell students to say they do the opposite of what you do. T: **Yo canto siempre.** S1: **Nosotros no cantamos nunca.** T: **Leo todo.** S2: **No leemos nada.** (etc.)
2. Have students describe what they do and what their brothers and sisters do: **Yo estudio mucho y él no estudia nada.**
3. Do questions and answers: **¿Estudias mucho? ¿Corres con frecuencia? ¿Hablaste con alguien?** (etc.)

Palabras afirmativas	Palabras negativas
todo/a everything ⎫ **algo** something ⎭	**nada** nothing
alguien someone	**nadie** no one
siempre always	**nunca** never

1. When the words **nada, nadie,** or **nunca** follow the verb in a sentence, the double negative is mandatory. You need to apply the following formula:

no + verb + negative word

—¿Tienes algo para mí?
—¿Llamó alguien?
—¿Siempre estudia tu hermana?

—No, **no** tengo **nada.**
—No, **no** llamó **nadie.**
—No, **no** estudia **nunca.**

Review use of the personal **a**, Ch. 4.

However, no double negative = negative word + verb: **Nadie llamó.** Note: **Alguien** and **nadie** require the personal **a** when they function as direct objects: **—¿Llamaste a alguien? —No, no llamé a nadie.**

Do mechanical drills, Workbook, Part II.

Actividad 27: Las próximas actividades

Describe las actividades que van a hacer estas personas la semana que viene. Forma oraciones con elementos de cada columna: Yo voy a preguntarle algo indiscreto a Julieta.

yo	explicar	un trabajo	a la psicóloga
el paciente	contestar	algo indiscreto	a Julieta
Avianca	mandar	una carta de amor	a nosotros
Romeo	ofrecer	su problema	a ti
ellos	pedir	varios telegramas	al piloto
	preguntar	cien dólares	al médico
		su nombre	a mí

Actividad 28: Los regalos

En parejas, pregúntenle a su compañero/a qué les regaló a cinco personas el año pasado. Piensen en ocasiones especiales y en personas como sus abuelos, su novio/a, un/a amigo/a especial, su hermano/a, etc. Luego, pregúntenle qué le dieron a él/ella el año pasado esas cinco personas.

Actividad 29: El optimista y el pesimista

En parejas, imagínense que uno de Uds. es una persona optimista y la otra es pesimista. Uno siempre contradice al otro.

ı●ı   El optimista: Alguien me escribe cartas.
El pesimista: Nadie me escribe cartas. / No me escribe cartas nadie.

Optimista	Pesimista
Voy a comer algo.	
_____	No conozco a nadie.
Siempre me regalan todo.	_____
_____	Nunca voy a fiestas.
Alguien me habla siempre.	_____
_____	Mis padres nunca me dieron nada.

Actividad 30: La Dra. Ruth

Act. 31: Explain the differences in nuance if necessary. **Es casado** = he is a married man; **está casado** = he is married. (**Está casado con Ana.**) **Es soltero** = he is a single man; **está soltero** = he is single. (**Todavía está soltero.**) **Es divorciado** = he is a divorced man; **está divorciado** = he is divorced. (**Ahora está divorciado.**)

En parejas, una persona es la Dra. Ruth y la otra es el/la invitado/a *(guest)* al programa. El tema de hoy es la educación sexual. La doctora quiere saber . . .

1. si le preguntó a alguien de dónde vienen los niños.
2. si alguien le explicó la verdad *(truth)*.
   Si contesta que sí, ¿quién? ¿Qué le dijo *(say)*?
3. si estudió la sexualidad humana en la escuela.
4. si les va a decir a sus hijos de dónde vienen los niños.

Actividad 31: La familia de tu compañero

Write the family-tree information in note form to help you give an oral report to the class.

Have some students talk about their partner's family to the class or, in groups of 4, have them inform one other. The latter would maximize participation.

En parejas, averigüen datos sobre la familia de su compañero/a y dibujen *(draw)* el árbol de la familia. Incluyan información sobre cada persona. Luego informen al resto de la clase. Las siguientes palabras pueden ser útiles: **es soltero/a** *(single)*, **está casado/a** *(married)*, **está divorciado/a** *(divorced)*, **la madrastra** *(stepmother)*, **el padrastro** *(stepfather)*. Usen preguntas como las siguientes: **¿Qué hace tu hermano . . . ? ¿Cuándo se casó tu tío? ¿Alguien de tu familia habla español? ¿Quién te escribe cartas?**

Vocabulario funcional

Los números del cien al millón

Ver página 150

Expresiones de tiempo pasado

Ver página 153

Verbos

abrir to open
asistir a to attend (class, church, etc.)
buscar to look for
casarse con to get married (to)
contar (o > ue) to tell; to count
contestar to answer
dar to give
decidir to decide
dejar to leave behind; to let, allow
entrar en to enter
explicar to explain
gritar to shout, scream

llegar to arrive
llorar to cry
mandar to send
ofrecer to offer
pagar to pay (for)
preguntar to ask (a question)
regalar to give (a present)
sacar to get a grade; to take out
salir de to leave
terminar to finish
tomar to eat, have food or drink; to take (a bus, etc.)
viajar to travel

La familia

el/la abuelo/a grandfather/grandmother
el/la cuñado/a brother-in-law/sister-in-law
el/la esposo/a husband/wife
el/la hermano/a brother/sister
el/la hijo/a son/daughter
la madrastra stepmother
el padrastro stepfather
los padres/papás parents
los parientes relatives

el/la primo/a cousin
el/la sobrino/a nephew/niece
el/la suegro/a father-in-law/mother-in-law
el/la tío/a uncle/aunt
está casado/a is married
está divorciado/a is divorced
es soltero/a is single
mayor older
menor younger

Preposiciones de lugar

Ver página 151

Medios de transporte

Ver página 160

Palabras afirmativas y negativas

Ver página 167

Palabras y expresiones útiles

bellísimo very beautiful
la boda wedding
la luna de miel honeymoon
en/por + barco/tren/etc. by boat/train/etc.
¡Qué + noun + **más** + adjective! What a + *adjective* + *noun!*
el regalo present
tener ganas de + infinitive to feel like + *-ing*

¿Cuál crees que es la ocupación de estas dos personas? ¿Por qué dices eso?

Hotel en Barranquilla, Colombia.

Capítulo 7

¿Para cuántas personas es una habitación doble? ¿Cuánto cuesta una habitación doble en este hotel? (Precio en bolívares—Venezuela)

After studying this chapter, you will know how to:

- make hotel and plane reservations
- describe past actions and occurrences

- place phone calls
- state how long ago an action took place and specify its duration

Desde el aeropuerto

al centro de Pto. Ordaz .... Bs. 60,00

a San Felix .... Bs. 70,00

COMIDAS (Diario)
Criolla .... Bs. 200,00
Internacional .... Bs. 250,00 - 370,00

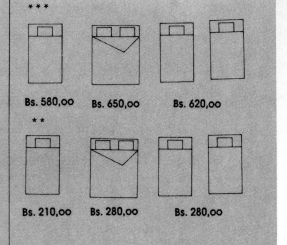

* * *

Bs. 580,00   Bs. 650,00   Bs. 620,00

* *

Bs. 210,00   Bs. 280,00   Bs. 280,00

¿En un "banco" de Segovia?

Estación de autobuses, Caracas, Venezuela.

Perdimos el autobús.	We missed the bus.
quisiera/quisiéramos	I/We would like
Lo siento.	I'm sorry.

Juan Carlos y Claudia están en Segovia, adonde fueron a comer, y allí tienen problemas.

Actividad 1: Escoge la opción

Escucha la conversación y escoge la opción correcta.

1. Claudia y Juan Carlos perdieron . . . .
   a. el tren   b. el autobús   c. el carro
2. Ellos tuvieron que buscar . . . .
   a. una habitación   b. un autobús   c. a don Andrés

3. Claudia llamó a . . . .
   a. Isabel   b. don Andrés   c. Teresa
4. Claudia habló con . . . .
   a. Isabel   b. don Andrés   c. Teresa
5. Finalmente tuvieron que dormir . . . .
   a. en un parque   b. en una habitación doble   c. no se sabe dónde

Juan Carlos	Bueno, perdimos el autobús a Madrid y no hay más trenes. ¿Qué vamos a hacer?
Claudia	Pues, buscar o un hotel o un hostal, ¿no?
Juan Carlos	Mira, allí hay uno . . .
Juan Carlos	Buenas noches, señor.
Recepcionista	Hola, buenas noches. ¿Qué desean?
Juan Carlos	Quisiéramos dos habitaciones sencillas.
Recepcionista	Lo siento, pero no hay.
Juan Carlos	Y, ¿una habitación doble?
Claudia	¿Doble?
Juan Carlos	No te preocupes. Ya nos arreglamos.
Claudia	Mmm . . .
Recepcionista	No hay nada, pero si quiere, puedo llamar a otros hoteles.
Juan Carlos	Sí, por favor.
Claudia	¿No sabe dónde hay un teléfono público? Quisiera llamar a Madrid.
Recepcionista	Sí, hay uno en el bar de enfrente.
Claudia	Ahora vuelvo. Voy a llamar a Teresa . . .
Don Andrés	Colegio Mayor. Dígame.
Claudia	¿Quién habla? ¿Don Andrés?
Don Andrés	Sí, ¿quién habla?
Claudia	Habla Claudia. ¿Está Teresa?
Don Andrés	No, hace dos horas que la vi salir.
Claudia	¿Le puedo dejar un mensaje?
Don Andrés	Sí, cómo no.
Claudia	¿Le puede decir que Juan Carlos y yo perdimos el autobús y estamos en Segovia? Nos dijeron que no hay autobuses hasta mañana.
Don Andrés	Vale. Vale. Adiós, Claudia.
Claudia	Gracias. Hasta mañana.
Claudia	Bueno, ¿pudo encontrar habitación para nosotros?
Recepcionista	No, lo siento . . .
Juan Carlos	Bueno Claudia, ¿sabes qué? Hay un parque muy bonito cerca de aquí . . . y tiene unos bancos muy buenos . . .

Explain that **hostal** does not mean *youth hostel* in Spain, but *small hotel.*

Making a request

Negating

Discuss the sound effects of the phone. In some countries there is a long beep in the receiver if the phone is ringing and short beeps if the line is busy.

Identifying oneself on the phone

Leaving a message

Apologizing

Actividad 2: Preguntas

Después de escuchar la conversación, contesta estas preguntas.

1. ¿Cuáles son los problemas que tienen Juan Carlos y Claudia?
2. ¿Tienen solución estos problemas?
3. ¿Perdiste alguna vez un autobús, un tren o un avión? ¿Qué ocurrió? ¿Fue en tu ciudad o en otro lugar?
4. En tu opinión, ¿qué hicieron Claudia y Juan Carlos? ¿Durmieron? ¿Dónde?

Actividad 3: Llamada a la operadora

En parejas, el/la estudiante "A" cubre la Columna B y el/la estudiante "B" cubre la Columna A. Llamen al/a la operador/a para averiguar el teléfono de los lugares que aparecen en su columna y escriban el número. Después cambien de papel.

A: Información.
B: Quisiera el número (de teléfono) de . . .
A: Es el . . . / Lo siento pero no tengo ese número.

A

Averigua el teléfono de:

1. el Restaurante El Hidalgo
2. la Librería Compás

Usa esta información cuando eres el/la operador/a:

MINICINES
ASTORIA 1 - 2
Pl. Carmen, 16 ------------------- 521 5666

B

Averigua el teléfono de:

1. Peluquero Pedro Molina
2. los Minicines Astoria

Usa esta información cuando eres el/la operador/a:

Restaurante
EL HIDALGO
San Fernando, 8 ------------------ 520 0392
RESTAURANTE FIESTA S. A.
Av. Denia, 47 ------------------ 526 4426

PELUQNERS'S
PEDRO MOLINA
ESTETICA - MAQUILLAJE - DEPILACION
Padre Espla, 15 ent.
☎ 521 94 21
No cerramos al mediodía

COMPAS LIBRERIA

LIBRERIA
COMPAS
COMPAS UNIVERSIDAD
Torre de Mando - Rabasa

ALICANTE
Alcalde Alfonso Rojas, 5
☎ 521 16 79
San Vte. del Raspeig ☎ 566 30 77

Lo esencial

I. En el hotel

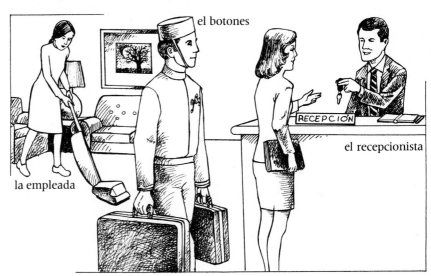

el botones

el recepcionista

la empleada

★★ Hotel Los Arcos

	Precio
Habitación sencilla con baño y con desayuno	3.100 ptas.
Con **media pensión**	3.900 ptas.
Con **pensión completa**	4.700 ptas.
Habitación doble sin baño y con desayuno	3.900 ptas.
Con media pensión	5.500 ptas.
Con pensión completa	7.100 ptas.
Habitación doble con baño y con desayuno	4.400 ptas.
Con media pensión	6.000 ptas.
Con pensión completa	7.600 ptas.

Actividad 4: ¿Quién es o qué es?

Basándote en la información presentada en **Lo esencial,** p. 175, di qué es o quién es . . .

1. la persona que lleva las maletas a la habitación del hotel.
2. el lugar donde te bañas o te lavas los dientes.
3. cuando tomas el desayuno y una comida más en el hotel.
4. la persona que te dice los precios de las habitaciones.
5. cuando tomas el desayuno y dos comidas en el hotel.
6. la persona que hace las camas.
7. una habitación para una persona.
8. el lugar del hotel donde está el/la recepcionista.
9. una habitación para dos personas.

The Tourist Office provides free folders about the **paradores.**

¿Lo sabían?

El gobierno español tiene muchos hoteles que se llaman Paradores Nacionales. La mayor parte está en monumentos históricos como castillos, monasterios o conventos. El gobierno puertorriqueño tomó la idea de los españoles e hizo paradores, pero no en castillos ni en monasterios sino en lugares de atractivo turístico típicos de Puerto Rico: cerca del mar, al lado de una bahía, en lugares de aguas termales, etc.

PARADOR "MARQUES DE VILLENA"
ALARCON • CUENCA
Teléfono: (966) 33 13 50.
Categoría: ***

PARADOR "ALCAZAR DEL REY DON PEDRO"
CARMONA • SEVILLA
Teléfono: (954) 14 10 10.
Categoría: ****

Interior del Parador "Marqués de Villena" en Alarcón, España. ¿Le gustaría a un niño este parador?

PATRIMONIO CULTURAL

Colombia, Perú y Ecuador

(1/2) Máscara funeraria y cuchillo ceremonial, Museo del Oro, Bogotá, Colombia   (3) La iglesia de la Compañía, Quito, Ecuador

Actividad
Los españoles llegaron a América en busca de riquezas. ¿Qué encontraron? ¿Qué hicieron con lo que encontraron?

1

2

3

4

Guatemala y Perú

(4) Fiestas de Inti-Raymi, Sacsahuaymán, Perú   (5) El claustro de Santa Clara y la iglesia de San Francisco, Antigua, Guatemala   (6) Tikal, Guatemala

Actividad

En parejas, digan qué culturas precolombinas vivieron en estos países. Luego, comenten qué cambios produjo la conquista española en la vida de estas culturas.

7

8

España

9

(7) La Giralda, Sevilla (8) El parque Güell, del arquitecto Gaudí, Barcelona (9) El castillo de Vélez-Blanco, Andalucía (10) La Dama de Elche (11) Detalle, La Alhambra, Granada (12) Toledo

Actividad

En grupos de tres, comenten la variedad de culturas que han formado lo que hoy en día se llama España.

10

11

12

13

México

14

(13) Sacerdote maya, Yaxchilán
(14) Estatua de Chac Mool, Chichén Itzá

Actividad
Miren estos ejemplos del patrimonio cultural hispano y después, en grupos de cuatro, escojan dos lugares que representan el patrimonio cultural de su país. Defiendan su elección.

Act. 5: Have the receptionist stand behind his/her desk to simulate a hotel.

Encourage students to invent prices for types of rooms not described in the brochure.

Actividad 5: Busca habitación

En parejas, imagínense que están en el Hotel Los Arcos. Una persona es el/la recepcionista y la otra es un/a viajero/a que busca habitaciones (una doble y otra sencilla) para tres personas por dos noches. El/La viajero/a averigua precios y tiene que decidir si quiere las habitaciones con o sin baño y con o sin pensión completa.

|●| El/La viajero/a: Buenas tardes.
El/La recepcionista: ¿En qué puedo servirle?
El/La viajero/a: . . .

II. El teléfono

Tipos de llamadas telefónicas

local

de larga distancia $\left\{\begin{array}{l}\textbf{marcar directo}\\ \text{con ayuda del/de la operador/a}\\ \quad\text{teléfono a teléfono}\\ \text{persona a persona}\\ \textbf{a cobro revertido}\end{array}\right.$

II. Answering the phone: **¿Bueno?** (Mexico), **¿Hola?** (Argentina).

Have students simulate phone conversations: wrong numbers, finding out that the person they want to speak to is not there, getting local information, etc.

If you have a phone book from a Hispanic country, create activities using the phone book. Have operators look for numbers.

Cómo hablar cuando . . .

contestas el teléfono $\left\{\begin{array}{l}\textbf{¿Aló?}\\ \textbf{Diga. / Dígame.} \text{ (España)}\end{array}\right.$

preguntas por alguien $\left\{\begin{array}{l}\textbf{¿Está Álvaro, por favor?}\\ \textbf{Quisiera hablar con}\\ \quad\textbf{Álvaro, por favor.}\end{array}\right.$

te identificas $\left\{\begin{array}{l}\textbf{—¿Quién habla?}\\ \textbf{—Habla Claudia.}\\ \\ \textbf{—¿De parte de quién?}\\ \textbf{—(De parte) de Claudia.}\end{array}\right.$

hay un número equivocado $\left\{\begin{array}{l}\textbf{—¿Está Marisel, por}\\ \quad\textbf{favor?}\\ \textbf{—No, tiene el número}\\ \quad\textbf{equivocado.}\end{array}\right.$

hay problemas de comprensión $\left\{\begin{array}{l}\textbf{¿Puede hablar más}\\ \quad\textbf{despacio, por favor?}\end{array}\right.$

To avoid confusion with **cero,** the conjuction **o** has a written accent when it appears between 2 numbers: **2 ó 3.**

¿Lo sabían?

En muchas ciudades y pueblos del mundo hispano, los números de teléfono tienen sólo 5 ó 6 cifras, y no siete como en los Estados Unidos. También es importante saber que, en muchos países, las llamadas locales se pagan según la cantidad de minutos, el número de llamadas y la distancia.

Actividad 6: Una llamada a Teresa

Vicente llama por teléfono a Teresa a su trabajo. Pon *(Put)* esta conversación en orden lógico.

__4__	¿De parte de quién?
__1__	Todos nuestros agentes están ocupados *(busy)* en este momento. Espere por favor. ♪♩♪♩
__11__	Bueno. Muchas gracias, don Alejandro. Adiós.
__6__	Hola Vicente. Habla Alejandro, el tío de Teresa. Ella no está.
__12__	De nada. Adiós.
__2__	Traveltur, buenos días. Dígame.
__7__	Bueno, quisiera dejarle un mensaje.
__3__	Buenos días. ¿Está Teresa?
_8 or 10_	Sí, por supuesto.
__5__	De parte de Vicente.
__9__	¿Puede decirle que la llamé y que voy a llamar mañana?
_10 or 8_	Sí, claro.

Act. 7: The word for *area code* varies from country to country: **prefijo** (Spain), **indicativo** (Colombia), **código** (El Salvador).

Act.'s 7,8: Have students sit back-to-back to simulate a phone conversation.

Give students other students' phone numbers, if possible, and have them read these numbers aloud while dialing. The student whose number is dialed must answer and carry on a conversation.

Actividad 7: Llamada de larga distancia

En parejas, una persona está en Montevideo, Uruguay, y necesita llamar a un pariente en los Estados Unidos. Necesita la ayuda del/de la operador/a. La otra persona es el/la operador/a y le pregunta qué tipo de llamada quiere, el área *(area code)* y el número. Después cambien de papel.

▶ **A:** Operador/a internacional, buenos días.
  B: Quisiera . . .

Actividad 8: La agencia de viajes

En parejas, una persona trabaja en una agencia de viajes y la otra persona es un/a cliente que llama por teléfono para hablar con alguien, pero no está. El/La cliente deja un mensaje y el/la agente de viajes escribe el mensaje.

MENSAJE TELEFÓNICO

Para: _____

De parte de: _____

Teléfono: _____

Asunto: _____

Recibido por:	Fecha:	Hora:

Hacia la comunicación

Gramática

I. Talking About the Past: Irregular Verbs and Stem-changing Verbs in the Preterit

1. Some common irregular verbs share similar patterns in the preterit.

Verbs whose irregular preterit stems end in **-j** add **-eron**, not **-ieron** in the third-person plural form.

Tener	
tuve	**tuv**imos
tuviste	**tuv**isteis
tuvo	**tuv**ieron

Decir	
dije	**dij**imos
dijiste	**dij**isteis
dijo	**dij**eron

Irregular verbs like **tener** have the same endings in the preterit as **hacer: -e, -iste, -o, -imos, -isteis, -ieron.**

Verbs that have endings like **tener: estar → estuve; poder → pude; poner → puse; querer → quise; venir → vine; saber → supe.**

Verbs that have endings like **decir: traducir* → traduje; traer → traje.**

—¿**Tuv**iste que trabajar anoche?　*Did you have to work last night?*
—Sí, **tuv**e que trabajar mucho.　*Yes, I had to work a lot.*

—¿Quién te **dij**o la verdad?　*Who told you the truth?*
—Me la **dij**o Andrés.　*Andrés told it to me.*

*Note: Most verbs that end in **-ucir** follow the same pattern as trad**ucir**: prod**ucir** → prod**uje**, etc.

I. Discuss the accent to dissolve diphthongs. Write on the board:
hoy = oi   ley = lei;
hoy ≠ oí   ley ≠ leí.

2. Verbs with stems ending in a vowel (except the silent **u** as in **seguir**) + **-er** or **-ir** take **y** in the third-person singular and plural. These verbs include **leer, creer, construir** *(to build),* and **oír** *(to hear).*

Note that the accent dissolves diphthongs.

Leer	
le**í**	le**í**mos
le**í**ste	le**í**steis
le**y**ó	le**y**eron

Oír	
o**í**	o**í**mos
o**í**ste	o**í**steis
o**y**ó	o**y**eron

¿Por qué no le**y**eron el artículo?　*Why didn't you read the article?*
Él o**y**ó las noticias.　*He heard the news.*

Review **-ir** stem-changing verbs, Ch. 5.

Note that the **nosotros** form is the same in the preterit and present indicative. Context will help you determine meaning.

3. Stem-changing verbs ending in **-ir** have a stem change in the third-person singular and plural of the preterit, that is, stem-changing **-ir** "boot verbs" become "shoe verbs" in the preterit.

Preferir (e > ie > i)		Pedir (e > i > i)		Dormir (o > ue > u)	
preferí	preferimos	pedí	pedimos	dormí	dormimos
preferiste	preferisteis	pediste	pedisteis	dormiste	dormisteis
prefirió	prefirieron	pidió	pidieron	durmió	durmieron

—¿**Du**rmieron en el parque Claudia y Juan Carlos?

Did Claudia and Juan Carlos sleep in the park?

—No, creo que prefirieron no dormir.

No, I think they preferred not to sleep.

4. These are some common stem-changing **-ir** verbs:

e > ie > **i**	e > i > **i**	o > ue > **u**
m**e**ntir *to lie*	p**e**dir *to ask for*	d**o**rmir/se *to sleep/to fall*
pref**e**rir *to prefer*	rep**e**tir *to repeat*	m**o**rir/se *to die*
s**e**ntirse *to feel*	s**e**guir *to follow*	

I. Generally **morir** = impersonal; **morirse** = personal: **Franco murió en el año 1975./Se murió mi abuelo el año pasado.**

II. Changes of Meaning in the Preterit

Review the uses of the preterit, Ch. 6.

Since the preterit expresses a completed past action, certain verbs convey a special meaning when used in the preterit.

Drill irregular preterit forms:
1. Do completion drills from present to past: **Hoy no tengo que leer el capítulo porque ayer ...**
2. Do questions and answers: **¿Oíste algo interesante ayer? ¿Qué cosas trajiste a la universidad cuando saliste de tu casa? ¿Qué te trajo tu padre la última vez que vino?** (etc.)
3. Do chain drills based on the last book students read, how students came to class (**vine en coche, en bicicleta**), famous people who died and in what year, etc.

	Present	Preterit
conocer	to know	met
poder	to be able	was/were able and succeeded in doing something
no poder	not to be able	was/were not able and didn't do something
querer	to want	tried but didn't do something
no querer	not to want	refused to do something
saber	to know	found out
tener que	to have to, be supposed to	had to and did something

II. Clarify that **pudo** indicates success, whereas **no pudo** indicates failure; **quiso** implies "tried and really wanted to do it," while **intentó/trató** implies "actively tried."

Conocí al padre de mi novia.

*I **met** my girlfriend's father.*

Por fin, **pude** ir a la fiesta.

*At last, I **was able to (and did)** go to the party.*

Ella **quiso** ir a la fiesta, pero **no pudo.**

*She **tried** to go to the party, but couldn't (**wasn't able to and didn't**).*

Él **no quiso** ir a la fiesta.

*He **refused** to go to the party.*

Él **tuvo que** estudiar.

*He **had to (and did)** study.*

Ayer **supe** la verdad.

*Yesterday, I **found out** the truth.*

III. Drill **hace** + time expression + **que** + verb in the preterit: Have students brainstorm activities they have done and list them on the board. Then have them ask a partner, **¿Cuánto tiempo hace que ... ?**

Note: Another way of asking this question is, **¿Hace cuánto (tiempo) que ... ?**

Review negatives, Ch. 6.

IV. The adjective **alguno** can be used after a noun only in negative sentences: **No tengo libro alguno.**

Remind students to use the double negative with **ningún/ninguno/a.**

Drill affirmative and negative words:
Ask students for things you know they don't have.
T: **¿Tienes nietos?** S1: **No, no tengo ninguno.** Have students invent absurd questions.

Do mechanical drills, Workbook, Part I.

III. Expressing the Time of Past Actions: *Hace* + time expression + *que* + verb in the preterit

To express *how long ago* an action took place, apply the following formula:

Hace + time expression + **que** + verb in the preterit

—¿Cuánto (tiempo) hace que ella llegó? — *How long ago did she arrive?*

—**Hace dos horas que** ella llegó. — *She arrived two hours **ago**.*

IV. Using More Affirmative and Negative Words

Affirmative and negative adjectives		Affirmative and negative pronouns	
algún/alguna/algunos/as	some/any	**alguno/a/os/as**	some/any
ningún/ninguna	(not) any	**ninguno/a**	none/no one

¿Necesitas **algún** libro sobre Segovia? — *Do you need any books on Segovia?*

Aquí tengo **algunas** camisas para ti. — *I have some shirts for you here.*

No vamos a visitar **ninguna** ciudad.* — *We're not going to visit any cities.*

—¿Vinieron tus invitados? — *Did your guests come?*
—Sí, **algunos** vinieron. — *Yes, some came.*

—¿Tienes todos los libros? — *Do you have all the books?*
—No, no tengo **ninguno.** — *No, I don't have any.*

*Note: The adjectives **ningún/ninguna** and the pronouns **ninguno/a** are seldom used in the plural.

Actividad 9: Tus actividades de la semana pasada

Haz dos listas: las cosas que tuviste que hacer la semana pasada y las cosas que quisiste hacer, pero no pudiste hacer. Luego, en grupos de tres, comparen las listas y expliquen por qué no pudieron hacer estas cosas.

Act. 10: Don't let students
peek.

Actividad 10: La habitación desordenada

En parejas, el/la estudiante "A" cubre la Columna B y el/la estudiante "B" cubre la Columna A. El dibujo de la Columna A está incompleto y el dibujo de la Columna B está completo. "A" debe averiguar qué cosas de las que están debajo de su dibujo se necesitan para completarlo, y dónde están. Cuando averigüe, "A" debe dibujar las cosas en los lugares apropiados.

A: ¿Hay algunas camisas en esta habitación?
B: Sí, hay una. / No, no hay ninguna.
A: ¿Dónde está? / ¿Hay algún televisor?
B: . . .

Act. 11: 1. 1968   2. 1963
3. 1865   4. 1972   5. 1980
6. 1989

Actividad 11: ¿Sabes mucha historia?

Di cuánto tiempo hace que murieron estas personas.

Hace más o menos 15 años que Francisco Franco murió. (Francisco Franco murió en 1975.)

Franco fue dictador de España desde 1939 hasta 1975.

1. Martin Luther King y Robert Kennedy
2. John Kennedy
3. Abraham Lincoln
4. Roberto Clemente
5. John Lennon
6. Salvador Dalí

Act. 12: You are the boss. Encourage your employees to tell you about the absent person.

El/la soplón/ona = el/la acusetas (some Latin American countries).

Act. 13: Encourage students to read with a news announcer's voice. Since props lower anxiety, have students use pens as microphones.

Remind students to use words such as **después, más tarde,** etc. to connect their sentences.

La policía = the police; **el/la policía** = the policeman/woman.

Manejar = conducir (Spain).

Actividad 12: Los soplones

En grupos de tres, imagínense que Uds. trabajan en una fábrica y ayer _____ (nombre de un/una estudiante de la clase) no vino a trabajar. ¿Dónde estuvo? ¿Con quién? ¿Qué hizo? ¿Cómo supieron Uds. todo esto? Decidan la historia y después, como Uds. son unos soplones *(tattletales)*, díganle a su jefe/a todo lo que saben.

Actividad 13: Las noticias

En parejas, Uds. van a narrar las noticias *(news)* de ayer. El/la estudiante "A" cubre la Parte B y el/la estudiante "B" cubre la Parte A. "A" comienza describiendo la noticia "La bomba" y "B" ordena y numera los dibujos de esta noticia que tiene en su parte. Después "B" narra "Lulú Camacho" y "A" ordena y numera los dibujos de su parte.

A

La bomba

1. terrorista / poner / bomba / aeropuerto
2. terrorista / llamar / policía
3. policía / manejar / aeropuerto
4. personas / salir / aeropuerto
5. perros / encontrar / bomba
6. policía / poder detener / terrorista

Lulú Camacho

There are several possible ways to number the drawings for the story of Lulu Camacho.

B

Lulú Camacho

1. Lulú Camacho / recibir / título de Miss Cuerpo
2. anoche / llorar de alegría
3. dar / las gracias / a sus padres, etc.
4. perder / título
5. su agente / decir / que / tomar / esteroides / la semana pasada
6. Lulú / preferir / no hacer comentarios

La bomba

Nuevos horizontes

Estrategia de lectura: *Reading for Main Ideas and Supporting Evidence*

As you saw in Chapter 3, when skimming you read quickly to find only the main ideas of a text. If the topic interests you, you may want to learn more about it, that is, read the evidence that supports the topic in question. Main ideas are usually found in the first sentence of a paragraph, and the supporting evidence is found in successive sentences.

You will have a chance to practice identifying main ideas and supporting evidence when you read the selection.

Actividad 14: Mira y contesta

Antes de leer el texto, contesta las siguientes preguntas.

1. Mira las fotos en la página 186. ¿Son construcciones modernas?
2. ¿En tu opinión, cuál es la conexión entre las fotos y el título del texto?
3. Se dice que para entender el presente hay que mirar el pasado. ¿Estás de acuerdo con esta idea? En tu opinión, ¿qué cosas de la historia de un país son importantes para entender el presente?

Actividad 15: Ideas principales y detalles

1. En una hoja aparte *(separate sheet)*, prepara un esquema como el siguiente, pero más grande.

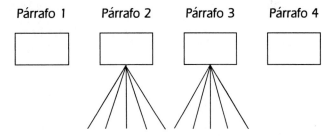

2. Lee el texto rápidamente y busca las cuatro ideas principales que se presentan. Pon cada idea en la caja *(box)* correspondiente.
3. Ahora, lee el texto otra vez y busca los detalles que apoyan *(support)* las ideas de los párrafos dos y tres y escríbelos en las líneas que salen de las cajas. Por ejemplo, un detalle del párrafo dos es la construcción de puentes.

España: Una historia variada

El estudio de las diferentes civilizaciones que vivieron en España nos ayuda a entender no solamente a los españoles sino también a los habitantes de todos los países hispanoamericanos, porque estos países recibieron, de algún modo, influencias de la "madre patria".

Una de las culturas que más influyó en España fue la cultura romana. Durante seis siglos, II a.C. - V d.C., España fue la provincia más importante del Imperio Romano. Los romanos introdujeron la base del sistema educativo actual[1]: escuela primaria, secundaria y escuelas profesionales. Su influencia fue muy importante en la lengua y la religión:

Bring in pictures of Spain: Sagunto, Mérida, Tarragona, etc. to show Roman ruins; Córdoba, Granada, Sevilla, etc. to show the Moorish influence. You may also want to show Visigothic and Jewish influences; or U.S. influence in present-day Spain: McDonalds, Wendy's, music stores, TV, jeans, etc.

a.C. = antes de Cristo
d.C. = después de Cristo

---

1. present

(izquierda) Alcázar de Segovia, España. (derecha) Acueducto romano, Segovia, España.

más o menos el 70% del idioma español proviene de su lengua, el latín, y los romanos también llevaron a España la religión cristiana. Los romanos construyeron anfiteatros, puentes, como el puente de Salamanca, que todavía se usa, y acueductos como el Acueducto de Segovia, que se hizo hace dos mil años y se usó hasta mediados de los años setenta de este siglo.

Otra influencia importante en España fue la de los moros, árabes del norte de África que vivieron principalmente en el sur de España por unos ocho siglos (711–1492). Ellos llevaron a España el concepto del "cero", el álgebra y su idioma, el árabe, que también influyó en el español. Esta influencia se ve en palabras como **alcohol, álgebra,** y **algodón**. Los moros fundaron ciudades esplendorosas como Granada y Córdoba. En esta última, instalaron la primera escuela de científicos donde se hizo cirugía cerebral. Los moros dejaron en España algo más: el aspecto físico que tienen muchos españoles, en especial los que viven en el sur (morenos, bajos, de pelo negro).

En 1492 los Reyes Católicos (Fernando de Aragón e Isabel de Castilla) lograron expulsar[2] a los moros de España y unificaron el país política y religiosamente. Al terminar la guerra con los moros, los reyes pudieron utilizar el dinero de España para financiar los viajes de los conquistadores al Nuevo Mundo, empezando con el viaje de Cristóbal Colón. Los viajes de Colón iniciaron una época de exploración y dominación española en el Nuevo Mundo y, al extender su poder por América, los españoles transmitieron el idioma español, su cultura y la religión cristiana.

2. **lograron . . .** managed to expel

Actividad 16: Completa las oraciones

Después de leer el texto, completa las siguientes oraciones usando información de la lectura. Hay varias posibilidades.

1. Para los países hispanoamericanos, la "madre patria" es . . .
2. Algo importante que introdujeron los romanos . . .
3. Hace cinco siglos que . . .
4. Una de las ciudades fundadas por los moros . . .
5. Los Reyes Católicos . . .
6. Los conquistadores . . .

Estrategia de escritura: *Writing a Paragraph*

A paragraph consists of a topic sentence and supporting sentences. The topic sentence usually appears first and introduces the theme of the text. The sentences that follow give additional or supporting information. As you saw in **Actividad 15,** the main idea of the second paragraph was the Roman influence in Spain. Examples of supporting sentences were those about the introduction of the educational system and the construction of bridges.

Actividad 17: Tu herencia familiar

Escribe un párrafo sobre el aspecto de tu herencia biológica, histórica o cultural que más influye en tu vida y explica por qué. Usa la información que acabas de leer sobre la estructura de un párrafo para presentar tus ideas de forma clara.

Act. 17: Remind students to identify the main idea and to give supporting evidence. Clarity in writing should be stressed. Have students peer edit first for content and then for grammar and vocabulary.

Lo esencial

I. Ask students when was the last time they flew and whether the plane left late or on time.

I. En el aeropuerto

Llegadas internacionales

Línea Aérea	Número de vuelo	Procedencia	Hora de llegada	Comentarios
Iberia	952	Lima	09:50	a tiempo
VIASA	354	Santo Domingo	10:29	11:05
LAN Chile	988	Santiago/Miami	12:45	a tiempo
Lacsa	904	México/N.Y.	14:00	14:35

Note the use of the 24-hour clock.

LLEGADAS

Salidas internacionales

Línea Aérea	Número de vuelo	Destino	Hora de salida	Comentarios	Puerta	S A L I D A S
TWA	750	San Juan	10:55	1115	2	
Avianca	615	Bogotá	11:40	a tiempo	3	
VIASA	357	Miami/N.Y.	14:20	a tiempo	7	
Aeroméxico	511	México	15:00	1605	9	

Act 18: 1. **11:05**   2. **Lacsa; hay retraso**   3. **Lima**   4. **11:40**
5. **3; no hay retraso**
6. **Bogotá**

Actividad 18: Información

En parejas, una persona necesita información sobre vuelos y la otra persona trabaja en el aeropuerto. Miren la información previa sobre los vuelos y usen preguntas como las siguientes.

1. ¿A qué hora llega el vuelo número 354 de Santo Domingo?
2. ¿De qué línea aérea es el vuelo 904? ¿Llega a tiempo o hay retraso?
3. ¿De dónde viene el vuelo 952?
4. ¿A qué hora sale el vuelo 615 para Bogotá?
5. ¿De qué puerta sale? ¿Hay retraso?
6. ¿Adónde va el vuelo 615 de Avianca?

II. Some synonyms for **pasaje:** **billete** (Spain), **boleto** (Mexico).

In **Lo esencial**, active vocabulary words are in blue.

II. El pasaje

Su pasaje de ida y vuelta **está confirmado.**
Puede llevar dos maletas y un bolso de mano
pero hay un límite de 64 kilos.

Ask students, ¿Qué prefieres, la sección de fumadores o de no fumadores? ¿Un asiento en el pasillo o al lado de la ventana? ¿Vuelos directos o con escalas? Para ir de *[your city]* a *[another city]*, ¿hay que hacer escala o hay vuelos directos?

Discuss customs: the type of questions you are asked, what you can bring into the country, and what you can't.

```
IDA
VIASA 357 de Caracas a Nueva York
    Salida de Caracas: 14:20 26/VIII/91
      Escala y aduana en Miami
    Llegada a Nueva York (JFK):
  22:15 26/VIII/91

VUELTA
VIASA 358 de Nueva York a Caracas
    Salida de Nueva York (JFK) 13:15 1/IX/91
      Escala en Miami
    Llegada a Caracas 21:00 1/IX/91
Aduana en Caracas
```

Actividad 19: ¿Qué es?

Usando el vocabulario del pasaje del Sr. Vega, contesta estas preguntas.

1. ¿Qué significa "pasaje de ida y vuelta"?
2. ¿Cómo se dice en español *a one-way ticket*?
3. ¿Tiene el Sr. Vega un vuelo directo o con escala?
4. ¿Cuántas maletas puede llevar el Sr. Vega? ¿Cuántos kilos como máximo?
5. ¿Cuál es el número del asiento del Sr. Vega? ¿Fuma él? ¿Qué prefieres tú, la sección de fumar o de no fumar?
6. ¿Sabes qué cosas no se pueden pasar por la aduana?
7. ¿Hay aduanas en aeropuertos que no son internacionales? ¿En cuáles de estos aeropuertos hay aduanas: La Guardia, Newark o Kennedy?

Actividad 20: La reserva

En parejas, Uds. están en México en una agencia de viajes. El/La estudiante "A" es el/la cliente que habla con el/la estudiante "B", un/a agente de viajes. Lean el papel que les corresponde y mantengan una conversación en la agencia.

A

Necesitas viajar de México a Lima el 23 de diciembre para volver el 2 de enero. No puedes salir por la mañana. No quieres hacer escala. No fumas. Necesitas saber la aerolínea, la hora de salida y de llegada y el precio.

B

De México a Lima hay vuelos de Mexicana y AeroPerú. AeroPerú hace escala en Bogotá y sale por la tarde. Mexicana sale por la mañana y vuela directo. Necesitas saber si el/la cliente quiere un pasaje de ida y vuelta, las fechas y si fuma.

Un día normal en el aeropuerto

darse cuenta de algo	to realize something
No me di cuenta de la hora.	I didn't realize the time.
¿Cómo que . . . ?	What do you mean . . . ?
¿Cómo que no hay nada?	What do you mean there isn't anything?

Antes de regresar a España Teresa va a la República Dominicana para trabajar por una semana en el aeropuerto. Ahora Teresa está ayudando en el mostrador *(check-in counter)* del aeropuerto de Santo Domingo y habla con algunos pasajeros *(passengers)* que salen hacia Miami; como siempre, hay problemas.

Actividad 21: ¿Cierto o falso?

Escucha las conversaciones y marca si estas oraciones son ciertas o falsas.

1. ___F___ El señor es paciente.
2. ___F___ El señor fuma.
3. ___C___ El niño viaja solo.
4. ___F___ Al final, el niño no lleva el ron.
5. ___F___ La señora perdió el pasaje.
6. ___C___ La señora llegó con un día de retraso.

Aeropuerto internacional, Buenos Aires, Argentina.

Expressing how long an action has been taking place

Apologizing

Tell students that in some countries it is possible for children to purchase alcoholic beverages for their families. A 12-year-old Hispanic child may be sent to buy wine, just as an American child is sent to buy milk.

Giving a reason

Narrating a series of past actions

After listening to the dialogue, ask students, **¿Cómo son físicamente el señor, el niño, la madre y la señora? Usen la imaginación.**

Teresa	Siguiente, por favor.
Señor	¡Por fin! Hace media hora que estoy en esta fila. Aquí está el pasaje, mi pasaporte, la maleta y quiero un asiento en la sección de no fumar.
Teresa	Lo siento, pero no hay nada.
Señor	¿Cómo que no hay nada?
Teresa	Perdón señor, pero es tarde y sólo hay asiento en la sección de fumadores. ¡Que tenga buen viaje!
Señor	Pues, va a ser difícil tener un buen viaje . . .
Teresa	Siguiente.
Madre	Aquí está el pasaje y el pasaporte de mi hijo, Ramoncito.
Teresa	¿Y su hijo viaja solo o con Ud.?
Madre	Solo, pero lo espera su tío Ramón en Miami. Yo regreso a casa.
Niño	Mamá, ¿dónde pongo las botellas de ron?
Madre	Las llevas en la mano.
Teresa	Pero señora, su hijo no puede entrar en los Estados Unidos con alcohol porque no tiene veintiún años.
Madre	Pero no lo va a beber él; es para su tío.
Teresa	Señora, tiene que darse cuenta de que es ilegal.
Madre	¡Bueno! Las ponemos en el bolso de mano. Ramoncito, si te preguntan en la aduana qué llevas, ¿qué les dices?
Niño	Les digo que no llevo nada, que no hay ron.
Teresa	Siguiente.
Señora	Por fin llegué. Es que estaba en la peluquería y no me di cuenta de la hora y es que vine en taxi y el taxista manejó muy rápidamente. Casi tuvimos un accidente, ¡qué nervios! Y luego dejé la maleta en el taxi. Tuve que hablar con un policía, muy simpático por cierto . . .
Teresa	Su pasaje y pasaporte, por favor.
Señora	Sí, aquí están . . . bueno el policía muy simpático . . .
Teresa	Ejem . . . señora, lo siento pero su vuelo salió hace 24 horas . . .

Actividad 22: Los problemas de los pasajeros

Después de escuchar las conversaciones, identifica cuáles son los problemas del señor, del niño y su madre y de la señora.

Hacia la comunicación

Gramática

Remember: Direct objects indicate *what* or *who* receives the action of the verb.

I. Point out that direct-object pronouns are the same as indirect-object pronouns except for third-person forms.

Elicit the placement rule for reflexive and indirect-object pronouns so students can apply it to direct-object pronouns.

Although **leísmo** may be seen in realia, it will not be practiced in this text.

Contrast **lo escribí** *(I wrote it)* with **le escribí,** *(I wrote him/her/you).*

Drill direct-object pronouns:
1. Demonstrate the use of the direct object by putting masculine, feminine, singular, and plural objects in front of a student and asking, **¿La tienes?** Have a student hold up an object and say, **Sí, la tengo.**
2. Ask students which of the following sentences contains a direct object: (a) **Voy a ir al parque.** (b) **Voy a visitar a mi abuelo.** (c) **Me gusta la música.** (d) **Te necesito; ¿puedes venir ahora?**
3. Send a student out of the room and give his/her belongings to other students to hide. To get things back, he/she must ask questions. S1: **¿Tienes mi mochila?** S2: **No, no la tengo.** (etc.)

I. Using the Direct Object

Before studying the grammar explanation, answer these questions based on the dialogue:

- To what do the boldfaced words in the following sentences refer?
  a. "**Las** llevas en la mano."   b. "**Lo** espera su tío . . ."
  c. "Pero no **lo** va a beber él . . ."

- Do the preceding words in boldface perform the action indicated by the verb?

- In the sentence "**. . .¿dónde pongo las botellas . . .?**" the noun phrase **las botellas** is not the subject but the object. If you had to replace this noun phrase with a pronoun, where in the sentence would you place it?

A direct object names the person or thing that directly receives the action of the verb. In Spanish, the direct object may be expressed by the direct-object pronoun. It follows the same placement rules as the reflexive and the indirect-object pronouns.

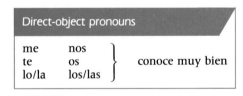

Direct-object pronouns		
me	nos	
te	os	conoce muy bien
lo/la	los/las	

Me gustó el vestido y **lo** compré.

Juan Carlos está enamorado de Claudia; **la** quiere muchísimo.

The following verbs can take direct objects.

amar	to love	**odiar**	to hate
ayudar	to help	**poner**	to put
creer	to believe	**querer**	to want; to love
esperar	to wait for; to hope	**tener**	to have
invitar	to invite	**ver**	to see
necesitar	to need	**visitar**	to visit

—¿Dónde pusiste el pasaje?   *Where did you put the ticket?*
—**Lo** puse en la maleta.   *I put it in the suitcase.*

II. You may want to mention that *verb in the present* + **desde hace** + *time expression* indicates the same idea.

Las invité a mi casa.	*I invited them to my home.*
Nuestros padres **nos** quieren.	*Our parents love us.*

II. Expressing the Duration of an Action: *Hace* + time expression + *que* + verb in the present

To express the duration of an action that began in the past and continues into the present, apply the following formula:

Hace + time expression + **que** + verb in the present

Do mechanical drills, Workbook, Part II.

—¿Cuánto (tiempo) hace que vives aquí?	*How long have you lived here?*
—**Hace tres años que vivo** aquí.	*I have lived here for three years.*

Actividad 23: Las cosas para el viaje

Drill **hace** + time expression + **que** + verb in the present:
1. Contrast: **Hace 5 años que como en este restaurante.** / **Hace 5 años que comí en este restaurante.**
2. Have students brainstorm things they began in the past and are still doing. In pairs, have them ask their partners questions: **¿Hace cuánto tiempo que ... ?**

En parejas, una persona es el esposo y la otra es su esposa. Van a hacer un viaje y quieren saber dónde puso su pareja las siguientes cosas. Altérnense haciendo preguntas.

A: ¿Dónde pusiste el radio?
B: Lo puse en la maleta.

Cosas: champú, gafas de sol, trajes de baño, máquina de afeitar, peine, zapatos de tenis, cepillo de dientes, pasaporte, regalos, niño
Lugares: la maleta, el carro, el bolso de mano

Actividad 24: Las cosas de tu compañero

En parejas, averigüen si su compañero/a tiene estas cosas y cuánto hace que las tiene: estéreo, carro, bicicleta, radio, apartamento, motocicleta, computadora, guitarra, novio/a, problemas, etc.

A: ¿Tienes grabadora?
B: Sí, tengo. / No, no tengo.
A: ¿Cuánto tiempo hace que la tienes?
B: Hace cinco años que la tengo.

Actividad 25: Romeo y Julieta

Act. 25: If your students enjoy exaggerated dramatization, have the women stand on chairs and the men kneel to simulate the balcony scene.

Have a few groups perform for the class.

En parejas, inventen un diálogo romántico entre los protagonistas de una telenovela *(soap opera)*: María Julieta y José Romeo. Usen en la conversación un mínimo de tres de estos verbos en oraciones o preguntas: **querer, necesitar, odiar, creer** y **esperar.**

José Romeo: María Julieta, te quiero.
María Julieta: Yo también te quiero, pero mi padre te odia.

Actividad 26: Los anuncios comerciales

En grupos de tres, imagínense que Uds. trabajan para una agencia de publicidad. Tienen que escribir anuncios *(ads)* para estos productos.

▶ el agua de colonia "Atracción": Hace un año que uso el agua de colonia "Atracción" y ahora tengo muchos amigos.

1. el jabón para la cara "Radiante"
2. el champú para hombres "Hércules"
3. el jabón de ropa "Blancanieves"
4. el perfume "Gloria"
5. el desodorante "Frescura Segura"

Actividad 27: El contestador automático

En parejas, Uds. tienen un contestador automático *(answering machine)* para la oficina de reclamos *(complaints office)* de una tienda. Los clientes llaman para quejarse de las cosas que compraron. Hagan el mensaje *(outgoing message)* en el que deben preguntarle al/a la cliente la siguiente información.

1. nombre del/de la cliente
2. teléfono
3. qué producto / comprar
4. cuánto (tiempo) hace
5. qué problema / tener
6. cómo / ocurrir

Terminen el mensaje con la frase "espere el tono antes de hablar".

Actividad 28: El problema

En parejas, una persona es el/la cliente que llama a la oficina de reclamos de esta tienda porque tiene problemas con algo que compró. Quiere dejar un mensaje describiendo su problema. La otra persona es el contestador automático.

Actividad 29: Conoce a tu compañero/a

En parejas, el/la estudiante "A" cubre la Parte B y el/la estudiante "B" cubre la Parte A. Lean sus instrucciones y completen el dibujo con la información necesaria. Al terminar, miren las respuestas de su compañero/a y háganle preguntas sobre lo que escribió.

A

1. En la línea que está arriba del triángulo, escribe el nombre y el apellido de la persona que te dio el primer beso *(first kiss)*.
2. En la línea que está abajo del rectángulo, escribe qué quieres para tu cumpleaños este año.
3. En el rectángulo, escribe el nombre de un político importante.

Act.'s 27, 28: Have students brainstorm complaints people may have. When doing Act. 28, have students use the outgoing message from Act. 27. If possible, tape the outgoing message and have the clients tape the incoming message.

Act. 29: Give students ample time to discuss their answers. Supply any needed vocabulary.

4. En la línea que está abajo del triángulo, escribe el nombre de una ciudad donde no quisieras vivir nunca.
5. En el triángulo, escribe cuánto cuesta tu carro ideal.
6. En la línea que está arriba del rectángulo, escribe el año en que empezaste a leer.
7. En el círculo, escribe tu nombre.
8. En las líneas que salen del círculo, escribe cuatro adjetivos que te describen.

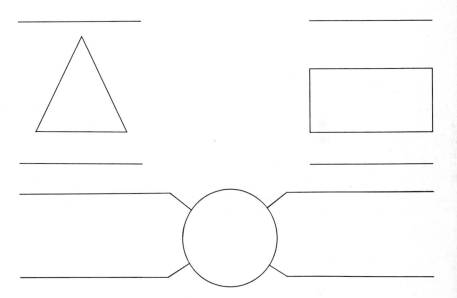

B
1. En la línea que está arriba del triángulo, escribe el nombre de tu actor o actriz favorito/a.
2. En la línea que está abajo del rectángulo, escribe una cosa que no te gustaría tener nunca.
3. En el rectángulo, escribe el nombre y el apellido de una persona que tuvo mucha influencia en tu vida.
4. En la línea que está abajo del triángulo, escribe el nombre de una ciudad que te gustaría conocer.
5. En el triángulo, escribe cuántos hijos quisieras tener.
6. En la línea que está arriba del rectángulo, escribe el año en que entraste en la universidad.
7. En el círculo, escribe tu nombre.
8. En las líneas que salen del círculo, escribe cuatro adjetivos que no te describen.

Vocabulario funcional

El hotel

el baño   bathroom
el botones   bellboy
la comida   meal
el desayuno   breakfast
la empleada (de servicio)   maid
la habitación doble   double room
la habitación sencilla   single room

media pensión   breakfast and one meal included
pensión completa   all meals included
la recepción   front desk
el/la recepcionista   receptionist

El teléfono

¿Aló?/Diga/Dígame   Hello?
¿De parte de quién?   Can I ask who is calling?
(De parte) de . . .   It/This is . . .
¿Está . . ., por favor?   Is . . . there, please?
Habla . . .   It/This is . . .
llamada a cobro revertido   collect call
llamada local   local call
marcar directo   to dial direct

No, tiene el número equivocado.   No, you have the wrong number.
¿Puede hablar más despacio, por favor?   Can you speak more slowly, please?
¿Quién habla?   Who is speaking/calling?
Quisiera hablar con . . ., por favor.   I would like to speak with . . ., please.

Verbos

amar   to love
ayudar   to help
construir   to build
creer   to believe
esperar   to wait (for); to hope (for)
invitar   to invite
manejar   to drive
mentir (ie, i)   to lie

morir/se (ue, u)   to die
odiar   to hate
oír   to hear
producir   to produce
repetir (i, i)   to repeat
seguir (i, i)   to follow
sentir/se (ie, i)   to feel

El aeropuerto

a tiempo   on time
la aduana   customs
el asiento   seat
el bolso/bolso de mano   purse/hand luggage
el destino   destination; destiny
hacer escala   to make a stop
la hora de llegada   time of arrival
la hora de salida   time of departure
ida y vuelta   round trip

la línea aérea (aerolínea)   airline
la maleta   suitcase
las maletas/el equipaje   luggage
el pasaje   (plane) ticket
el/la pasajero/a   passenger
la puerta (de salida) número . . .   gate number . . .
el retraso   delay
la sección de (no) fumar   (no) smoking section
el vuelo   flight

Palabras afirmativas y negativas

Ver página 181

Palabras y expresiones útiles

¿Cómo que . . .? What do you mean . . . ?
darse cuenta de algo to realize something
Lo siento. I'm sorry.

por fin at last
Perdimos el autobús. We missed the bus.
quisiera/quisiéramos I/We would like

¿Hay oficinas o aparta-
mentos en este edificio?
¿Cómo sabes?

Edificio en el pueblo de Castro
Urdiales, provincia de
Cantabria, España.

Capítulo 8

Chapter Objectives

After studying this chapter you will know how to:

- describe the layout of a house and its furnishings
- describe household items you want to buy
- express preferences, advise, and make requests
- indicate sequence

¿Hay patios como éste en el estado donde vives? ¿Qué diferencia hay entre la palabra "patio" en inglés y en español?

Discuss the importance of the inner patio.

Típico patio andaluz, Córdoba, España. El patio está en el centro y es el corazón de la casa.

Buscando apartamento

Portero de un edificio de apartamentos en Colombia.

¡Vaya!	Wow!
o sea	that is

In Spain, **piso** = large apartment or condominium; **apartamento** is a similar space but smaller. In various Latin American countries, **condominio/propiedad horizontal** = condominium (in ads), but people refer to their condos as **apartamentos** or **departamentos**.

While discussing the **portero**, you may want to mention the defunct institution of the **sereno** and the security they gave to a neighborhood.

Las cinco chicas buscan apartamento porque el colegio mayor se cierra en el mes de agosto durante las vacaciones. Ahora están hablando Diana, Marisel y Teresa sobre qué tipo de apartamento quieren.

Actividad 1: Marca qué buscan

Escucha la conversación y marca qué cosas buscan las chicas en un apartamento.

dormitorios	2 ③ 4		aire acondicionado	sí (no)
teléfono	(sí) no		balcón	(sí) no
patio	sí (no)		muchas ventanas	sí (no)
muebles	sí (no)		cocina grande	(sí) no
portero	(sí) no			

Describing what you are looking for

Marisel	Entonces necesitamos un apartamento que tenga tres dormitorios.
Teresa	También debemos tener una cocina grande porque cocinamos mucho.
Marisel	Y es muy importante que tenga teléfono porque, claro, Teresa y Claudia tienen que hablar con sus novios . . .
Diana	Recuerden que el apartamento debe ser barato, y ¿no lo queremos amueblado?
Teresa	No, sin muebles porque mi tío tiene muebles de segunda mano que podemos usar. O sea, tres dormitorios, cocina grande, teléfono y barato. ¿Algo más?
Marisel	Sí, que tenga portero.
Diana	¿Por qué?

Giving a reason

Marisel	Porque un portero es una ayuda enorme. Limpia la entrada, recibe las cartas, saca la basura, abre la puerta y además es el policía del edificio.
Diana	¡Qué curioso! En mi país no hay muchos porteros. Generalmente hay teléfonos para abrir la puerta.
Teresa	En Puerto Rico también tenemos teléfono: el intercomunicador. Sólo los apartamentos más caros tienen portero.
Marisel	Aquí en España también hay teléfono y se le llama portero automático. Se usa por la tarde o por la noche cuando el portero no está.

Expressing preference

Teresa	Prefiero tener portero porque normalmente vive en el edificio y, si tienes problemas, siempre está para ayudarte.

Expressing a desire

Diana	Y a mí me gustaría tener balcón.
Marisel	Si tiene balcón no debe estar en el primer piso porque puede entrar alguien de la calle fácilmente.
Diana	¡Vaya! Entonces buscamos un apartamento que esté en un segundo piso o más alto, con tres dormitorios, balcón, teléfono, una cocina grande, con portero y que sea barato. ¡Uf! ¡No pedimos nada!

In most Hispanic countries, **la planta baja/el bajo** = first or ground floor; **el primer piso** = second floor.

Actividad 2: ¿Comprendiste?

Después de escuchar la conversación, contesta estas preguntas.

1. ¿Cuáles son dos cosas importantes para Diana, para Teresa y para Marisel?
2. ¿Qué es un portero? ¿Es común tener portero en Puerto Rico? ¿Y en los Estados Unidos? ¿Te gustaría vivir en un edificio con portero?
3. Cuando Diana dice, "¡No pedimos nada!", ¿quiere decir que va a ser fácil o difícil encontrar apartamento?
4. ¿Prefieres vivir en un apartamento o en una residencia estudiantil?

Apartamento = departamento (some Latin American countries).

¿Lo sabían?

Cuando se busca apartamento en un país hispano, a veces las necesidades son diferentes de las de los Estados Unidos. En un país hispano es usual tener portero automático; también es común tener portero en los edificios. Asimismo en los Estados Unidos nadie se preocupa si hay línea de teléfono o no porque es fácil instalarla, pero en muchos países hispanos hay que esperar meses y cuesta mucho dinero obtener una línea de teléfono. Entonces, es importante encontrar un apartamento que tenga teléfono. ¿Te imaginas viviendo en un apartamento sin teléfono?

Act. 3: Discuss how these priorities might be different in another culture.

Actividad 3: ¿Qué prefieren Uds.?

En grupos de cinco, decidan cuáles son las cosas más importantes para Uds. en un apartamento. Clasifiquen las siguientes cosas en una escala de uno a tres. Después informen al resto de la clase.

(1) no es importante   (2) es importante   (3) es muy importante

_____ el número de dormitorios   _____ la parte de la ciudad en
_____ que sea barato   que esté
_____ que tenga teléfono   _____ que tenga garaje
_____ que tenga balcón   _____ que tenga cocina grande
_____ que esté amueblado   _____ el piso en que esté
_____ que tenga portero

Lo esencial

I. Discuss abbreviations: 1er, 2°, 2ª.

Ask students what floor they live on.

I.   Los números ordinales

1°	primero	6°	sexto
2°	segundo	7°	séptimo
3°	tercero	8°	octavo
4°	cuarto	9°	noveno
5°	quinto	10°	décimo

1. Ordinal numbers are used to refer to things such as floor numbers, grade levels in elementary school, and finishing positions in races. It is not common to use ordinal numbers above **décimo**; cardinal numbers are used instead.

Felipe II (segundo) construyó El Escorial.
BUT: Alfonso XIII (trece) murió en 1941.

Felipe II and Alfonso XIII are former Spanish kings. Alfonso XIII is the grandfather of the present king, Juan Carlos I.

2. The ordinal numbers agree in gender and number with the nouns they modify. **Primero** and **tercero** drop the final **o** when modifying a masculine singular noun.

Ella vive en el **primer** apartamento del **tercer** piso.
La esquiadora chilena llegó **primera**.

Actividad 4: La carrera de ciclismo

En una carrera *(race)* de ciclismo este fin de semana participaron seis ciclistas de Hispanoamérica. En parejas, lean las pistas *(clues)* y adivinen el número de llegada (primero, segundo, etc.), nombre, nacionalidad y color de camiseta de cada ciclista.

1. Claudio Vardi, con camiseta roja, es de un país suramericano.
2. El uruguayo llegó en tercer lugar.
3. El hombre de la camiseta amarilla se llama Augusto Terranova y no es uruguayo.
4. El colombiano que llegó primero tiene una camiseta roja.
5. Hernando Calasa, con camiseta morada, no llegó cuarto.
6. Francisco Lara, que tiene camiseta azul, es el único que no es suramericano.
7. Silvio Scala, de nacionalidad chilena, llegó justo después del boliviano de camiseta amarilla.
8. El peruano de camiseta morada llegó último.
9. El guatemalteco llegó justo después del colombiano.
10. La camiseta del uruguayo Marcelo Ruso es verde y no negra como la del ciclista chileno.

La Vuelta a España empezará en Tenerife y terminará en Madrid.

When the **vueltas** are taking place they are as popular as the World Series baseball championship in the U.S.

Ask students if they know the name of the American who won the Tour de France in 1989. (Greg LeMond)

¿Lo sabían?

El ciclismo es un deporte muy popular en muchos países y cada año hay carreras internacionales de bicicletas. Quizás las más interesantes sean las de Colombia y España, no sólo por la habilidad de los participantes sino también porque son muy difíciles, pues hay muchas montañas. La carrera más importante del mundo es la Vuelta a Francia que tiene lugar todos los años en el mes de julio. En 1985, Fabio Parra de Colombia ganó la carrera y en 1988, la ganó Pedro Delgado de España. Los ciclistas hispanos se encuentran entre los mejores del mundo. ¿Sabes los nombres de algunos ciclistas norteamericanos?

II. Las habitaciones de la casa

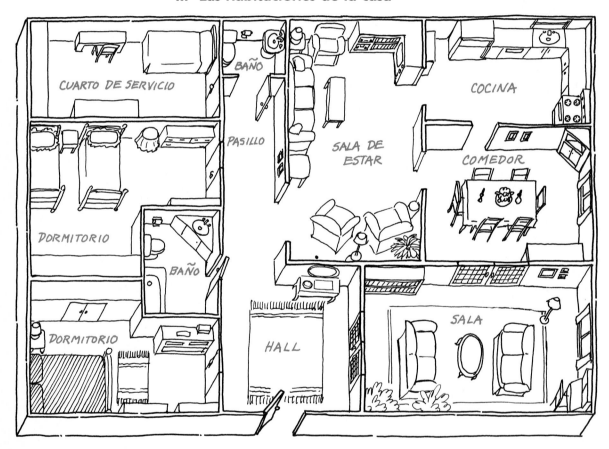

Dormitorio = habitación, alcoba, cuarto, recámara.

II. In small groups, have students design the interior layout of a house.

Actividad 5: ¿Cómo es tu casa?

En grupos de tres, cada persona les describe la casa de su familia a sus compañeros. Digan si es grande o pequeña, qué tipo de habitaciones hay, cuántos dormitorios, etc., y si tiene alguna característica especial.

Actividad 6: Pidiendo información

En grupos de tres, los estudiantes "A" y "B" están estudiando en Madrid por un semestre y necesitan alquilar *(to rent)* un apartamento. El/La estudiante "C" es un/a amigo/a y les dice que hay un apartamento para alquilar en su edificio. "A" y "B" quieren información sobre el apartamento y le hacen preguntas a "C". Lean sólo las instrucciones para su papel.

● URB EL ALAMO: Mirador para matrimonio, amueblado, agua, luz, teléfono. $600. Apto Estudio para 1 persona, amuebl., agua, luz, tel. $325. Tels. **789-6600, 790-1322**

● URB.MUÑOZ RIVERA: Estudio. Persona sola. Incluye agua, luz, nevera, estufa, parking. Renta $225. mensual. Inf.: **789-1809**

SANTIAGO IGLESIAS: Cómodo apt. Incluye agua y luz, nevera, estufa. Para información llamar 783-7174.

HATO REY: Amueblado, 1 dorm. y sala-com., parking privado con portón electrónico. Guayama 136. Incluye luz-agua. $375. 765-0045.

UNIVERSITY GDNS: Céntrico, remodelado, 1 hab., sala, comedor, coc. equip., patio, marq., abanicos techo, agua, luz. $450. **789-8792**

Act. 6: Point out that frequently bills are paid at a bank, not by mailing a check.

"A" y "B" quieren saber:

1. cuánto es el alquiler
2. si hay fianza (depósito)
3. si está amueblado
4. si hay calefacción
5. si hay teléfono
6. si hay otros gastos *(expenses)*, como gas, agua y luz (electricidad)

"C" sabe:

1. el alquiler es 58.000 ptas. al mes
2. un mes de fianza (depósito)
3. está amueblado (con muebles viejos)
4. hay calefacción central
5. hay teléfono
6. los gastos *(expenses)* incluyen gas, agua y luz (electricidad)

Hacia la comunicación

Gramática

An independent clause can stand alone as a complete sentence: *I'm looking for a house.* A dependent clause cannot stand alone: *... that has a garage.*

Remember: the subjunctive forms are normally in dependent clauses and are therefore almost always preceded by **que.**

Talking About the Unknown: The Present Subjunctive

Before studying the grammar explanation, answer these questions based on the dialogue:

● When Marisel says, **"Necesitamos un apartamento que tenga tres dormitorios,"** is she describing an apartment she has seen?

● The word **tenga** is used in two other instances in the dialogue. Is it used to describe what the women are looking for or what they have found?

Up to now, you have used the verbs in the indicative mood. There is another verbal mood called the subjunctive, which is used to express things such as doubt, uncertainty, hope, possibility, influence, and lack of existence. Subjunctive constructions contain both an independent and a dependent clause. The independent clause contains the verb in the indicative and the dependent clause contains the verb in the subjunctive. The two clauses are usually linked by the word **que.**

Buscamos un apartamento **que** tenga teléfono.
independent clause   dependent clause
(indicative)   (subjunctive)

A. Forms of the Present Subjunctive

1. To conjugate a verb in the subjunctive, apply the following rules:

 a. take the present indicative **yo** form: **hablo, como, salgo**
 b. drop the **-o** from the verb ending: **habl-, com-, salg-**
 c. add **-e** for **-ar** verbs; add **-a** for
   -er and **-ir** verbs: habl**e**, com**a**, salg**a**
 d. add the endings for the other persons as shown in the following charts:

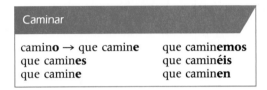

Caminar	
camin**o** → que camin**e**	que camin**emos**
que camin**es**	que camin**éis**
que camin**e**	que camin**en**

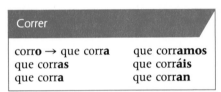

Correr	
corr**o** → que corr**a**	que corr**amos**
que corr**as**	que corr**áis**
que corr**a**	que corr**an**

Salir	
salg**o** → que salg**a**	que salg**amos**
que salg**as**	que salg**áis**
que salg**a**	que salg**an**

Note:
a. Verbs ending in **-car**, **-gar**, **-zar**, and **-ger** require spelling changes in all persons.

bus**car**   busco → que bus**que**   empe**zar**   empiezo → que empie**ce**
pa**gar**   pago → que pa**gue**   esco**ger**   escojo → que esco**ja**

b. Remember that reflexive pronouns precede a conjugated form: **que se levante, que se bañen.**

2. In the subjunctive, stem-changing verbs ending in **-ar** and **-er** have the same stem change as in the present indicative: **que yo piense, que él quiera, que nosotros almorcemos.** Stem-changing verbs ending in **-ir** have the same change in the stem as the present indicative, and **nosotros** and **vosotros** require a stem change from **e** to **i** or from **o** to **u**.

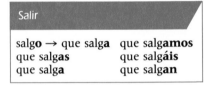

Mentir	
que m**ie**nta	que m**i**ntamos
que m**ie**ntas	que m**i**ntáis
que m**ie**nta	que m**ie**ntan

Dormir	
que d**ue**rma	que d**u**rmamos
que d**ue**rmas	que d**u**rmáis
que d**ue**rma	que d**ue**rman

Note: The subjunctive of **hay** is **haya.**

Haber will be presented in Ch. 13.

The accent distinguishes **dé,** the subjunctive, from **de,** the preposition. Accents on **estar** reflect pronunciation.

Review other word pairs with accents that change meaning: **sí/si, él/el, sólo/solo, más/mas.**

B. Drill subjunctive in adjective clauses:
1. Have students identify the antecedents in the examples given or in sentences you create.
2. Do male and female chain drills: **Busco un/a novio/a que ...**
3. Have students create sentences: **Tengo un carro que no funciona. Necesito un carro que funcione, pero que sea barato.**

Quechua is a language spoken by many Andean Indians. Basque is a language spoken in a region of northern Spain and in southwestern France. It is unrelated to other modern European languages.

Do mechanical drills, Workbook, Part I.

3. The following verbs are irregular in the present subjunctive:

dar → que **dé**	**estar** → que **esté**	**ser** → que **sea**
ir → que **vaya**	**saber** → que **sepa**	

Here is the complete conjugation of **dar** and **estar:**

Dar		Estar	
que d**é**	que d**emos**	que est**é**	que est**emos**
que d**es**	que d**eis**	que est**és**	que est**éis**
que d**é**	que d**en**	que est**é**	que est**én**

B. Using the Present Subjunctive

1. The subjunctive is used in dependent adjective clauses to describe something that may or may not exist.

¿Hay algún apartamento **que sea** grande?	*Is there an apartment (any apartment) that is big? (It may or may not exist.)*
Busco un apartamento **que tenga** balcón.	*I am looking for an apartment (any apartment) that has a balcony.*
Busco una persona **que sepa** hablar quechua.*	*I'm looking for a person (any person) who can speak Quechua.*

However, when you talk about something that you know exists, you use the indicative mood.

Vivo en un apartamento que **tiene** balcón.	*I live in an apartment that has a balcony. (I know it exists, where it is, what it looks like, etc.)*

*Note: The personal **a** is not used when the direct object refers to a person that may or may not exist, unless it is **alguien** or **nadie: Busco a *alguien* que sepa hablar quechua.**

2. The subjunctive is also used in adjective clauses to describe something that does not exist from the point of view of the speaker.

No hay ningún apartamento **que tenga** balcón.	*There are no apartments (not a one) with a balcony.*
No conozco a nadie **que hable** vasco en esta universidad.	*I don't know anyone at this university who speaks Basque.*

If something exists, use the indicative. If something may/may not exist, use the subjunctive.

Actividad 7: Por teléfono

En parejas, una persona busca apartamento y llama a una agencia de alquiler. La otra persona trabaja en la agencia y le da información.

▮◉▮ **A:** Busco un apartamento que tenga . . . que sea . . . que esté . . .
B: Tenemos un apartamento que tiene . . . que es . . . que está . . .

Nonexistence from the speaker's point of view = subjunctive.

Actividad 8: El eterno pesimista

Imagínate que eres una persona pesimista. Completa estas oraciones de forma original.

1. No hay nadie que . . .
2. No tengo nada que . . .
3. No conozco a nadie que . . .
4. El presidente no hace nada que . . .
5. En las tiendas no encuentro nada que . . .
6. No tengo ningún profesor que . . .

Act. 9: Explain the title: **Se busca** = wanted. Practice some questions before starting the activity.

Tell students to ask each person 1 question and then to move on to the next person. Set a time limit. Check by asking questions and by encouraging students to use the subjunctive when reporting back to the class: ¿**Hay alguien que sepa hablar catalán?** S1: **No, no hay nadie que sepa hablar catalán.**

Actividad 9: Se busca

Tienes cuatro minutos para encontrar personas que tengan o hagan las siguientes cosas.

▮◉▮ **A:** ¿Tienes dos hijos?
B: Sí, tengo dos hijos. / No, no tengo dos hijos.

1. que trabaje en un restaurante
2. que termine los estudios este año
3. que vaya a viajar a Bolivia este verano
4. que tenga tres hermanos
5. que sepa hablar catalán
6. que sea de Illinois
7. que hable japonés
8. que piense casarse este año
9. que tenga perro
10. que sepa preparar mole poblano

Catalán is a language spoken in **Cataluña** (northeastern Spain). Capital of **Cataluña**: Barcelona.

Mole poblano = a spicy Mexican sauce made with chocolate.

Act. 10: Have some pairs act out the conversation in front of the class.

Actividad 10: Los consejos

En parejas, una persona va a graduarse de escuela secundaria y busca una universidad para el año próximo. La otra persona es un/a consejero/a (counselor) de la escuela.

▮◉▮ **A:** Quiero/Busco una universidad que . . .
B: Hay muchas universidades que . . . (No hay ninguna universidad que . . .)
A: En Stanford, ¿tienen computadoras para los estudiantes?
B: . . .

Actividad 11: La perfección

En grupos de cuatro, describan a una persona ideal. El/La secretario/a del grupo toma apuntes *(takes notes)*. Después, comparen su descripción con las de otros grupos. Escojan uno de esta lista: profesor/a, doctor/a, secretario/a, padres o amigo/a.

|●| Queremos tener un profesor que . . .
    Buscamos un médico que . . .

Actividad 12: Bienvenidos a Radio Tienda

Uds. van a hacer un programa de radio de compra-venta de cosas de segunda mano. Cada persona tiene dos minutos para escribir la descripción de una cosa que quiere vender o comprar. Después, en parejas, mantengan una conversación telefónica. No olviden cambiar de papel.

|●| **A:** Bienvenido/a a Radio Tienda. ¿Compra o vende?
    B: Quiero comprar un televisor que tenga . . .

Actividad 13: Eso es lo que quiero

Ahora escoge algunas de las cosas que escuchaste en el programa Radio Tienda que te interesa comprar o vender y llama a la persona que ofreció o pidió ese producto.

|●| **A:** ¿Aló?
    B: Buenos días. Llamo porque tengo un televisor que tiene . . .

¿Lo sabían?

En los países hispanos no es común vender cosas de segunda mano delante de la casa o en el garaje *(tag or garage sales)*. Generalmente, la gente no vende la ropa de segunda mano sino que la regala a miembros de la familia, a la iglesia o a personas pobres. Cosas usadas como estéreos, computadoras y libros se anuncian en la sección de avisos clasificados del periódico o en revistas o periódicos especializados como *Segunda Mano*. ¿Conoces algún periódico como éste en los Estados Unidos?

COMPRA & VENTA ■ ANUNCIOS GRATIS

segundamano

Mercado entre Particulares
Todos los martes y viernes en su kiosco

del martes

Nº **502**

MADRID, 26 Julio 1988. 150 Pts.

Actividad 14: Se necesita

EE.UU. = Estados Unidos.

Lee estos anuncios y decide cuáles pueden combinarse. Después, en parejas, una persona llama para pedir más información y la otra da información adicional.

The infinitive is frequently used to give impersonal commands: **Llamar a Javier.**

| | **A:** ¿Aló? |
| | **B:** Sí, llamo por la moto . . . |

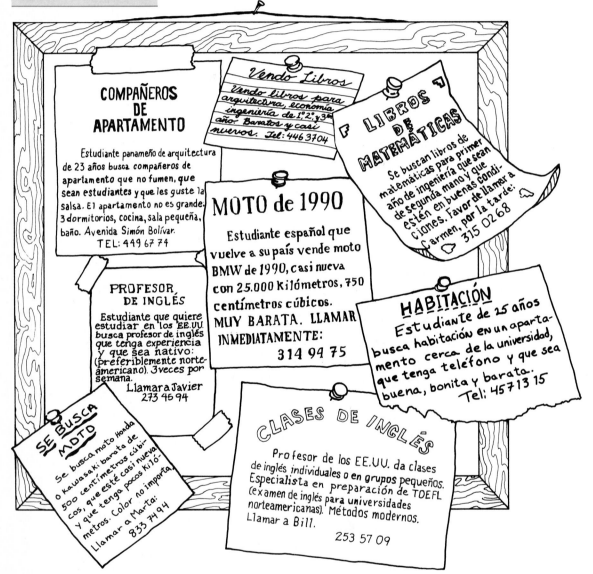

COMPAÑEROS DE APARTAMENTO

Estudiante panameño de arquitectura de 23 años busca compañeros de apartamento que no fumen, que sean estudiantes y que les guste la salsa. El apartamento no es grande: 3 dormitorios, cocina, sala pequeña, baño. Avenida Simón Bolívar.
TEL: 449 67 74

Vendo Libros

Vendo libros para arquitectura, economía, ingeniería de 1°, 2°, y 3° año. Baratos y casi nuevos. Tel: 446 3704

LIBROS DE MATEMÁTICAS

Se buscan libros de matemáticas para primer año de ingeniería que sean de segunda mano y que estén en buenas condiciones. Favor de llamar a Carmen, por la tarde: 315 0268

MOTO de 1990

Estudiante español que vuelve a su país vende moto BMW de 1990, casi nueva con 25.000 kilómetros, 750 centímetros cúbicos.
MUY BARATA. LLAMAR INMEDIATAMENTE:
314 94 75

PROFESOR DE INGLÉS

Estudiante que quiere estudiar en los EE.UU. busca profesor de inglés que tenga experiencia y que sea nativo (preferiblemente norteamericano). 3 veces por semana.
Llamar a Javier
273 45 94

HABITACIÓN

Estudiante de 25 años busca habitación en un apartamento cerca de la universidad, que tenga teléfono y que sea buena, bonita y barata.
Tel: 457 13 15

SE BUSCA MOTO

Se busca moto Honda o Kawasaki barata de 500 centímetros cúbicos, que esté casi nueva y que tenga pocos kilómetros. Color no importa. Llamar a Marta:
833 74 94

CLASES DE INGLÉS

Profesor de los EE.UU. da clases de inglés individuales o en grupos pequeños. Especialista en preparación de TOEFL (examen de inglés para universidades norteamericanas). Métodos modernos. Llamar a Bill.
253 57 09

Nuevos horizontes

Estrategia de lectura: *Using the Dictionary*

Although many of the words that you encounter when reading Spanish are cognates or are guessable from context, there are usually some words that require the use of a dictionary. The following guidelines will help you make better use of the dictionary.

a. Check the grammatical form of the word.
b. Try to guess its meaning from context.
c. Look up the word to confirm your guess. Remember that a word may have more than one meaning, so you should check the context in which it appears to make your choice.
d. If the word you are looking up is part of an idiom, you will find it referenced under the main word of the idiom.
e. Adjectives and nouns are usually presented in their masculine singular form.
f. Important grammar abbreviations are: **m.** (masculine noun), **f.** (feminine noun), **adj.** (adjective), **adv.** (adverb), **v. tr.** (transitive verb), **v. intr.** (intransitive verb), and **reflex.** (reflexive verb).

You will have a chance to practice this strategy after you read the selection.

Actividad 15: Mira y contesta

Antes de leer el texto, contesta las siguientes preguntas.

1. Describe los mercados que ves en las fotos en las páginas 212 y 213. ¿Qué tipo de cosas se venden?
2. ¿Qué diferencias y semejanzas *(similarities)* ves entre estos dos tipos de mercado?
3. ¿Conoces mercados como éstos?
4. ¿Qué tipo de mercados hay en la ciudad donde vives?
5. ¿En qué lugares, que no sean tiendas, se venden cosas en tu ciudad o pueblo?

Actividad 16: Ideas y detalles

Lee el texto y busca las ideas principales y los detalles que apoyan estas ideas.

El Rastro, Madrid, España.

Los mercados en el mundo hispano

Si viajas a un país hispano, un lugar interesante para visitar, es el mercado al aire libre. Hay muchas clases de mercados: mercados de artesanía, de antigüedades, de comida y también de cosas en general. Algunos de estos mercados son especialmente para turistas y otros son para la gente del lugar. Vas a encontrar mercados que están abiertos todos los días y otros que sólo abren en días específicos.

En general, se pueden conseguir buenos precios en los mercados y, a veces, se puede inclusive regatear, pero tienes que tener cuidado con el regateo. En algunos lugares el regateo es común: el comerciante espera que el cliente no acepte el primer precio que se le dé, sino que haga una contraoferta o pida un precio más bajo. Por otro lado, hay mercados donde no se regatea y si lo haces puedes insultar al comerciante. Para no meter la pata es una buena idea ver qué hace la gente del lugar. Si ellos no regatean, pues entonces es mejor no hacerlo.

Los mercados de artesanía y de comidas más conocidos de Hispanoamérica están en México, Guatemala y Perú. Allí prevalecieron las culturas azteca, maya e incaica y hoy día sus descendientes venden al público la artesanía que aprendieron a hacer de sus antepasados.

En México, Guatemala y Perú están, por ejemplo, los mercados de Oa- 20
xaca, Chichicastenango y Huancayo respectivamente, donde la gente local vende telas típicas, hamacas, cerámica, especias y comidas. Para saber
si los precios que tienen son buenos o no, es buena idea ir a las tiendas
artesanales del gobierno, donde tienen productos similares, para comparar precios.

En la ciudad de México y en Buenos Aires puedes encontrar mer- 25
cados con antigüedades como la Lagunilla y el mercado de San Telmo
respectivamente. Allí es posible regatear. Los días más interesantes para
ir son los sábados y domingos cuando hay mucha gente.

Para comprar cosas en general, hay mercados como el Rastro en
Madrid. Este mercado es enorme y está dividido en diferentes zonas 30
donde se venden cosas como antigüedades, ropa, artesanía moderna y
hay además una zona para comprar animales domésticos. En este mercado normalmente no se regatea.

Si estás en un país hispano y quieres saber si hay mercados como los
que se mencionan aquí, puedes averiguar en la oficina de turismo local 35
o simplemente preguntarle a alguien del lugar.

Mercado al aire libre en Pisac, Perú.

ar·te·sa·ní·a f. *(habilidad)* craftsmanship; *(producto)* crafts.

con·se·guir §64 tr. *(obtener)* to obtain; *(llegar a hacer)* to attain; *(lograr)* to manage.

es·pe·cia f. spice.

pa·ta f. ZOOL. *(pie)* paw, foot; *(pierna)* leg; COLL. *(pierna humana)* leg; *(base)* leg <*las patas de la mesa* the legs of the table>; ORNITH. female duck ✝ **a cuatro patas** on all fours • **a p.** COLL. on foot • **estirar la p.** COLL. to kick the bucket • **meter la p.** COLL. to put one's foot in it • **p. de gallo** crowfoot

pre·va·le·cer §17 intr. *(sobresalir)* to prevail; BOT. to take root.

Act. 17: Answers: 1. crafts 2. to obtain 3. to put one's foot in it 4. prevailed 5. spices.

Act. 18: It is interesting to note that in the U.S. one bargains for cars, electrical appliances, a house, etc., all of which are expensive items.

Remind students that it is important to be sure of the word they are searching for in English to avoid sentences such as, **El niño Jesús está mintiendo en la cuna.**

cof·fee·pot (:pŏt') s. cafetera.

smart (smärt) **I.** adj. *(intelligent)* listo; *(witty)* ingenioso; *(impertinent)* impertinente; *(quick)* rápido; *(fashionable)* de moda **II.** intr. *(to sting)* escocer.

Actividad 17: Usa el diccionario

Adivina qué significan las siguientes palabras del texto. Luego confirma tu predicción buscando sus significados en las secciones del diccionario que se presentan.

1. línea 3 **artesanía**
2. línea 7 **conseguir**
3. línea 13 **meter la pata**
4. línea 16 **prevalecieron**
5. línea 21 **especias**

Actividad 18: Preguntas

Después de leer el texto, contesta las siguientes preguntas.

1. ¿Cuáles son algunos de los consejos que da el autor para la persona que visita los mercados hispanos?
2. ¿Cuáles de estos mercados te gustaría visitar?
3. ¿Tienes artesanía de algún país hispano?
4. ¿En qué situaciones regateas en los Estados Unidos?

Estrategia de escritura: *Using the Dictionary*

When writing in a foreign language, you often need to consult the dictionary. The following are some clues to help you use the dictionary appropriately:

a. Remember that some words have more than one translation. Make sure you choose the one that suits the context.
b. Abbreviations such as (coll.) or (pop.) indicate that the choice of word is colloquial or popular.
c. Abbreviations such as (Guat.) or (C. Rica) indicate that the word is a regionalism used only in that country.
d. When looking up a verb, check whether it is irregular. This is indicated in the Spanish-English section by the abbreviation **irreg.** or **irr.** and the forms are usually given in a table of irregular verbs.

To make the best use of the dictionary, it is advisable to look at the user's guide included in it.

Actividad 19: Completa las oraciones

Completa estas oraciones buscando las palabras entre paréntesis en las secciones del diccionario que se presentan.

1. Mario quiere ir a la Lagunilla a comprar una ___cafetera___ *(coffeepot)*.
2. Ese cliente que regatea es un hombre muy ___listo___ *(smart)*.

closed (klōzd) adj. cerrado; *(finished)* concluido; *(season)* vedado; *(restricted)* reservado; *(mind)* estrecho.

in·hab·it (ĭn-hăb′ĭt) tr. habitar, vivir en.

low·er¹ (lou′ər) intr. *(to scowl)* fruncir el ceño; *(to cloud over)* nublarse, encapotarse.

low·er² (lō′ər) **I.** adj. más bajo, inferior ♦ **I. case** IMPR. minúsculas **II.** tr. & intr. bajar; *(to diminish)* disminuir, reducir.

3. Hay mercados que están ____cerrados____ *(closed)* durante la semana.

4. A los comerciantes del mercado del Rastro no les gusta ____reducir, bajar____ *(to lower)* los precios.

5. Los incas ____habitaron____ *(inhabited)* gran parte de Suramérica.

Actividad 20: El mercado al aire libre

Use the strategies explained in Ch. 7 on paragraph writing.

En grupos de tres, hagan un *brainstorming* sobre las ventajas y desventajas *(advantages and disadvantages)* de comprar cosas en un mercado al aire libre. Después, individualmente, escriban dos párrafos: uno sobre las ventajas y otro sobre las desventajas.

Lo esencial

I. Más muebles

1. la alfombra
2. el armario/el ropero
3. la cómoda
4. el estante
5. el sillón
6. el tocador

Actividad 21: Asociaciones

1. Di qué muebles y objetos asocias con estas habitaciones: la sala, el dormitorio y el comedor.
2. Di qué muebles asocias con estas acciones: dormir, leer, escribir, comer y sentarse.
3. Di qué muebles asocias con estas cosas: suéteres, vestidos, peine y diccionario.

Actividad 22: Casa amueblada

Mira el plano *(diagram)* de la casa en la página 204 y describe los muebles que ves y en qué parte de la casa están.

II. Los electrodomésticos y otras cosas necesarias

1. la cafetera
2. la estufa/cocina eléctrica (de gas)
3. el fregadero
4. el horno (de) microondas
5. la lavadora
6. el lavaplatos
7. la nevera
8. el congelador
9. la tostadora
10. la aspiradora

Las cosas del baño

la bañera	bathtub	**el inodoro**	toilet
el bidé	bidet	**el lavabo**	bathroom sink
la ducha	shower		

Actividad 23: Asociaciones

Asocia estas marcas con el vocabulario de electrodomésticos y de las cosas del baño:

Maytag, Melitta, Mr. Bubble, Hoover, Frigidaire, Saniflush, Toastmaster, Kenmore, Amana

Actividad 24: Describe y dibuja

En parejas, el/la estudiante "A" le describe a "B" su cocina, sala o baño. "A" debe indicar qué muebles y electrodomésticos tiene en la habitación y dónde están. "B" dibuja un plano del lugar con muebles y electrodomésticos. Después cambien de papel.

Actividad 25: El apartamento nuevo

En grupos de cuatro, imagínense que Uds. acaban de alquilar un apartamento semiamueblado. El apartamento tiene cuatro dormitorios, un teléfono, un sofá, dos camas, dos cómodas, una mesa grande en el comedor y solamente tres sillas para la mesa. Miren la siguiente lista y
decidan qué más necesita cada persona y qué cosas no necesitan.

alfombras	estantes	sillones
una aspiradora	un estéreo	un televisor
una cafetera	un horno (de) microondas	tocadores
camas	una lavadora	una tostadora
cómodas	sillas para el comedor	

Todos son expertos

Turistas con las tortugas gigantes de las Islas Galápagos,
Ecuador.

ojalá (que) + subjunctive	I hope (that) . . .
Ojalá que quiera venderla.	I hope he wants to sell it.
la plata	slang for "money" (literally "silver")
¡Por el amor de Dios!	For heaven's sake! (literally "For the love of God!")

Pronunciation: [h]
1. Model and have students repeat after you words that contain [h]: **manejar, equipaje, pasajero, gimnasia, Argentina,** etc.
2. Contrast [g] and [h]: **guerra** vs. **gente, seguir** vs. **gira, jefe,** etc.
3. Practice the following sentences: **Juan José trabaja en Jalapa. El general José de San Martín fue el jefe de su regimiento.**
4. Have students find 5 words in the dialogue that contain [h] and dictate them to their partners.
5. Have students make new sentences with 2 of the words they found in the dialogue.

Asking an opinion

Expressing influence

To practice **ojalá** have students discuss going to a party: **Ojalá que esté Paco/que tengan cerveza/que Felipe traiga la guitarra,** etc.

Ojalá = may God grant (from Arabic).

Giving an implied command

Matrimonial = de matrimonio, grande, doble.

Don Alejandro, el tío de Teresa, tiene algunos muebles para el apartamento que acaban de alquilar las chicas, pero ellas tienen que comprar algunas cosas. Vicente y Alejandro le están dando consejos a Teresa sobre los muebles de la casa.

Actividad 26: Marca los muebles

Escucha la conversación y marca sólo las cosas que necesitan las chicas.

_____ sofá	✔ estantes	
_____ escritorio	✔ lavadora	
_____ cómoda	✔ cama	
_____ alfombra	✔ lámparas	

Tío	Entonces, con los muebles que voy a darles, ya tienen casi amueblado el apartamento.
Teresa	¡Sí, es fantástico!
Vicente	Pero todavía necesitan una cama y unas lámparas, ¿no?
Teresa	Sí, y también dos estantes para los libros.
Vicente	¿Crees que en el Rastro puedas encontrar unos estantes que no cuesten mucha plata?
Teresa	Buena idea, porque no tenemos mucho dinero.
Tío	Oye Teresa, creo que es necesario que tengan lavadora, ¿no?
Teresa	Es verdad, pero nos va a costar un ojo de la cara.
Vicente	¿Sabes? Ayer me dijo Juan Carlos que la semana que viene Francisco se va a Ecuador para trabajar en el Instituto Darwin de las Islas Galápagos.
Teresa	¿Francisco? ¿Quién es Francisco?
Vicente	Un amigo que tiene un apartamento con lavadora. Podemos llamarlo para preguntarle si la va a vender.
Teresa	¡Perfecto! Ojalá que quiera venderla. Y podemos preguntarle si también quiere vendernos una cama.
Tío	Pero, Teresa, ¡cómo que una cama de segunda mano! No quiero que compres una cama usada.
Teresa	Entonces, ¿quieres que duerma en la alfombra?
Tío	No, ¡por el amor de Dios! Tu tío Alejandro te compra una cama nueva.
Vicente	(En voz baja) ¿Matrimonial?

Actividad 27: ¿Hay soluciones?

Después de escuchar la conversación, explica cómo va a obtener Teresa estas cosas: una cama, unas lámparas, dos estantes y una lavadora.

¿Lo sabían?

Las Islas Galápagos, que están en el Océano Pacífico, pertenecen a *(belong to)* Ecuador. Se conocen en todo el mundo por su gran variedad de animales y plantas. Charles Darwin fue a estas islas por primera vez en el año 1835 y fue allí donde hizo estudios para su teoría de la evolución. Hoy, las Islas Galápagos son un santuario para conservar la naturaleza. Allí está el Instituto Darwin, donde los biólogos estudian muchas especies de animales que no existen en otras partes del mundo.

Actividad 28: Los deseos de año nuevo

Uds. están celebrando el año nuevo y están brindando *(toasting)* por el año que comienza. Hagan un deseo para el año nuevo. Por ejemplo: Ojalá que este año pueda ir de vacaciones a México.

Hacia la comunicación

Gramática

I.   Influencing: Other Uses of the Subjunctive

Before studying the following grammar explanation, answer these questions based on the dialogue:

- How many subjects are there in the following sentences: **"No quiero que compres una cama usada"** and **"¿ . . . quieres que duerma en la alfombra"?**
- What is present in one of the following sentences that helps to indicate the use of the subjunctive: **"Es mejor ir al Rastro . . ."** and **". . . es necesario que tengan lavadora"?**

The subjunctive is used in dependent noun clauses when the verb in the independent clause expresses a desire to influence someone's actions. Influence may be expressed by stating preference, by requesting, hoping, advising, or giving an implied command. There are two ways of expressing influence: personal and impersonal.

1. To express influence in a personal way:

   a. The independent clause contains a subject that wants to influence and a verb of influence such as **querer** or **aconsejar**.

   b. The dependent clause contains a different subject, which is the person or thing being influenced, and a verb in the subjunctive.

I. Have students practice identifying the 2 subjects in other
sentences with the subjunctive.

Discuss other ways to give advice and implied commands:
deber + infinitive, **tener
que** + infinitive, **necesitar** +
infinitive.

Drill subjunctive:
1. Do a transformation drill:
Debes comer. → **Quiero que
comas.**
2. Have S1 finish this sentence:
**El jefe quiere que su em-
pleado ...** Have S2 negate
S1's response and correct it:
**No, el jefe no quiere que su
empleado ... Él quiere que
su empleado ...**
3. Have students decide what
advice a psychiatrist gives a
married couple, a lonely young
man, a perfectionist, a pessimist, parents of a drug addict, etc.
4. Create situations and have
students give advice and express hope: **Pete perdió su
tarjeta de Visa.** S1: **Él espera
que ...** (etc.)

Yo quiero **que** **tú** com**as** en la cocina.
influencing   influenced
  subject   subject

Quiero que (tú) vayas al Rastro.	*I want you to go to the Rastro.*
Siempre **me pide que me levante** temprano.	*He/She always asks me to get up early.*
Te aconsejo que te compres una cama nueva.	*I advise you to buy a new bed.*
Ella espera que compres éste.	*She hopes you buy this one.*
Te prohíbe que fumes.	*He/She forbids you to smoke.*

2. To express influence in an impersonal way:

a. The independent clause contains an impersonal expression such as **es bueno, (no) es necesario, (no) es importante,** or **es mejor.**

b. The dependent clause contains the subject being influenced and a verb in the subjunctive.

Es necesario que la casa tenga una cocina grande.	*It's necessary that the house have a big kitchen.*
No **es importante que vuelvas** pronto.	*It isn't important that you return soon.*
Es mejor que te acuestes.	*It's better that you go to bed.*

However, when you want to express influence, but not over someone in particular, use a verb in the infinitive.

Es necesario **volver** mañana.	*It's necessary to return tomorrow.* (no **que** and no subject in the dependent clause)

II. Using *ya* and *todavía*

A. Ya

Are you coming? =
¿Vienes?
I'm coming = **Ya voy.**

II. A./B. Drill **ya** and **todavía**:
Ask questions regarding the
class: **¿Escribiste la composición? ¿Entiendes la forma-
ción del subjuntivo?** (etc.)

1. When used in an affirmative sentence, **ya** means *already* or *now*. Context helps determine which meaning is being conveyed.

—¿Te explico la lección?	*Should I explain the lesson to you?*
—No, gracias. **Ya** la entiendo.	*No thanks. I **already** understand it.*
—¿Ves? Así se hace una tortilla.	*See? This is how a tortilla is made.*
—¡Ah! ¡**Ya** entiendo!	*Now I understand!*

2. When used in a negative sentence, **ya** means *no longer, not any more.*

Ya no tengo que estudiar porque   *I **don't** have to study **any more***
terminé los exámenes.   *because I finished my exams.*

B. Todavía

1. When used in an affirmative sentence, **todavía** means *still* or *yet.*

Todavía tengo problemas.   *I **still** have problems.*

2. When used in the negative, **todavía** means *not yet.*

—¿Estudiaste?   *Did you study?*
—**Todavía no.**   ***Not yet.***

Note that **todavía no** is used as an isolated expression or, depending on dialect, followed by the present perfect or the preterit.

Do mechanical drills, Workbook, Part II.

Influencing = subjunctive.

Actividad 29: Quiero que . . .

Di qué quieres que hagan y qué no quieres que hagan las siguientes personas. Usa frases como **prefiero que . . . , quiero que . . . , espero que . . . , le/s pido que . . . , es importante que . . . , y es necesario que . . . .**

el presidente de los Estados Unidos   tus profesores
el/la decano/a de la universidad   tu mejor amigo/a

Act. 30: In some areas of Spain, **¿Ya has estudiado?** would be used. Otherwise, **¿Ya estudiaste?** is more prevalent in the Spanish-speaking world.

Actividad 30: ¿Ya estudiaste?

En parejas, el/la estudiante "A" cubre la Columna B y el/la estudiante "B" cubre la Columna A. "A" y "B" viven en la misma casa y cada persona tiene sus responsabilidades. El problema es que "B" es muy perezoso/a y hace las cosas a última hora. "A" le pregunta a "B" si ya hizo las tareas que le corresponden.

A: ¿Ya estudiaste?
B: Sí, ya estudié. / Todavía no.
A: ¿Ya fuiste al correo? / ¿Cómo que todavía no?
B: . . .

✔ indicates a completed task

A   B
limpiar el baño   Tareas para hoy:
comprar el periódico   ☐ comprar el periódico
dar de comer al perro   ✔ pagar la luz
pagar la luz   ☐ comprar detergente
comprar detergente   ✔ limpiar el baño
                           ✔ dar de comer al perro

Actividad 31: Dando consejos

En parejas, el/la estudiante "A" es un padre o una madre que tiene que darle consejos a su hijo/a sobre las drogas y el alcohol. El/La estudiante "B" es el/la hijo/a y debe reaccionar a los consejos. "A" usa frases como **te aconsejo (que) . . . , te prohibo (que) . . . ,** y **es importante (que) . . . .**

Actividad 32: El conflicto

En parejas, Uds. van a compartir un apartamento y tienen que amueblarlo. El/La estudiante "A" es muy práctico/a y "B" es muy excéntrico/a. Deben tratar de influir en la otra persona (**es mejor . . . , te aconsejo . . . ,** etc.) para comprar los muebles y ponerlos en el lugar que cada uno quiere.

A: Es mejor que compremos unas sillas para el comedor.
B: No, yo creo que es mejor sentarse en la alfombra.

Actividad 33: Querida Esperanza

Act.'s 33, 34: Students can play the role of editor by peer editing these letters, first for content, and then for grammar and vocabulary.

Eres Esperanza, una señora que trabaja para un periódico y contesta cartas dando consejos. Lee estas cartas y escribe unas respuestas apropiadas usando la imaginación. Usa expresiones como **es necesario que . . . , le aconsejo que . . . ,** etc.

Querida Esperanza:

Soy un hombre de 35 años y tengo un problema: hace una semana compré una crema especial y muy cara para cambiarme el color del pelo, pero mi pelo no solamente cambió de color sino que también empezó a caerse. Después de una semana ya no tengo pelo.

¡Imagínese! Me da vergüenza salir de casa. ¿Qué puedo hacer? ¿Comprar un sombrero? ¿Qué es mejor: que escriba a la compañía que hizo la crema o que hable con un abogado?

Calvo y sin plata

Querida Esperanza:

Hace un mes se murió mi suegra y ahora tenemos problemas con la herencia. Ella estuvo enferma durante tres años y yo la llevé al médico, le di de comer y cuando ya no pudo caminar, le compré una silla de ruedas. El hermano de mi esposa no hizo nada, pero recibió todo el dinero y a nosotros mi suegra nos dejó solamente el perro y un álbum de fotos. ¿Qué nos aconseja que hagamos?

Responsable pero pobre

Actividad 34: Con esperanza, de Esperanza

En parejas, lean la respuesta que escribió Esperanza a una carta. Inventen la carta que recibió.

Queridos niños tristes:
Quiero que sepan que sus padres los quieren. Ellos solamente les prohiben que hagan algunas cosas porque pueden ser malas para Uds. Yo también les aconsejo que estudien y que estén en casa a las diez de la noche. Es mejor que estén con sus padres y no en la calle donde hay violencia y drogas. Ojalá que Uds. entiendan las intenciones de sus padres.

Con esperanza de, Esperanza

Vocabulario funcional

Los números ordinales

Ver página 202

Las habitaciones de la casa

Ver página 204

Palabras relacionadas con una casa o apartamento

el agua water	**la fianza/el depósito** security
alquilar to rent	deposit
el alquiler rent	**el garaje** garage
amueblado/a furnished	**la luz/electricidad** electricity
amueblar to furnish	**el piso** floor
el apartamento apartment	**el portero** doorman; janitor
la calefacción heat	**el portero automático** intercom;
el edificio building	electric door opener

Más muebles

Ver página 215

Los electrodomésticos y otras cosas necesarias

Ver páginas 216-217

Más verbos

aconsejar to advise	**limpiar** to clean
escoger to choose, select	**prohibir** to prohibit

Palabras y expresiones útiles

la calle   street
el consejo   advice
es bueno   it's good
es importante   it's important
es mejor   it's better
es necesario   it's necessary
la esperanza   hope
o sea   that is
ojalá (que) + subjuntivo   I hope
 that . . .
la plata   slang for "money" (literally
 "silver")

¡Por el amor de Dios!   For
 heaven's sake! (literally "for the
 love of God!")
de segunda mano   secondhand,
 used
todavía   still
todavía no   not yet
¡Vaya!   Wow!
ya   already; now
ya no   no longer

Mercado en Valencia, España.

Capítulo 9

Chapter Objectives

After studying this chapter, you will know how to:

- express doubt and certainty
- tell how an action is done (quickly, etc.)
- express emotion
- indicate time and age in the past
- discuss leisure-time activities
- give instructions
- identify food items

Monedas del mundo hispano. ¿Coleccionas monedas? ¿Tienes dinero de otros países?

Un fin de semana activo

Practice **¿No sabías?** by talking about bizarre news events that students may or may not have heard. Use the expression when appropriate.

Ask students: **¿Cuántos son en tu familia?**

Tal vez and quizás don't use que; they are followed directly by the subjunctive.

¿No sabías?	Didn't you know?
tal vez/quizás + subjunctive	perhaps/maybe
Somos tres.	There are three of us.
¡Qué mala suerte!	What bad luck!

Juan Carlos, Álvaro y Vicente llegan al apartamento para ayudar a las chicas a poner los muebles, pero ellas todavía no están allí. Entonces, ellos deciden ir al bar de enfrente a esperarlas y hablan del fin de semana pasado.

Act. 1: 1. C   2. C   3. F   4. F
5. F   6. F

Actividad 1: ¿Cierto, falso o no se sabe?

Escucha la conversación y di si estas oraciones son ciertas, falsas o no se sabe.

1. Todos los muchachos piden café.
2. Vicente compró monedas de Cuba.
3. Vicente tiene una colección de monedas de cincuenta países.
4. A Juan Carlos le gustan los animales.
5. Álvaro tuvo un fin de semana muy divertido.
6. Álvaro fue a hablar con un policía porque alguien le robó el coche.

Discuss influence from international markets in different countries. Use Donkey Kong and Stephen King novels as examples.

Ask students why they think Juan Carlos wanted a table next to the window.

Discussing past actions	

Indicating possibility	

Stating age in the past	

Narrating a series of past events	

ventana = window
ventanilla = car window

Expressing certainty	

Juan Carlos	Oiga, por favor. ¿Podemos sentarnos en aquella mesa al lado de la ventana?
Camarero	¿Cuántos son?
Juan Carlos	Somos tres.
Camarero	Vale.
Vicente	Gracias. Tres cafés con leche y un vaso de agua para mí, por favor . . . . ¿Saben que por fin el domingo fui al Rastro con Teresa?
Álvaro	¿Y? . . . ¿Compraron algo?
Vicente	Sí. Ella compró unos estantes baratos para su apartamento y yo tuve mucha suerte porque encontré unas monedas viejísimas de Cuba con la imagen de José Martí.
Álvaro	¿Qué? ¿Coleccionas monedas?
Vicente	¿No sabías? Es posible que tenga unas quinientas monedas de cuarenta países diferentes. Las empecé a coleccionar cuando tenía diez años. Pero bueno, ¿qué hicieron Uds. el fin de semana?
Juan Carlos	Yo jugué en la computadora con una versión nueva de Donkey Kong que me dio un amigo y es buenísima. ¡Ay! Esta cuchara está sucia. ¡Camarero!
Camarero	¿Sí?
Juan Carlos	¿Puede darme otra cuchara?
Camarero	Sí . . . Aquí tiene.
Juan Carlos	Gracias. Y tú, Álvaro, ¿qué hiciste?
Álvaro	Tuve miles de problemas. Primero dejé las llaves dentro del coche y tuve que romper la ventanilla. Alguien me vio y llamó a la policía. Entonces llegó un policía y me quiso detener por robar el coche. Le expliqué el problema y por fin entendió.
Vicente	¡Qué mala suerte! Bueno, quizás exista alguien que te odie. ¿Crees que alguien te esté echando el mal de ojo?[1]
Álvaro	¡Hombre! Deja de tonterías que no creo en esas cosas. ¡Qué imaginación! Es evidente que lees demasiadas novelas de Stephen King.
Juan Carlos	¡Miren! Ahí llegan las chicas. Vamos a ayudarlas.

---

1. **te . . .** is putting a curse on you

Act. 2: In pairs, have students ask each other what they did last weekend.

Actividad 2: El fin de semana

Después de escuchar el diálogo, di qué hicieron los chicos el fin de semana.

> **¿Lo sabían?**
>
> José Martí (1853–1895) fue un famoso poeta, escritor y revolucionario cubano. Su sueño era ver a Cuba independiente de España, pero murió en una batalla contra los españoles antes de ver su sueño realizado. A Martí lo llaman "el apóstol de la independencia de Cuba". Su poesía *Versos sencillos* fue la inspiración para la famosa canción "Guantanamera".

Act. 3: Point out the use of the subjunctive in the model.

Note the use of the subjunctive.

Common Hispanic superstitions include: **Si te barren los pies, te casas con un viudo. Si cantas mal va a llover.** Se pone una escoba detrás de la puerta para que la gente se vaya pronto. En la mesa, no le das el salero a nadie en la mano sino que lo pones en la mesa enfrente de la persona porque si no, trae mala suerte.

Act. 4: Have students note the use of the subjunctive in the model.

Actividad 3: ¿Qué piensas?

En parejas, háganle a su compañero/a las siguientes preguntas.

▶ **A:** ¿Crees que exista la reencarnación?
  B: Sí, creo que existe. / Es posible que exista. / No, no creo que exista.

1. ¿Crees que exista la suerte?
2. ¿Crees que se pueda ver el futuro en la palma de la mano?
3. ¿Crees que vivan personas en otros planetas (Venus, Marte, Pluto, Urano)?
4. ¿Crees que exista la percepción extrasensorial (*extrasensory perception, i.e., ESP*)?
5. ¿Crees que alguien te pueda echar el mal de ojo?

Actividad 4: Quizás . . . quizás . . . quizás

En parejas, uno de Uds. tiene problemas y quiere hablar con un/a amigo/a porque necesita ayuda. El/La estudiante "A" le explica sus problemas (que están en la Columna A) a su compañero/a para ver qué piensa. Después cambien de papel.

▶ **A:** Dejé las llaves dentro del coche.
  B: Tal vez debas tener dos. / Tal vez tengas que romper la ventanilla. / Quizás debas llamar a la policía.

A	B
1. No funciona el televisor nuevo que compraste.	1. Acabas de empezar un trabajo nuevo y tu jefe/a quiere salir contigo.
2. Acabas de recibir tu cuenta de teléfono por $325. Hay tres llamadas de larga distancia a Japón y no llamaste a nadie allí.	2. Un buen amigo bebe mucho y crees que es alcohólico.

Lo esencial

I. Los pasatiempos

1. hacer rompecabezas
2. jugar con juegos de computadora/vídeos
3. jugar (a las) cartas
4. jugar (al) billar
5. jugar (al) dominó
6. ser radioaficionado/a

Otros pasatiempos

arreglar el carro   to fix the car
coleccionar   to collect
  estampillas   stamps
  monedas   coins
coser   to sew

cuidar plantas (jardinería)
  to take care of plants
  (gardening)
escribir cartas/poesías
  to write letters/poems

hacer crucigramas   to do crossword puzzles

Tejer = hacer punto (to knit).

jugar   to play
   (al) ajedrez   chess
   (al) pool (billar americano) pool

pescar   to fish
pintar   to paint
tejer   to knit; to weave
trabajar con madera   to work with wood

Actividad 5: Los pasatiempos

Habla con tus compañeros para ver qué hacen en su tiempo libre. Haz preguntas como **¿Te gusta cocinar?, ¿Pintas en tu tiempo libre?** Luego, marca la columna apropiada.

le gusta:	mucho	poco	nada
1. coser	————	————	————
2. la jardinería	————	————	————
3. pintar	————	————	————
4. pescar	————	————	————
5. . . .	————	————	————

Actividad 6: Los intereses

Habla con varias personas y pregúntales si hacen las siguientes actividades en su tiempo libre.

1. jugar a las cartas
   Si contestan que sí: ¿A qué juegan? ¿Con quiénes? ¿Juegan por dinero? ¿En general, pierden o ganan dinero?
   Si contestan que no: ¿Por qué no?
2. tener colecciones
   Si contestan que sí: ¿De qué? ¿Cuántos? ¿Hace cuánto tiempo que coleccionan?
   Si contestan que no: ¿Les gustaría tener una colección? ¿Qué les gustaría coleccionar?
3. hacer crucigramas o rompecabezas
   Si contestan que sí: ¿Dónde? ¿Cuándo? ¿Son expertos?
   Si contestan que no: ¿Por qué? ¿Son interesantes o frustrantes estos juegos?
4. jugar con juegos electrónicos
   Si contestan que sí: ¿Cuáles? ¿Dónde? ¿Son expertos? ¿Hace cuánto tiempo que juegan?
   Si contestan que no: ¿Qué piensan de las máquinas? ¿Tienen computadora?
5. hacer otra actividad en su tiempo libre

II. Cosas de la cocina

II. Bring in kitchen items and use TPR to practice vocabulary: **¿Quién tiene el cuchillo? ¿Dónde está la servilleta? ¿Qué hay encima de la servilleta? Pete, dale la olla a Janet.** (etc.)

Discuss cultural differences in table manners: not changing the knife and fork from hand to hand, keeping hands above the table, etc.

1. la cuchara ⎫
2. el cuchillo ⎬ los cubiertos
3. el tenedor ⎭
4. la servilleta
5. la olla

6. el plato
7. el/la sartén
8. la taza
9. el vaso

Actividad 7: ¿Qué están haciendo?

Mira el dibujo de la tienda y di qué están haciendo las personas.

Actividad 8: ¿Dónde?

En grupos de cuatro, hagan una lista y digan para qué son las cosas que hay en el dibujo de la tienda. Luego nombren tiendas de su ciudad donde se pueden comprar estas cosas.

Hacia la comunicación

Gramática

I. Expressing Doubt and Certainty: Contrasting the Subjunctive and the Indicative

Before studying the following grammar explanation, answer these questions based on the dialogue:

- When Vicente says, **"Es posible que tenga unas quinientas monedas . . . ,"** is he *sure* that he has about five hundred or is it a possibility?
- When Álvaro says, **"Es evidente que lees demasiadas novelas . . . ,"** is he showing certainty or doubt?

I. Note: In this text, students will be asked to use the subjunctive after **creer** and **pensar** in questions. **Creer** and **pensar** in questions followed by the indicative is presented passively in direction lines.

The subjunctive is used in dependent noun clauses when the verb in the independent clause expresses doubt or disbelief about something or someone. Doubt may be expressed in a personal or an impersonal way.

1. To express doubt in a personal way:
   a. the independent clause contains the subject or person expressing doubt and a verb of doubt such as **dudar, no creer** and **no pensar** or **¿pensar?** and **¿creer?**
   b. the dependent clause contains a different subject and a verb in the subjunctive.

Note: **Creer** and **pensar** in an affirmative statement do not imply doubt.

Dudo que ellas **tengan** muebles.	*I doubt that they have furniture.*
No creo que a las chicas les **guste** el apartamento.	*I don't believe (think) that the girls are going to like the apartment.*

Quizás and **tal vez** imply doubt.

The indicative is used in affirmative sentences when no doubt is expressed.

Creo que a las chicas les **gusta** el apartamento.	*I believe (think) that the girls like the apartment.*
Estoy seguro de que Vicente **va** a venir.	*I'm sure Vicente is coming.*

Drill verbs and expressions of doubt:
1. Have students express doubt about things you say: **Mi padre es millonario.** S1: **Dudo que su padre sea millonario.**
2. Discuss items from the news: **Dudo que ... Es posible que ... No es probable que ...** (etc.)
3. Have students predict the future: **Es evidente que tú ... Es posible que ...** (etc.)
4. Do questions and answers using **pensar** and **creer.**

2. To express doubt or denial in an impersonal way:
   a. the independent clause contains an impersonal expression such as **no es cierto, no es evidente, no es verdad, (no) es posible, posiblemente, (no) es probable,** and **es dudoso.**
   b. the dependent clause contains the subject and a verb in the subjunctive, which expresses the action that is being doubted or denied.

Es posible que Teresa **necesite** platos.	*It's possible that Teresa may need dishes.*
No es cierto que vivan en Guatemala.	*It isn't true that they live in Guatemala.*
Es probable que Diana no **se sienta** bien.	*It's probable that Diana doesn't feel well.*
Es dudoso que Juan Carlos **pueda** ir con nosotros hoy.	*It's doubtful that Juan Carlos can come with us today.*

If the impersonal expression indicates certainty, the indicative is used.

Es verdad que viven en Nicaragua.	*It is true that they live in Nicaragua.*

Other impersonal expressions that express certainty and do not require the subjunctive are **es cierto, es claro, es evidente, no hay duda (de),** and **es obvio.**

II. Saying How an Action Is Done: Adverbs Ending in *-mente*

An adverb of manner indicates how the action expressed by the verb is done. English adverbs of manner that end in *-ly* are formed in Spanish by adding **-mente** to the feminine singular of the adjectives. If the adjective ends in a consonant or **-e**, add **-mente**. If the adjective has an accent, it is retained when **-mente** is added.

rápida → rápid**amente**	general → general**mente**
Speedy González corre **rápidamente.**	*Speedy González runs rapidly.*

Common adverbs include **constantemente, continuamente, divinamente, fácilmente, frecuentemente, generalmente, inmediatamente, posiblemente, probablemente, solamente*,** and **tranquilamente.**

*Note: **solamente = sólo** *(only)*, but **solo/a** *(alone)*

¡SUS PREGUNTAS SERÁN RÁPIDAMENTE CONTESTADAS! ¡SUS DUDAS SERÁN INMEDIATAMENTE ACLARADAS! Este es un nuevo servicio que Editorial América, S.A. quiere ofrecerle a todos sus actuales suscriptores para que se sientan satisfechos y felices.

III. Drill **ser** and **tener** in the imperfect:
Do questions and answers:
¿Qué hora era cuando empezaste a estudiar anoche?
¿Qué hora era cuando terminó (un partido)? ¿Cuántos años tenías cuando te dieron tu primera bicicleta? (etc.)

III. Indicating Time and Age in the Past: *Ser* and *tener*

You already know one way to express the past, the *preterit*. There is another way called the *imperfect*, which has its own uses.

1. When you want to indicate the time an action took place, you use the imperfect form of the verb **ser: era** or **eran**.

Era la una de la mañana
cuando mi novia me llamó.
Eran las ocho cuando salí de
mi casa.

*It was one in the morning when
my girlfriend called me.*
It was eight when I left my house.

2. When you want to indicate age in the past, you use one of the following forms of the verb **tener.**

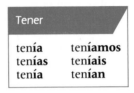

Tener	
tenía	tení**amos**
tenías	tení**ais**
tenía	tení**an**

Do mechanical drills, Workbook, Part I.

Álvaro **tenía** diez años cuando
empezó a coleccionar monedas.
Una vez, cuando **tenía** quince
años, fui a la Isla de Pascua.

*Álvaro was ten when he began
collecting coins.*
*Once, when I was fifteen, I went
to Easter Island.*

Actividad 9: La política

Da tus opiniones sobre el presidente de los Estados Unidos, formando oraciones con frases de las tres columnas.

Doubt = subjunctive; certainty = indicative.

Es evidente		ser inteligente
Dudo		proteger el país
(No) creo		vivir en Washington
(No) es cierto	que el presidente	ser liberal
Es obvio		ser bueno
(No) es posible		trabajar mucho
(No) es probable		decir la verdad
(No) es verdad		saber hablar con los rusos

Actividad 10: ¿Conoces bien a tu compañero?

¿Crees que conoces bien a tu compañero/a? En parejas, escriban oraciones describiendo las costumbres de su compañero/a usando las palabras que se presentan. Después tienen que leerse las oraciones para ver si se conocen bien o no. Por ejemplo: Tú duermes constantemente.

comer	frecuente
correr	divino
conducir	tranquilo
Tú (no) dormir	constante
leer	general
bailar	continuo
estudiar	inmediato
	fácil
	rápido

Actividad 11: El horóscopo

En grupos de cuatro, lean el horóscopo de Uds. para hoy y coméntenlo. Usen frases como **es evidente que hoy debo . . . porque . . . , no creo que sea verdad porque . . . , es posible que . . . , es necesario que . . . , es probable que . . . , dudo que . . . , es mejor que . . . ,** etc.

ARIES 21 de marzo 20 de abril — Días muy propicios para renovar a fondo tu vida afectiva y ponerla en orden. Tu mente estará muy inspirada y pondrás en marcha buenas ideas profesionales. Suerte: días 12 y 16.	**LEO** 23 de julio 23 de agosto — Días de renovación y de gran vitalidad para ti en los que serás la reina de la fiesta allá donde vayas. Estarás muy observadora de ti misma. Suerte: días 17 y 18.	**SAGITARIO** 23 de noviembre 20 de diciembre — Continúas en pleno ritmo de expansión afectiva a lo que se van a unir muchas facilidades para hacer un viaje largo. No te excedas en cuanto al físico. Suerte: días 16 y 18.
TAURO 21 de abril 21 de mayo — Te sentirás muy segura de tus planteamientos y tendrás mucha fuerza creativa a tu disposición. Un amor pasajero te hará pasar momentos inolvidables. Suerte: días 17 y 18.	**VIRGO** 24 de agosto 23 de septiembre — Saldrás de dudas respecto a tu futuro profesional y tendrás muchos deseos de relajar tu mente y descansar. Te aproximarás afectivamente a un amigo. Suerte: días 16 y 18.	**CAPRICORNIO** 21 de diciembre 20 de enero — Días de contraste entre tu vida afectiva y tus retos profesionales. Querrás romper barreras en la intimidad y todo dependerá de tus iniciativas. Suerte: días 15 y 16.
GEMINIS 22 de mayo 21 de junio — Tu expansión afectiva sigue viento en popa y empezarás a madurar proyectos en común con tu pareja. Recibirás dinero y regalos de forma imprevista. Suerte: días 12 y 15.	**LIBRA** 24 de septiembre 23 de octubre — Por medio de un amigo conocerás a una persona que te cautivará afectivamente. En tu empresa te harán hacer el trabajo de varios, pero podrás con el reto. Suerte: días 13 y 15.	**ACUARIO** 21 de enero 19 de febrero — Días de mucho movimiento y de multitud de contactos en los que encontrarás a alguien que te dará una confianza inmediata. No temas lo que te suceda. Suerte: días 17 y 18.
CANCER 22 de junio 22 de julio — Días muy positivos para tu vida profesional en los que te comunicarán buenas noticias. Tu economía mejorará notablemente por cobrar algo pendiente. Suerte: días 12 y 16.	**ESCORPION** 24 de octubre 22 de noviembre — Toda la energía que has puesto en tu trabajo te dará resultados inesperados e inusuales. Tendrás en tus manos una oportunidad única, no la dejes escapar. Suerte: días 12 y 17.	**PISCIS** 20 de febrero 20 de marzo — Alguien que te rondaba secretamente se va a manifestar y te quedarás gratamente sorprendida por su forma de hacer. Gastarás de forma excesiva. Suerte: días 12 y 13.

Actividad 12: ¿Cuántos años tenían?

En parejas, averigüen cuántos años tenía su compañero/a o alguien de su familia cuando hicieron estas cosas.

1. casarse
2. terminar la escuela secundaria
3. tener su primer trabajo
4. empezar a jugar a (un deporte)
5. tener novio/a por primera vez
6. empezar a leer

Actividad 13: Era medianoche cuando . . .

En parejas, lean la siguiente historia y después digan a qué hora ocurrieron las cosas indicadas, empezando cada oración con **Era/Eran** (+ hora) cuando . . . .

Era medianoche cuando Pablo llegó a casa. Una hora más tarde, alguien llamó por teléfono, pero él no contestó porque diez minutos antes había empezado *(had started)* a bañarse. Estuvo allí por media hora. Justo cuando salió de la bañera empezó un episodio de "Viaje a las estrellas", donde el Sr. Spock casi se enamora de la enfermera del *Enterprise*. Cuando terminó el programa, Pablo se acostó.

Act. 13: 1. **12:00**   2. **1:00**
3. **12:50**   4. **1:20**   5. **2:20**
("Star Trek" is a 1-hour show)

1. él / llegar / a casa
2. alguien / llamar
3. él / empezar a bañarse
4. el programa / empezar
5. él / acostarse

Actividad 14: La visita de un primo

Act. 14: Remind students that **gusta** is used when **gustar** is followed by an infinitive because the infinitive is considered a singular subject.

Walk around spot-checking these paragraphs since they will be used for Act. 15.

Completa esta información sobre tu primo con su edad y sus gustos.

Mi primo va a pasar el fin de semana conmigo. Él tiene _____ años y le gusta mucho _____ , _____ y _____ . Nunca _____ y tampoco le gusta _____ . Creo que le gusta _____ . No creo que le guste _____ .

Actividad 15: Planeando el fin de semana de tu primo

En parejas, una persona cubre el Papel A y la otra persona cubre el Papel B. Lean las instrucciones para su papel y planeen el fin de semana del primo de su compañero/a, usando la información de la Actividad 14. Después cambien de papel.

Papel A

Tu primo viene a visitarte este fin de semana. Pídele ayuda a tu compañero/a para planear algunas actividades. Si no estás seguro/a de que le gusten ciertas actividades, usa **dudo que . . .** o **no creo que . . . .**

Papel B

El primo de tu compañero/a viene este fin de semana. Debes ayudarle a planear algunas actividades y para eso necesitas saber qué cosas le gusta hacer a él. Dale consejos a tu compañero/a sobre lo que pueden hacer, usando **te aconsejo que . . . , es posible que . . .** o **quizás/tal vez . . . .**

Nuevos horizontes

Estrategia de lectura: *Recognizing Prefixes*

One way of improving your understanding of unfamiliar words is by using your knowledge of prefixes. A prefix is a letter or group of letters preceding the stem of a word (un- + familiar = unfamiliar). Prefixes modify the meaning of a word. Many prefixes of Greek or Latin origin are the same or similar in Spanish and English. Can you identify the prefixes in **ilimitado, premeditar,** and **anticuerpo** and tell what they mean?

The following chart lists some common Spanish prefixes.

Prefix	Meaning	Example
ante-	before	**anteanoche, antepasado**
anti-/contra-	against, counter	**antídoto, contrarrevolución**
auto-	self	**autorrespeto, autoservicio**
bi-	two	**bilateral, bicicleta**
co-	with	**cooperación, coautor**
extra-	beyond	**extraordinario, extrasensorial**
i-, in-, im-	not	**ilegal, increíble**
mal-	bad	**malhumor, malpensado**
pre-	before	**premonición, preposición**
re-	again	**renovación, repasar**
sobre-	over, super	**sobredosis, sobrehumano**
sub-	under	**subterráneo, subdesarrollo**

Act. 17: You may want to have the title and the first lines from each paragraph on a transparency. Encourage students to form hypotheses by asking probing questions: **¿Qué curiosidades pueden ser éstas? ¿Por qué decimos que una cosa es curiosa o misteriosa? ¿Sabes algo sobre Nazca? ¿Conoces otras cosas inexplicables? ¿Hay razón lógica para todas las cosas que ocurren?** (etc.) It is important to follow the students' leads. The idea is to brainstorm beforehand; later, when reading the text itself, accept or reject hypotheses.

Actividad 16: Mira y contesta

Antes de leer el texto, contesta estas preguntas.

1. Mira la foto de Nazca en la página 240. ¿Sabes quién hizo esas líneas? ¿Qué piensas que son esas líneas?
2. Describe la foto de la página 241. ¿Qué crees que pueda ser este lugar? ¿Hay tiendas así en tu ciudad o pueblo?

Actividad 17: Predicción

Después de leer el título y la primera oración de cada párrafo, escribe tres ideas que piensas que se van a tratar en el texto. Luego lee el texto y confirma tu predicción.

Detalle de las líneas de Nazca, Perú. ¿Qué crees que represente el dibujo?

At home analyze why the following words have accents: **fenómenos, época, arqueológicos, lógica, and sólo.**

Curiosidades del mundo hispano

En algunos países hispanos se encuentran enigmas difíciles de comprender. Hay enigmas arqueológicos intrigantes que se están investigando y quizás nunca se encuentre una explicación para ellos. Por otro lado, hay fenómenos religiosos curiosos que tienen su origen en civilizaciones pasadas. 5

Uno de los fenómenos arqueológicos inexplicables está en Nazca, Perú. Allí, en la tierra, hay dibujos gigantescos de animales y flores que sólo pueden verse en su totalidad desde el aire. También hay unas líneas muy derechas que tal vez sean pistas de aterrizaje[1] que se hicieron en la época prehistórica para visitantes extraterrestres. 10

Otro enigma arqueológico, que contradice toda lógica, está en la Isla de Pascua, Chile. Allí, al lado del mar, hay unas cabezas enormes de piedra volcánica. Hay mucha controversia sobre el origen de estos monolitos, pero se cree que se construyeron unos cuatrocientos años antes de Cristo. Hoy en día, todavía es inexplicable cómo una pequeña 15 población pudo mover estas cabezas, que pesan más de veinte toneladas cada una, tantos kilómetros, desde el volcán hasta la costa. Hay gente que afirma que es un fenómeno sobrenatural.

Toneladas = toneladas métricas. Una tonelada métrica = 2204 libras.

---

1. **pistas . . .** landing strips

En el mundo hispano no sólo hay fenómenos arqueológicos intrigantes sino que existen también algunas costumbres religiosas que
muestran aspectos fascinantes de la cultura. Una de estas costumbres es
el uso de la hoja de coca por los indios de Bolivia y Perú. Ellos le ofrecen
la coca a la diosa Pachamama para que ella les dé buena suerte; también
mascan[2] la coca para evitar el hambre y el cansancio que causa la alti-
tud. La hoja de coca se usa además en esa zona para predecir el futuro y
para diagnosticar enfermedades.

Un fenómeno religioso que coexiste con el catolicismo es la santería,
común en varios países del Caribe. Es de origen africano y consiste en la
identificación de dioses africanos con santos cristianos. Cuando los españoles trajeron a los esclavos a América, los forzaron a adoptar el cris-
tianismo, pero ellos no abandonaron totalmente su propia religión y el
resultado fue una mezcla de las dos religiones. La santería que se practica hoy en día varía de país en país. En Cuba, por ejemplo, los *orishas*
(dioses) corresponden a los santos cristianos: Babalú es el nombre de
San Lázaro y es el protector de los enfermos; Changó, el dios del rayo[3],
es Santa Bárbara. Hay símbolos especiales asociados con cada orisha y
rituales para honrarlos.

Estos fenómenos arqueológicos y religiosos nos muestran varios aspectos de la cultura hispana. Desafortunadamente, algunas prácticas o

Elicit from students the kinds of articles sold at a **botánica** (from photo). Mention that many people other than *santeros* buy at these stores.

Botánica en Harlem, Nueva York.

2. they chew   3. lightning

costumbres pueden ser malinterpretadas, en vez de ser aceptadas como   4C
formas de expresión de un grupo determinado.

Actividad 18: Los prefijos

Escribe qué significan las siguientes palabras del texto, usando tu
conocimiento de prefijos. Consulta el texto si es necesario.

1. línea 6 **inexplicables**
2. línea 10 **extraterrestres**
3. línea 11 **contradice**
4. línea 18 **sobrenatural**
5. línea 25 **predecir**
6. línea 40 **malinterpretadas**

Act. 18: 1. inexplicable   2. extraterrestrials   3. contradicts   4. supernatural   5. to predict   6. misinterpreted

Actividad 19: Preguntas

Contesta estas preguntas.

1. En tu opinión, ¿se construyeron las líneas de Nazca para extraterrestres?
2. ¿Cuál es el fenómeno inexplicable de la Isla de Pascua?
3. ¿Conoces otros fenómenos inexplicables?
4. ¿Para qué usan la coca los indios de Perú y Bolivia?
5. ¿Cuál es el origen de la santería?
6. ¿Crees que existan los malos espíritus? ¿Crees que los seres humanos tengamos energía positiva y energía negativa *(good and bad vibes)*?

Act. 19: If possible, give the history of the use of **coca.** Discuss its religious significance. Point out that the Indians are not drug addicts. Explain how the importance of cocaine in the 19th century created a "gold rush" in the Andes and that until recently, cocaine was not considered harmful.

Ask students what practices or phenomena in the U.S. might be either inexplicable to or misinterpreted by foreigners. Discuss the Bermuda Triangle.

Examples of expressing personal opinion: Line 3: "**quizás nunca se encuentre**"   Line 9: "**tal vez sean**"   Line 14: "**se cree que**"   Line 17: "**Hay gente que afirma**"
Using words such as **difíciles, curiosos,** etc., also show the authors' point of view.

Estrategia de escritura: *Describing and Giving Your Opinion*

When describing something—a situation, a theory, etc.—first you must establish the main idea you want to convey by answering the question *what?* To describe supporting details and to give your reader the necessary background information for understanding, you should also address questions such as *who?*, *where?*, *how?*, and *why?*. In formal writing, expressions such as **es interesante, se dice, tal vez, es bueno/malo que,** etc., introduce the author's point of view. In informal writing, you may express your point of view or interpretation of the topic with phrases such as **pienso que, dudo que, en mi opinión, creo que,** and **tal vez.**

Although the previous text is written in a formal manner, can you find two examples where the author expresses a personal opinion?

La suerte = good luck.

Actividad 20: La suerte

Hay muchas personas que dicen que la suerte no existe. Entonces, ¿por qué hay personas que, por ejemplo, usan el mismo par de medias para todos los partidos de basquetbol? En grupos de cuatro, hablen sobre el tema de la suerte. Si creen que la suerte existe, describan algunas costumbres que tienen Uds. que piensan les traen suerte. Después, cada persona escoge la costumbre de uno de sus compañeros, escribe un párrafo con su descripción y da su opinión.

I. Discuss the importance of bread in Hispanic culture.

Lo esencial

I. La comida

Practice vocabulary at the supermarket, when making up your shopping list, and when cooking.

1. el aceite
2. la cebolla
3. la fruta
4. los huevos
5. el jamón
6. la lechuga
7. el pan
8. la pimienta
9. el queso
10. la sal
11. el tomate
12. el vinagre

Actividad 21: Una ensalada

Prepared salad dressings are not normally used; Hispanics prefer **aceite y vinagre.**

En grupos de tres, imagínense que Uds. van a preparar una ensalada *(salad)*. Digan qué ingredientes van a ponerle.

Actividad 22: El menú

En parejas, planeen un picnic usando las cosas que compraron en la tienda de comida.

¿Lo sabían?

En el mundo hispano, por lo general, la comida más importante del día es la del mediodía, que en muchos países se llama el almuerzo. A esa hora mucha gente va a casa a comer con su familia; por eso, en algunos lugares es normal que se cierren casi todas las tiendas durante unas dos horas. La hora de las comidas varía de país en país, pero generalmente se come unas horas más tarde que en los Estados Unidos. En este país, ¿cuánto tiempo tienen para almorzar las personas que trabajan y por qué? ¿Dónde almuerzan generalmente? ¿Cuál es la comida más importante del día?

II. Preparando la comida

Freír is an irregular verb. See Appendix A.

1. añadir	3. darle la vuelta	5. poner la mesa
2. cortar	4. freír	6. revolver

Actividad 23: Los cocineros

Di qué cosas de la siguiente lista de comida se pueden cortar, freír, revolver, añadir, etc.

	la sal
se corta	un huevo
se fríe	el pan
se añade	el jamón
se le da la vuelta a	la pimienta
se revuelve	el aceite
	el queso
	la cebolla

Act. 24: Encourage students to be outrageous and creative.

Actividad 24: El "chef"

Use the passive and impersonal **se** to give instructions: **Primero, se cortan las patatas.**

Eres cocinero/a y vas a inventar un plato nuevo. Escribe la receta *(recipe)* y después explícale la receta a un/a amigo/a. Por ejemplo: Primero se cortan . . . . Después se . . . , etc. Se llama . . . y es delicioso.

Después de un día de trabajo, una cena ligera

La cena = evening meal (Spain and some countries in Latin America); in other countries, supper is called **la comida.**

hay que + infinitive	one/you must + *verb*
mientras tanto	meanwhile
No puedo más.	I can't take it anymore.

Después de arreglar el apartamento, los chicos están cansados y tienen hambre. Ahora están hablando sobre la cena.

Actividad 25: Ponlas en orden

Escucha la conversación y pon en orden estas instrucciones para hacer una tortilla española.

_6_ Añades la sal.
_1_ Cortas las patatas y la cebolla.
_2_ Fríes las patatas y la cebolla.
_9_ Le das la vuelta a la tortilla.
_8_ Pones todo en la sartén.
_5_ Revuelves las patatas y la cebolla con los huevos.
_7_ Quitas casi todo el aceite de la sartén.
_3_ Revuelves los huevos.
_4_ Pones las patatas y la cebolla en un recipiente.

Una familia española prepara
la cena. ¿Quiénes están partici-
pando?

Make a tortilla in class, if possible, or assign as homework. Follow the recipe in the dialogue.

Vicente	¡Qué hambre tengo!
Isabel	Y yo también; ¡no puedo más! ¿Quién va a preparar la comida?
Juan Carlos	Álvaro, el gran cocinero cordobés, nos va a preparar una tortilla española, ¿no es verdad Álvaro?
Diana	¡Ay, qué bueno! Si tú me das instrucciones puedo aprender a hacerla yo.
Álvaro	Vale, yo te enseño, pero espero que Teresa y Vicente preparen la ensalada y los otros pongan la mesa.
Diana	¿Y cómo se hace la tortilla?
Álvaro	Primero, se cortan unas cuatro patatas grandes y un poco de cebolla y . . .
Diana	¿Se cortan en trozos grandes o pequeños?
Álvaro	No, no, pequeños; y luego se fríen en aceite. Mientras tanto, revuelves los huevos, o sea, bien revueltos.
Diana	Y después, ¿qué hago? ¿Pongo los huevos en la sartén?

Expressing a desire

Giving instructions

246

Álvaro	No, se ponen las patatas y la cebolla en un recipiente, se revuelven con los huevos y se añade un poco de sal. Después, se quita casi todo el aceite de la sartén dejando sólo un poco.
Diana	Y luego, ¿se pone todo en la sartén?
Álvaro	Exactamente. Pero hay que esperar unos minutos antes de darle la vuelta.
Diana	Pero, ¿cómo se le da la vuelta?
Álvaro	Pues, se pone un plato encima.
Diana	Ay, tengo miedo de que salga mal. ¿Por qué no la haces tú?
Álvaro	Bueno. Te voy a ayudar pero no la voy a hacer por ti.
Teresa	A ver. De primer plato tenemos ensalada; de segundo plato, la tortilla de papas a la Diana, jamón y queso y de postre, fruta.
Vicente	Y café, ¿no?
Teresa	¡Ay, no! No lo compramos. ¡Qué lástima que no tengamos café!
Álvaro	No importa. Salimos después a tomarlo en algún lugar.

Expressing fear

Expressing regret

Actividad 26: Preguntas

Después de escuchar el diálogo, contesta estas preguntas.

1. ¿Quién es un buen cocinero?
2. ¿Quién va a preparar la tortilla y por qué?
3. ¿Qué van a comer de primer plato los chicos? ¿Quién va a prepararlo?
4. ¿Qué van a comer de segundo plato? ¿Y de postre?
5. ¿Van a tomar el café con la comida o después de comer?
6. ¿Sabes cuál es la diferencia entre la tortilla española y la tortilla mexicana?

Pronunciation: [s]: **c, s, z**
Discuss **ceceo** vs. **seseo** if you wish.
1. Model and have students repeat after you words that contain [s]: **tal vez, quizás, hacer, saber,** etc.
2. Have students read aloud 5 words from the dialogue that contain [s].

El primer plato is frequently called **la entrada.**

Discuss how coffee-drinking habits differ in the U.S. and in Hispanic countries. Mention the lack of refills, the preference for expresso and/or strong coffee, etc.

Compare lunch hour in the U.S. with the longer lunch break in Hispanic countries.

¿Lo sabían?

En los países hispanos las comidas normalmente tienen tres platos o más. El primer plato puede ser una sopa o una ensalada; el segundo plato es el plato principal, que varía de país en país. Éste puede ser comida picante *(hot, spicy)* como se come en México y en Perú, por ejemplo, o no picante, como se come en muchos otros países hispanos. El último plato es el postre, que a menudo es fruta. En algunos países es usual tomar vino y agua con o sin gas con las comidas. El café no se toma normalmente con la comida sino después y en taza pequeña porque es mucho más fuerte que el café que se toma en los Estados Unidos. ¿Qué tomas tú con las comidas? ¿Te gusta la comida picante?

Actividad 27: Las necesidades

Termina estas frases, usando **hay que**.

1. Para el examen de mañana . . .
2. La casa está en desorden; . . .
3. Para hacer un viaje . . .
4. No hay huevos para la tortilla; . . .
5. Para tener dinero . . .
6. Para jugar al fútbol . . .

Hacia la comunicación

Gramática

Note: **Ojalá (que)** takes the subjunctive because it expresses emotion.

I. Drill verbs of emotion:
1. Contrast **tener miedo** with and without subjunctive by having students finish these sentences: **Tenemos miedo de** + infinitive and **Tenemos miedo de que ...**
2. Use famous people in sentences: **Liz Taylor se sorprende de que ... Me sorprendo de que Liz Taylor ... Dan Quayle tiene miedo de que ...** (etc.)
3. Give situations and have students give rejoinders: **Mi niño está en el hospital.** S1: **Siento que esté enfermo. Es una pena ...** Encourage multiple responses.
4. Give the response and have students create the initial statement: **Es una lástima que no tengas más tiempo.** S1: **Tengo que irme.** (etc.)

I. Expressing Emotions: More Uses of the Subjunctive

Up to now, you have seen that the subjunctive is used in dependent noun clauses after verbs that express influence and doubt. In addition, it is used in dependent clauses after verbs that express emotion.

1. To express emotion in a personal way:
   a. the independent clause contains the subject expressing the emotion and a verb of emotion such as **alegrarse de** *(to be happy about)*, **esperar, sentir, tener miedo de,** or **sorprenderse de** *(to be surprised about).*
   b. the dependent clause contains a different subject and a verb in the subjunctive.

¿Te **alegras de que vengan** los muchachos?	*Are you happy that the guys are coming?*
Siento que no **quieras** ir conmigo.	*I'm sorry that you don't want to go with me.*
Me sorprendo de que no te **afeites**, Álvaro.	*I'm surprised that you don't shave, Álvaro.*
Nos alegramos de que te **guste** la tortilla.	*We're glad that you like the tortilla.*

2. To express emotion in an impersonal way:
   a. the independent clause contains an impersonal expression of emotion such as **qué lástima, es una pena, qué pena,** or **es fantástico.**
   b. the dependent clause contains a subject and a verb in the subjunctive.

¡**Qué lástima que** no **tengas** lavadora!	*What a shame that you don't have a washer.*
¡**Qué pena que** no **podamos** salir esta noche!	*What a pity that we can't go out tonight!*

Review uses of **para** and **por,** Ch. 5.

II. Other Uses of *para* and *por*

You have already learned some uses of **para** and **por** in Chapter 5. Here are some other uses.

A. Para

To give a personal opinion.

Para Gabriel, el carro español Seat es el coche perfecto.	*For Gabriel, the Spanish car Seat is the perfect car.*

II. Demonstrate **por: Camino por la clase. Salgo por la puerta. El hombre invisible pasa por la pared.** Reenter: **Voy a viajar por/en tren.**

Drill **para** and **por:**
1. Have students negotiate with peers to trade items: **Te doy mi lápiz por tu pluma.**
2. Make controversial statements and have students give opinions: **La astrología es una ciencia ...** S1: **Para mí, no es una ciencia.**

B. Por

a. To indicate that a person is replacing someone.

Muchas veces Jay Leno trabaja **por** Johnny Carson.	*Jay Leno often works for Johnny Carson. (He takes his place.)*

b. To indicate exchange.

¿Cuánto pagaste **por** tu raqueta de tenis?	*How much did you pay for your tennis racket? (Payment indicates exchange.)*
Te doy mis esquíes **por** tus patines.	*I'll give you my skis for your skates.*

c. To indicate *along, by, through.*

Do mechanical drills, Workbook, Part II.

Caminaron **por** la playa.	*They walked along the beach.*
Mandé la carta **por** correo.	*I sent the letter by mail.*
Van a entrar **por** la puerta principal.	*They are going to come in through the main door.*

Emotion = subjunctive.

Actividad 28: El miedo y la esperanza

Todos tenemos esperanzas y miedos sobre el futuro. En dos minutos escribe tres cosas que te dan miedo y tres esperanzas que tienes. Después, pregúntales a tus compañeros de qué tienen miedo y qué esperanzas tienen. Puedes contestar de dos formas.

Act. 28: Point out to students that the subjunctive is used when there are two subjects.

¿De qué tienes miedo?
$\begin{cases} \text{Tengo miedo de una guerra nu-} \\ \quad \text{clear.} \\ \text{Tengo miedo de que tengamos una} \\ \quad \text{guerra nuclear.} \end{cases}$

¿Qué esperas para el futuro?
$\begin{cases} \text{Espero tener un trabajo bueno.} \\ \text{Espero que me den un trabajo} \\ \quad \text{bueno.} \end{cases}$

Actividad 29: El pesimista y el optimista

En parejas, imagínense que una persona es pesimista y la otra persona es optimista. Están haciendo comentarios sobre una comida que está preparando un amigo por primera vez. Terminen las siguientes oraciones de forma original.

El/La pesimista

1. Tengo miedo de que . . .
2. ¡Qué pena que . . . !
3. Es una lástima que . . .
4. Espero que . . .
5. Me sorprendo de que . . .

El/La optimista

1. Me alegro de que . . .
2. Es fantástico que . . .
3. Me sorprendo de que . . .
4. Estoy contento/a de que . . .
5. Me gusta que . . .

Actividad 30: ¿Por o para quién?

Forma oraciones para las siguientes situaciones usando **para** o **por.**

Marcos trabaja en la oficina de su tío.

Marcos trabaja **para** su tío.

Fueron a América en el Titanic.

Fueron **por** barco.

1. Oscar compra doce rosas rojas porque es el cumpleaños de su novia.
2. Todas las noches ella corre diez kilómetros. Corre en el parque.
3. Pablo es estudiante de ingeniería, pero no le interesan sus estudios. Su padre es ingeniero y quiere que su hijo estudie esa carrera.
4. Ayer Carlos estuvo enfermo y por eso no pudo jugar fútbol. Felipe tuvo que jugar en su lugar.
5. Pepe Morales tiene un banco y su nieto Pepito es cajero allí.
6. El profesor Fernández está en el hospital y la Sra. Ramírez da las clases en su lugar.

Actividad 31: El viaje a Cancún

Uno de Uds. acaba de recibir la siguiente carta pero no sabe qué pensar. En parejas, hablen con su compañero/a para ver qué piensa de la carta. Usen frases como **tengo miedo de que . . . , es posible que . . . , (no) creo que . . . , me sorprendo de que . . . , no hay duda (de) que . . . , siento que . . . , espero que . . . , es evidente que . . . ,** etc.

Estimado/a señor/señora:

Tengo el gusto de informarle que Ud. acaba de recibir un viaje para dos personas a Cancún, México, por una semana. Es posible que sea una segunda luna de miel, un regalo para su persona favorita o simplemente una manera de dejar el frío del invierno para ir al calor del Caribe. En Cancún, van a estar en los Condominios Miramar que se acaban de

Playa y ruinas de Tulum, cerca de Cancún, México.

Act. 31: Ask students if they receive letters like this. If they say yes, ask if they answer them. Ask, ¿Creen Uds. que cartas como ésta deban ser ilegales?

construir. Tienen playa, piscina, restaurante, bar, casino, discoteca y campo de golf de 18 hoyos. Van a recibir además un jeep gratis por esa semana para que viajen por el área.

Hay solamente una condición: es necesario que pasen una mañana visitando los Condominios Miramar con un representante del lugar.

El vuelo no está incluido pero es posible hacer la reserva en vuelos especiales organizados por Maya Tours.

Para hacer la reserva en Cancún y para comprar sus pasajes de avión, llame al número 1-314-555-7859 y pregunte por Antonio González.

Ojalá que no pierdan esta oportunidad única en su vida. Esperamos que se diviertan en Cancún.

El agente de la felicidad,

Antonio González

Antonio González
Maya Tours

P.D. Una cosita más . . . Esperamos que Ud. nos permita usar su nombre y su foto para hacer publicidad de los Condominios Miramar.

Autorizo. _____
Firma

No autorizo el uso ni de mi nombre ni de mi foto para publicidad.

_____
Firma

251

Act. 32: Assign this the night before to be read at home.

Point out the title: **tomar** (not **hacer**) **decisiones.** Set a time limit.

Actividad 32: Tomando decisiones

Adrián Molina Durán es un hombre de negocios que viaja mucho. Tiene treinta y ocho años y estuvo casado por cinco años, pero nunca tuvo hijos. En general, está muy contento con su vida y su trabajo, pero quiere ser papá. Quiere casarse pero no sabe con quién. A Adrián le gustan las mujeres que son activas, independientes y que tienen buen sentido del humor. Piensa que una mujer debe dedicarse a los hijos, pero también cree que es importante que trabaje. Conoce a tres mujeres que viven en tres ciudades diferentes que tal vez quieran casarse con él. En grupos de tres, decidan a quién debe preguntarle si quiere ser su esposa. Usen frases como **es posible que . . . , dudo que . . . , es una lástima que . . . , es mejor que . . . , creo que . . . ,** etc. Aquí están las opciones de Adrián.

Carolina
Es una actriz de cine de veintinueve años muy rica y que viaja mucho. Es muy romántica y la última vez que Adrián estuvo con ella, fueron a una fiesta en Hollywood; allí Adrián conoció a muchas personas famosas. Carolina sólo quiere tener un hijo, pero le gustaría adoptar más. Quiere continuar con su trabajo después de casarse.

Alejandra
Es profesora de escuela secundaria. Tiene treinta y dos años, es muy simpática y quiere tener muchos hijos porque le gustan los niños. Baila muy bien y va a clases de gimnasia aeróbica. Después de tener hijos quiere trabajar, pero no tiempo completo porque cree que los hijos necesitan a la madre en casa. También cree que es importante que el padre pase mucho tiempo con los niños.

Camila
Es una mujer de negocios que tiene cuarenta años. Es divorciada, tiene tres hijos y no quiere tener más. Sus hijos son muy simpáticos y quieren mucho a Adrián. Tiene una boutique de ropa que es muy famosa y toda la gente importante compra en su tienda. A ella le gusta la ropa exclusiva y siempre lleva vestidos de diseñadores famosos como Oscar de la Renta y Carolina Herrera.

Act. 33: Have some students read opposing viewpoints and have the students decide as a class on the best woman for Adrián.

Use phrases from the **Estrategia de escritura** section to help you state your opinions.

Actividad 33: El hombre feliz

En grupos de tres, escriban un párrafo diciendo por qué Carolina, Alejandra o Camila es la mujer ideal para Adrián. Deben estar preparados para leerle el párrafo a la clase.

Vocabulario funcional

Los pasatiempos
Ver página 231

La comida
Ver página 243

Otro vocabulario relacionado con la comida

la ensalada salad
el primer plato first course

el segundo plato second course
el postre dessert

Preparando la comida
Ver página 244

Verbos

alegrarse de to be happy about
dudar to doubt
sentir to feel sorry

sorprenderse de to be surprised about

Cosas de la cocina
Ver página 233

Adverbios
Ver página 235

Expresiones impersonales

es cierto it's true
es claro it's clear
es dudoso it's doubtful
es evidente it's evident
es fantástico it's fantastic
es obvio it's obvious
es posible it's possible

es probable it's probable
es una pena it's a pity
es verdad it's true
no hay duda (de) there's no doubt
¡Qué lástima! What a shame!
¡Qué pena! What a pity!

Palabras y expresiones útiles

estar seguro/a (de) to be sure
hay que + infinitive one/you must + *verb*
el mal de ojo a curse
mientras tanto meanwhile
No puedo más. I can't take it anymore.
¿No sabías? Didn't you know?

¡Qué mala suerte! What bad luck!
quizás/tal vez + subjunctive perhaps/maybe
Somos tres. There are three of us.
tener suerte to be lucky
la ventana window

¿Para qué es esta carreta (*cart*)? En tu opinión, ¿se usan estas carretas hoy día para trabajar o crees que sean sólo una parte del folklore?

Un hombre pinta la rueda *(wheel)* de una carreta en Sarchí, Costa Rica.

Capítulo 10

Chapter Objectives

After studying this chapter, you will know how to:

- avoid redundancies in everyday speech
- describe actions, situations, people, and things in the past
- talk about sports
- make use of postal services

El jai alai es un deporte del país vasco en el norte de España. Es el deporte más rápido del mundo. También es popular en la Florida, Estados Unidos. (Guernica, España)

It is common to bet on jai alai games.

If this is the beginning of the semester and you have students who did not use the first half of the text, have former students summarize the plot and describe the characters. This will provide a review of key functions.

You may want to refer new students to p. 13.

¡Feliz día!

echar de menos	to miss (someone or something)
a lo mejor	perhaps
quedarse en + place	to stay in + *place*

Después de pasar dos años en España sin ver a su familia, Vicente regresa a Costa Rica de vacaciones para ver a sus padres y para celebrar su cumpleaños.

Actividad 1: ¿Cierto o falso?

Escucha la conversación entre Vicente y sus padres y escribe una **C** si la oración es cierta y una **F** si la oración es falsa.

1. ___C___ Hace un mes que Vicente le mandó una tarjeta a su madre.
2. ___F___ A la madre le gustó la tarjeta.
3. ___C___ Hoy es el cumpleaños de Vicente.
4. ___C___ Los padres de Vicente le compraron un regalo.
5. ___F___ Vicente y sus padres van a ir a Sarchí.
6. ___C___ Es posible que Vicente le compre un regalo a Teresa.

El Teatro Nacional de San José (al centro) es uno de los edificios más apreciados de la capital de Costa Rica.

Discuss how saints' days are often celebrated like birthdays. Calendars normally list the saints for each day.

Complaining

Expressing likes

Discussing memories

Avoiding redundancies

Vos is commonly used in Costa Rica and in other parts of Latin America instead of **tú**. It was omitted from the dialogue, but could be discussed in class.

Vicente	No saben cuánto me gusta estar en Costa Rica otra vez; siempre los echo de menos a Uds. y a mis amigos.
Madre	Y a nosotros nos encanta tenerte en casa, hijo.
Vicente	Por cierto, mamá, no dijiste nada sobre la tarjeta que te mandé para tu santo.
Madre	Pero, ¿qué tarjeta? Yo no recibí nada.
Vicente	Te la mandé hace un mes por avión.
Padre	Es que el correo es terrible. Mandas cosas y tardan un siglo en llegar, si llegan.
Madre	No te preocupes; ya va a llegar. Además, mi mejor regalo es tener a mi hijo aquí con nosotros, gracias a Dios.
Vicente	Gracias, mamá. Bueno, ¿qué vamos a hacer hoy?
Padre	Primero, vamos a darte tu regalo de cumpleaños; aquí lo tienes. Te lo compramos porque sabemos que es algo que necesitas. ¡Feliz cumpleaños!
Vicente	. . . ¡Una raqueta de tenis! Hace mucho tiempo que no juego. Muchas gracias mamá . . . papá.
Padre	¿Te gusta?
Vicente	¡Me fascina!
Padre	Bueno, ahora vamos a ir a Sarchí para ver las carretas.
Vicente	¿Para el festival?
Padre	Sí, lo celebran hoy.
Vicente	¡Pura vida![1] Echo de menos el "canto" de las carretas. Tenía tres años cuando subí a la carreta del abuelo por primera vez y me fascinó. ¿Vienes con nosotros, mamá?
Madre	No, me quedo en casa porque me duele la cabeza y quiero dormir un poco.
Vicente	Pero mamá . . .
Madre	No, es mejor que vayan Uds. solos. ¡Ah! ¡Oye! Sarchí es un buen lugar si quieres comprarle algo de artesanía típica a Teresa.
Vicente	A lo mejor le regalo una carreta pequeña.
Padre	Yo conozco un lugar perfecto donde se la puedes comprar.
Vicente	Bueno, voy a echarle gasolina al carro. Ahorita vengo, papá. Adiós mamá; espero que te mejores.
Madre	Hasta luego mi amor; que Dios te acompañe.
Padre	. . . ¿Ya llamaste a todos sus amigos?
Madre	Sí, vienen como a las ocho. A Vicente le va a encantar verlos a todos. Tengo mucho que hacer mientras Uds. están en Sarchí. No pueden llegar hasta las 9:00, ¿eh?

---

1. That's great! (Costa Rican expression)

Actividad 2: Preguntas

Después de escuchar la conversación, contesta estas preguntas.

1. ¿Por qué le mandó Vicente una tarjeta a su madre?
2. Según el padre de Vicente, ¿qué ocurre cuando se mandan cosas por correo?
3. ¿Qué van a hacer Vicente y su padre en Sarchí?
4. ¿Qué va a pasar esta noche en la casa de Vicente?
5. ¿Es verdad que a la madre de Vicente le duele la cabeza?
6. ¿Es muy religiosa la madre de Vicente? ¿Por qué sí o por qué no?

¿Lo sabían?

En español las palabras **Dios** y **Jesús** se oyen con frecuencia en las conversaciones y esto no significa que la persona que las usa sea religiosa o irrespetuosa. Algunas expresiones comunes que se usan son **¡Por Dios!, ¡Dios mío!, Con la ayuda de Dios, ¡Sabe Dios . . .!** *(Who knows . . .!)*, **Dios mediante** *(God willing)* y **que Dios te acompañe** *(May God go with you)*. ¿Es común usar el nombre de Dios en los Estados Unidos?

Actividad 3: Las carretas de Sarchí

En parejas, escojan el papel A o B y cubran las instrucciones para el papel de su compañero/a. Lean las instrucciones para su papel y conversen según las indicaciones.

Papel A

Eres Vicente y estás en Sarchí con tu padre mirando y comentando sobre las carretas. Después de un rato *(while)*, estás cansado y quieres volver a tu casa.

Papel B

Eres el padre de Vicente y estás con tu hijo en Sarchí mirando las carretas. Tienes que tratar de distraer *(distract)* a tu hijo para que tu esposa pueda preparar la fiesta de cumpleaños para tu hijo. Recuerda que conoces el lugar ideal donde Vicente puede comprarle un regalo a su novia.

¿Lo sabían?

Hace unos ochenta años en Sarchí, Costa Rica, empezaron a pintar las carretas de trabajo de colores muy brillantes. Las mejores carretas son las que tienen los colores más fuertes y las que "cantan" mejor. El canto de las carretas es un ruido especial que hacen cuando se mueven. Hoy en día todavía se usan las carretas para trabajar en el campo, por ejemplo, para transportar el café por los caminos donde los carros no pueden pasar fácilmente.

Lo esencial

El correo

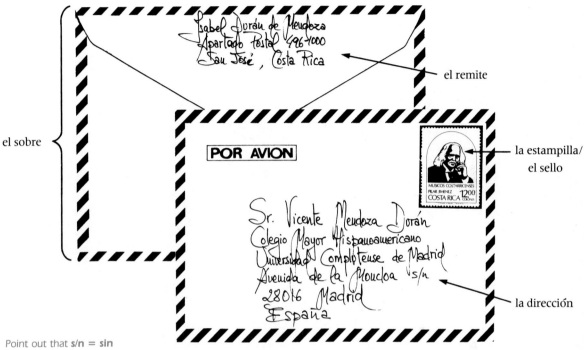

el sobre

el remite

la estampilla/
el sello

POR AVION

la dirección

Point out that **s/n = sin
número.**

Point out **la** with **cartero.**

Ask students to name other
places where one stands in line.

Practice this vocabulary
while receiving and send-
ing letters.

Act. 4: Make sure students take
turns.

Otras palabras relacionadas con el correo

el aerograma	aerogram	**hacer cola**	to stand in line
el buzón	mailbox	**mandar una carta**	to send a letter
la carta	letter	**el paquete**	package
el/la cartero	letter carrier	**la (tarjeta) postal**	postcard
certificado/a	certified	**el telegrama**	telegram
el giro postal	money order		

Actividad 4: Definiciones

En parejas, una persona define palabras que tienen que ver con el
correo y la otra adivina qué palabras son. Altérnense frecuentemente.

A: Si quiero mandarte dinero por correo te mando esto.
B: Un giro postal.

Act. 5: Encourage students to bring in stamps if they are collectors.

Actividad 5: ¿Coleccionas estampillas?

Uds. coleccionan estampillas y van a intercambiarlas. Quieren saber de dónde son y qué representan las estampillas de su compañero/a. En parejas, el/la estudiante "A" cubre la Columna B y el/la estudiante "B" cubre la Columna A. "A" colecciona estampillas de personas famosas y a "B" le gustan las estampillas de flores o animales.

A   B

Junípero Serra, a missionary and one of the colonizers of California.
Santa Teresa, a 16th century writer, mystic, and reformist nun.
Christopher Columbus (Cristóbal Colón), this stamp commemorates the establishment of the first Spanish colony in the Americas in the Dominican Republic.
Simón Bolívar, "el Libertador," the George Washington of northern South America.
Oscar Arias, president of Costa Rica, recipient of the Nobel Peace Prize, 1988.

Oficina de correos en Cuzco, Perú. ¿Qué crees que significa "terrestre"?

Actividad 6: En orden, por favor

En parejas, pongan estas oraciones sobre el correo en orden lógico.

_____ Busco un buzón.

_____ Escribo el remite en el sobre.

_____ Le pongo una estampilla.

_____ Echo la carta en el buzón.

_____ Escribo la carta.

_____ La pongo en un sobre.

_____ Escribo la dirección en el sobre.

Hacia la comunicación

Gramática

> The verb agrees with what is loved, hurt, etc. The indirect-object pronoun tells who is affected.

I. Drill verbs like **gustar:**
1. Do a chain drill. S1: **Odio ... , pero me fascina/n ...** S2: **Ralph odia ... , pero le fascina/n ... Yo odio ... , pero me fascina ...** (etc.)
2. Air complaints about the university: **Me molesta/n ...** Others react by saying: **A mí no me importa/n ... / También me importa/n ...**
3. Ask opinions: **¿Qué te pareció el último examen? ¿Qué les parecieron ...?**
4. Ask students to be chronic complainers: **Me duele la cabeza. Me falta dinero.** (etc.) Others can give advice or show indifference: **A lo mejor debes ... /No me importa.**

I. Using Verbs Like *gustar*

In Chapter 2, you learned how to use the verb **gustar.**

> ¿**Te gusta** el festival?
> **Nos gustan** las carretas de Sarchí.

1. Here are some other verbs that work like **gustar:**

doler(ue)	to hurt	**fascinar**	to like a lot;
encantar	to like a lot, love		to fascinate
faltar	to lack; to be missing	**importar**	to matter
		molestar	to bother

> ¿**Le duelen** los pies a la madre de Vicente?
> A Vicente **le encanta** visitar a su familia.

> *Do Vicente's mother's feet hurt? (Literally: Her feet hurt her.)*
> *Vicente loves to visit his family. (Literally: Visiting his family is really pleasing to him.)*

2. The verb **parecer** *(to seem)* is used much like **gustar,** except that it must be immediately followed by either an adjective or a clause introduced by **que.**

> **Me parecen** bonitas esas estampillas.
> A él **le parece** que va a llover.

> *Those stamps seem pretty to me.*
> *It seems to him it's going to rain.*

When **parecer** is used in a question with the word **qué,** its meaning changes to *how do/does/did . . . like . . . ?*

> ¿Qué **te pareció** el regalo?

> *How did you like (What did you think of) the present?*

II. Avoiding Redundancies: Combining Direct- and Indirect-Object Pronouns

Before studying the grammar explanation, answer this question based on the dialogue:

• When Vicente and his father say the following, to what do the words in boldface refer?   "**Te la** mandé hace un mes . . ." / "**Te lo** compramos porque sabemos . . ."

In Chapters 6 and 7 you learned how to use the indirect- and the direct-object pronouns separately. The indirect object tells for whom or to whom the action is done and the direct object is the person or thing that directly receives the action of the verb.

Indirect-object pronouns		Direct-object pronouns	
me	nos	me	nos
te	os	te	os
le	les	lo, la	los, las

Le mandé un regalo a mi amiga.	*I sent a gift to her (to my friend).*
—Mandaste un regalo?	*Did you send a gift?*
—Sí, **lo** mandé.	*Yes, I sent it.*

II. Clarification of the indirect-object pronoun can only be done with an a-phrase: **Se lo mandé a él.**

Remember: Indirect before direct (I.D.).

1. When you use both an indirect- and a direct-object pronoun in the same sentence, the indirect-object pronoun immediately precedes the direct-object pronoun.

Mi amigo me dio un libro.   ¿Quién te mandó la carta?

Mi amigo **me lo** dio.   ¿Quién **te la** mandó?
My friend gave it to me.   *Who sent it to you?*

Drill direct- and indirect-object pronouns:
1. Do transformation drills: **Le escribí una carta.** → **Se la escribí.**
2. Do questions and answers: **¿Me escribiste un memo? ¿Le compraste un regalo?**
3. Have students write questions and answers, then have them quiz each other.

The indirect-object pronouns **le** and **les** become **se** when combined with the direct-object pronouns **lo, la, los,** and **las**.

$$\text{le/les} \rightarrow \text{se} + \text{lo/la/los/las}$$

Le voy a pedir un café (a Inés). → **Se lo** voy a pedir (a Inés/a ella).
Les escribí las instrucciones (a ellos). → **Se las** escribí (a ellos).

2. As you have learned before, object pronouns can either precede a conjugated verb or be attached to the end of an infinitive or present participle.

Remember to add accents when needed.

Se lo voy a mandar.	Voy a mand**ár**selo.
Se la estoy escribiendo.	Estoy escrib**ié**ndosela.

Do mechanical drills, Workbook, Part I.

Actividad 7: Los dolores

Ask students what would
change if **codos** instead of
codo were in the example.

Después de jugar un partido de fútbol, los atletas profesionales siempre tienen problemas. Mira el dibujo de estos atletas y di qué les duele.

◖●◗ Al número 34 le duele el codo.

Act. 8: Find out class preferences by comparing the completed polls. Make generaliza-
tions: **A muchos no les gusta la
música clásica.**

Actividad 8: ¿Lo odias, te gusta o te encanta?

Vas a hacer una encuesta *(poll)*. Pregúntales a tus compañeros si les gustan estas cosas. Anota *(Jot down)* sus respuestas.

	odiar	gustar	encantar
la comida picante	_____	_____	_____
los postres	_____	_____	_____
la música clásica	_____	_____	_____
cocinar	_____	_____	_____
montar en bicicleta	_____	_____	_____
fumar	_____	_____	_____
tomar vino	_____	_____	_____
hacer gimnasia	_____	_____	_____

Actividad 9: Las cosas que te faltan

Imagina que acabas de mudarte a un apartamento semiamueblado. Escribe una lista de cinco cosas que te faltan. Después, en parejas, comparen sus listas.

|●| Me falta una lavadora para lavar la ropa.

Actividad 10: ¿Qué te pareció?

En parejas, Uds. son Siskel y Ebert y en su programa de hoy van a hablar de películas de los años ochenta. Usen verbos como **encantar, fascinar, gustar, parecer**, etc.

Act. 10: *Raiders of the Lost Ark* was also translated as ***En busca del arca perdida.*** Titles translated into Spanish may vary depending on where the dubbing or subtitles were done.

|●| **A:** ¿Qué te pareció *Los cazadores del arca perdida*?
   B: Me fascinó. Hay mucha acción y Harrison Ford es un actor sensacional.

1. *Atracción fatal*
2. *Tres hombres y un bebé*
3. *Regreso al futuro*
4. *El último emperador*
5. *Un pez llamado Wanda*
6. *Los cazafantasmas*
7. *El beso de la mujer araña*
8. *Rambo IV*

Actividad 11: ¿Ya lo hiciste?

Act. 11: Have students listen, read, memorize, look up, and say their line, while maintaining eye contact with their partner. Change situations; for example, "A" and "B" are in a movie theater. Despite the circumstances, "B" is hard of hearing and speaks loudly.

En parejas, el/la estudiante "A" cubre la Columna B y el/la estudiante "B" cubre la Columna A. Mantén (*Carry on*) una conversación con tu compañero/a, escogiendo la oración apropiada de cada caja en tu columna. Hay dos conversaciones posibles.

A

¿Me compraste el champú? ¿Me compraste la cinta?

Sí, se lo di. No, no se las di.

Ya te las di, ¿no? Ya te lo di, ¿no?

B

Sí, te lo compré. ¿Y tú? ¿Le diste las cartas al cartero? Sí, te la compré. ¿Y tú? ¿Le diste el paquete al cartero?

¿Puedes mandarlas mañana, por favor? ¿Y cuándo vas a darme el dinero del alquiler? Perfecto. ¿Puedes darme las llaves del carro?

Ah, es cierto. Lo tengo en mi habitación. Ah, es verdad. Las tengo en la chaqueta.

Act. 12: Have selected pairs read aloud the mini-dialogues. Discuss possible variations.

Actividad 12: La redundancia

Estos diálogos tienen mucha repetición innecesaria. En parejas, arreglen los diálogos para que sean más naturales.

1. A: ¿Piensas comprarle un regalo a tu hermano?
   B: Sí, pienso comprarle un regalo a mi hermano mañana.
   A: ¿Cuándo vas a mandarle el regalo a tu hermano?
   B: Voy a mandarle el regalo a mi hermano mañana por la tarde.

2. A: Vicente, ¿le trajiste los cubiertos a Teresa?
   B: No, no le traje los cubiertos a Teresa. ¿Quieres que le traiga los cubiertos a Teresa mañana?
   A: Claro que mañana puedes traerle los cubiertos.

3. A: ¿Cuándo vas a prepararme la comida?
   B: Voy a prepararte la comida más tarde.
   A: Siempre dices que vas a prepararme la comida y nunca me preparas la comida. No me quieres.
   B: ¡Cómo molestas! Ya estoy preparándote la comida.

Actividad 13: En la oficina

Use **Ud.** when speaking to your boss.

En parejas, una persona es el/la empleado/a y cubre la Columna A y la otra persona es el/la jefe/a y cubre la Columna B. Los dos quieren saber si la otra persona hizo las cosas que tenía que hacer. El/La jefe/a hace preguntas primero, basándose en la información de la Columna A.

A: ¿Le mandaste el telegrama a la directora de la compañía M.O.L.A.?
B: Sí, ya se lo mandé. / No, no se lo mandé.

Act. 13: A check mark indicates that the task was completed.

A	B
Esto es lo que tiene que hacer tu empleado/a:	Esto es lo que tienes que hacer hoy:
☐ pedirle los documentos al Sr. Lerma	☐ pedirle los documentos al Sr. Lerma
☐ mandarle un giro al Dr. Fuentes	✔ mandarle un giro al Dr. Fuentes
☐ llamar a la agente de viajes	☐ llamar a la agente de viajes
☐ darte la información del banco	✔ darle la información del banco a tu jefe/a
☐ comprar estampillas	✔ comprar estampillas

Ahora, el/la empleado/a hace las preguntas, basándose en la información de la Columna B.

A

Cosas que debes hacer hoy:

☑ mandarle la carta a la
    Srta. Pereda
☐ escribirle a la Sra.
    Hernández
☑ darle las instrucciones
    a la secretaria nueva
☑ preguntarles su dirección a
    los Sres. Montero
☐ darle a tu empleado/a el
    dinero para la gasolina

B

Cosas que debe hacer tu jefe/a
    hoy:

☐ mandarle la carta a la Srta.
    Pereda
☐ escribirle a la Sra.
    Hernández
☐ darle las instrucciones
    a la secretaria nueva
☐ preguntarles su dirección a
    los Sres. Montero
☐ darte el dinero para la
    gasolina

Nuevos horizontes

Estrategia de lectura: *Finding Relationships Between Words and Sentences*

Understanding the relationship between words and sentences can help improve your understanding of a text. A text is usually full of references that are used to avoid redundancies. Common reference words used are possessive adjectives; personal, indirect-, and direct-object pronouns; demonstrative adjectives; and pronouns. Furthermore, as you have seen, subject pronouns are generally omitted where the context allows it.

You will have a chance to practice identifying references after you read the selection.

Actividad 14: Mira y contesta

1. Mira el mapa de la contratapa *(inside cover)* del libro y di qué países forman Centroamérica.
2. Mira la foto del Canal de Panamá. ¿Sabes quién lo construyó? ¿Sabes quién lo administra?
3. ¿Qué aprendiste sobre Costa Rica en este capítulo?
4. ¿Qué sabes sobre la situación política de Centroamérica?

Actividad 15: Lee y adivina

1. Lee el título de la lectura que sigue y escribe una lista de cuatro ideas que piensas que va a tratar el texto.
2. Compara tu lista con la de un/a compañero/a.
3. Lee el texto para confirmar tu predicción y busca algunos detalles de las ideas principales que se presentan.

Centroamérica: Mosaico geográfico y cultural

Uniendo dos gigantes, Norteamérica y Suramérica, y separando el Océano Atlántico del Océano Pacífico están los siete países que forman Centroamérica. Seis de ellos son países hispanos; el otro, Belice, es una antigua colonia británica.

Belize used to be British Honduras. English is the official language.

Centroamérica es un mosaico de tierras y de pueblos.[1] En esa región 5 se encuentran playas blancas, selvas tropicales, montañas de clima fresco, sabanas fértiles y gigantescos volcanes. Su población incluye indios con lenguas y costumbres precolombinas, descendientes de europeos, negros y mestizos.

Aunque los países centroamericanos están unidos físicamente por la 10 Carretera Panamericana, no hay verdadera unión entre ellos. Los esfuerzos de unificación con el Mercado Común Centroamericano en los años sesenta no tuvieron éxito y hoy en día ésta es una región de conflictos y de inestabilidad económica y política.

Barcos en las esclusas *(locks)* de Miraflores del Canal de Panamá.

---

1. peoples

El país más austral[2] de Centroamérica es Panamá, que tiene la   15
mayor población negra de los países hispanos de la región. El recurso
económico más importante de este país es el Canal de Panamá que construyeron los Estados Unidos. El gobierno estadounidense lo va a admi-
nistrar hasta el año 2000, cuando pase a manos de Panamá. Este canal es
de gran importancia comercial porque al conectar el Océano Pacífico con   20
el Océano Atlántico, es la ruta ideal para los barcos que van no sólo de
Nueva York a California sino también de Asia a Europa.

En Costa Rica, la mayoría de la población es de origen europeo y el
porcentaje de analfabetismo es bajo (10%). Es el único país centroamericano que no tiene ejército[3]; además no tiene grandes conflictos políticos   25
internos. En 1987, el presidente Oscar Arias recibió el Premio Nóbel de
la Paz por su iniciativa en buscar un fin a las guerras de Centroamérica.
Desafortunadamente, a pesar de tener paz, hoy en día Costa Rica tiene
problemas económicos muy serios.

Nicaragua, Honduras y El Salvador, por otro lado, son países de
grandes conflictos políticos internos, pero a la vez de grandes riquezas   30
naturales. Nicaragua es un país de volcanes y lagos donde sólo se cultiva
el 10% de la tierra. Honduras es un país de montañas y su población
vive principalmente en el campo; sus exportaciones principales son el
banano, el café y la madera. El Salvador, a pesar de ser el país más pequeño de la zona, es el tercer exportador de café del mundo, después de   35
Brasil y Colombia. El Salvador es además un país muy densamente
poblado. La población de Nicaragua, Honduras y El Salvador tiene un
alto porcentaje de mestizos (70%–90%).

Al norte de El Salvador está Guatemala. Allí se encuentran ruinas de
una de las civilizaciones indígenas más avanzadas, la civilización maya.   40
Más de un 50% de los guatemaltecos son descendientes directos de los
mayas y hablan una variedad de lenguas indias; ellos forman la población indígena de sangre pura más grande de Centroamérica.

A pesar de las grandes diferencias que existen entre los países centroamericanos, también hay muchas semejanzas[4]. Éstas forman la base   45
de lo que es Centroamérica, pero, realmente, es la diversidad la que le
da riqueza a la zona.

---

2. **más . . .** southernmost   3. army   4. similarities

Honduran mahogany is known worldwide.

Because of the population density, all arable land in El Salvador is used for agriculture, including craters of volcanos.

Actividad 16: Referencias

Mira el texto nuevamente y di a qué se refieren las siguientes frases o palabras.

1. línea 5 **esa región**
2. línea 11 **ellos**
3. línea 18 **lo**
4. línea 27 **su**
5. línea 33 **sus**
6. línea 39 **allí**
7. línea 42 **ellos**
8. línea 45 **Éstas**

Act. 16: 1. **Centroamérica** 2. **países centroamericanos** 3. **el Canal de Panamá** 4. de **Oscar Arias** 5. de **Honduras** 6. **en Guatemala** 7. **los mayas** 8. **semejanzas**

Mercado al aire libre en Sololá, Guatemala. ¿Puedes reconocer lo que venden?

Actividad 17: Preguntas

Después de leer el texto contesta las siguientes preguntas.

1. ¿Cuál es la importancia del Canal de Panamá?
2. ¿En qué se diferencia Costa Rica de los otros países centroamericanos?
3. ¿Qué peculiaridad caracteriza a Nicaragua, Honduras y El Salvador?
4. ¿Cuál es una característica de Guatemala?

Estrategia de escritura: *Avoiding Redundancies*

When writing, one should avoid repetition, particularly of nouns. Try to use the same kind of references that you saw in the reading when you write: possessive pronouns, object pronouns, and demonstrative adjectives and pronouns.

Actividad 18: El Canal de Panamá

Act. 18: Have students compare their versions of the text and account for their choices.

La siguiente historia del Canal de Panamá tiene muchas redundancias. Lee el texto y después escribe la historia nuevamente evitando por lo menos cuatro redundancias. Hay varias posibilidades.

En 1881 una compañía francesa inició la construcción del Canal de Panamá. Pero en 1889 la compañía francesa decidió abandonar la construcción del canal por la malaria y la fiebre amarilla de esta zona. La malaria y la fiebre amarilla causaron muchas muertes. En 1901, la compañía francesa les ofreció los derechos del proyecto de la compañía francesa a los Estados Unidos, pero Panamá en esa época era parte de Colombia y Colombia rehusó la oferta. Entonces, los Estados Unidos ayudaron a Panamá a independizarse de Colombia. Así los Estados Unidos pudieron construir el canal y terminaron el canal en 1914.

269

Lo esencial

Los artículos de deporte

El Estadio del Deporte
312 ALCALÁ   TEL. 456 33 42

Se Cierra el Negocio   Grandes Rebajas

Tenemos todo lo que Ud. necesite para los deportes: en el campo de fútbol, en la cancha de tenis, en el gimnasio. Uniformes de todos los equipos.

1. pelotas de fútbol, fútbol americano, basquetbol, tenis, squash, golf y béisbol
2. raqueta de tenis y de squash (de metal o de grafito)
3. palos de golf
4. cascos de bicicleta, moto y fútbol americano
5. pesas
6. bolas de bolos
7. patines de hielo y de ruedas
8. esquíes de agua y de nieve
9. bates
10. guantes de béisbol, boxeo y ciclismo
11. uniformes de todo tipo

> Jugar a los bolos = jugar al boliche.

Act. 19: Possible answers include: 1. **la raqueta de tenis** ... 2. **la pelota de fútbol** ... 3. **la pelota de basquetbol** ... 4. **los guantes de béisbol** ... 5. **las bolas de bolos** ... 6. **los patines de hielo** ... 7. **las pesas** ... 8. **los guantes de boxeo** ... 9. **los palos de golf** ... 10. **los cascos de fútbol americano** ...

Diego Maradona is a famous soccer player from Argentina.

Actividad 19: Asociaciones

Asocia estas personas con los objetos que usan en sus deportes y si es posible, con el deporte que juegan.

1. Martina Navratilova y Guillermo Vilas
2. Diego Maradona y Pelé
3. Larry Bird
4. Fernando Valenzuela
5. Laverne y Shirley
6. Katarina Witt y Dorothy Hamill
7. Arnold Schwarzenegger
8. Mike Tyson y Sugar Ray Leonard
9. Nancy López y Seve Ballesteros
10. Joe Montana y Joe Namath

Actividad 20: Rebajas

En parejas, imagínense que Uds. están casados y tienen cuatro hijos. Acaban de leer en el periódico un anuncio de rebajas en el Estadio del Deporte y, ahora cuando todo está barato, van a comprar algunas cosas para sus hijos. Usen la información que tienen sobre los gustos de sus hijos para decidir qué les van a comprar. Usen frases como **es mejor que, dudo que, es posible que,** etc.

> Miguel: 18 años; siempre está en el gimnasio, es muy fuerte, juega al squash y practica boxeo
> Felipe: 16 años; le encanta el ciclismo y juega al fútbol
> Ángeles: 14 años; le gusta patinar en el verano y juega al béisbol
> Patricia: 10 años; juega al tenis, pero todavía no juega muy bien; le gusta montar en bicicleta

Act. 21: Within each group, students may not know all the answers. They can discuss possibilities and make choices. During the check phase, they should be able to get the remaining answers as a class.

Actividad 21: ¿Son Uds. deportistas?

En grupos de cuatro, identifiquen estos equipos (*teams*) y digan de dónde son, qué deporte juegan, cómo se llama el estadio donde juegan y cuáles son los colores de su uniforme.

◖◗ El equipo de los Packers es de Green Bay, Wisconsin. Ellos juegan al fútbol americano en el Estadio Lombardi. Los colores de su uniforme son verde y amarillo.

1. Yankees
2. Bears
3. Broncos
4. Dodgers
5. Padres
6. Redskins

Actividad 22: ¿Y tú?

En parejas, pregúntenle a su compañero/a qué deportes practica y qué equipo (*gear*) tiene para jugarlos.

Act. 23: Encourage students to debate which sport is the most popular in the U.S. Remind them to consider how many players are in the game, attendance by fans, bets placed, athletes' salaries, etc.

Other popular sports include volleyball (Cuba), boxing (Cuba and Panama), and basketball (Spain).

Explain that soccer is not a violent sport, but that at times the fans (hinchas) become so involved that violence may erupt. Ask students if they know of any outbreaks at soccer games outside the U.S., or of fan violence within the U.S.

Actividad 23: Opiniones

Los deportes favoritos cambian de país en país. En grupos de cuatro, hablen sobre cuáles piensan que son los deportes más populares de los Estados Unidos, de Argentina y del Caribe y por qué creen que sean populares. Después de terminar, comparen con otros grupos.

¿Lo sabían?

En la mayoría de los países hispanos el fútbol es el deporte más popular. Es un deporte muy económico porque sólo se necesita una pelota y se puede jugar en cualquier lugar. En el Caribe el deporte más popular es el béisbol. Los norteamericanos lo llevaron a esta zona porque tiene un clima ideal que permite practicar el deporte todo el año.

En países como España, México y Perú, otro deporte popular es la corrida de toros. A mucha gente le gusta la corrida y la considera un arte, pero también hay muchas personas a quienes no les gusta. ¿Crees que la corrida de toros sea cruel? ¿Por qué crees que algunos la consideran un arte?

Teresa, campeona de tenis

cambiando de tema	changing the subject
dejar de + infinitive	to stop, quit + *-ing*
Te va a salir caro.	It's going to cost you.

Vicente acaba de volver de sus vacaciones en Costa Rica y está hablando con Teresa.

Actividad 24: ¿Qué hizo?

Escucha la conversación y marca las cosas que Vicente hizo en Costa Rica.

1. ___✔___ Pasó tiempo con sus padres.
2. ___✔___ Salió con sus amigos.
3. _____ Votó en las elecciones.
4. ___✔___ Fue a la playa.
5. _____ Jugó un partido de fútbol.
6. ___✔___ Fue a un partido de fútbol.
7. ___✔___ Notó una situación tensa a causa de los problemas políticos de la zona.
8. ___✔___ Jugó al tenis.

Juego de fútbol en el Estadio Azteca de la Ciudad de México.

Teresa	¿Qué tal todo por Costa Rica?
Vicente	¡Pura vida!, como se dice allí.
Teresa	¿Qué hiciste?
Vicente	Visité a mis padres, salí con mis amigos, fui al interior y a la playa . . .
Teresa	O sea . . . un viaje típico.
Vicente	¡Ah! ¿No te dije que fui a un partido de fútbol en que jugó Maradona? Fue estupendo. Me divertí mucho.
Teresa	¡Qué bueno! Y tu familia, ¿cómo está?
Vicente	Todos bien, pero hay muchos problemas en Centroamérica y aun en Costa Rica se siente la tensión.
Teresa	Pero Costa Rica se mantiene neutral en estas guerras, ¿no?
Vicente	Sí, es cierto, pero todavía así hay tensión.
Teresa	Bueno, pero cambiando de tema, ¿qué hiciste con tus amigos?
Vicente	Pues . . . salir, nadar, jugar al tenis; mis padres me regalaron una raqueta de tenis fenomenal para mi cumpleaños.
Teresa	¡Ah! ¿Te gusta el tenis? No sabía que jugabas.
Vicente	Sí, empecé a jugar cuando tenía ocho años. Practicaba todos los días, pero dejé de jugar cuando vine a España.
Teresa	Yo también jugaba mucho.

Telling about completed past actions

Discussing a series of completed past events

Discussing habitual past actions

Discussing the end of an action

Vicente	¿Y ya no juegas?
Teresa	Muy poco, pero me encanta. ¿Sabes? Fui campeona de mi club en Puerto Rico hace tres años, pero dejé de jugar cuando tuve problemas con una rodilla.
Vicente	Pero, vas a jugar conmigo, ¿no?
Teresa	Claro que sí . . . y te voy a ganar.
Vicente	¿Y qué pasa si le gano a la campeona?
Teresa	Dudo que puedas. Pero, si ganas tú, te invito a comer y si gano yo, tú me invitas, ¿de acuerdo?
Vicente	De acuerdo, pero creo que debes ir al banco ya para sacar dinero porque la comida te va a salir muy cara.

Actividad 25: ¿Entendiste?

A veces, para entender una conversación se necesita saber algo de política, deportes, arte, cine, etc. Para entender la conversación entre Vicente y Teresa es importante saber algunas cosas. En parejas, discutan estas preguntas.

1. ¿Quién es Maradona? ¿Sabes de dónde es?
2. ¿Sabes en qué países de Hispanoamérica hay democracia estable?
3. ¿Qué tipos de problemas hay en Centroamérica?
4. Si Costa Rica es un país democrático y neutral, ¿por qué crees que existe tensión?

Act. 26: Encourage students to speculate, and support their ideas: **Dudo que gane ... Espero que ...**

Actividad 26: ¿Quién va a ganar?

En parejas, usando la información del diálogo, decidan quién va a ganar el partido de tenis entre Teresa y Vicente y por qué.

Act. 27: Draw attention to the verb forms.

Actividad 27: Los deportes que jugabas

Habla con un mínimo de cinco personas para averiguar a qué deportes jugaban cuando estaban en la escuela secundaria.

⦿ **A:** ¿A qué deportes jugabas?
  B: Jugaba al fútbol, al béisbol, . . .

Actividad 28: Problemas económicos

Uds. acaban de recibir la cuenta de Visa y no tienen dinero para pagarla. En parejas, decidan qué van a dejar de hacer para ahorrar (save) el dinero.

⦿ Ahora fumo mucho, pero puedo dejar de fumar.

Hacia la comunicación

I. Describing in the Past: The Imperfect

Before studying the grammar explanation, answer this question based on the dialogue:

- Do the sentences **"Practicaba todos los días . . ."** and **"Yo también jugaba mucho"** refer to actions that occurred only once in the past or to habitual actions in the past?

As you have already learned, the preterit in Spanish talks about completed past actions. There is another past form, the imperfect, whose main function is to describe.

A. Formation of the Imperfect

1. To form the imperfect of *all* **-ar** verbs, add **-aba** to the stem.

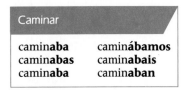

Caminar	
camin**aba**	camin**ábamos**
camin**abas**	camin**abais**
camin**aba**	camin**aban**

2. To form the imperfect of **-er** and **-ir** verbs, add **-ía** to the stem.

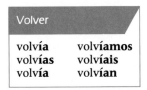

Volver	
volv**ía**	volv**íamos**
volv**ías**	volv**íais**
volv**ía**	volv**ían**

Salir	
sal**ía**	sal**íamos**
sal**ías**	sal**íais**
sal**ía**	sal**ían**

3. There are only three irregular verbs in the imperfect.

Ir	
iba	íbamos
ibas	ibais
iba	iban

Ser	
era	éramos
eras	erais
era	eran

Ver	
veía	veíamos
veías	veíais
veía	veían

B. Using the Imperfect

1. As you learned in Chapter 9, the imperfect is used when telling time and one's age in the past. The imperfect is also used to describe people, actions, situations, weather, or things in the past as well as states of mind and feelings.

Mi abuela **era** pequeña y **tenía** pelo blanco.
My grandmother was small and had white hair. (description of a person)

John Lennon **cantaba** muy bien.
John Lennon sang very well. (description of an action)

Había mucha gente en la fiesta de Vicente.*
There were many people at Vicente's party. (description of a situation)

Hacía mucho calor en la playa.
It was very hot at the beach. (description of the weather)

Vicente **estaba** contento de ver a sus padres.
Vicente was happy to see his parents. (description of feelings)

*Note: **Había** means both *there was* and *there were*.

2. Another use of the imperfect is to describe habitual or repeated actions in the past.

Diana **iba** a clase todos los días.
Diana used to go to class every day. (habitual action)

Se **levantaban** temprano, se **desayunaban** y **leían** el periódico.
They used to get up early, eat breakfast, and read the newspaper. (a series of habitual actions)

Actividad 29: El extraterrestre

Uds. vieron a un extraterrestre. En grupos de tres, contesten estas preguntas para describirlo. Después, léanle su descripción al resto de la clase.

1. ¿Dónde estaban ustedes cuando lo vieron?
2. ¿Día?
3. ¿Hora?
4. ¿Qué tiempo hacía?
5. ¿Cómo era?
6. ¿Color?
7. ¿Cuántos ojos?
8. ¿Llevaba ropa?
9. (etc.)

Actividad 30: La rutina diaria

En parejas, describan un día típico de su vida cuando tenían quince años. Digan qué hacían con sus amigos.

Actividad 31: ¿Tenías razón?

En grupos de tres, piensen en las ideas que tenían sobre la universidad antes de comenzar el primer año y digan si estas ideas cambiaron o no. ¿Qué pensaban y qué encontraron al llegar a la universidad?

▮●▮ Yo pensaba que las clases eran difíciles, pero ahora me parece que son fáciles.

Actividad 32: Ilusiones y desilusiones

En parejas, pregúntenle a su compañero/a (1) qué fantasías tenía cuando era niño/a y cuándo dejó de creer en ellas, y (2) si hacía ciertas cosas y cuándo dejó de hacerlas. Usen las siguientes listas.

¿Creías en estas cosas?	¿Hacías estas cosas?
en Santa Claus	odiar a los chicos/las chicas
en el Coco *(boogie man)*	dormir con la luz encendida *(lit)*
en el ratoncito *(tooth fairy)*	jugar con pistolas/muñecas
que había monstruos *(monsters)* debajo de la cama	*(dolls)*
que la cigüeña *(stork)* traía a los bebés	

Ahora comenten esta pregunta: ¿Es bueno que los niños tengan fantasías? ¿Por qué sí o no?

¿Lo sabían?

Por influencia de Alemania y de los Estados Unidos, en muchos países hispanos se habla de Santa Claus o Papá Noel. En algunos países, como Argentina, Uruguay y Puerto Rico, los niños reciben los regalos de Papá Noel o del Niño Jesús a la medianoche del veinticuatro de diciembre (Nochebuena).

En España, México y otros países hispanos, de la misma manera que en Bélgica y Francia, los Reyes Magos *(Three Wise Men)* les traen los regalos a los niños el 6 de enero. En los Estados Unidos, Santa Claus llega en trineo *(sled)*, entra por la chimenea, deja los regalos y pone dulces en los calcetines que los niños cuelgan *(hang)* allí. En cambio, en otros países los Reyes Magos llegan en camello y dejan los regalos en los balcones o cerca de las ventanas. Con frecuencia, los niños ponen los zapatos en las ventanas y al día siguiente encuentran los regalos al lado de ellos.

Act. 33: Encourage students to
be very specific and to ask questions for clarification or expansion. Have some students report
back to the class on their partners' schools.

Act. 34: Before assigning this
activity as homework, you may
want to do a class group-writ-
ing describing the bedroom of a
familiar TV character, such as
Beaver Cleaver. Encourage students to use a variety of adjectives. Review prepositions of
location if necessary. Students
may use this as a model on
which to base their own
compositions.

Have students peer edit completed compositions, discuss
them between partners, and
rewrite before handing in.

Póster is a common Anglicism
for **cartel;** in many countries,
afiche is used.

Actividad 33: La escuela

En parejas, Uds. van a hablar de su niñez *(childhood)*. Describan cómo
era su escuela primaria (grande, pequeña, pública, privada, número de
estudiantes), dónde estaba, cómo eran los estudiantes y los maestros
(teachers), quién era su maestro/a favorito/a, qué programas deportivos
había en la escuela, si les gustaba la comida, etc.

Actividad 34: Mi dormitorio

Escribe una composición sobre cómo era tu dormitorio cuando tenías
diez años. Sigue este bosquejo.

Título: _____

  I. Descripción física
    Muebles
    1. Cama/s (dormir solo/a o con hermano/a)
    2. Tocador/es
    3. Silla/s
    4. Cómoda/s
    5. Armario/s
    6. Escritorio/s

 II. Decoración y diversión
    A. Color
    B. Carteles *(Posters)*
    C. Juguetes *(Toys)*
    D. Televisión, estéreo, radio, etc.

III. Actividades y cuándo
    A. Con amigos
      1. Jugar
      2. Hablar
      3. Dormir
    B. Solo/a
      1. Leer
      2. Escuchar música
      3. Estudiar
      4. Mirar la televisión

 IV. Conclusión
    Por qué me gustaba/no me gustaba

Vocabulario funcional

El correo

Ver página 259

Otros verbos

Ver página 261

Artículos de deporte

Ver página 270

Palabras relacionadas con los deportes

los bolos   bowling
el boxeo   boxing
el campeón/la campeona   champion
el campeonato   championship
el/la deportista   athlete
el equipo   team; equipment
el estadio   stadium
ganar   to win; to earn
montar en bicicleta   to ride a bicycle
el partido   game
patinar   to skate

Palabras y expresiones útiles

a lo mejor   perhaps
cambiando de tema   changing the subject
dejar de + infinitive   to stop, quit + *-ing*
echar de menos   to miss (someone or something)
quedarse en + place   to stay in + *place*
Te va a salir caro.   It's going to cost you.

¿Es Bogotá una ciudad
grande?
¿Cómo es la arquitectura
de Cartagena?

Bogotá, Colombia.

Capítulo 11

Chapter Objectives

After studying this chapter you will know how to:

- explain medical problems
- name the parts of a car and items associated with it
- describe the past and narrate past events

- discuss two actions that occurred at the same time
- tell about ongoing actions in the past and what interrupted them

Cartagena de Indias, Colombia.

De vacaciones y enfermo

Using TPR, practice **ahora mismo: Levántate ahora mismo.** (etc.)

(No) vale la pena.	It's (not) worth it.
(no) vale la pena + infinitive	it's (not) worth + *-ing*
ahora mismo	right now
además	besides

Alejandro, el tío de Teresa, tuvo que ir a Bogotá en un viaje de negocios y decidió llevar a toda su familia para hacer turismo. Cuando estaban allí, su hijo, Carlitos, no se sentía bien y lo llevaron al médico para ver qué tenía.

Actividad 1: Marca los síntomas

Escucha la conversación en el consultorio de la doctora y marca los síntomas que tenía Carlitos.

_____	diarrea	✓	fiebre
_____	hemorragia	✓	náuseas
✓	falta de apetito	_____	dolor de cabeza
✓	dolor de estómago	✓	dolor de pierna

Explaining symptoms

Discussing a series of completed past actions

Explain that 39°C = 102.2°F.

Expressing pain

Speculating

Expressing desires

Bogotá is at an altitude of 8600 feet. To get a panoramic view of the city, one can ride a cable car (funicular) which climbs approximately 3000 feet to the top of Monserrate.

Have students find expressions in the dialogue that are used to calm down Carlitos. Review diminutives such as hombrecito.

Enfermera	Pasen Uds.
Alejandro	Gracias . . . Buenos días, doctora.
Doctora	¿Cómo están Uds.?
Alejandro	Mi esposa y yo bien, pero Carlitos nos preocupa. Ayer, el niño estaba bien cuando se levantó; fuimos a visitar la Catedral de Sal, y cuando caminábamos en la mina, de repente el niño empezó a quejarse de dolor de estómago, tenía náuseas, vomitó una vez y no quiso comer nada en todo el día.
Carlitos	Me sentía muy mal. Hoy me duele la pierna derecha y casi no puedo caminar.
Doctora	¿También tenía fiebre o diarrea?
Rosaura	Ayer tenía 39 de fiebre por la noche.
Doctora	A ver, Carlitos, ¿puedo examinarte?
Carlitos	¿Me va a doler?
Doctora	No, y tú eres muy fuerte . . . ¿Te duele cuando te toco aquí?
Carlitos	No.
Doctora	¿Y aquí?
Carlitos	¡Ay, ay, ay!
Doctora	Bueno, creo que debemos hacerle un análisis de sangre ahora mismo. Pero por los síntomas, es muy posible que tenga apendicitis.
Alejandro	¿Hay que operarlo?
Doctora	Si es apendicitis, hay que ingresarlo en el hospital y mientras tanto, hay que darle unos antibióticos para combatir la infección.
Rosaura	Entonces, quizás tengamos que quedarnos unas semanas en Bogotá.
Alejandro	Claro, y Cristina y Carlitos van a perder el comienzo de las clases. Tal vez valga la pena buscarles un profesor particular.
Carlitos	¡Ay mamá! No quiero que me operen. Y, además, yo quería ir a Monserrate y subir en funicular y . . . y ahora no voy a poder.
Alejandro	Vamos, Carlitos. Tú eres un hombrecito y ya vas a ver que la operación no es tan mala. Te prometo que antes de regresar a España te vamos a llevar a Monserrate; dicen que desde allí, la vista de la ciudad es muy bonita.
Carlitos	Bueno, pero, también puedo . . . y quisiera . . . y . . .

Pronunciation: h
1. Model and have students repeat after you words that contain h: **hombre, humor, hospital, hermano.**
2. Have students find words in the Spanish-English Vocabulary that contain h and dictate them to their classmates.

Actividad 2: ¡Pobre Carlitos!

Después de escuchar la conversación, pon esta lista en orden cronológico. Luego, en parejas, cuéntenle a su compañero/a qué le pasó a Carlitos.

_5_	antibióticos
_1_	tener dolor de estómago, náuseas y no querer comer
_6_	operación
_2_	dolor de pierna
_3_	39°C de fiebre
_4_	análisis de sangre

Actividad 3: Avisando

En parejas, una persona es Alejandro y la otra persona es Teresa. Alejandro llama a Teresa a España para explicarle qué le pasó a Carlitos.

¿Lo sabían?

En Colombia hay muchos lugares de atracción turística. La Catedral de Sal, que está cerca de Bogotá, es uno de ellos. Es una iglesia muy grande que se construyó en 1954 debajo de la tierra en una mina de sal que los indios ya explotaban antes de la llegada de los españoles a América.

Catedral de Sal, Zipaquirá, Colombia.

Actividad 4: ¿Vale la pena?

Habla de las cosas que vale o no vale la pena hacer, formando oraciones con frases de las tres columnas.

		trabajar
si no estás enamorado/a		ir a la playa
si buscas trabajo		estudiar mucho
si eres gordo/a		hacer ejercicio
si hace mucho frío		tomar clases
si te gusta Dustin Hoffman	(no) vale la pena	ver su última película
		casarte
si necesitas dinero		correr todos los días
si quieres saber esquiar bien		alquilar unos esquíes
		ir a Puerto Rico
		hablar con tu jefe/a

Lo esencial

I. La salud

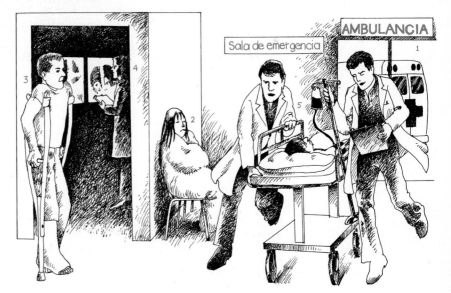

Sala de emergencia

AMBULANCIA

1. la ambulancia
2. tener escalofríos
3. la fractura
4. la radiografía
5. la sangre

Otras palabras útiles

el calambre cramp	**tener buena salud** to be in good health
la enfermedad sickness, illness	**un resfrío/catarro** to have a cold
estar resfriado/a to have a cold	
estornudar to sneeze	**diarrea** to have diarrhea
la gripe flu	**fiebre** to have a fever
la herida injury, wound	**tos** to have a cough
la infección infection	**toser** to cough
el mareo dizziness	**vomitar/devolver (o > ue)** to vomit
las náuseas nausea	
sangrar to bleed	

The article Tu salud *comes from a Spanish magazine. Before reading it, look at the titles and pictures and have students guess the content. Then read the article and ask comprehension questions.*

Pregnant **(embarazada)** is a false cognate.

Actividad 5: Los síntomas

Di qué síntomas puede tener una persona que

1. tiene hepatitis
2. tuvo un accidente automovilístico
3. está embarazada
4. tiene mononucleosis

TU SALUD *Por Antonio Calvo Roy*

■ **Hipertensión**

De tiempo en tiempo hay que recordarlo. En nuestro país el 20 por ciento de la población, cinco millones de personas, sufren de hipertensión, pero sólo el 10 por ciento lo sabe y toma las medidas oportunas. Hágase medir la tensión de vez en cuando, no olvide que tener la tensión alta es como llevar una espada de Damocles sobre la cabeza, y, por cierto, con muchos filos, entre ellos el peligro de infarto.

■ **¡Olé la siesta!**

La siesta pasa por ser una de las grandes contribuciones hispanas a la calidad de vida mundial. En verano la costumbre se extiende como una benéfica bendición propiciada por el calor. Su sueño puede estar partido, seis horas nocturnas y dos vespertinas, no es perjudicial para su salud. Muy al contrario, pasar las horas de máximo calor entre dulces sueños puede reportarle beneficios.

Actividad 6: Una emergencia

Víctima is always feminine, even when referring to males.

En parejas, una persona es el/la doctor/a y la otra persona es la esposa de la víctima. El/La doctor/a llama a la señora para explicarle qué le pasó a su esposo, basándose en la información de la ficha médica.

■) **A:** ¿Aló?

B: Buenos días. ¿Habla la Sra. Porta?

A: Sí . . .

B: Señora, le habla el Dr. Torres del Hospital Fulgencio Yegros . . .

Sala de Emergencias   Hospital Centro Médico Fulgencio Yegros

Fecha: 14/X/90
Hora: 6:30 P.M.
Paciente: Mariano Porta Lerma
Dirección: Avenida Bolívar, 9
Ciudad: Asunción
Teléfono: 26-79-08
Estado civil: casado
Alergias: penicilina
Diagnóstico: contusiones; fractura de la tibia izquierda
Tratamiento: 5 puntos en el codo derecho
Causa: accidente automovilístico

Puntos = stitches.

II. Las medicinas

¿Tiene tos? ¿No puede respirar?
¿Tiene fiebre? ¿Estornuda?

Para matar el catarro use
Respira Libre
2 cápsulas cada 8 horas

Si tose y no puede dormir,
busque una noche de tranquilidad

con el jarabe
Noche de Paz

II. Have students associate medical remedies with symptoms.

el antibiótico antibiotic
la aspirina aspirin
la cápsula capsule
la inyección injection

el jarabe (cough) syrup
la píldora/pastilla pill
la receta médica prescription
el vendaje bandage

¿Lo sabían?

Si viajas a un país hispano y te enfermas a las tres de la mañana, ¿adónde vas para comprar medicinas? En muchas ciudades hispanas hay farmacias de turno, o de guardia, adonde puedes ir durante la noche. Éstas se anuncian en el periódico o en la puerta de las farmacias mismas.

Actividad 7: Asociaciones

Di qué medicinas asocias con estas marcas: Bayer, Contac, Formula 44, ACE, Valium, NICE, NyQuil.

Actividad 8: Consejos

En parejas, una persona se siente mal y llama a su compañero/a para pedirle consejos. Dile qué te pasa y él/ella va a aconsejarte algo. Después cambien de papel.

> **A:** Hola, habla . . . ¿Qué tal?
> **B:** La verdad, no muy bien. Tengo fiebre y no tengo mucho apetito.
> **A:** ¡Qué lástima! Te aconsejo que tomes una aspirina y te acuestes. / Debes tomar una aspirina y acostarte.

Hacia la comunicación

Gramática 🔑

I. Review uses of the imperfect from Ch. 10.

Drill the imperfect:
1. Prepare a silent Gouin series with a student ahead of time. Perform it for the class and then ask, **¿Qué hice yo? ¿Qué hizo él? ¿Qué hacía él mientras yo leía?** (etc.)
2. Contrast the preterit and imperfect by having students explain a well-known movie such as *Psycho,* to someone who hasn't yet seen it. Remind students to set the scene with the imperfect. Ask them to tell what the characters did, how the plot thickens, how the main characters change, and what happens at the end. Encourage people in the class who haven't seen the movie to ask questions when anything is unclear.

I. Past Action in Progress: The Imperfect

Before studying the grammar explanation, answer these questions:

- In the dialogue between the Domínguez family and the doctor, do the boldfaced actions in the following sentence indicate two consecutive actions or one action in progress interrupted by another?
  ". . . y cuando **caminábamos** en la mina, de repente el niño **empezó a quejarse** de dolor de estómago . . ."
- Look at the following sentences and identify the uses of the imperfect that you have practiced.
  a. **Eran** las 11:00 de la mañana.   b. El niño **tenía** cuatro años.
  c. **Era** un día horrible, **llovía** y **hacía** frío.
  d. Él siempre **se levantaba** temprano.

1. In addition to the uses you have seen, the imperfect is used to express a past action in progress that lasted for an indefinite period of time; the duration of the action is unimportant.

   Ella **trabajaba** mucho.   *She worked (was working) a lot.*

2. The imperfect is also used to express two actions in progress that occurred simultaneously in the past.

   Tú **leías** mientras ella **trabajaba**.   *You read (were reading) while she worked (was working).*

Mention that the preterit is used when an action occurring over a period of time is viewed in its entirety.

Note: A past action in progress can also be expressed by using the past continuous tense.

$$\textbf{estaba} + \text{present participle} = \text{imperfect}$$

Estaba llov**iendo.** = Llovía.
Estábamos viv**iendo** en Panamá. = Vivíamos en Panamá.

II. Narrating and Describing: Contrasting the Preterit and the Imperfect

As you have already learned, the preterit is used to talk about or *narrate* completed actions in the past, and the imperfect is used to *describe* in the past. If you think of the preterit as a polaroid camera that gives you individual, separate shots of events, you can think of the imperfect as a video camera that gives a series of continuous shots of a situation or a picture that is prolonged over an indefinite period of time.

En la fiesta la gente **cantaba** y **bailaba.**　　　Por eso el señor **llamó** a la policía.

1. The preterit narrates a specific action in the past, an action that occurred over a limited period of time, or a series of unrelated, completed past actions. The imperfect describes a past action in progress or a series of past actions not limited by time.

En 1988 mi familia **visitó** España.　　　Antes **visitábamos** España todos los años.
Mi familia **vivió** en España seis años.　　　Mi familia **vivía** en España.

Fuimos al Vaticano y **vimos** la fuente de Trevi.

Nosotros **íbamos** a casa de mi abuela y **mirábamos** televisión.

Ayer Carlitos **estuvo** enfermo.
Carlitos **tosió** durante dos horas.
Ayer el niño **tosió, tuvo** fiebre y **estuvo** en cama todo el día.

Carlitos **estaba** enfermo.
Carlitos **tosía** mucho.
El niño **tosía, tenía** fiebre y **estaba** en cama.

2. When talking about the past, the imperfect sets or describes the background and tells what was going on. The preterit narrates what occurred or what interrupted an action that was in progress.

Ella **leía** (estaba leyendo) cuando él **entró.**

Viajaban por Colombia cuando Carlitos **se enfermó.**
Hacía un día magnífico; por eso **fuimos** a la playa y **nadamos.**
Cuando yo **tenía** ocho años, **vivimos** en Bélgica por seis meses.

Actividad 9: Descripciones

En grupos de tres, describan cómo piensan que eran las siguientes personas u otros personajes famosos.

⌐●⌐ George Washington tenía pelo blanco, era alto, tenía dientes de madera, . . .

Winston Churchill	Don Quijote	Napoleón
Cleopatra	Abraham Lincoln	Romeo y Julieta

Repeated habitual actions
in the past.

Act.'s 9, 10: Substitute or add
any names you prefer.

Act.'s 11, 12: Ask some students
to recount what their partners
told them.

Past actions over an
indefinite period of time.

Act. 13: Ask students if they
have any funny personal or family anecdotes to share.

Ongoing action interrupted
by another action.

Act. 14: Set a time limit and instruct students to read all questions before beginning. Monitor
and have some of the better or
unique conversations done for
the class.

Actividad 10: Las costumbres

En grupos de tres, describan qué hacían estas personas en sus programas
de televisión.

Gilligan   Batman y Robin   Archie Bunker
Herman Munster   Marcia Brady   "Hawkeye" Pierce

Actividad 11: ¿Qué tiempo hacía?

En parejas, digan adónde fueron el verano pasado, qué hicieron y qué
tiempo hacía.

Actividad 12: La historia médica

En parejas, hablen con su compañero/a sobre las enfermedades que tuvo
durante el último año y los síntomas que tenía.

Actividad 13: ¿Qué pasó?

En parejas, pregúntenle a su compañero/a si le ocurrió alguna de estas
cosas y averigüen qué estaba haciendo cuando le ocurrió.

A: ¿Alguna vez dejaste las llaves en el carro?
B: Sí.
A: ¿Qué pasó?
B: . . .

1. encontrar dinero
2. tener un accidente automovilístico
3. romperse una pierna/un brazo
4. perder una maleta
5. quemarse (to burn oneself)
6. caerse de una bicicleta

Actividad 14: ¿Aló?

Aquí tienen la mitad (half) de una conversación telefónica. En parejas,
inventen la otra mitad y presenten la conversación a la clase.

¿Dónde estaba José?
¿Con quién?
¿Qué estaban haciendo ellos mientras tú esperabas?
¿Qué ocurrió?
¡Por Dios! ¿Y después?
¿Qué hizo la policía?
¿De verdad?
¿Qué hacían ellos mientras la policía hacía eso?
¿Cómo se sentían?
¿Adónde fueron?

Act. 15: The person who is claiming a lost object should not look at the form to be filled out.

Have students phrase their questions carefully: *¿Cuál es su número de teléfono?*

Remind students: description = imperfect.
Interrupted action = **estaba ... cuando ...**

Actividad 15: Objetos perdidos

En parejas, una persona perdió algo y va a la oficina de objetos perdidos para ver si está allí. La otra persona es el/la dependiente/a que trabaja en la oficina y tiene que llenar este formulario haciendo las preguntas apropiadas.

Nombre: _____

Dirección: _____

Ciudad: _____

Teléfono: _____

Artículo perdido: _____

   Dónde: _____

   Cuándo: _____

   Descripción: _____

Act. 16: Actors/actresses should have books closed.

Actividad 16: La entrevista

En parejas, una persona es Rona Barrett y va a entrevistar a un actor famoso/una actriz famosa. El actor/La actriz tiene que usar la imaginación para contestar.

    Nombre original
    Trabajos extras que hacía cuando buscaba trabajo de actor/actriz
    Primer trabajo de actor/actriz
      Descripción del trabajo
      Director
      Otros actores
    Cirugía plástica   sí/no
      Si contesta que sí: doctor/a
      Cómo era antes y después
    Cuántas veces se casó   Por qué se divorció
      Descripción de sus esposos/as
    Trabajo actual *(current)*
      Director   Cine/Teatro/Televisión   Comedia/Drama/etc.
    Planes para el futuro

Ana Belén is a famous Spanish singer.

La entrevista

ANA BELEN	«NUNCA ME HA GUSTADO ESCANDALIZAR. NO ME LO PIDE EL CUERPO»

Nuevos horizontes

Estrategia de lectura: *Recognizing Suffixes*

Suffixes are syllables that are attached to the end of a word and can alter the grammatical form of the word (manage + -able → manageable). They can help you understand the relationship between words in a sentence. For example, consider the following nonsense sentence: "The murer mured murelly." Even though this sentence is made up of nonsense words, you can probably tell which word indicates the action, which word indicates the way the action is done, and which is the thing or person doing the action. This is because of your unconscious knowledge of suffixes. Now try finding the subject, verb, and adverb in the following nonsense sentence in Spanish: **"El melulidero maró lenemente."**

The following is a list of common Spanish suffixes and word endings that will help you determine the grammatical form of the words.

Nouns	Adjectives	Adverbs
-ancia elegancia	**-ante** elegante	**-mente** tranquilamente
-ción cooperación	**-ble** amable	
-ad amistad	**-ísimo** rapidísimo/a	**Verbs**
-ismo comunismo	**-ivo** primitivo/a	**-ar, -er, -ir,** and
-ista pianista	**-oso** peligroso/a	their conjugations

Actividad 17: Mira y contesta

Diana le escribe la siguiente carta a un colega de la escuela secundaria donde ella enseña en los Estados Unidos.

1. Mira la foto en la página 294. En tu opinión, ¿cuál es la conexión entre esta foto y la carta de Diana?
2. Lee rápidamente el texto para encontrar las ideas principales. Luego, en parejas, comparen sus resultados con los de un/a compañero/a.

Madrid, 6 de octubre

Querido Craig:

Recibí tu carta hace unos días, pero no tuve tiempo de contestarte antes porque estaba ocupadísima con mis clases de literatura en la universidad. Por fin comencé mis vacaciones y ahora tengo tiempo para escribirte unas líneas. ¿Cómo estás? ¿Cómo va tu clase de español? ¿Mucho trabajo?

5

Biblioteca de la Universidad Autónoma de México (UNAM).

En tu carta me pides información sobre el sistema educativo hispano para usar en tu clase de español. Bueno, a nivel universitario, los estudiantes deben pasar primero un examen para entrar en la universidad, pero desde el momento que entran comienzan a especializarse. Por ejemplo, si quieres estudiar psicología, entras en esa facultad (lo que nosotros llamamos *department*) y estudias materias de esa área desde el primer día, no como en los Estados Unidos, donde cursas materias de varias áreas. Aquí los estudiantes tienen una preparación más global en la secundaria. Por lo que me contaron unos amigos, este sistema de educación es parecido en casi toda Hispanoamérica.

Es interesante que la gente, en general, va a la universidad en el lu-

10

15

gar donde vive y no se muda a otra parte del país. Aunque muchas ciudades grandes tienen ciudades universitarias (*campuses*), en otras las diferentes facultades están en distintas partes de la ciudad. Esto no es ningún problema porque en general sólo necesitas ir a una facultad. ¡Y 20 el tamaño de algunas de estas universidades! ¡Una sola facultad puede tener alrededor de veinte mil estudiantes! Increíble, ¿no? Algunas universidades importantes son la UNAM en México, la Central en Venezuela, la Universidad de Costa Rica y, por supuesto, la Complutense de Madrid. 25

¿Qué más te puedo contar? ¡Ah, sí! La educación generalmente es gratis; mejor dicho, los ciudadanos pagan impuestos que ayudan a mantener las universidades. En otros lugares como en Cuba, por ejemplo, los estudiantes universitarios trabajan en el campo para devolver ese dinero al gobierno. También hay universidades donde sí tienes que pagar, pero 30 es algo mínimo; yo, por ejemplo, pago cien dólares por año. Naturalmente, también existen las universidades privadas donde los estudiantes pagan la matrícula y a veces es cara.

Bueno, no se me ocurre qué más decirte sobre el sistema educativo. Pero si tienes alguna pregunta puedes escribirme. ¿No te gustaría venir a 35 estudiar aquí? Para mí ésta es una experiencia fabulosa: estoy aprendiendo cantidades, no sólo del idioma sino de la cultura y de la gente; además, la comida española es deliciosa. Siempre pienso en ti cuando como paella. Tienes que venir a probarla.

Espero entonces noticias tuyas. 40

Saludos,

Diana

P.D. Saludos a tus estudiantes de español.

The oldest university in the Americas is San Marcos in Lima.

The UNAM in Mexico has over 270,000 students.

Explain that a **paella valenciana** is a rice-based dish, cooked with saffron, sausage, chicken, seafood, and vegetables.

Act. 18: 1. **-ísima; adjetivo** 2. **-ivo; adjetivo** 3. **-ción; sustantivo** 4. **-ad; sustantivo** 5. **-antes; adjetivo** 6. **-mente; adverbio** 7. **-osa; adjetivo**

Act. 18: Discuss the false cognate **facultad.**

Actividad 18: Los sufijos

Subraya los sufijos de estas palabras; luego indica si las palabras son sustantivos, verbos, adjetivos o adverbios. Refiérete al texto si es necesario.

1. línea 2 **ocupadísima**
2. línea 6 **educativo**
3. línea 10 **facultad**
4. línea 13 **preparación**
5. línea 23 **importantes**
6. línea 31 **naturalmente**
7. línea 37 **cantidades**
8. línea 38 **deliciosa**

Actividad 19: Comparaciones

1. En grupos de tres, comparen el sistema educativo universitario hispano con el sistema norteamericano en las siguientes áreas: tamaño de las universidades, número de estudiantes y los cursos.

Act. 19: Compare and contrast an obligatory curriculum vs. one with options. Discuss separating college-bound from noncollege-bound students in high school. Discuss grading in Spain: **sobresaliente, notable, bien.**

2. Aquí tienes las notas *(grades)* de un estudiante de escuela secundaria de España. La mayoría de las materias que aparecen son los cursos obligatorios que estudió esta persona durante el segundo año de la escuela secundaria. En parejas, comparen estas materias con las que Uds. estudiaron en el segundo año de la secundaria.

1	Lengua española y Literatura ..	BIEN
2	Latín	Sobresaliente
3	Lengua extranjera (*Inglés*).	Notable
4	Geografía	Notable
5	Formación Política, Social y Económica	
6	Formación religiosa	Notable
7	Matemáticas	Notable
8	Física y Química	Notable
9	Educación física y deportiva ...	BIEN
10	E. A. T. P. (*Diseño*).	Notable
	Euskera	Sobresaliente

In post-Franco Spain, the Basque language, *Euskera,* became an obligatory subject in the Basque provinces.

Estrategia de escritura: *Writing a Personal Letter*

The format of a personal letter in Spanish differs slightly from English. The heading includes the name of the city where the writer is, as well as the date. The salutation usually begins with **Querido/a** followed by the name and a colon instead of a comma. The closing can include phrases such as **espero que me escribas, espero noticias tuyas, te extraño, recuerdos a . . . .** The letter may end with phrases such as **Saludos, Un abrazo,** or **Un beso** (more personal). To give additional information after the signature, use **P.D. (posdata).**

Actividad 20: Tu carta

Act. 20: You may want to begin by brainstorming what a foreign student needs to do to enter a university in the U.S.

Ustedes tienen un amigo uruguayo que quiere venir a estudiar a los Estados Unidos y necesita información sobre cómo entrar en la universidad. En parejas, hagan una lista de las cosas que se necesitan para entrar en la universidad. Después, individualmente, escríbanle la carta a su amigo.

Lo esencial

El carro

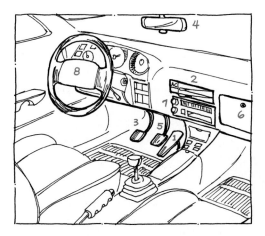

1. el acelerador
2. el aire acondicionado
3. el embrague
4. el (espejo) retrovisor
5. el freno
6. la guantera
7. el/la radio
8. el volante

1. el baúl
2. las direccionales
3. el limpiaparabrisas
4. las luces
5. la llanta
6. el parabrisas
7. el parachoques
8. la puerta
9. el tanque de gasolina

While in a car, practice vocabulary by quizzing yourself on car parts.

Use mime to elicit vocabulary words. Have students do the same in pairs.

Use TPR to drill useful verbs. Have students do the actions.

To spark a controversial discussion, recite this saying: **Mujer al volante, peligro constante.** Ask students if they think the generalization is true. Discuss why men, ages 18-25, pay higher insurance premiums.

Otras palabras relacionadas

el aceite oil
la batería battery
el cinturón de seguridad seat belt

la matrícula/placa license plate
el motor engine

Verbos útiles

abrocharse el cinturón to buckle the seat belt
apagar to turn off
chocar to crash
girar/doblar to turn

manejar to drive
pisar to step on
arrancar to start the car
revisar to check

Actividad 21: Definiciones

En grupos de cuatro, una persona da definiciones de diferentes partes del carro y las otras personas tienen que adivinar cuál es.

—Es un líquido que cambias cada dos meses.
—El aceite.

Actividad 22: Alquilando un carro

En grupos de tres, dos personas son amigos que van a alquilar un carro y la otra persona es el/la agente de alquiler. Tienen que decidir qué tipo de carro van a alquilar: **¿baúl grande/pequeño, aire acondicionado, radio, automático/con cambios?,** etc.

REQUISITOS DE ALQUILER
- Tarjeta de Crédito
- Cédula o Pasaporte
- Libreta Militar
- Pase vigente
- Edad mínima 25 Años

Act. 23: Brainstorm expressions used to persuade: **Usa poquísma gasolina. Cuesta sólo ...** (etc.) Remind students that people make a lot of small talk when buying a car.

Actividad 23: La persuasión

En parejas, una persona es un/a vendedor/a de carros en Los Ángeles, California y la otra persona quiere comprar un carro. El/La vendedor/a tiene que convencer al/a la cliente de que debe comprar este carro; el/la cliente quiere un buen precio.

A: Buenos días. ¿En qué puedo servirle?
B: Me interesa comprar este carro.
A: ¡Ah! Es un carro fantástico. Tiene llantas Michelín. . . .

Because of Michelin tire ads, people often say, **tiene michelines** to describe someone who is a little plump around the middle. In some countries, **tiene llanta** is used, just as some Americans would say that someone has a "spare tire."

radiocassette estéreo	estándar
llantas Michelín	estándar
cinturones de seguridad	estándar
limpiaparabrisas trasero	estándar
motor de seis cilindros	estándar
frenos hidráulicos	estándar
retrovisor diurno y nocturno	estándar
transmisión automática	$799
aire acondicionado	$599
ventanillas y cierre automático	$249
asientos de cuero	$489

In the metric system, one measures kilometers per liter, not miles per gallon.

Precio total sin impuestos ni matrícula	$18.995

Garantía: 7/70.000
35 millas por galón de gasolina

Si manejas, te juegas la vida

¡Qué lío!	What a mess!
¡Qué va!	No way!
para colmo	to top it all off
jugarse la vida	to risk one's life

Operaron a Carlitos y don Alejandro todavía tiene negocios que hacer. Por eso deja a la familia en Bogotá y se va en un carro alquilado hacia el sur del país. Alejandro tiene una conversación de larga distancia con su esposa.

Actividad 24: ¿Cierto o falso?

Escucha la conversación y marca C si estas oraciones son ciertas o F si son falsas. Corrige las oraciones falsas.

1. __C__ Cuando don Alejandro llamó, su esposa estaba preocupada.
2. __F__ Don Alejandro llegó muy tranquilo a Cali.
3. __C__ El carro alquilado era un desastre.
4. __F__ Las gasolineras estaban cerradas porque era jueves.
5. __C__ Carlitos va a salir mañana del hospital.
6. __F__ Don Alejandro va a regresar en carro.
7. __F__ A don Alejandro le fascina viajar por carro en Colombia.

Los Andes, Bolivia. ¿Te gustaría manejar en esta carretera?

Stating intentions

Discuss how the terrain in parts of South America — mountains, jungles, etc. — makes travel difficult.

Describing

Describing a series of completed actions

Explain that although Bogotá is near the equator, it is cool because of the altitude.

Expressing an unfulfilled obligation

Rosaura	¿Aló? ¿Alejandro? ¡Por Dios! ¡Qué preocupada estaba! ¿Qué te pasó? ¿Por qué no me llamaste?
Alejandro	Iba a llamarte ayer, pero no pude. No sabes cuántos problemas tuve con este carro que alquilé. Pero, ¿cómo sigue Carlitos?
Rosaura	Sigue mejor; no te preocupes. Pero, ¿qué te pasó con el carro? ¿Dónde estás ahora?
Alejandro	Pues, ya llegué a Cali, gracias a Dios, pero creí que nunca iba a llegar. ¡Qué lío! Manejar por los Andes es muy peligroso y, para colmo, el carro que alquilé casi no tenía frenos: Y como ya era tarde, las gasolineras estaban cerradas.
Rosaura	Entonces, ¿qué hiciste?
Alejandro	Pues seguí hasta que por fin encontré una gasolinera que estaba abierta. El mecánico era un hombre muy simpático y eficiente que arregló los frenos pronto, le echó gasolina al carro y revisó las llantas y el aceite.
Rosaura	¡Virgen Santa! Pero, ¿estás bien?
Alejandro	Sí, sí. Por fin llegué esta mañana con los nervios destrozados y dormí unas horas.
Rosaura	Ojalá que ya no tengas más problemas. ¿Qué tal Cali?
Alejandro	Muy agradable; tiene un clima ideal que es un alivio después del frío constante de Bogotá. Y tú, ¿estás bien?
Rosaura	Sí, sólo un poco cansada. Carlitos tenía que salir del hospital hoy, pero los médicos dicen que debemos esperar hasta mañana. ¿Cuándo regresas?
Alejandro	El jueves, si Dios quiere.
Rosaura	¿Y piensas manejar?
Alejandro	¡Qué va! Me voy por avión. Ahora entiendo por qué Colombia fue el primer país del mundo en tener aviación comercial. Si viajas en carro, ¡te juegas la vida!

Act. 25: Explain the idiomatic usage of **vaya** + noun. **¡Vaya problemas!** = What problems!

It is customary to tip a gas station attendant.

Besides being more economical, small cars are necessary in some cities due to narrow streets and lack of parking. They are also more manageable in the mountains.

Actividad 25: ¡Vaya problemas!

Después de escuchar la conversación, di los problemas que tuvo don Alejandro.

¿Lo sabían?

Si viajas vas a encontrar que en muchos países hispanos no es común tener autoservicio en las gasolineras sino que hay personas que atienden a los clientes. También es más común encontrar carros pequeños y con cambios (gears). ¿Por qué crees que es común tener carros pequeños en muchos países hispanos?

Gasolinera en Bogotá, Colombia.

Actividad 26: Casi me muero

En grupos de cinco, cuéntenles *(tell)* a sus compañeros una situación donde se jugaron la vida.

 Javier bebió muchas cervezas, pero yo decidí ir con él en el carro. Él estaba manejando cuando, de repente, perdió el control y chocamos contra otro carro. Abrí la puerta con la cabeza y terminé en un hospital. ¡Qué tonto fui! Aprendí que nunca se le debe permitir manejar a una persona después de beber.

Hacia la comunicación

I. Expressing Past Intentions: *Iba a* + infinitive

1. To express what you were going to do, but didn't, use **iba a +** *infinitive*.

   Iba a llamarte.   *I was going to call you (but I didn't).*

2. To tell what you actually did, use the preterit.

   Ayer te **llamé.**   *I called you yesterday.*
   Iba a llamarte, pero **me olvidé.**   *I was going to call you, but I forgot.*

301

II. Change of Meaning in the Preterit and the Imperfect

The following verbs have different meanings depending on whether they are used in the preterit or the imperfect. Note that the imperfect retains the original meaning of the verb.

	Preterit	Imperfect
conocer	met (for the first time)	knew
poder	was/were able (and succeeded in doing something)	was/were able, had the ability*
no poder	was/were not able (and didn't do something)	was/were not able*
querer	tried something (but failed)	wanted to do something*
no querer	refused to do something	didn't want to do something*
saber	found out	knew
tener que	had to and did something	had to do something*

*Note: The actions that follow these verbs may or may not have occurred. Context will help you decide.

Don Alejandro **podía** llamar a su esposa, pero estaba cansado.	*Don Alejandro was able (had the ability) to call his wife, but he was tired.*
Don Alejandro **pudo** llamar a su esposa.	*Don Alejandro was able to call his wife (and did).*
Carlitos **tenía que salir** del hospital hoy pero no salió.	*Carlitos was supposed to leave the hospital today, but didn't.*
Carlitos **tuvo que quedarse** en el hospital.	*Carlitos had to stay in the hospital (and did).*

After studying the grammar explanation, answer the following questions:

- In the sentences that follow, who actually went to buy a present,
- the man or the woman?
  Ella fue a comprarle un regalo. / Él iba a comprarle un regalo.
- If someone said, **"Tenía que comprarle un regalo,"** what would
- be a logical response? **¿Qué compraste?** or **¿Lo compraste al fin?**

III. Irregular past participles will be presented in Ch. 12.

Remind students of some past participles they have been using: **encantado, enojado,** etc.

Drill past participles:
1. Ask students how they would write in Spanish these signs from a car lot: Closed for vacation, Sold, Used.
2. Ask students where they would expect to see these signs: **Prohibido fumar, Recién casados, Apartamento amueblado.**
3. Mention sayings that include past participles: **A caballo regalado, no se le mira el diente/colmillo. En boca cerrada no entran moscas.** Discuss situations where one would use these sayings. Ask students for English equivalents, if necessary.

Do mechanical drills, Workbook, Part II.

III. Describing: Past Participle As an Adjective

The past participle can function as an adjective to describe a person, place, or thing. To form the past participle *(rented, done, said)* in Spanish, add **-ado** to the stem of all **-ar** verbs, and **-ido** to the stem of most **-er** and **-ir** verbs. When the past participle functions as an adjective it agrees in gender and number with the noun it modifies.

alquilar → alquil**ado**   perder → perd**ido**   servir → serv**ido**

Él fue a Cali en un carro **alquilado.**	*He went to Cali in a rented car.*
Sólo encontró gasolineras **cerradas.**	*He only found gas stations that were closed.*

When the past participle is used to emphasize a condition resulting from an action, it functions as an adjective and is used with the verb **estar.**

estar + past participle

Cerraron las gasolineras. ↓ Las gasolineras **están cerradas** ahora.	*They closed the gas stations.* ↓ *The gas stations are closed now.*
Ella se sentó. ↓ Ya **está sentada.**	*She sat down.* ↓ *She is already sitting/seated.*

Actividad 27: Buenas intenciones

En español, como en inglés, hay un refrán que dice "No dejes para mañana lo que puedas hacer hoy". Pero, con frecuencia, todos dejamos para mañana lo que podemos hacer hoy. En parejas, digan qué acciones iban a hacer la semana pasada pero no hicieron.

🔊 Iba a visitar a mi hermana, pero no fui porque no tenía carro.

Act. 28: Act upset and accept only the inventive excuses; look angry and hurt when you are given poor excuses.

Actividad 28: ¿Mala memoria?

Su profesor/a organizó una fiesta para la clase, pero nadie fue. Uds. tienen vergüenza y tienen que inventar buenas excusas. Empiecen diciendo: "Lo siento. Iba a ir pero tuve que . . ."

Actividad 29: ¿Eres responsable?

Escribe tres cosas que tenías que hacer el fin de semana pasado pero que no hiciste y tres cosas que tuviste que hacer. Luego, en parejas, comenten por qué las hicieron y por qué no.

Actividad 30: ¿Qué pasó?

Participio pasivo = past participle.

Past participles as adjectives agree in gender and number with the nouns they modify.

Terminen estas oraciones usando **estar +** *el participio pasivo* de un verbo apropiado: **aburrir, levantar, pagar, dormir, encantar, terminar, beber, vender, decidir, preocupar, resfriar, vestir** y **sentar.** Hay más verbos de los que necesitas.

1. El carro iba haciendo eses *(zig-zagged)* porque el conductor _____.
2. La chica estaba en una clase de matemáticas y el profesor hablaba y hablaba y ella _____.
3. Salí a comer con mi amigo y cuando iba a pagar la cuenta, el mozo me dijo que la cuenta ya _____.
4. Queríamos comprar entradas para el cine, pero no había porque todas _____.
5. El tenor, José Carreras, no pudo cantar porque _____.
6. Mi padre _____ en el sillón cuando terminó el programa de televisión.
7. Mi novio llegó temprano y tuvo que esperar porque todavía yo no _____.
8. Mi esposo debía de llegar a las 8:00 y era la medianoche. Yo _____.

Actividad 31: Un poema

Act. 31: Compare the poem to the folk song about conformity, "Little Boxes." Ask if the poem relates to yuppies today. Discuss the effect of mass media and advertising on the public. Discuss the importance of repetition in the poem.

Give students poetry to recite. Poems or parts of poems by Rubén Darío, Federico García Lorca, Gabriela Mistral, Pablo Neruda, and Rosalía de Castro make good selections.

Alfonsina Storni (1892-1938), una poetisa argentina, escribió este poema para hacer un comentario social. En grupos de cuatro, contesten estas preguntas: ¿Qué critica Storni con este poema? ¿Tenemos los mismos problemas hoy?

Cuadrados y ángulos

Casas enfiladas,[1] casas enfiladas,
casas enfiladas.
Cuadrados,[2] cuadrados, cuadrados.
Casas enfiladas.
Las gentes ya tienen el alma[3] cuadrada,
ideas en fila
y ángulo en la espalda.
Yo misma he vertido[4] ayer una lágrima,[5]
Dios mío, cuadrada.

1. in rows 2. squares 3. soul 4. shed 5. tear

LAS ARTES

Música y danza

(1) El tango, Buenos Aires, Argentina   (2) Conjunto de rock, Madrid, España   (3) Ballet folklórico de Cuba

Actividad

En parejas, hagan una lista de tipos de bailes hispanos y de los instrumentos musicales que asocian con estos bailes.

Pintura

4

(4) El Greco, El entierro del Conde de Orgaz
(5) Frida Kahlo, Autorretrato con mono
(6) Rufino Tamayo, Danza de la alegría
(7) Velázquez, La reina María Teresa de
Austria   (8) Picasso, Guernica

Actividad

Escoge uno de estos cuadros: descríbelo y di qué te
sugiere. ¿Conoces algún pintor norteamericano que
tenga un estilo similar? Luego, comenta tu cuadro
con dos compañeros.

5

9

10

11

12

Artesanías

(9) Chaqueta bordada, Guatemala   (10) Autobús panameño   (11) Pintura, El Salvador   (12) Indios Otavalos hilando, Ecuador   (13) Tapices colombianos

Actividad

En grupos de cuatro, digan por qué creen que estas obras de artesanía tienen colores tan vivos. ¿Se puede encontrar artesanía hispana como ésta en su ciudad?

13

14

Literatura

(14) Monumento a Cervantes con Don Quijote y Sancho Panza, Madrid, España
(15) Gabriel García Márquez firmando sus novelas

Actividad

Las siguientes palabras y expresiones en inglés tienen su origen en la literatura española: *to dream the impossible dream; he's a Don Juan; fighting windmills; quixotic.* En grupos de cuatro, comenten el significado de cada una y hagan una lista de frases famosas que tienen su origen en la literatura escrita en inglés.

15

Act. 32: Example poem:
Perro
viejo y amado.
Corría, jugaba, duerme.
Compañero de mi juventud,
amigo.

The poem could be assigned as homework and read as warmup the next day.

Actividad 32: Músicos, poetas y locos

"De músico, poeta y loco, todos tenemos un poco" dice el refrán. Escribe un poema, siguiendo las instrucciones. Después, lee tu poema al resto de la clase.

primera línea: un sustantivo
segunda línea: dos adjetivos (es posible usar participios)
tercera línea: tres acciones (verbos)
cuarta línea: una frase relacionada con el primer sustantivo
                            (cuatro o cinco palabras máximo)
quinta línea: un sustantivo que resuma la idea del primer
                            sustantivo

Vocabulario funcional

La salud
Ver páginas 285-286

El carro
Ver página 297

Las medicinas
Ver página 287

Palabras y expresiones útiles

además   besides
ahora mismo   right now
casi   almost
jugarse la vida   to risk one's life
mientras   while
(No) vale la pena.   It's (not) worth it.

(No) vale la pena + infinitive
 It's (not) worth + -ing
para colmo   to top it all off
¡Qué lío!   What a mess!
¡Qué va!   No way!

Restaurante en Barcelona, España.

Capítulo 12

Chapter Objectives

After studying this chapter, you will know how to:

- discuss past occurrences
- make comparisons
- describe people and things
- order food and plan a meal
- discuss music
- describe the climate and geographical features of a place

¿Quién escribió este poema? ¿Para quién lo escribió?

Demonstrate the meanings of **clavar** and **pupila.**

Leyendas by Bécquer, a Spanish poet (1836– 1870) have an eerie tone, much like the short stories of Poe. His *Rimas* show personal agony and deal mainly with love, art, and death.

¿Qué es poesía?–dices mientras clavas

en mi pupila tu pupila azul,

¿Qué es poesía? ¿Y tú me lo preguntas?

Poesía...¡eres tú!

Gustavo Adolfo Bécquer

¡Qué música!

¡Qué chévere!	Great! (Caribbean expression)
cursi	overly cute, tacky, in bad taste
¿Algo más?	Something/Anything else?

Teresa ganó el partido de tenis y por eso Vicente la invitó a comer. Están en un restaurante argentino donde hay un conjunto de música.

Actividad 1: ¿Cierto o falso?

Escucha la conversación y di si estas oraciones son ciertas o falsas.

1. ___C___ Teresa aprendió a jugar al tenis en un parque de Puerto Rico.
2. ___C___ Vicente juega bien al tenis.
3. ___F___ Teresa pide sopa, una ensalada y churrasco.
4. ___C/F___ Vicente es un hombre muy romántico.
5. ___F/C___ A Teresa le gusta mucho cuando los músicos le tocan una canción.

	Camarero	Su mesa está lista . . . Aquí tienen el menú.
	Vicente	Muchas gracias.
	Teresa	¡Qué chévere este restaurante argentino! ¡Y con conjunto de música!
Being facetious	Vicente	Espero que a la experta de tenis le gusten la comida y los tangos argentinos con bandoneón y todo.
	Teresa	Me fascinan. Pero, juegas bastante bien, ¿sabes?
	Vicente	Eso es lo que pensaba antes de jugar contigo; pero, ¿cómo aprendiste a jugar tan bien?
Discussing habitual past actions	Teresa	Cuando era pequeña aprendí a jugar con mi hermano mayor. Todas las tardes, después de la escuela, íbamos a un parque donde había una cancha de tenis y allí nos encontrábamos con unos amigos de mi hermano para jugar dobles. Seguí practicando y después de mucha práctica, empezamos a ganar.
	Vicente	¿Así que aprendiste con tu hermano?
	Teresa	No exactamente; mi padre se dio cuenta de que yo tenía talento y me buscó un profesor particular. Yo jugaba al tenis a toda hora; era casi una obsesión, no quería ni comer ni dormir.
	Vicente	¡Por eso! Ya decía yo . . .
	Camarero	¿Qué van a comer?
	Teresa	Ay, no sé todavía. Perdón, ¿cuál es el menú del día?
	Camarero	De primer plato, hay sopa de verduras o ensalada mixta; de segundo, churrasco y de postre, flan con dulce de leche.
Ordering a meal	Teresa	Me parece perfecto. Quiero el menú con sopa, por favor.
	Camarero	¿Y para Ud.?
	Vicente	También el menú, pero con ensalada. ¿El churrasco viene con papas fritas?
	Camarero	Sí. ¿Y de beber?
	Vicente	Vino tinto, ¿no?
	Teresa	Sí, claro.
	Camarero	¿Algo más?
	Vicente	No, nada más, gracias. Teresa, este restaurante es fantástico. No sabes cuánto me gusta estar aquí contigo. Estoy con una chica no solamente inteligente y bonita sino también buena atleta. ¿Me quieres?
Discuss the concept of the serenata, still done today in countries like Venezuela and Mexico.	Teresa	Claro que sí, ¿y tú a mí?
	Vicente	Por supuesto que sí . . . Mira, aquí vienen los músicos.

Músicos	*En mi viejo San Juan*
	cuántos sueños forjé
	en mis años de infancia . . .
Teresa	¡¡¡VICENTE!!! ¡Te voy a matar! ¡Qué cursi! ¿Cuánto les pagaste?

Actividad 2: Preguntas

Después de escuchar la conversación, contesta estas preguntas.

1. ¿Qué tipo de música se asocia con Argentina?
2. ¿Por qué es buena jugadora de tenis Teresa?
3. ¿Qué van a comer Vicente y Teresa?
4. ¿Por qué le gusta Teresa a Vicente?
5. ¿Crees que la última canción que tocan los músicos sea un tango?
6. ¿Por qué crees que los músicos fueron a la mesa de Vicente y Teresa a tocar esa canción?

Actividad 3: ¿Cursi o chévere?

Di si las siguientes cosas son cursis o chéveres.

⦿ ¡Qué chévere es/son . . . ! / ¡Qué cursi es/son . . . .!

jugar al bingo	unas vacaciones en el Caribe
ganar la lotería	el concurso de Miss Universo
Star Trek	Graceland y Elvis

Actividad 4: Los tiempos de antes

Di las cosas que hacían habitualmente tus padres o tus abuelos cuando eran jóvenes.

UN DÍA COMO HOY

1973
El negociador norteamericano Henry Kissinger y el vietnamita Le Duc Tho se preparan para reanudar las conversaciones de paz sobre Vietnam en París.

1983
El pacto de Varsovia pide un acuerdo con la OTAN para renunciar al uso de la fuerza militar.

1986
Tras elecciones legislativas en Estados Unidos, se inicia la 100 sesión del Congreso, con dominio del Partido Demócrata en el Senado y la Cámara de Representantes.

Lo esencial

I. Los instrumentos musicales

1. la batería
2. el clarinete
3. la flauta
4. el saxofón

5. el trombón
6. la trompeta
7. el violín
8. el violonchelo

Other instruments: **el sintetizador, el oboe, la guitarra eléctrica, el bajo, el flautín, el piano.**

Act. 5: Brainstorm names of musical instruments before doing this activity.

Actividad 5: ¿Qué sabes de música?

En parejas, decidan qué instrumentos musicales necesitan estos grupos musicales.

una orquesta sinfónica
una banda municipal

un conjunto de rock ácido

Tuna en Segovia, España.

Bring in music by a **tuna**. Teach the **tuna** song "**Sebastopol**" with the superlative in the second part of this chapter.

Discuss the custom of marching bands in the U.S.

Act. 6: Before doing this activity, find out which students play instruments. Review the subjunctive when checking: **¿Hay alguien que toque la trompeta?** This will help you pair students who don't play an instrument with those who do.

¿Lo sabían?

En España, muchas facultades de las diferentes universidades tienen **tunas** formadas por estudiantes que cantan y tocan guitarras, bandurrias *(mandolins)* y panderetas *(tambourines)*. Los tunos, o miembros de la tuna, llevan trajes al estilo de la Edad Media y cantan canciones tradicionales en restaurantes, en las plazas y por las calles.

Actividad 6: ¿Tocas?

En grupos de tres, descubran el talento musical de sus compañeros. Pregúntenles qué instrumentos tocan o tocaban y averigüen algo sobre su experiencia musical, según las indicaciones.

Nombre _____
Instrumento _____
   Si no toca ningún instrumento, pregúntale cuál le gustaría tocar.
Toca/Tocaba   muy bien   bien   un poco
Cuándo empezó a tocar _____
Dónde aprendió a tocar _____
Quién le enseña/enseñaba _____
Cuánto tiempo practica/practicaba _____
Si ya no toca, cuándo dejó de tocar y por qué _____

Actividad 7: Preferencias

En parejas, planeen la música para una boda en una iglesia y para la recepción en un restaurante sin preocuparse por el dinero. ¿Qué tipo de música quieren? ¿Qué instrumentos van a tocar los músicos?

¿Lo sabían?

Dos músicos españoles famosísimos del siglo XX son **Andrés Segovia** (1893–1987) y **Pablo Casals** (1876–1973). Segovia llevó la guitarra de la calle y de los bares a los teatros del mundo y la convirtió en un instrumento de música clásica. Pablo Casals tocaba el violonchelo; era maestro, compositor, director y organizador de festivales musicales. Salió de España en 1939 por no estar de acuerdo con la dictadura de Franco. Vivió en Francia y después en Puerto Rico hasta su muerte. Segovia y Casals dieron conciertos en lugares como el Lincoln Center y la Casa Blanca. Cuando murieron, el mundo perdió a dos músicos extraordinarios. ¿Te gusta la guitarra clásica? ¿Tienes algún disco de Segovia o de Casals?

II. La comida

II. Have students list the foods they most commonly eat. Ask students to tell which foods from the vocabulary they like or dislike.

Think of the names of food items when you eat.

1. el ajo
2. la coliflor
3. los espárragos
4. las habichuelas/judías verdes

5. el pollo
6. el cordero
7. el cerdo
8. la carne de res

Verduras (Vegetables)

los frijoles beans   **las lentejas** lentils
los guisantes/las arvejas peas

Aves (Poultry)

el pavo turkey

Carnes (Meats)

el bistec (churrasco in   **el filete** fillet; sirloin
  Argentina) steak   **la ternera** veal
la chuleta chop

Postres

el flan Spanish egg custard   **el helado** ice cream

Discuss the variety of tropical fruits in the Caribbean. Mention that there are different types of bananas and different ways to prepare them, such as, **tostones.**

¿Lo sabían?

La comida básica en los países hispanos varía de región a región según la geografía. Por ejemplo, en la zona del Caribe la base de la comida son el plátano *(plantain)*, el arroz *(rice)*, y los frijoles. El maíz *(corn)* es importante especialmente en México y Centroamérica y la papa en la región andina de Suramérica. En el Cono Sur se come mucha carne, producto de las pampas argentinas. El nombre de muchas comidas también varía según la región; por ejemplo, judías verdes, habichuelas, porotos verdes, vainas y ejotes son diferentes maneras de decir *"green beans"*.

Actividad 8: Una comida especial

Have studentes scan the menu to find food items that they recognize.

En parejas, Uds. necesitan planear una comida muy especial, porque Uds. invitaron a su jefe a comer. Usen vocabulario de este capítulo y de otros: **primer plato, segundo plato, postre, bebida,** etc.

MENU

Mousse de queso frío

INGREDIENTES:
2 cajas de queso «Boursin»,
1 caja de queso Filadelfia,
2 latas de consomé de buey
«Campbells» y
2 sobres de gelatina en polvo
«Aspic».

Lomo de cerdo en hojaldre

INGREDIENTES:
1 lomo de cerdo de 3/4 de kilo,
1 kg. de manzanas,
1 paquete de hojaldre
congelado,
2 cucharadas soperas de
mantequilla,
1 yema,
1/2 vaso de aceite,
sal y pimienta.

Tarta de ciruelas y nueces

INGREDIENTES:
1 kilo de nueces,
1 taza de azúcar,
8 huevos,
1/2 kilo de ciruelas secas y
16 cucharadas soperas de
azúcar.

Actividad 9: ¡Camarero!

Act. 9: "**Mi Buenos Aires Querido**" is the name of a famous tango.

En grupos de cuatro, una persona es el/la camarero/a y las otras tres son clientes que van a comer juntos en el restaurante Mi Buenos Aires Querido. Tienen que pedir la comida. Antes de empezar, miren la lista de frases útiles que está a continuación.

Camarero/a	Clientes
¿Qué van a comer?	¿Está bueno/a el/la . . . ?
¿De primer plato?	¿Cómo está el/la . . . ?
¿De segundo plato?	Me gustaría . . .
¿Qué desean beber?	¿Qué hay de primer/segundo plato?
El/La . . . está muy bueno/a hoy.	¿Viene con papas?
El/La . . . está muy fresco/a hoy.	¿Hay . . . ?
El menú del día es . . .	¿Cuál es el menú del día?
De postre tenemos . . .	¿Qué hay de postre?
Aquí tienen la cuenta *(bill)*.	La cuenta *(bill)*, por favor.

Although this restaurant is in Madrid, the terminology used is typically Argentine. Prices are in **pesetas.**

Mi Buenos Aires Querido

Casa del churrasco
Castellana 240, Madrid

Primer plato	pts.	Ensaladas	pts.
Sopa de verduras	400	Mixta	400
Espárragos con mayonesa	600	Zanahoria y huevo	400
Melón con jamón	650	Waldorf	600
Tomate relleno	550	**Bebidas**	
Ensalada rusa	400	Agua con o sin gas	225
Provoleta (queso		Media botella	125
provolone con orégano)	450	Gaseosas	125
Segundo plato		Té	100
Churrasco	1400	Café	100
Bistec de ternera con puré		Vino tinto, blanco	125
de papas	1200	**Postres**	
Medio pollo al ajo con		Helado de vainilla,	
papas fritas	900	chocolate	350
Ravioles	850	Flan con dulce de leche	350
Lasaña	850	Torta de chocolate	400
Pan	75	Frutas de estación	350

Menú del día: ensalada mixta, medio pollo al ajo con papas, postre, café y pan   1500 pts

Hacia la comunicación

Gramática

Review uses of the
preterit and imperfect,
Ch.'s 9, 10, and 11.

I. Drill preterit and imperfect:
Supply the first part of sentences and have students complete them: **Ayer Pablo ...**
**Todos los días el presi-
dente ...** (etc.)

I. Narrating and Describing: Preterit and Imperfect

Before studying the grammar explanation, answer these questions:

• In the following sentences, some of the verbs in boldface indicate actions that occurred more than once in the past or refer to past actions in progress. Identify these verbs. Are there any words that help
   indicate this? If so, which?
   a. Cuando era pequeño **jugaba** con mi hermano mayor.
   b. El sábado pasado **jugué** al tenis.
   c. Todos los días **íbamos** al parque.
   d. Ellas siempre **salían** con sus amigos, **hacían** fiestas y **bailaban**
      mucho.
   e. Teresa **jugaba** al tenis mientras Claudia **estudiaba**.
   f. Don Alejandro **pensaba** en Teresa cuando ella lo **llamó** por
      teléfono.

Since the preterit is used to narrate completed past actions, or actions
limited by time in the past, and since the imperfect is used to describe
habitual or ongoing past actions unlimited by time, certain expressions
are often used with the preterit and other expressions with the imperfect.

Some expressions associated with the preterit that you saw in Chapter 6 are **anoche, ayer, anteayer, de repente, el sábado/mes/año
pasado,** and **la semana pasada.**

The following expressions are often associated with the imperfect:

a menudo frequently	**muchas veces** many times
a veces at times	**siempre** always
algunas veces sometimes	**todos los días/meses** every
con frecuencia frequently,	day/month
often	
de vez en cuando once in a	
while, from time to time	

La semana pasada fuimos	**Íbamos con frecuencia**
a la playa.	a la playa.
Anteayer comí paella.	**A menudo comía** paella.
El mes pasado Vicente **jugó**	En Costa Rica, Vicente **jugaba**
al tenis dos veces.	al tenis **de vez en cuando**.

II. Describing: Irregular Past Participles

As you saw in Chapter 11, a past participle can be used as an adjective to describe a noun. The following verbs have irregular past participles:

abrir → **abierto**	morir → **muerto**
cubrir → **cubierto**	poner → **puesto**
decir → **dicho**	romper → **roto**
escribir → **escrito**	ver → **visto**
hacer → **hecho**	volver → **vuelto**

—¿Abriste la puerta?	*Did you open the door?*
—No, ya **estaba abierta**.	*No, it was already open.*
La guitarra **estaba rota.**	*The guitar was broken.*
Mi abuelo **está muerto**.	*My grandfather is dead.*

III. Negating: *ni . . . ni*

To express *neither . . . nor* use **ni . . . ni.** If **ni . . . ni** is part of the subject, a plural form of the verb is used.

Ni él **ni** ella asist**en** a la clase.	*Neither he nor she attends the class.*
No como **ni** carne **ni** pollo.	*I eat neither meat nor chicken.*

Actividad 10: Antes y después

En grupos de tres, hagan un anuncio para la dieta "Kitakilos" usando los dos dibujos del Sr. Delgado. Expliquen cómo era y qué hacía cuando estaba gordo, cuándo empezó la dieta y qué tuvo que hacer para perder peso *(lose weight)*. También expliquen qué hace hoy y cómo está cambiando su vida.

Actividad 11: ¿Qué hiciste ayer?

En parejas, hablen de las cosas que hicieron ayer. Usen palabras como **primero, después, a las 8:30, mientras,** etc.

🔊   Ayer me levanté a las . . . . Después . . .

Actividad 12:   Una carta

Diana le escribe una carta a otra colega que es profesora de español en los Estados Unidos. Completa la carta con la forma y el tiempo correctos de los verbos que aparecen después de cada párrafo.

Madrid, 12 de octubre

Querida Vicky:

Ya hace cinco meses que ___lleguè___ a España y por fin hoy, ___tengo___ unos minutos libres para ___escribir___. Las cosas aquí me van de maravilla. Primero, ___vivía___ en un colegio mayor, pero ahora ___alquilo___ un apartamento con cuatro amigas hispanoamericanas. ___Son___ muy simpáticas y no sólo estoy ___aprendiendo___ mucho de España sino también de Hispanoamérica.

(alquilar, aprender, escribir, llegar, ser, tener, vivir)

Durante el verano, ___tenía___ clases todos los días. Por las mañanas, nosotros ___íbamos___ a la universidad y por las tardes, ___visitábamos___ museos y lugares históricos como la Plaza Mayor, el Palacio Real y el Convento de las Descalzas Reales. Cuando ___entré___ por primera vez en el Museo del Prado, me ___pareció___ grandísimo, ¡y solamente ___vi___ las salas de El Greco y de Velázquez!

(entrar, ir, parecer, tener, ver, visitar)

___Estoy___ enamorada de España. La música me ___fascina___ porque tiene mucha influencia de los árabes y de los gitanos *(gypsies)*. El otro día ___caminaba___ por la calle cuando ___vi___ a unos niños gitanos cantando y bailando; ___tenían___ unos diez años y me ___dijeron___ que, con frecuencia, ellos ___cantaban___ en la calle para ___ganar___ dinero.

(caminar, cantar, decir, fascinar, ganar, tener, ver, estar)

Mis clases ___terminaron___ hace dos meses; después ___tuve___ cinco semanas de vacaciones y las clases ___empezaron___ otra vez la semana pasada. Además de tomar clases, ___estoy___ enseñando inglés desde el junio pasado para ___ganar___ dinero.

(empezar, ganar, estar, tener, terminar)

Act. 12: Discuss the fact that gypsies are victims of prejudice, but form a vital, ever-present part of what Spain is.

Bueno, ya tengo que irme a la clase de Cervantes. Espero que
__tengas__ un buen año en la escuela y ojalá que me
__escribas__ pronto.

(escribir, tener)

Un abrazo desde España de tu amiga,

Diana

P.D. Saludos a todos los profesores.

Actividad 13:   Detectives

En parejas, Uds. son el detective Sherlock Holmes y su ayudante Watson. Entran en una habitación donde ocurrió un asesinato. Describan la escena usando participios pasivos. Incluyan los participios de estos verbos: **abrir, cubrir, escribir, servir, romper, morir, poner, preparar** y **hacer.**

◖●◗   La lámpara estaba rota . . .

Act. 14: Ask some of the actors to give their pitch. Have students vote for the most convincing.

Actividad 14: Ayuda a la víctima

En parejas, una persona es un actor famoso y habla con una señora que perdió todo en un huracán. La víctima no tiene nada, no recibe ayuda de nadie y está sola. Ella contesta usando **ni . . . ni.**

1. ¿Sabe Ud. dónde está su esposo o sus hijos?
2. ¿Tiene ropa o comida?
3. ¿Dónde durmió anoche, en una iglesia o en una escuela?
4. ¿Le van a dar dinero o apartamento?
5. ¿Fue a un hospital o a una clínica?
6. ¿Habló con la policía o con la Cruz Roja?

Ahora, el actor quiere ayudar a la víctima. Pide donaciones en un programa de televisión y explica los problemas terribles de la señora.

|●| Ayer conocí a una señora que perdió todo y necesita su ayuda. No sabe dónde están ni su esposo ni sus hijos . . .

Actividad 15: Inventando historias

En grupos de cinco, Uds. están haciendo camping en una noche de luna llena. Terminen el cuento que sigue entre los cinco. Usen palabras como **a menudo, a veces, algunas veces, con frecuencia** y **siempre** con el imperfecto. Usen palabras como **una vez, de repente, primero, después** y **a la medianoche** con el pretérito.

|●| Era un martes 13. Era de noche y no había luces; hacía mucho frío y viento. La pareja estaba llegando a casa cuando oyó un ruido. Siempre cerraban la puerta con llave, pero al llegar a la casa, la puerta estaba abierta y una ventana estaba rota. Iban a ir por la policía, pero el carro no funcionaba . . .

Act. 16: This can be done in pairs in class or individually as a homework assignment, to be shared in small groups the next day. Have each group select the most imaginative story to read to the class.

Actividad 16: Un cuento

En un libro de texto normalmente lees un cuento y después contestas preguntas para ver si entendiste o no el contenido. Ahora vas a hacer esta actividad pero al revés *(backwards)*. Contesta estas preguntas y escribe un cuento basado en las contestaciones. Usa la imaginación.

1. ¿Adónde fueron Ricardo y su esposa de vacaciones?
2. ¿Cómo era el lugar y qué tiempo hacía?
3. ¿Qué hacían durante las vacaciones?
4. ¿Cómo se murió la esposa de Ricardo?
5. ¿Qué estaba haciendo cuando se rompió la pierna Ricardo?
6. La policía no dejó a Ricardo volver a su ciudad. ¿Por qué?
7. ¿Qué le dijo Ricardo a la policía?

8. ¿Quién era la señora del abrigo negro y los diamantes? ¿Puedes describirla?
9. ¿Qué importancia tiene ella?
10. Al fin, los policías descubrieron la verdad. ¿Cuál era?

Nuevos horizontes

Discuss the drawings and where each instrument is from.

Estrategia de lectura: *Reading an Interview Article*

Here are a few tips that can help you in reading an interview article:

1. Read the headline and subheadline; these usually contain or summarize in a few words the main ideas of the article.
2. Look at the pictures, tables, or graphs that may accompany the text; they illustrate themes in the article.
3. Scan the text to read only the interviewer's questions, which will clue you in to the main ideas. These steps provide you with background knowledge before actually reading the whole text.

Flamenco has influences from the Middle East and India, however it is only representative of Andalucía.

Actividad 17: Lee y adivina

1. Lee el título y el subtítulo del texto y adivina la idea principal.
2. Mira las fotos y los dibujos que aparecen con el texto y lee las preguntas de la entrevistadora para confirmar tu predicción.
3. Finalmente lee la entrevista completa.

Pablo Cuerda is a fictitious character.

El mundo de la música hispana
Entrevista con el cantante boliviano Pablo Cuerda
Por Laura Rógora

Entré en la sala de su casa y allí me esperaba sentado con su guitarra, compañera inseparable. Charlamos un poco sobre su gira musical por Europa y luego comencé así.

—**¿Me puedes contar un poco sobre las influencias que hubo en la música hispana**?

—Bueno, la influencia fundamental en España fue la de los árabes. Su música fue la base del flamenco de hoy día.

—**Y el flamenco influyó en la música hispanoamericana, ¿verdad?**

—Exactamente. El instrumento principal del flamenco es la guitarra y los españoles la trajeron al Nuevo Mundo.

—**¿Y los indios adoptaron este instrumento?**

—Bueno, es decir, lo adaptaron porque crearon instrumentos más pequeños como el cuatro y el charango, que está hecho del caparazón del armadillo. Y, naturalmente, la música indígena es la base de gran parte de la música moderna hispanoamericana.

—**Muy interesante. ¿Y qué otra influencia importante existe?**

—Pues, la más importante para la zona caribeña fueron los ritmos africanos de los esclavos que fueron la inspiración para la cumbia colombiana, el joropo de Venezuela, el merengue dominicano, el jazz y los blues americanos y también para la salsa.

—**La salsa. ¡Qué ritmo!**

—Por supuesto, ¿y sabes que Cuba, Puerto Rico y Nueva York se disputan su origen? Pero, es verdad que fue en Nueva York donde se hizo famosa la salsa.

—**¿Hay otros movimientos musicales recientes?**

—Era justo lo que iba a decir. Un movimiento es el de la "Nueva Trova Cubana" con Silvio Rodríguez y Pablo Milanés que cantan canciones de temas políticos, sociales y sentimentales. El otro movimiento importante fue el nacimiento, en Chile, de la "Nueva Canción" en la década de los sesenta. Este tipo de canción se conoció en el mundo cuando Simon y Garfunkel incluyeron en un álbum "El cóndor pasa" del conjunto Los Incas que pertenece a este movimiento.

—**Pero ¿qué es la Nueva Canción?**

—Es un estilo de música que tiene como elementos esenciales el uso de los ritmos e instrumentos tradicionales de los indios de los Andes y son canciones de protesta, o sea, de tema político y que critican la situación socioeconómica de los países hispanos. Este estilo de música se conoce ahora en todo el mundo.

—**. . . que nos lleva a mi última pregunta. ¿Qué escucha la gente joven hoy día?**

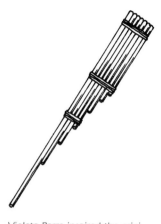

Violeta Parra inspired the originators of the **Nueva Canción**. After the 1973 coup in Chile, some members of the **Nueva Canción** were forced into exile, and instruments associated with this movement were banned. Their music evolved as musicians in exile were exposed to new influences.

(Izquierda) Rubén Blades, panameño. (Derecha) Pablo Milanés, cubano.

Bring in music: flamenco, cumbia, joropo, salsa, Silvio Rodríguez, Paco de Lucía, Quilapayún, Victor Jara, etc.

—La gente joven escucha de todo: la Nueva Canción, rock nacional y extranjero, la Nueva Trova . . . En el Caribe los jóvenes escuchan también salsa y la bailan muchísimo. Permíteme ahora tocarte una canción de Inti-Illimani, un conjunto chileno.

Y así terminó nuestra entrevista: con un ritmo y una melodía maravillosos.

Actividad 18: Completa las ideas

Después de leer el texto, di una o dos oraciones sobre cada una de las siguientes ideas relacionadas con el texto: **la guitarra, la salsa, los esclavos africanos, "El cóndor pasa"** y **la Nueva Trova Cubana.**

Actividad 19: ¿Y tú?

Contesta las siguientes preguntas sobre la música.

1. ¿Qué tipo de música te gusta? ¿Qué tipo de música no te interesa?
2. ¿Conoces algún conjunto (norteamericano, inglés, hispano) que toque canciones de protesta? ¿Cuáles son los temas de sus canciones?
3. ¿Por qué crees que en Hispanoamérica es popular la música de protesta?

Estrategia de escritura: *Writing an Interview Article*

Here are a few tips that can help you in writing a short interview article:

1. Organize the points that you plan to cover in the interview.
2. Interview the subject.
3. Edit the piece. When editing, try to leave out repetitions people have made in the interview because they sound awkward in a written text.
4. Provide a setting for the beginning and the end of the interview.
5. Write a catchy heading to attract the reader.

Look at the way the writer of the interview keeps the conversation flowing. What techniques other than questions does she use?

Remember that certain time expressions are frequently used with the preterit or imperfect.

Actividad 20: La entrevista imaginaria

Escribe una entrevista imaginaria con tu cantante favorito/a sobre cómo él/ella se convirtió en cantante (si no lo sabes, puedes inventar). Sigue los pasos mencionados para escribir una entrevista.

Lo esencial

I. La geografía

Occidente/oeste = west;
oriente/este = east.

1. la carretera	3. la montaña	5. el puente	7. el valle
2. el lago	4. el pueblo	6. el río	

Otras palabras de geografía

la autopista freeway, expressway	**la isla** island
el bosque woods	**el mar** sea
el campo countryside	**el océano** ocean
la catarata waterfall	**la playa** beach
la ciudad city	**el puerto** port
la colina hill	**la selva** jungle
la costa coast	**el volcán** volcano

Agua salada = salt water.

In Chile, there are frequent tremors.

Discuss other world disasters.

¿Lo sabían?

La variedad geográfica de Hispanoamérica incluye fenómenos naturales como el Lago de Nicaragua que, aunque es de agua dulce *(fresh water)* tiene tiburones *(sharks)* y el Lago Titicaca, entre Bolivia y Perú, que es el lago navegable más alto del mundo. En los Andes está el Aconcagua, la montaña más alta del hemisferio. También hay erupción de volcanes y terremotos causados por una falla *(fault line)* que va de Centroamérica a Chile. Dos desastres que tuvieron eco en todo el mundo ocurrieron en 1985. El primero fue un terremoto que destruyó parte del centro y suroeste de México, y en el que murieron unas 25.000 personas. El segundo fue la erupción de un volcán en Colombia que destruyó un pueblo de más de 20.000 habitantes.

Actividad 21: Asociaciones

Asocia estos nombres con las palabras de geografía presentadas.

Amazonas, Cancún, Pacífico, Cuba, Mediterráneo, Titicaca, Andes, Iguazú, Pascua, Quito

Actividad 22: ¿Dónde naciste tú?

En parejas, descríbanle a su compañero/a la geografía de la zona donde nacieron.

Act. 23: Have groups pick different areas. Set a time limit for the ad.

Actividad 23: La publicidad

En grupos de tres, preparen un anuncio para la radio hispanoamericana para atraer más turismo a una zona de los Estados Unidos. Después, presenten los anuncios a la clase. Escojan una zona de la lista siguiente:

el suroeste, el noroeste, el noreste, la zona central *(Midwest)*, el sur, la Florida, Alaska, Hawai

II. Review weather expressions previously studied.

II. El tiempo

1. caer granizo
2. haber niebla
3. haber tormenta
4. haber relámpagos/ relampaguear
5. haber truenos

Actividad 24: La geografía y el tiempo

En parejas, piensen en las expresiones del tiempo y en las diferentes zonas de los Estados Unidos. Decidan qué tiempo hace en distintas zonas durante cada estación del año.

ı●ı   En California llueve mucho en el invierno. En las montañas . . .

Actividad 25: El viaje horrible

> Remember: Completed action = preterit; actions continued over an indefinite period of time = imperfect.

En parejas, una persona acaba de llegar a la casa de la otra. El viaje en carro fue horrible; casi tuvo un accidente por el tiempo. El/La conductor/a le explica a la otra persona qué tiempo hacía. Después cambien de papel.

Actividad 26: Mapas

Mira el mapa de Suramérica e interpreta los símbolos para describir el tiempo que hizo el fin de semana pasado.

El Dorado

Discuss the **Museo del Oro** in Bogotá, which houses the largest pre-Columbian gold exhibit in the world. Explain that each group of Indians had their own style and employed techniques still used by goldsmiths today.

Figuras de oro precolombinas, Museo del Oro, Colombia.

Practice **hoy (en) día** by making statements such as, **En los años 30, la gente escuchaba la radio.** The students respond, **Hoy en día, la gente mira la televisión.**

sin embargo	however, nevertheless
verdadero/a	real, true
hoy (en) día	today; nowadays

Mientras Carlitos está en el hospital, tiene que seguir con sus estudios. Su padre encontró un profesor particular y él le manda a leer un cuento sobre El Dorado, una leyenda del tiempo de la conquista de América.

Actividad 27: Motivos

Antes de leer la leyenda, di por qué crees que vinieron los españoles a América y qué querían encontrar. Coméntalo con la clase.

El Dorado = gilded; covered with gold.

El Dorado

¿Qué es El Dorado?

Cuando los españoles llegaron a América, oyeron hablar de El Dorado. Les preguntaban a los indígenas qué era El Dorado y ellos

Comparing

les decían que era el país legendario del hombre de oro,[1] el hombre más fabuloso del mundo. Como decían que allí había más oro que en ninguna otra parte del mundo, los españoles empezaron a buscar El Dorado desde México hasta el Río Amazonas, pasando por valles, montañas y ríos. Muchos perdieron la vida por el oro; sin embargo, nunca lo encontraron porque era sólo una leyenda.

Se cree que la leyenda de El Dorado comenzó porque desde muchos años antes de la llegada de los españoles el jefe de los indios chibchas (de la región que hoy en día es Colombia) se cubría el cuerpo de oro y se bañaba en las aguas de una laguna sagrada[2] para adorar al Sol.

Describing habitual actions

Los españoles no encontraron El Dorado porque no existía, pero sí encontraron una tierra fértil y rica, Hispanoamérica, que era y sigue siendo hoy en día un verdadero El Dorado.

---

1. gold   2. sacred

Actividad 28: El examen

Cuando volvió el profesor le hizo unas preguntas a Carlitos. Después de leer la leyenda, ¿puedes tú contestar las preguntas?

1. ¿Cómo era El Dorado que buscaban los españoles?
2. ¿Encontraron El Dorado finalmente?
3. ¿Por qué crees que murieron muchas personas buscando El Dorado?
4. ¿Hay un El Dorado en tu vida? ¿Cuál es?
5. ¿Qué pasó en California en el año 1849?

Act. 28: In 1849, the California gold rush occurred. Discuss what life was like then.

Actividad 29: El Dorado de hoy día

En el pasado los hombres buscaban El Dorado y nosotros seguimos buscándolo hoy. ¿Qué busca la gente hoy día? ¿Cuál es "El Dorado" de hoy día?

Some American legends include Paul Bunyan, Johnny Appleseed, and Big Foot.

¿Lo sabían?

Ponce de León, explorador español, vino a América en busca de la mítica Fuente de la Juventud. No la encontró; sin embargo, descubrió la Florida y le dio este nombre porque llegó allí durante la Pascua Florida (Easter). ¿Conoces otras leyendas como la de La Fuente de la Juventud?

Hacia la comunicación

I. Describing: Comparisons of Inequality

1. When you want to compare two things by indicating that one is *more . . . than* the other one or when you want to indicate that there is more than a certain amount, use the following formulas:

$$\textbf{más} + \text{noun/adjective/adverb} + \textbf{que}$$
$$\textbf{más de} + \text{number}$$

Hablamos **más** español **que** ellos.	*We speak more Spanish than they do.*
Mis clases son **más** difíciles **que** tus clases.	*My classes are more difficult than your classes.*
Me acosté **más** tarde **que** tú.	*I went to bed later than you.*
Hay **más de** veinte lenguas indígenas en Guatemala.	*There are more than twenty native languages in Guatemala.*

2. When you want to compare two things by indicating that one is *less/fewer . . . than* the other one or when you want to indicate that there is less than a certain amount, use the following formulas:

$$\textbf{menos} + \text{noun/adjective/adverb} + \textbf{que}$$
$$\textbf{menos de} + \text{number}$$

Hoy tengo **menos** clases **que** ayer.	*Today I have fewer classes than yesterday.*
Carlos es **menos** diligente **que** su hermana.	*Charles is less diligent than his sister.*
Me costó **menos de** 20.000 pesos.	*It cost me less than 20,000 pesos.*

3. Some adjectives have both a regular and an irregular comparative form, as well as a change in meaning in some cases.

bueno → **más bueno** = better*	bueno → **mejor** = better
malo → **más malo** = worse*	malo → **peor** = worse
grande → **más grande** = larger in size	grande → **mayor** = older; greater
pequeño → **más pequeño** = smaller in size; younger	pequeño → **menor** = younger; lesser

Las playas del Caribe son **mejores que** las playas del Pacífico.	*The Caribbean beaches are better than the Pacific beaches.*
Pablo es **menor que** Juan.	*Pablo is younger than Juan.*

*Note: **Más bueno** and **más malo** usually refer to *goodness* or lack of it.

Pablo es **más bueno que** Juan.	*Pablo is kinder/a better person than Juan.*
Pablo es **mejor** estudiante **que** Juan.	*Pablo is a better student than Juan.*
Esta tortilla está **más buena que** la tortilla que preparó mi tía.	*This tortilla tastes better than the tortilla that my aunt prepared.*

After studying the grammar explanation, answer these questions:

- How would you express **"En mi familia, el más pequeño es el más alto"** in English?
- What is another way of saying the same sentence in Spanish?

II. Describing: The Superlative

1. When you want to compare three or more things by indicating that one is *the most/least*, use the following formula:

$$\left.\begin{array}{l}\text{el/la/los/las (noun) \textbf{más}}\\ \text{el/la/los/las (noun) \textbf{menos}}\end{array}\right\} + \text{adjective}$$

Toño es **el** (chico) **más** optimista.	*Toño is the most optimistic (young man).*
Raquel es **la mejor** (cantante) **del** conjunto.*	*Raquel is the best singer **in** the group.*

*Note:

a. In the superlative, *in* = **de: El fútbol es el deporte más popular *de* Suramérica.**

b. **Mejor** *(best)* and **peor** *(worst)* usually precede the nouns they modify: **Lucía es mi *mejor* amiga. Luquillo es *la mejor* playa *de* Puerto Rico.**

2. As you saw in Chapter 6, the absolute superlative of an adjective (very, extremely) can be expressed by attaching **-ísimo/a/os/as** to the adjective. When the adjective ends in a vowel, drop the final vowel and add **-ísimo**. Necessary spelling changes occur when **c, g** or **z** are present in the last syllable.

especial → especial**ísimo**	largo → larg**uísimo**
grande → grand**ísimo**	feliz → feli**císimo**
rico → ri**quísimo**	

Después de trabajar tanto, estamos **cansadísimas.**	*After working so much, we are very, very tired.*
El churrasco está **riquísimo**.	*The steak is delicious.*

Do mechanical drills, Workbook, Part II.

Note: When **-ísimo** is added to an adjective that has a written accent, the accent in the adjective is dropped, for example: **fácil→ facilísimo.**

Act. 30: You may want to add other comparisons of your choosing.

Actividad 30: Comparaciones

Comparen estas personas, lugares o cosas.

◖●◗ un disco compacto y un cassette   Un disco compacto es más caro que un cassette.

1. el lago Superior, el lago Michigan y el lago Erie
2. Nel Carter y Twiggy
3. Alaska, California y Panamá
4. un Mercedes Benz y un Volkswagen
5. el Nilo, el Amazonas y el Misisipí
6. Ronald Reagan y George Bush
7. El Salvador, Colombia y México
8. las Cataratas del Iguazú y las del Niágara

¿Lo sabían?

En español hay muchos dichos que son comparaciones. Es común oír expresiones como "Es más viejo que (la moda de) andar a pie", "Es más viejo que Matusalén", "Es más largo que una cuaresma *(Lent)*" o "Es más largo que una semana sin carne". Para hablar de la mala suerte se dice, "Es más negra que una noche". ¿Puedes inventar otras comparaciones?

Actividad 31: Las vacaciones

En parejas, el/la estudiante "A" cubre la Columna B y el/la estudiante "B" cubre la Columna A. Uds. deben decidir adónde quieren ir de vacaciones. Describan y comparen con su compañero/a cuál de los dos lugares les parece mejor. Comparen el precio del viaje, el clima, etc.

◖●◗ **A:** El Hotel Casa de Campo tiene tres canchas de tenis.
   B: Pues el Hotel El Caribe tiene seis canchas.
   A: Entonces el Hotel Caribe tiene más canchas de tenis que el Hotel Casa de Campo.

A	B
La Romana, República Dominicana	Cartagena, Colombia
Hotel Casa de Campo*****	Hotel El Caribe****
Una semana	Una semana
Media pensión	Pensión completa
Temperatura promedio 30°C	Temperatura promedio 27°C
Increíble playa privada	Playas fabulosas
Tres canchas de tenis	Seis canchas de tenis
Golf, windsurfing	Golf, pesca, esquí acuático
Discoteca	Casino
$2.199 por persona en habitación doble	$2.599 por persona en habitación doble

Act. 32: Once you have nominated the movies, place students in groups of five. Ask them to determine who gets the Oscars. Then as a class, have each group defend their nomination.

Act. 33: Discuss the saying, Latin America is a land of contrasts. Discuss contrasts in the U.S. Mention the homeless. Discuss the saying, "The rich get richer and the poor get poorer."

Actividad 32: El Óscar

En parejas, hagan una lista de las mejores películas de este año y hagan nominaciones para estas categorías: **película dramática, película cómica, actor,** y **actriz.** Discutan por qué cada película o persona es mejor que las otras y por qué debe ganar. Después, hagan una votación *(vote).*

Actividad 33: Los extremos

En grupos de tres, comparen estas dos partes de México. Después, individualmente, escriban un párrafo comparando las dos fotos.

Dos áreas de la Ciudad de México.

Vocabulario funcional

Instrumentos musicales

Ver página 311

Vocabulario relacionado con la música

la banda band
el conjunto group (as in rock group)

la orquesta sinfónica symphony orchestra

La comida

Ver páginas 313–314

Vocabulario de restaurante

La cuenta, por favor. The check, please.
¿Cómo está el/la . . .? How is the . . .?

Me gustaría el/la . . . I would like . . .
el menú/la carta menu

Adverbios usados con el imperfecto

Ver página 316

Más verbos

continuar to continue
cubrir to cover

romper to break

La geografía

Ver página 324

Los puntos cardinales

el este east
el norte north

el oeste west
el sur south

El tiempo

Ver página 325

Palabras y expresiones útiles

¿Algo más? Something/Anything else?
¡Qué chévere! Great! (Caribbean expression)
cursi overly cute; tacky; in bad taste

hoy (en) día today; nowadays
sin embargo however, nevertheless
verdadero real, true

El Carnaval Miami se celebra
cada año en la Calle Ocho de
la Pequeña Habana. Actualmente es el festival hispano
más grande de los Estados
Unidos.

¿Por qué crees que los hispanos crearon este carnaval
en Miami?

Capítulo 13

Chapter Objectives

After studying this chapter, you will know how to:

- discuss travel plans
- express preferences about jewelry
- talk about past experiences in relation to the present
- talk about unplanned occurrences
- give directions and commands
- make comparisons

Playa en Horcón, Chile.

¿Qué están haciendo estas personas en la playa? ¿Crees que son turistas o que son del pueblo?

La oferta de trabajo

Pronunciation: Intonation
1. Model and have students repeat after you sentences with a rising intonation (**¿Eres soltera?**) and sentences with a falling intonation (**Soy soltero. ¿Qué hora es?**)
2. Say sentences and have students guess whether they are questions or statements.
3. Have students read sentences from the dialogue with the appropriate intonation.
4. Have students turn some of the dialogue sentences into questions with a rising intonation.

Ask, **¿Quién fue la última persona que te sacó de un apuro? ¿Cuándo fue la última vez que sacaste a alguien de un apuro? ¿Qué hiciste?**

ya que	since
¿De acuerdo?	O.K.?, Agreed?
sacar de un apuro (a alguien)	to get (someone) out of a jam

Don Alejandro ya regresó de Colombia y quiere hablar con Juan Carlos y con Álvaro para ofrecerles un trabajo.

Actividad 1: ¿Qué oferta?

Escucha la conversación y di cuál es la oferta que hace don Alejandro, y si los muchachos la aceptan.

Juan Carlos	Buenos días, don Alejandro.
Alejandro	¡Entren, entren muchachos! Buenos días. Encantado de verlos.
Álvaro	Igualmente, don Alejandro. ¿Cómo está?
Alejandro	Bien, pero muy ocupado. Los invité a la oficina porque quiero hablarles sobre un posible trabajo y

espero que todavía no hayan planeado sus vacaciones de Semana Santa.

Juan Carlos Yo no tengo ningún plan en particular. ¿Y tú, Álvaro?

Álvaro No, yo tampoco. ¿De qué se trata?

Alejandro Pues necesito ayuda con un grupo de cuarenta turistas que va a viajar por América. He contratado a un guía, pero necesito a alguien más. Teresa me mencionó que Uds. tenían alguna experiencia de ese tipo. ¿Pueden darme más detalles?

Juan Carlos Yo fui guía turístico en Machu Picchu.

Álvaro Y yo he acompañado a algunos grupos de estudiantes a las Islas Canarias.

Alejandro Bueno, me parece experiencia suficiente, ya que no van a tener Uds. toda la responsabilidad. El trabajo consiste en llevar al grupo de los aeropuertos a los hoteles, ir en las excursiones y ayudar al guía a resolver problemas. El tour va a los Estados Unidos, México, Guatemala y Venezuela. ¿Les interesa?

Álvaro ¡Me parece buenísimo! ¿Y a ti, Juan Carlos?

Juan Carlos Me encanta la idea.

Alejandro Entonces . . . ah, casi se me olvida decirles algo importante. El viaje es gratis para Uds., por supuesto, y también reciben un pequeño sueldo. Mi secretaria puede darles más detalles. Luego podemos reunirnos la próxima semana para hablar con más calma. ¿De acuerdo?

Juan Carlos Cómo no, don Alejandro, y gracias por la oferta.

Alejandro ¡Uds. son los que me sacan de un apuro! Fue un placer verlos.

Álvaro Adiós, don Alejandro. Gracias nuevamente.

Juan Carlos Hasta luego, don Alejandro.

Álvaro ¡Vamos a América! No lo puedo creer.

Juan Carlos Vamos a hablar con la secretaria y luego te invito a tomar una cerveza para celebrarlo.

Actividad 2: En el bar

En grupos de tres, Uds. son Juan Carlos, Álvaro y un camarero amigo que trabaja en un bar adonde van a celebrar su nuevo trabajo. Cuéntenle al camarero sobre la oferta que acaban de aceptar.

A y B: ¡Hola!

 C: ¡Hola chicos! ¿Qué hay de nuevo?

A y B: . . .

¿Lo sabían?

Las Islas Canarias, provincias españolas, son siete islas volcánicas, que están en el Océano Atlántico cerca de África. Son una meca para el turismo por su belleza natural. En las islas hay una gran variedad de paisajes: unas playas doradas y otras negras por la lava de los volcanes, montañas con valles fértiles de vegetación tropical y hasta desiertos con camellos. En las ciudades de Santa Cruz de Tenerife y Las Palmas de Gran Canaria, el turista tiene la oportunidad de gastar sus dólares, francos o marcos en las numerosas tiendas libres de impuestos.

Actividad 3: De viaje

Haz una lista de lugares interesantes donde has estado. Después de escribirla, pregúntales a algunos de tus compañeros si han estado en esos lugares. Si contestan que sí, pregúntales cuándo fueron, cómo fueron, con quién, por cuánto tiempo estuvieron allí y qué hicieron.

En el 85 = en 1985.

A: ¿Has estado en el parque de Yellowstone?
B: Sí, he estado.
A: ¿Cuándo fuiste?
B: Fui en el 85.
A: . . .

Lo esencial

In **Lo esencial,** active vocabulary words are in blue.

El viaje

Itinerario e instrucciones especiales para Juan Carlos y Alvaro

Primer día
   10:45 Llegada a Miami del vuelo charter 726 de Iberia
   Traslado del aeropuerto al hotel en autobús ($10,00 de propina para el chofer)
   13:00 Almuerzo en el hotel
   Tarde libre para ir a la playa

Discuss tipping customs in Hispanic countries.

Explíquenle al grupo que en los Estados Unidos no es como en España donde la propina está incluida en el precio, o se deja muy poco. Hay que dar un 15% a los camareros en los restaurantes y a los taxistas. A los botones en los hoteles, como en España,

se les da $1 por cada maleta. A los guías y al chofer
del autobús los pasajeros no tienen que darles
nada; Traveltur les da propinas.

Segundo día
9:00 Tour por la ciudad en autobús con guía
turístico
($25.00 propina para el guía)
Visita a Vizcaya (museo y jardines), el
Seaquarium y el Metro Zoo
Entradas incluidas en el tour de la ciudad
Almuerzo libre
Sugerencias: el comedor del hotel; hay muchas
cafeterías cerca del hotel
Tarde: Excursión opcional a los Everglades
Precio: $15.00
Cena libre
Sugerencias: Joe's Stone Crab (mariscos),
Los Ranchos (nicaragüense), Versailles
(cubano), La Carreta (cubano), Monserrate
(colombiano)

Tercer día
Traslado del hotel al aeropuerto en autobús
($10.00 de propina para el chofer)
Tiempo para ir de compras en el aeropuerto
Los impuestos de los aeropuertos están incluidos
en el precio del tour.
13:00 Salida del vuelo 356 de Aeroméxico para
México
Almuerzo a bordo

El/la guía is a person who guides; **la guía** is a book that guides.

La entrada = admission ticket; **el billete**(Spain)/**el boleto** (Hispanic America) = ticket for transport; **el ticket/tiquete** = ticket stub.

Call attention to the different countries represented in the list of restaurants in Miami. Discuss what this indicates about immigration to the city.

Point out the need to pay airport taxes in some countries.

Act. 4: Have students look at the itinerary and say what is and what isn't included in the price of the tour.

Actividad 4: Las responsabilidades

En grupos de tres, contesten las siguientes preguntas según el itinerario y el primer diálogo del capítulo.

1. ¿Cuáles son tres cosas que Juan Carlos y Álvaro tienen que explicarle al grupo?
2. ¿A quiénes les tienen que dar ellos propina? ¿A quiénes les tienen que dar propina los pasajeros?
3. ¿Cómo van a ir del aeropuerto al hotel y viceversa?
4. Ya que Álvaro y Juan Carlos tienen que ir en todas las excursiones, ¿qué cosas van a ver ellos?

Actividad 5: Decidan

En parejas, el/la estudiante "A" quiere ir a México y el/la estudiante "B" quiere visitar las islas del Caribe para pasar las vacaciones. Miren estos dos itinerarios de viaje y después cada persona intenta convencer a su compañero/a de que debe ir al lugar que él/ella prefiere.

ESTE ITINERARIO INCLUYE:	
VISITAS	Incluidas en el itinerario.

- Billete de avión de línea regular.
- Traslados aeropuerto-hotel y viceversa.
- Estancia en régimen de alojamiento.
- Seguro turístico.
- Bolsa de viaje.

Noches	C I U D A D	H O T E L
4	MEXICO D. F.	CROWNE PLAZA
2	GUADALAJARA	FIESTA AMERICANA
3	MANZANILLO	LAS HADAS

ITINERARIO DEL CRUCERO:

FECHA	PUERTO DE ESCALA	LLEGADA	SALIDA
Día 1.º (Sáb.)	SAN JUAN P. RICO .... (Embarque 16.00 h.)	—	24.00
Día 2.º (Dom.)	Navegación	—	—
Día 3.º (Lun.)	CURAÇAO (Ant. Holandesas)....	10.00	20.00
Día 4.º (Mar.)	LA GUAYRA (Venezuela)	08.00	16.00
Día 5.º (Mié.)	GRANADA	12.30	18.00
Día 6.º (Jue.)	MARTINICA (Ant. Francesas)..	07.00	12.00
Día 7.º (Vie.)	ST. TOMAS (I. Vírgenes)	09.00	24.00
Día 8.º (Sáb.)	SAN JUAN P. RICO	08.00	—

Hacia la comunicación

Gramática

Acabar de + *infinitive* is another way to express the recent past: **Acabo de comprar una entrada.**

Review past participles, Ch.'s 11 and 12.

I. Drill present perfect: Have students ask and answer nagging questions. S1: **¿Has hecho la cama? ¿Has escrito la composición?** (etc.) S2: **Sí, ya la hice. / No, no la he hecho todavía.** Mention that in Spain, many speakers would say, **Sí ya la he hecho.**

I. Speaking About Past Experiences: The Present Perfect

In Spanish, the perfect tenses are formed with the auxiliary verb **haber** and a past participle. One of these tenses is the present perfect, which is primarily used in Spain. The present perfect is used to express an action that occurs in the past but is related to the present. It is formed as follows:

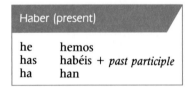

Haber (present)	
he	hemos
has	habéis + *past participle*
ha	han

—**¿Han ido** Uds. a Suramérica alguna vez?
—No, nunca **hemos ido** a Suramérica.

Have you (ever) gone to South America?
No, we have never gone to South America.

Review the subjunctive, Ch.'s 8 and 9.

II. Drill **haya** + past participle:
1. Contrast: **Espero que vuelva. / Espero que haya vuelto.**
2. Have students express their hopes and wishes, given situations such as these: (a) Your boyfriend/girlfriend had a job interview today with a firm in Alaska. (b) You go to the train station to meet some friends and they aren't on the train. (c) You and your friends just auditioned for "Star Search" and are waiting for results. (etc.)

II. Expressing Feelings About the Past: *Haya* + Past Participle

The present perfect subjunctive is used to express doubt, emotion, etc. in the present about something that may have happened in the past. This tense is formed as follows:

que + present subjunctive of **haber** + past participle

Haber (present subjunctive)		
que **haya**	que **hayamos**	
que **hayas**	que **hayáis**	+ *past participle*
que **haya**	que **hayan**	

Espero que **haya vuelto**.	*I hope that he/she has returned.*
Dudamos que **hayan ido** de viaje.	*We doubt that they have gone on a trip.*
¿Crees que **haya comido** ya?	*Do you think that he/she has eaten already?*
Busco una persona que **haya estado** en Perú.	*I'm looking for someone who has been in Peru.*

III. Talking About Unintentional Occurrences: *Se me olvidó* and Similar Constructions

To express events that happened accidentally or unintentionally, use the following construction with verbs like **caer, olvidar, perder, quemar,** and **romper**:

se me	se nos		
se te	se os	+	verb
se le	se les		

Remember: RID (Reflexive before Indirect; Indirect before Direct).

III. Drill **se me olvidó** and similar constructions:
1. Do a silent Gouin series to show breaking, dropping, losing something, etc. Have students identify actions.
2. Tell students you have a friend who is really clumsy **(torpe)** and has horrible luck. Ask them to invent things that happened to him: **Se le quemó el carro. Se le perdieron los cheques de viajero.** (etc.)
3. Ask students, **¿Qué cosas se te olvidaron la semana pasada?**

Quemamos la carta.	*We burned the letter (intentionally).*
Se nos quemó la tortilla.	*We burned the tortilla (unintentionally).*

To form this construction remember:

1. The verb agrees with what is lost, dropped, etc.

   Se me perd**ieron las entradas**.　　*I lost the tickets.*

2. The person who accidentally does the action is represented by an indirect-object pronoun, which may be clarified or emphasized by a phrase with **a: a mí, a él,** etc.

   Se **le** perdió la maleta (**a Juan**).　　*He lost the suitcase.*

(A mí) siempre se **me** olvida traer los
libros a clase.

*I always forget to bring my
books to class.*

(A Jorge) se **le** rompieron las gafas.

*George's glasses broke
(unintentionally).*

Act. 6: Use the third person
subjunctive while checking:
**¿Hay alguien que haya es-
quiado en Utah?** S1: **Sí, Juan
ha esquiado en Utah. / No, no
hay nadie que haya esquiado
en Utah.**

Actividad 6: Las experiencias

Pregúntales a un mínimo de cuatro compañeros si han hecho las cosas
de la lista que sigue. Si contestan que sí, pregúntales cuándo, cuántas
veces, con quién, si les gustó, etc. Si contestan que no, pregúntales si les
gustaría hacerlas algún día.

A: ¿Has piloteado un avión?
B: No, nunca.
A: ¿Te gustaría hacerlo?
B: ¡Qué va! No estoy loco/a. / Sí, me gustaría porque . . .

1. ganar algo en la lotería
2. nadar en el Caribe
3. ver un OVNI (objeto volador no identificado = *UFO*)
4. hacer un viaje por barco
5. jugar en un campeonato de basquetbol
6. escribir un poema
7. visitar un país donde se habla español
8. estudiar francés

Actividad 7: El Club Med

El Club Med de Punta Cana, República Dominicana, está entrevistando
gente para el puesto *(position)* de director de actividades. Ésta es la persona que entretiene a todos los huéspedes *(guests)* durante una semana,
organizando bailes, competencias deportivas, etc. En parejas, escojan el
papel A o B y sigan las instrucciones para su papel.

Papel A

Trabajas para el Club Med y vas a entrevistar a una persona para el
puesto de director de actividades. La persona que buscas debe haber hecho las siguientes cosas: trabajar para el Club Med antes, tener experiencia con adultos o con niños y primeros auxilios *(first aid)*. Buscas una
persona que sea enérgica. Haz preguntas como la siguiente: ¿Has traba-
jado para el Club Med antes?

Papel B

Estás en una entrevista para el puesto de director de actividades del Club
Med y estás muy cansado/a porque ayer te acostaste muy tarde. Ésta es
la información sobre ti que puede ayudarte a conseguir este trabajo:
fuiste huésped en el Club hace dos años, tienes cuatro hermanos pequeños y enseñas educación física en una escuela.

Actividad 8: No te preocupes

En parejas, tú y tu esposo/a se van de viaje con sus siete hijos a la playa de Puerto Vallarta, México. El/La estudiante "A" preparó una lista de cosas que cada persona de la familia tenía que hacer y ahora quiere comprobar si hicieron las cosas. El/La estudiante "B" sabe qué hicieron todos y qué no. Miren sólo su parte.

ɪ●ɪ Juan: hacer la maleta

A: Espero que Juan haya hecho la maleta.
B: La hizo ayer. / Todavía no la ha hecho, pero va a hacerla hoy.

Act. 8: Point out the use of **todavía.**

A

1. Pablo: comprar los pasajes
2. Pepe y Manuel: conseguir cheques de viajero
3. Victoria y Ángela: comprar las gafas de sol
4. Elisa: cambiar dólares por pesos mexicanos
5. Guillermo y Manuel: obtener sus pasaportes
6. Tú: poner el Pepto-Bismol en la maleta
7. Victoria: conseguir su tarjeta de crédito nueva
8. Todos: poner los trajes de baño en la maleta

B

Tú sabes que tus hijos y tú han hecho las cosas que tenían que hacer, pero que tus hijas no.

Puerto Vallarta, México, ciudad, puerto y centro turístico en la costa del Pacífico.

Actividad 9: Una llamada urgente

En parejas, Uds. son hermanos y acaban de volver a casa. Vieron que había un mensaje en el contestador automático diciendo que sus padres están en el hospital y que Uds. deben ir allí. Reaccionen a esta llamada usando: **Dudo que hayan . . . , Es posible que . . . , No creo que . . . ,** etc.

➡ Es posible que hayan tenido un accidente.

Actividad 10: La mala suerte

En grupos de cuatro, diles a tus compañeros si alguna vez has tenido uno de los siguientes problemas inesperados *(unexpected)* en un viaje y da detalles.

➡ Una vez se me olvidó el pasaporte en el avión . . .

1. perder la maleta
2. acabar el dinero
3. olvidar cosas en un hotel
4. romper algo en una tienda
5. perder las tarjetas de crédito
6. abrir el Pepto-Bismol en la maleta

Actividad 11: Dichos

En español hay muchos dichos. Se usa la construcción **se me, se te,** etc. para formar algunos de estos dichos. Unos muy populares son los siguientes.

Se le hace agua la boca.   Se le acabó la paciencia.
Se le fue la lengua *(tongue)*.   Se le fue el alma *(soul)* a los pies.
Se le hizo tarde.   Se le cae la baba *(drool)*.

En parejas, adivinen el significado de cada dicho y digan qué dichos se pueden usar en estas situaciones.

Act. 11: English equivalents: 1. He/She was running late. 2. He/She talked too much (spilled the beans). 3. He's/She's drooling over him/her, etc. 4. It makes his/her mouth water. 5. He/She ran out of patience. 6. His/Her heart sank.

1. Tenía que ir a la biblioteca por un libro; iba a ir a las siete, pero llegué a las ocho y ya estaba cerrada. ___Se le hizo tarde.___
2. El niño no debía decir nada a nadie, pero le dijo a su abuela que sus padres tenían problemas económicos. ___Se le fue la lengua.___
3. Miguel está muy enamorado de Marcela y tiene ganas de salir con ella. ___Se le cae la baba.___
4. El domingo pasado mi madre hizo un pan buenísimo . . . UMMMM . . . ___Se me hace agua la boca.___
5. Al final, la mujer se enfadó y le tiró toda la comida encima a su esposo. ___Se le acabó la paciencia.___
6. Ramón tuvo un accidente y su madre recibió una llamada del hospital. ___Se le fue el alma a los pies.___

Nuevos horizontes

Estrategia de lectura: *Linking Words*

In a text, phrases and sentences are linked with connectors, or linking words, to provide a smooth transition from one idea to another. Furthermore, they establish relationships between parts of a text. For example, in the sentence *My house is more beautiful than yours, more* expresses a comparison. In the sentences *I went to the movies, Next I had dinner,* sequence is established by the word *next.* The following list contains common Spanish linking words.

Function	Linking Words
Adding	**y, también, así como (también), aparte de, asimismo** *(likewise),* **a la vez**
Contrasting and Comparing	**a diferencia de, pero, sin embargo, por otro lado** *(on the other hand),* **a pesar de que** *(in spite of),* **sino, sino también, aunque** *(although),* **más/menos . . . que, diferente de, al igual que, como**
Exemplifying	**por ejemplo**
Generalizing	**en general, generalmente**
Showing Results	**por lo tanto** *(therefore),* **por eso, como consecuencia/resultado, entonces**
Showing Sequence	**primero, después/luego, finalmente**

Actividad 12: Preguntas

Contesta estas preguntas antes de leer el texto.

1. ¿Quiénes fueron los primeros inmigrantes que llegaron a los Estados Unidos?
2. ¿Por qué vinieron?
3. ¿Dónde hay inmigrantes hispanos en los Estados Unidos?
4. ¿Piensas que la cultura hispana es heterogénea u homogénea?
5. ¿Piensas que los inmigrantes que vienen a los Estados Unidos pierden sus costumbres en las sucesivas generaciones?

Actividad 13: Ideas principales

Lee el texto que está a continuación y busca la idea principal de cada párrafo y los detalles que la apoyan.

En busca de un nuevo mercado

La población de los Estados Unidos está formada en su gran mayoría por inmigrantes o descendientes de inmigrantes que han venido no sólo de Europa, sino también de muchas otras partes del mundo. Los hispanos forman parte de estos inmigrantes; hay 19 millones de hispanos en el país y se predice que para el año 2015 esta población va a exceder los 40   5 millones de habitantes, sobrepasando a los negros como la minoría más grande del país. Muchas compañías comerciales están investigando e invirtiendo en este creciente mercado hispano.

A diferencia de los norteamericanos, los hispanos gastan una mayor parte de su sueldo en productos para el hogar, a pesar de tener un   10 sueldo promedio menor. Y aunque la mayoría de los inmigrantes hispanos van asimilándose al idioma inglés y a la cultura estadounidense a través de las generaciones, mantienen a la vez su idioma y su identidad

Stress that there are Hispanics throughout the U.S., but that some states have a higher percentage than others. Ask students to name the states where there are the greatest number of Cubans, Puerto Ricans, Chicanos or Mexicans.

Note that many Hispanic families have lived on U.S. soil for hundreds of years.

Roberto Goizueta, cubano, presidente de Coca-Cola. ¿Conoces a algún hispano que ocupe una posición importante en tu estado o en el país?

130 mil millones = 130 billion

hispana. Muchos de ellos (mexicanos, puertorriqueños, cubanos y centroamericanos) viven relativamente cerca de sus países de origen y esto les permite mantenerse en contacto con sus familias, sus amigos y su cultura. Otra forma que tiene casi el 80% de los hispanos de mantener este contacto con su lengua y con su cultura es a través de las dos cadenas hispanas de televisión en los Estados Unidos: Telemundo y Univisión. 15 20

Basadas en sus investigaciones, las compañías comerciales hacen dos tipos de propaganda para los hispanos. Por un lado, hay propaganda dirigida a la comunidad hispana en general y por otro lado, debido a las diferencias entre hispanos de diferentes países, hay propaganda dirigida hacia grupos en particular. Por ejemplo, una propaganda de la cerveza Coors basada en un rodeo puede ser muy popular entre los mexicanos de Los Ángeles, San Antonio y Houston, pero no entre otros grupos de hispanos. Asimismo, la compañía Goya Foods presenta una propaganda de frijoles rojos para la comunidad puertorriqueña de Nueva York y otra de frijoles negros, para la comunidad cubana de Miami. 25 30

El creciente poder adquisitivo de la población hispana en los Estados Unidos, unos 130 mil millones de dólares, ha hecho que el mundo de los negocios tome conciencia de la importancia de este mercado. Las compañías comerciales, con la ayuda de expertos norteamericanos e hispanos, comienzan a comprender que la cultura hispana se basa en una multitud de culturas diferentes, con puntos en común, pero también con características y sutilezas propias. 35

Actividad 14: Conecta

Después de leer el texto, contesta estas preguntas sobre las palabras que conectan (*linking words*). Consulta el texto.

1. ¿Qué ideas contrasta **sino también** en la línea 3?
2. ¿Qué grupos contrasta **a diferencia de** en la línea 9?
3. ¿Qué añade **a la vez** en la línea 13?
4. ¿Qué compara **por otro lado** en la línea 23?
5. ¿Qué ejemplifica **por ejemplo** en la línea 25?

Actividad 15: ¿Qué sabes?

Di qué sabes sobre los siguientes temas.

1. La diferencia entre la inmigración europea e hispana
2. Los factores que motivan a las compañías norteamericanas a invertir en el mercado hispano
3. Algunos aspectos de la vida diaria en que notas influencia hispana
4. Algunos lugares de los Estados Unidos que tengan nombres hispanos y qué significan

Estrategia de escritura: *Comparing and Contrasting*

To compare or contrast two ideas is to present their similarities and differences. This may be done by presenting one idea and then the other or by presenting the similarities of both ideas followed by the differences. Look at the text on the Hispanic market and tell which of the two approaches is used by the author.

Actividad 16: La inmigración

Act. 16: You may want to brainstorm similarities and differences as a pre-writing activity.

Have students read a few of their peers' paragraphs, then have a discussion about the similarities and differences between the 2 consumer groups.

En grupos de cuatro, comparen el mercado consumidor norteamericano y el mercado hispano en los Estados Unidos. Después, escriba cada uno un párrafo presentando las diferencias y semejanzas y utilizando una de las técnicas de comparación y contraste. Para unir sus ideas, recuerden el uso de las palabras que conectan.

Lo esencial

I. Las joyas

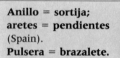

**Anillo = sortija;
aretes = pendientes
(Spain).
Pulsera = brazalete.**

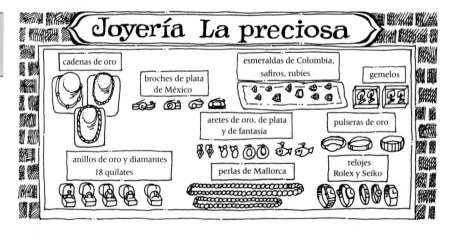

Actividad 17: Dos horizontal y cuatro vertical

En parejas, el/la estudiante "A" cubre el Crucigrama *(crossword puzzle)* B y el/la estudiante "B" cubre el Crucigrama A. Para completar el crucigrama, Uds. tienen que darle pistas *(clues)* a la otra persona. "A" tiene las palabras verticales y "B" las horizontales. Altérnense haciendo preguntas.

A: ¿Qué es el quince horizontal?
B: Es una joya verde de Colombia que se usa en anillos y aretes.
A: ¡Ah! Es una esmeralda.

Wrist = **muñeca;**
neck = **cuello.**

Crucigrama A

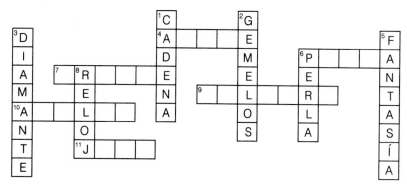

Crucigrama B

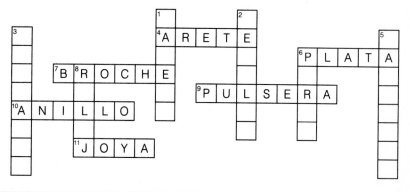

¿Lo sabían?

Colombia es el primer productor de esmeraldas del mundo y las exporta a todas partes. En Venezuela y en partes de Centroamérica se producen perlas verdaderas, que pueden ser de agua salada (de mar) o de agua dulce (de río). Si son de agua salada, son redondas, y si son de agua dulce, son de formas irregulares. Venezuela también produce diamantes. En la isla española de Mallorca se producen perlas cultivadas *(cultured)*, que por su buen precio y su excelente calidad se venden en todo el mundo.

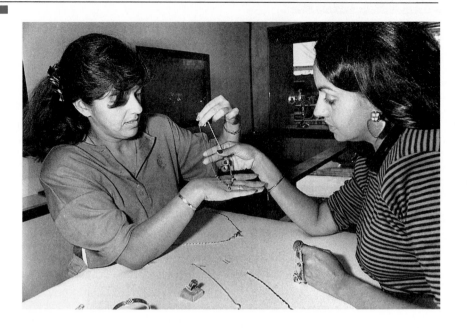

En una joyería, Colombia.

Actividad 18: Los regalos

En grupos de tres, una persona es el/la dependiente/a y las otras personas son hermanos que van a comprar algo en la Joyería La Preciosa para el aniversario de sus padres. Tienen tarjetas de crédito y mucho dinero, pero una persona no quiere gastar mucho. Decidan con la ayuda del/de la dependiente/a qué van a comprar para sus padres.

A: Buenos días. ¿Puedo ayudarles?
B: Buenos días. Quisiéramos comprar algo para el aniversario de nuestros padres. ¿Tiene alguna sugerencia?
A: . . .

Considere
que tendrá que mirarlo
varias veces al día.

Christian Duvenet
SWISS MADE

Bañado en Oro de 18 quilates. Hecho a mano.

II. Las direcciones

Ayer un detective pasó todo el día observando los movimientos de un sospechoso *(suspect)*. Mira el dibujo y lee el informe del detective.

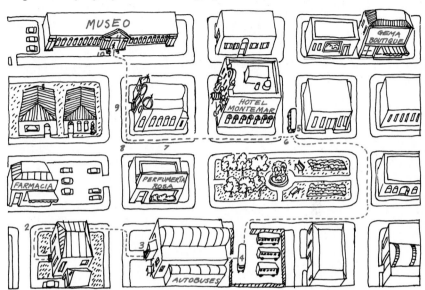

II. In **Lo esencial,** active vocabulary words are in boldface.

Cuadra = manzana (Spain), **bloque** (Puerto Rico).

Derecho = recto.

1. El criminal salió de su casa y caminó hasta **la esquina.**
2. En la esquina dobló a la derecha.
3. Caminó hasta la estación de autobuses.
4. **Tomó** el autobús.
5. **Bajó** del autobús.
6. **Cruzó** la calle.
7. **Siguió derecho** dos **cuadras.**
8. Dobló a la derecha en la esquina.
9. **Pasó por** la iglesia.
10. **Subió las escaleras.**
11. Entró en el museo.

Act. 19: The same pair activity can be done by having 1 student give directions while the other guesses the location. This can also be a warm-up activity.

You may want to have students use the impersonal **se** to give directions.

Actividad 19: Las direcciones

En parejas, explíquenle a su compañero/a cómo se va al correo, al banco o a otro lugar desde su clase. Luego su compañero/a le explica cómo llegar a otro sitio.

A: ¿Cómo se llega a . . .?
B: Primero, sales de la clase, después bajas la escalera y . . .

Actividad 20: ¿Adónde fue?

Ayer la Dra. Llanos, que está en la excursión de Juan Carlos y Vicente, salió del hotel y fue a comprar un perfume, unos pantalones y unas tarjetas postales. Mira el mapa que usó el detective y di qué camino tomó la señora. Comienza así: **La Dra. Llanos salió del hotel y . . .**

Impresiones de Miami

así	like this/that
todo el mundo	everybody, everyone
volver a + infinitive	to (do something) again

Juan Carlos y Álvaro llegaron ayer a Miami con el grupo de turistas españoles y ahora regresan al hotel en el autobús después de hacer el tour de la ciudad.

Actividad 21: Cierto o falso

Escucha la conversación y di si estas oraciones son ciertas o falsas.

1. ___C___ A los turistas les sorprendió ver que Miami no fuera una ciudad típica de los Estados Unidos.
2. ___F___ La Dra. Llanos estuvo en Cuba.
3. ___F___ Los Estados Unidos están bien representados en las películas.
4. ___C___ El Sr. Ruiz y la Dra. Llanos no son muy buenos amigos.
5. ___F___ El Sr. Ruiz tiene que ir a la oficina de American Express mañana.

Discuss Hispanic influence in Miami: **la Calle Ocho, la Pequeña Habana,** banks from Hispanic countries, the rising importance of Miami as a port for exports to Latin America, etc.

Making comparisons

Discuss the movement to keep English as the official language.

Giving a direct command

Expressing annoyance

Álvaro	Esperamos que les haya gustado el tour de la ciudad. Para mí fue una verdadera sorpresa.
Dra. Llanos	Es cierto. ¡Qué sorpresa encontrar una ciudad tan hispana en los Estados Unidos!
Juan Carlos	Y Miami no es la única; hay hispanos en el suroeste, en California, en Nueva York . . .
Sr. Ruiz	¡Y la Calle Ocho! ¡Qué interesante! Todo el mundo hablando con acento caribeño. Al cerrar los ojos me parecía volver a estar en La Habana. ¿Sabían que yo estuve allí hace muchos años? Me fascina, sencillamente, ¡me fascina! Y . . .
Álvaro	¿Vieron qué interesante pasear por las calles y ver restaurantes de tantos países hispanos? Hay muchos centroamericanos, ¿no?
Juan Carlos	¡Cómo no! Y suramericanos también.
Dra. Llanos	De veras, los Estados Unidos es un país increíble. No creo que haya otro país tan variado como éste, con tal mezcla de gentes y costumbres. Para nosotros es difícil comprender este pluralismo cultural.
Álvaro	Y qué distinta es la realidad del estereotipo que se ve en las películas. Pero los estereotipos son siempre así . . .
Juan Carlos	Bueno, ¡atención! Ya hemos llegado al hotel. Escuchen, por favor. Ahora hay un rato libre para el almuerzo, pero por favor, si quieren ir a los Everglades regresen a la una y media porque volvemos a salir a las dos.
Sr. Ruiz	¡Virgen Santísima! ¡No encuentro mis cheques de viajero y los tenía en el bolsillo. ¿Ahora qué voy a hacer?
Álvaro	Pero, los tiene Ud. en la mano, Sr. Ruiz.
Dra. Llanos	¡Qué hombre, Dios mío, qué hombre!

Actividad 22: ¿Comprendiste?

Después de escuchar la conversación, contesta las siguientes preguntas.

1. Según Juan Carlos, ¿en qué parte de los Estados Unidos hay muchos hispanos?
2. Según el Sr. Ruiz, ¿a qué ciudad se parece Miami y por qué?
3. Menciona dos cosas que le sorprendieron a la Dra. Llanos.
4. Álvaro menciona los estereotipos que se ven en las películas. ¿Cuáles son? ¿Cómo es el estereotipo del hispano? ¿Y del norteamericano? ¿Qué piensas de los estereotipos en general?

Actividad 23: Una tarjeta postal

Eres la Dra. Llanos y les escribes una tarjeta postal a tus colegas del hospital hablando de Miami y quejándote del Sr. Ruiz. Usa la imaginación.

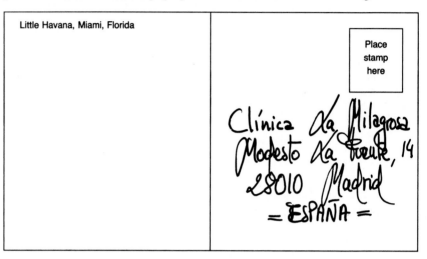

Little Havana, Miami, Florida

Place stamp here

Clínica La Milagrosa
Modesto La Fuente, 14
28010 Madrid
= ESPAÑA =

Actividad 24: Volver a empezar

Di las cosas que tienes que volver a hacer, completando estas frases.

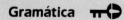 Si no entiendo las instrucciones, tengo que **volver a** leerlas.

1. Si no sale bien la foto, . . .
2. Si estás contando dinero y te interrumpen, . . .
3. Si el teléfono está ocupado, . . .
4. Si el profesor no está en su oficina, . . .
5. Si te devuelven una carta por no tener estampillas, . . .

Hacia la comunicación

Gramática

I. Describing: Comparisons of Equality

When you want to compare things that are equal, you can apply the following formulas:

tan + adjective/adverb + **como**

Mi hermano es **tan** alto **como** mi mamá.	*My brother is **as** tall **as** my mother.*
Llegaste **tan** tarde **como** tus hermanos.	*You arrived **as** late **as** your brothers.*

I. Explain countable and un-countable nouns. Contrast: **Voy a comprar cerveza. / Voy a comprar cervezas.** Some un-countable nouns: **champú, pasta de dientes, chicle,** etc.

Drill comparisons:
Use students as models, and compare them. Review comparatives and superlatives while doing this: **Pete es más alto que John pero John es tan alto como Paul. Pete es el más alto.** (etc.)

II. Review that object pronouns are positioned *before* a conjugated verb and a negative command; *after* and attached to present participles, infinitives, and affirmative commands.

Drill commands:
1. Do transformation drills: **Levántese.** → **No se levante.**
2. Have students write commands for government pamphlets on different topics: What to Do If a Child is Choking, What to Do If There Is a Fire in Your Apartment, etc.

Remember to use accents if needed.

Do mechanical drills, Workbook, Part II.

Act. 25: Encourage multiple responses.

tanto/a/os/as + noun + como

Tienes **tanto** trabajo **como** yo.	*You have as much work as I do.*
Hay **tantas** mujeres **como** hombres en el tour.	*There are as many women as men in the tour group.*

II. Making Requests and Giving Commands: Commands With *Usted* and *Ustedes*

Before studying the grammar explanation, answer the following question based on the dialogue:

- In the paragraph that begins, **"Bueno, ¡atención! . . ."**, which two verbs are used to give instructions?

1. To make a request or to give a command **(Ud., Uds.)**, use the corresponding verb forms, which are identical to the subjunctive.

¡Hable (Ud.)!* **¡Hablen (Uds.)!**	*Speak!*
¡No **lleguen** tarde al concierto, por favor!	*Don't come late to the concert, please!*

*Note: Subject pronouns are seldom used with requests and commands, but if they are, they follow the verb.

2. When reflexive or object pronouns are used with commands, follow these rules:
   a. When the command is affirmative, the pronouns are attached to the end of the verb.

¡Levánte**se** temprano!	*Get up early!*
¡Dígan**selo** a él!	*Tell it to him!*

   b. When the command is negative, the pronouns immediately precede the verb.

¡No se levante tarde!	*Don't get up late!*
¡No se lo digan a él, por favor!	*Please, don't say it to him!*

Actividad 25: ¿Quién dice qué?

En parejas, decidan en qué situaciones se dicen estas frases.

1. No hable en voz alta.
2. No tiren papeles.
3. No fumen.
4. No toque.
5. Abróchense el cinturón de seguridad.
6. Llame a la policía.
7. Compre camisas . . .

Actividad 26: Las comparaciones

En parejas, comparen a Adela y Consuelo, dos buenas amigas que tienen muchas cosas en común. Una persona cubre la Columna A y la otra cubre la Columna B. Altérnense dando información.

> **A:** Adela tiene 28 años. ¿Y Consuelo?
> **B:** 29. Entonces Adela es menor que Consuelo. / Entonces Consuelo es mayor que Adela.

A	B
Adela	Consuelo
mide: 1, 70 (uno setenta)	mide: 1, 65 (uno sesenta y cinco)
pesa: 59 kilos	pesa: 59 kilos
bonita	bonita
jugar bien al tenis	jugar bien al tenis
tener dos carros	tener dos carros
tener $10.000 en el banco	tener $1.000 en el banco

1,70 = 1 meter 70 centimeters.

Actividad 27: Sigan las instrucciones

Act. 27: You can read this, or have students read it to one another in pairs as a listening-comprehension activity.

Have students invent instructions for American gestures. Then have the class follow the instructions.

Escuchen las instrucciones y hagan las acciones de los siguientes gestos *(gestures)* hispanos.

Para indicar que una persona es tacaña *(stingy)*:
1. Levántense.
2. Doblen el brazo derecho con la mano hacia arriba.
3. Abran la mano izquierda.
4. Pongan la mano izquierda debajo del codo derecho.
5. Con la palma de la mano izquierda, tóquense el codo varias veces.

Para indicar "no, no, no":
1. Levanten la mano derecha y pónganla enfrente del cuerpo con la palma de la mano hacia enfrente.
2. Cierren la mano.
3. Saquen el dedo índice hacia arriba.
4. Muevan el dedo índice de izquierda a derecha como un limpiaparabrisas.

¿Lo sabían?

Otros gestos comunes en los países hispanos son los siguientes:
1. Poner el dedo índice debajo del ojo y tirar hacia abajo para indicar que se debe tener cuidado.
2. Cerrar la mano y levantar el dedo meñique *(little finger)* para significar que una persona es delgada.
3. Cerrar la mano con la punta de los cinco dedos tocándose para significar que hay muchas personas.

Actividad 28: Los asistentes de vuelo

Eres asistente de vuelo de la aerolínea VIASA y vas a demostrar las instrucciones de seguridad en un avión. Lee individualmente las instrucciones que hay a continuación. No vas a entender todas las palabras, pero no importa. Intenta comprender las ideas principales. Después, escucha a tu profesor/a y demuestra las acciones para los pasajeros.

Buenos días y bienvenidos a bordo. Ahora unas medidas de seguridad. Abróchense el cinturón de seguridad. Mantengan el respaldo del asiento en posición vertical, la mesa en posición inicial y pongan su equipaje de mano completamente debajo del asiento de enfrente o en uno de los compartimientos de arriba. Por favor, obedezcan el aviso de no fumar. En el respaldo del asiento enfrente de Uds. hay una tarjeta con información. Esta tarjeta les indica su salida de emergencia más cercana. Tomen unos minutos para leerla. En este avión hay dos puertas en cada extremo de la cabina y dos salidas sobre las alas. En caso de que sea necesario, el cojín del asiento puede usarse como flotador: pasen los brazos por los tirantes que están debajo del cojín. Si hay un cambio brusco de presión en la cabina, los compartimientos que contienen las máscaras de oxígeno se abren automáticamente. Entonces, apaguen los cigarrillos, pónganse la máscara sobre la nariz y la boca y respiren normalmente. Después, tomen la cinta elástica y póngansela sobre la cabeza. Después de ponerse la máscara, ajusten bien las máscaras de sus niños. Gracias por su atención y esperamos que tengan un buen viaje a bordo de VIASA.

VIASA is the largest Venezuelan airline.

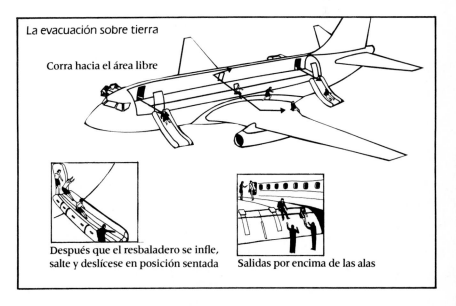

La evacuación sobre tierra

Corra hacia el área libre

Después que el resbaladero se infle, salte y deslícese en posición sentada

Salidas por encima de las alas

Actividad 29: En la calle

En parejas, una persona cubre la Columna A y la otra cubre la Columna B. Mira tu mapa de la ciudad y pregúntale a tu compañero/a (una persona que va por la calle) cómo llegar a los lugares que aparecen en tu columna. Las dos personas están donde se indica en el mapa. Alternen preguntando y respondiendo.

- **A:** ¿Puede decirme cómo llegar a . . . ? / ¿Sabe dónde está . . . ?
  B: Siga derecho dos cuadras . . .

A	B
el Hotel San Jorge	el Museo de Arqueología
el correo	el Consulado de los Estados Unidos
el Cine Sol	la Biblioteca Nacional

Actividad 30: Buen ejercicio

Te dieron un puesto como profesor/a de gimnasia aeróbica. Tienes que dar buenas instrucciones. Escribe las instrucciones y, si es posible, practica la rutina con un grupo de amigos. Usa frases como **corran; con la mano derecha tóquense el pie izquierdo diez veces; siéntense en el suelo con las piernas enfrente de Uds.; tóquense las rodillas con la cabeza;** etc.

Note the use of the reflexive with **tocar.**

Vocabulario funcional

El viaje

el chofer   driver, chauffeur
la entrada   entrance ticket
la excursión   excursion, side trip
el/la guía turístico/a   tour guide
los impuestos   taxes
el itinerario   itinerary

libre   free (with nothing to do)
opcional   optional
la propina   tip, gratuity
el/la taxista   taxi driver
el tour   tour
el traslado   transfer

Las joyas

Ver página 348

Las direcciones

bajar   to go down
cruzar   to cross (the street)
la cuadra   city block
la(s) escalera(s)   stairs
la esquina   corner
pasar por   to pass by/through
seguir derecho   to keep going straight ahead

subir   to go up
¿Puede decirme cómo llegar a . . . ?   Can you tell me how to get to . . . ?
¿Sabe dónde está . . . ?   Do you know where . . . is?

Más verbos

caer   to fall; to drop
conseguir   to get, obtain
haber   to have (auxiliary verb)
olvidar   to forget

pasar   to spend (time)
perder   to lose
quemar   to burn

Palabras y expresiones útiles

así   like this/that
¿De acuerdo?   O.K.?, Agreed?
sacar de un apuro (a alguien)   to get (someone) out of a jam
tan   so
tan . . . como   as . . . as
tanto . . . como   as much . . . as

tantos/as . . . como   as many . . . as
todo el mundo   everybody, everyone
volver a + infinitive   to (do something) again
ya que   since

Detalle de un mural de Diego
Rivera.

Bring in pictures by other mural-
ists — Rivera, Siqueiros, Orozco,
etc. — and have students discuss the content. Discuss the
artists.

¿De qué país crees que sea
este mural?
¿Qué crees que represente
el mural?

Capítulo 14

Chapter Objectives

After studying this chapter, you will know how to:

- explain simple dental problems
- make some bank transactions
- give informal and implied commands
- avoid repetition
- express possession in an emphatic way
- order and discuss breakfast

Banco en Tegucigalpa, Honduras.

En una calle de la Zona Rosa

Pronunciation: Review of [p], [t], [k]
1. Write the following tongue twisters on the board for students to practice: **Paco compra papas pero paga poco. Toto tomó té de tilo Tatetí. Carmen come comida cara.**
—**Compadre, cómpreme coco.**
—**Compadre, no compro coco porque como poco coco como poco coco compro.**
2. Have students work in pairs to create their own tongue twisters, then have other students read them aloud.

La Zona Rosa es un distrito de tiendas y restaurantes elegantes en la Ciudad de México.

Give students sentences and have them respond: **¿Te espero o vienes más tarde? ¿Quieres saltar de un avión? Para mañana tienen que escribir 3 páginas en el libro de ejercicios, pasar una hora en el laboratorio, escribir una composición de 6 páginas ...**

¡Basta (de . . .)!	(That's) enough (. . .)!
¡Ya voy!	I'm coming!
una enciclopedia ambulante	a walking encyclopedia
¡Ni loco/a!	Not on your life!

Mientras el grupo de turistas tiene unas horas libres en México, Álvaro y Juan Carlos dan un paseo.

Actividad 1: Por la calle

Escucha la conversación que tienen los muchachos al salir del hotel y contesta estas preguntas.

1. ¿Qué es una "sala de torturas" para Álvaro?
2. ¿Adónde va a ir Juan Carlos?
3. ¿Por qué llama Álvaro a Juan Carlos una enciclopedia ambulante?

Juan Carlos	Vamos Álvaro, ya es tarde.
Álvaro	¡Ya voy! ¡Ay, ay, ay!
Juan Carlos	¿Qué te pasa? Ya son las nueve y sólo tenemos dos horas.
Álvaro	¡Ay! Mi muela, ¡qué dolor de muela!
Juan Carlos	Te digo que vayas a un dentista.
Álvaro	¿A una sala de torturas? ¡Ni loco!
Juan Carlos	Te lo dije en España. ¿Por qué no fuiste al dentista allá?
Álvaro	Porque no me gusta y pensé que . . .
Juan Carlos	¡Basta de tonterías! Allí veo el consultorio de un dentista y por última vez te digo que vayas ahora mismo o que dejes de quejarte.
Álvaro	Bueno, bueno, voy. Mientras tanto, ve tú al banco para cambiar dinero.
Juan Carlos	No olvides que tenemos que estar en el hotel a las once para acompañar al grupo en el tour de la ciudad.
Álvaro	¿Qué vamos a ver hoy? Lo leí en el itinerario anoche, pero se me olvidó.
Juan Carlos	Tienes tanto dolor que te está afectando la mente, ¿no?
Álvaro	Vamos, ¡dime!
Juan Carlos	Vamos a ir por la Avenida de la Reforma hasta el Zócalo, que es la plaza principal, ¿te acuerdas? Allí vamos a ver la Catedral y los murales de Diego Rivera en el Palacio Nacional. Después vamos al Parque de Chapultepec a ver el castillo de Maximiliano y Carlota y por último, vamos a la Plaza de las Tres Culturas, donde hay edificios de apartamentos modernos, una iglesia colonial y ruinas de una pirámide azteca. ¿Y qué? ¿Ya se te va pasando la amnesia?
Álvaro	¡Cuánto sabes! ¿Para qué le pagamos a un guía si tú eres una enciclopedia ambulante?
Juan Carlos	¡Deja de molestar! Ve al dentista mientras yo voy al banco y luego nos encontramos en el hotel. ¡Chau!

Side notes:
- Giving an implied command
- Giving a negative command
- Insisting
- If possible, show pictures or slides of Mexico City. Bring in a map to show different locations. Discuss the history of Mexico and its present-day problems: pollution, population density, etc.
- Giving a command

Actividad 2: ¿Comprendiste?

Después de escuchar la conversación, contesta estas preguntas.

1. ¿Adónde va a ir Álvaro? ¿Por qué no fue antes?
2. ¿A qué hora tienen que estar Álvaro y Juan Carlos en el hotel y por qué?
3. ¿Qué hay alrededor del Zócalo?

4. ¿Qué van a visitar en el Parque de Chapultepec?
5. ¿Cuáles son las culturas representadas en la Plaza de las Tres Culturas?

¿Lo sabían?

Maximiliano y Carlota fueron emperadores de México, enviados allí por Napoleón III en 1864. Su imperio fue corto y desastroso. Cuando Napoleón retiró su ayuda, Carlota fue a Europa para buscar apoyo, pero nadie quiso ayudarla; frustrada y desesperada, se volvió loca cuando los mexicanos capturaron y ejecutaron *(executed)* a Maximiliano. Carlota vivió sesenta años más en Italia.

Point out the use of the historical present. Ask students what was happening in the U.S. at that time.

HISTORIA

1862 Las tropas francesas de Bazaine entran en la capital.

1864 El archiduque Fernando Maximiliano, hermano del emperador Francisco José, acepta la corona mexicana que le ofrece una Junta de Notables a instancias de Napoleón III, emperador de los franceses.

1866 Las dificultades de la política exterior de Napoleón III y las que halla Maximiliano en México provocan el comienzo de la evacuación de las tropas francesas.

1867 Prosigue el éxito de la ofensiva republicana. Maximiliano, que había pretendido abdicar contra la oposición, queda sitiado en Querétaro. Entregada la plaza, es fusilado junto a los generales mexicanos Miramón y Mejía, que habían luchado a su favor. Benito Juárez es reelegido presidente constitucional.

Act. 3: Answers: **Te digo que vayas a un dentista. ¡Basta de tonterías!** ... **que dejes de quejarte. Tienes tanto dolor que te está afectando la mente, ¿no? Vamos, ¡dime! ... ¿te acuerdas? ¿Y qué? ¿Ya se te va pasando la amnesia? ¿ ... tú eres una enciclopedia ambulante? ¡Deja de molestar!**

Actividad 3: Un buen amigo

Cuando hablan dos amigos, como Juan Carlos y Álvaro, no es igual que cuando hablan dos personas que no se conocen bien. En parejas, indiquen qué oraciones y comentarios de la conversación muestran que son amigos y por qué.

Actividad 4: Una enciclopedia ambulante

Si una persona sabe muchos datos, coloquialmente se dice que es "una enciclopedia ambulante". Para formar expresiones como éstas, por lo general se usa un sustantivo relacionado con las palabras indicadas y se añade "ambulante". ¿Cómo se puede describir a estas personas?

Act. 4: 1. **una joyería ambulante** 2. **una farmacia ambulante** 3. **una biblioteca ambulante** 4. **un diccionario ambulante** 5. **un atlas ambulante**

1. una persona que lleva muchas **joyas**
2. una persona que tiene muchas **medicinas**
3. una persona que siempre lleva muchos **libros**
4. una persona que sabe **la definición de muchas palabras**
5. una persona que sabe mucha **geografía**

Lo esencial

I. El consultorio del dentista

BIENVENIDO
REACH†

El cepillo más efectivo para prevenir caries.

CERDAS EN DOS NIVELES.
CORTAS: para cepillar profundamente la superficie dental, y dejarla limpia y brillante.
LARGAS: para limpiar y dar masaje a las encías.

CABEZA COMPACTA.
Cerdas concentradas y redondeadas para cepillar uniforme y firmemente cada diente, sin irritar las encías.

CUELLO ANGULADO.
En forma de instrumento dental para alcanzar perfectamente todas las piezas, incluso las posteriores.

MANGO ANATOMICO.
(Moldeado).
Permite un cepillado más efectivo y cómodo.

caerse un empaste to lose a filling
la carie cavity
el diente tooth
el dolor de muela toothache
el empaste filling

el hilo dental dental floss
la limpieza de dientes teeth cleaning
la muela molar
la muela de juicio wisdom tooth

Actividad 5: La historia dental

Vas a ver a un nuevo dentista por primera vez y tienes que darle tu historia dental a su ayudante. En parejas, habla con el/la ayudante, que necesita saber la siguiente información.

|●| número de empastes

    A: ¿Cuántos empastes tiene?
    B: No tengo ninguno. / Tengo . . .

1. fecha de la última limpieza dental
2. frecuencia de las visitas al dentista
3. higiene dental
4. número de muelas de juicio
5. problemas dentales recientes
6. sensibilidad al frío o al calor

Actividad 6: El dolor de muela

En parejas, una persona cubre el Papel A y la otra cubre el Papel B. Conversen por teléfono según las indicaciones.

Papel A

Tienes *uno* de estos problemas: un dolor de muela terrible y casi no puedes hablar; una muela sensible al calor y al frío y crees que pueda ser una carie; se te cayó un empaste. Llamas al dentista para hacer una cita urgente. Eres una persona muy insistente.

Papel B

Eres recepcionista en el consultorio de un dentista. Hoy estás pasando un mal día y estás de mal humor. Un/a paciente te llama por teléfono pero a ti no te parece nada urgente. El dentista está ocupado hasta el mes que viene.

II. En la casa de cambio

II. Drill vocabulary: Do a Gouin series based on changing money: **Miro el dinero. Le digo al cajero que quiero cambiar dinero. Le digo cuánto. Firmo los cheques de viajero. Le enseño el pasaporte. Le digo mi dirección. Recojo el recibo. Paso por la caja. Espero. Espero. Recibo el dinero en efectivo. Lo cuento.**

El cambio de monedas internacionales, Banco Central de Madrid.

el billete   bill (paper money)
la caja   cashier's desk
cambiar (dinero)   to exchange; to change (money)
el cambio   exchange rate; change
el cheque de viajero   traveler's check

el (dinero en) efectivo   cash
la firma   signature
firmar   to sign
el giro bancario   money order
la moneda   currency; coin
sacar   to take out
la tarjeta de crédito   credit card

Juan Ramón Jiménez (1881–1958), Spanish poet.
Juan Pablo Duarte, considered to be the founder of the Dominican Republic.
Rafael Yglesias Castro, president of Costa Rica in 1894, the year the country entered its modern period of progress and democracy.
Francisco Indalecio Madero, Mexican revolutionary and president of the Republic from 1911–1913.

¿Lo sabían?

Si viajas por un país hispano, siempre es mejor que cambies dinero en un banco o en una casa de cambio y no en una tienda ni en un hotel porque cobran una comisión alta. También es bueno que uses cheques de viajero, pues son más seguros y puedes recibir mejor cambio en los bancos. En algunos países no se puede cambiar dinero en todos los bancos; hay que hacerlo en casas de cambio o en bancos que tienen un aviso que dice "CAMBIO". Tampoco es común pagar con cheques personales en tiendas, restaurantes o supermercados; las compras se hacen con dinero en efectivo o con tarjeta de crédito.

Actividad 7: ¿Cómo pagas?

En parejas, decidan cómo explicarle a un/a visitante hispano/a dónde se paga con dinero en efectivo, con cheque personal, con cheque de viajero o con tarjeta de crédito en los Estados Unidos.

Actividad 8: El dinero

Los billetes de los Estados Unidos son todos del mismo color y tamaño *(size)*, pero en otros países, unos billetes son más grandes y otros más pequeños y de diferentes colores. En grupos de cinco, miren e identifiquen de dónde son estos billetes. ¿Quién o qué aparece en el dibujo? ¿Creen Uds. que sea bueno o malo tener billetes de diferentes tamaños y colores?

Act. 9: As some students may be unfamiliar with how to change currency, review this procedure before beginning the activity.

Actividad 9: El cambio

En parejas, el/la estudiante "A" va a una casa de cambio en Puerto Rico a cambiar dólares por moneda de un país hispano; el/la estudiante "B" trabaja en la casa de cambio. "B" le pregunta si quiere comprar o vender, qué moneda quiere, cuánto dinero quiere cambiar y le dice a cuánto está el cambio.

1 U.S. dollar = **1.8155 marcos**

Option 1: Bring in a current exchange-rate table to use in class. To reenter large numbers, have students calculate how much of a particular currency they will get for different amounts in dollars.

Option 2: Bring in ads from Hispanic newspapers and catalogs, and have students calculate the equivalent prices in dollars.

cambio	$		
		España/Peseta	114.00
		Francia/Franco	6.1430
Alemania Occ./Marco	1.8155	Gran Bretaña/Libra	.5624
fArgentina/Austral	16.3000	Hong Kong/Dólar	7.8080
Brasil/Cruzado	801.58	Italia/Lira	1329.50
Canadá/Dólar	1.1956	Japón/Yen	126.00
Colombia/Peso	335.00	México/Peso	2280.00
Chile/Peso	248.90	zVenezuela/Bolívar	37.2000

Hacia la comunicación

Gramática ⊤⊙

Drill **tú** commands:
1. Use TPR to give individual students a series of commands. Some can be cultural, such as the test given to people in Spain to see if they are "under the influence": **Levanta la pierna derecha y haz un cuatro con la rodilla. Pon el dedo pequeño en la rodilla y el pulgar en la nariz. ¡No te caigas!**
2. Put students in groups of 5 and have them give singular commands.
3. Have students write a series of commands that lead to the completion of an action. Have them do this in pairs.

I. Making Requests and Giving Commands: Commands with *tú*

Before studying the grammar explanation, answer the following question based on the dialogue:

• When Juan Carlos says to Álvaro, **"¡Deja de molestar!"**, is he making a suggestion or giving a command? Do you think Juan Carlos is using the **Ud.** or the **tú** form when talking to Álvaro?

1. In this book you have seen the singular familiar command (tú) used in the directions for many activities. To give an affirmative familiar command or to make a request, use the verb form corresponding to **él/ella/Ud.** in the present indicative for most verbs.

practicar → practi**ca**   traer → tra**e**   subir → sub**e**

Sube a mi habitación y **trae** el libro que está allí.

Go up to my room and bring the book that is there.

¡Espera un momento!

Wait a minute!

The familiar commands for the following verbs are irregular:

decir → **di**   salir → **sal**
hacer → **haz**   ser → **sé**
ir → **ve**   tener → **ten**
poner → **pon**   venir → **ven**

Ven acá y **haz** el trabajo.   *Come here and do the work.*
Sé bueno y **di** siempre la verdad.   *Be good and always tell the truth.*

Sé is a familiar command; **se** is a reflexive pronoun and an object pronoun.

2. To give a negative familiar command or request, the form used is identical to the **tú** form of the present subjunctive.

No vayas al dentista todavía.   *Don't go to the dentist yet.*
No salgas esta tarde.   *Don't go out this afternoon.*

Review formation of the subjunctive, Ch. 8.

Note: Subject pronouns are seldom used with familiar commands, but if they are, they follow the verb: **Estoy ocupado; ven tú. No lo hagas tú; yo voy a hacerlo.**

3. In familiar commands, as in formal commands, the reflexive and the object pronouns immediately precede the verb in a negative command and are attached to the end of an affirmative command.

No se lo digas.   *Don't tell it to her.*
Levánta**te.**   *Get up.*

4. The following chart summarizes the forms used for formal and familiar commands:

Vosotros affirmative commands: deci̶r̶ + d → **decid.**
Reflexive affirmative **vosotros** commands: lava̶r̶s̶e̶ + os → **lavaos.**
Negative **vosotros** commands: Use subjunctive forms.

Mandatos		
	Afirmativo	Negativo
(tú)	come*	no comas
(Ud.)	coma	no coma
(Uds.)	coman	no coman

*Note: All forms are identical to the subjunctive except the affirmative command form of **tú.**

II. Giving Implied Commands: *Decir* + subjunctive

To give an implied command, you can use the verb **decir** in the independent clause and a verb in the subjunctive in the dependent clause.

Te **digo** que **vayas** al dentista.   *I tell you to go to the dentist.*
¡Oigan! Les **estoy diciendo** que   *Listen! I'm telling you to come.*
  vengan.

Do mechanical drills, Workbook, Part I.

However, when the verb **decir** is used to give information the verb in the dependent clause is in the indicative.

Él dice que **no va** a llover.	*He says that it's not going to rain.*
Le digo que **vamos** al Zócalo.	*I tell her that we're going to the Zócalo.*
Ella dice que no **tienes** que venir mañana.	*She says that you don't have to come tomorrow.*

Actividad 10: En el programa de David Letterman

Tú tienes un perro muy inteligente y lo llevas al programa de David Letterman. Dale órdenes comunes y después mándale hacer "un truco estúpido". Usa verbos como **sentarse, levantarse, dar la pata** *(paw)*, **hablar, correr, saltar** *(to jump)*, **hacerse el muerto, traer,** etc.

Hacerse el/la + adjective = to pretend to be + *adjective.*

Act. 11: Encourage students to be creative!

Actividad 11: ¡Cuántas órdenes!

En grupos de tres, Uds. son tres hermanos que viven juntos. Sus padres acaban de llamar y dicen que van a llegar dentro de una hora. El apartamento es un desastre y Uds. no tienen nada de comer ni de beber. Tienen que darse órdenes uno al otro para tener el apartamento presentable para sus padres.

◖●◗ ¡Corre a la tienda y compra café!
¡No compres café, compra té!

Act. 12: Because there is some overlap, students will have to negotiate to decide who will do what.

Actividad 12: ¿Quién hace qué?

En parejas, Uds. son Juan Carlos y Álvaro y tienen muchas cosas que hacer. Lean primero todas las instrucciones para su papel solamente; luego denle órdenes a la otra persona.

Juan Carlos	Álvaro
Quieres que Álvaro:	Quieres que Juan Carlos:
–mande tarjetas postales	–compre las entradas para el Ballet Folklórico
–compre las entradas para el Ballet Folklórico	–ponga un anuncio sobre el Ballet en el hotel
–llame al guía para ver la hora de salida mañana	–haga una reserva en un restaurante
–no le pague al guía todavía	–pregunte cómo llegar al Ballet
Tú ya:	Tú ya:
–hiciste una reserva en un restaurante	–llamaste al guía y sabes que el grupo sale mañana a las 7:30
	–mandaste las tarjetas postales

Actividad 13: Los mensajes

Tú eres secretario/a. Tu jefe, el Sr. Beltrán, te da algunos mensajes *(mes-sages)* para el mensajero *(messenger boy)*. Dile al mensajero qué tiene que hacer.

El jefe dice que . . .

tú usar el coche y no la moto porque va a llover hoy
tú llevar un mensaje al Sr. Piera
tú comprar sobres y estampillas
tú avisarle a la compañía de teléfonos que el teléfono no funcionar
tú depositar el dinero de la oficina en el banco
tú deber trabajar el sábado
tú tener que venir mañana a las 8:00
tú no llegar tarde

Act. 14: To practice **vosotros**, do this activity with 2 Spaniards who are coming to visit.

Actividad 14: Consejos

En grupos de tres, hagan una lista de cosas que debe o no debe hacer una amiga hispana que viene a visitar su ciudad. Hay diferentes maneras de dar consejos: **Es necesario que . . . , (No) debes . . . , Te aconsejamos que . . . ,** etc.

|●| Visita el museo.
No camines sola por los parques de noche.

Nuevos horizontes

Estrategia de lectura: *Recognizing False Cognates*

Throughout the readings in this book, you have probably noticed how many English cognates there are in Spanish. You have also seen that there are false cognates, that is, words that are spelled similarly in both languages, but have different meanings. The following is a list of commonly used false cognates.

Discuss and practice other common false cognates.

actual   present-day
asistir a   to attend
comprensivo/a   understanding
discutir   to argue
embarazada   pregnant
gracioso/a   funny
la librería   bookstore

la noticia   news item
real   royal; true
realizar   to accomplish
sensible   sensitive
simpático/a   pleasant, nice
soportar   to tolerate

Use a dictionary to find the Spanish equivalent for these false cognates in English:

actual	embarrassed	to realize
to assist	gracious	sensible
comprehensive	library	to support
to discuss	notice	sympathetic

Actividad 15: Preguntas

Antes de leer el texto, contesta estas preguntas.

1. De acuerdo con el diálogo entre Juan Carlos y Álvaro, ¿qué visitaron en México?
2. ¿Qué sabes sobre los lugares que ellos mencionaron?
3. ¿Has estado en México alguna vez? ¿Qué lugares visitaste?
4. ¿Sabes qué civilizaciones indias vivieron en México?

Actividad 16: Ideas principales

Lee el diario de Juan Carlos y busca las ideas principales que él menciona.

For further information, consult *Mexico: A History in Art* by Bradley Smith (New York: Doubleday, 1971) and *Pre-Columbian Art*, edited by Elizabeth P. Benson (Chicago: University of Chicago Press, 1976).

Bring in photos of Mexico.

martes, 25 de marzo

Hoy discutí con Álvaro pues me tenía loco con su dolor de muela. Finalmente fue al dentista, así que ahora está mejor. Hoy dimos una vuelta por la ciudad. Fuimos por el Paseo de la Reforma hasta el Zócalo y visitamos la Catedral y el Palacio Nacional, donde se ve la historia de México en los murales de Diego Rivera. De allí fuimos al Parque de Chapultepec y visitamos el Museo de Antropología. ¡Qué maravilla! La cantidad de objetos olmecas, mayas, toltecas y aztecas que había era impresionante: joyas, instrumentos musicales, cerámica, ropas y, por supuesto, el calendario azteca. Nos contó la guía de la excursión que ya en el siglo XIV los aztecas eran capaces de calcular el año solar.

El imperio azteca consistía en una confederación de tres ciudades —una de ellas era Tenochtitlán, la capital que estaba donde actualmente está la Ciudad de México. Es increíble lo bien planeada que estaba la ciu-

(Izquierda) Pirámide del Sol, Teotihuacán, México.
(Derecha) El Palacio Nacional en el Zócalo, Ciudad de México.

dad: tenía agua potable y sistemas sanitarios mucho mejores que los que Europa llegó a tener en el siglo XVIII. (Esto yo ya lo sabía; lo aprendí en la facultad.)

Salimos del museo (demasiado corta la visita; tengo que regresar algún día) y fuimos a la Plaza de las Tres Culturas: ruinas aztecas, una iglesia colonial y rascacielos del siglo XX. ¡Qué buen ejemplo de la mezcla de culturas hay en el México actual!

miércoles, 26 de marzo
Anoche fuimos a ver el Ballet Folklórico y me fascinó. Me acosté muy tarde y estaba muerto de cansancio. Hoy llegamos a Mérida, Yucatán. El viaje en autobús me cansó mucho pero, por suerte, me divertí charlando con el Sr. Ruiz, porque es muy gracioso. Es una lástima que la Dra. Llanos ya no lo soporte. Llegamos al hotel tardísimo. Ahora a dormir, porque mañana salimos temprano para visitar Chichén Itzá.

jueves, 27 de marzo
Hoy fuimos a las ruinas de Chichén Itzá, donde vivieron muchos de los mayas entre los años 300 y 900 d.C. No se sabe bien dónde comenzó

esta civilización: algunos dicen que en el Petén, Guatemala; otros creen que fue en Palenque, México. Los mayas eran muy avanzados en astronomía y matemáticas y conocían el uso del cero antes de que los árabes lo introdujeran en Europa. Cultivaban no sólo el maíz como los aztecas, sino también el cacao, la batata y el chile. Estos genios también inventaron un sistema de escritura jeroglífica. Todo esto es tan fascinante que ahora quiero conocer otras ciudades mayas como Copán en Honduras y Tikal en Guatemala.

Bueno, de Chichén Itzá lo que más me gustó fue el templo de Kukulkán. Es un lugar impresionante; al entrar sentí una sensación de temor y me salí pronto. En este templo hay un jaguar rojo con ojos de jade pintado en la pared. Es bellísimo.

Mañana partimos para Uxmal. A ver si les grabo un cassette a las chicas porque no he tenido tiempo para escribirles.

Actividad 17: Explícalo

Después de leer el texto, explica con otras palabras las siguientes ideas relacionadas con cognados falsos.

1. Juan Carlos dice que discutió con Álvaro.
2. La ciudad de Tenochtitlán estaba en el lugar donde actualmente está la ciudad de México.
3. Juan Carlos dice que el Sr. Ruiz es gracioso.
4. La Dra. Llanos no soporta al Sr. Ruiz.

Actividad 18: Impresiones

En grupos de tres, comenten las impresiones de Juan Carlos sobre los lugares que vio en los tres días.

|●| **A:** El primer día Juan Carlos vió . . .
B: Y le gustó mucho . . .
C: . . .

Estrategia: *Journal Writing*
Discuss the writing strategies apparent in Juan Carlos's journal entries.

Act. 19: Encourage students to continue writing in their journals for as long as you feel is productive. Suggest they use a small notebook, rather than separate sheets of paper, for journals to be kept over time. Collect entries sporadically and in small groups. Correction of grammar and vocabulary use is important, but may be secondary with this type of writing. Responding in a personal way to what the student has written is strongly suggested.

Estrategia de escritura: *Journal Writing*

Writing a journal is a way to record the main events of your day. To write a journal or diary, concentrate on the day's highlights, making comments and jotting down your impressions about what happened. Write down your thoughts freely, focusing on the content of the writing, not its form. This spontaneous style of writing helps ideas flow and minimizes writer's block.

Actividad 19: Mi diario

Escribe un diario sobre un mínimo de tres días. Incluye las cosas importantes que ocurrieron y haz comentarios libremente.

Lo esencial

El desayuno

Practice these words when cooking, eating breakfast, etc.

1. el croissant   3. el jugo/zumo   5. la mermelada   7. el yogur
2. el café   4. la mantequilla   6. la tostada

Otras cosas para el desayuno

los churros y el chocolate   Spanish crullers and hot chocolate
las galletas   cookies; crackers
los huevos (fritos, revueltos, duros)   eggs (fried, scrambled, hard-boiled)
la salchicha   sausage
el tocino   bacon

Huevos tibios/pasados por agua = soft-boiled eggs.

Point out that café con leche is approximately about half coffee and half steamed milk, not cream.

¿Lo sabían?

En los países hispanos es normal tomar un desayuno ligero *(light)* que consiste en café con leche y tostadas, croissants o galletas con mantequilla o mermelada. No es común comer huevos y tocino para el desayuno. Por lo general, no mucha gente come cereal, con la excepción de los niños pequeños. En España, si se desayuna fuera de casa es común desayunarse con churros y chocolate.

Actividad 20: Las preferencias

Habla con algunos compañeros para averiguar con qué se desayunan durante la semana y el fin de semana. Si comen huevos, pregúntales cómo los prefieren.

Actividad 21: ¡Una tostada, ya va!

En grupos de cuatro, el/la estudiante "A" es el/la camarero/a y los estudiantes "B", "C" y "D" son clientes que entran en la cafetería para tomar el desayuno. Antes de pedir, cada persona debe leer solamente las instrucciones de su papel, que están a continuación.

A   No hay tocino, pero hay salchichas. No hay croissants, ni churros ni jugo de naranja *(orange)*; sólo hay jugo de tomate.

B   Hoy quieres un desayuno fuerte, porque no vas a poder almorzar.

C   Estás a dieta, así que quieres algo ligero y un café con leche para despertarte.

D   Te encantan los churros y el chocolate. Siempre comes algo dulce *(sweet)* por la mañana.

¿Lo sabían?

En español hay muchos dichos relacionados con la comida.

1. **Se vende como churros** se usa cuando una cosa es muy popular y se vende mucho en las tiendas.
2. **Estoy hecho una sopa** se dice después de caminar en la lluvia.
3. **Estoy aburrido como una ostra** *(oyster)* quiere decir que uno está muy aburrido.
4. **No sabe ni papa** se usa cuando una persona es ignorante.

¿Hay equivalentes en inglés para estos dichos? ¿Que dichos relacionados con la comida conoces en inglés?

En Yucatán

Practice **pasarlo bien/mal.** Ask, **¿Lo pasas bien en las reuniones de tu familia? ¿Adónde fuiste/Qué hiciste este fin de semana? ¿Lo pasaste bien?**

Ask students to brainstorm phobias, then ask if they have any phobias.

pasarlo bien/mal	to have a good/bad time
por un lado/por otro (lado)	on the one hand/on the other (hand)
tenerle fobia a . . .	to have a fear of . . .; to hate

Juan Carlos está en Yucatán, México, y no tiene tiempo para escribirles una carta a sus amigas de España; por eso, les graba un cassette.

Kukulkán is the name used in the Yucatán for Quetzalcóatl, the Feathered Serpent.

Templo de Kukulcán, Chichén Itzá, México.

Act. 22: Have students correct the false statements.

Actividad 22: Cierto o falso

Escucha la grabación de Juan Carlos y di si estas oraciones son ciertas o falsas.

1. __C__ Juan Carlos y Álvaro lo están pasando muy bien en México.
2. __C__ Álvaro tenía una carie.
3. __F__ El grupo de Álvaro tiene gente divertida.
4. __C__ El Sr. Ruiz llega tarde para el desayuno.
5. __F__ Las ruinas de Yucatán son aztecas.

Hola, chicas. ¿Cómo están? Por aquí todo bien. Con todas las responsabilidades de la excursión, no he tenido tiempo para escribirles y es más fácil y rápido mandarles un cassette. Estamos bien y muy contentos conociendo lugares interesantísimos, aunque Álvaro estuvo mal de la muela que ya le molestaba en España y, claro, . . . por fin tuvo que ir al dentista y . . . y le pusieron un empaste enorme. Pues, yo le digo que es un cobarde, pero es que el pobre les tiene fobia a los dentistas. Je, je . . .

Expressing extreme interest

Displaying false sympathy

377

Confiding

es un secreto y no se lo digan a Álvaro, pero . . . yo les tengo fobia a los ascensores.[1]

Bueno, aquí lo estamos pasando muy bien. O sea, por un lado, es una responsabilidad, pero por otro . . . pues nos encanta el trabajo de líderes y aprendemos mucho en cada lugar. Dividimos a la gente en dos grupos: el de Álvaro tiene personas un poco sosas, pero el mío es muy divertido. Este . . . en mi grupo hay un señor, el Sr. Ruiz, que es excéntrico y, a veces, algo desconsiderado. Siempre llega tarde para tomar el desayuno y lo tenemos que esperar para ir a las excursiones. ¡Un día de éstos lo vamos a dejar en el hotel!

México me fascina. En algunos aspectos es como Perú, y se ve bastante la cultura india, pero en otros es totalmente distinto y la influencia de los Estados Unidos es fuerte. México, la ciudad, es increíblemente grande con gente y tráfico por todas partes. Este . . . el grupo se ha divertido aprendiendo mexicanismos como **jale** en vez de "tire" y **camión** en vez de "autobús".

Ya hace dos días que estamos en Yucatán. Las ruinas mayas y toltecas son diferentes de las de Perú, pero . . . claro . . . también fascinantes. Ayer estuvimos en, ¿cómo se llama? eh . . . eh . . . este . . . ¡ah! Chichén Itzá; es un lugar misterioso donde se practicaban ritos de sacrificios humanos. Lo que más me gustó fue el Caracol, una torre redonda y . . . y también me fascinó el Castillo, el templo principal del dios Kukulkán. Saben que . . .

¡Ah! Me está llamando Álvaro. ¡Un momento, ya voy! . . . Pues, tengo que irme corriendo con el grupo. Álvaro les manda besos y yo también. Oye, Claudia, ¡te echo de menos! Sigo esto luego, tal vez esta noche, si no llegamos muy tarde . . . Un beso y chau.

Discuss different lexical items: **durazno/melocotón, aparcar/ estacionar,** etc.

Have students identify what Juan Carlos says instead of *um . . .* or *you know.* Some examples: **y ... y, pues, pero ... , o sea, este, eh ... eh.**

---

1. elevators

Actividad 23: ¿Comprendiste?

Después de escuchar el cassette de Juan Carlos, contesta estas preguntas.

1. Sabemos que Álvaro les tiene fobia a los dentistas. ¿A qué le tiene fobia Juan Carlos? ¿Tienes tú alguna fobia?
2. ¿Por qué dice Juan Carlos que el Sr. Ruiz es desconsiderado?
3. ¿Qué piensa hacerle Juan Carlos al Sr. Ruiz?
4. ¿Dónde están ahora los turistas? ¿Qué visitaron?
5. ¿Por qué crees que Juan Carlos dice que las ruinas mayas son diferentes de las ruinas de Perú?
6. ¿Has viajado alguna vez en tour? ¿Adónde fuiste? ¿Había alguien como el Sr. Ruiz en el grupo?

Actividad 24: Los pros y los contras

Di cuáles son los pros y los contras de las siguientes acciones.

 Por un lado es bueno leer el periódico porque sabes qué pasa en el mundo, pero **por otro (lado)** las noticias son muy tristes.

1. tomar café	5. ir a la universidad
2. correr	6. viajar en un tour
3. mirar televisión	7. trabajar como guía
4. trabajar con una computadora	8. visitar lugares históricos

Hacia la comunicación

I. Avoiding Repetition: Nominalization

Before studying the grammar explanation, answer the following question based on Juan Carlos' recording:

● In the second paragraph of the tape, when Juan Carlos says " . . . **el de Álvaro . . . pero el mío . . .**" is he referring to **las responsabilidades, los grupos,** or **el trabajo**?

Nominalization consists of avoiding the repetition of a noun by using only its corresponding article and the words that modify the noun.

Nos gustan las faldas azules y **las faldas negras** también.	→ Nos gustan las faldas azules y **las negras** también.
Pon unas mesas aquí y **unas mesas** allí.	→ Pon unas mesas aquí y **unas** allí.
La casa que quería comprar y **la casa que compré** son muy diferentes.	→ La casa que quería comprar y **la que compré** son muy diferentes.
Tu sobrino y **los sobrinos de ella** llegaron ayer.	→ Tu sobrino y **los de ella** llegaron ayer.

Note: The indefinite article **un** becomes **uno** when the noun is eliminated.

Tengo un carro negro y **un carro blanco.**	→ Tengo un carro negro y **uno blanco.**

II. Expressing Possession: Long Forms of Possessive Adjectives and Pronouns

1. Possessive adjectives have corresponding long forms that are used for emphasis. The long forms agree in gender and in number with the noun being modified and they *always* follow the noun.

(un amigo) **mío/a/os/as**   (un pariente) **nuestro/a/os/as**
tuyo/a/os/as   **vuestro/a/os/as**
suyo/a/os/as   **suyo/a/os/as**

Un amigo **mío** vino a verme.   *A friend of mine came to see me.*

Esa habitación **tuya** siempre está sucia.*   *That room of yours is always dirty.*

*Note: Except for **ese amigo mío**, if the long forms of possessive adjectives are used with a demonstrative adjective, the connotation is usually pejorative.

2. The possessive pronouns, which have the same forms as the possessive adjectives, are an example of nominalization.

Adjective		Pronoun
Mi grupo es divertido pero	→	**el tuyo** es aburrido.
Ella tiene su casa y	→	nosotros tenemos **la nuestra**.
¿Es su maleta?		No, es **mía.***

*Note: After **ser,** the definite article may be omitted: **Esta es tu maleta, pero ésa es (la) mía.**

Actividad 25: ¿Qué prefieres?

En parejas, pregúntenle a su compañero/a qué cosas prefiere de la siguiente lista.

A: ¿Te gusta más/Prefieres la sopa de verduras o la de pescado?
B: Me gusta más/Prefiero la de verduras.

1. la clase de geografía/la clase de cálculo
2. los carros grandes/los carros pequeños
3. las ruinas de Machu Picchu/las ruinas de Chichén Itzá
4. el equipo de los Yanquis/el equipo de los Mets
5. un restaurante vegetariano/un restaurante chino
6. un reloj de oro/un reloj de plata
7. un tour organizado/un tour independiente
8. (etc.)

Act. 26: Make sure students maintain eye contact when saying their lines. Have students repeat the activity with different characterizations: the clerk is hard of hearing, so the customer must speak up; the customer is embarrassed to make the purchase and whispers; the customer is 90 years old, etc.

Actividad 26: En la tienda

En parejas, el/la estudiante "A" es un/a dependiente/a en una tienda de ropa y cubre la Columna B; el/la estudiante "B" es un/a cliente y cubre la Columna A. Conversen en la tienda.

A

B

¿Desea ver una camisa?   ¿Quiere ver un vestido?

Sí. Una azul, por favor.   Sí, el azul, por favor.

¿Le gusta? Tengo el mismo en blanco.   ¿Le gusta? Tengo una igual en blanco.

Déjeme ver la blanca.   Quiero ver el blanco.

¿Le gusta más el blanco o el azul?   ¿Prefiere más la blanca o la azul?

Voy a llevar las dos.   Prefiero el azul.

Actividad 27: Hijos perdidos

En grupos de tres, los estudiantes "A" y "B" son dos amigos que perdieron a sus hijos en el aeropuerto y van a hablar con el/la estudiante "C", un/a policía. Sigan las instrucciones para su papel.

A Tienes una hija de cuatro años. Mira el dibujo para describirla.

B Tienes un hijo de cinco años. Mira el dibujo para describirlo.

C Eres policía y necesitas la siguiente información: edad, color de pelo y ojos, ropa, cosas que tienen, etc. Usa oraciones como **¿Cuántos años tiene su hijo? ¿y la suya?**

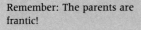

Remember: The parents are frantic!

Actividad 28: La confusión

En grupos de seis, imagínense que están desayunando en un restaurante; uno de Uds. es un/a camarero/a nuevo/a y está un poco confuso/a. Sigan las instrucciones para su papel.

Clientes:

Escojan entre los siguientes platos para contestar las preguntas del/de la camarero/a (dos personas pidieron la misma cosa):

huevos revueltos, tostadas y jugo de naranja
croissant con mermelada y café con leche
churros y chocolate
huevos fritos, tocino y café

Contesten las preguntas del/de la camarero/a con frases como **es mío, es de él,** etc.

Camarero/a:

The waiter should use **Ud.** with customers.

Mira los platos que aparecen en la lista de los clientes y pregúntales cosas como **¿Para quién son los churros? ¿Son suyos?**

Actividad 29: El orgullo

Act. 29: Instruct students to be inventive and to try to impress their partners by bragging. Encourage physical description of the family members.

En parejas, imagínense que Uds. son dos mujeres de negocios que están en un avión y se ponen a hablar sobre sus familias. Para hablar de las "fotos" que están abajo, usen oraciones como las siguientes: —**Mi esposo es abogado.** —**El mío es ingeniero.**

Actividad 30: Una carta

Mientras estás en el avión vas a escribir una carta a un amigo. Basándote en la conversación que tuviste, escríbele algo sobre esa persona tan interesante que acabas de conocer y sobre su familia.

¡En un avión! _____ de _____

Querido _____ :

¿Qué tal todo en _____ ? Espero que tu familia esté bien. Ahora mismo estoy en un avión y voy a aprovechar el tiempo para escribirte unas líneas. Es un vuelo muy largo, pero acabo de conocer a una persona muy interesante que . . .

Vocabulario funcional

En el consultorio del dentista

Ver página 365

En la casa de cambio

Ver página 366

El desayuno

Ver página 375

Palabras y expresiones útiles

¡Basta (de . . .)! (That's) enough (. . .) !
la cita appointment; date
dulce sweet
una enciclopedia ambulante a walking encyclopedia
¡Ni loco/a! Not on your life!

pasarlo bien/mal to have a good/bad time
por un lado/por otro (lado) on the one hand/on the other (hand)
tenerle fobia a . . . to have a fear of . . . , to hate
¡Ya voy! I'm coming!

En los capítulos 4, 14 y 15 hay fotos de ruinas incas, aztecas y mayas. ¿Puedes compararlas?

Templo del Gran Jaguar, Tikal, selva de El Petén, Guatemala.

Capítulo 15

Chapter Objectives

After studying this chapter, you will know how to:

- express indefinite future actions
- make suggestions and extend invitations
- request clarification and information

- express a past action that preceded another past action
- discuss animals, the environment, and ecology
- describe personality traits

Pasándolo muy bien en Guatemala

To practice **al** + *infinitive*, give students result clauses and have them form complete sentences. T: **Encontré a mi profesor de historia.** S1: **Al entrar en el supermercado encontré a mi profesor de historia.** Other result clauses: **me caí, empezó a llorar, me reí, gritamos,** etc.

al + infinitive	upon + *-ing*
Me cae (la mar de) bien.	I like him/her a lot.
Me cae mal.	I don't like him/her.

El grupo de turistas está en Guatemala y hoy se dividieron en dos grupos para hacer diferentes excursiones. Juan Carlos fue con un grupo y Álvaro con el otro. Acaban de regresar al hotel.

Una de las muchas iglesias en Antigua, Guatemala. ¿Has visto alguna vez una iglesia de este estilo arquitectónico?

Actividad 1: ¿Qué dices?

Escucha la conversación y contesta estas preguntas.

1. ¿Adónde fue el grupo de Álvaro?
2. ¿Adónde fue el grupo de Juan Carlos?
3. En tu opinión, ¿quiénes se divirtieron más y por qué?

Discuss the geographic variety of Hispanic America as well as the ecological problems.

Dra. Llanos	¡Qué cansada estoy!
Álvaro	Yo también, pero valió la pena hacer el viaje a Tikal.
Juan Carlos	O sea, que les gustó, ¿eh?
Dra. Llanos	Fue interesantísimo; imagínate, ruinas mayas en medio de una selva tropical tan verde y con tal variedad de pájaros cantando por todos lados. Fue maravilloso.
Álvaro	Después de ver tanta belleza no entiendo por qué destruyen la selva.
Dra. Llanos	Sí, es triste. Parece que el hombre no va a estar sa-tisfecho hasta que lo destruya todo. Es una pena que seamos así.
Álvaro	. . . ¿Y vosotros en Antigua y Chichicastenango?
Juan Carlos	Fue fantástico. Antigua es una ciudad colonial bella, con muchas iglesias y muy tranquila.
Dra. Llanos	¿Y Chichicastenango?
Juan Carlos	El pueblo nos encantó porque es muy pintoresco y el mercado tiene unas artesanías fabulosas. El grupo compró de todo; creo que ya no queda nada en el mercado.
Dra. Llanos	¿Y qué hizo el Sr. Ruiz esta vez?
Juan Carlos	Cada día está más gracioso. Al llegar al mercado, se puso a regatear con un indio por un vestido que quería comprar para su hija.
Álvaro	¿Y qué pasó?
Juan Carlos	No lo van a creer. Le pidió ayuda a una mujer que, según él, tenía la misma talla que su hija y siguió regateando quince minutos más. ¡Hasta la mujer, con el vestido puesto, empezó a ayudarle a regatear!
Dra. Llanos	¡Qué vergüenza!
Juan Carlos	Nada de vergüenza. Fue divertidísimo. Al final el vendedor le dio un descuento y también le regaló un cinturón. Se hicieron amigos.

Speculating about future actions

Discuss colonial architecture in cities like Antigua, Quito, Popayán, Arequipa, Cuzco, etc.

Requesting information

Discuss the variety of indigenous populations in Hispanic America and the implications of this with regard to government policy.

Showing disgust

Introduce the phrase **el payaso del grupo**. Ask students if they think Sr. Ruiz or Dra. Llanos is playing the clown.

Suggesting

Stating future intentions

Explain "**no lo quiero volver a ver ni pintado en la pared.**"

Act. 2: 1. b   2. b   3. b   4. a

Pronunciation: Rhythm and intonation
1. Write the following exchange between Juan Carlos and Dr. Llanos on the board. Have students repeat each line at normal speed, while maintaining the rhythm and correct intonation.
Dra.: **¡Qué vergüenza!** JC: **Nada de vergüenza. Fue divertidísimo.** Dra.: **¡Ay! Ese pesado me cae tan mal . . .** Á: **Pues a mí me cae la mar de bien.**
2. Divide students into 2 groups, each takes a role and reads in chorus. Make sure students keep to the rhythm.

Dra. Llanos	¡Ay! Ese pesado me cae tan mal . . .
Álvaro	Pues a mí me cae la mar de bien. Cuando llegue a España, quiero conocer a su familia. Deben ser todos tan graciosos como él. Seamos justos, es un hombre inofensivo.
Dra. Llanos	Por mi parte, cuando yo vuelva a España no lo quiero volver a ver ni pintado en la pared.

Actividad 2: ¿Comprendiste?

Después de escuchar la conversación, escoge la respuesta correcta.

1. Según Álvaro la selva tropical está . . . .
   a. intacta   b. destruida   c. llena de animales
2. La ciudad de Antigua . . . .
   a. tiene ruinas mayas   c. está en la selva
   b. es de la época colonial
3. La Dra. Llanos usa la palabra "pesado" para referirse al Sr. Ruiz. Ella quiere decir que el Sr. Ruiz . . . .
   a. es gordo   b. molesta mucho   c. es divertido
4. El vendedor le regaló un cinturón al Sr. Ruiz porque él . . . .
   a. le cayó bien   b. compró mucho   c. a y b

¿Lo sabían?
Guatemala, México, Ecuador, Perú y Bolivia son los países de Hispano-américa que tienen la población indígena más numerosa y donde todavía se ven más aspectos de la cultura y las tradiciones indias. Alrededor de la mi-tad de los guatemaltecos son indios que conservan las costumbres y las lenguas de sus antepasados *(ancestors)*. En Guatemala se hablan todavía más de veinte lenguas indígenas y hoy en día, el gobierno está estableciendo programas educativos en las escuelas para enseñarles a los indios en sus propias lenguas.

Act. 3: Ask students to justify their choices.

Actividad 3: ¿Cómo te cae?

Haz una lista de cinco actores y actrices que te caen bien y cinco que te caen mal. Al terminar, en parejas, pregúntenle a su compañero/a qué piensa de los actores de su lista.

¡●¡ **A:** ¿Te cae bien Roseanne Barr?
      B: Me cae (muy/la mar de) bien/(muy) mal porque es . . .

Lo esencial

I. Los animales

1. el elefante
2. el león
3. el mono
4. el oso

5. el pájaro
6. el pez
7. la serpiente

1. el caballo
2. la gallina
3. el gato

4. el perro
5. el toro
6. la vaca

I. Discuss the feminine forms of these animals.

Act. 4: Have students justify some of their choices. You could debate which animal is the prettiest, fastest, etc.

The word *pet* has a Spanish equivalent in a few countries only. For example, in Mexico and Puerto Rico, **la mascota** is used.

Actividad 4: Características

En parejas, clasifiquen los animales de los dibujos anteriores según los siguientes adjetivos.

◖●◗ grande → El animal más grande es el elefante.

1. feo
2. gracioso
3. rápido
4. tímido
5. valiente *(brave)*

6. simpático
7. tonto
8. bonito
9. inteligente
10. cobarde *(cowardly)*

Trabajando en Cuzco, Perú.

¿Lo sabían?

La llama, la vicuña, la alpaca y el guanaco son animales de la familia del camello que viven en los altiplanos de los Andes. Tanto el guanaco como la vicuña son salvajes y están en peligro de extinción, pues los indios andinos los cazan para usar su piel *(hide)* y su lana, que es muy fina y muy cara. La llama y la alpaca han sido domesticadas por los indios, y se emplean como animales de carga en las zonas muy elevadas de los Andes. Pueden llevar cargas hasta de cuarenta y cinco kilos (100 libras). De la llama y la alpaca se usan también su leche y su carne, además de su lana y su piel.

Actividad 5: ¿Iguales o diferentes?

En parejas, el/la estudiante "A" cubre la Columna B y el/la estudiante "B" cubre la Columna A. "A" describe los números impares *(odd)* de su lista y "B" describe los pares *(even)* de la suya. Al escuchar cada descripción de tu compañero/a, decide si el animal es igual al animal del mismo número en tu columna. Para dar estas descripciones necesitan saber que un pájaro tiene dos **alas**, que come con el **pico** y que los animales tienen **patas**, no piernas.

A		B	
1. caballo	5. pájaro	1. vaca	5. gallina
2. perro	6. oso	2. gato	6. mono
3. león	7. toro	3. león	7. toro
4. pez		4. serpiente	

Act. 6: Brainstorm domestic animals before doing this activity.

Ask students if their opinions would change if they lived in an apartment rather than a house.

Actividad 6: ¿Te gustan los animales?

En grupos de tres, pregúntenles a sus compañeros si tienen o tuvieron un animal doméstico alguna vez. Luego comenten los pros y los contras de tener un animal en una casa y compartan sus ideas con el resto de la clase.

II. El medio ambiente

1. la basura
2. la contaminación
3. la fábrica
4. la lluvia ácida

5. la conservación; conservar
6. la energía solar
7. el reciclaje; reciclar

II. Ask students which city they would like to live in and why. Ask which picture is most like their city and why.

Otras palabras relacionadas con el medio ambiente

la destrucción; destruir
la ecología

la energía nuclear
la extinción

Actividad 7: Salvar el planeta

En grupos de tres, miren estos artículos y anuncios. Hablen sobre el mensaje de cada uno.

Señor Turista:
Bariloche le ofrece
sus bellezas.
Colabore conservándolas.

Use y disfrute los bosques, playas y lagos.
Manténgalos limpios.

Las flores son para mirarlas.
¡No las corte!

De la arena nace el vidrio
del vidrio la botella...
Pero la botella no se
convierte en arena.
¡No insista!

VECINO DE SAN MARTIN

NO PODE LOS ARBOLES

La contaminación provoca muertes prematuras

Unos 18.000 suecos mueren anualmente de forma prematura a causa de diversas enfermedades provocadas por la contaminación del medio ambiente. Así se afirma en el libro recientemente publicado por el biofísico norteamericano Arthur Tamplin «Asesinato con permiso estatal». Según este libro, la cifra mayor de mortalidad se registra entre las edades de cuarenta y cinco y sesenta y nueve años.

Actividad 8: La conservación, ¿sí o no?

Act. 8: When finished, compile the data and decide if the class conserves or wastes natural resources. Ask for suggestions on how people can improve their habits.

Hazles una encuesta sobre ecología a algunos de tus compañeros y después comenta los resultados con la clase.

1. ¿Estás a favor o en contra de estas fuentes de energía?

    nuclear   a favor _____   en contra _____

    solar   a favor _____   en contra _____

    carbón   a favor _____   en contra _____

2. Las armas nucleares son . . . para un país.

esenciales _____   importantes _____
peligrosas _____   inútiles _____

3. ¿Haces algún esfuerzo por reciclar materiales?

latas de aluminio   sí _____   no _____
periódicos   sí _____   no _____
papel   sí _____   no _____
botellas   sí _____   no _____

4. En cuanto a la contaminación, el control del gobierno sobre las fábricas es . . . .

excesivo _____   adecuado _____
no sé _____   insuficiente _____

5. ¿Le has escrito una carta a algún político sobre la contaminación?

sí _____   no _____

6. La extinción de especies de animales . . . .

afecta mucho al hombre _____
afecta poco al hombre _____

7. ¿Haces algo por reducir la cantidad de contaminación?

no usar plástico _____
tener un coche económico _____
no usar fluorocarburos (productos aerosoles) _____
no quemar al aire libre _____
otras cosas _____

Act. 9: Discuss the phrase "throwaway society."

Actividad 9: La basura

Hay gente que dice que se conoce un país por su basura. En grupos de cuatro, hablen sobre los siguientes temas:

1. ¿Cuál es la multa (*fine*) por tirar basura en las calles o en las carreteras de su estado?
2. Alaska y otros estados han sufrido grandes derrames (*spills*) de petróleo que han afectado la ecología del área. ¿Qué sugerencias pueden dar Uds. para evitar estos desastres? ¿Quién debe tener la responsabilidad de limpiar los derrames que ocurran?
3. Una compañía en Beverly Hills, California, empaca (*packs*) y vende la basura de muchos de sus vecinos famosos. ¿Qué piensan Uds. de esto? ¿Creen que es diferente esa basura a la de otros lugares? ¿Por qué?

Hacia la comunicación

Gramática

I. Drill the subjunctive in adverbial clauses:
Ask students to finish these phrases: **Después de que termine el semestre ... Voy a estudiar hasta que ... Después de ... Cuando me paguen ... Cuando me pagaron ...** (etc.)

I. Expressing Indefinite Future Actions: The Subjunctive in Adverbial Clauses

Before studying the grammar explanation, answer this question:

- Which of the following sentences refers to an action that may occur in the future?
  a. **Cuando llegue a España quiero conocer a su familia.**
  b. **Cuando llegué a España quería conocer a su familia.**

1. Adverbial conjunctions such as **cuando, después de que,** and **hasta que** are used with the indicative to express actions that normally happen or have happened.

Todos los días **cuando llego** a casa, preparo la cena.	*When I come home every day, I prepare dinner.*
Después de que hablé contigo, me acosté.	*After I talked to you, I went to bed.*

2. **Cuando, después de que,** and **hasta que** require the subjunctive when they refer to an indefinite future action, that is, an action that has not happened yet and therefore may or may not occur.

Esta noche, **cuando llegue** a casa, voy a cenar.	*When I get home tonight, I'm going to eat dinner. (The future is not certain: I may be detained, have an accident, etc.)*
¿Qué vas a hacer mañana **después de que me llames**?	*What are you going to do tomorrow after you call me? (You may not have the chance to call me.)*
Vamos a trabajar **hasta que terminemos**.	*We'll work until we finish. (It is unknown when and whether we will finish.)*

Note: No change of subject is necessary when these adverbial conjunctions are followed by the subjunctive.

II. Suggesting and Inviting: Let's . . .

1. When you want to invite someone or suggest that someone do something with you, use a **nosotros** command, which is identical to the subjunctive form.

Ya es tarde. **Volvamos** a casa.   *It's late already. Let's go home.*
¡Hagámoslo!   *Let's do it!*
No le **digamos** nada a Isabel.   *Let's not tell Isabel anything.*

2. When the **nosotros** command is followed by **se** or by the reflexive pronoun **nos,** drop the final **-s.**

¿Vamos a prepararle la comida?   —→   Sí, **¡preparémosela!**
¿Quieres que nos levantemos?   —→   Bien, **¡levantémonos!**

However:
¿Quieres que lo **levantemos**?   —→   Sí, **¡levantémoslo!**
¿Vamos a preparar la comida?   —→   Sí, **¡preparémosla!**

III. Requesting Clarification and Information: *¿Qué?* and *¿Cuál/es?*

1. In most cases, the uses of **¿qué?** *(what?)* and **¿cuál/es?** *(which?)* are similar in Spanish and English.

¿Qué pasa?	*What's going on?/What's up?*
¿Qué tienes?	*What do you have?/What's the matter?*
¿Cuál de estos prefieres?	*Which of these do you prefer?*
¿Cuáles de tus amigas son uruguayas?	*Which of your friends are Uruguayan?*

2. Both **¿qué?** and **¿cuál?** may be followed by the verb **ser.**
Use **¿qué + ser . . .?** when asking for a *definition*, an *identification*, or a *classification*.

¿Qué es antropología?	*What is anthropology? (definition)*
¿Qué es?	*What is it? (identification)*
¿Qué eres, demócrata o republicano?	*What are you, a Democrat or a Republican? (classification)*

Use **¿cuál/es + ser . . .?** when asking for a *clarification*.

¿Cuál es el país más grande de Hispanoamérica?	*What/Which is the largest country in Hispanic America?*
¿Cuáles son tus pasatiempos favoritos?	*What/Which are your favorite pastimes?*

Note: **Cuál** + noun is often used by native speakers, especially in the Caribbean.

Do mechanical drills, Workbook, Part I.

3. Use **qué** when a noun follows: **¿qué +** noun . . .?

¿Qué idiomas hablas?	*What/Which languages do you speak?*
¿En qué país nacieron tus padres?	*In what/which country were your parents born?*

Actividad 10: Tus planes futuros

Termina estas frases y después, pregúntales a algunos compañeros cuáles son sus planes para el futuro.

1. Después de que termine los estudios universitarios . . .
2. Voy a trabajar hasta que . . .
3. Cuando tenga cincuenta y cinco años . . .

Actividad 11: Los padres de Juan Carlos

Juan Carlos le describe su familia al Sr. Ruiz. Completa el párrafo que sigue con la forma y tiempo correctos de los verbos entre paréntesis.

Remember: After a preposition, use the infinitive.

Mis papás se casaron cuando ___tenían___ (tener) veinticinco años. Yo nací cuando mi mamá ___tenía___ (tener) veintinueve años. Después de ___tener___ (tener) a mis cuatro hermanos menores, mi mamá ___dejó___ (dejar) de trabajar. Mi papá es abogado y trabajó quince años con la misma compañía hasta que ___cambió___ (cambiar) de trabajo y empezó a trabajar para el gobierno. Dice que cuando ___cumpla___ (cumplir) sesenta y dos años va a dejar de trabajar, pero hasta que yo no lo ___vea___ (ver) no voy a creerlo porque es un hombre que vive para el trabajo. Dice que después de que ___deje___ (dejar) de trabajar, va a hacer cruceros por el Caribe en los inviernos.

Act. 11: If students are confused by the phrase **hasta que yo no lo vea,** explain that in English, the **no** is not translated.

Actividad 12: ¿Y tu familia?

En parejas, después de leer la descripción de la familia de Juan Carlos, hablen con su compañero/a sobre su familia y sus planes para el futuro.

Actividad 13: ¡Sorpresa!

En grupos de tres, Uds. van a planear una fiesta de sorpresa *(surprise)* para un/a amigo/a que se va a casar. Den sugerencias.

◖●◗ Invitemos a todo el mundo.
Alquilemos un salón en un restaurante.

Actividad 14: Un día de viaje

En grupos de tres, lean el folleto sobre Caracas y decidan qué van a hacer en un solo día allí. Tienen que aprovechar *(take advantage of)* el tiempo que tienen.

⦿ Veamos . . .
    Visitemos . . .

MUSEOS Y GALERIAS DE ARTE
Museums and Art Galeries

- CASA AMARILLA
  Torre Banco Nacional de Descuento, Carmelitas.
  Telf.: 81.85.21, Ext. 29
- CASA NATAL DEL LIBERTADOR
  San Jacinto a Traposos.
  Telf.: 545.76.93
  Martes a Domingo: de 9 a 12 m. y de 2:30 a 5:30 pm.

RESTAURANTES
Restaurants

- LA CHURRASQUERIA
  Av. Río de Janeiro, Las Mercedes.
  Telf.: 752.65.21
- MAUTE GRILL
  Av. Río de Janeiro, Las Mercedes
  Telf.: 91.08.92
- TARZILANDIA
  Av. San Juan Bosco, Altamira Norte.
  Telf.: 261.84.19

ARTESANIAS
Handicrafts

- ARTE MURANO C.A. - ICET
  Urbanización Potrerito, vía La Mariposa.
  Telf.: (032) 71.02.94
- ARTE VENEZOLANO CRISTALART
  Carretera Panamericana.

IGLESIAS   CENTRO HISTORICO
Churchs   Historic Places

- BASILICA DE SANTA TERESA
  Esq. de Santa Teresa, fte. al Centro Simón Bolívar.
- DIVINA PASTORA
  Esq. Urapal, La Pastora.
  7:00 am. a 9:00 am y 4:00 pm. a 6:00 pm. Lunes a Viernes. Domingo: 6:30 am. a 12 m. y 3:30 a 7:00 pm.

Actividad 15: La entrevista estudiantil

Qué + ser = definition, identification, classification. **Cuál + ser** = clarification.

De carrera = undergraduate; **de posgrado** = graduate student.

Act. 15: Check answers before doing the pair part of the activity.

Completa las siguientes preguntas usando **qué** o **cuál/es.** Luego entrevista a tres compañeros de la clase que no conozcas bien sobre sus estudios académicos, usando las preguntas que completaste. Háblale sobre las respuestas al resto de la clase.

1. ¿___Qué___ eres, estudiante de carrera o de posgrado?
2. ¿___Qué___ clases estás estudiando?
3. ¿___Cuál___ es tu clase favorita?
4. ¿___Cuáles___ son las clases más difíciles?
5. ¿___Qué___ problemas tuviste al llegar a la universidad?
6. ¿___Qué___ piensas hacer cuando termine el semestre?
7. ¿___Cuáles___ son tus planes para el futuro?

Actividad 16: Cultura general

En parejas, preparen un examen de quince preguntas sobre cultura general para luego averiguar el nivel de cultura de la clase. Después de preparar el examen, dénselo a algunos compañeros para que lo hagan.

|●| ¿Cuál es la capital de Honduras?
   ¿Qué idiomas se hablan en Guatemala?

Nuevos horizontes

Estrategia de lectura: *Mind mapping*

Mind mapping is a way of brainstorming before you read a text, in order to activate your background knowledge and predict the contents of a reading selection. To apply this technique, you start with a key concept and jot down related ideas in different directions radiating from this key concept. This technique lets your mind run freely to tap whatever is stored in it. In the following example you can see how the mind mapping technique was applied to the word **hogar** *(home)*.

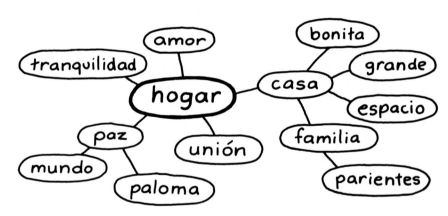

Actividad 17: El mapa mental

En parejas, hagan un mapa mental con la palabra **ecología** y luego compártanlo con el resto de la clase. Después piensen en los temas relacionados con este concepto que puedan aparecer en el siguiente texto sobre la ecología en Hispanoamérica. Finalmente, lean el texto para confirmar sus predicciones.

(Izquierda) Esta gasolinera argentina ofrece alconafta, combustible hecho de caña de azúcar. (Derecha) Cascada en la selva de Costa Rica, país que se preocupa por la ecología.

Carta abierta a los hermanos hispanoamericanos

Como ciudadano de Hispanoamérica considero que tengo la obligación de pedirles a los gobernantes que hagan algo para salvar nuestra tierra antes de que sea demasiado tarde. Para modernizarnos e intentar convertirnos en países desarrollados necesitamos la tecnología, pero esta tecnología que trae avances constantes muchas veces destruye nuestros recursos naturales.

Tomemos Guatemala, por ejemplo. ¿Por cuánto tiempo vamos a continuar destruyendo la selva tropical? Decimos que necesitamos esa área para criar animales y tener comida. ¿Pero a qué precio? Matamos las especies que ya habitan esa zona y así provocamos la extinción de animales y de plantas. Uds. dirán que nosotros, los guatemaltecos, no somos los únicos que destruimos el ambiente y hay que reconocer que es verdad. Sin embargo, Costa Rica, que también tiene este problema, lo admite y está intentando salvar su selva con la ayuda de científicos estadounidenses.

Usemos los recursos naturales, pero con moderación. ¿Qué va a ocurrir, por ejemplo, el día que se termine el petróleo mundial? El petróleo es un recurso, sí, pero como todo recurso tiene un límite. Si países latinoamericanos como Brasil y Argentina pueden obtener combustible para carros de la caña de azúcar, Guatemala, Honduras, Cuba y la República Dominicana pueden hacer lo mismo con su exceso de caña de azúcar y así reducir notablemente el consumo de petróleo. La fuente de energía que puede reemplazar de forma parcial el petróleo es la energía hidroeléctrica y su posibilidad de desarrollo en Hispanoamérica es gigantesca. Países ejemplares como Perú y Costa Rica lograron duplicar su producción entre 1980 y 1985.

Debemos también tener cuidado con el uso de productos químicos que pueden destruir nuestro medio ambiente. Si seguimos abusando del uso de fluorocarburos (aire acondicionados, neveras, etc.) y se expande el agujero de ozono sobre la Antártida, entonces Chile y Argentina van a ser los primeros en sufrir un aumento de radiación ultravioleta. ¿Qué significa esto? Miles de casos de enfermedades como cáncer de la piel y cataratas de los ojos. Debemos eliminar este peligro antes de que sea demasiado tarde.

¿Es éste el mundo que les queremos dejar a nuestros hijos? Por favor, tomemos conciencia.

Un ser humano preocupado

Costa Rica offers tax incentives for planting trees and for other actions that help preserve the environment.

Discuss environmental issues in the U.S., such as acid rain. Discuss how international cooperation is needed.

Actividad 18: Tus preguntas

Prepara un mínimo de cuatro preguntas sobre las ideas principales que menciona el texto. Luego haz estas preguntas a la clase.

Estrategia de escritura: *Mind mapping*

The mind mapping technique described under the **Estrategia de lectura** section can also be used as a prewriting strategy. This is a useful way of generating ideas in a nonlinear, nonstructured way. Once you finish your mind map, you choose the main ideas and organize them.

Actividad 19: La contaminación

En parejas, hagan un mapa mental con la palabra **progreso.** Luego escojan las ideas más interesantes y escriban individualmente un párrafo con estas ideas.

Lo esencial

I. La personalidad

> ¿Cómo eres? ¿Te conoces bien a ti mismo?
> 1. Cuando tienes un problema, ¿lo confrontas o lo ignoras?
> 2. Cuando cometes un error, ¿lo admites?
> 3. Cuando un amigo te habla de sus problemas, ¿lo escuchas?
> 4. Si necesitas un trabajo, ¿lo buscas activamente?

Associate these adjectives with friends or relatives to help you remember them.

agresivo/a aggressive
amable nice
ambicioso/a ambitious
cobarde cowardly
honrado/a honest
ignorante ignorant

orgulloso/a proud
perezoso/a lazy
sensato/a sensible
sensible sensitive
valiente brave

Actividad 20: ¿Cómo somos?

Escoge de la lista anterior la característica que más te describa, la que menos te describa y escríbelas; después en parejas, escojan dos características que describan a su compañero/a. Luego comparen las palabras y digan por qué las seleccionaron.

Actividad 21: ¿Positivo o negativo?

En grupos de cinco, decidan qué palabras de la lista anterior representan defectos y cuáles representan cualidades. ¿Es positivo o negativo ser orgulloso o ambicioso? ¿Creen que sea igual en otras culturas?

Actividad 22: Libertad de palabra

En los Estados Unidos hay democracia y por eso, se puede hablar libremente sobre los políticos. En parejas, den su opinión sobre el presidente, la primera dama y el vicepresidente del país.

Sí, mi capitán

| dar una vuelta | to take a ride; to go for a stroll/walk |
| llevarse bien/mal (con alguien) | to get along/not to get along (with someone) |

El grupo de turistas salió desde Guatemala para hacer un crucero por el Mar Caribe.

Actividad 23: Cierto o falso

Escucha el anuncio del capitán y di si estas oraciones son ciertas o falsas.

1. __C__ Hace buen tiempo.
2. __F__ Durante la conquista se exportaba plata desde La Guaira.
3. __F__ La Guaira es una ciudad muy moderna.
4. __F__ El Sr. Ruiz va a invitar a las personas del grupo a cenar esta noche porque es su cumpleaños.

Ciudad y puerto de La Guaira, cerca de Caracas, Venezuela.

Identifying oneself

Describing weather

Informing

La Guaira is commonly referred to as **la playa de Caracas.**

It is common in Spain for the person celebrating a birthday to invite others out.

Thanking

Explain that cocoa and chocolate are made from the seeds of the **cacao,** or chocolate tree. Inform students that during the Spanish colonization of the Americas, chocolate was considered to be a delicacy by the European upper class.

Today Venezuela relies heavily on the exportation of petroleum and imports many products from abroad.

Colorado means "reddish," Nevada means "snowfall" or "covered with snow", Arizona means "arid zone," Montana means "mountain" (from **montaña**), and Texas means "tiles" (from **tejas**).

¡Atención! ¡Atención! Señores pasajeros: Les habla el capitán Leyva. Espero que estén disfrutando del crucero y del agradable clima caribeño. Avanzamos a una velocidad promedio de quince nudos (knots) y, como les había prometido ayer, hoy tenemos un día claro y despejado, de sol brillante y poco viento y una temperatura de veintiocho grados centígrados: un día ideal para hacer una parada en La Guaira, Venezuela. La Guaira era el puerto exportador de cacao más importante durante la conquista, antes de convertirse en un centro no sólo de exportación sino también de importación. Hoy día, además de ser el puerto más importante del país, es una bella ciudad del siglo XVI y un lugar de mucho turismo. Tenemos un día para ir de compras, descansar en las playas y dar una vuelta por la ciudad antes de seguir para Caracas, que queda a una hora y media por autobús.

Este . . . ¿cómo? . . . Un momento por favor . . . ¡Atención! Acaban de informarme que es el cumpleaños del Sr. Pancracio Ruiz, un miembro del grupo que se lleva muy bien con todo el mundo. Él quiere invitarnos a todos a tomar una copa esta noche en el Club Tanaguarenas de La Guaira. Le damos las gracias y le deseamos un feliz cumpleaños.

Gracias por la atención prestada y espero que pasen un día muy agradable.

Actividad 24: ¿Comprendiste?

Después de escuchar el anuncio del capitán, contesta estas preguntas.

1. ¿Adónde van a hacer escala hoy?
2. ¿Cuál es la importancia de este lugar?
3. ¿Qué va a hacer el grupo allí?
4. ¿Por qué piensas que el capitán dice que el Sr. Ruiz se lleva muy bien con todo el mundo?
5. ¿Has viajado alguna vez en crucero? ¿Adónde fuiste? ¿Con quién?

¿Lo sabían?
El origen de los nombres de algunos países hispanoamericanos es muy variado. Por ejemplo, cuando llegaron los españoles a Venezuela, vieron las casas construidas sobre pilotes (stilts) en el agua y recordaron a Venecia, en Italia. Por eso, llamaron a esa tierra Venezuela, que quiere decir "pequeña Venecia". Colón les dio su nombre a Puerto Rico y a Costa Rica porque cuando llegó a esos lugares vio que tenían una rica vegetación. Uruguay es una palabra india que quiere decir "río de los pájaros". Nicaragua lleva el nombre del jefe indio que los españoles encontraron en esa región. ¿Sabes qué significan las palabras Colorado, Nevada, Arizona, Montana y Texas?

Actividad 25: ¿Bien o mal?

En parejas, pídanle a su compañero/a los nombres de dos personas con quienes se lleva bien y dos personas con quienes se lleva mal y por qué. Pueden ser amigos, compañeros de trabajo, profesores, vecinos (neighbors), etc.

Hacia la comunicación

Gramática

Review formation of the past participle, Ch.'s 11 and 12.

I. Drill the past perfect:
1. Ask students what they had already done today before arriving in class.
2. Have students look at the Table of Contents and tell in what sequence they learned particular grammar topics:
Cuando aprendimos el imperfecto ya habíamos estudiado el pretérito.

I. Talking About the Past: The Past Perfect

Before studying the grammar explanation, answer the following question:

• In the following sentence, which of the two actions in bold happened first?
La Dra. Llanos, a quien **conocí** ayer cuando ya **había salido** el barco, es española.

The past perfect tense is used to express a past action that occurred prior to another past action. To express this tense use the following formula:

Haber (imperfect)		
había	habíamos	
habías	habíais	+ *past participle*
había	habían	

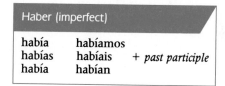

Ellos ya **habían llegado** *They had already arrived*	cuando *when*	los llamé. *I called them.*
¿**Habías estudiado** para el examen de ayer?		*Had you studied for yesterday's exam?*
El barco ya **había salido** cuando llegaste.		*The ship had already left when you arrived.*

II. Other Uses of *por*

1. **Por** is used to express rate or measurement.

Compramos los huevos **por** docena.
We buy eggs by the dozen.

La velocidad máxima es de 110 km **por** hora.
The speed limit is 110 km an hour.

2. **Por** is used with many common expressions.

por (pura) casualidad	by (pure) chance
por eso	that's why
por lo menos	at least
por si acaso	(just) in case
por suerte	luckily
por supuesto	of course

Llevemos abrigo **por si acaso** hace frío.
Let's take coats in case it's cold.

Por suerte llegué a tiempo.
Luckily I arrived in time.

Ellos tienen **por lo menos** un millón de dólares.
They have at least a million dollars.

¿**Por casualidad**, tienes tiempo para ayudarme?
Do you, by any chance, have time to help me?

III. Relating Ideas: The Relative Pronouns *que, lo que,* and *quien*

1. Relative pronouns connect or relate two clauses and refer to a person or thing in the first clause. The most common relative pronoun is **que,** which is used to refer both to persons and things.

La llama es un animal.
La llama vive en los Andes. } La llama es un animal **que** vive en los Andes.

El señor llamó.
El señor es ingeniero. } El señor **que** llamó es ingeniero.

2. To refer to a situation or occurrence in its entirety, use **lo que.**

Lo que me dijiste no es verdad.
What (the thing that) you told me isn't true.

Nos molestó **lo que** pasó esta mañana.
What happened this morning bothered us. (The speaker knows what happened.)

Do mechanical drills, Workbook, Part II.

3. The relative pronoun **quien/es** is preferred after a preposition when referring to people.

No conozco al chico con **quien** sales.

I don't know the young man you are dating.

Actividad 26: La historia

En parejas, completen las dos oraciones que siguen. Después inventen cinco oraciones más que presenten una acción que ya había ocurrido cuando ocurrió otra.

1. John F. Kennedy ya ____había muerto____ (morir) cuando Neil Armstrong ____llegó____ (llegar) a la luna.
2. La Guerra de Vietnam ya ____había terminado____ (terminar) cuando yo ____nací____ (nacer).

Actividad 27: ¿Una vida interesante?

En parejas, cuéntenle a su compañero/a tres cosas interesantes que ya habían hecho antes de empezar los estudios universitarios.

Act. 28: When checking, ask for different possibilities for each item.

Actividad 28: Por supuesto

Completa estas situaciones de forma lógica, usando una expresión con **por.**

1. Odio a mi jefe/a y . . .
2. Para vivir bien económicamente hay que tener . . .
3. Mi hermana quiere ser una buena arquitecta . . .
4. No sé si va a nevar, pero . . .
5. Mi moto es muy rápida; puede ir a . . .
6. Yo sé que tengo razón y . . .
7. ¡Qué bueno! No tenía la tarea y . . .

Actividad 29: 1492

Completa este párrafo sobre los conquistadores españoles con **que, lo que** o **quien/es.**

Quienes is also acceptable, but this use is not presented in the book.

En el primer viaje __que__ Cristóbal Colón hizo a América, llegó a una isla __que__ él llamó La Española. Colón y sus hombres, para __quienes__ fue una sorpresa encontrar una tierra fértil y bella, tomaron posesión de la isla en nombre de los Reyes de España __que__ habían pagado los gastos de la expedición. Hoy en día, en la isla hay dos países __que__ son la República Dominicana y Haití. __Lo que__ es interesante es que en Haití no se habla español sino francés, aunque la isla es el lugar donde comenzó la dominación española de América.

Act. 30: If you want to practice specific vocabulary items, you may prepare 2 lists or have students draw items from an envelope.

Actividad 30: Esa cosa

Cuando no recuerdas o no sabes la palabra exacta para algo, necesitas describirlo. En parejas, usen **que** o **lo que** para explicar las palabras que buscan. Describan palabras de estas categorías: animales, medicina, partes del carro, ropa y comida.

> **A:** Es un líquido que le echamos al carro.
> **B:** Ah, la gasolina.
>
> **A:** Es lo que usas en el carro cuando llueve.
> **B:** Ah, el limpiaparabrisas.

Actividad 31: Describiendo

En parejas, cuéntenle a su compañero/a sobre un/a nuevo/a amigo/a que tienen, completando las siguientes frases. Usen la imaginación.

Conocí a un/a chico/a que . . .
Lo que más me gusta de
  él/ella . . .
Es una persona que . . .

No sé lo que . . .
Creo que es una persona a
  quien . . .

Actividad 32: Comentando

En grupos de tres, hablen sobre la conservación del medio ambiente. Usen frases como **lo que más me preocupa es/son . . . , los países que . . . , los animales que . . .** y **lo que hay que hacer es . . .** , etc.

Actividad 33: Antes, ahora y después

Act. 33: Have students brainstorm ideas in groups of 3 before doing this activity.

En los últimos cincuenta años la tecnología ha avanzado muy rápidamente. Cuando nuestros abuelos tenían quince años no había ni calculadoras electrónicas ni personas viajando por el espacio ni teléfonos en los carros. Escribe una composición sobre la tecnología. Sigue este bosquejo.

Hay = there is/are;
había = there was/were.

  I. La tecnología que ya existía cuando tú naciste
      Usa oraciones como **Cuando nací ya habían inventado las computadoras, pero no había computadoras personales.**

 II. La tecnología actual
      Usa oraciones como **Ahora es muy común tener una computadora personal que nos ayude en el trabajo.**

III. La tecnología del siglo XXI
      Usa oraciones como **En el año 2010, cuando tenga . . . años, es posible que no exista el dinero en efectivo. Lo que vamos a tener son tarjetas de crédito de láser.**

Vocabulario funcional

Los animales

Ver página 389

El medio ambiente

Ver página 391

Expresiones con **por**

Ver página 404

La personalidad

Ver página 400

Palabras y expresiones útiles

al + infinitive   upon + -*ing*
dar una vuelta   to take a ride; to go for a stroll/walk
llevarse bien/mal (con alguien)   to get along/not to get along (with someone)

Me cae (la mar de) bien.   I like him/her a lot.
Me cae mal.   I don't like him/her.
nacer   to be born
tan   so

Vista de Caracas, Venezuela.

¿Sabes cuál es la mayor
fuente de riqueza de
Venezuela?

Capítulo 16

¿Cuál es la ocupación del señor Pérez de Arce?

GONZALO PÉREZ de ARCE
Ventas

E.V. y T. - D.N.S.T. 1109/86
Av. Córdoba 838 - 8º Piso - Of. 16
1054 - Buenos Aires, República Argentina
☎ 325-8824 / 9153
R. Llamada 311-0056 / 312-6383 Cód. 3941
Telex: 25735 PALTOU AR

Ya nos vamos . . .

Practice **boquiabierto** by giving situations. T: **Le dije que acababa de ganar la lotería y ...** S1: **Lo dejó boquiabierto.** Have students create situations.

Practice **es hora de** and **antes que nada** by giving situations: **Los invitados ya van a llegar; es hora de sacar los aperitivos. Antes que nada debes ...**

dejar boquiabierto (a alguien)	to leave (someone) dumbfounded
es hora de + infinitive	it's time + *infinitive*
antes que nada	before anything else

Es el último día del tour y Juan Carlos y Álvaro están en la playa de La Guaira aprovechando los últimos momentos de descanso antes de regresar esta noche a España con el grupo de turistas.

Actividad 1: Temas principales

Escucha la conversación e indica cuatro temas que se mencionan.

Speaking hypothetically

Discussing the future

Generalizing

Before listening to the dialogue, have students describe the trip in detail, including the itinerary, places the group visited, and different events that occurred. This will also provide a good review of narrating and describing in the past.

Discuss how the economy of Venezuela is dependent on the exportation of oil. Point out the word **petrodólares.**

Expressing amazement

Juan Carlos	Y se acaban las vacaciones . . . ¿Tú tienes ganas de regresar a España? Por mi parte, yo preferiría quedarme aquí, disfrutando unos días más de la playa y el sol del Caribe.
Álvaro	Yo tampoco tengo ganas de volver a la rutina diaria y, además, me ha encantado conocer estos países. Tendré que volver pronto para conocer otros.
Juan Carlos	Ya sabía yo que te gustaría. Pero, dime, ¿qué fue lo que más te gustó?
Álvaro	No sé . . . Sería difícil decidir. Lo más fascinante y lo nuevo para mí fueron las ruinas indígenas de México y Guatemala. México me pareció increíble por su variedad en todo: comida, gente . . . y los colores . . . colores por todas partes. Pero me encantó todo. Por ejemplo, ayer en Caracas lo que más . . .
Juan Carlos	¿Sabes lo que me sorprendió a mí? Yo nunca me había dado cuenta de que en Venezuela la industria nacional es algo relativamente nuevo y que . . .
Álvaro	Pero, hombre, es lógico, porque con los petrodólares antes podían importarlo todo; en cambio, ahora que el precio del petróleo ha bajado tienen que diversificar su economía; pero, como te iba a decir, lo que me dejó boquiabierto fue ver lo cosmopolita que es Caracas. ¡Qué de restaurantes y vida nocturna! Y . . . toda esta experiencia gracias a don Alejandro.

En el Lago Maracaibo de Venezuela hay muchos pozos de petróleo.

Juan Carlos	Trabajar con el grupo ha sido una experiencia magnífica, aunque hay que ser muy diplomático.
Álvaro	¡Ya lo creo! Especialmente con la Dra. Llanos y el Sr. Ruiz . . . , pero, es hora de volver. Cuando llegue a España, antes que nada tengo que ir al oculista . . .
Juan Carlos	De verdad, ¡qué mala suerte tienes! Primero te molesta la muela y ahora se te pierde el lente de contacto . . . Sí, será mejor que lleguemos pronto porque quién sabe qué más te pasará. ¡Ay, Dios mío! Mira qué hora es y yo le prometí al Sr. Ruiz que iría . . .
Álvaro	Y hablando del rey de Roma . . . Ahí viene el Sr. Ruiz.
Juan Carlos	¡Por Dios! Mira el traje de baño que lleva y como siempre, sacándoles fotos a las chicas.
Álvaro	¡Qué barbaridad! ¡Ese traje tiene más colores que todo México!

Reporting

Actividad 2: ¿Comprendiste?

Después de escuchar la conversación, contesta estas preguntas.

1. ¿Quieren volver a España Juan Carlos y Álvaro?
2. ¿Qué es lo que más le gusta a Álvaro?
3. ¿Por qué ha tenido que diversificar su industria Venezuela?
4. ¿Qué tiene que hacer Álvaro en cuanto llegue a España?
5. ¿Crees que les gustó a los muchachos viajar con el grupo? ¿Te gustaría viajar a Hispanoamérica con un grupo de turistas?

Act. 2: Have students list the advantages and disadvantages of an organized tour.

411

¿Lo sabían?

A lo largo de este texto se han visto muchos dichos y refranes *(proverbs)* porque los dichos son parte de la cultura. Cuando Álvaro y Juan Carlos están hablando del Sr. Ruiz, Álvaro lo ve venir y usa el dicho **"Hablando del rey de Roma (pronto asoma** *[he soon shows up])*". Usa la imaginación y trata de explicar los siguientes dichos.

1. En boca cerrada no entran moscas.
2. Dime con quién andas y te diré quién eres.
3. Ojos que no ven, corazón que no siente.
4. Del odio al amor hay sólo un paso.
5. Quien mucho duerme poco aprende.

Actividad 3: Predicciones

Di quiénes van a hacer estas acciones cuando el grupo de turistas regrese a España.

1. Irá al oculista.
2. Llamará a Claudia.
3. Saldrá con Juan Carlos.
4. Hablarán con don Alejandro.
5. Le dará un vestido a su hija.
6. No volverá a ver al Sr. Ruiz.

Actividad 4: Lo mejor

En grupos de cuatro, decidan qué fue lo mejor y lo peor de todo el viaje para los muchachos y para los turistas. Usen frases como **lo más divertido fue . . . ; ahora, lo triste es . . . ; lo peor era que . . . ;** etc.

UNICENTRO de la Visión

tiene la recomendación cariñosa: regale ANTEOJOS.
Los tenemos de todas las marcas y de todos los precios
para DAMAS o CABALLEROS.
¡Venga antes de que sea tarde!
vea nuestra colección de anteojos de sol y monturas.

Lo esencial

En la óptica

In some Hispanic countries it is common for optical stores to sell cameras and develop film.

If possible, bring in items to use in the presentation of vocabulary.

Mention alternate vocabulary words: **las gafas/los anteojos = los lentes, los espejuelos; los lentes de contacto = las lentillas.**

1. el álbum (de fotos)
2. la cámara/máquina de fotos
3. la cámara de vídeo
4. el flash
5. las gafas/los anteojos
6. el rollo/carrete
7. el/la oculista

Otras palabras relacionadas

blanco y negro; color   black and white; color
la diapositiva   slide
enfocar   to focus
el enfoque   focus
los lentes de contacto (blandos/duros)   contact lenses (soft/hard)

la pila   battery
revelar (fotos)   to develop (photos)
sacar fotos   to take pictures

Act. 5: Set a time limit. Have students try to speak to as many people as possible.

Actividad 5: Entrevistas

Habla con diferentes personas de la clase y escribe el nombre de las personas que usen o necesiten las siguientes cosas. Usa preguntas como **¿Cuándo usas anteojos?, ¿Usas anteojos sólo para leer?,** etc.

Busca a las personas que . . .

1. usen anteojos sólo para leer
2. usen lentes de contacto blandos
3. usen lentes de contacto duros
4. usen anteojos para ver a distancia
5. usen anteojos para manejar
6. no usen anteojos

Actividad 6: Los consejos fotográficos

En grupos de cuatro, escriban un mínimo de cuatro consejos para sacar una buena foto.

|●| Hay que chequear las pilas.

Actividad 7: Las quejas

En parejas, el/la estudiante "A" trabaja en una óptica y cubre el Papel B. El/La estudiante "B" es un/a cliente y cubre el Papel A. El/La cliente recibe unas fotos que salieron bastante mal.

Papel A

Trabajas en una óptica en México y revelas fotos. A veces los clientes te culpan *(blame)* por revelar mal las fotos, pero usas máquinas automáticas para hacer el revelado. Muchas veces son ellos los que no sacan bien las fotos. Ahora, viene un/a cliente a buscar sus fotos que no son muy buenas. Es evidente que la persona que las sacó, las sacó mal: una foto tiene poca luz y otra está borrosa *(blurry)*.

Papel B

Estás haciendo turismo en México y ayer dejaste un rollo de fotos para revelar en una óptica. Hoy, al recibirlas, ves que las fotos salieron mal y tú piensas que las revelaron mal. Habla con el/la dependiente/a para quejarte; empieza diciendo **Estas fotos están horribles . . .**

Read the following sentence to show students how odd it sounds in English when a set phrase is reversed: I just bought a white-and-black TV.

¿Lo sabían?

En todas las lenguas hay "frases hechas" que a menudo son iguales o parecidas en varios idiomas. Sin embargo, si miras la lista que sigue, verás unas diferencias curiosas entre algunas frases hechas del español y del inglés.

agua y jabón	huevos y jamón	besos y abrazos	perros y gatos
blanco y negro	de pies a cabeza	vivo o muerto	tarde o temprano

¿Sabes cuáles son las expresiones correspondientes en inglés?

Hacia la comunicación

I. Expressing the Future: The Future Tense

Before studying the grammar explanation, answer the following question based on the dialogue:

● Álvaro says, **"Tendré que volver pronto . . ."** and Juan Carlos says, **"Sí, será mejor que lleguemos pronto . . ."** Can you think of another way to say these sentences?

I. Point out that in Spanish, the future tense is often used for actions occurring in the distant future.

As you have already seen, the future may be expressed with the present indicative or with the construction **ir + a +** *infinitive:* **Te veo mañana./ Voy a ver a mi padre mañana.** The future may also be expressed with the future tense. To form this tense, add the following endings to all verbs **(-ar, -er, -ir):**

Mirar	
miraré	miraremos
mirarás	miraréis
mirará	mirarán

Traer	
traeré	traeremos
traerás	traeréis
traerá	traerán

Ir	
iré	iremos
irás	iréis
irá	irán

*Note that the **nosotros** form has no accent.*

Drill the future tense:
1. Have students tell 5 things they will do next year.
2. Have students say what they will do in 20 years.
3. Have students say what technical advances will occur in the future.
4. Have students predict the political future of the U.S.
5. Have students be fortune tellers and read each others' palms.

El año que viene, Teresa y Marisel **irán** a Suramérica.
Si el vuelo llega a tiempo, Juan Carlos **comerá** con Claudia.

Teresa and Marisel will go to South America next year.
If the flight arrives on time, Juan Carlos will eat with Claudia.

The following groups of verbs have an irregular stem in the future tense.

Drop **e** from infinitive	Change **e** or **i** in infinitive to **d**	Drop **e** and **c** from infinitive
hab**e**r → **habr**é	poner → **pondr**é	de**c**ir → **dir**é
pod**e**r → **podr**é	salir → **saldr**é	ha**ce**r → **har**é
quer**e**r → **querr**é	tener → **tendr**é	
sab**e**r → **sabr**é	venir → **vendr**é	

*Inform students that **habrá** means there will be and that **habré/habrás/habrá**/etc. + past participle = future perfect.*

Habrá muchos amigos esperando a los turistas.
Si Álvaro llega hoy, él y Diana **saldrán** a cenar esta noche.

There will be many friends waiting for the tourists.
If Álvaro arrives today, he and Diana will go out to eat tonight.

II. Expressing Hypothetical Actions and Reporting: The Conditional

The conditional tense may be used to express something that you *would* do in a hypothetical situation. It is also used to report what someone has said. This tense is similar to the future tense in that it adds the same endings to all verbs **(-ar, -er, -ir).**

Mirar	
miraría	miraríamos
mirarías	miraríais
miraría	mirarían

Traer	
traería	traeríamos
traerías	traeríais
traería	traerían

Ir	
iría	iríamos
irías	iríais
iría	irían

Yo creía que **irías** al aeropuerto a esperar a Juan Carlos.

I thought you would go to the airport to wait for Juan Carlos.

Álvaro me dijo que me **traería** unos aretes de jade mexicano.

Álvaro told me that he would bring me some Mexican jade earrings.

The following groups of verbs have the same irregular stems in the conditional as they do in the future.

Infinitive	Stem	Conditional
haber	habr-	**habr**ía
poder	podr-	**podr**ía
querer	querr-	**querr**ía
saber	sabr-	**sabr**ía
poner	pondr-	**pondr**ía
salir	saldr-	**saldr**ía
tener	tendr-	**tendr**ía
venir	vendr-	**vendr**ía
decir	dir-	**dir**ía
hacer	har-	**har**ía

Con el dinero que gana en la agencia, Teresa **podría** ir a Puerto Rico.

With the money she earns at the agency, Teresa could (would be able to) go to Puerto Rico.

—No sé qué **haría** sin ella—
dijo Juan Carlos.

*"I don't know what I would do
without her," said Juan Carlos.*

III. Drill **lo** + masculine singular adjective: Have students finish sentences about the university: **Lo bueno ... Lo malo ... Lo interesante ... Lo divertido ... Lo raro ...**

Differentiate between **lo bueno, el bueno,** and **lo bueno que es: Lo bueno es que ... El bueno es Antonio. No sabes lo bueno que es.**

III. Using *lo* + Masculine Singular Adjective

To characterize something in an abstract way, use the neutral article **lo** with a masculine singular adjective.

Lo bueno es que regresaron
sin problemas.
Lo más **interesante** del viaje
fue la gente.
Lo difícil para los españoles
era la comida mexicana
picante.

*The good thing is that they
returned without any problems.*
*The most interesting part of the
trip was the people.*
*The difficult thing for the Spaniards
was the hot Mexican food.*

After studying the preceding examples, answer the following question:

• What does the title of the movie, *Lo bueno, lo malo y lo feo* with Clint Eastwood mean in English? What would it mean if it were *El bueno, el malo y el feo*?

Do mechanical drills, Workbook, Part I.

Act. 8: If necessary, brainstorm names of famous people.

Actividad 8: ¿Qué pasará?

Todos los años Jean Dixon hace sus predicciones para el año que viene. ¿Qué va a predecir Jean Dixon para este año? En parejas, preparen diez predicciones para personas famosas y para el país en general.

◖●◗ El presidente firmará un tratado de paz.

Act. 9: Discuss the significance of **el qué dirán** in Hispanic culture and the difference between this saying and "keeping up with the Joneses."

Actividad 9: El "qué dirán"

La opinión de otros afecta a muchas personas. En muchos países hispanos, como en los Estados Unidos, la opinión de los vecinos es importante. En parejas, imagínense que Uds. viven en un pueblo pequeño. Si hacen las siguientes cosas, ¿qué harán los vecinos?

◖●◗ si cuelgan *(hang)* la ropa enfrente de la casa
Si colgamos la ropa enfrente de la casa, los vecinos se enojarán.

1. si tienen muchas fiestas en su casa
2. si pintan el exterior de la casa de color morado
3. si ponen flamencos rosados de plástico delante de la casa
4. si sus hijos tienen un conjunto de rock y ensayan *(rehearse)* en el garaje con la puerta abierta
5. si tienen un gran danés que ladra *(barks)* a toda hora

Actividad 10: Mentiras inocentes

¿Has mentido alguna vez para evitar problemas o por el bien de otra persona? Decide qué harías en las siguientes situaciones. Después, en parejas, compartan las respuestas con su compañero/a.

◖ Acabas de comprar algo y el dependiente te da el cambio; te das cuenta de que hay $10 de más.
   a. decírselo al dependiente   c. algo diferente
   b. darle las gracias

> For hypothetical situations, use the conditional.

Yo le diría que me dio $10 de más. / Sería honesto/a y devolvería el dinero. / Le daría las gracias y saldría. / (etc.)

1. Vuelves de un viaje por México y traes diez botellas de tequila en el carro y el agente de aduanas te pregunta si traes alcohol.
   a. decirle que sí   c. algo diferente
   b. decirle que no

2. Tu esposo/a se está muriendo de cáncer, pero él/ella no lo sabe.
   a. decirle la verdad   c. algo diferente
   b. no decirle nada

> 125 kilómetros por hora = 80 mph

3. Un policía te detiene porque tú ibas manejando a 125 kilómetros por hora y el límite de velocidad es 100.
   a. pedirle perdón por tu error   c. algo diferente
   b. decirle que ibas a 105

4. Un niño de cuatro años te dice que su hermana mayor le dijo que Santa Claus no existía.
   a. explicarle la verdad   c. algo diferente
   b. decirle que su hermana le mintió

5. Sabes que un amigo casado está saliendo con otra mujer.
   a. no hacer nada   c. algo diferente
   b. hablar con él

6. Tu mejor amigo/a va a estar en tu ciudad el viernes y Uds. quieren pasar el día juntos pero tú tienes que trabajar.
   a. explicarle la verdad a tu jefe/a   c. algo diferente
   b. llamar al trabajo por la mañana y decir que estás enfermo/a

Actividad 11: Los críticos

En parejas, escojan una película muy interesante que Uds. dos hayan visto y comenten los aspectos de la película. Usen expresiones como **lo bueno, lo malo, lo inesperado, lo interesante, lo cómico, lo triste, lo peor de todo**, etc.

◖ Lo mejor fue el final porque . . .
   Lo más divertido fue cuando . . .

Actividad 12: El dilema

Hay problemas con el motor de un avión y el avión se está cayendo. Hay ocho pasajeros y un piloto, pero sólo hay cuatro paracaídas *(parachutes)*. En grupos de cuatro, lean las descripciones de las personas y decidan a quiénes les darían Uds. los paracaídas y por qué.

1. Antonio Sánchez: 44 años, piloto, casado y con tres hijos
2. Pilar Tamayo: 34 años, soltera, doctora famosa por sus investigaciones sobre métodos anticonceptivos
3. Lola del Rey: 23 años, soltera, actriz; fue Miss Ecuador y salió segunda en el concurso de Miss Universo; hizo viajes con Bob Hope cantando para los soldados
4. Tommy González: 10 años, estudiante de cuarto grado, jugador de fútbol
5. Angustias Ramírez: 63 años, casada, con cinco hijos y siete nietos, abuela de Tommy González; ayuda a los pobres en un programa de la iglesia
6. Enrique Vallejo: 46 años, divorciado, con tres hijos, político importante, liberal, líder del movimiento laboral
7. El padre Pacheco: 56 años, cura católico de una iglesia para trabajadores migratorios, fundador del programa E.S.D. (Escuela sin drogas) que es una escuela para jóvenes que eran drogadictos
8. Lulú Camacho y Víctor Robles: 25 y 28 años, dos atletas que se dedican a levantar pesas y participan en competencias internacionales; hacen anuncios en la televisión para el Club Cuerposano

Nuevos horizontes

Estrategia de lectura: *Understanding the Writer's Purpose*

In writing a text, the writer chooses a purpose (informing, convincing, entertaining, etc.) and an audience (teachers, researchers, teenagers, etc.). He/She usually keeps the purpose and audience in mind when writing the text, in order to both achieve this purpose and to gear the level of discussion to the reader's knowledge. Therefore, when choosing to read a text, it is advisable to skim it to find out whether you are part of the intended audience.

Actividad 13: Preguntas

🔘 Antes de leer los artículos, contesta estas preguntas.

1. ¿Sabes qué exportan los Estados Unidos?
2. ¿Cuáles son los principales recursos económicos de este país?
3. ¿Sabes cuáles son algunos de los recursos económicos de los países hispanos?
4. ¿Cuál es el recurso más importante de Venezuela?
5. ¿Sabes cuál es el problema económico que más afecta a Hispanoamérica?

Act. 14: Brainstorm different motives and tones used in texts.

La Señora ... : Discuss the rate of inflation in certain countries. Show examples by comparing rates with those of the previous year.

Actividad 14: Propósito y tono

Lee los diferentes textos relacionados con la economía hispana y busca cuál es el propósito de los diferentes autores (informar, entretener, convencer, etc.) y qué tono usan (serio, gracioso, irónico, etc.). Luego, di cuáles serían algunos posibles lectores de estos textos.

La Señora Inflación

La gente se pregunta cómo podemos vivir con la Señora Inflación y nosotros contestamos: "No sé, pero con ella vivimos." Es verdad, la vemos todos los días por todos lados. Si vemos algo que nos gusta en una tienda, no dudamos en comprarlo inmediatamente porque sabemos que mañana viene la señora y le sube el precio. Por la mañana hay que estar bien despierto al tomar al autobús porque no es extraño que el día anterior la señora haya decidido aumentar el precio y que el conductor nos mire con cara de "¡Ufa! Otro que no se enteró todavía del aumento." ¿Cómo vivimos con esta señora? No sé, pero sobrevivimos.

La deuda externa

La gran crisis de la deuda externa, que se originó en 1982, es uno de los problemas económicos más graves que tiene Latinoamérica. Países como Argentina, Brasil, México y Perú tienen una deuda que sobrepasa los miles de millones de dólares. Este problema afecta seriamente a los países deudores, pues el dinero que en épocas normales se usaría para crear industrias y reinvertir en el país, se utiliza ahora para pagar la deuda. Es por eso que muchas personas piensan que no deberían pagarla, o que podrían pagarla dentro de unos años cuando los países tengan más dinero. El temor de mucha gente es que, si no pagan la deuda, sus países queden aislados económicamente del mundo.

La deuda ... : Discuss current news items dealing with international debts.

El turismo ... : The number of tourists in Spain is at least equal to the number of inhabitants. Main attractions are the Canary Islands, the Balearic Islands, and coastal beaches.

El turismo en el mundo hispano

El turismo internacional es la principal fuente de ingresos para España, donde entra un promedio de 53 millones de turistas por año. Para México, el turismo es la segunda fuente de ingresos después del petróleo y entra en el país un promedio anual de cinco o seis millones de turistas. Otros países que han estado fomentando la industria turística son Puerto Rico, la República Dominicana y Cuba, tres países caribeños que se caracterizan por sus bellísimas playas y clima tropical.

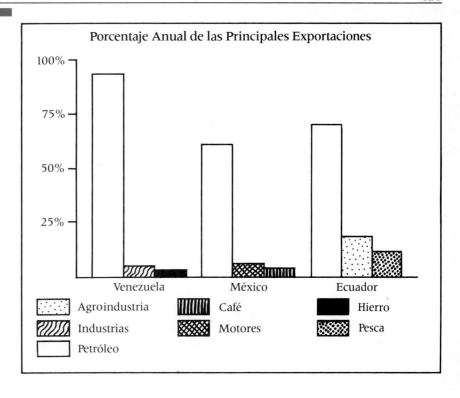

Porcentaje Anual de las Principales Exportaciones

Agroindustria — Café — Hierro
Industrias — Motores — Pesca
Petróleo

Actividad 15: Preguntas

Después de leer los artículos, contesta estas preguntas.

1. En el primer artículo, ¿cómo se refiere el autor a la inflación? ¿Por qué?
2. ¿Cuáles son algunos de los problemas diarios de la inflación?
3. ¿Cómo afecta la deuda externa a algunos países hispanos?
4. ¿Cuáles pueden ser las consecuencias de que un país exporte un solo producto principal?
5. Nombra los países que tienen un alto índice de turismo.

Estrategia de escritura: *Writing a Summary*

A summary includes the main points of a text, without details. As with a description, you address the questions *who?, what?, where?, when?,* and *why?.* In order to do a summary, it is helpful to list the main points of the text first and then to use connectors or linking words to join the ideas.

Actividad 16: Un resumen

Completa este párrafo con las palabras de la lista para obtener un resumen de las ideas principales de los textos presentados.

por un lado	por otro lado	ni . . . ni
como consecuencia	en general	también

La economía hispana, _____en general_____ , sufre algunas crisis graves. _____Por un lado_____ está el problema de la deuda externa y _____como consecuencia_____ de este problema no hay dinero ___ni___ para crear industrias ___ni___ para reinvertir en estos países. _____Por otro lado_____ está el problema de la inflación galopante que afecta a muchos países. Entre las principales fuentes de ingresos de algunos países hispanos están las exportaciones de petróleo y _____también_____ el turismo.

Lo esencial

Buscando trabajo

E X T R A N J E R O S

REGISTRO

(Régimen General)

SOLICITUD DE PERMISO DE TRABAJO Y RESIDENCIA

ESPAÑA

NUMERO DE IDENTIFICACIÓN

POR FAVOR, NO ESCRIBA EN LOS ESPACIOS SOMBREADOS. VEA
INSTRUCCIONES AL DORSO. RELLÉNELO A MAQUINA O CON
BOLIGRAFO NEGRO Y LETRA DE IMPRENTA

DATOS DEL TRABAJADOR

Apellido(s)

Nombre

Apellido de nacimiento

País de nacionalidad

Lugar de nacimiento (localidad)

País de nacimiento

Fecha de nacimiento (día, mes y año)   Sexo   Estado civil   Profesión habitual

Núm. de afiliación a la Seguridad Social española (1)   Titulación y conocimientos especiales

Apellido(s) y nombre de la madre   Apellido(s) y nombre del padre

¿TUVO PERMISO DE RESIDENCIA Y TRABAJO CON ANTERIORIDAD A ESTA SOLICITUD? (2) No ☐   Sí ☐   ¿Por cuenta propia? ☐   ¿Por cuenta ajena? ☐

SI YA TRABAJA O VA A TRABAJAR: Dependencia laboral (2)   Cuenta propia ☐   Cuenta ajena ☐

la carta de recomendación
letter of recommendation
contratar to contract, to hire
el contrato contract
el curriculum (vitae) résumé,
curriculum vitae
el desempleo unemployment
despedir to fire
el empleo/el puesto job/
position; employment
la entrevista interview
la experiencia experience

rellenar to fill out
el seguro médico medical
insurance
solicitar to apply for
la solicitud application
el sueldo salary
el título title; (university)
degree
**trabajar medio tiempo/
tiempo completo** to work
part time/full time

¿Lo sabían?

En muchos países hispanos se divide el sueldo anual en catorce o quince
pagos en vez de doce. De esta forma, una persona recibe normalmente el
doble del sueldo mensual en julio y en diciembre. Mucha gente usa este
dinero, «el bono», para las vacaciones y para las compras de Navidad. ¿Te
gustaría recibir bonos, o prefieres repartir el dinero igualmente en doce
pagos?

Actividad 17: Definiciones

Termina estas frases con una palabra lógica de la lista presentada en la
sección **Buscando trabajo.**

1. Antes de una entrevista, tienes que rellenar una . . .
2. Para solicitar un trabajo es bueno pedirle a varias personas una . . .
3. Sólo trabajas veinte horas por semana; no trabajas . . . sino . . .
4. La cantidad de dinero que recibes por semana o por mes es tu . . .
5. Tu historia profesional se llama . . .
6. Un beneficio que te pueden dar es . . .

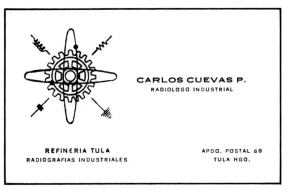

Actividad 18: Buscando trabajo

En parejas, el/la estudiante "A" busca empleo y el/la estudiante "B" es un/a consejero/a en la agencia de empleos de la universidad. "A" quiere saber qué posibilidades de empleo hay, qué beneficios tienen, qué documentos tendrá que presentar, y qué debe incluir en su curriculum. Lean sólo las instrucciones para su papel.

Papel A

Tienes un título universitario en economía y estás empezando tus estudios de posgrado; por eso, necesitas un trabajo de medio tiempo. Tu idioma es el inglés pero hablas francés y español. Durante tus años de escuela secundaria trabajaste en McDonald's y mientras estudiabas en la universidad trabajabas en una compañía de importación escribiendo las cartas dirigidas a países hispanos y a Francia.

Papel B

Los siguientes son dos puestos disponibles *(available)*. Averigua las cosas que sabe hacer "A" y recomiéndale uno de estos puestos.

> Camarero/a en el restaurante elegante El Charro; lunes, martes, fines de semana; 25 horas semanales; sueldo según experiencia; propinas; 2 semanas de vacaciones; sin seguro médico.
> Requisitos: buena presencia; con experiencia; una carta de recomendación del último jefe; curriculum; conseguir la solicitud en el restaurante. Avenida Guanajuato 3252.

> Traductor/a para compañía de seguros; bilingüe (español/inglés); horario variable — más o menos 20 horas por semana; $25 la página; seguro médico incluido.
> Requisitos: un año de experiencia; examen de español e inglés; 3 cartas de recomendación; curriculum; título universitario; para conseguir la solicitud, llamar al 467 43 89.

Actividad 19: El puesto ideal

Ahora, el/la consejero/a quiere simular una entrevista. "A" y "B" deben practicar entrevistas para los puestos presentados en la Actividad 18. Cambien de papel después de la primera entrevista.

¿A trabajar en la Patagonia?

Have students invent **chismes**.

Tell students they are going to have a quiz, then say, **Les estoy tomando el pelo.**

Ask students, **¿Les ha pasado algo por (pura) casualidad?**

los chismes	gossip
fue pura casualidad	it was by pure chance
resultó ser . . .	it/he/she turned out to be . . .
tomarle el pelo (a alguien)	to pull someone's leg

Patagonia

Juan Carlos y Álvaro acaban de regresar de su viaje, y mientras estaban en Venezuela Juan Carlos conoció a un señor que le habló de un posible empleo. Ahora él está otra vez en Madrid con Teresa y Claudia contándoles sobre el viaje y rellenando la solicitud.

Actividad 20: Escucha y responde

Escucha la conversación y contesta estas preguntas.

1. ¿Dónde conoció Juan Carlos al señor?
2. ¿Por qué tiene el señor interés en ayudar a Juan Carlos?
3. ¿Qué tiene que hacer Juan Carlos?
4. ¿Está contento don Alejandro con el trabajo de Juan Carlos y Álvaro?
5. Si Juan Carlos consigue el trabajo, ¿adónde irá?

La Patagonia es una región apartada de gran belleza natural.

Debate the saying, **Del odio al amor hay sólo un paso.**

Expressing urgency

Approximating

Discuss **mala suerte** and **suerte loca.**

Wondering

Teresa	¿Por qué no sigues contándonos de la Dra. Llanos y el Sr. Ruiz? Ayer no terminaste de explicarnos por qué ella lo odiaba a muerte. No me sorprendería verlos después muy amigos.
Juan Carlos	¿Amigos, ellos? Nunca. ¡Estás loca! Tú no los viste en el viaje.
Claudia	Y, ¿por qué no? Del odio al amor hay sólo un paso . . .
Juan Carlos	Bueno, dejémonos de chismes, y ayúdenme a terminar esta solicitud, pues quiero mandarla antes de que cierren el correo esta tarde.
Teresa	Lo que no entiendo es que te fuiste de viaje y llegaste con una oferta de trabajo. ¿Cómo es posible?
Juan Carlos	Fue pura casualidad. Estábamos en Venezuela celebrando el cumpleaños del Sr. Ruiz en un club y me puse a hablar con un señor peruano que tendría unos cuarenta años. Resultó ser gerente de una empresa de ingenieros e íntimo amigo de un tío mío.
Claudia	Para mala suerte, Álvaro, y para suerte loca, Juan Carlos.
Juan Carlos	Bueno, entonces cuando supo quién era mi tío y que yo estudiaba ingeniería, me dijo que por qué no solicitaba un puesto con su empresa. Y ahora tengo que mandarles esta solicitud a los jefes de personal.
Claudia	O sea, conoce a tu tío, ¿eh? . . . A eso se le llama tener palanca.
Juan Carlos	Bueno, pero también tengo un buen curriculum, ¿no? Oye, Teresa, ¿crees que tu tío me escribiría una carta de recomendación?
Teresa	Por supuesto. Él está feliz con los comentarios de la gente del tour, pues todo lo que dicen de ti y de Álvaro son maravillas. Lo malo es que esta tarde sale para Londres y no sé dónde estará ahora . . . Lo llamo ahora mismo a ver si está en la oficina.
Juan Carlos	Con la recomendación de don Alejandro es posible que me den el puesto sin entrevistarme, ¿no crees?
Claudia	¡Un momento, un momento! Lo que yo quisiera saber es dónde es ese trabajo . . . Creo que yo tengo derecho a saber . . . ¿eh?
Juan Carlos	Pues . . . Lo único es que . . . es que es . . . es en la Patagonia . . .

| Claudia | ¿La Patagonia? pero, ¡eso está muy lejos! |
| Juan Carlos | Calma, calma. Te estoy tomando el pelo. La oferta de trabajo es para Caracas, no para la Patagonia y ¡con un buen sueldo . . . ! |

Actividad 21: Un resumen

Di cinco oraciones que resuman lo que pasó en la conversación entre Juan Carlos y las dos chicas.

Actividad 22: Prediciendo

Escribe las respuestas a las siguientes preguntas y después, en parejas, comparen sus respuestas con las de su compañero/a. Deben estar preparados para defender sus predicciones.

1. Algún día, ¿serán amigos el Sr. Ruiz y la Dra. Llanos?
2. ¿Qué va a decir don Alejandro en la carta de recomendación?
3. ¿Le van a dar el empleo a Juan Carlos?
4. ¿Qué va a pasar con Claudia y Juan Carlos?

¿Lo sabían?

En español se dice que si una persona está debajo de un árbol grande, está protegida por su sombra *(shade)*. Este dicho se refiere a lo importante que es conocer a personas de influencia para obtener un buen puesto o, a veces, para recibir favores. Esta costumbre tiene diferentes nombres en diferentes países hispanos: el enchufe, la corbata, la conexión, la palanca, tener padrino, etc. ¿Crees que esta costumbre sea común en muchos países? ¿Puedes pensar en algunas palabras o expresiones en inglés que se relacionen con esta costumbre? ¿Sabes de alguien que haya obtenido su puesto con "palanca"?

Actividad 23: Al fin

Di qué ocurrió en las siguientes situaciones, usando la frase "resultó ser" para terminar las oraciones.

1. Abraham Lincoln perdió varias elecciones pero al final . . .
2. Compré un coche nuevo y . . .
3. Conseguí un puesto con la ONU (Organización de las Naciones Unidas) y . . .
4. Cuando Pablo conoció a su primera novia, ella era simpática, trabajadora y tenía ambiciones, pero después de unos años . . .
5. Para Juan Carlos el viaje . . .

Hacia la comunicación

I. Expressing Probability: The Future and the Conditional

The future and the conditional tenses are often used to express probability or to wonder about a situation. When you wonder about the present, use the future tense. When you wonder about the past, use the conditional.

—¿Cuántos años **tendrá** ese muchacho?	*I wonder how old that guy is.*
—**Tendrá** unos diecinueve.	*He's probably (He must be) about nineteen.*
—¿Qué hora **será**?	*I wonder what time it is.*
—**Serán** las 3:00.	*It must be (it's probably) 3:00.*
—¿Cuántos años **tendría** cuando se casó?	*I wonder how old he was when he got married. (How old could he have been when he got married?)*
—**Tendría** unos veinticinco.	*He probably was (must have been) about twenty-five.*
—¿Qué hora **sería** cuando llegaron los chicos?	*What time could it have been when the guys arrived?*
—**Serían** las 3:00 de la mañana.	*It must have been (It probably was) 3:00 A.M.*

II. Expressing Indefinite Future Actions: The Subjunctive in Adverbial Clauses

The following adverbial conjunctions, which may be used to talk about the present or the indefinite future, are *always* followed by the subjunctive.

E	en caso (de) que	in the event that; in case
S	sin que	without
C	con tal (de) que	provided that
A	antes (de) que	before
P	para que	in order that, so that
A	a menos que	unless

En caso de que llueva, no iremos al parque.	*In the event that it rains, we won't go to the park.*

Van a entrar **sin que** nadie los **oiga**.
Yo voy, **con tal de que** tú no me **molestes** más.
Llámame **antes de que salgas** para Caracas.
El profesor explica **para que** los alumnos **entiendan.**
Juan Carlos no aceptará el puesto **a menos que** Claudia **vaya** con él.

They're going to come in without anybody hearing them.
I'll go provided that you don't bother me any more.
Call me before you leave for Caracas.
The teacher explains in order that (so that) the students understand.
Juan Carlos won't accept the job unless Claudia goes with him.

Remember the acronym **SEPA.**

Do mechanical drills, Workbook, Part II.

Act. 24-26: Encourage multiple responses for the next 3 exercises.

There are multiple possibilities.

Note: **Sin que, en caso de que, para que, antes de que** take the subjunctive when there is a change of subject. If there is no change of subject, use an infinitive immediately after the preposition.

Trabajo **para que mi familia viva** bien.
Trabajo **para vivir** bien.

Actividad 24: Situaciones

Imagínate qué están haciendo las personas que dicen estas oraciones.

◖●◗ "Me encanta esta música."
Estará en un concierto.

1. "Está excelente. Realmente eres un genio."
2. "No puedo continuar. Estoy cansadísima."
3. "No me interrumpas. Debo terminar esto lo antes posible."
4. "Justo ahora que estoy aquí, suena el teléfono."

Actividad 25: Los misterios de la vida

En parejas, digan por qué creen que ocurrieron estas cosas.

◖●◗ Gloria no fue a la entrevista de trabajo.
Estaría enferma.

1. No aceptaron a tu amigo Alfredo, un estudiante excelente, en la facultad de medicina.
2. Se desaparecieron misteriosamente tus amigos Mariano y Rosa.
3. Tu amigo Felipe nunca tenía dinero y la semana pasada compró un carro nuevo.
4. Tu perra estaba más gorda. Siempre tenía hambre y no hacía más que comer y dormir.

Actividad 26: Usa la imaginación

Completa las siguientes frases de forma original usando expresiones como **antes de que, sin que, para que,** etc.

◖●◗ Juan Carlos no irá a Caracas a menos que le den el trabajo.

1. Don Alejandro entrevista a personas . . .
2. Teresa estudia turismo . . .
3. Claudia piensa casarse con Juan Carlos . . .
4. No le van a dar el trabajo a Juan Carlos . . .
5. Vicente y Teresa irán de vacaciones a Centroamérica . . .
6. Claudia le pregunta a Juan Carlos sobre sus planes . . .
7. Diana quiere quedarse en España . . .

Act. 27: Before doing this activity, brainstorm problems group leaders may encounter with a group of teenagers in a foreign country. As each item in the list is discussed, clarify how misunderstandings or unexpected reactions could result from cultural differences.

After doing this activity, discuss the validity of the phrase "the ugly American."

Actividad 27: La diplomacia

Uds. van a llevar a un grupo de estudiantes norteamericanos de dieciséis años a México para vivir con familias durante un mes y no quieren que el grupo tenga problemas por razones culturales. Aquí hay algunas cosas que les preocupan. Comenten la lista y sus ramificaciones.

Habrá problemas con el alcohol.
No querrán probar la comida.
Llegarán tarde por la noche.
Saldrán sin pedir permiso.
No hablarán en español.
Aprenderán malas palabras en la calle y las usarán en la casa.
(etc.)

Act. 28: This can be written in small groups, pairs, or individually as homework. When finished, compare the reasons given and create a composite letter.

Actividad 28: Evitando problemas

Después de haber hablado sobre los posibles problemas, intenten evitarlos con una carta a los estudiantes dándoles razones que ellos puedan entender. Usen oraciones como **No deben salir de casa sin que sus padres mexicanos les den permiso. Hay que recordar que son sus padres en México y Uds. están en sus casas como invitados.**

Empiecen la carta así:

Querido grupo:

Pronto pasaremos un mes juntos en México. Uds. van a estar en un país extranjero y tienen que recordar que no son un grupo de turistas sino representantes de los Estados Unidos. Como todos queremos que la experiencia sea maravillosa, tanto para Uds. como para los mexicanos que los van a aceptar en sus casas, tienen que recordar algunas cosas: . . .

Vocabulario funcional

En la óptica

Ver página 413

Buscando trabajo

Ver página 423

Palabras y expresiones útiles

antes que nada before anything
else
los chismes gossip
dejar boquiabierto (a alguien)
to leave (someone) dumbfounded
es hora de + infinitive it's time
to + *infinitive*

fue pura casualidad it was by
pure chance
resultó ser . . . it/he/she turned
out to be . . .
tomarle el pelo (a alguien) to
pull someone's leg

¿Sabes qué hizo Velázquez?

Velázquez, a Spanish court painter, is considered one of the best Spanish painters of all time. His famous works include *Las meninas, La rendición de Breda, Los borrachos, Las hilanderas,* and *Los bufones.*

Bring in photos or slides of Velázquez's work.

Estatua de Diego Rodríguez de Silva y Velázquez (1599–1660), Museo del Prado, Madrid.

HACIA EL SIGLO XXI

Forjando el futuro

(1) Carolina Herrera, diseñadora venezolana
(2) Oscar Arias, presidente de Costa Rica y Premio Nóbel de la Paz   (3) Astronauta Franklin Chang Díaz, costarricense

Actividad
En parejas, ¿cómo piensan que estas tres fotos se relacionan con el futuro del mundo hispano?

1

2

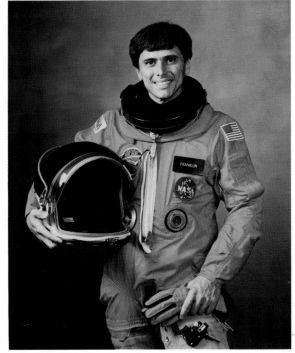

3

4

5

6

7

8

9

El comercio, la industria y los recursos naturales

(4) Fábrica de Ford, México   (5) Cortando caña,
Cuba   (6) Presa, Itapúa, Paraguay   (7) Torre de
perforación, México   (8) La Bolsa, Santiago, Chile
(9) Vendiendo café, Colombia

Actividad
El futuro económico internacional depende de la comunicación entre los países. En grupos de cuatro,
comenten cómo el uso del español puede ayudarles
a Uds. en su futuro profesional.

El tiempo libre

(10) Plácido Domingo filmando la película *Carmen*, España (11) Filmando para la televisión, Barcelona, España (12) Aranxa Sánchez, tenista española (13) Partido de béisbol entre los Estados Unidos y la República Dominicana (14) La Copa Mundial de fútbol, México

Actividad

En grupos de tres, preparen una lista de personajes hispanos asociados con las siguientes categorías: actores, músicos, deportistas.

12

13

14

La familia y la educación

(15) Nuevo Laredo, México
(16) Buenos Aires, Argentina

Actividad

En parejas, comenten el futuro de la familia y la educación en el siglo XXI. ¿Seguirá siendo la familia un núcleo esencial en la sociedad? ¿Qué papel tendrá la tecnología en la educación?

15

16

Capítulo 17

Chapter Objectives

After studying this chapter, you will know how to:

- express doubts and emotions in the past
- give implied commands in the past
- describe hypothetical situations
- express reciprocal actions
- discuss and give opinions about art
- express your ideas on love and romance

museo de arte
prehispánico
de méxico
rufino tamayo

Nº 008575

morelos 503 oaxaca, oax.

¿Te gusta visitar museos?
¿Te gustaría visitar éste?

El arte escondido

Francisco de Goya y Lucientes was a prolific Spanish painter from the province of Zaragoza. He is known as a precursor of modern painting. His early paintings were cheerful depictions of the times. Years later, while still a court painter, he went deaf, a change that added a somber, new dimension to his work. ***Los fusilamientos del 3 de mayo,*** for instance, is Goya's disturbing vision of the Napoleonic invasion of Spain. It is said that Goya went crazy in old age, during the period of his "black paintings."

Bring in photos or slides of Goya's paintings to show his great variety of style.

Los fusilamientos del tres de mayo, Francisco de Goya y Lucientes (1746–1828), España.

Practice **en seguida** by giving commands and having students respond, **En seguida ...**

It is also acceptable to write **enseguida** as 1 word.

no veo la hora de + infinitive	I can't wait + *infinitive*
dar a conocer	to make known
en seguida	at once, right away

Diana y Álvaro van en el carro escuchando la radio cuando oyen una noticia increíble.

Actividad 1: Buscando información

Escucha la conversación y la noticia y contesta las siguientes preguntas.

1. ¿Cuándo tendrá examen Álvaro?
2. ¿Qué encontraron en la casa de la señora?
3. ¿Qué le pasó a la señora?
4. ¿Qué le molesta a Álvaro?
5. ¿Cuántas veces ha ido Álvaro al Museo del Prado?

Álvaro No veo la hora de terminar el trimestre. A propósito, quería preguntarte, ¿qué tal van tus clases?
Diana Pronto tendré exámenes.
Álvaro Sí, yo tengo uno de derecho penal el martes que viene.
Diana Y yo, uno de literatura.
Álvaro ¡Uy! literatura, ¡qué aburrido!
Diana De aburrido, nada. A mí me encanta.
Álvaro Pero la literatura es . . .
El locutor ¡Atención! Interrumpimos para dar una noticia de última hora . . .
Diana ¡Calla, calla! Escucha.
El locutor La dirección del Museo del Prado dio a conocer hoy el hallazgo de un cuadro de Goya que nadie sabía que existiera. Se trata de una de las pinturas de su época negra. El cuadro se encontró en la casa de una señora de noventa y ocho años que murió en la provincia de Zaragoza. Cuando sus hijos estaban sacando los muebles de la casa, encontraron la pintura debajo de la cama. Al principio se dudaba que fuera un original, pero al examinarla, los expertos en seguida se dieron cuenta de que era una obra maestra del gran pintor español. Al pedirle una declaración al director del museo, sólo ha dicho que valoran el cuadro en cientos de millones de pesetas . . .
Álvaro Un loco del siglo XVIII pintó algo para que otro loco del siglo XX pagara millones de pesetas por su cuadro.
Diana ¡Qué poco entiendes! El loco serás tú.
Álvaro Es que el arte me aburre, la arquitectura me fascina, pero los cuadros . . .
Diana ¿Has visitado el Museo del Prado alguna vez?
Álvaro No, pero . . .
Diana Eres un inculto, mañana te llevo porque tengo que ir allí. Y vas a recibir una lección de arte.

Actividad 2: ¿Comprendiste?

Después de escuchar la conversación y la noticia, completa estas oraciones.

1. Diana y Álvaro tienen exámenes porque . . .
2. La pintura de Goya se encontró . . .
3. El valor de la obra . . .
4. Diana llama loco a Álvaro porque . . .
5. Álvaro prefiere . . .
6. Mañana Álvaro . . .

¿Lo sabían?

Uno de los mejores museos de arte del mundo es el Museo del Prado de Madrid. El Prado tiene una colección artística de más de tres mil pinturas y unas cuatrocientas esculturas de artistas de todo el mundo. Además de obras de El Greco, Velázquez, Goya, Ribera y muchos otros artistas españoles, el Prado tiene la segunda colección de pintores flamencos del mundo, con obras de Rubens, El Bosco, Van Dyck y Brueghel, para mencionar unos pocos. En un edificio aparte, el Casón del Buen Retiro, se encuentra representada la historia del arte español y allí se puede ver la obra más política de Picasso, *Guernica*, y el estudio completo de dibujos que hizo el pintor cuando preparaba esta famosa obra.

Actividad 3: No veo la hora . . .

Escribe una lista de cuatro cosas que deseas que ocurran muy pronto. Después, en parejas, comparen su lista con la de su compañero/a y pregúntenle por qué quiere que pasen estas cosas.

⦿ No veo la hora de terminar el semestre.

Lo esencial

La exhibición de arte

1. el/la artista
2. el cuadro/la pintura
3. el dibujo
4. el/la escultor/a
5. la escultura

Otras palabras relacionadas con el arte

el bodegón still life	**el original** original
la copia copy	**el paisaje** landscape
dibujar to draw, sketch	**pintar** to paint
la escena scene	**el/la pintor/a** painter
la estatua statue	**el retrato** portrait
la obra maestra masterpiece	

Actividad 4: ¿Hay artistas en la clase?

En parejas, háganle las siguientes preguntas a su compañero/a para ver si es una persona artística o una persona a quien le gusta el arte.

1. Cuando eras más joven, ¿dibujabas o pintabas mucho?
2. Hoy día, ¿dibujas en tus cuadernos durante tus clases o cuando hablas por teléfono?
3. ¿Te gusta dibujar? ¿Pintar? ¿Has hecho alguna escultura?
4. ¿Has tomado clases de arte?
5. ¿Hay cuadros en tu casa o apartamento? ¿Son originales o copias?
6. ¿Te gusta visitar museos? ¿Cuál fue el último museo que visitaste?
7. ¿Qué pintores/artistas te gustan y por qué?

¿Lo sabían?

Muchos artistas hacen comentarios sociales como hizo Goya hace doscientos años. El arte chicano es un comentario social importante en los Estados Unidos. Los chicanos comenzaron a pintar murales urbanos en Chicago en 1968 y hoy en día hay murales en otras ciudades del país, especialmente en Los Ángeles. Estos murales representan, de forma a veces satírica, la historia mexicana, el movimiento de los trabajadores agrícolas y la experiencia mexicana en los Estados Unidos; en ellos se ve la influencia de los grandes muralistas mexicanos.

La antorcha (torch) *de Quetzalcóatl,* Leo Tanguma, chicano. Este mural muestra la historia del chicano y su lucha por mantener sus costumbres dentro de la sociedad norteamericana.

Actividad 5: Críticos de arte

En grupos de cuatro, miren los cuadros de este capítulo y de otras partes del libro y coméntenlos dando sus impresiones. Usen oraciones como **lo interesante es . . . , lo curioso es . . . , lo que (no) me gusta es . . . ,** etc. Incluyan el nombre del artista y del cuadro.

Actividad 6: Usando la imaginación

En parejas, escojan uno de los siguientes cuadros para inventar una historia sobre lo que ocurrió y ocurría fuera del cuadro que no se puede ver.

(Izquierda) *Antes del juego,* Claudio Bravo, Chile. (Derecha) *Gallos y gente,* Francisco Amighetti, Costa Rica.

Hacia la comunicación

I.   Speaking About the Past: The Imperfect Subjunctive

Before studying the grammar explanation, answer this question:

- What is the difference between the following pairs of sentences?
  a. **Se duda que el cuadro sea de Goya** and **Se dudaba que el cuadro fuera de Goya.**
  b. **Diana quiere que Álvaro vaya al museo** and **Diana quería que Álvaro fuera al museo.**

A. Formation of the Imperfect Subjunctive

You have already seen how to use the present subjunctive. The imperfect subjunctive is used in the same circumstances as the present subjunctive, except that you are referring to the past. To conjugate any verb in the imperfect subjunctive, apply the following rules:

1. Put the verb in the **Uds.** form of the preterit: **cerrar** ⟶ **cerraron**
2. Drop the final **-ron:**   **cerra-**
3. Add the appropriate **-ra** endings: **cerrara, cerraras,** etc.

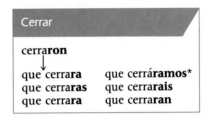

Cerrar

cerra**ron**

que cerra**ra**	que cerrá**ramos***
que cerra**ras**	que cerra**rais**
que cerra**ra**	que cerra**ran**

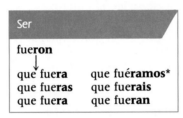

Ser

fue**ron**

que fue**ra**	que fué**ramos***
que fue**ras**	que fue**rais**
que fue**ra**	que fue**ran**

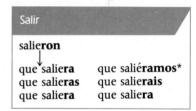

Salir

salie**ron**

que salie**ra**	que salié**ramos***
que salie**ras**	que salie**rais**
que salie**ra**	que salie**ra**

*Note: The **nosotros** form always takes an accent.

Quería que **vinieras** temprano.	*I wanted you to come early.*
Busqué un cuadro que **fuera** famoso.	*I looked for a painting that was famous.*
Teresa **iba** a llevar a Carlitos al museo para que **viera** un cuadro de Goya.	*Teresa was going to take Carlitos to the museum so that he could see one of Goya's paintings.*

B. Using the Subjunctive Tenses

In order to decide which form of the subjunctive to use (**hable, haya hablado** or **hablara**), follow these two guidelines:

1. If the first clause refers to the present or future, use the present or present perfect subjunctive in the dependent clause.

    Dudo que Álvaro **hable** mucho de arte.
    Le **pedirá** que **vaya** al museo mañana.
    Es posible que Álvaro no **haya estado** en el Museo del Prado.
    Dile que **vaya** al museo.

For other tenses in the subjunctive, see Appendix A.

2. If the first clause refers to the past or to a hypothetical situation, use the imperfect subjunctive in the dependent clause.

Dubaba que Álvaro **hablara** mucho de arte.
Le **pediría** que **fuera** al museo, pero no sé si aceptará.
Diana le **aconsejó** que **aprendiera** algo de arte.

II. Asking and Requesting: *Preguntar* versus *pedir*

1. Use the verb **preguntar** when asking for information.

Me **preguntaron** cuántos años tenía.	*They asked me how old I was.*
Le voy a **preguntar** si quiere ir al museo conmigo.	*I'm going to ask him if he wants to go to the museum with me.*

2. Use the verb **pedir** when asking for things or requesting somebody to do something.

Vamos a **pedirles** el dinero.	*We are going to ask them for the money.*
Ellos me **pidieron** que viniera.	*They asked me to come.*

II. Drill **preguntar** vs. **pedir**: Tell students what is being asked for and have them express the request as a complete sentence. T: **un dólar** S1: **Me pidió un dólar.** T: **el precio** S2: **Me preguntó el precio.** Possible requests: **las capitales de Bolivia, las llaves del carro, ayuda, mi nombre, si podía ir, que fuera a su casa,** etc.

Do mechanical drills, Workbook, Part I.

Actividad 7: La indecisión

Tú tienes un jefe que siempre cambia de ideas. Lee estas oraciones que explican qué quiere hoy y compáralo con lo que quería ayer.

1. Hoy mi jefe quiere que yo aprenda a usar una computadora IBM, pero ayer . . .
2. Hoy mi jefe me aconseja que tome las vacaciones, pero ayer . . .
3. Hoy mi jefe me dice que le prepare café, pero ayer . . .
4. Hoy mi jefe quiere una recepcionista nueva que sepa hablar francés, pero ayer . . .
5. Hoy mi jefe pide que los documentos estén listos para mañana, pero ayer . . .
6. Hoy mi jefe busca un sistema de teléfono que tenga cuatro líneas, pero ayer . . .
7. Hoy mi jefe quiere ir a Quito antes de que termine la semana, pero ayer . . .

Actividad 8: Consejos

Be careful with imperfect and preterit!

En parejas, hablen de los consejos que les dieron sus padres, otros parientes o sus maestros cuando Uds. eran pequeños. ¿Cómo se comparan estos consejos con los consejos que les dan esas personas hoy día? Usen oraciones como **Antes me aconsejaban que . . . , pero ahora pien-**

san que es mejor que yo . . . ; **Cuando tenía diez años me dijeron que . . . para que . . . , pero ahora . . . ;** etc.

Actividad 9: En el consultorio

Usando **me preguntó** y **me pidió,** forma oraciones que diría un paciente al explicar su visita al médico.

1. cómo me sentía
2. si tenía fiebre
3. que explicara los síntomas
4. cuántos años tenía
5. qué me dolía
6. mi historia médica
7. qué comía
8. si prefería píldoras o inyecciones
9. que comiera más frutas
10. que volviera la semana que viene

Act. 10: Except for #1, the sentences are based on information in the **Nuevos horizontes** sections. Discuss Bolívar, Martí, San Martín, and O'Higgins.
Possible answers: 1. **pudiera independizarse** 2. **la malaria y la fiebre amarilla los forzaran a abandonar el proyecto**
3. **el dios de los indios supiera**
4. **lo supiera** 5. **sea demasiado tarde** 6. **vivamos mejor**
7. **llegaran los moros**

Act. 11: Before doing this activity, ask students what they know about 1492.

You may want to teach the words **redondo** and **las Indias.**

Actividad 10: ¿Qué sabes?

En parejas, terminen las oraciones de forma lógica; si no saben, inventen una respuesta posible.

1. Simón Bolívar, José Martí, José de San Martín y Bernardo O'Higgins lucharon contra los españoles para que el pueblo hispanoamericano . . .
2. Los franceses intentaron construir el Canal de Panamá antes de que . . .
3. La leyenda de las Cataratas del Iguazú dice que los enamorados se fueron de la tribu sin que . . .
4. Miguel Littín entró en Chile en 1985 sin que el gobierno de Pinochet . . .
5. Todo el mundo tiene que ayudar a salvar la selva antes de que . . .
6. Hay que conservar el medio ambiente para que . . .
7. Los romanos vivieron seis siglos en España antes de que . . .

Actividad 11: La duda

Siempre hay gente que duda de los nuevos descubrimientos. En grupos de tres, imagínense cuáles eran las dudas que tenían los españoles a finales del siglo XV cuando oyeron que los Reyes Isabel y Fernando le habían dado dinero a Cristóbal Colón. Usen frases como **dudaban que . . . , era imposible que . . . , no creían que . . . , pensaban que estaba loco porque . . . ,** etc.

Remember: Present or future → present subjunctive or present perfect subjunctive.
Past → imperfect subjunctive.

Nuevos horizontes

Estrategia de lectura: *Timed Reading*

One of the ways of improving your reading speed is by timing yourself when you read. The advantage of this technique is that it forces you not to stop and wonder about individual words. You will have a chance to practice this strategy while you read the selection.

Actividad 12: Mira y contesta

Antes de leer el texto, contesta estas preguntas.

1. ¿Qué piensas que representan las obras de arte de la página 443? ¿Por qué crees que sean tan gordas las personas?
2. ¿Qué crees que quiera expresar el artista?
3. ¿Por qué piensas que se pinta un cuadro o se hace una escultura?

Actividad 13: Lectura veloz

En dos minutos, lee los siguientes textos sobre el artista Fernando Botero. Concéntrate en buscar las ideas principales que se presentan.

FERNANDO BOTERO
Pinturas Dibujos Esculturas

Del 22 de Junio al 15 de Agosto de 1987
Sala A-O

MINISTERIO DE CULTURA
Centro de Arte Reina Sofía
C/. Santa Isabel, 52-28012 MADRID

"Después de haber estado colonizados durante siglos, nosotros los artistas hispanoamericanos sentimos con especial fuerza la necesidad de encontrar nuestra propia autenticidad. El arte ha de ser independiente... Quiero que mi pintura tenga raíces, porque estas raíces son las que dan sentido y verdad a lo que se hace. Pero, al mismo tiempo, no quiero pintar únicamente campesinos sudamericanos. Quiero poder pintar de todo, así también a María Antonieta, pero siempre con la esperanza de que todo lo que toque reciba algo del alma sudamericana..."

Fernando Botero, (1932–   ), realistic and satirical Colombian painter and sculptor, known for his oversized depiction of figures.

Ask students if they have seen any works by this artist and, if so, which ones and where.

Bring in slides or reproductions of works.

Discuss where in the U.S. students can see paintings and sculptures by Hispanic artists.

Esta es la primera gran exposición individual de Fernando Botero en España. Organizada por la Kunsthalle de Munich, se ha exhibido ya en Bremen y Frankfurt, de donde llega a Madrid, ciudad en que finaliza su itinerario.

Junto al casi centenar de obras que integran la exposición itinerante, procedentes de Galerías, Museos y Colecciones privadas de E.E.U.U. y Europa, se presentarán unas 30 obras más entre pinturas, dibujos y esculturas de la colección del artista, que quiere subrayar así la importancia que concede a su exposición en Madrid.

El mundo creado por Botero—nutrido del arte de Piero della Francesca, Velázquez, Rubens, Ingres o Bonard entre otros—es un mundo imaginario, una distorsión poética de lo cotidiano, en donde subyace la realidad latinoamericana que Botero transforma.

Sus temas surgen de las ciudades de su juventud, padres e hijos, curas, monjas, cardenales, militares, etc., que no sólo quedan plasmados en los óleos, sino también en sus monumentales esculturas; "gigantismo" no exento de inocencia que provoca en el espectador una respuesta de acercamiento a su obra, por otro lado difícil de olvidar, ya que la originalidad de su estilo la convierte inmediatamente en reconocible.

Botero ha realizado desde 1951 exposiciones individuales y colectivas, en las más importantes galerías y museos, en muchos de los cuales sus obras se encuentran en la colección permanente.

Los Músicos; Hombre a caballo, Fernando Botero (1932–), Colombia.

Actividad 14: Preguntas

Después de leer el texto, contesta las siguientes preguntas.

1. ¿Dónde está la exposición de las obras de Botero?
2. ¿De dónde son las pinturas de esta exhibición?
3. ¿Qué influencias tuvo este artista?
4. ¿Cuáles son los temas de sus pinturas?
5. Botero dice que "El arte ha de ser *(should be)* independiente." ¿Independiente de qué?

Estrategia de escritura: *Describing a Scene*

To describe a scene for an audience who will not see it, you should look carefully at all the details and make a list of those that are essential to include. A description can include not only the physical characteristics but also the feelings that the scene evokes in you. The idea is to try to recreate a picture using words.

Act. 15: Inform students that this etching **(aguafuerte/ grabado al aguafuerte)** is from *Los caprichos,* a satirical series about corrupt society.

Actividad 15: Descripción de un cuadro

En parejas, observen detenidamente el siguiente grabado *(etching)* de Francisco de Goya. Coméntenlo y luego interpreten la frase que acompaña el grabado. Finalmente escriban un párrafo con una descripción y su interpretación de la frase.

El sueño de la razón produce monstruos, Francisco de Goya.

Lo esencial

La expresión del amor

Y EN EL SUEÑO APRENDEN LA FELICIDAD DE LARGOS INSTANTES DE AMOR.

abrazar/el abrazo

UN BESO QUE PARECE NO ACABAR NUNCA.

besar/el beso

CIERTAMEN- TE NUNCA HA HABIDO ESPOSA TAN TRISTE.

He tenido gran suerte en casarme con Guido. Es muy bueno. Se ocupará de nosotros...

la boda

Amante = lover (of a married person).

Discuss **fotonovelas** and **telenovelas**.

Have students invite each other out on a date and use words such as **cariño,** etc.

Have students gossip and invent stories about romances in the news.

Otras palabras relacionadas con el amor

el/la amante   lover *(usually a negative connotation)*
la aventura amorosa   affair
el cariño   affection
comprometido/a   engaged
el compromiso   engagement
el corazón   heart
divorciarse   to get divorced
el divorcio   divorce
enamorarse de   to fall in love with
feliz   happy
la novia   girlfriend; fiancée
el novio   boyfriend; fiancé
odiar   to hate
la pareja   couple; lovers *(positive connotation)*
pelear   to fight
querer   to love; to want

querido/a, cariño   dear *(terms of endearment)*
salir con   to date
separarse   to separate
ser celoso/a   to be jealous
la soledad   loneliness
tener celos (de)/estar celoso/a (de)   to be jealous (of)

14 de Febrero

Día de los Enamorados

Actividad 16: Opiniones

Lee estas oraciones y marca **sí** o **no.** Después, en grupos de cuatro, comparen las respuestas y coméntenlas.

Act. 16: In #2, the reciprocal **se** is present for recognition only; it will be discussed and practiced in the second part of this chapter.

1. _____ Te enamoras fácilmente.
2. _____ Te molesta ver parejas que se besan y se abrazan en público.
3. _____ Es importante salir con una persona por lo menos un año para conocerla bien antes de casarse.
4. _____ Te gustaría casarte en una iglesia, sinagoga, etc.
5. _____ Para casarse, es más importante que exista amistad que amor.
6. _____ Te casarías con una persona que no supiera besar bien.
7. _____ Es mejor vivir juntos antes de casarse.
8. _____ Muchas parejas se divorcian rápidamente sin intentar solucionar sus problemas.
9. _____ En la televisión hay demasiadas aventuras amorosas y esto no refleja la realidad.
10. _____ Te gusta usar palabras como "cariño", "querido/a" y "mi amor" cuando hablas con tu novio/a.

Explain the saying in #11. If necessary, ask students for an English equivalent. Compare the saying in #12 to, Still waters run deep.

11. _____ El refrán que dice, "Más vale solo que mal acompañado", es verdad.
12. _____ El refrán, "Donde hubo fuego, cenizas *(ashes)* quedan", es verdad.

Actividad 17: La boda

En parejas, Uds. están comprometidos y van a casarse dentro de un mes. Escojan el papel A o B, y lean solamente las instrucciones para su papel. Después conversen según las indicaciones.

Papel A

El fin de semana pasado fuiste a una fiesta sin tu novio/a y conociste a otro/a. Esta persona te gusta muchísimo y has decidido no casarte. Ve a casa de tu novio/a para decirle que no quieres casarte, pero sé diplomático/a para no herir *(hurt)* mucho sus sentimientos.

Papel B

Estás planeando todos los detalles de tu boda y justo en ese momento llega tu novio/a. Pregúntale a quién invitó él/ella y si reservó el salón para la fiesta.

Act. 18: Instruct students to write a brief outline that is concise, yet easy to follow. Set a time limit.

Actividad 18: Una telenovela

Las telenovelas siempre tienen un argumento *(plot)* muy complicado. Aquí tienen Uds. seis personajes que necesitan nombre, profesión y personalidad. En grupos de tres, descríbanlos y escriban una sinopsis breve del argumento de tres episodios de la telenovela para publicarla en una revista. Usen las palabras de la lista **La expresión del amor**.

La pregunta inesperada

Invitar = convidar. Explain that the person who extends the invitation pays.

Mention that *Dutch treat* is sometimes translated as **a la americana.**

Note that **por** implies reason.

invitar	to invite; to treat
por algo será	there must be a reason

Juan Carlos invitó a Claudia a pasar el día en Alcalá de Henares, una pequeña ciudad que está a media hora de Madrid.

Actividad 19: Busca la información

Escucha la conversación y di qué hay en Alcalá de Henares y por qué están allí Juan Carlos y Claudia.

> Claudia   ¿Por qué quisiste venir a Alcalá de Henares? No me dices nada, ¿eh? Tú te andas con unos misterios como si tuvieras algún secreto . . .

Don Quijote, Pablo Ruiz Picasso (1881–1973), España.

Alcalá de Henares: city to the northeast of Madrid, Spain. During the Golden Age, the university was one of the most prestigious in the country. Its students include Tirso de Molina, Quevedo, Lope de Vega, and Calderón de la Barca.

Juan Carlos	Pero, ¿no te parece romántico estar aquí, en el lugar donde nació Cervantes? Si no fuera por él, no habría existido Dulcinea y entonces yo no te podría llamar "mi Dulcinea".
Claudia	Por favor, Juan Carlos, no seas cursi y vamos a almorzar que me estoy muriendo de hambre.
Juan Carlos	Bueno, vamos a comer en la Hostería del Estudiante.
Claudia	¡Uy, uy, uy! ¿A qué se debe tanta elegancia? ¿Qué vamos a celebrar, tu nuevo puesto en Caracas? Supongo que me vas a invitar, ¿no?
Juan Carlos	Claro que te voy a invitar. Si venimos a Alcalá de Henares, por algo será . . .

En la Hostería del Estudiante (después de la comida)

Claudia	La comida estaba deliciosa. ¿Tomamos el café en otro lugar?
Juan Carlos	No, mejor nos quedamos aquí porque quiero hablarte. Claudia . . . este . . . nosotros nos queremos, ¿no?
Claudia	Claro que nos queremos. ¿A qué viene esa pregunta? No sé qué te pasa hoy; estás tan . . . tan no sé qué . . .

Popping the question

Showing disbelief

Hypothesizing

Juan Carlos	Pues es que . . . ya casi se acaba el año . . . y . . . yo me voy a Venezuela y tú te vuelves a Colombia.
Claudia	No me lo recuerdes . . . Pero vamos a estar cerca . . . Vas a ir a visitarme, ¿no?
Juan Carlos	Por supuesto, pero . . . ya nos conocemos desde hace un año y . . . ¿Sabes que mi abuelo le propuso matrimonio a mi abuela aquí mismo hace cincuenta y cuatro años? Y . . . estaba pensando que . . . ¿Por qué no nos casamos tú y yo?
Claudia	¿Cómo! . . . ¿Me estás tomando el pelo?
Juan Carlos	Claudia, ¡por favor! Hablo en serio. Quiero que te cases conmigo, que te vayas a Caracas conmigo y que pasemos el resto de nuestras vidas juntos.
Claudia	Juan Carlos . . .
Los clientes	Si fuera más jóven yo me casaría con él. . . . ¡Di que sí! . . . ¡Contesta que sí! ¡Acepta! . . . ¡No lo hagas sufrir! ¡Cásate!

Actividad 20: ¿Comprendiste?

Después de escuchar la conversación, contesta estas preguntas.

1. ¿Por qué es romántico Alcalá de Henares para Juan Carlos?
2. ¿Qué sabes de Cervantes?
3. ¿Qué van a hacer Juan Carlos y Claudia ahora que casi se acaba el año?
4. ¿Por qué fueron a la Hostería del Estudiante y no a otro restaurante?
5. ¿Va a decir que sí o que no Claudia? ¿Por qué crees eso?
6. En tu opinión, ¿Cómo es Juan Carlos? ¿Romántico? ¿Cursi? ¿Cómo?

¿Lo sabían?

Alcalá de Henares fue un centro cultural muy importante en siglos pasados. Por su universidad pasaron muchas personas famosas, incluyendo al escritor más famoso de la lengua española, Miguel de Cervantes Saavedra. Cervantes escribió *Don Quijote de la Mancha*, la novela cumbre de la literatura española. La figura de Don Quijote representa el idealismo y Sancho Panza, su fiel compañero, el realismo. Del *Quijote* viene la palabra "Dulcinea" que tiene una connotación parecida a la de "Julieta" en inglés.

Actividad 21: Los estereotipos

La gente hispana tiene fama de ser muy romántica. En cambio, los norteamericanos tienen fama de ser fríos y poco apasionados. En grupos de cuatro, hablen sobre esta pregunta: ¿Creen que sean ciertos estos estereotipos? Justifiquen su opinión.

Hacia la comunicación

I. Expressing Hypothetical Situations: The Imperfect Subjunctive and the Conditional

1. The imperfect subjunctive and the conditional tense are used together to express hypothetical situations. Notice in the examples that the **si** clause expresses a contrary-to-fact statement.

Clause stating condition		Conclusion clause
si + imperfect subjunctive	. . .	conditional
Si **fueras** presidente	. . .	¿qué **harías**?
If you were president (but in fact you aren't)	. . .	*what would you do?*

Si yo **viviera** en España, **viajaría** por todas las provincias.	*If I lived in Spain (but I don't), I would visit all the provinces.*
Si **fueras** Claudia, ¿**te casarías** con Juan Carlos?	*If you were Claudia (but you aren't), would you marry Juan Carlos?*

2. *Always* use the imperfect subjunctive after **como si** *(as if)* because it always indicates a contrary-to-fact statement.

Él gasta dinero **como si fuera** rico.	*He spends money as if he were rich (but he isn't rich).*
Te portas **como si estuvieras** enamorado.	*You act as though you were in love (but you aren't).*

3. When **ojalá** is used with the imperfect subjunctive, it has a contrary-to-fact connotation.

¡**Ojalá estuviera** enamorado!	*If only/I wish I were in love (but I'm not).*
¡**Ojalá pudiéramos** ir a Europa!	*If only/I wish we could go to Europe (but we can't).*

After studying the grammar explanation, answer these questions:

- What is the difference in meaning between **Si tengo dinero, iré al cine** and **Si tuviera dinero, iría al cine**?
- How would you say the following sentence in Spanish: *I would (do it) if I could, but I can't, so I won't?*

II. Expressing Reciprocal Actions

Él la besa.

Ella lo besa.

Ellos se besan.

To indicate a reciprocal action, use the reflexive pronouns **nos, os, se** with the corresponding form of the verb. You may use **el uno al otro** *(each other)* for clarification. The phrase **el uno al otro** is changed to agree in gender and number with the nouns being modified. Some common verbs used reciprocally are **abrazar, amar, besar, escribir, mirar, odiar,** and **querer.**

Las amigas **se** escriben (la una a la otra/las unas a las otras) a menudo.

The friends write to each other often.

Cuando entró mamá, **nos** estábamos besando.

When Mom entered, we were kissing (each other).

After studying the grammar explanation, answer this question:

- How many interpretations can you give for the sentence, **Nosotros nos miramos**?

Actividad 22: ¿Qué pasaría?

En parejas, discutan qué pasaría en estas situaciones.

1. si no tuviéramos electricidad
2. si no existiera el teléfono
3. si pudiéramos viajar a través del tiempo
4. si los jóvenes no pudieran mirar la televisión
5. si no existiera una edad mínima para beber en los Estados Unidos
6. si hubiera una mujer como presidenta de los Estados Unidos

Act. 23: Explain the title: **a lo loco** = without rhyme or reason.

Sentences that make any sense whatsoever are valid. The absurd possibilities of this activity will help students understand contrary-to-fact statements.

Actividad 23: A lo loco

En grupos de seis, preparen situaciones hipotéticas. Tres personas lean la Parte A y tres personas lean la Parte B. Sigan las instrucciones.

A

Usen la imaginación y escriban cinco situaciones como las siguientes (cuanto más exageradas las ideas, mejor): Si ganara $100 por hora . . .; Si tuviera un león en casa . . .; Si estuviera en Siberia . . . , etc.

B

Usen la imaginación y escriban cinco resultados como los siguientes (cuanto más exageradas las ideas, mejor): . . . tendría ocho carros, . . . sería feliz, . . . pondría mis zapatos en el armario, etc.

Cuando estén listos, miren todas las frases del grupo y hagan combinaciones para formar oraciones. Compartan las que más les gusten con la clase.

◖●◗   Si estuviera en Siberia, tendría ocho carros.

Actividad 24: La felicidad matrimonial

Explica qué pasa en cada dibujo, usando los verbos que se dan.

gritar   no/hablar/mirar   mirar   mirar

mirar, reír   besar   abrazar   hablar

Act. 25: Explain the title: **Mi media naranja** = my better half (a husband, wife, girlfriend, or boyfriend).

Tell students they can assume a role or answer truthfully.

Actividad 25: Mi media naranja

Tu vida romántica está muy mal últimamente y por eso, decides ir a la agencia "Corazones solitarios" para encontrar a la persona de tus sueños. Tienes que completar un formulario:

Nombre _____

Edad _____

Soltero/a _____ Divorciado/a _____

Fumas: Sí _____ No _____

Intereses: _____

Estás feliz cuando _____

Crees que la inteligencia de una persona es tan importante como su apariencia física.   Sí _____ No _____

Termina estas frases: Si la persona que me selecciona . . .

fuera quince años mayor que yo, _____

tuviera otra religión, _____

fuera mucho más baja que yo, _____

no tuviera dinero, _____

no quisiera hijos, _____

no tuviera estudios universitarios, _____

viviera a más de cinco horas de mi casa, _____

Pienso que una noche perfecta es cuando _____

Act. 26: Set a time limit for each interview. Encourage the interviewer to probe and learn as much as possible about the client.

Actividad 26: La entrevista

En parejas, después de completar el formulario, vas a tener una entrevista con un/a empleado/a de la agencia. Basen la entrevista en las respuestas del formulario de arriba. Después, cambien de papel.

🔊 —Veo que Ud. no fuma. ¿Le molestaría salir con alguien que fume?
   —Sí, me molestaría porque le tengo alergia al cigarrillo.

Vocabulario funcional

La exhibición de arte

Ver página 436–437

Palabras y expresiones útiles

dar a conocer   to make known
en seguida   at once, right away
invitar   to invite; to treat
no veo la hora de + infinitive
  I can't wait + *infinitive*

La expresión del amor

Ver página 445

por algo será   there must be a
  reason

¿Quién era Juan Domingo
Perón?
¿Qué sabes de su primera
esposa, Evita?

Discuss recent changes of government in Hispanic countries.
Bring in headlines from Hispanic
newspapers, if possible. Ask students to name Hispanic leaders,
past and present.

Juan Domingo y Eva Perón (1951), Buenos Aires, Argentina.

Capítulo 18

After studying this chapter, you will have reviewed many of the language functions that you have practiced throughout the book, such as:

- narrating and describing in the past
- discussing past, present, and future intentions
- You will also be able to discuss politics.

- stating one's opinion and giving supporting evidence
- hypothesizing
- agreeing and disagreeing

Toma forma la oposición a Pinochet

Histórico para Venezuela el déficit en su balanza de pago

Dilema sandinista

El gobierno sandinista, agobiado por la inflación más elevada de la historia, pone en vigor severas medidas económicas.

¿Participación o apatía?

Make statements such as, **La energía solar es barata y limpia.** Have students react using **desde luego, por mi parte,** and **al fin y al cabo.**

desde luego	of course
por mi parte	as far as I'm concerned
al fin y al cabo	after all

Se acerca el final del año escolar y el momento de despedirse de los amigos. Claudia y Juan Carlos han decidido casarse y pronto se irán a Colombia donde se celebrará la boda. Ahora Juan Carlos, Álvaro, Diana e Isabel están hablando sobre sus planes para el futuro.

Actividad 1: Preguntas

Escucha la conversación y contesta estas preguntas.

1. ¿Quién no va a ir a la boda y por qué?
2. ¿Qué planes tienen Diana y Marisel?
3. ¿Qué van a hacer de despedida?

Discuss **la tertulia** and the importance of political discussions in daily life.

Indicating future plans

Reporting

Giving an excuse

Describing habitual past actions

Álvaro	Felicitaciones, Juan Carlos. ¿Ya saben vuestros padres que os vais a casar?
Juan Carlos	Desde luego. Anoche los llamamos y les dimos la noticia. Y Uds. van a ir, ¿no, Diana?
Diana	Yo no me perdería tu boda por nada del mundo. Voy a ir a Colombia y después regreso a los Estados Unidos porque no me dan más tiempo libre en el colegio donde enseño, pero regreso a España el verano que viene.
Álvaro	Sí, y Marisel me dijo que también iría a la boda antes de volver definitivamente a Venezuela. ¿Y tú, Isabel?
Isabel	Por mi parte, yo no voy a poder ir porque no tengo plata y mis papás quieren que termine los estudios en España. Siempre se preocupan por la inestabilidad política en Chile.
Juan Carlos	¡Qué pena que no puedas ir! Pero entiendo lo que dices; por la inestabilidad política mis papás insistieron en que yo estudiara fuera de Perú. Cuando había huelgas de estudiantes, a menudo se cancelaban las clases y como yo participaba en los movimientos estudiantiles, ellos siempre estaban preocupados.

Stating reasons

Álvaro	Es lógico que se preocupen. Al fin y al cabo son nuestros padres; pero es que participar en la política te hace sentir que estás haciendo algo para que cambien las cosas.
Diana	En mi país, hoy en día, muchos jóvenes no se preocupan por los asuntos internacionales, pero, en cambio, sí hay interés en asuntos como la ecología. ¿Saben? Mi padre estaba en Berkeley en los años sesenta y siempre cuenta de las manifestaciones estudiantiles que había contra la Guerra de Vietnam.
Isabel	No sé . . . Yo creo que en muchos lugares hay apatía por lo que ocurre en el mundo; a veces por falta de interés, a veces por no tener ni voz ni voto o tal vez porque mucha gente tiene que preocuparse por sobrevivir . . . quién sabe . . . .
Juan Carlos	Bueno, bueno . . . ya es tarde. Recuerden que tenemos la reserva en el restaurante para nuestra comida de despedida. No se olviden de avisarles a Teresa y a Marisel que pasaremos por ellas a las 9:00.

Hay un gran interés en la política entre los jóvenes chilenos. ¿Te interesa a ti la política?

Actividad 2: Preguntas

Después de escuchar la conversación, contesta estas preguntas.

1. ¿Quiénes van a ir a la boda?
2. ¿Por qué se preocupan los padres de Isabel y Juan Carlos?
3. ¿Recientemente, has oído alguna noticia sobre protestas estudiantiles en otros países?
4. ¿Te parece importante participar activamente en la política?
5. Isabel dice que a veces la gente no participa por no tener "ni voz ni voto". ¿Qué crees que significa esta frase?

Act. 3: In many Hispanic countries, as much as 90 percent of the population votes. Point out that in Argentina, for instance, voting is obligatory.

Actividad 3: ¡Felicitaciones!

En grupos de cinco, uno de Uds. es Claudia, y los otros tienen que felicitarla *(congratulate)* y decir si pueden ir a la boda o no. Si dicen que no, tienen que decir por qué.

Actividad 4: La participación del pueblo

En grupos de tres, consideren por qué sólo vota más o menos un 50% de los votantes en las elecciones presidenciales de los Estados Unidos. ¿Qué significa esto para el país? ¿Sería posible hacer el voto obligatorio en los Estados Unidos?

Lo esencial

La política

Toda Europa contra el terrorismo
Juicio a la dictadura en el referéndum uruguayo

El terrorismo y la crisis económica atenazan a Perú

Situaciones políticas y económicas

Associate vocabulary words with people and places. Examples: **la democracia = los Estados Unidos; el dictador = Pinochet.**

la anarquía	el comunismo	el partido (político)
la campaña (electoral)	la democracia	el socialismo
el/la candidato/a	la dictadura	votar
el capitalismo	las elecciones	el voto
el/la ciudadano/a	el fascismo	

If necessary, give English equivalents for **el juez, el alcalde/la alcaldesa, el golpe de estado, la huelga,** and **la manifestación.** Point out that **manifestación** is a false cognate.

Practice vocabulary:
Option 1: Use word association to elicit vocabulary. T: **George Washington** S1: **presidente** T: **el gobierno de Mussolini** S2: **fascismo** (etc.)
Option 2: Ask students to explain the main characteristics of socialism, communism, democracy, fascism, and anarchy. If students have trouble, help them out by associating ideologies with specific countries or leaders: **el fascismo de Franco,** etc.
Option 3: In small groups, have students discuss the latest protest at the university. Ask, **¿Contra qué protestaban? ¿Fueron Uds.? ¿Están de acuerdo o no con la gente que participaba? ¿Por qué sí o no?**

Personas, grupos o ideas relacionados con la política

el/la presidente/a	la libertad de palabra/prensa
el/la primer/a ministro/a	la censura
el/la dictador/a	censurar
el/la congresista	las fuerzas armadas
el congreso	el/la guerrillero/a
el senado	los militares
el/la senador/a	el golpe de estado
la Corte Suprema	la huelga
el/la juez	la manifestación
el/la gobernador/a	la protesta
el alcalde/la alcaldesa	protestar

¿Lo sabían?

En algunos países hispanos, las campañas electorales son relativamente cortas. En España, por ejemplo, las campañas duran solamente tres semanas y terminan veinticuatro horas antes del día de la votación. Este día se llama "día de reflexión" y es ilegal hacer campaña política. ¿Qué opinas de esta idea? ¿Sería posible o conveniente hacer lo mismo en los Estados Unidos?

Actividad 5: ¿Participación o no?

Habla con algunos de tus compañeros para ver si son políticamente activos o no. Usa las preguntas que siguen.

1. ¿Saben los nombres de estas personas?
   un/a congresista o senador/a federal, el/la gobernador/a del estado, el/la secretario/a de defensa, el alcalde/la alcaldesa de la ciudad donde estudian, un/a juez de la Corte Suprema de los Estados Unidos
2. ¿Han hecho estas cosas?
   votar en las últimas elecciones presidenciales, escribir una carta a un/a representante, participar en una campaña política, ir a una manifestación
   si no han hecho estas cosas, ¿las piensan hacer en el futuro?

Actividad 6: La libertad de expresión

En grupos de cuatro, hablen sobre la libertad de prensa y la libertad de palabra que existe en los Estados Unidos. Mencionen las ventajas y desventajas. ¿Creen que un neonazi o una persona de extrema izquierda deba poder hablar libremente? ¿Creen que se debería prohibir a los cantantes cantar canciones llenas de violencia y con referencias a drogas?

Actividad 7: Americanos todos

En grupos de cuatro, hagan una lista de tres cosas específicas que pueden hacer los Estados Unidos para mejorar las relaciones con Hispanoamérica y tres cosas que pueden hacer los países hispanoamericanos para lograr ese mismo objetivo. Tengan en cuenta lo que aprendieron estudiando la lengua española y la cultura hispana en este curso y lo que sepan de noticias recientes.

Hacia la comunicación

This chapter introduces no new grammar points.

The activities that follow provide general review practice.

Act. 8: Comment on any recent political jokes you have heard.

Actividad 8: El humor

En grupos de tres, miren los siguientes chistes *(jokes)* políticos e intenten explicar la ironía.

1. A Maximiliano, el Emperador de México del siglo pasado, lo llamaban los mexicanos, "el Em**peor**ador".
2. En Chile bajo Pinochet, alguien escribió enfrente de una prisión: "Los derechos del hombre son tres: ver, oír y callarse".

© Joaquín Salvador Lavado (Quino), from *Potentes, prepotentes e impotentes*

© Joaquín Salvador Lavado (Quino), from *Potentes, prepotentes e impotentes*

Quino is an Argentine cartoonist famous for his social and political comments.

Actividad 9: El papel de la religión

La constitución de los Estados Unidos dice que hay separación entre la Iglesia y el Estado, pero en las monedas dice *In God We Trust* y cuando una persona se presenta ante un juez comúnmente tiene que poner la mano encima de la Biblia. ¿A qué se debe esto? En grupos de tres, decidan si la religión juega un papel en el gobierno de los Estados Unidos.

¿Lo sabían?

La Iglesia católica es una fuerza activa y participante en la política hispana. Por la importancia de la religión en la vida diaria, los gobiernos tratan de tener buenas relaciones con la Iglesia y, en algunos países, hay una cláusula en la constitución que habla del papel de la Iglesia. Sin embargo, en otros países hay separación entre la Iglesia y el Estado, como por ejemplo en México, donde desde el siglo pasado estos dos poderes son independientes.

Actividad 10: Monolingüe, bilingüe, trilingüe, políglota

Hay gente que dice que es más fácil aprender un idioma de pequeño, en parte porque los niños no tienen miedo de cometer errores. Sin embargo, otros afirman que es mejor aprender cuando uno es adulto porque tiene mejor memoria y mejor habilidad mental. En grupos de cuatro, consideren si es bueno que el estudio de lenguas sea obligatorio en las escuelas primarias. ¿Les gustaría que sus hijos aprendieran una lengua extranjera en la escuela primaria? Hablen también sobre cómo creen que les pueda servir a Uds. su conocimiento de la lengua española en futuros empleos y en la vida en general.

Act. 11: In groups of 3, have students prepare a newscast about recent national or international news. You may want to assign particular news topics ahead of time.

Actividad 11: Problemas del momento

En grupos de tres, hablen sobre estas preguntas:

1. ¿Qué ha hecho el gobierno que les haya afectado personalmente?
2. ¿Cuáles son las responsablilidades del gobierno hacia los ciudadanos en cuanto a la salud, el medio ambiente y la defensa nacional?

Ask students what the American government is doing to combat AIDS.

Act. 12: Make sure both groups have some opinionated and lively students. If there is a controversy on campus, use this as the debate topic instead. Assist students, as needed, while they prepare their argument. Run this as a real debate with time limits or allow just enough time for students to make their points.

As a follow-up activity, have students write a newspaper article about the debate and the points made.

Actividad 12: Un debate

En dos grupos grandes, hagan un debate sobre la violencia y el sexo en los programas de televisión. El Grupo A va a defender la libertad de expresión y el Grupo B piensa que los programas están destruyendo la moral del país y que los más afectados son los niños. Tomen cinco minutos para prepararse antes del debate.

Grupo A

Hay libertad de palabra
Puedes mirar o no mirar los programas
La televisión sólo es un reflejo de la sociedad
(etc.)

Grupo B

Ver la violencia produce violencia
Los niños no saben qué es ficción y qué es realidad
Hay gente que imita lo que ve en los programas
(etc.)

Nuevos horizontes

You may wish to have students apply one or more of these strategies while reading.

Resumen de estrategias de lectura

In this book, you have seen strategies that can help you in your comprehension of a written text. Among other strategies, you have learned to brainstorm before reading to activate your background knowledge, to predict the contents of a passage, to scan a text to look for specific information, to skim a passage to get its basic ideas, as well as to recognize prefixes, suffixes, and false cognates. In this final chapter, apply the strategies you feel would be most helpful as you read the selection.

Actividad 13: Preguntas

Antes de leer el artículo, contesta estas preguntas.

1. ¿Qué movimientos o protestas ha habido en tu universidad este año?
2. ¿Hablas de política con tus amigos?
3. ¿Cuáles son los temas políticos actuales?

Actividad 14: Ideas principales

Lee el artículo sobre política en la próxima página y busca las ideas principales. Luego escribe un título para este artículo.

El Universal   Primera sección   Por Hugo Torres

El Universal is the name of a Mexican newspaper.

Compare the problems the author finds in Hispanic America with those students see in the U.S.

Como todos sabemos, uno de los temas de conversación diaria en los países hispanoamericanos es la política: "¿Viste lo que ocurrió en Chile?" "Con este gobierno no vamos a llegar a ningún lado." "¿Se enteró del golpe de estado en . . . ?" Todos hablamos de política, algunos con más conocimiento del tema, otros con menos, pero todos tenemos algo que decir.

Por un lado están los estudiantes universitarios que, por ser jóvenes, tienen mucha energía e ilusiones de que "las cosas van a cambiar". Los partidos políticos intentan conquistar su simpatía, ya que estos jóvenes serán mañana el futuro de los países. Por otro lado están los escritores como participantes políticos activos, pues ellos influyen en el destino de sus países con sus libros y ensayos que con frecuencia critican la situación actual.

Aunque sea solamente con la palabra y no con actos, todos intentamos arreglar el mundo y predecir su futuro. ¿Y qué futuro le espera a Hispanoamérica? Es muy difícil predecirlo, pero en gran parte dependerá de su situación económica y lo que ocurra con la deuda externa. El pago de esta deuda presiona económicamente a países como México, Perú y Argentina y puede causar inestabilidad no sólo económica sino también política. La inestabilidad política en algunos países ha provocado golpes de estado y dictaduras militares, y también ha motivado a países hermanos a seguir sus pasos. Debido a la inestabilidad política y económica es imposible predecir qué ocurrirá en muchos países tales como Nicaragua y El Salvador, pero sí se puede prever que su recuperación política y económica será dolorosa.

Es momento de que hablemos menos y hagamos más por tratar de solucionar los problemas del mundo hispanoamericano.

Una pareja española se pone al día con las últimas noticias.

Actividad 15: Tus preguntas

Prepara un mínimo de cuatro preguntas sobre el texto, y luego hazles estas preguntas a tus compañeros.

Act. 16: You may want to ask students to do the last step of this activity at home.

Actividad 16: Escritura libre

En grupos de cuatro, imagínense cómo será el mundo en el año 2010 y hagan un *brainstorming* de las diferentes ideas. Luego, individualmente, escoge una idea y escribe libremente sobre esa idea durante diez minutos. Finalmente, escoge las oraciones que prefieres, organízalas y revisa la gramática y puntuación.

La despedida

| dentro de poco | in a while |
| ni siquiera | not even |

Después de un año en España, los amigos se despiden. Hoy Claudia y Juan Carlos salen para Colombia y por eso los chicos están juntos por última vez en la cafetería del aeropuerto.

Actividad 17: Siguiendo el hilo

Escucha la conversación y busca información sobre estos temas.

1. el papel de don Alejandro en la vida de los chicos
2. cómo se siente Isabel y por qué
3. qué le pasa a Isabel

Act. 17: Explain the title: **siguiendo el hilo** = following the story line.

Claudia	Teresa, no te olvides de darle a tu tío las gracias otra vez por toda la ayuda que nos dio a Juan Carlos y a mí este año.
Isabel	De veras, él ha sido como un papá para todos nosotros.
Camarero	¿Van a tomar algo?
Teresa	Sí, a mí tráigame un café, por favor.
Juan Carlos	A mí también, un café. ¿Vas a comer algo, Claudia?
Claudia	No sé, estoy nerviosa. Lo único que quiero es un café con leche.
Teresa	¿Ni siquiera una tostada? Deberías comer algo antes del viaje.
Claudia	Es que no puedo, estoy muy nerviosa.
Isabel	Para mí, también un café. ¡Cómo quisiera ir a tu matrimonio! Pero tú entiendes, ¿no, Claudia? Yo estaré muy cerca de ti ese día con mi pensamiento.
Claudia	Claro que entiendo, pero te voy a echar de menos y tienes que prometerme que cuando regreses a Chile, vas a pasar por Venezuela a visitarnos.
Isabel	Eso sí te lo prometo . . . y por eso, no te voy a decir "adiós" sino "hasta luego".
Teresa	Miren, ahí viene Diana con Álvaro, Marisel y Vicente.
Diana	Ay, casi no llegamos . . . Pero traemos dos botellas de champán para la despedida y un pasaje para Isabel . . .
Isabel	¡Qué? . . . ¿Un pasaje?
Álvaro	Sí, hemos hablado con don Alejandro y entre todos te hemos comprado un pasaje para que puedas ir a la boda.
Isabel	Pero . . . pero . . .
Claudia	¡Qué felicidad! Dentro de poco, estaremos todos juntos otra vez.

Comparing

Expressing a desire

Promising

Discuss the saying, **Hasta luego no es adiós ni hasta mañana tampoco.**

Expressing surprise

Actividad 18: Tus reacciones

Después de escuchar la conversación, contesta estas preguntas.

1. Si estuvieras en un país extranjero, ¿considerarías a un pariente como tu padre?

2. Si fueras Claudia, ¿estarías nervioso/a? ¿Por qué sí o no?
3. ¿Por qué dice Isabel que le va a decir "hasta luego" a Claudia y no "adiós"?
4. Si te despides de una persona querida, ¿prefieres despedirte en el aeropuerto o antes de ir al aeropuerto? ¿Por qué?

Hacia la comunicación

Act. 19: Assign the play as homework, or practice in class. You may want to have all groups or just some present it at an end-of-the-semester party.

Actividad 19: Una obra de teatro

Lean el siguiente minidrama. Luego, en grupos de tres, prepárenlo para hacer una representación en clase. Una persona es ELLA, otra persona es ÉL, y la otra persona es el/la director/a que va a ayudar a los actores a hacer el mejor papel posible. Es importante que Uds. exageren los papeles.

A la luz de la luna
Anónimo

Personajes: Él, Ella, La luna

Acto único

La escena representa un lugar apartado de un parque público, en Madrid. Un banco, a la derecha. Es una noche de luna clarísima de primavera. ELLA, sentada en el banco, lee con un abanico[1] en una mano; hay varios libros al lado, en el banco. Por la izquierda entra ÉL, vestido de viaje. La mira, sonríe, tose[2] . . . y pasa. Ella no lo mira; lee medio

---

1. fan   2. coughs

dormida y bosteza[3] frecuentemente. Al ver que ÉL se va, ELLA suspira[4] y deja caer el libro . . . ÉL, como es muy educado, se detiene, se atusa[5] el bigote, se sonríe otra vez y recoge el libro.

---

3. yawns   4. sighs   5. strokes

ELLA	*(Sorprendida.)* ¡Ah . . . !	ELLA	¿Granada?
ÉL	*(Dándole el libro.)*	ÉL	No.
	¡Ejem . . . !	ELLA	¿Barcelona?
ELLA	Gracias.	ÉL	Sí.
ÉL	Ah . . .	ELLA	¿Negocios?
ELLA	*(Sonríe.)* Ah . . .	ÉL	Sí.
ÉL	*(Indicando el libro.)*	ELLA	¡Bien!
	¿Bueno?	ÉL	¿Contenta?
ELLA	Bastante.	ELLA	Bastante.
ÉL	¿Me quedo?	ÉL	¿Por qué?
ELLA	*(Sorprendida.)* ¿Cómo?	ELLA	Porque . . .
ÉL	¿Me quedo?	ÉL	¡Amo . . .
ELLA	Sí . . .	ELLA	¿Cómo?
ÉL	*(Sentándose.)* Gracias.	ÉL	. . . Luna! *(Señalando la*
ELLA	*(Se abanica.)* ¡Uf . . . !		*luna.)*
ÉL	¿Calor?	ELLA	Ah . . .
ELLA	Mucho.	ÉL	Pues . . .
ÉL	*(Mirando hacia el parque.)*	ELLA	¿Pues?
	¡Bonito!	ÉL	Bonita. *(Mirando la luna,*
ELLA	Sí.		*pero hablándole a ELLA.)*
ÉL	¿Con frecuencia?	ELLA	¡Fresco!
ELLA	Bastante.	ÉL	¡Bonita!
ÉL	¿Dónde . . . ?	ELLA	¿Cómo!
ELLA	¿Cómo . . . ?	ÉL	¡Adorable!
ÉL	¿ . . . vive?	ELLA	¡No!
ELLA	¿Yo?	ÉL	¡Preciosísima!
ÉL	Sí.	ELLA	¡Señor!
ELLA	Cerca.	ÉL	Luna. *(Inocente.)*
ÉL	¿Dónde?	ELLA	¡Ah . . . ! *(Levantándose.)*
ELLA	Ciudad.	ÉL	¿Cómo?
ÉL	¿Dónde?	ELLA	¡Adiós!
ELLA	Allá. *(Los dos se ríen.)*	ÉL	¿Por qué?
ÉL	Ah . . .	ELLA	Casa.
ELLA	¿Usted?	ÉL	¿Por qué?
ÉL	Ciudad.	ELLA	Esposo. *(Coqueta.)*
ELLA	¿Segovia?	ÉL	¡¡¡CARAMBA!!!
ÉL	No.	ELLA	Síííííí . . .

ÉL   ¡Demonios!
ELLA   Sí.
ÉL   ¡Cielos!
ELLA   No.
ÉL   ¿Qué . . . ?
ELLA   Chiste.
ÉL   ¡Ah . . . !
ELLA   Mire . . .
ÉL   ¿Qué?
ELLA   Luna.
ÉL   ¿Nueva?
ELLA   Sí.
ÉL   Yo . . .
ELLA   Ah . . .
ÉL   . . . amo . . .
ELLA   ¿Luna?
ÉL   ¡¡No!!
ELLA   ¿A quién? *(Coqueta.)*
ÉL   ¡A usted!
ELLA   ¡Cómo!
ÉL   ¡A ti!
ELLA   Aaaah . . .
ÉL   ¿Cómo?
ELLA   Adiós.
ÉL   No.
ELLA   Sí.
ÉL   ¿Por qué?
ELLA   Tarde.
ÉL   ¿A casa?
ELLA   Necesario.
ÉL   ¡Quédate!
ELLA   No puedo.
ÉL   ¿Por qué?
ELLA   Madre.
ÉL   Aaaah . . .
ELLA   Síííí . . .
ÉL   Yo . . .
ELLA   ¿Cómo?
ÉL   . . . voy . . .
ELLA   ¿Cómo?

ÉL   . . . contigo.
ELLA   ¡¡NO!!
ÉL   ¿Por qué?
ELLA   Padre.
ÉL   ¿Cruel?
ELLA   Sí.
ÉL   Oh.
ELLA   Sí.
ÉL   Mira . . .
ELLA   ¿Qué?
ÉL   Luna.
ELLA   Magnífica.
ÉL   Y tú.
ELLA   Estupenda.
ÉL   Como tú.
ELLA   Preciosa.
ÉL   ¡Divina!
ELLA   ¿Luna?
ÉL   ¡No!
ELLA   ¿Quién?
ÉL   ¡Tú!
ELLA   Ah . . .
ÉL   ¿Mañana?
ELLA   ¿Cómo?
ÉL   ¿Vendrás?
ELLA   ¿Y usted?
ÉL   Sí.
ELLA   Pues . . .
ÉL   ¿Vendrás?
ELLA   Tal vez.
ÉL   ¿¿¿Cómo???
ELLA   Sí.
ÉL   ¡¡Ah!!
ELLA   ¿Contento?
ÉL   ¡Muchísimo!
ELLA   Pues . . .
ÉL   ¿Pues?
ELLA   ¿Hasta . . .
ÉL   . . . mañana?

Have students discuss the role of **la luna** in the drama.

Discuss why she insists on using **Ud.** while he uses **tú.**

(ÉL sale por la derecha y ELLA sale por la izquierda.)
FIN

Actividad 20: Análisis

En grupos de tres, hablen sobre el juego que hay entre los dos personajes del drama: ¿Cuáles son algunos adjetivos que describen a los personajes? ¿Conocen a algunas personas que actúen así en la vida real? ¿Creen que cuando una persona sale con otra exista a veces un juego? Si contestan que sí, ¿hay reglas *(rules)* para este juego? ¿Cuáles son? ¿Eran estas reglas iguales para sus padres?

Actividad 21: A la luz de la luna II

Act. 21: Have students present their written work in class or hand it in to be checked as a major composition. You may want to count this as part of their final-exam grade. If used as part of the final, have students complete the work individually.

En parejas, después de haber presentado el drama, escojan una de estas actividades.

1. Reescriban una parte de la conversación extendiendo las líneas para incluir frases u oraciones completas sin cambiar el tono del diálogo.
2. Con frases u oraciones completas, escriban la escena del encuentro de la noche siguiente en el parque.
3. Escriban una escena donde él conoce a los padres de ella. Usen frases u oraciones completas. Recuerden cómo son los padres de ella.
4. Escriban una escena que tenga lugar veinte años más tarde cuando ellos les explican a sus hijos cómo se conocieron.

Actividad 22: Tu futuro

Contesta estas preguntas y después compara y comenta tus respuestas con las de un/a compañero/a.

1. Di cinco cosas que quieres hacer antes de tener cincuenta años.
2. Di una cosa que tus padres quieren que hagas, pero que no piensas hacer. Di por qué.
3. Di una cosa que has hecho que sea poco común.
4. Di algo que nunca harías en tu vida.

Actividad 23: Preparación necesaria

Contesta las siguientes preguntas y luego, en parejas, hablen sobre sus metas *(goals)* para el futuro, la preparación que ya tienen y denle sugerencias a la otra persona sobre otras cosas que puede hacer para estar mejor preparada.

1. ¿Qué estarás haciendo en el año 2005?
2. ¿Qué cosas ya has hecho que te preparen para tu futuro?
3. ¿Qué estás haciendo ahora mismo para prepararte?
4. ¿Qué necesitas hacer todavía?

Act. 24: When students finish the pair work, make a master list of the class's responses.

Actividad 24: No lo sabía antes

Escribe diez cosas que aprendiste en esta clase que no tengan nada que ver con la lengua española. Puedes incluir datos históricos, costumbres, diferencias entre países, etc. Después, en parejas, comparen y comenten las listas.

Vocabulario funcional

Situaciones políticas y económicas

Ver página 458

Personas, grupos o ideas relacionadas con la política

Ver página 459

el alcalde/la alcaldesa mayor
el golpe de estado coup d'état
la huelga strike

el/la juez judge
la manifestación demonstration

Palabras y expresiones útiles

al fin y al cabo after all
dentro de poco in a while
desde luego of course

ni siquiera not even
por mi parte as far as I'm concerned

Reference Section

Appendix A: Verb Charts

Note: In the sections on stem-changing and spelling-changing verbs, only tenses in which a change occurs are shown.

Regular verbs

Infinitive	hablar	comer	vivir
Present participle	hablando	comiendo	viviendo
Past participle	hablado	comido	vivido

Simple tenses

	hablar	comer	vivir
Present indicative	habl**o**	com**o**	viv**o**
	as	**es**	**es**
	a	**e**	**e**
	amos	**emos**	**imos**
	áis	**éis**	**ís**
	an	**en**	**en**
Imperfect indicative	habl**aba**	com**ía**	viv**ía**
	abas	**ías**	**ías**
	aba	**ía**	**ía**
	ábamos	**íamos**	**íamos**
	abais	**íais**	**íais**
	aban	**ían**	**ían**
Preterit	habl**é**	com**í**	viv**í**
	aste	**iste**	**iste**
	ó	**ió**	**ió**
	amos	**imos**	**imos**
	asteis	**isteis**	**isteis**
	aron	**ieron**	**ieron**
Future indicative	hablar**é**	comer**é**	vivir**é**
	ás	**ás**	**ás**
	á	**á**	**á**
	emos	**emos**	**emos**
	éis	**éis**	**éis**
	án	**án**	**án**

	hablar	comer	vivir
Conditional	hablar**ía**	comer**ía**	vivir**ía**
	ías	**ías**	**ías**
	ía	**ía**	**ía**
	íamos	**íamos**	**íamos**
	íais	**íais**	**íais**
	ían	**ían**	**ían**
Affirmative and negative commands	**tú:** habl**a**, no habl**es**	com**e**, no com**as**	viv**e**, no viv**as**
	Ud.: habl**e**, no habl**e**	com**a**, no com**a**	viv**a**, no viv**a**
	Uds.: habl**en**, no habl**en**	com**an**, no com**an**	viv**an**, no viv**an**
	vosotros, -as: habl**ad**, no habl**éis**	com**ed**, no com**áis**	viv**id**, no viv**áis**
Present subjunctive	que habl**e**	que com**a**	que viv**a**
	es	**as**	**as**
	e	**a**	**a**
	emos	**amos**	**amos**
	éis	**áis**	**áis**
	en	**an**	**an**
Imperfect subjunctive	que habl**ara**	que com**iera**	que viv**iera**
	aras	**ieras**	**ieras**
	ara	**iera**	**iera**
	áramos	**iéramos**	**iéramos**
	arais	**ierais**	**ierais**
	aran	**ieran**	**ieran**

Compound tenses

	hablar	comer	vivir
Present perfect indicative	he hablado	he comido	he vivido
	has hablado, *etc.*	has comido, *etc.*	has vivido, *etc.*
Pluperfect indicative	había hablado	había comido	había vivido
	habías hablado, *etc.*	habías comido, *etc.*	habías vivido, *etc.*
Future perfect	habré hablado	habré comido	habré vivido
	habrás hablado, *etc.*	habrás comido, *etc.*	habrás vivido, *etc.*
Conditional perfect	habría hablado	habría comido	habría vivido
	habrías hablado, *etc.*	habrías comido, *etc.*	habrías vivido, *etc.*
Present perfect subjunctive	que haya hablado	que haya comido	que haya vivido
	que hayas hablado, *etc.*	que hayas comido, *etc.*	que hayas vivido, *etc.*
Pluperfect subjunctive	que hubiera hablado	que hubiera comido	que hubiera vivido
	que hubieras hablado, *etc.*	que hubieras comido, *etc.*	que hubieras vivido, *etc.*

Stem-changing verbs

	-ar verbs: **e > ie**		**-er** verbs: **e > ie**	
Infinitive	**pensar** to think		**entender** to understand	
Present indicative	**pienso**	pensamos	**entiendo**	entendemos
	piensas	penséis	**entiendes**	entendéis
	piensa	**piensan**	**entiende**	**entienden**
Affirmative commands	**piensa**	pensad	**entiende**	entended
	piense	**piensen**	**entienda**	**entiendan**
Present subjunctive	que **piense**	pensemos	que **entienda**	entendamos
	pienses	penséis	**entiendas**	entendáis
	piense	**piensen**	**entienda**	**entiendan**

	-ar verbs: **o > ue**		**-er** verbs: **o > ue**	
Infinitive	**contar** to count		**volver** to return	
Present indicative	**cuento**	contamos	**vuelvo**	volvemos
	cuentas	contáis	**vuelves**	volvéis
	cuenta	**cuentan**	**vuelve**	**vuelven**
Affirmative commands	**cuenta**	contad	**vuelve**	volved
	cuente	**cuenten**	**vuelva**	**vuelvan**
Present subjunctive	que **cuente**	contemos	que **vuelva**	volvamos
	cuentes	contéis	**vuelvas**	volváis
	cuente	**cuenten**	**vuelva**	**vuelvan**

	-ir verbs: **e > i**	
Infinitive	**servir** to serve	
Present participle	**sirviendo**	
Present indicative	**sirvo**	servimos
	sirves	servís
	sirve	**sirven**
Affirmative commands	**sirve**	servid
	sirva	**sirvan**
Present subjunctive	que **sirva**	**sirvamos**
	sirvas	**sirváis**
	sirva	**sirvan**
Preterit	serví	servimos
	serviste	servisteis
	sirvió	**sirvieron**
Imperfect subjunctive	que **sirviera**	
	sirvieras, *etc.*	

	-ir verbs: **e > ie** or **i**		-ir verbs: **o > ue** or **u**	
Infinitive	**sentir** to regret, to feel		**dormir** to sleep	
Present participle	**sintiendo**		**durmiendo**	
Present indicative	**siento**	sentimos	**duermo**	dormimos
	sientes	sentís	**duermes**	dormís
	siente	**sienten**	**duerme**	**duermen**
Affirmative commands	**siente**	sentid	**duerme**	dormid
	sienta	**sientan**	**duerma**	**duerman**
Present subjunctive	que **sienta**	**sintamos**	que **duerma**	**durmamos**
	sientas	**sintáis**	**duermas**	**durmáis**
	sienta	**sientan**	**duerma**	**duerman**
Preterit	sentí	sentimos	dormí	dormimos
	sentiste	sentisteis	dormiste	dormisteis
	sintió	**sintieron**	**durmió**	**durmieron**
Imperfect subjunctive	que **sintiera**		que **durmiera**	
	sintieras, *etc.*		**durmieras,** *etc.*	

Verbs with spelling changes

	Verbs in **-car:** c > **qu** before **e**		Verbs in **-gar:** g > **gu** before **e**	
Infinitive	**buscar** to look for		**llegar** to arrive	
Preterit	**busqué**	buscamos	**llegué**	llegamos
	buscaste	buscasteis	llegaste	llegasteis
	buscó	buscaron	llegó	llegaron
Affirmative commands	busca	buscad	llega	llegad
	busque	**busquen**	**llegue**	**lleguen**
Present subjunctive	que **busque**	**busquemos**	que **llegue**	**lleguemos**
	busques	**busquéis**	**llegues**	**lleguéis**
	busque	**busquen**	**llegue**	**lleguen**

	Verbs in **-ger** and **-gir**: g > j before **a** and **o**		Verbs in **-guir**: gu > g before **a** and **o**	
Infinitive	**coger** to pick up		**seguir** to follow	
Present indicative	**cojo**	cogemos	**sigo**	seguimos
	coges	cogéis	sigues	seguís
	coge	cogen	sigue	siguen
Affirmative commands	coge	coged	sigue	seguid
	coja	**cojan**	**siga**	**sigan**
Present subjunctive	que **coja**	**cojamos**	que **siga**	**sigamos**
	cojas	**cojáis**	**sigas**	**sigáis**
	coja	**cojan**	**siga**	**sigan**

	Verbs in **-zar**: z > c before **e**	
Infinitive	**empezar** to begin	
Preterit	**empecé**	empezamos
	empezaste	empezasteis
	empezó	empezaron
Affirmative commands	empieza	empezad
	empiece	**empiecen**
Present subjunctive	que **empiece**	**empecemos**
	empieces	**empecéis**
	empiece	**empiecen**

	Verbs in **-eer**: unstressed i > y	
Infinitive	**creer** to believe	
Present participle	**creyendo**	
Preterit	creí	creímos
	creíste	creísteis
	creyó	**creyeron**
Imperfect subjunctive	que **creyera**	**creyéramos**
	creyeras	**creyerais**
	creyera	**creyeran**

Irregular verbs

	caer to fall	**conducir** to drive
Present indicative	caigo, caes, cae, caemos, caéis, caen	conduzco, conduces, conduce, conducimos, conducís, conducen
Preterit	caí, caíste, cayó, caímos, caísteis, cayeron	conduje, condujiste, condujo, condujimos, condujisteis, condujeron
Imperfect	caía, caías, *etc.*	conducía, conducías, *etc.*
Future	caeré, caerás, *etc.*	conduciré, conducirás, *etc.*
Conditional	caería, caerías, *etc.*	conduciría, conducirías, *etc.*
Present subjunctive	que caiga, caigas, caiga, caigamos, caigáis, caigan	que conduzca, conduzcas, conduzca, conduzcamos, conduzcáis, conduzcan
Imperfect subjunctive	que cayera, cayeras, cayera, cayéramos, cayerais, cayeran	que condujera, condujeras, condujera, condujéramos, condujerais, condujeran
Participles	cayendo, caído	conduciendo, conducido
Affirmative commands	cae, caed caiga, caigan	conduce, conducid conduzca, conduzcan

	conocer to know, be acquainted with	**dar** to give
Present indicative	conozco, conoces, conoce, conocemos, conocéis, conocen	doy, das, da, damos, dais, dan
Preterit	conocí, conociste, conoció, conocimos, conocisteis, conocieron	di, diste, dio, dimos, disteis, dieron
Imperfect	conocía, conocías, *etc.*	daba, dabas, *etc.*
Future	conoceré, conocerás, *etc.*	daré, darás, *etc.*
Conditional	conocería, conocerías, *etc.*	daría, darías, *etc.*
Present subjunctive	que conozca, conozcas, conozca, conozcamos, conozcáis, conozcan	que dé, des, dé, demos, deis, den
Imperfect subjunctive	que conociera, conocieras, conociera, conociéramos, conocierais, conocieran	que diera, dieras, diera, diéramos, dierais, dieran
Participles	conociendo, conocido	dando, dado
Affirmative commands	conoce, conoced conozca, conozcan	da, dad dé, den

	decir to say	**estar** to be
Present indicative	digo, dices, dice, decimos, decís, dicen	estoy, estás, está, estamos, estáis, están
Preterit	dije, dijiste, dijo, dijimos, dijisteis, dijeron	estuve, estuviste, estuvo, estuvimos, estuvisteis, estuvieron
Imperfect	decía, decías, *etc.*	estaba, estabas, *etc.*
Future	diré, dirás, *etc.*	estaré, estarás, *etc.*
Conditional	diría, dirías, *etc.*	estaría, estarías, *etc.*
Present subjunctive	que diga, digas, diga, digamos, digáis, digan	que esté, estés, esté, estemos, estéis, estén
Imperfect subjunctive	que dijera, dijeras, dijera, dijéramos, dijerais, dijeran	que estuviera, estuvieras, estuviera, estuviéramos, estuvierais, estuvieran
Participles	diciendo, dicho	estando, estado
Affirmative commands	di, decid diga, digan	está, estad esté, estén

	haber to have	**hacer** to make, to do
Present indicative	he, has, ha, hemos, habéis, han	hago, haces, hace, hacemos, hacéis, hacen
Preterit	hube, hubiste, hubo, hubimos, hubisteis, hubieron	hice, hiciste, hizo, hicimos, hicisteis, hicieron
Imperfect	había, habías, *etc.*	hacía, hacías, *etc.*
Future	habré, habrás, *etc.*	haré, harás, *etc.*
Conditional	habría, habrías, *etc.*	haría, harías, *etc.*
Present subjunctive	que haya, hayas, haya, hayamos, hayáis, hayan	que haga, hagas, haga, hagamos, hagáis, hagan
Imperfect subjunctive	que hubiera, hubieras, hubiera, hubiéramos, hubierais, hubieran	que hiciera, hicieras, hiciera, hiciéramos, hicierais, hicieran
Participles	habiendo, habido	haciendo, hecho
Affirmative commands	———	haz, haced haga, hagan

	construir to build	**ir** to go
Present indicative	construyo, construyes, construye, construimos, construís, construyen	voy, vas, va, vamos, vais, van
Preterit	construí, construiste, construyó, construimos, construisteis, construyeron	fui, fuiste, fue, fuimos, fuisteis, fueron
Imperfect	construía, construías, *etc.*	iba, ibas, íbamos, íbais, iban
Future	construiré, construirás, *etc.*	iré, irás, *etc.*
Conditional	construiría, construirías, *etc.*	iría, irías, *etc.*
Present subjunctive	que construya, construyas, construya, construyamos, construyáis, construyan	que vaya, vayas, vaya, vayamos, vayáis, vayan
Imperfect subjunctive	que construyera, construyeras, construyera, construyéramos, construyerais, construyeran	que fuera, fueras, fuera, fuéramos, fuerais, fueran
Participles	construyendo, construido	yendo, ido
Affirmative commands	construye, construid construya, construyan	ve, id vaya, vayan

	oír to hear	**poder** to be able, can
Present indicative	oigo, oyes, oye, oímos, oís, oyen	puedo, puedes, puede, podemos, podéis, pueden
Preterit	oí, oíste, oyó, oímos, oísteis, oyeron	pude, pudiste, pudo, pudimos, pudisteis, pudieron
Imperfect	oía, oías, *etc.*	podía, podías, *etc.*
Future	oiré, oirás, *etc.*	podré, podrás, *etc.*
Conditional	oiría, oirías, *etc.*	podría, podrías, *etc.*
Present subjunctive	que oiga, oigas, oiga, oigamos, oigáis, oigan	que pueda, puedas, pueda, podamos, podáis, puedan
Imperfect subjunctive	que oyera, oyeras, oyera, oyéramos, oyerais, oyeran	que pudiera, pudieras, pudiera, pudiéramos, pudierais, pudieran
Participles	oyendo, oído	pudiendo, podido
Affirmative commands	oye, oíd oiga, oigan	———

	poner to put	**querer** to wish, to love
Present indicative	pongo, pones, pone, ponemos, ponéis, ponen	quiero, quieres, quiere, queremos, queréis, quieren
Preterit	puse, pusiste, puso, pusimos, pusisteis, pusieron	quise, quisiste, quiso, quisimos, quisisteis, quisieron
Imperfect	ponía, ponías, *etc.*	quería, querías, *etc.*
Future	pondré, pondrás, *etc.*	querré, querrás, *etc.*
Conditional	pondría, pondrías, *etc.*	querría, querrías, *etc.*
Present subjunctive	que ponga, pongas, ponga, pongamos, pongáis, pongan	que quiera, quieras, quiera, queramos, queráis, quieran
Imperfect subjunctive	que pusiera, pusieras, pusiera, pusiéramos, pusierais, pusieran	que quisiera, quisieras, quisiera, quisiéramos, quisierais, quisieran
Participles	poniendo, puesto	queriendo, querido
Affirmative commands	pon, poned ponga, pongan	quiere, quered quiera, quieran

	saber to know (how)	**salir** to leave
Present indicative	sé, sabes, sabe, sabemos, sabéis, saben	salgo, sales, sale, salimos, salís, salen
Preterit	supe, supiste, supo, supimos, supisteis, supieron	salí, saliste, salió, salimos, salisteis, salieron
Imperfect	sabía, sabías, *etc.*	salía, salías, *etc.*
Future	sabré, sabrás, *etc.*	saldré, saldrás, *etc.*
Conditional	sabría, sabrías, *etc.*	saldría, saldrías, *etc.*
Present subjunctive	que sepa, sepas, sepa, sepamos, sepáis, sepan	que salga, salgas, salga, salgamos, salgáis, salgan
Imperfect subjunctive	que supiera, supieras, supiera, supiéramos, supierais, supieran	que saliera, salieras, saliera, saliéramos, salierais, salieran
Participles	sabiendo, sabido	saliendo, salido
Affirmative commands	sabe, sabed sepa, sepan	sal, salid salga, salgan

	ser to be	**tener** to have
Present indicative	soy, eres, es, somos, sois, son	tengo, tienes, tiene, tenemos, tenéis, tienen
Preterit	fui, fuiste, fue, fuimos, fuisteis, fueron	tuve, tuviste, tuvo, tuvimos, tuvisteis, tuvieron
Imperfect	era, eras, era, éramos, erais, eran	tenía, tenías, *etc.*
Future	seré, serás, *etc.*	tendré, tendrás, *etc.*
Conditional	sería, serías, *etc.*	tendría, tendrías, *etc.*
Present subjunctive	que sea, seas, sea, seamos, seáis, sean	que tenga, tengas, tenga, tengamos, tengáis, tengan
Imperfect subjunctive	que fuera, fueras, fuera, fuéramos, fuerais, fueran	que tuviera, tuvieras, tuviera, tuviéramos, tuvierais, tuvieran
Participles	siendo, sido	teniendo, tenido
Affirmative commands	sé, sed sea, sean	ten, tened tenga, tengan

	traer to bring	**valer** to be worth
Present indicative	traigo, traes, trae,	valgo, vales, vale,
	traemos, traéis, traen	valemos, valéis, valen
Preterit	traje, trajiste, trajo,	valí, valiste, valió,
	trajimos, trajisteis, trajeron	valimos, valisteis, valieron
Imperfect	traía, traías, *etc.*	valía, valías, *etc.*
Future	traeré, traerás, *etc.*	valdré, valdrás, *etc.*
Conditional	traería, traerías, *etc.*	valdría, valdrías, *etc.*
Present subjunctive	que traiga, traigas, traiga,	que valga, valgas, valga,
	traigamos, traigáis, traigan	valgamos, valgáis, valgan
Imperfect subjunctive	que trajera, trajeras, trajera,	que valiera, valieras, valiera,
	trajéramos, trajerais, trajeran	valiéramos, valierais, valieran
Participles	trayendo, traído	valiendo, valido
Affirmative commands	trae, traed	val, valed
	traiga, traigan	valga, valgan

	venir to come	**ver** to see
Present indicative	vengo, vienes, viene,	veo, ves, ve,
	venimos, venís, vienen	vemos, veis, ven
Preterit	vine, viniste, vino,	vi, viste, vio,
	vinimos, vinisteis, vinieron	vimos, visteis, vieron
Imperfect	venía, venías, *etc.*	veía, veías, veía,
		veíamos, veíais, veían
Future	vendré, vendrás, *etc.*	veré, verás, *etc.*
Conditional	vendría, vendrías, *etc.*	vería, verías, *etc.*
Present subjunctive	que venga, vengas, venga,	que vea, veas, vea,
	vengamos, vengáis, vengan	veamos, veáis, vean
Imperfect subjunctive	que viniera, vinieras, viniera,	que viera, vieras, viera,
	viniéramos, vinierais, vinieran	viéramos, vierais, vieran
Participles	viniendo, venido	viendo, visto
Affirmative commands	ven, venid	ve, ved
	venga, vengan	vea, vean

Reflexive verbs

	levantarse to get up
Present indicative	me levanto, te levantas, se levanta
	nos levantamos, os levantáis, se levantan
Participles	levantándose, levantado
Affirmative **tú:**	levántate, no te levantes
and negative **Ud.:**	levántese, no se levante
commands **Uds.:**	levántense, no se levanten
vosotros, -as:	levantaos, no os levantéis

Appendix B: Answers to Grammar Questions

Chapter 1, page 20

I.   • El se llama = *His name is.* Ella se llama = *Her name is.*
   • Me llamo . . . /Soy . . .
   • ¿Cómo te llamas? / ¿Cómo se llama Ud.?
   • ¿Cómo se llama Ud.?

Chapter 1, page 21

II.   • ¿De dónde eres?
   • ¿De dónde es Ud.?
   • Mi madre es de . . .
   • Mi novio/novia es de . . .

Chapter 1, page 31

III.   • a. ¿De dónde eres?; ¿De dónde es Ud.? b. ¿Eres de Lima/Caracas . . . ?;
   ¿Es Ud. de Lima/Caracas . . . ? Eres de Lima/Caracas . . . ¿no?; Ud. es de
   Lima/Caracas . . . ¿no? c. Eres de Quito, ¿no?/¿verdad?; Ud. es de Quito,
   ¿no?/¿verdad?; ¿Eres de Quito?; ¿Es Ud. de Quito?
   • Sí, son de Guatemala.; No, no son de Guatemala.; No, son de . . .

Chapter 2, page 44

II.   • Tengo/tenemos radio.
   • Tenemos televisor.
   • ¿Tiene Ud. estéreo?
   • Mis amigos no tienen radiorreloj.

Chapter 2, page 44

II.   • 's = de
   • El disco es de Carlos; El disco es del Sr. González; El disco es de la Srta.
   López; El disco es de los estudiantes.
   • ¿De quién/es es la toalla?
   • ¿De quién/es son las plantas?

Chapter 2, page 45

III.   • Me gusta la revista; Me gustan los periódicos de Nueva York; Me gusta el
   vídeo; Me gusta el estéreo de Carmen.

Chapter 2, page 45

II.   • A Raúl no le gusta la novela. A Raúl no le gustan las novelas.
   • You (sir, madam) like tea; John/he likes tea; Ann/she likes tea.
   • A Tomás le gusta la música.
   • Al señor Porta le gusta la Coca-Cola y a la señora Bert no (le gusta la
   Coca-Cola).

Chapter 2, page 57

   • Alvaro is referring to a future action.

Chapter 3, page 83

I. • Carmen está cansada.
    • ¿Cómo es ella? = *What is she like?* ¿Cómo está ella? = *How is she (feeling, doing)?*
    • Use **ser** with generous, courageous, interesting, honest. Use **estar** with upset, elated.

Chapter 6, page 166

I. • **Les** refers to Olga and Nando; **Le** refers to nadie; **Les** refers to Olga and Nando.
    • No.

Chapter 7, page 192

I. • a. las botellas; b. el niño; c. el ron
    • No, they receive the action.
    • ¿Dónde las pongo?

Chapter 8, page 205

I. • No.
    • What the women are looking for.

Chapter 8, page 220

I. • *Two:* yo, tú; *Two:* tú, yo.
    • que

Chapter 9, page 234

I. • Possibility
    • Certainty

Chapter 10, page 262

II. • **Te** refers to **tú** (the mother) and **la** refers to **la tarjeta. Te** refers to **tú (Vicente)** and **lo** refers to **el regalo.**

Chapter 10, page 275

I. • Habitual actions in the past

Chapter 11, page 288

I. • One action in progress interrupted by another.
    • a. Telling time in the past. b. Telling age in the past. c. Describing in the past (weather). d. Habitual or repeated action in the past.

Chapter 11, page 302

II. • The woman
    • ¿Lo compraste al fin?

Chapter 12, page 316

I. • a. jugaba c. íbamos d. salían, hacían, bailaban e. jugaba, estudiaba f. pensaba *Words that help:* c. todos los días d. siempre e. mientras

Chapter 12, page 330

II. • In my family, the youngest is the tallest.
    • En mi familia, el menor es el más alto.

Chapter 13, page 355
II.   • Escuchen, regresen.

Chapter 14, page 368
I.   • He is giving a command and he is using the **tú** form.

Chapter 14, page 379
I.   • He is refering to **los grupos**

Chapter 15, page 394
I.   • The first sentence

Chapter 15, page 403
I.   • Había salido *happened first.*

Chapter 16, page 415
I.   • Tengo que/Voy a tener que volver pronto. Sí, es/va a ser mejor que lleguemos pronto.

Chapter 16, page 417
III.   • First title: Whatever is good, whatever is bad and whatever is ugly. Second title: The good one, the bad one and the ugly one.

Chapter 17, page 438
I.   • a. Doubt in the present vs. doubt in the past. b. Influence (wish) in the present vs. influence in the past

Chapter 17, page 451
II.   • We look at ourselves. We look at each other. We looked at ourselves. We looked at each other.

Appendix C: Accentuation and Syllabication

Diphthongs

1. A diphthong is the combination of a weak (i, u) and a strong vowel (a, e, o) or the combination of two weak vowels. When two vowels are combined, the strong or the second of two weak vowels takes a slightly greater stress in the syllable:

   vuelvo   *a*utomático   tiene   conciencia   ciudad

2. When the stress of the word falls on the weak vowel of a strong-weak combination, no diphthong occurs and the weak vowel takes a written accent mark to break the diphthong:

   pa-ís   dí-a   tí-o   en-ví-o

Stress

1. If a word ends in **n, s** or a **vowel,** the stress falls on the *next-to-last syllable.*

   lava**pla**tos   e**xa**men   **ho**la   aparta**men**to

2. If a word ends in any **consonant** other than **n** or **s,** the stress falls on the *last syllable.*

   espa**ñol**   us**ted**   regu**lar**   prohi**bir**

3. Any exception to rules 1 and 2 has a written accent mark on the stressed vowel.

   televisi**ó**n   tel**é**fono   **á**lbum   cent**í**metro

4. Question and exclamation words, **cómo, dónde, cuál, qué,** etc., always have accents.

5. Certain words change meaning when written with an accent although pronunciation remains the same.

cómo	how	como	like	sí	yes	si	if
dé	give	de	of/from	sólo	only	solo	alone
él	he/him	el	the	té	tea	te	you
más	more	mas	but	tú	you	tu	your
mí	me	mi	my				

6. Demonstrative pronouns have a written accent to distinguish them from demonstrative adjectives (except for **esto, eso,** and **aquello,** which are always neuter pronouns).

   éste   este niño   éstas   estas blusas

Syllabication

1. Syllables usually end in a vowel.

   ca-sa   ba-su-ra   dro-ga

2. A diphthong is never separated unless the stress of the word falls on the weak vowel of a strong-weak vowel combination.

   a-mue-blar   ciu-dad   ju-lio   BUT: dí-a

3. Two consonants are usually separated. Remember that **ch, ll** and **rr** are each a single consonant in Spanish.

   al-qui-ler   por-te-ro   ca-le-fac-ción   BUT: pe-rro

4. The consonants **l** and **r** are never separated from the preceding consonant, except from the letter **s.**

   po-si-ble   a-cla-rar   a-bri-go   BUT: ais-lar

5. When there is a cluster of three consonants, the first two stay with the preceding vowel unless the third consonant is an **l** or an **r,** in which case the last two consonants stay with the vowel that follows.

   ins-ti-tu-ción   BUT: ex-pli-car   des-crip-ción

6. When there is a cluster of four consonants, they are always divided between the second and third consonants.

   ins-crip-ción   ins-truc-ción

Spanish-English Vocabulary

This vocabulary includes both the active and passive vocabulary found throughout the lessons. The definitions are limited to the context in which the words are used in the book. Active words are followed by a number that indicates the chapter in which the word appears as an active item; the abbreviation Pre. refers to the *Capítulo preliminar*. Names of cities, countries and other obvious cognates have been eliminated.

The following abbreviations are used:

adj. adjective	*inf.* infinitive	*subj.* subjunctive
adv. adverb	*m.* masculine	*v.* verb
f. feminine		

a to; at; **al (a+el)/a la** to the; **A la/s . . .** At . . . o'clock 5; ~ **lo mejor** perhaps 10; ~ **menudo** often 12; ~ **partir de** starting from; ~ **pesar de que** in spite of; ¿~ **qué hora . . . ?** At what time . . . ? 5; ¿ ~ **quién?** to whom; ~ **tiempo** on time 7; in time; ~ **veces** at times 12; ~ **ver** let's see

abajo below

abierto/a open

el/la abogado/a lawyer 1

abrazar to hug 17

el abrazo hug 17

el abrigo coat 5

abril April 4

abrir to open 6;

abrochar/se el cinturón to buckle the seat belt 11

el/la abuelo/a grandfather/ grandmother 6

aburrido/a boring; bored 3

acabar de + *inf.* to have just + *past participle* 5

académico/a academic

acaso: por si ~ in case 15

el accidente accident

la acción action

el aceite oil 9

el acelerador accelerator 11

el acento accent

aceptado/a accepted

aceptar to accept, agree to do

el acercamiento closeness

acercar/se to approach, come near

acompañar to accompany

aconsejar to advise 8

acordarse (o > ue) de to remember

acostarse (o > ue) to go to bed 5

acostumbrar/se a to become accustomed to

la actividad activity Pre.

activo/a active, lively

el actor/la actriz actor/actress 1

actual present-day

acuerdo: de ~ agreed, O.K.

adecuado/a adequate

además besides 11

Adiós. Good-by. Pre.

la adivinanza guessing game

adivinar to guess

la admisión admission

¿Adónde? Where? (with verb of motion); ¿~ **vas?** Where are you going? 3

adorar to adore

la aduana customs 7; **el/la agente de aduanas** customs official

el aerograma aerogram 10

la aerolínea airline 7

el/la aeromozo/a steward/ess, flight attendant

el aeropuerto airport

afectar to affect

afeitar/se to shave 4

la afición liking, fondness

el/la aficionado/a enthusiast, fan

africano/a African 3

la agencia de viajes travel agency 3

la agenda agenda

el/la agente: ~ **de aduanas** customs official; ~ **de viajes** travel agent 1

agosto August 4

agradable pleasant

agresivo/a aggressive 15

agrícola agricultural

el agua (*f.*) water 8; ~ **de colonia** cologne 2

el agujero hole

ahora now; ~ **mismo** right now 11

ahorrar to save

el aire acondicionado air conditioning 11

aislado/a isolated

el ajedrez chess 9

el ajo garlic 12

ajustar to adjust; to fasten

al + *inf.* upon + *-ing* 15

el ala (*f.*) wing

el álbum (de fotos) (photo) album 16

el alcalde/la alcaldesa mayor 18

alcanzar to reach
alcohólico/a alcoholic
la alconafta fuel made of sugar cane
alegrarse de to be happy about 9
la alegría happiness
alemán/alemana German 3
la alfombra rug 8
algo something 6; ¿~ **más?** Something/Anything else? 12; **por ~ será** there must be a reason 17
el algodón cotton 5
alguien someone 6
algún/alguno/a/os/as some/any 7; **algunas veces** sometimes 12
el alivio relief
el alma (*f.*) soul
el almacén department store
almorzar (o > ue) to have lunch 5
el almuerzo lunch
¿Aló? Hello? 7
alquilar to rent 8
el alquiler the rent 8
alrededor around
alternar to alternate
el altiplano high plateau
alto/a tall 3
allá over there 4
allí there 4
el ama de casa (*f.*) housewife 1
amable nice 15
el/la amante lover (*usually a negative connotation*) 17
amar to love 7
amarillo/a yellow 5
ambicioso/a ambitious 15
ambiente: el medio ~ the environment
la ambulancia ambulance 11
ambulante: una enciclopedia ~ a walking encyclopedia 14
el/la amigo/a friend
la amnesia amnesia
el amor love; **¡Por ~ de Dios!** For heaven's sake! (literally "for the love of God!") 8
amueblado/a furnished 8
amueblar to furnish 8

el analfabetismo illiteracy
anaranjado/a orange 5
la anarquía anarchy 18
el/la anciano/a old man/woman
andar to go, walk, travel
andinismo: hacer ~ mountain climbing, mountaineering
andino/a Andean
la anexión annexation
el anillo ring 13
el aniversario anniversary
anoche last night 6
anotar to take notes, jot down
anteayer the day before yesterday 6
los anteojos eyeglasses 16
el/la antepasado/a ancestor
anterior former, previous, front part
antes before; **~ de** (+ *inf.*) before + -*ing*; **~ que nada** before anything else 16
el antibiótico antibiotic 11
el anticonceptivo contraceptive
antipático/a unpleasant, disagreeable 3
la antorcha torch
anunciar to advertise; announce
el anuncio advertisement, notice, announcement
añadir to add 9; to increase
el año year 1; **~ pasado** last year 6; **~ Nuevo** New Year's Day
apagar to turn off 11
aparecer to appear
apartado/a remote
el apartamento apartment 8
aparte separate
la apatía apathy
el apellido: el primer apellido first last name (father's name) 1; **el segundo apellido** second last name (mother's maiden name) 1
apoyar to support
apreciado/a esteemed
aprender to learn 3
aprovechar to make use of, take advantage of
la apuesta bet, wager

aquel/aquella that (over there) 4; **aquellos/aquellas** those (over there) 4
aquél/aquélla that one (over there) 4; **aquéllos/aquéllas** those ones (over there) 4
aquí here 4
árabe Arab 3
el árbol tree
el arete earring 13
el armario closet 8
el/la arqueólogo/a archaeologist
el/la arquitecto/a architect
arquitectónico/a architectural
arrancar to start the car 11
arreglar to fix, arrange; **~ el carro** to fix the car 9
el arreglo arrangement
arriba above, up
el arroz rice
la artesanía craftsmanship, handicraft
el artículo article
el/la artista artist 17
la arveja pea 12
el asesinato murder
así like this/that 13
asiático/a Asian, Asiatic 3
el asiento seat 7
la asignatura subject
asimilar/se to assimilate
asimismo likewise
asistir a to attend (class, church, etc.) 6
la asociación association
asociar to associate
la aspiradora vacuum cleaner 8
la aspirina aspirin 11
el asunto matter, subject
el/la atleta athlete 1
atraer to attract
atrás back, behind, rear
atrasar to slow down, delay; to be late
aumentar to increase
el aumento increase
aun even
aún still, yet
aunque although
el auto car 6
el autobús bus 6
la autopista freeway, expressway 12

el autorretrato self-portrait
auxilios: primeros ~ first aid
el ave (*f.*) bird
la aventura amorosa affair
17
averiguar to find out (about)
el avión airplane 6; **por
avión** air mail
ayer yesterday 6
la ayuda help
el/la ayudante helper, assistant
ayudar to help 7; **~ a** to
help to
la azafata flight attendant
azteca Aztec
el azúcar sugar
azul blue 5

bailar to dance 2
el bailarín/la bailarina dancer
el baile dance
bajar to go down 13
bajo/a short (in height) 3; low
(voice)
el balcón balcony
el banano banana
el banco bank 3; bench
la banda band 12
el bandoneón concertina, type
of accordion
bañar/se to bathe 4
la bañera bathtub 8
el baño bathroom 7; **el traje
de baño** bathing suit 5
barato/a cheap, inexpensive 5
la barba beard 4
barbaridad: ¡Qué ~ ! How
awful!
el barco boat 6
el barrio neighborhood
basado/a based
basar to base
¡Basta (de . . .) ! (That's)
enough (. . .) ! 14
bastante enough
la basura garbage, waste 15;
sacar ~ to take out the
garbage
la batata sweet potato
el bate bat 10
la batería battery 11;
drums 12
el baúl trunk 11

beber to drink 2
la bebida drink
el béisbol baseball
la belleza beauty
bello/a beautiful; **bellísimo/a**
very beautiful 6
besar to kiss 17
el beso kiss 17
la biblioteca library 3
la bicicleta bicycle 6
el bidé bidet 8
bien O.K. Pre.; well
bienvenido/a welcome
el bigote mustache 4
el billar billiards 9;
~ americano pool 9
el billete bill (paper money)
14; ticket
la biología biology 3
el bistec steak 12
blanco/a white 5; **blanco y
negro** black and white 16
blando/a soft 16
la blusa blouse 5
la boca mouth 4
la boda wedding 6
el bodegón still life 17
la bola: ~ de bolos bowling
ball 10
el boleto ticket
el bolígrafo ball-point pen
Pre.
los bolos bowling 10
la bolsa stock exchange
el bolso purse 7; **~ de mano**
hand luggage 7
bonito/a pretty 3
**boquiabierto: dejar ~ (a
alguien)** to leave (someone)
dumbfounded 16
bordado/a embroidered
borracho/a drunk 3
el bosque woods 12
el bosquejo outline
la bota boot 5
la botánica store that sells can-
dles, books, and other religious
articles
la botella bottle
el botones bellboy 7
el boxeo boxing 10
brasileño/a Brazilian 3
el brazo arm 4
breve brief

el broche brooch 13
bueno/a good 3; **es ~** it's
good 8; **Buenas noches.**
Good night. Good evening.
Pre.; **Buenas tardes.** Good
afternoon. Pre.; **Buenos
días.** Good morning. Pre.
buscar to look for 6
el buzón mailbox 10

el caballero gentleman
el caballo horse 15
la cabeza head 4
cabo: al fin y al ~ after all
18
cada each, every
la cadena chain 13; network
caer to fall; to drop 13;
~ granizo to hail 12; **caerse
un empaste** to lose a filling
14; **Me cae (la mar de) bien.**
I like him/her a lot. 15; **Me
cae mal.** I don't like him/
her. 15
el café coffee 2
la cafetera coffeepot 8
la cafetería cafeteria, bar,
short-order restaurant 1
la caída fall, drop
la caja cashier's desk 14; box
el/la cajero/a cashier
el calambre cramp 11
la calculadora calculator 2
el cálculo calculus
la calefacción heat 8
el calendario calendar
cálido/a warm, hot
calor: hace ~ it's hot 4;
tener ~ to be hot 5
los calzones/calzoncillos
women's/men's underwear 5
¡Calla! Quiet!
callarse to be silent, keep quiet
la calle street 8
la cama bed 2
la cámara camera 2; **~ de
vídeo** video camera 16
el/la camarero/a waiter/wait-
ress 1
cambiar to change; **~ (dinero)**
to exchange; to change (money)
14; **cambiando de tema**
changing the subject 10

el cambio exchange rate; change 14; exchange; **en cambio** in exchange; on the other hand; instead

el camello camel

caminar to walk 2

el camino road, path

el camión truck 6

la camisa shirt 5

la camiseta T-shirt 5

la campaña (electoral) (electoral) campaign 18

el campeón/la campeona champion 10

el campeonato championship 10

el/la campesino/a peasant, farmer

el campo countryside 12; ~ **de fútbol** soccer field

canadiense Canadian 3

el canal de televisión TV channel

la canción song

la cancha (tennis, basketball) court

el/la candidato/a candidate 18

cansado/a tired 3

el cansancio fatigue, tiredness, weariness

el/la cantante singer

cantar to sing 2

la cantidad quantity

el canto singing, song

la caña (de azúcar) (sugar)cane

el caparazón shell

capaz capable

la capital capital (city); **¿Cuál es ~ de . . . ?** What is the capital of . . . ? Pre.

el capitalismo capitalism 18

el capítulo chapter

la cápsula capsule 11

la cara face 4

la carga load, cargo, burden

cargar to carry, transport

la carie cavity 14

el cariño affection; **cariño** dear *(term of endearment)* 17

la carne meat 12; ~ **de res** beef 12

caro/a expensive 5; **Te va a salir caro.** It's going to cost you. 10

la carrera course of study; career; race

la carreta wagon, cart

el carrete film 16

la carretera road, highway 12

el carro car 6

la carta letter 4; menu 12; ~ **de recomendación** letter of recommendation 16

las cartas: jugar a ~ to play cards 9

el/la cartero letter carrier 10

la casa house/home 3

casado/a: está ~ is married 6

casarse con to get married (to) 6

el casco de bicicleta, moto, fútbol americano bicycle, motorcycle, football helmet 10

casi almost

caso: en ~ (de) que in case that

el cassette tape, cassette 2

casualidad: fue pura ~ it was by pure chance 16; **por (pura) ~** by (pure) chance 15

la catarata waterfall 12; cataract (of the eyes)

catarro: tener ~ to have a cold 11

catorce fourteen 1

el/la cazador/a hunter

cazar to hunt

la cebolla onion 9

la celebración celebration

celebrar to celebrate

celos: tener ~ (de) to be jealous (of) 17

celoso/a: estar ~ (de) to be jealous (of) 17; **ser ~** to be jealous 17

la cena dinner

la censura censorship 18

censurar to censor 18

el centenar hundred

centígrados centigrade/Celsius 4

cepillarse: ~ el pelo to brush one's hair 4; ~ **los dientes** to brush one's teeth 4

el cepillo: ~ de dientes toothbrush 2; ~ **de pelo** hairbrush 2

cerca de near 6

el cerdo pork 12; pig

cero zero 1

cerrado/a closed

la cerradura lock

cerrar (e > ie) to close 5

certificado/a certified 10

la cerveza beer 2

el ciclismo cycling 10

el/la ciclista cyclist

cien one hundred 1

la ciencia science

cierto/a sure, certain, true; **es cierto** it's true 9; **por cierto** by the way

la cifra numeral

la cigüeña stork

cinco five 1

cincuenta fifty 1

el cine movie theater 3

la cinta tape, cassette 2

el cinturón belt; ~ **de seguridad** seatbelt 11

la cirugía surgery

la cita appointment; date 14

la ciudad city 12

el/la ciudadano/a citizen 18

el clarinete clarinet 12

claro/a light 5; clear; **es claro** it's clear 9

Claro. Of course. 2; **¡ ~ que sí!** Of course! 2

la clase lesson, class 3

la cláusula clause

el claustro cloister

clavar to fix upon; to nail down

el/la cliente client

cobarde cowardly 15

cobrar to charge; to collect

cobro: llamada a ~ revertido collect phone call 7

la cocina kitchen 8; ~ **eléctrica/de gas** electric/gas stove 8

cocinar to cook

el/la cocinero/a cook

el coche car 6

el código postal postal code, zip code

el codo elbow 4

el cognado cognate

cola: hacer ~ to stand in line 10

la colección collection
coleccionar to collect 9; ~ **estampillas** to collect stamps 9; ~ **monedas** to collect coins 9
el colegio mayor dormitory 1
colgar (o > ue) to hang
la coliflor cauliflower 12
la colina hill 12
colmo: para ~ to top it all off 11
colocado/a positioned, arranged
colombiano/a Colombian 3
la colonia cologne 2; colony
el color color 16; **¿De qué color es?** What color is it? 5
combatir to combat, fight
combinar to combine
el combustible fuel
la comedia comedy
el comedor dining room 8
comentar to comment on; to gossip
el comentario comment
comenzar (e > ie) to begin 5
comer to eat 2
la comida meal 7
como like, as; ~ **consecuencia** as a consequence; ~ **resultado** as a result
¿Cómo? What? / What did you say? 1; ¿ ~ **estás?** How are you? Pre.; ¿ ~ **que . . . ?** What do you mean . . . ? 7; ¿~ **se dice _____ en español?** How do you say _____ in Spanish? Pre.; ¿ ~ **se escribe _____ ?** How do you spell _____ ? Pre.; ¿ ~ **se llama (usted)?** What's your name? (formal) Pre.; ~ **si** as if; ¿ ~ **te llamas?** What's your name? (informal) Pre.
la cómoda chest of drawers 8
el/la compañero/a companion
la compañía comercial company, business
comparar to compare
compartir to share
completar to fill out; to complete, finish
comprar to buy 2
comprender to understand Pre.

comprensivo/a understanding
comprobar to check
comprometido/a engaged 17
el compromiso engagement 17
la computadora computer 2
común common; **en** ~ in common
la comunicación communication
la comunidad community
el comunismo communism 18
con with 3; ~ **cuidado** carefully; ~ **frecuencia** frequently, often 12; ~ **mucho gusto** with pleasure; ~ **tal (de) que** provided that
la concordancia concordance, harmony
conducir to drive
conectar to connect
la conferencia lecture, talk
el congelador freezer 8
el/la congresista congressman/woman 18
el congreso congress 18
el conjunto group (as in rock group) 12
conocer to know (a person/place/thing) 4; **dar a** ~ to make known
conocido/a known
el conocimiento knowledge
conquistar to win, conquer, overcome
la consecuencia consequence; **como consecuencia** as a consequence
conseguir to get, obtain 13
el consejo advice 8
la conservación conservation 15
conservar to conserve 15
consistir en to consist of
constante constant
constantemente constantly 9
constituida made of
construir to build 7
consultar to consult
el consultorio doctor's office
el consumidor consumer
el consumo consumption
la contaminación pollution 15

contar (o > ue) to tell; to count 6
contemporáneo/a contemporary
el contenido content
contento/a happy 3
el contestador automático answering machine
contestar to answer 6
continuamente continually 9
continuar to continue 12
contra: estar en ~ to be against
contratado/a contracted, hired
contratar to contract, hire 16
la contratapa inside cover
el contrato contract 16
la conversación conversation
conversar to converse, talk
convertir (e > ie > i) to convert
la copa stemmed glass, goblet; ~ **Mundial** World Cup (soccer)
la copia copy 17
el corazón heart 17
la corbata tie 5
el cordero lamb 12
corregir (e > i > i) to correct
el correo post office; mail 10
correspondiente corresponding
correr to run 2
la corrida de toros bullfight
cortar to cut 9
la Corte Suprema Supreme Court 18
corto/a short (in length) 3
la cosa thing
coser to sew 9
la costa coast 12
costar (o > ue) to cost 5; **Cuesta un ojo de la cara.** It costs an arm and a leg. 5
costarricense Costa Rican 3
la costumbre custom, habit
cotidiano/a daily
crear to create
creciente growing, increasing
creer to believe 7
la crema de afeitar shaving cream 2
criar breed, rear, raise
el croissant croissant 14
el crucero cruise
el crucigrama crossword puzzle

cruzar to cross (the street) 13
la cuadra city block 13
el cuadro painting 17
¿Cuál? Which? 1; ¿ ~ **es tu/ su número de . . . ?** What is your . . . number? 1; ¿ ~ **es el origen de tu familia?** Where is your family from? 3 ¿ ~ **es la capital de . . . ?** What is the capital of . . . ? Pre.
cualquier any; whichever
cuando when
¿Cuándo? When? 2
¿Cuánto? How much?; ~ **cuesta/n . . . ?** How much is/are . . . ? 5
¿Cuántos? How many?; ¿ ~ **años tiene él/ella?** How old is he/she? 1
cuarenta forty 1
el cuarto room 8; ~ **de hora** quarter (of an hour) 5; ~ **de servicio** maid's bedroom 8
cuarto/a fourth 8
cuatro four 1
el cuatro four-stringed guitar used in Andean and Caribbean music
los cubiertos silverware 9
cubrir to cover 12
la cuchara spoon 9
el cuchillo knife 9
la cuenta check; account; ~**, por favor.** The check, please. 12; **darse cuenta de algo** to realize something 7; **tener en cuenta** to take into account, bear in mind
el cuento story
el cuero leather 5
el cuerpo body
el cuestionario questionnaire
el cuidado care; **con cuidado** carefully; **tener cuidado** to be careful
cuidar to care for, take care of; ~ **plantas** to take care of plants 9
cultivado/a cultured, cultivated
la cultura culture
la cumbre summit, height

el cumpleaños birthday 4; **feliz cumpleaños** happy birthday
el/la cuñado/a brother-in-law/ sister-in-law 6
el cura priest
curar to cure, treat
la curiosidad curiosity; indiscretion; question
el curriculum (vitae) résumé, curriculum vitae 16
cursar to study, take
cursi overly cute; tacky; in bad taste 12
el curso course

el champú shampoo 2
Chao. By. / So long. Pre.
la chaqueta jacket 5
el charango small, five-stringed guitar
la charla talk, conversation
charlar to chat, talk
Chau. By. / So long. Pre.
el cheque check; ~ **de viajero** traveler's check 14
chévere: ¡Qué chévere! Great! (Caribbean expression) 12
el/la chico/a boy/girl 1
el chile chili pepper
chileno/a Chilean 3
la chimenea chimney
los chismes gossip 16
el chiste joke, funny story
chocar to crash 11
el chocolate chocolate, hot chocolate 14
el chofer driver, chauffeur 13
la chuleta chop 12
el churrasco steak (in Argentina) 12
el churro Spanish cruller 14

la danza dance
dar to give 6; ~ **a conocer** to make known; ~ **un paseo** to take a walk; ~**le la vuelta** to turn over 9; ~ **una vuelta** to take a ride; to go for a stroll/ walk 15; **dar vergüenza** to make ashamed; **darse cuenta**

de algo to realize something 7
el dato fact, piece of information
de of; from 1; ¿ ~ **acuerdo?** O.K.?, Agreed? 13; ~ **compras** shopping; ¿ ~ **dónde eres?** Where are you from? (informal) Pre.; ~ **nada.** You're welcome. Pre.; (~ **parte**) ~ **. . .** It/This is . . . 7; ¿ ~ **parte de quién?** Can I ask who is calling? 7; ¿ ~ **qué color es?** What color is it? 5; ¿ ~ **qué material/ tela es?** What material is it made out of? 5; ~ **quien** about whom; ¿ ~ **quién/es?** Whose? 2; ~ **repente** suddenly 6; ~ **segunda mano** secondhand, used 8; ¿ ~ **veras?** Really? 2; ~ **vez en cuando** once in a while, from time to time 12
debajo de below 6
deber to owe; ~ + *inf.* should/must + *inf.* 4
debido/a due; **debido a** due to, because of
el/la decano/a dean
decidir to decide 6
décimo/a tenth 8
decir (e > i) to say; to tell 5; **¿Qué quiere ~ ____ ?** What does ____ mean? Pre.; **¡No me digas!** No kidding! 5; **Diga/ Dígame** Hello? (on telephone) 7; **dile a . . .** tell . . . Pre.
el dedo finger 4; ~ **meñique** little finger; ~ **del pie** toe 4
dejar to leave behind; to let, allow 6; ~ **de** + *inf.* to stop, quit + *-ing* 10; ~ **boquiabierto (a alguien)** to leave (someone) dumbfounded 16
del = de + el of
delante de in front of 6
delgado thin 3
demás remaining, rest
demasiado too much 3
la democracia democracy 18

democrático/a democratic
¡Demonios! Damn! What the devil!
demostrar to demonstrate
el/la dentista dentist 1
dentro: ~ **de** within, inside; ~ **de poco** in a while 18
depender de to depend on
el/la dependiente/a store clerk 1
el deporte sport
el/la deportista athlete 10
el depósito security deposit 8
la derecha right-hand side; **a** ~ **de** to the right of 6
el derecho right; law; ~ **penal** criminal law
derecho: seguir ~ to keep going straight
el derrame de petróleo oil spill
desafortunadamente unfortunately
desarrollado/a developed
desarrollar to develop
el desastre disaster
desayunar/se to have breakfast 4
el desayuno breakfast 7
el/la descendiente descendant
describir to describe
la descripción description
el descubrimiento discovery
descubrir to discover
el descuento discount
desde since, from; ~ **hace** for (time duration); ~ . . . **hasta** from . . . until; ~ **luego** of course 18
deseable desirable
desear to want; to desire 3
el desempleo unemployment 16
el deseo wish, desire
desesperado/a desperate
el desierto desert
desnudo/a naked
despacio slow, slowly; **Más** ~**, por favor.** More slowly, please. Pre.; **¿Puede hablar más** ~**, por favor?** Can you speak more slowly, please? 7

la despedida farewell
despedir to fire 16; ~**se** to say good-by
despejado/a clear, sunny; spacious
despertar/se (e > ie) to wake someone up/to wake up 5
después after 3; ~ **de que** after
el destino destination; destiny 7
destrozado/a ruined, destroyed
la destrucción destruction 15
destruido/a destroyed
destruir to destroy 15
la desventaja disadvantage
el detalle detail
detener to detain
detenidamente thoroughly
determinado/a specific
detrás de behind 6
la deuda debt
el/la deudor/a debtor
devolver (o > ue) to vomit 11; to return, send back
el día day; **Buenos días.** Good morning. Pre.; **ponerse al día** to bring up to date; **todos los días** every day 12
el diálogo dialogue
el diamante diamond 13
la diapositiva slide 16
diario/a daily
diarrea: tener ~ to have diarrhea 11
dibujar to draw 17
el dibujo drawing, sketch 17
el diccionario dictionary 2
diciembre December 4
el/la dictador/a dictator
la dictadura dictatorship 18
el dicho saying
el diente tooth 14; **cepillarse los dientes** to brush one's teeth 4
diez ten 1
la diferencia difference; **a diferencia de** unlike; in contrast to
diferente different; ~ **de** different from
difícil difficult

el dinero money
la dirección address 1
las direccionales blinkers 11
las direcciones directions
directamente directly
el/la director/a director 1
dirigido/a directed
el disco record 2; ~ **compacto** compact disc 2
discutir to argue; to discuss
el/la diseñador/a designer
disfrutar to enjoy
disparar to fire, shoot
disponible available
la distancia distance; **larga distancia** long distance
el distrito district
diurno/a diurnal, daytime
diversificar to diversify
la diversión amusement, entertainment, recreation
divertido/a entertaining, amusing
divertir/se (e > ie > i) to have fun 5
divinamente divinely 9
divino/a divine, wonderful
divorciado/a: está ~ is divorced 6
divorciar/se to get divorced 17
el divorcio divorce 17
doblar to turn 11; to fold
doble: la habitación ~ double room 7
doce twelve 1
el/la doctor/a doctor 1
el documental documentary
doler (o > ue) to hurt 10
el dolor de muela toothache 14
doméstico/a domestic
el domicilio residence
domingo Sunday 2; **el** ~ on Sunday 2
dominicano/a Dominican 3
el dominó dominoes 9
don/doña title of respect used before a man/woman's first name
donde where
¿dónde? where?; **¿** ~ **estás?** Where are you? 3; **¿de** ~

eres? where are you from? (informal) Pre.
dormir/se (o > ue > u) to sleep/to fall asleep 5
el dormitorio bedroom 8
dos two 1
dramático/a dramatic
la ducha shower 8
duchar/se to take a shower 4
duda: no hay ~ (de) there is no doubt 9
dudar to doubt 9
dudoso: es ~ it's doubtful 9
el/la dueño/a de un negocio owner of a business 1
dulce sweet 14
el dulce: ~ de leche custard cream
durante during
duro/a hard 16; **huevo duro** hard-boiled egg 14

e and
la ecología ecology 15
la economía economics 3; economy
el/la economista economist 1
ecuatoriano/a Ecuadoran 3
echar to throw; to put in, add; to throw out; **~ de menos** to miss (someone or something) 10; **~ la casa por la ventana** to go all out; **~ el mal de ojo** to put a curse on
la edad age; **~ Media** Middle Ages
el edificio building 8
el (dinero en) efectivo cash 14
ejemplar exemplary, model
el ejemplo example; **por ejemplo** for example
el ejercicio exercise Pre.
el ejército army
el the (masculine singular) 2
él/ella he/she 1
las elecciones election 18
la electricidad electricity 8
el elefante elephant 15
elegir (e > i > i) to choose, select
ellos/as they 1

embarazada pregnant
embargo: sin ~ however, nevertheless 12
el embrague clutch 11
la emergencia emergency
la emisora radio station
empacar to pack
el empaste filling 14; **caerse un empaste** to lose a filling 14
empezar (e > ie) to begin 5
el/la empleado/a employee; **~ (de servicio)** maid 7
emplear to employ, use
el empleo job/position; employment 16
la empresa enterprise; company
en in; on; at; **~ + barco/tren/** etc. by boat/train/etc. 6; **~ general** in general; **¿~ qué página, por favor?** What page please? Pre.; **¿~ qué puedo servirle?** How can I help you?; **~ realidad** really, actually; **~ seguida** at once, right away 17
enamorado/a in love 3
enamorarse de to fall in love with 17
Encantado/a. Nice to meet you. 1
encantar to like a lot, love 10
enciclopedia: una ~ ambulante a walking encyclopedia 14
encima de on top of 6
encontrar (o > ue) to find 5
el encuentro encounter, meeting
la encuesta inquiry, poll
la energía energy; **~ nuclear** nuclear energy 15; **~ solar** solar energy 15
enero January 4
enfadar/se to get angry
la enfermedad sickness, illness 11
el/la enfermero/a nurse
enfermo/a sick 3
enfocar to focus 16
el enfoque focus 16

enfrente de facing, across from 6
enfurecer/se to become enraged, angry
enojado/a angry, mad 3
enojarse to become angry
la ensalada salad 9
ensayar to rehearse
el ensayo essay
enseñar to teach; to indicate, point out
entender (e > ie) to understand 5
el entierro burial
entonces then 1
la entrada entrance ticket 13; entrance
entrar (en) to enter 6
entre between, among
entrenar to train
entretener to entertain
la entrevista interview 16
el/la entrevistador/a interviewer
entrevistar to interview
enviado/a sent
el equipaje luggage 7
el equipo team; equipment 10
equivocado: el número ~ wrong number 7
la escala scale; **hacer escala** to make a stop 7
escalar to climb
la escalera stairs 13
escalofríos: tener ~ to have the chills 11
la escena scene 17
el/la esclavo/a slave
la esclusa lock (canal gate)
escoger to choose, select 8
escondido/a hidden
escribir to write 2
el/la escritor/a writer
el escritorio desk 2
escuchar to listen 2
la escuela school 3
el/la escultor/a sculptor 17
la escultura sculpture 17
ese/a that 4
ése/a that one 4
esencial essential

el esfuerzo effort
la esmeralda emerald 13
eso that 4; **por eso** therefore 2; that's why 15
esos/as those 4
ésos/as those ones 4
el espacio blank, space
la espalda back 4
los espárragos asparagus 12
la especia spice
especial special
la especie species
específico/a specific
el (espejo) retrovisor rearview mirror 11
la esperanza hope 8
esperar to wait (for); to hope (for) 7
el/la esposo/a husband/wife 6
el esquema diagram; sketch; outline
el esquí skiing
esquiar to ski 2
los esquíes: ~ de agua water skis 10; **~ de nieve** snow skis 10
la esquina corner 13
estable stable
establecer to establish
la estación season 4
el estadio stadium 10
el estado state; **~ civil** marital status
estadounidense from the U.S. 3
la estampilla stamp 9
el estándar standard
el estante shelf 8
estar to be 3; **~ celoso/a (de)** to be jealous (of) 17; **~ en** to be in/at 3; **~ embarazada** to be pregnant; **~ listo/a** to be ready 3; **~ resfriado/a** to have a cold 11; **~ seguro/a (de)** to be sure 9; **está casado/a** is married 6; **está divorciado/a** is divorced 6; **está nublado** it's cloudy 4; **¿Está . . . , por favor?** Is . . . there, please? 7
la estatua statue 17

el este east 12
este/a this 4
éste/a this one 4
el estéreo stereo 2
el esteroide steroid
el estilo style
estimado/a esteemed, respected
estimar to estimate
esto this 4
el estómago stomach 4
estornudar to sneeze 11
estos/as these 4
éstos/as these ones 4
la estrategia strategy
la estrella star
el/la estudiante student 1
estudiar to study 2
el estudio study
la estufa stove 8
estúpido/a stupid 3
europeo/a European 3
evidente: es ~ it's evident 9
evitar to avoid
exactamente exactly
exceder to exceed
excéntrico/a eccentric
la excepción exception
la excursión excursion, side trip 13
la excusa excuse
exento/a exempt
existir to exist
éxito: tener ~ to be successful
el éxodo exodus
la experiencia experience 16
explicar to explain 6
la expresión expression
externo/a external, outside
la extinción extinction 15
el/la extranjero/a foreigner
extrañar/se to miss/to find strange
extraño/a strange

la fábrica factory 15
fabuloso/a fabulous
fácil easy
fácilmente easily 9
la facultad department of a university
la falda skirt 5

falso/a false
la falta lack
faltar to lack; to be missing 10
la familia family 3
famoso/a famous
fantasía: de ~ costume (jewelry) 13
fantástico/a fantastic, great; **es ~** it's fantastic 9
la farmacia drugstore 3
fascinar to like a lot; to fascinate 10
el fascismo fascism 18
favor: ~ de + inf. please . . . 4; **por ~** please 1
favorito/a favorite
febrero February 4
la fecha date 4
la felicidad happiness
feliz happy 17; **~ cumpleaños** happy birthday
feo/a ugly 3
la fianza security deposit 8
la ficción fiction
la ficha record card, index card
la fiebre fever 11; **tener ~** to have a fever 11
fiel faithful, loyal
la fiesta party
la figura figure
el filete fillet; sirloin 12
el fin end; **~ de semana** weekend 2; **al fin y al cabo** after all 18; **por fin** at last 7
finalmente finally
fino/a fine, elegant
la firma signature 14
firmar to sign 14
flaco/a skinny 3
el flan Spanish egg custard 12
el flash flash (in photography) 16
la flauta flute 12
la flor flower
el flujo flow, stream
fobia: tenerle ~ a . . . to have a fear of . . . , to hate . . . 14
el folleto brochure, pamphlet
fomentar to promote, foster, encourage
el fondo bottom
forjar to forge, shape, make

formado/a formed
formar to form
el formulario form
la foto(grafía) photograph; photography; **sacar fotos** to take pictures 16
la fractura fracture, break 11
francés/francesa French 3
la frase phrase
frecuencia: con ~ frequently, often
frecuente frequent
frecuentemente frequently 9
el fregadero kitchen sink 8
freír (e > i > i) to fry 9
el freno brake 11
fresco/a fresh, cool; **hace fresco** it's chilly 4
frío/a cold; **hace frío** it's cold 4; **tener frío** to be cold 5
el frijol bean 12
frito/a fried 14; **los huevos fritos** fried eggs 14
frustrado/a frustrated
frustrante frustrating
la fruta fruit 9
el fuego fire
la fuente fountain; source
fuerte strong
la fuerza strength, power, force; **las fuerzas armadas** armed forces 18
fuga: la ~ de cerebros brain drain
fumar to smoke 7; **la sección de (no) ~** (no) smoking section 7
funerario/a funeral, funerary
el fusilamiento shooting, execution
el futuro future

las gafas eyeglasses 16; **~ de sol** sunglasses 5
galopante runaway; galloping
la galleta cookie; cracker 14
la gallina chicken 15
el gallo rooster
ganar to win; to earn 10; to gain
ganas: tener ~ de + inf. to feel like + -ing 6

la ganga bargain
el garaje garage 8
la gasolinera gas station
gastar to spend
el gasto expense; use
el gato cat 15
el gemelo cufflink 13; twin
general: en ~ in general 13
generalmente generally 9
el/la genio genius
la gente people
la geografía geography
la geología geology
el/la gerente manager
el/la gigante giant
la gira tour
girar to turn 11
el giro: ~ bancario money order 14; **~ postal** money order 10
el/la gobernador/a governor 18
el/la gobernante person in power, ruler, governor
el gobierno government
el gol goal, point
el golpe: ~ de estado coup d'état 18
gordo/a fat 3
la grabación recording
el grabado etching
la grabadora tape recorder 2
grabar to record
Gracias. Thank you. Pre.
gracioso/a funny
el grado degree; **Está a ____ grados (bajo cero).** It's ____ degrees (below zero). 4
graduar/se to graduate
la gramática grammar
grande large, big 3; great
el granizo hail 12; **caer granizo** to hail 12
la gripe flu 11
gris gray 5
gritar to shout, scream 6
el grupo group
la guantera glove compartment 11
el guante de béisbol, boxeo, ciclismo baseball, boxing, racing glove 10
guapo/a good-looking 3

guatemalteco/a Guatemalan 3
la guayabera specific style of men's shirt
la guerra war
el/la guerrillero/a guerrilla 18
el/la guía guide; **~ turístico/a** tour guide 13
el guisante pea 12
la guitarra guitar 2
gustar to like, be pleasing 2; **me gustaría** I would like 3
el gusto taste; pleasure

haber to have (auxiliary verb) 13; **~ niebla** to be foggy 12; **~ relámpagos** to flash with lightning 12; **~ tormenta** to storm 12; **~ truenos** to thunder 12
la habichuela green bean 12
la habitación room 2; **~ doble** double room 7; **~ sencilla** single room 7
el/la habitante inhabitant
hablar to speak 2; **Habla . . .** It/This is . . . 7; **¿Puede hablar más despacio, por favor?** Can you speak more slowly, please? 7; **¿Quién habla?** Who is speaking/calling? 7
hace (weather): **~ buen tiempo** it's nice out 4; **~ calor** it's hot 4; **~ fresco** it's chilly 4; **~ frío** it's cold 4; **~ mal tiempo** it's bad out 4; **~ sol** it's sunny 4; **~ viento** it's windy 4
hacer to do 2; to make; **~ cola** to stand in line 10; **~ escala** to make a stop 7
hacia toward
el hall entrance hall 8
el hallazgo discovery, finding
el hambre hunger; **tener hambre** to be hungry 5
hasta until; **~ luego.** See you later. Pre.; **~ mañana.** See you tomorrow. Pre.; **~ que** until
hay there is/there are 4; **~ que + inf.** one/you must + verb 9; **No ~ de qué.** Don't

mention it/You're welcome. 1;
no ~ duda (de) there's no
doubt 9
el helado ice cream 12
la herencia heritage
la herida injury, wound 11
el/la herido/a injured man/
woman
el/la hermano/a brother/sis-
ter 6
el hielo ice 10; **los patines
de hielo** ice skates 10
el hierro iron
el/la hijo/a son/daughter 6
hilar to spin (thread)
el hilo thread; theme;
~ **dental** dental floss 14;
seguir ~ to follow (a story)
hispano/a Hispanic
hispanoamericano/a Hispanic
American
la historia history 3
el hogar home; fireplace,
hearth
la hoja leaf; sheet (of paper)
Hola. Hi. Pre.
el hombre man; ~ **de
negocios** businessman 1
el hombro shoulder 4
hondureño/a Honduran 3
honrado/a honest 15
la hora hour 5; ~ **de salida**
time of departure 7; ~ **de llegada** time of arrival 7; **es ~
de** + *inf.* it's time to + *inf.*
16; **No veo ~ de** + *inf.* I
can't wait + *inf.*; **¿A qué
hora . . . ?** At what time . . . ?
5; **¿Qué hora es?** What time
is it? 5
el horario schedule
el horizonte horizon
el horno oven; ~ **(de) microondas** microwave oven 8
el hospedaje lodging
el hospital hospital 3
hoy today 2; ~ **(en) día** today; nowadays 12
el hoyo hole
la huelga strike 18
el huésped guest
el huevo egg 9; **los huevos
(fritos, revueltos, duros)**

(fried, scrambled, hard-boiled)
eggs 14

ida y vuelta round trip 7
la idea idea
la identidad identity
la identificación identification
identificar to identify
el idioma language
la iglesia church 3
ignorante ignorant 15
igual equal, (the) same; **al
~ que** just like, whereas
Igualmente. Nice to meet you,
too./Same here. 1
imaginar/se to imagine
importante important; **es ~**
it's important 8
importar to matter 10; **No
importa.** It doesn't matter. 2
impresionante impressive
el impuesto tax 13
incaico/a Incan
incierto/a uncertain
incluido/a included
incluir to include
inca Incan; **el/la ~** Inca
el inculto uncivilized person
indicar to indicate
el índice index
indígena indigenous, native
indio/a Indian 3; **el/la ~**
Indian man/woman; **el/la indio/a
americano/a** American Indian
la inestabilidad instability
la infección infection 11
la influencia influence
influir to influence
la información information
el informe report
el/la ingeniero/a engineer 1
el inglés English language
inglés/inglesa English 3
ingresar to admit (as a patient)
los ingresos income, revenue
iniciar to initiate, start
la injusticia injustice
inmediatamente immediately
el inodoro toilet 8
inofensivo/a harmless
instalar to install
integrar to make up, compose

inteligente intelligent 3
intentar to try
interno/a internal
interrumpir to interrupt
la introducción introduction
las instrucciones instructions,
directions Pre.
introducir to introduce
inútil useless
inventar to invent
la inversión investment
invertir (e > ie > i) to invest
el invierno winter 4
la invitación invitation
invitar to invite 7; to treat 17
la inyección injection 11
ir to go; ~ **a** + *inf.* to be going to . . . 2; ~ **de compras**
to shop 5
irlandés/irlandesa Irish 3
irrespetuoso/a disrespectful
la isla island 12
italiano/a Italian 3
el itinerario itinerary 13
la izquierda left-hand side;
a ~ de to the left of 6

el jabón soap 2
el jamón ham 9
el jarabe (cough) syrup 11
el jardín flower garden
la jardinería gardening 9
el/la jefe/a boss, chief
joven young 3
las joyas jewelry
la joyería jewelry store
la judía verde green bean 12
el juego game; ~ **de com-
putadora/vídeo** computer/
video game 9
jueves Thursday 2; **el ~** on
Thursday 2
el/la juez judge 18
jugar (u > ue) to play (a sport
or game) 5; **~se la vida** to
risk one's life 11
el jugo juice 14
julio July 4
junio June 4
junto/a together
justo/a just, fair
la juventud youth

el kleenex Kleenex 2
el kilómetro kilometer

la the (feminine singular) 2
el labio lip 4
el lado side; **al lado de** beside 6; **por otro (lado)** on the other (hand) 14; **por un lado** on the one hand 14
el lago lake 12
la lámpara lamp 2
la lana wool 5
el lápiz pencil Pre.
largo/a long 3; **a lo largo de** alongside; **larga distancia** long distance
las the (feminine plural) 2
lástima: es una ~ it's a shame/pity
la lata: ~ de aluminio aluminum can
el lavabo bathroom sink 8
la lavadora washing machine 8
el lavaplatos dishwasher 8
lavarse to wash up, wash (oneself) 4
la lección lesson
la lectura reading
la leche milk
la lechuga lettuce 9
leer to read 2
lejos de far from 6
la lengua tongue 4; language
la lenteja lentil 12
los lentes de contacto (blandos/duros) (soft/hard) contact lenses 16
el león lion 15

levantarse to stand up Pre.; to get up 4
la ley law
la leyenda legend
la libertad de palabra/prensa freedom of speech/the press 18
libre free (with nothing to do) 13
la librería bookstore 3
el libro book Pre.
ligero/a light

limitar con to border on
el limpiaparabrisas windshield wiper 11
limpiar to clean 8
la limpieza de dientes teeth cleaning 14
lindo/a pretty
la línea line; **~ aérea** airline 7
la lista list
listo/a: ser ~ to be clever 3; **estar ~** to be ready 3
la literatura literature 3
lo que what (the thing that)
Lo siento. I'm sorry. 7
loco/a crazy; **¡Ni ~!** Not on your life! 14
el/la locutor/a commentator
lograr to get, obtain, achieve
los the (masculine plural) 2
la lucha fight, struggle
luego later; **Hasta ~.** See you later. Pre.
el lugar place
lujoso/a luxurious
la luna moon; **~ de miel** honeymoon 6
el lunar mole
lunes Monday 2; **el ~** on Monday 2; **los ~** on Mondays 2
las luces headlights 11
la luz electricity, light 8

la llamada telephone call; **~ a cobro revertido** collect call 7; **~ local** local call 7
llamar to call; to phone; **llamarse** to be called; **Me llamo . . .** My name is . . . Pre.
la llanta tire 11
la llave key
llegada: la hora de ~ time of arrival 7
llegar to arrive 6
lleno/a full
llevar to carry, take along; to wear 2; **llevarse bien/mal (con alguien)** to get along/not to get along (with someone) 15
llorar to cry 6

llover (o > ue) to rain 4; **llueve** it's raining 4
la lluvia rain; **~ ácida** acid rain 15

la madera wood 9
la madrastra stepmother 6
la madre mother 1
la madrina godmother
el/la maestro/a teacher; **la obra maestra** masterpiece 17
el maíz corn
mal lousy, awful Pre.; **el ~ de ojo** a curse 9
la maleta suitcase 7; **las maletas** luggage 7
malo/a bad 3
la mamá mom 1
mami mom, mommy
mandar to send 6; to command
manejar to drive 7
la manera way, manner
la manga sleeve
la manifestación demonstration 18
manifestar to demonstrate
la mano hand 4; **de segunda mano** secondhand 8
la mantequilla butter 14
mantener to maintain
la manzana apple
mañana tomorrow 2; **Hasta mañana.** See you tomorrow. Pre.; **la ~** morning 2
el mapa map
maquillarse to put on make-up 4
la máquina machine; **~ de afeitar** electric razor 2; **~ de escribir** typewriter 2; **~ de fotos** camera 16
el mar sea 12
la maravilla wonder, marvel
maravilloso/a wonderful
marcar to mark; to dial; **~ directo** to dial direct 7; **~ un gol** to score a goal/point
el mareo dizziness 11
el mariachi mariachi musician/group

los mariscos shellfish
marrón brown 5
martes Tuesday 2; **el ~** on Tuesday 2
marzo March 4
más more 2; **~ de +** number more than; **~ +** *n./adj./v.* **+ que** more . . . than; **~ o menos.** So, so. Pre.
matar to kill
el mate maté (tea, plant), maté vessel
las matemáticas mathematics 3
la materia class; subject; material
la matrícula license plate 11; tuition
el matrimonio marriage
maya Mayan
mayo May 4
la mayonesa mayonnaise
mayor older 6; **la ~ parte de** most of
la mayoría majority
mediados middle, halfway through
la medianoche midnight 5
las medias stockings 5
el médico doctor 1
medio/a half; **media (hora)** half (an hour) 5; **media pensión** breakfast and one meal included 7; **en medio de** in the middle of; **el medio de transporte** means of transportation
el mediodía noon 5
medir to measure
mejor better 12; **a lo ~** perhaps 10; **es ~** it's better 8
melón melon
la memoria memory
memorizar to memorize
mencionar to mention
menor younger 6
menos less; **~ de** less than; **a ~ que** unless; **por lo ~** at least 15
mensual monthly
la mente mind

mentir (e > ie > i) to lie 7
la mentira lie
el menú menu
menudo: a ~ often 12
meñique: el dedo ~ little finger
el mercadeo marketing
el mercado market
la mermelada marmalade, jam, jelly 14
el mes month 4; **~ pasado** last month 6; **todos los meses** every month 12
la mesa table 2; **poner ~** to set the table 9
mestizo/a of mixed Indian and European blood
el metal metal 10
meter la pata to put one's foot in it, meddle, interfere
el metro subway 6
mexicano/a Mexican
mi/s my 1
el miedo fear; **tener miedo** to be scared 5
el miembro member
mientras while 11; **~ tanto** meanwhile, in the meantime 9
miércoles Wednesday 2; **el ~** on Wednesday 2
mil one thousand 6
los militares military 18
la milla mile
un millón one million 6
el mínimo minimum
ministro/a: el/la primer/a ~ prime minister 18
la minoría minority
el minuto minute 5
mío/a mine 14; **el/la ~** mine 14
mirar to look (at) 2
el/la mismo/a the same; **ahora mismo** right now 11
el misterio mystery
misterioso/a mysterious
la mitad half
mítico/a mythical
el modelo model; **el/la modelo** (fashion) model
moderno/a modern
el mole (poblano) black chili sauce

molestar to bother 3
momento: un ~ just a moment
la moneda currency; coin 14
el mono monkey 15
el monstruo monster
la montaña mountain 12
montar to ride; **~ en bicicleta** to ride a bicycle 10; **~ en carro** to ride in a car
morado/a purple 5
moreno/a brunet/te; dark skinned 3
morir/se (o > ue > u) to die 7
la mosca fly
mostrar (o > ue) to show
motivar to motivate
la moto/motocicleta motorcycle 6
el motor engine 11
el mozo waiter; young man
el/la muchacho/a boy/girl, young man/woman
mucho/a many, a lot (of) 2; **muchas veces** many times 12; **Mucho gusto.** Nice to meet you. 1
mudar/se to move
muebles furniture
la muela molar 14; **~ de juicio** wisdom tooth 14; **el dolor de muela** toothache 14
la muerte death
muerto/a dead
la mujer woman; **~ de negocios** businesswoman 1
la multa fine
el mundo world; **todo ~** everybody, everyone 13
el museo museum
muy very 3; **¡ ~ bien!** Very well! Pre.

nacer to be born 15
nacido/a born
el nacimiento birth
la nación nation
la nacionalidad nationality
nada nothing 6; **antes que ~** before anything else 16; **De ~.** You're welcome. Pre.

nadar to swim 2
nadie no one 6
el nailon nylon 5
la naranja orange
la nariz nose 4
la náusea nausea 11
navegable navigable
la navidad Christmas
necesario/a necessary; **es necesario** it's necessary 8
necesitar to need 3
el negocio business; **el hombre/la mujer de negocios** businessman/woman 1
negro/a black 5
nervioso/a nervous
nevar to snow 4; **nieva** it's snowing 4
la nevera refrigerator 8
ni . . . ni neither . . . nor
ni siquiera not even 18
nicaragüense Nicaraguan 3
la niebla fog 12; **haber niebla** to be foggy 12
el/la nieto/a grandson, granddaughter
la nieve snow
el nilón nylon
ningún/ninguno/a (not) any; none/no one 7
el/la niño/a boy/girl
el nivel level
no no 1; **¿ ~ ?** right?; isn't it? 1
la noche night, evening; **Buenas noches.** Good evening. Pre.
el nombre (de pila) first name 1
el norte north 12
nosotros/as we 1
la nota grade; note
la noticia news item
la novela novel
noveno/a ninth 8
noventa ninety 1
noviembre November 4
el/la novio/a boyfriend/girlfriend 1; fiancé/fiancée; groom/bride 17
nublado: está ~ it's cloudy 4
el nudo knot (nautical)

nuestro/a our 3; ours; **el/la nuestro/a** ours 14
nueve nine 1
nuevo/a new
el número number; **~ equivocado** wrong number 7
nunca never 6
nutrido/a de full of, abounding in

o or 2; **~ sea** that is 8
o . . . o either . . . or
el objeto object
la obra maestra masterpiece 17
obtener to obtain
obvio: es ~ it's obvious 9
el océano ocean 12
octavo/a eighth 8
octubre October 4
el/la oculista optometrist, eye doctor 16
la ocupación occupation
ocupado/a busy 4
ocupar to fill (a position)
ocurrir to happen, occur
ochenta eighty 1
ocho eight 1
odiar to hate 7
el oeste west 12
la oficina office 3
ofrecer to offer 6
el oído inner ear 4
oír to hear 7
ojalá (que) + *subj.* I hope that . . . 8
el ojo eye 4; **Cuesta un ~ de la cara.** It costs an arm and a leg. 5; **el mal de ~** a curse 9; **¡Ojo!** Watch out!
la ola wave
el óleo oil (paint)
olvidar/se to forget 13
la olla pot 9
once eleven 1
la opción option
opcional optional 13
el/la operador/a operator
la óptica optician's shop
la oración sentence
el órden order
la oreja ear 4

organizar to organize
el orgullo pride
orgulloso/a proud 15
el origen origin 3; **¿Cuál es ~ de tu familia?** Where is your family from? 3
el original original 17
el oro gold 13; **de oro** made of gold 13
la orquesta (sinfónica) (symphony) orchestra 12
oscuro/a dark 5
el oso bear 15
el otoño fall, autumn 4
otro/a other; **el uno al otro** each other; **otra vez** again 10
¡Oye! Hey! 1

el padrastro stepfather 6
el padre father 1
los padres/papás parents 6
los padrinos best man and maid of honor; godparents
pagar to pay (for) 6
la página page Pre.; **¿En qué página, por favor?** What page, please? Pre.
el país country
el paisaje landscape 17
el pájaro bird 15
la palabra word
palanca: tener ~ to know people in the right places
el palo de golf golf club 10
la pampa Argentine prairie
el pan bread 9
panameño/a Panamanian 3
los pantalones pants 5
la pañoleta scarf 5
la papa potato; **las papas fritas** potato chips; french fries 2
el papel paper Pre.
el papá dad 1
papi Dad
el paquete package 10
un par (de) a pair (of)
para for; **~ colmo** to top it all off 11; **~ + *inf.*** in order to; **~ que** in order that; **¿ ~ qué?** why? for what purpose?; **¿~ quién?** for whom?

el parabrisas windshield 11
el parachoques bumper 11
la parada stop
el parador inn, hotel
paraguayo/a Paraguayan 3
parecer to seem 10
parecido/a similar
la pared wall
la pareja couple; lovers *(positive connotation)* 17; pair
el/la pariente relative 6
el parque park 3
el párrafo paragraph
la parte: De parte de . . . It/This is . . . (telephone) 7; **¿De parte de quién?** Can I ask who is calling? 7; **por mi parte** as far as I'm concerned 18
participar to participate
particular private
el partido game 10; **~ (político)** political party 18
partir: a ~ de starting from
pasado/a: el (sábado) pasado last (Saturday) 6; **la semana pasada** last week 6
el pasaje (plane) ticket 7
el/la pasajero/a passenger 7
el pasaporte passport 1
pasar to spend (time) 13; **~ por** to pass by/through 13; **pasarlo bien/mal** to have a good/bad time 14
el pasatiempo pastime, hobby
paseo: dar un to take a walk
el pasillo hallway 8
el paso step
la pasta de dientes toothpaste 2
la pastilla pill 11
la pata paw, foot
la patata potato (Spain) 2
patinar to skate 10
los patines de hielo/de ruedas ice skates/roller skates 10
el patrimonio heritage
el pavo turkey 12
la paz peace
pedir (e > i > i) to ask for 5
peinarse to comb one's hair 4
el peine comb 2

pelear to fight 17
la película movie 5
el peligro danger
peligroso/a dangerous
el pelo hair 4; **tomarle ~ (a alguien)** to pull someone's leg 16; **cepillarse ~** to brush one's hair 4
la pelota ball 10
la peluquería hairdresser's
la pena grief, sorrow; **(no) vale ~** it's (not) worth it 11; **es una pena** it's a pity 9; **¡Qué pena!** What a pity! 9
el pendiente earring
el pensamiento thought
pensar (e > ie) to think 5; **~ (en)** to think (about) 5; **~ + inf.** to plan to 5
la pensión boarding house; **media pensión** breakfast and one meal included 7; **pensión completa** all meals included 7
peor worse
pequeño/a small 3
perder to lose 13; **perder + means of transportation** to miss the . . . 7
perdido/a lost
Perdone. I'm sorry.
perezoso/a lazy 15
perfecto/a perfect
la perforación drilling
el perfume perfume 2
la perfumería perfume shop
el periódico newspaper 2
el/la periodista journalist
la perla pearl 13
la permanencia stay
pero but 3
el perro dog 15
el personaje character
la personalidad personality
personalmente personally
pertenecer a to belong to
peruano/a Peruvian 3
pesado/a heavy
la pesa weight 10
pesar to weigh; **a ~ de que** in spite of
la pesca fishing

pescar to fish 9
el peso weight
el petrodólar petrodollar (a unit of hard currency held by oil-producing countries)
el petróleo oil
el pez fish 15
picante spicy
el pico beak
el pie foot 4
la piedra rock, stone
la piel skin, hide
la pierna leg 4
la pila battery 16
la píldora pill 11
pilotear to fly a plane
la pimienta pepper 9
pintar to paint 9
el/la pintor/a painter 17
pintoresco/a picturesque
la pintura painting 17
pisar to step on 11
la piscina pool 3
el piso floor 8
la pizarra chalkboard
la placa license plate 11
el placer pleasure
el plan plan; diagram
planear to plan
la planta plant 2
plasmado/a formed, created
la plata slang for "money" (literally "silver") 8; **de plata** made of silver 13
el plato course, plate 9; dish
la playa beach 3
la pluma pen
la población population
poblado/a populated
poco/pocos a little/few 3; **dentro de poco** in a while 18; **poco a poco** little by little
el poder power; **~ adquisitivo** purchasing power
poder (o > ue > u) to be able, can 5; **¿podrías + inf.?** could you + verb? 4; **¿Puede decirme cómo . . . ?** Can you tell me how . . . ? 13; **¿Puede hablar más despacio, por favor?** Can you speak more slowly, please? 7;

No puedo más. I can't take it anymore. 9
la poesía poem 9; poetry
el/la políglota polyglot, a person who knows several languages
la política politics
el/la político/a politician
el pollo chicken 12
poner to put 4; ~ **la mesa** to set the table 9; **~se al día** to bring up to date; **~se la ropa** to put on one's clothes 4; **~se rojo/a** to blush
por for; by 5; ~ **algo será** there must be a reason 17; ~ **aquí** around here; ~ **avión** airmail; ~ + **barco/tren**/etc. by boat/train/etc. 6; ~ **cierto** by the way; ~ **ejemplo** for example; **¡~ el amor de Dios!** For heaven's sake! (literally "for the love of God!") 8; ~ **eso** therefore 2; that's why 15; ~ **falta de** for lack of; ~ **favor** please 1; ~ **fin** at last 7; ~ **lo general** in general; ~ **lo menos** at least 15; ~ **lo tanto** therefore; ~ **mi parte** as far as I'm concerned 18; ~ **otro (lado)** on the other (hand) 14; ~ **(pura) casualidad** by (pure) chance 15; ~ **si acaso** (just) in case 15; ~ **suerte** luckily 15; ~ **supuesto.** Of course. 2; ~ **última vez** for the last time; ~ **un lado** on the one hand 14
¿Por qué? Why? 3
el porcentaje percentage
porque because 3
el portero doorman; janitor 8; ~ **automático** intercom; electric door opener 8
portugués/portuguesa Portuguese 3
el posgrado graduate studies
posible possible 7; **es ~** it's possible 9
posiblemente possibly 9
postal: la (tarjeta) ~ postcard 10

el postre dessert 9
el pozo well
la práctica practice
practicar to practice
el precio price
precolombino/a pre-Columbian
predecir to predict
la preferencia preference
preferir (e > ie > i) to prefer 5
el prefijo prefix
la pregunta question
preguntar to ask (a question) 6
preocupado/a worried 3
preocuparse to worry; **No te preocupes.** Don't worry. 3
el premio prize
preparar to prepare
la presa dam
la presentación introduction
presentado/a presented
presidencial presidential
el/la presidente/a president 18
prestado/a loaned; borrowed
prevalecer to prevail
prever to foresee
la primavera spring 4
primero/a first 8; **el/la primer/a ministro/a** prime minister 18; **el primer plato** first course 9; **los primeros auxilios** first aid
el/la primo/a cousin 6
el principio beginning
prisa: tener ~ to be in a hurry
probable: es ~ it's probable 9
probablemente probably 9
probar/se (o > ue) to taste/to try on (clothes) 5
la procedencia (point of) origin
procedente de coming from, originating in
producir to produce 7
el/la profesor/a teacher 1
el programa program
el/la programador/a de computadoras computer programmer 1
prohibir to prohibit 8

el promedio average
prometedor/a promising
pronto soon
la propaganda advertising
la propina tip, gratuity 13
proponer to propose
el propósito purpose, intention
el/la protagonista main character
protegido/a protected
la protesta protest 18
protestar to protest 18
provenir de to come from
la provincia province
próximo/a next
el proyecto project
el/la psicólogo/a psychologist
el pueblo town, village 12
el puente bridge 12
la puerta door 11; ~ **(de salida) número . . .** gate number . . . 7
el puerto port 12
puertorriqueño/a Puerto Rican 3
pues well
el puesto job/position; employment 16
la pulgada inch
la pulsera bracelet 13
el punto point
la pupila pupil (of the eye)

que that, who
Qué: ¿~? What? 2; **¡~ + adj.!** How + adj.! 4; **¡~ + noun + más + adj.!** What a + adj. + noun!; **¡~ barbaridad!** How awful!; **¡~ chévere!** Great! (Caribbean expression) 12; **¿~ hay?** What's up? 1; **¿~ hora es?** What time is it? 5; **¡~ lástima!** What a shame! 9; **¡~ lío!** What a mess! 11; **¡~ mala suerte!** What bad luck! 9; **¡~ pena!** What a pity! 9; **¿~ quiere decir . . . ?** What does . . . mean? Pre.; **¿~ tal?** How are you? (informal) Pre.; **¿~ tiempo hace?** What's the weather like? 4; **¡~ va!** No way! 11

quedar: Te queda bien. It looks good on you. / It fits you well. 5
quedarse en + *place* to stay in + *place* 10
quejarse to complain
quemar to burn 13
querer (e > ie > i) to want; to love 5; **quisiera/quisiéramos** I/we would like 7; **Quisiera hablar con . . . , por favor.** I would like to speak with . . . , please. 7
querido/a dear (*term of endearment*) 11
el queso cheese 9
quien who; **de ~** about whom
¿Quién/es? Who? 1; **¿De ~?** Whose? 2; **¿~ habla?** Who is speaking/calling? 7
quince fifteen 1
quinto/a fifth 8
quitarse la ropa to take off one's clothes 4
quizás + *subj.* perhaps/maybe 9

el/la radio radio 2
el/la radioaficionado/a radio buff, ham radio operator
la radiografía x-ray 11
el radiorreloj clock radio 2
la raíz root
la ranchera a type of Mexican song
rápido/a fast
la raqueta racquet 10
el rascacielos skyscraper
el rato period of time
el ratón mouse
la raya stripe
el rayo beam of light
la razón reason; **tener razón** to be right
real royal; true
la realidad reality; **en realidad** really, actually
realizar to accomplish
realmente really
la rebaja discount, sale
la recepción front desk 7

el/la recepcionista receptionist 1
la receta recipe; **~ médica** prescription 11
recibir to receive 3
el reciclaje recycling 15
reciclar to recycle 15
reciente recent
el reclamo complaint
recoger to pick up, gather
recomendación: carta de ~ letter of recommendation 16
reconocer to recognize
reconocible recognizable
recordar (o > ue) to remember
recorrer to traverse, tour; to look over
recreativo/a recreational
el recuerdo memory; memento
el recurso resource
redondo/a round
referir/se (e > ie > i) to refer to
el reflejo reflection; reflex
regalar to give (a present)
el regalo present, gift
regatear to haggle over, bargain for
regresar to return 3
regular not bad Pre.
rehusar/se to refuse
la reina queen
reinvertir (e > ie > i) reinvest
la relación relation
relacionado/a related
el relámpago lightning 12; **haber relámpagos** to flash with lightning 12
relampaguear to flash with lightning 12
relativamente relatively
el reloj watch 13; clock
rellenar to fill out 16
relleno/a filled
el remite return address 10
repente: de ~ suddenly
repetir (e > i > i) repeat 7
el/la reportero/a reporter
representar to represent
el requisito requirement
la reserva reservation

resfriado/a: estar ~ to have a cold 11
la residencia (estudiantil) dormitory 1
respirar to breathe
responder to answer, respond
la responsabilidad responsibility
la respuesta answer Pre.
el restaurante restaurant 3
el resultado result; **como resultado** as a result
resultó ser . . . it/he/she turned out to be . . . 16
el resumen summary
resumir to summarize
el retraso delay 7
el retrato portrait 17
el (espejo) retrovisor rearview mirror 11
revelar (fotos) to develop (photos) 16
revertido: la llamada a cobro ~ collect call 7
revisar to check 11
la revista magazine 2
revolver (o > ue) to stir; to scramble 9
revuelto/a scrambled 14; **los huevos revueltos** scrambled eggs 14
el rey king
rico/a rich
el río river 12
la riqueza wealth, riches, richness
rítmico/a rhythmic
robar to steal
la rodilla knee 4
rocoso/a rocky
rojo/a red 5; **ponerse ~** to blush
el rollo film 16
el rompecabezas jigsaw puzzle 9
romper/se to break 12
el ron rum
la ropa clothes; **ponerse ~** to put on one's clothes 4; **quitarse ~** to take off one's clothes 4
el ropero closet 8
rosa/rosado/a pink 5

el rubí   ruby   13
rubio/a   blond/e   3
la rueda   wheel; **los patines de ruedas**   roller skates   10
el ruido   noise
la ruina   ruin
ruso/a   Russian   3

sábado   Saturday   2; **el sábado**   on Saturday   2; **los sábados**   on Saturdays   2
saber   to know (facts/how to do something)   4; **¿Sabe(s) dónde está . . . ?**   Do you know where . . . is?   13; **¿No sabías?**   Didn't you know?   9; **No sé (la respuesta).**   I don't know (the answer).   Pre.
sacar   to get a grade; to take out   6; **~ de un apuro (a alguien)**   to get (someone) out of a jam   13; **~ la basura**   to take out the garbage; **~ fotos**   to take pictures   16
el sacerdote   priest
el saco   sports coat   5
el safiro   sapphire   13
sagrado/a   sacred
la sal   salt   9
la sala   living room   8; **~ de estar**   family room   8; **~ de emergencia**   emergency room
la salchicha   sausage   14
salida: la hora de ~   time of departure   7
salir   to leave, go out   2; **~ con**   to date   17; **~ de**   to leave   6; **Te va a ~ caro.**   It's going to cost you.   10
el salón   hall, room for a large gathering; formal living room
la salsa   music from the Caribbean
saltar   to jump
el salto   waterfall; jump, dive
la salud   health
el saludo   greeting
salvadoreño/a   Salvadorian   3
salvaje   wild   15
salvar   to save
sangrar   to bleed   11
la sangre   blood   11

la sangría   sangria (a wine punch)   2
el/la santo/a   saint
el/la sartén   frying pan   9
el saxofón   saxophone   12
secar   to dry
la sección   section; **~ de (no) fumar**   (no) smoking section   7
el/la secretario/a   secretary   1
secundario/a   secondary
sed: tener ~   to be thirsty   5
la seda   silk   5
seguida: en ~   at once, right away   17
seguir (e > i > i)   to follow   7
según   according to
segundo/a   second   8; **de segunda mano**   secondhand, used   8; **el segundo apellido**   second family name, mother   1; **el segundo plato**   second course   9
el segundo   second (time)   5
la seguridad   security
seguro/a: estar ~ (de)   to be sure   9
el seguro médico   medical insurance   16
seis   six   1
seleccionar   to select
la selva   jungle   12
el sello   stamp   10
la semana   week; **~ pasada**   last week   6; **~ que viene**   next week   2; **~ Santa**   Holy Week
la semejanza   similarity
el senado   senate   18
el/la senador/a   senator   18
sencillamente   simply
sencillo/a   simple, easy; **la habitación sencilla**   single room   7
la sensación   feeling
sensato/a   sensible   15
la sensibilidad   sensitivity
sensible   sensitive   15
sentarse (e > ie)   to sit down   5
sentir/se (e > i > i)   to feel   7; **sentir**   to feel sorry   9; **Lo siento.**   I'm sorry.   7

señor/Sr.   Mr.   1; **el señor**   the man   1
señora/Sra.   Mrs./Ms.   1; **la señora**   the woman   1
señorita/Srta.   Miss./Ms.   1; **la señorita**   the young woman   1
separarse   to separate   17
septiembre   September   4
séptimo/a   seventh   8
ser   to be   3; **~ + de**   to be from   1; **~ celoso/a**   to be jealous   17; **Somos tres.**   There are three of us.   9; **Son las . . .**   It's . . . (time)   5
la serpiente   snake   15
serrano: el jamón ~   a type of ham
la servilleta   napkin   9
servir (e > i > i)   to serve   5; **¿En que puedo servirle?**   How can I help you?
sesenta   sixty   1
setenta   seventy   1
el sexo   sex
sexto/a   sixth   8
si   if   3
sí   yes   1
siempre   always   3
siete   seven   1
el siglo   century
significar   to mean
siguiente   following
silenciosamente   silently
la silla   chair   2; **~ de ruedas**   wheelchair
el sillón   easy chair, arm chair   8
la similitud   similarity
simpático/a   nice   3
sin   without; **~ embargo**   however, nevertheless   12; **~ que**   without
sino   but rather; **~ que**   but rather; on the contrary; but instead
el síntoma   symptom
siquiera: ni ~   not even   18
el sitio   place
la situación   situation
sobre   about
el sobre   envelope   10
sobrepasar   to surpass

sobrevivir to survive
el/la sobrino/a nephew/niece 6
el socialismo socialism 18
la sociología sociology 3
el sofá sofa, couch 2
sol: hace ~ it's sunny 4
solamente only 9
el/la soldado soldier
la soledad loneliness 17
solicitar to apply for 16
la solicitud application 16
solitario/a lonely, solitary
solo/a alone 3
sólo only
soltero/a: es ~ is single 6
el sombrero hat 5
sonar (o > ue) ring/make a loud noise, sound
soñar con to dream of/about
la sopa soup
el soplón/la soplona tattletale
soportar to tolerate
sorprenderse de to be surprised about 9
la sorpresa surprise
soso/a dull
el sostén bra 5
el squash squash 10
su/s his/her/your (in/formal)/their 1
subir to go up 4; to climb, raise
subrayar to underline, emphasize
el subtítulo subtitle
el/la suegro/a father-in-law/mother-in-law 6
el sueldo salary 16
el suelo ground; floor
suelto/a separate, unmatched
el sueño dream; **tener sueño** to be tired 5
la suerte luck; **por suerte** by chance 15; **¡Qué mala suerte!** What bad luck! 9; **tener suerte** to be lucky 9
el suéter sweater 5
sufrir to suffer
la sugerencia suggestion
sugerido/a suggested
sugerir (e > ie > i) to suggest

sumar to summarize; to add up, total
el supermercado supermarket 3
supuesto: por ~ of course 2
el sur south 12
surgir to emerge, arise
el suspenso suspense
la sutileza subtlety
suyo/a his/her/your/their 14; **el/la suyo/a** his/hers/yours/theirs 14

tacaño/a stingy, cheap
el tacón heel
tal vez + _subj._ perhaps/maybe 9
la talla size 5
el tamaño size
también too, also 1
el tambor drums
tampoco neither, nor
tan so 13; **~ . . . como** as . . . as 13
el tanque de gasolina gas tank 11
tanto: por lo ~ therefore; **tanto/a . . . como** as much . . . as 13
tantos/as . . . como as many . . . as 13
el tapiz tapestry
tardar to be late, to take a long time
tarde afternoon 2; **Buenas tardes.** Good afternoon. Pre.
la tarea homework 2
la tarjeta: ~ de crédito credit card 14; **~ postal** postcard 10
el taxi taxi 6
el/la taxista taxi driver 13
la taza cup 9
el té tea 2
el teatro theater 3
tejer to knit; to weave 9
la tela cloth, fabric, material; **¿De qué tela es?** What material is it made out of? 5
el/la teleadicto/a television addict

el teléfono telephone 2
el telegrama telegram 10
la telenovela soap opera
la televisión television (programming)
el televisor television set 2
el tema theme
el temor fear
la temperatura temperature 4
temprano early
tender to hang
el tenedor fork 9
tener to have 2; **~ . . . años** to be . . . years old 1; **~ buena salud** to be in good health 11; **~ calor** to be hot 5; **~ un catarro** to have a cold 11; **~ celos (de)** to be jealous (of) 17; **~ diarrea** to have diarrhea 11; **~ en cuenta** to take into account, bear in mind; **~ escalofríos** to have the chills 11; **~ éxito** to succeed; **~ fiebre** to have a fever 11; **~ frío** to be cold 5; **~ ganas de + _inf._** to feel like -_ing_ 6; **~ hambre** to be hungry; **~ lugar** to take place 5; **~ miedo** to be scared 5; **~ palanca** to know people in the right places; **~ prisa** to be in a hurry; **~ que + _inf._** to have to . . . 2; **~ razón** to be right; **~ un resfrío** to have a cold 11; **~ sed** to be thirsty 5; **~ sueño** to be tired 5; **~ suerte** to be lucky 9; **~ tos** to have a cough 11; **~ vergüenza** to be ashamed 5; **No tengo idea.** I don't have any idea. 3; **tenerle fobia a . . .** to have a fear of . . . , to hate 14; **No, tiene el número equivocado.** No, you have the wrong number. 7
tercero/a third 8
terminar to finish 6
la ternera veal 12
el terremoto earthquake
terrestre terrestrial

el tesoro treasure
el texto text
el tiempo weather 4; time; tense; **a tiempo** on time 7; in time; **hace buen (mal) tiempo** 4; **medio tiempo** part-time 16; **¿Qué tiempo hace?** What's the weather like? 4; **tiempo completo** full-time 16
la tienda store 3
la tierra earth
tinto: el vino ~ red wine
el tío uncle 3; **la tía** aunt 6
típico/a typical
el tipo type
tirar to pull; throw out
el título title; (university) degree 16
la toalla towel 2
el tocador dresser, vanity 8
tocar to play (an instrument); to touch 3
el tocino bacon 14
todavía still 8; **~ no** not yet 8
todo/a everything 6; **todo el mundo** everybody, everyone 13; **todos** all 1; **~ los días** every day 12; **~ los meses** every month 12
tomar to eat, have food or drink; to take (a bus, etc.) 6; **tomarle el pelo (a alguien)** to pull someone's leg 16
el tomate tomato 9
el tono tone
la tontería foolishness
tonto/a stupid 3
tormenta: haber ~ to storm 12
el torneo tournament 5
el toro bull 15
la tortilla omelette (in Spain) 2
la tortuga tortoise
tos: tener ~ to have a cough 11
toser to cough 11
la tostada toast 14
la tostadora toaster 8
totalmente totally

el tour tour 13
trabajar to work 2; **~ con madera** to work with wood 9; **~ medio tiempo** to work part-time 16; **~ tiempo completo** to work full-time 16
el trabajo work
traducir to translate 4
traductor/a translator
traer to bring 4
el traje suit 5; **~ de baño** bathing suit 5
tranquilamente quietly 9
tranquilo/a quiet, tranquil
transporte: el medio de ~ means of transportation
trasero/a back, rear
el traslado transfer 13
el tratado treaty
el tratamiento treatment
tratar de to try to
tratarse de to be about
a través de across, through
trece thirteen 1
treinta thirty 1
el tren train 6
tres three 1
triste sad 3
el trombón trombone 12
la trompeta trumpet 12
tronar (o > ue) to thunder
el trozo piece
el trueno thunder 12; **haber truenos** to thunder 12
tu/s your (informal) 1
tú you 1
el turismo tourism
tuyo/a yours 14; **el/la ~** yours 14

Ud. (usted) you (formal) 1
Uds. (ustedes) you (formal/informal) 1
últimamente lately/recently
último/a last, most recent
un, una a, an 2
el uniforme uniform 10
unir to unite, join together
la universidad university 3
uno one 1; **el ~ al otro** each other
unos/as some 2

urbano/a urban
uruguayo/a Uruguayan 3
usar to use 3

la vaca cow 15
las vacaciones vacation
Vale. O.K. 2; **(No) ~ la pena.** It's (not) worth it.; **~ + inf.** It's (not) worth + -ing. 11
valiente brave 15
el valor value
valorar to value, price
el valle valley 12
variar to vary
la variedad variety
varios/as several
vasco/a Basque
el vaso glass 9
Vaya! Wow! 8
veces: a ~ at times 12; **algunas ~** sometimes 12; **muchas ~** many times 12
el/la vecino/a neighbor
veinte twenty 1
el vendaje bandage 11
el/la vendedor/a seller; sales person
vender to sell 3
venezolano/a Venezuelan 3
venir (e > ie > i) to come 5
la ventaja advantage
la ventana window 9
ver to see 4; **a ~** let's see; **no veo la hora de + inf.** I can't wait + inf. 17
el verano summer 4
veras: ¿de ~? really 2
¿verdad? right? 1; **es verdad** it's true 9
verdadero real, true 12
verde green 5
la verdura vegetable
la vergüenza shame; **tener vergüenza** to be ashamed 5
el vestido dress 5
vestirse (e > i > i) to get dressed 5
la vez point in time; **a ~** at the same time; **de vez en cuando** once in a while, from time to time 12; **en vez de**

instead of; **por última vez** for the last time
viajar to travel 6
el viaje trip; **el/la agente de viajes** travel agent 1
el/la viajero/a traveller
la vida life
el vídeo VCR; videocassette 2
viejo/a old 3
viento: hace ~ it's windy 4
viernes Friday 2; **el ~** on Friday 2
el vinagre vinegar 9
el vino wine 2; **~ tinto** red wine
el violín violin 12
el violonchelo cello 12
la visita visit

la vista view
el/la visitante visitor
visitar to visit 2
vivir to live 3
vivo/a bright 5; alive
el volante steering wheel 11
el volcán volcano 12
volver (o > ue) to return, come back 5; **~ a +** *inf.* to (do something) again 13
vomitar to vomit 11
vosotros/as you (plural, informal) 1
la votación vote
el/la votante voter
votar to vote 18
el voto vote 18
la voz voice
el vuelo flight 7

vuelta: darle la ~ to turn over 9; **dar una ~** to take a ride; to go for a stroll/walk 15
vuestro/a your 3; **el/la ~** yours 14

y and 1
ya already; now 8; **~ no** no longer 8; **~ que** since 13; **¡~ voy!** I'm coming! 14
yo I 1
el yogur yogurt 14

la zanahoria carrot
el zapato shoe 5
la zona zone
el zumo juice 14

Index

Credits

Black and White Photographs

Preliminary Chapter: page 0, Peter Menzel/Stock Boston; 4, left, Robert Frerck/Odyssey Productions; 4, right, Owen Franken; **Chapter 1:** page 14, Sid and Mary Nolan/Taurus Photos; 16, Javier Merino Bartrina; 33, top left to right, Peter Menzel; Owen Franken; Stuart Cohen/Comstock; bottom left to right, Peter Menzel; Carl Frank/Photo Researchers; Owen Franken/Stock Boston; Robert Frerck/Odyssey Productions; **Chapter 2:** page 36, Stuart Cohen/Comstock; 56, Zoe Dominic; 59, Luis Villota; 60, Robert Frerck/Odyssey Productions; **Chapter 3:** page 62, Peter Menzel/Stock Boston; 66, Eugene Gordon; 75, Stuart Cohen/Comstock; 83, Peter Menzel/Stock Boston; **Chapter 4:** page 90, Beryl Goldberg; 92, Charlie Fowler/Adventure Photo; 103, Stuart Cohen/Comstock; 108, Hugh Rogers/Monkmeyer; **Chapter 5:** page 118, Robert Frerck/Odyssey Productions; 120, Javier Merino Bartrina; 132, both, Lee Malis/Picture Group; 137, Victor Englebert; 138, Peter Menzel/Stock Boston; **Chapter 6:** page 146, Stuart Cohen/Comstock; 147, Luis Villota; 148, Peter Menzel/Stock Boston; 150, 158, Peter Menzel; 159, Victor Englebert; 163, Paul Conklin; **Chapter 7:** page 170, Will McIntyre/Photo Researchers; 172, 176, Peter Menzel; 186, left, Dick Huffman/Monkmeyer; 186, right, 190, Peter Menzel; **Chapter 8:** page 198, Mark Antman/Image Works; 199 Robert Frerck/Odyssey Productions; 200, Victor Englebert; 212, Robert Frerck/Odyssey Productions; 213, David Ball/Picture Cube; 218, Luis Villota; **Chapter 9:** page 226, Joe Viesti/Viesti Associates; 240, Mary Altier/Picture Cube; 241, Eugene Gordon; 246, Robert Frerck/Odyssey Productions; 251, Bob Daemmrich/Stock Boston; **Chapter 10:** page 254, Max & Bea Hunn/D. Donne Bryant; 255, Mark Antman/Image Works; 256, Joe Viesti/Viesti Associates; 260, Peter Menzel; 267, Robert Frerck/TSW/Click Chicago; 269, Jim Harrison/Stock Boston; 273, Peter Menzel; **Chapter 11:** page 280, Peter Menzel; 281, Victor Englebert; 284, Stuart Cohen/Comstock; 294, Dagmar Fabricius/Stock Boston; 299, Olaf Soot; 301, Robert Frerck/Odyssey Productions; **Chapter 12:** page 306, Owen Franken/Stock Boston; 308, Beryl Goldberg; 312, Peter Menzel/Stock Boston; 322, left, 1988 Elektra Records, a division of Warner Communications Inc.; 322, right, Pablo Milanés/Center for Cuban Studies; 327, Victor Englebert; 332, top, Robert Frerck/Odyssey Productions; 332, bottom, Allan Philiba; **Chapter 13:** page 334, Carnaval Miami/Kiwanis Club of Little Havana, Miami; 335, Peter Menzel; 343, Allan Philiba; 346, Rob Nelson/Picture Group; 350, Victor Englebert; **Chapter 14:** page 360, Peter Menzel; 361, Arlene Collins/Monkmeyer; 362, 366, Robert Frerck/Odyssey Productions; 373, left, Mike Mazzaschi/Stock Boston; 373, right, Joe Viesti/Viesti Associates; 377, Jim Fox/Photo Researchers; **Chapter 15:** page 384, George Holton/Photo Researchers; 386, Joe Viesti/Viesti Associates; 390, Bernard Silberstein/Photo Researchers; 399, left, Joe Viesti/Viesti Associates; 399, right, Al Buchanan/D. Donne Bryant; 401, Peter Menzel; **Chapter 16:** page 408, 411, Hugh Rogers/Monkmeyer; 425, Carl Frank/Photo Researchers; **Chapter 17:** page 433, Peter Menzel; 434, Alinari/Art Resource, N.Y.; 437, William A. Cotton/Colorado State Magazine; 438, left, Frederick R. Weisman Art Foundation, Los Angeles, California; 438, right, courtesy of the artist, Francisco Amighetti and El Museo de Arte Costarricense; 443, left, Hirshhorn Museum and Sculpture Garden, courtesy, Marlborough Gallery; 443, right, courtesy, Marlborough Gallery; 444, Gift of Mr. and Mrs. Burton S. Stern, Mr. and Mrs. Bernard S. Shapiro and the M. and M. Karolik Fund, courtesy, Museum of Fine Arts, Boston; 448, © ARS, New York/SPADEM; **Chapter 18:** page 454, UPI Bettmann Newsphotos; 457, Stuart Cohen/Comstock; 464, Peter Menzel

Color Photographs

Los contrastes y la diversidad: Page A: photo 1, Kirk/DDB Stock Photography; photo 2, Luis Villota; photo 3, Joe Viesti; Page B: photo 4, Walter Aguiar; photo 5, Frerck/Odyssey; photo 6, Victor Englebert; Page C: photo 7, Beryl Goldberg; photos 8 and 9, Frerck/Odyssey; Page D: photo 10, Ferrero/DDB Stock Photography; photo 11, Mangino/The Image Works; Page E: photo 12, Victor Englebert; photo 13, Wells/The Image Works; photo 14, Victor Englebert; Page F: photo 15, Luis Villota; photo 15, Victor Englebert; **Patrimonio cultural:** Page A: photo 1, Victor Englebert; photo 2, Frerck/Odyssey; photo 3, Luis Villota; Page B: photo 4, Altier/The Picture Cube; photo 5, Frerck/

Odyssey; Page C: photo 6, Bryant/DDB Stock Photography; Page D: photo 7, Peter Menzel; photo 8, Ball/The Picture Cube; photo 9, Everts/TSW/Click Chicago; Page E: photo 10, Scala/Art Resource; photo 11, Beryl Goldberg; photo 12, Luis Villota; Page F: photo 13, Frerck/Odyssey; photo 14, Kraus/TSW/Click Chicago; **Las artes:** Page A: photo 1, Frerck/Odyssey; photo 2, Peter Menzel; photo 3, Putnam/The Picture Cube; Page B: photo 4, Scala/Art Resource; photo 5, Art Resource; Page C: photos 6, 7, and 8, Art Resource; Page D: photo 9, Murphy/DDB Stock Photography; photo 10, Frerck/TSW/Click Chicago; photo 11, McNee/TSW/Click Chicago; Page E: photo 12, Victor Englebert; photo 13, Kirk/DDB Stock Photography; Page F: photo 14, Beryl Goldberg; photo 15, Charlon/Gamma Liaison; **Hacia el siglo XXI:** Page A: photo 1, Courtesy of Carolina Herrera; photo 2, Bleibtreu/Sygma; photo 3, NASA; Page B: photo 4, Abbas/Magnum; photo 5, Burri/Magnum; photo 6, Luis Villota; Page C: photo 7, Frerck/TSW/Click Chicago; photo 8, Peter Menzel; photo 9, Victor Englebert; Page D: photo 10, Scianna/Magnum; photo 11, Wells/The Image Works; Page E: photo 12, Iooss/Sports Illustrated/Time, Inc.; photo 13, Stoltman/Duomo; photo 14, Focus on Sports; Page F: photo 15, Daemmrich/Stock Boston; photo 16, Beryl Goldberg.

Art

Drawings by Joyce A. Zarins

Pages 1, 2, 3, 4, 6, 32, 48, 67, 69, 91, 97, 99, 101, 105, 106, 122, 123, 136, 151, 160, 182, 204, 215, 216, 231, 233, 244, 250, 270, 287, 289, 290, 297, 313, 315, 321, 322, 323, 324, 325, 326, 348, 351, 358, 382, 389, 391, 413, 425, 451, 452

Drawings by Will Winslow

Pages 5, 13, 26, 27, 28, 38, 40, 46, 52, 54, 64, 78, 79, 80, 81, 94, 95, 110, 114, 125, 134, 161, 175, 183, 184, 228, 243, 263, 282, 285, 311, 319, 336, 352, 375, 381, 436, 447, 465

Realia

Page 8, top left, Restaurante VégéTarien; 8, bottom, Instituto de estudios norteamericanos; 8, top right, *Venezuela Farándula*; 9, Gregory E. Robbins, D.D.S.; 19, Tomás Lozano Seisdedos; 23, Festejos M.A.R., C.A.; 36, Federación Nacional de Cafeteros de Colombia; 37, Ordenadores Atari, S.A.; 41, *El Nuevo Día*; 50, *Lecturas*; 106-107, Diario *El Mercurio*, Santiago, Chile; 119, *¿Qué pasa?*; 124, Revista *Estar Viva* / Editorial G + J; 132-133, Copyright *El País*; 135, *El País*, Diario Independiente de la mañana; 143, left, Fundación Banco Consolidado; 143, center, Fundación Ricardo Zuloaga; 143, right, Fundación Teresa Carreño; 165, The Muñoz-Torres and Montero-Salgado families; 171, Reportaje realizado por Douglas González, *Ida y Vuelta*; 174, top left, Minicines Astorias; 174, top right, Restaurante El Hidalgo; 174, bottom left, Peluqueros Pedro Molina; 174, bottom right, Librería Compás; 176, Administración Turística Española; 188, Venezuelan International Airways; 203, Copyright *El País*; 205, *El Nuevo Día*; 209, Periódico *Segundamano*; 217, Electroshop Sonidos, S.A.; 235, Editorial América, S.A.; 237, Diario *El Mercurio*; 286, Revista *Mucho Más*; 292, Revista *Diez Minutos*; 296, Fernando Revuelta; 298, Dollar Rent-a-Car; 310, *El Nuevo Día*; 314, Revista *Mucho Más*; 317, Slim International Esthetic Center de Argentina; 334, Courtesy of Burger King; 340, right, Pulmantur; 340, left, Aeroméxico; 347, Kentucky Fried Chicken; 350, Christian Duvenet; 357, Courtesy of United Airlines; 364, Espasa-Calpe, S.A.; 365, Johnson y Johnson de México, S.A. de C.V.; 368, *El Nuevo Día*; 372, Palacio Bellas Artes; 385, Fundación Vida Silvestre Argentina; 392, Asociación Conciencia-Folleto de Campaña "Vivamos en un paisaje limpio", Argentina; 392, bottom right, Revista *Mucho Más*; 397, Venezuelan International Airways; 409, Gonzalo Pérez de Arce; 412, Unicentro de la Visión; 423, left, Carlos Cuevas P.; 423, right, Gerardo Huidobro Ruiz; 433, Museo Rufino Tamayo; 445, top, Copyright © Lancio Film 1986; 445, bottom, Unicentro de la Visión; 455, Copyright *El País*; 458, *Cambio*; 460-461, © Joaquín Salvador Lavado (Quino) from *Potentes, Prepotentes e Impotentes*; 462, Center for Disease Control, Atlanta

Barranquilla
Cartagena
Maracaibo   La Guaira
San Carlos   Caracas
Río Magdalena
Río Orinoco
VENEZUELA
GUYANA
GUAYANA FRANCESA
Medellín
Bogotá
COLOMBIA
Cali
Popayán
Río Negro
SURINAM
ECUADOR
Amazonas
ECUADOR
Quito
Guayaquil
Río
PERÚ
CORDILLERA
Callao
Lima
Machu Picchu
Cuzco
Puno
La Paz
BRASIL
Brasilia
Lago Titicaca
BOLIVIA
Sucre
Potosí
DE LOS
Río Paraná
São Paulo
PARAGUAY
Río de Janeiro
Salta
Asunción
Iguazú
TRÓPICO DE CAPRICORNIO
CHILE
San Miguel de Tucumán
ANDES
ARGENTINA
Aconcagua
Mendoza
Viña del Mar
Valparaíso
Santiago
URUGUAY
OCÉANO ATLÁNTICO
OCÉANO PACÍFICO
Buenos Aires
La Plata
Montevideo
Río de la Plata
Concepción
PAMPAS
Mar del Plata
Río Colorado
Playa Blanca
Bariloche
PATAGONIA

0   400   800 km
0   200   400   600 mi

Punta Arenas   TIERRA DEL FUEGO
Estrecho de Magallanes   CABO DE HORNOS

AMÉRICA DEL SUR